Growth, Employment, and Poverty in Latin America

UNU World Institute for Development Economics Research (UNU-WIDER) was established by the United Nations University as its first research and training centre and started work in Helsinki, Finland, in 1985. The mandate of the institute is to undertake applied research and policy analysis on structural changes affecting developing and transitional economies, to provide a forum for the advocacy of policies leading to robust, equitable, and environmentally sustainable growth, and to promote capacity strengthening and training in the field of economic and social policy-making. Its work is carried out by staff researchers and visiting scholars in Helsinki and via networks of collaborating scholars and institutions around the world.

United Nations University World Institute for
Development Economics Research (UNU-WIDER)
Katajanokanlaituri 6B, 00160 Helsinki, Finland
<www.wider.unu.edu>

Growth, Employment, and Poverty in Latin America

Guillermo Cruces, Gary S. Fields, David Jaume,
and Mariana Viollaz

A study prepared by the United Nations University World Institute for Development Economics Research (UNU-WIDER)

OXFORD
UNIVERSITY PRESS

OXFORD
UNIVERSITY PRESS

Great Clarendon Street, Oxford, OX2 6DP,
United Kingdom

Oxford University Press is a department of the University of Oxford.
It furthers the University's objective of excellence in research, scholarship,
and education by publishing worldwide. Oxford is a registered trade mark of
Oxford University Press in the UK and in certain other countries

First Edition published in 2017
Impression: 2

Published in the United States of America by Oxford University Press
198 Madison Avenue, New York, NY 10016, United States of America

British Library Cataloguing in Publication Data
Data available

Library of Congress Control Number: 2016957034

ISBN 978–0–19–880108–5

Printed and bound by
CPI Group (UK) Ltd, Croydon, CR0 4YY

Foreword

The motivation behind this piece of research was cemented during a meeting attended by Professor Gary Fields—one of the co-authors of this book—and myself in mid-2013 where we discussed in depth the linkages between economic growth, changing employment conditions, and the reduction of poverty. Gary has been working on the frontier of our profession on employment and development issues all of his academic career, and he pointed to new inroads and data to be explored within the growth–employment–poverty nexus, focusing on Latin America.

At the time of our exploratory discussions the target date for completion of the UN Millennium Development Goals was looming, with the number one goal—to halve between 1990 and 2015 the proportion of people living on less than 1 dollar a day—having already been achieved. The new Post-2015 Development Agenda, since adopted, was under intense debate. Leading the charge among the Sustainable Development Goals is the aim to end poverty in all its forms everywhere, followed closely by the SDG to promote inclusive and sustainable economic growth, full and productive employment, and decent work for all. Thus the proposed research could not have been more timely for the international agenda. And more so as UNU-WIDER was then launching a new research programme—focusing on the three development challenges of transformation, inclusion, and sustainability—wherein work on the growth–employment–poverty nexus was a straightforward fit.

I hereby express my sincere appreciation of the four authors, Guillermo Cruces, Gary S. Fields, David Jaume, and Mariana Viollaz, for bringing this academic work to full fruition, and particularly for their analytical skills brought out so clearly in this book.

UNU-WIDER gratefully acknowledges the support and financial contributions to its research programme by the governments of Denmark, Finland, Sweden, and the United Kingdom.

Finn Tarp

Helsinki
September 2016

Acknowledgements

We would like to express our gratitude to UNU-WIDER for its generous support, and especially to its director, Finn Tarp, who encouraged us during the three years we worked on this book. We are also grateful to CEDLAS and its director, Leonardo Gasparini, for allowing us access to the SEDLAC database to construct most of the calculations presented in this book.

Many persons provided helpful comments throughout the process of writing this book. They include Leonardo Gasparini for comments on a first draft of this book, and the following colleagues for comments on country-specific chapters: Tim Gindling (Costa Rica), Robert Duval-Hernández (Mexico), José Rodríguez (Peru), and Verónica Amarante (Uruguay). We would also like to thank anonymous reviewers from Oxford University Press and UNU-WIDER whose comments helped us improve our work. Participants at the UNU-WIDER 30th Anniversary Conference 'Mapping the Future of Development Economics', held in Helsinki in September 2015, and the 2015 LACEA Meeting also provided useful suggestions and comments on previous versions of our manuscript.

A group of excellent research assistants contributed to the bibliographical review. They are Ivana Benzaquén, Jessica Bracco, Cynthia Marchioni, and Germán Reyes.

Guillermo Cruces, Gary S. Fields, David Jaume, and Mariana Viollaz

Contents

List of Figures

List of Tables

List of Abbreviations

CASEN	Encuesta de Caracterización Socioeconómica Nacional (Chile)
CCT	conditional cash transfer
CEDLAS	Centro de Estudios Distributivos, Laborales y Sociales
CSS	Caja del Seguro Social (Panama)
ECH	Encuesta Continua de Hogares (Bolivia, Colombia, Uruguay)
EH	Encuesta de Hogares (Bolivia, Panama)
EHPM	Encuesta de Hogares de Propósitos Múltiples (Costa Rica, El Salvador)
EIH	Encuesta Integrada de Hogares (Paraguay)
ENAHO	Encuesta Nacional de Hogares (Costa Rica, Peru)
ENEMDU	Encuesta de Empleo, Desempleo y Subempleo (Ecuador)
ENFT	Encuesta Nacional de Fuerza de Trabajo (Dominican Republic)
ENIGH	Encuesta Nacional de Ingresos y Gastos de los Hogares (Mexico)
EPH	Encuesta Permanente de Hogares (Argentina, Paraguay)
EPH-C	Encuesta Permanente de Hogares-Continua (Argentina)
EPHPM	Encuesta Permanente de Hogares de Propósitos Múltiples (Honduras)
EPM	Encuesta de Hogares por Muestreo (Venezuela)
FPS	Fondo de Pensiones Sociales (Peru)
GEIH	Gran Encuesta Integrada de Hogares (Colombia)
GIC	growth incidence curve
IESS	Instituto Ecuatoriano de Seguridad Social
IHSS	Instituto Hondureño de Seguridad Social
ILO	International Labour Organization
IMSS	Instituto Mexicano del Seguro Social
INJUPEMP	Instituto Nacional de Jubilaciones y Pensiones de los Empleados y Funcionarios del Poder Ejecutivo (Honduras)
INPREMA	Instituto Nacional de Previsión del Magisterio (Honduras)
IPM	Instituto de Previsión Militar (Honduras)
IPS	Instituto de Previsión Social (Paraguay)

IPSFA	Instituto de Prevision Social de las Fuerzas Armadas (Venezuela)
ISSFA	Social Security Institute of the Armed Forces (Ecuador)
ISSFAM	Instituto de Seguridad Social para las Fuerzas Armadas Mexicanas
ISSPOL	Instituto de Seguridad Social de la Policía Nacional (Ecuador)
ISSS	Instituto Salvadoreño de Seguridad Social
ISSSTE	Instituto de Seguridad y Servicios Sociales de los Trabajadores del Estado (Mexico)
IVSS	Instituo Venezolano de los Seguros Sociales
NAFTA	North American Free Trade Agreement
PISA	Programme for International Student Assessment
PNAD	Pesquisa Nacional por Amostra de Domicílios (Brazil)
PPP	purchasing power parity
PRAF	Programa de Asignación Familiar (Honduras)
RGPS	Regime Geral de Previdência Social (Brazil)
RJP IMSS	Régimen de Jubilaciones y Pensiones, Instituto Mexicano del Seguro Social
RPPS	Regime Próprio de Previdência Social (Brazil)
SDG	Sustainable Development Goal
SEDLAC	Socio-Economic Database for Latin America and the Caribbean
UN-ECLAC	United Nations Economic Commission for Latin America and the Caribbean

Notes on Authors

Guillermo Cruces (PhD in economics, LSE) is the deputy director of the Center for Distributive, Labor and Social Studies (CEDLAS) at the Universidad Nacional de La Plata, Argentina (UNLP) and a research fellow at IZA. His research is focused on labour economics and distributional analysis in Latin America and the Caribbean. He has published in journals such as the *Journal of Political Economy*, *Journal of Public Economics*, *Labour Economics*, *Journal of Population Economics*, *Brookings Papers on Economic Activity*, *Journal of Development Studies*, and *Economia*, and he has edited books and contributed to collective volumes and reports.

Gary S. Fields is the John P. Windmuller Professor of International and Comparative Labor and Professor of Economics at Cornell University, a research fellow at IZA, and a Non-Resident Senior Research Fellow at UNU-WIDER. At Cornell, he teaches and conducts research in labour economics, development economics, and public policy in the university-wide Department of Economics and the ILR School. He is the winner of the 2014 IZA Prize in Labor Economics, the top worldwide award in the field, and director of the IZA Program in Labor and Development. His most recent prior book is *Working Hard, Working Poor* (Oxford University Press).

David Jaume is an economics PhD student at Cornell University, and visiting researcher at CEDLAS. His work is focused on labour markets and income distribution in developing countries. He has published in the areas of economics of development and economics of education. He has also been a research fellow at CEDLAS, Universidad Nacional de La Plata, where he received his Master's degree in economics.

Mariana Viollaz has a PhD in economics from the Universidad Nacional de La Plata (UNLP), Argentina. She is a Senior Researcher at the Center for Distributive, Labor and Social Studies (CEDLAS) at the Universidad Nacional de La Plata. She has been a postdoctoral fellow at the ILR School of Cornell University where she researched on the growth–employment–poverty nexus in Latin America during the 2000s. Her research is focused on labour and development economics in Latin America and the Caribbean.

Part I
Introduction to the Volume

1

Introduction and Motivation for the Project

1.1 Context and Motivation

The year 2015 marked the conclusion of the United Nations' Millennium Development Goals and the beginning of the UN's 2030 Agenda for Sustainable Development. Foremost among the Sustainable Development Goals is to end poverty in all its forms everywhere. Another of the SDGs is to promote sustained, inclusive, and sustainable economic growth, full and productive employment, and decent work for all.

This book examines the links between economic growth, changing employment conditions, and the reduction of poverty in Latin America. The research project that led to this book had its origins in a mid-2013 meeting attended by the director of UNU-WIDER, Finn Tarp, and Gary Fields, one of the researchers on this project. At that time, the United Nations' Millennium Development Goals were nearing their target date for completion, and the number one goal—to halve, between 1990 and 2015, the proportion of people whose income is less than 1 dollar a day—had already been achieved. The new Post-2015 Development Agenda, since adopted, was under discussion.

UNU-WIDER, for its part, had just launched a four-year research programme with the three development challenges of transformation, inclusion, and sustainability. Fields has had a long-term research interest in improving labour market conditions as a means of helping the poor lead better material lives and had just published a book on this topic (Fields 2012). Other important works had just appeared as well—in particular, the World Bank's World Development Report 2013, entitled simply 'Jobs' (World Bank 2013a). What struck Tarp and Fields and their colleagues was how much was known about some aspects of the problem, but also how little was known about others. In particular, a priority for deeper analysis was the growth–employment–poverty nexus in the various countries of the world.

By then, the dismal growth–employment–poverty record of the United States and other OECD countries had been well-documented. In the case of the United States, Stiglitz (2012, 2015) showed: recent United States' economic growth took place primarily in the top 1 per cent of the income distribution; as a result, there was growing inequality of income and wealth; those at the bottom and in the middle are actually worse off now than they were in 2000; life is particularly harsh at the bottom, and the recession made it much worse; and there has been a hollowing-out of the middle class. Other OECD countries have not done much better. The OECD Employment Outlook (2012, 2015) tells us: economic growth has not been strong enough to make more than a small dent in OECD-wide unemployment; labour market conditions are improving but recovery is far from complete; employment is still growing too slowly to close the jobs gap induced by the crisis any time soon; the jobs mix has shifted towards more part-time work, making it harder for some unemployed to find full-time jobs; the OECD average unemployment rate is still 1.6 percentage points above its pre-crisis level; long-term unemployment also remains unacceptably high; and weak real wage growth also remains a concern, particularly in the euro area.

UNU-WIDER had a strong interest in learning about the links between growth, employment, and poverty in the poorer regions of the world. It would have been an impossibly ambitious task to analyse the entirety of the rest of the world. Fortunately, though, an exceptional database had been compiled for Latin America and was available for our use.

Household datasets have been processed by CEDLAS (Centro de Estudios Distributivos, Laborales y Sociales, Universidad Nacional de La Plata), compiled into the database SEDLAC—Socio-Economic Database for Latin America and the Caribbean (CEDLAS and World Bank 2014), and made available for us to analyse in this project.[1] The microeconomic data used in this project included more than 150 household surveys, comprising observations for five million households and eighteen million persons for sixteen Latin American countries: Argentina, Bolivia, Brazil, Chile, Colombia, Costa Rica, Dominican Republic, Ecuador, Honduras, Mexico, Panama, Paraguay, Peru, El Salvador, Uruguay, and Venezuela. Most countries offered annual household surveys, though a few were biennial, with sample sizes typically numbering in the tens of thousands of households. Further details are given in Chapter 2.

Our research project answers the following broad questions: Has economic growth resulted in gains in standards of living and reductions in poverty via improved labour market conditions in Latin America in the 2000s, and have

[1] Three of the researchers—Cruces, Jaume, and Viollaz—are affiliates of CEDLAS.

these improvements halted or been reversed since the Great Recession of 2008? How do the rate and character of economic growth, changes in the various employment and earnings indicators, and changes in poverty and inequality indicators relate to each other?

From the very outset of the study, we adopted broad conceptualizations of the three key terms: growth, employment, and poverty. *Economic growth* includes the usual measure: the growth of real gross domestic product (GDP) per capita. But growth goes beyond just the growth rate to include also attention to the type of growth being pursued. Are mechanisms in place making the economic growth inclusive in the sense that ordinary people can share in improved standards of living through the work they do and/or through the social programmes available to them? *Employment and unemployment* include the usual measures promulgated by the ILO—employed if working even one hour for pay or fifteen hours or more not for pay in the reference week; unemployed if not employed but actively looking for work; but in addition employment and unemployment also include other aspects of employment such as the amount earned in a month and the type of work performed. *Poverty* is gauged by 'income poverty', measured using a number of alternative absolute poverty lines.

The first stage of our research was a collection of sixteen detailed country studies completed in late 2014 and revised early in 2015 (Cruces et al. 2015a–2015p). We then compiled all of the individual country data and results into a new dataset on the rate of economic growth, changes in employment and earnings indicators, and changes in poverty and inequality indicators. With this dataset, we performed cross-country analysis of the growth–employment–poverty nexus and provided additional within-country evidence (Cruces et al. 2015q). This volume is based on these working papers.

1.2 The Analytical Framework Adopted

Following Fields (in press), the analytical framework adopted in this volume can be visualized schematically in the following way. Consider a policy action of interest and an outcome variable by which the policy action is judged—in this study, it is pursuing economic growth as a means for reducing poverty. For economic growth to contribute to poverty reduction, there must be at least one channel, maybe more, through which growth reduces poverty.

The channel emphasized in this research is the employment channel. Employment is understood to include not only wage and salaried employment but also self-employment. The issue is not just whether people are employed but also how much they earn for the work they do. Thus, besides employment/unemployment per se, the types of jobs people are working in and their labour market earnings are central to the analysis.

There are good reasons for concentrating on labour markets. One is that national accounts data show that labour incomes account for more of total income than do all other income sources combined. Another reason is that income and expenditure surveys indicate that most people derive most if not all of their income from the work they and other members of their households do. A third reason is that decomposition studies reveal that labour income inequality accounts for a larger share of total income inequality than do the inequalities of all other income sources combined.

But employment is not the only important channel. Economic growth may provide the tax revenues enabling countries to increase spending on existing social programmes and create new ones. Some of these social programmes work through the labour market, reaching people as workers (e.g. unemployment insurance, old-age pensions, and job-related health coverage). Others work in other ways, reaching people as consumers and citizens (e.g. free or subsidized transportation, food, or housing).

Consider Figure 1.1. Employment as a channel linking growth and poverty is the focal point of our analysis. For economic growth to reduce poverty via the employment channel, the growth must result in improved employment conditions (Channel A), and improved employment conditions must result in reduced poverty (Channel B). The growth–employment–poverty channel receives the bulk of the emphasis in what follows. But in addition, economic growth reduces poverty insofar as it results in improved social programmes (Channel C) and if the social programmes reach the poor (Channel D). These social programme channels are discussed in the specific country chapters, but they are not analysed from a cross-country perspective as this book is focused on the employment channel. Figure 1.1 displays the case in which all these channels are open, and consequently economic growth reduces poverty via both the employment channel and the social programmes channel.

Unfortunately, these channels may be blocked, because employment is created but the wages and hours of work offered are so limited that workers cannot escape poverty, or because the benefits of the social programmes go to the haves but not to the have-nots. This second case is depicted in Figure 1.2.

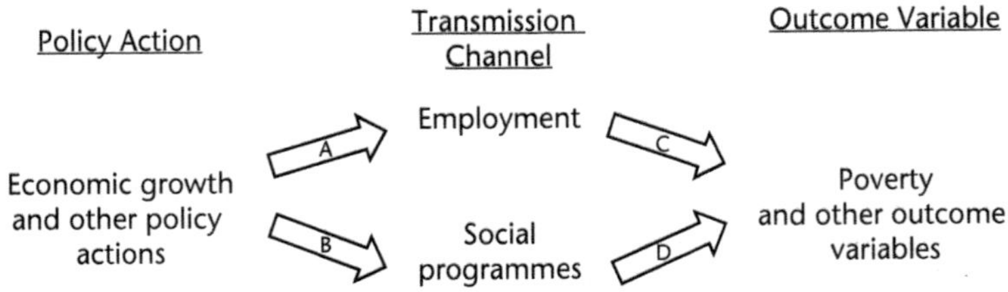

Figure 1.1 Open transmission channels
Source: The figure is taken from Fields (in press).

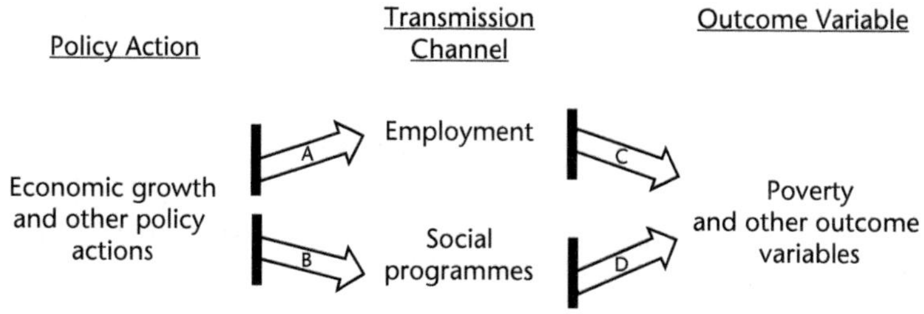

Figure 1.2 Blocked transmission channels
Source: The figure is taken from Fields (in press).

In such a case, economic growth may take place, but employment conditions may improve only for those at the very top of the income distribution but not for those in the middle or the bottom, and the same may be true for socially provided goods and services. Thus, although economic growth takes place, the poor may be left out, and thus poverty is not reduced.

Does economic growth benefit everyone? Or does it benefit just those at the top to the exclusion or even impoverishment of those further down in the income distribution? Neither answer can be assumed, especially in a region with as much inequality as Latin America has. A fruitful way to proceed is to examine which channels are open in Latin American countries, which are sluggish, and which are blocked. That is what the research in this book investigates.

1.3 Previous Literature and our Contributions

As detailed in our conceptual framework, we study the growth–employment–poverty nexus in Latin America. This work is related to several literatures dealing (mostly separately) with the growth–employment nexus, with the employment–poverty nexus, and with the growth–inequality nexus in the Latin American region. In the following pages, we highlight some of the most important multi-country contributions to these literatures. There are also country-specific studies covering growth patterns and changes in some labour market indicators on the one hand, and the relationship between changes in some labour market conditions and changes in poverty on the other hand. We provide more details about these studies in each of the corresponding country chapters.

In the latest of a series of papers, Weller (2014) studies mainly the growth–employment nexus in Latin America and the Caribbean for the years 2003 to 2012. He finds that, at the regional level, during the period of high economic growth from 2003 to 2012, the region experienced: an important reduction in the unemployment rate; an improvement in employment quality indicators, such as wages, share of workers registered with social security, share of self-employed and wage/salaried employees, sectoral composition of employment, and level of education of employed workers; and a reduction in the wage gap between highly and low educated workers. The paper focuses on the whole period under study, does not analyse in detail the impact of the international crisis of 2008–9 on labour markets in Latin America, and has little to say about changes in individual countries. In the discussion of the results, the author attributes the generalized improvement in labour market conditions in Latin America over this period to the role of labour market institutions.

Another recent multi-country study (World Bank 2015a) also covers the 2003–12 period but focuses on the employment–poverty nexus rather than on the growth–employment nexus. The report, based as ours is on the SEDLAC database for almost the same group of countries (excluding Venezuela and including Guatemala), emphasizes the post-international-crisis period. Based on different microeconomic decomposition approaches, the study highlights the importance of changes in labour earnings to explain poverty reduction in the region during the 2003–8 and 2008–13 periods, documenting that the magnitude of this effect was lower for the post-international-crisis period. The report relates the rise in mean labour earnings to improvements in the educational composition of the workforce. Finally, the report also documents a fall in wage skill premiums, which it attributes to external conditions (e.g. the commodity price boom) and government policies (e.g. minimum wage increases).

There are other studies of the employment–poverty nexus for the region based on microeconomic decompositions of household survey data. ECLAC (2014) uses a variation of this methodology and concludes that the most important factor for poverty reduction was the combined increase in employment and wages, although in general, labour earnings increases had a greater impact than employment growth on household income changes. This is consistent with results from Beccaria et al. (2011), World Bank (2013b), and Inchauste et al. (2014), who also decompose changes in the poverty rate and report increases in labour income as the main channel to poverty reductions. While not based on decompositions, ECLAC-ILO (2015) is another example of a study of the labour market determinants of the fall in poverty in Latin America for the period 2002–12. The study highlights the role of strong job creation, especially in wage/salaried positions, and public policies, such as minimum wages increases, formalization of workers, and expanded coverage of education and social protection systems.[2]

[2] Other less comprehensive multi-country studies have also been carried out which include a more limited group of countries or fewer labour market indicators, or focus on previous years and not on the whole decade of 2000. Pagés, Pierre, and Scarpetta (2009), for instance, discuss the

Another strand of the recent literature on Latin America deals with the well-documented fall in income inequality since 2002, and most of these studies cover the connection between labour markets and these changes in inequality. Some recent examples include López Calva and Lustig (2010), Gasparini and Lustig (2011), Gasparini et al. (2011), Alvaredo and Gasparini (2015), and Cornia (2014). The conclusion from these studies is that the fall in inequality in the region is attributable to global economic conditions, growth acceleration, and a rapid equitable accumulation of human capital. Others also speculate about the role of new policy approaches, including macroeconomic policies, fiscal and monetary policies, trade and financial policies, and labour and social expenditure policies (Cornia 2014).

Finally, a series of studies also cover the social programmes—poverty reduction nexus, dealing with the role of social policies in reducing poverty, highlighting conditional cash transfers (CCT), among others. The multi-country studies on these issues document an increase in the number of countries in the region adopting programmes of this type. They also find that the fiscal resources allocated to CCT programmes increased as a percentage of GDP from 2000 to 2010, which implied an increase in the percentage of the population covered by these programmes during the same period (Cecchini and Madariaga 2011; Stampini and Tornarolli 2012). While we do not cover this channel directly in our work, the country chapters discuss the specific initiatives adopted in each case during the period under study.

We build on these studies by analysing the growth–employment–poverty nexus in Latin America in the decade of the 2000s, which was only partially covered by the previous literature. Previous papers have only focused on the first part of the link (growth–employment and growth–poverty) or the second one (employment–poverty).

Building on what came before, our contribution is an in-depth study of the multi-pronged growth–employment–poverty nexus based on a large number of labour market indicators (twelve employment and earnings indicators and four poverty and inequality indicators) for a large number of Latin American countries (in our case, sixteen of them). Moreover, we present an exhaustive analysis of the growth–employment–poverty nexus which directly relates changes in all labour market indicators to economic growth, and changes in all employment

growth–employment nexus in Latin America, with data up to the year 2004, and found that many jobs were created during the 1990–2004 period in the Latin American and the Caribbean region, but they were of low productivity and low pay. Cho et al. (2012) document the fact that in Latin America, as in other low- and middle-income countries, employment increased apace of labour force growth in every country but one, although the study does not identify any single country by name. ILO (2014) reports an increase in the share of workers registered with social security in Argentina, Brazil, Colombia, the Dominican Republic, Ecuador, Jamaica, Mexico, Paraguay, Peru, and Uruguay, caused mainly by the favourable economic context and several government programmes.

and earnings indicators to changes in poverty. We also base our analysis on a broader set of labour market indicators than those used in other studies: the previous literature focused mainly on labour earnings, unemployment, and a limited set of job mix indicators (mainly, the share of workers registered with social security), whereas we offer a greater detail in terms of job mix and sectors. In terms of the period under study, we cover the whole decade of 2000, starting in 2000 up to 2012–13, but our analysis is not limited to the whole period only: we include the domestic economic crises that some of the countries suffered at the beginning of the 2000s, and we also study the generalized crisis that followed the Great Recession of 2008–9. Finally, while we present a cross-country analysis of broad patterns for the whole region, our multi-country analysis is based on a consistent and systematic review of the experience of each one of the sixteen countries in our sample.

1.4 Main Questions and Major Findings

This section proceeds in two stages: first, the principal questions asked, and second, our major findings.

Some of our questions about the growth–employment–poverty nexus in Latin America are on a country-by-country basis. If a country grows faster, what is the effect on the employment and earnings indicators and on poverty and inequality indicators? What is the relationship between employment and earnings indicators and poverty rates? How did earnings change over all deciles of each country's income distribution during the 2000s?

We also ask a set of cross-country questions. Do those countries that grew faster have larger and more widespread improvements in labour market conditions and consequently larger reductions in poverty? How tight is this cross-country relationship? To the extent that substantial variance is left unexplained by countries' rates of economic growth alone, what other factors might be responsible for improving labour market indicators? The other factors examined include initial GDP, the initial value of the labour market indicators, and a list of selected macroeconomic variables: agriculture as a percentage of GDP, industry as a percentage of GDP, services as a percentage of GDP, final consumption expenditure as a percentage of GDP, expenditure in education and health as a percentage of GDP, expenditure in social security as a percentage of GDP, terms of trade, foreign investments as a percentage of GDP, revenues from natural resources as a percentage of GDP, and stock of public debt as a percentage of GDP. Other questions we ask in this study are: are labour market indicators moving together—improving or worsening? Do those countries that enjoyed larger and more widespread improvements in labour market conditions have larger reductions in poverty? Regarding the economic crisis of 2008, how did labour market indicators change during the crisis and its aftermath in Latin America?

We turn now to the findings. Looking first at a comparison between each country's initial household survey (typically the year 2000) and the final year (typically 2012), we find remarkable progress in all three aspects of the growth–employment–poverty nexus:

Growth: National income accounts reveal that all sixteen countries achieved positive rates of growth of real GDP per capita. These annualized rates ranged from just below 1 per cent in the case of Mexico to 5.6 per cent in the case of Panama and Peru. The regional average (unweighted) for the sixteen Latin American countries was just under 3 per cent, well above the annualized rate of growth of GDP per capita in OECD countries, which was 1.0 per cent.

Labour market indicators: The rate of improvement in labour market indicators in Latin America was exceptional. All sixteen of the labour market indicators used in this study improved in Bolivia, Brazil, and Peru, fifteen of the sixteen improved in Panama, and the majority of the labour market indicators improved in all of the other countries except for one (Honduras).

Poverty rates: Using the 4 dollars-a-day poverty line ('poverty') and the 2.5 dollars-a-day poverty line ('extreme poverty'), we find reduced rates of poverty and extreme poverty in fifteen of the sixteen countries. Once again, Honduras was the only Latin American country to have registered an increase in its rate of poverty.

In short, the 2000s were a time of strong improvement in the growth–employment–poverty nexus in Latin America. The only exception to this pattern was Honduras, which was simultaneously affected by the international crisis and episodes of political instability that led to most of the deteriorations observed by the end of the period.

Of course, like the rest of the world, Latin America suffered from the global economic crisis of 2008. However, the downturns in Latin America were milder and more short-lived. Real GDP per capita in Latin America fell at a 1.5 per cent annual rate in 2008–9, but then grew at a near 3 per cent annual rate from 2009 to 2012. In the labour market, most countries in the region suffered a deterioration in at least some labour market indicators as a consequence of the international crisis of 2008, but the negative effects were reversed very quickly in most countries, with the result that nearly all labour market indicators showed improvements in 2012 compared to where they had been in 2008. And both poverty and extreme poverty rates fell monotonically, even during the global economic crisis.

In sum, in the great majority of Latin American countries, economic growth took place and brought about improvements in almost all labour market indicators and consequent reductions in poverty rates. But not all improvements were equal in size or caused by the same things. To understand why some countries progressed more in some dimensions than others, we performed a number of additional analyses, from which we draw the following lessons, detailed below:

- For the region as a whole, real GDP per capita grew during the 2000s, all employment and earnings indicators improved, and poverty and inequality fell.
- Country by country, real GDP per capita grew during the 2000s in all Latin American countries, the great majority of labour market indicators improved in all countries but one, poverty rates using the 2.5 and 4 dollars-a-day poverty lines fell in all countries but one.
- Looking across countries, faster growth was associated with larger improvements in labour markets indicators, but the relationships were not tight.
- Looking across countries, increases in some macroeconomic factors were associated with changes in labour market conditions in Latin America during the 2000s, some of them always in the welfare-improving direction and some others always in the welfare-reducing direction.
- Looking across countries, larger improvements in employment and earnings were associated with larger reductions in poverty.
- Looking at year-by-year changes within countries, when economic growth was faster, employment and earnings indicators and poverty and inequality indicators improved more rapidly, and the faster labour market conditions improved, the faster poverty was reduced. The magnitude of the effect and the pattern over time varied substantially from country to country.
- The patterns of changes in labour market earnings were strongly progressive.

In conclusion, the growth–employment–poverty nexus in Latin America changed much more favourably than was the case in the OECD countries in general and the United States in particular. It would be interesting to know about developing economies in other regions of the world. Such studies define the current research frontier.

1.5 Differences between Latin America and the United States and Other OECD Countries

Contrary to the Latin American experience, during the 2000s, inequality soared in developed countries even in the context of economic growth. Moreover, employment indicators have not yet recovered from the crisis of 2009, and wages at the bottom have not increased. The question that naturally follows is: why was it different in Latin America? We cannot provide an exact answer to this important question, but we explore below three possible interrelated explanations.

First, the rate of economic growth was higher in Latin America than in the OCED countries (including the United States and excluding Chile and Mexico). Between 2000 and 2012, average GDP per capita grew by 35.2 per cent in the Latin American region, a growth rate nearly three times larger than that of developed countries. The corresponding figures for high-income OECD countries and the United States in particular were 12.4 and 10.7 per cent respectively (World Bank 2014). As postulated in our framework, higher economic growth could lead to larger improvements in employment and earnings indicators and expansion of social programmes, and to a subsequent reduction in poverty if the channels relating them are open.

Second, Latin America experienced a different type of economic growth compared to that of the United States and other high-income OECD countries. In particular, South America enjoyed excellent external conditions that not only promoted economic growth but also endowed governments with increased fiscal revenues. This was translated into more stable macroeconomic environments and more resources being devoted to social programmes (such as conditional cash transfers). Countries in Central America did not enjoy these exceptional external conditions, and with the exception of Panama, they had a more mixed experience in terms of the number of labour market indicators that improved. In the United States and high-income OECD countries, economic growth during the same period was based on rapid productivity increases, built mainly on innovation and information technology. This process of economic growth led to job losses for workers in the middle of the wage distribution (see Acemouglu and Autor 2011 for the United States, and Goos, Manning, and Salomons 2010 for evidence on Europe). It also led to stagnant wages for unskilled workers and to increasing wages for high-skilled workers.

Third, political conditions seem to have changed significantly in Latin America. In the words of Roberts (2014: 67):

> Declining levels of inequality registered in most Latin American countries during the first decade of the twenty-first century coincided with a basic shift in the political and economic landscape—a shift from the politics of market-based structural adjustment to a new, post-adjustment era in which democratic competition has repoliticized social inequalities and placed redistributive policies at the forefront of the political agenda. Although new Leftist governments have increased the salience of redistributive politics and adopted innovative social welfare reforms, the renewed attention placed on social problems is hardly the exclusive preserve of the left. With heightened electoral competition from the left and

> widespread public sentiments for an active state role in the provision of social welfare, conservative governments have also taken significant steps to address the needs of low-income groups. Consequently, the institutionalization of electoral competition in contexts of egregious social and economic inequalities appears to be producing new forms of democratic accountability, as parties and governments of diverse ideological profiles struggle to respond to popular demands for equity and social inclusion. The historic tensions between universal rights of democratic citizenship and de facto social exclusion continue to exist, but they have clearly given rise to new political expressions and policy outputs in Latin America's post-adjustment era.

Although these ideas are hypotheses and as such difficult to test empirically, there is a widespread consensus that Latin America has advanced towards governments whose redistributive policies play a more important role, at least compared to the previous decade which was marked by widespread structural reforms. One example is that during these years every country in the region implemented or extended social programmes targeting the poor (in most cases, conditional cash transfers). A further sign of the increased importance of redistributive policies is the increase in minimum wages in real terms between 2002 and 2012 in most countries of the region, Mexico and the Dominican Republic being the exceptions.

These three factors are related to each other: high economic growth was possible because of favourable external conditions, which in turn made additional resources available for implementing social programmes.

1.6 Recent Developments

At the time that this research project was launched in 2014, the most recent labour market data available for Latin American countries came from surveys conducted in 2012 and 2013. It was not feasible to include an additional year or years of data and redo all the analysis for each of the countries or for all of them taken together. Nonetheless, it is worth noting some of the latest developments that have taken place in the interim.

Since 2012/13, the rate of economic growth has slowed down for a large number of countries in Latin America, especially those located in South America. Argentina, Brazil, and Venezuela were affected the most (World Bank 2015b). Argentina and Brazil practically did not grow from 2012 to 2014, while Venezuela entered a deep recession: GDP per capita decreased 5.3 per cent during this period. The other South American countries had a less marked deceleration in the rate of economic growth starting in 2013. The average rate of economic growth went from 5.3 per cent during 2012–13 to 2.5 during 2013–14. External conditions changed for these countries.

First, the commodity boom that most of these countries experienced during the first decade of the 2000s either slowed down or reversed after 2010, deteriorating their terms of trade. This affected the private sector, but it also reduced government revenues and increased pressure on government fiscal balances. The latter had not yet recovered from the deficits incurred to finance countercyclical policies during the international crisis of 2009. Projections for 2015 and 2016 indicate that this scenario of low growth is not likely to change (International Monetary Fund 2015). Our framework indicates that labour market conditions are likely to be affected, with a slowdown in the rate of improvement in some dimensions or even some worsenings, contrary to what happened in the first decade of the century. Furthermore, the tight relationship described in this book between improvements in employment conditions and poverty reduction indicates that the rate of poverty reduction is likely to slow down as well. Moreover, it might not be feasible to finance a further expansion of social programmes such as were implemented by most governments in the region in 2009, since the fiscal space has also diminished.

On the other hand, the experience since 2012 has been more positive for countries in Central America (Costa Rica, Dominican Republic, Honduras, Mexico, Panama, and El Salvador). These counties continued to experience rates of economic growth similar to the period 2000–12 (between 2 and 3 per cent a year on average). This process of growth was based on the service sector rather than commodities and on the economic recovery of the United States, which is the main trading partner of these countries. Our framework indicates that this group of countries is likely to continue to improve in terms of labour market indicators in the future at a similar rate as during the period 2000–12.

The post-2012 period seems to be marked by more heterogeneous country experiences than the period 2000–12 analysed in this book. Countries in the South will face the challenge of achieving economic growth without the tailwind of the commodity boom that took place at the beginning of the century. While policies to achieve economic growth are being put into place, the channels to improve employment conditions and social programmes should remain open and be enhanced: it is the only way economic growth will help reduce poverty, the single most important objective these countries can pursue.

1.7 Roadmap

The book is divided into three parts. Part I provides an overview of the project. In the two chapters in this part, the reader will learn about the principal questions, previous literature and our contributions, the analytical framework adopted, overview of the major findings, and data and methodology. Part II presents cross-country analysis across sixteen Latin American countries in the 2000s. This part consists of four textual chapters—'Changing Labour Market Indicators and the Rate of Economic Growth in Latin America during the 2000s', 'Cross-Country Analysis of the Growth–Employment–Poverty Nexus', 'Within-Country Analysis of the Growth–Employment–Poverty Nexus: Additional Evidence', and 'Conclusions from the Cross-Country Analysis'—plus two data chapters. Part III presents sixteen country chapters, each comprising a country study. These country chapters—for Argentina, Bolivia, Brazil, Chile, Colombia, Costa Rica, Dominican Republic, Ecuador, Honduras, Mexico, Panama, Paraguay, Peru, El Salvador, Uruguay, and Venezuela—follow a common format: introduction, economic growth, unemployment, job mix, labour earnings, poverty and inequality, and conclusions.

Overall, the book presents a positive and hopeful set of findings for the period 2000–12/13. Economic growth took place in all sixteen of the countries. The employment and earnings indicators and poverty and inequality indicators used in this study overwhelmingly moved in the welfare-increasing direction: in fifteen of the sixteen countries, most or all of the indicators improved, the only exception being Honduras. Thus, despite Latin America being one of the most unequal regions of the world (together with sub-Saharan Africa), economic growth brought about improvements in employment conditions and thereby reduced poverty.

References

Acemoglu, D. and D. Autor (2011). 'Skills, Tasks and Technologies: Implications for Employment and Earnings', in D. Card and O. Ashenfelter (eds), *Handbook of Labor Economics*. Amsterdam: Elsevier, 1043–171.

Alvaredo, F. and L. Gasparini (2015). 'Recent Trends in Inequality and Poverty in Developing Countries', in A. Atkinson and F. Bourguignon (eds), *Handbook of Income Distribution*. Amsterdam: North-Holland, 697–805.

Beccaria, L., R. Maurizio, A. L. Fernández, P. Monsalvo, and M. Álvarez (2011). 'Dynamics of Poverty, Labor Market and Public Policies in Latin America'. PMMA Working Paper 2011-05. Nairobi: Poverty and Economic Policy Research Network.

Cecchini, S. and A. Madariaga (2011). 'Conditional Cash Transfer Programs: The Recent Experience in Latin America and the Caribbean'. Cuadernos de la CEPAL 95. Santiago de Chile: Economic Commission for Latin America and the Caribbean.

CEDLAS and World Bank (2014). SEDLAC—Socio-Economic Database for Latin American and the Caribbean. Centro de Estudios Distributivos, Laborales y Sociales, Facultad de Ciencias Económicas, Universidad Nacional de La Plata and World Bank Poverty Group LCR. Available at <http://sedlac.econo.unlp.edu.ar/eng/index.php>, accessed 2014.

Cho, Y., D. Margolis, D. Newhouse, and D. Robalino (2012). 'Labor Markets in Low- and Middle-Income Countries: Trends and Implications for Social Protection and Labor Policies'. Social Protection and Labour Discussion Paper 1207. Washington, DC: World Bank.

Cornia, G. A. (ed.) (2014). *Falling Inequality in Latin America: Policy Changes and Lessons*. New York: Oxford University Press.

Cruces, G., G. S. Fields, D. Jaume, and M. Viollaz (2015a). 'The Growth–Employment–Poverty Nexus in Latin America in the 2000s: Argentina Country Study'. WIDER Working Paper 2015/069. Helsinki: UNU-WIDER.

Cruces, G., G. S. Fields, D. Jaume, and M. Viollaz (2015b). 'The Growth–Employment–Poverty Nexus in Latin America in the 2000s: Bolivia Country Study'. WIDER Working Paper 2015/070. Helsinki: UNU-WIDER.

Cruces, G., G. S. Fields, D. Jaume, and M. Viollaz (2015c). 'The Growth–Employment–Poverty Nexus in Latin America in the 2000s: Brazil Country Study'. WIDER Working Paper 2015/071. Helsinki: UNU-WIDER.

Cruces, G., G. S. Fields, D. Jaume, and M. Viollaz (2015d). 'The Growth–Employment–Poverty Nexus in Latin America in the 2000s: Chile Country Study'. WIDER Working Paper 2015/072. Helsinki: UNU-WIDER.

Cruces, G., G. S. Fields, D. Jaume, and M. Viollaz (2015e). 'The Growth–Employment–Poverty Nexus in Latin America in the 2000s: Colombia Country Study'. WIDER Working Paper 2015/073. Helsinki: UNU-WIDER.

Cruces, G., G. S. Fields, D. Jaume, and M. Viollaz (2015f). 'The Growth–Employment–Poverty Nexus in Latin America in the 2000s: Costa Rica Country Study'. WIDER Working Paper 2015/074. Helsinki: UNU-WIDER.

Cruces, G., G. S. Fields, D. Jaume, and M. Viollaz (2015g). 'The Growth–Employment–Poverty Nexus in Latin America in the 2000s: Dominican Republic Country Study'. WIDER Working Paper 2015/075. Helsinki: UNU-WIDER.

Cruces, G., G. S. Fields, D. Jaume, and M. Viollaz (2015h). 'The Growth–Employment–Poverty Nexus in Latin America in the 2000s: Ecuador Country Study'. WIDER Working Paper 2015/076. Helsinki: UNU-WIDER.

Cruces, G., G. S. Fields, D. Jaume, and M. Viollaz (2015i). 'The Growth–Employment–Poverty Nexus in Latin America in the 2000s: El Salvador Country Study'. WIDER Working Paper 2015/077. Helsinki: UNU-WIDER.

Cruces, G., G. S. Fields, D. Jaume, and M. Viollaz (2015j). 'The Growth–Employment–Poverty Nexus in Latin America in the 2000s: Honduras Country Study'. WIDER Working Paper 2015/078. Helsinki: UNU-WIDER.

Cruces, G., G. S. Fields, D. Jaume, and M. Viollaz (2015k). 'The Growth–Employment–Poverty Nexus in Latin America in the 2000s: Mexico Country Study'. WIDER Working Paper 2015/079. Helsinki: UNU-WIDER.

Cruces, G., G. S. Fields, D. Jaume, and M. Viollaz (2015l). 'The Growth–Employment–Poverty Nexus in Latin America in the 2000s: Panama Country Study'. WIDER Working Paper 2015/080. Helsinki: UNU-WIDER.

Cruces, G., G. S. Fields, D. Jaume, and M. Viollaz (2015m). 'The Growth–Employment–Poverty Nexus in Latin America in the 2000s: Paraguay Country Study'. WIDER Working Paper 2015/081. Helsinki: UNU-WIDER.

Cruces, G., G. S. Fields, D. Jaume, and M. Viollaz (2015n). 'The Growth–Employment–Poverty Nexus in Latin America in the 2000s: Peru Country Study'. WIDER Working Paper 2015/082. Helsinki: UNU-WIDER.

Cruces, G., G. S. Fields, D. Jaume, and M. Viollaz (2015o). 'The Growth–Employment–Poverty Nexus in Latin America in the 2000s: Uruguay Country Study'. WIDER Working Paper 2015/083. Helsinki: UNU-WIDER.

Cruces, G., G. S. Fields, D. Jaume, and M. Viollaz (2015p). 'The Growth–Employment–Poverty Nexus in Latin America in the 2000s: Venezuela Country Study'. WIDER Working Paper 2015/084. Helsinki: UNU-WIDER.

Cruces, G., G. S. Fields, D. Jaume, and M. Viollaz (2015q). 'The Growth–Employment–Poverty Nexus in Latin America in the 2000s: Cross-Country Analysis'. WIDER Working Paper 2015/110. Helsinki: UNU-WIDER.

ECLAC (2014). 'Social Panorama of Latin America, 2014'. LC/G 2635-P. Santiago de Chile: Economic Commission for Latin America and the Caribbean.

ECLAC-ILO (2015). 'Employment Situation in Latin America and the Caribbean: Universal Social Protection in Labour Markets with High Levels of Informality'. Report prepared jointly by the Economic Division of the Economic Commission for Latin America and the Caribbean and the Office for the Southern Cone of Latin America of the International Labour Organization. Santiago de Chile.

Fields, G. S. (2012). *Working Hard, Working Poor: A Global Journey*. New York: Oxford University Press.

Fields, G. S. (in press). *Employment and Development*. Oxford: Oxford University Press.

Gasparini, L., S. Galiani, G. Cruces, and P. Acosta (2011). 'Educational Upgrading and Returns to Skills in Latin America: Evidence from a Supply–Demand Framework, 1990–2010'. IZA Working Paper 6244. Bonn: Institute for the Study of Labor.

Gasparini, L. and N. Lustig (2011). 'The Rise and Fall of Income Inequality in Latin America', in J. A. Ocampo and J. Ros (eds), *The Oxford Handbook of Latin American Economics*. Oxford: Oxford University Press, 218–43.

Goos, M., A. Manning, and A. Salomons (2010). 'Globalization and Labour Market Outcomes'. CEP Discussion Paper 1026. London: Center of Economic Performance.

ILO (2014). 'Recent Experiences of Formalization in Latin America and the Caribbean'. Geneva: International Labour Organization, Regional Office for Latin America and the Caribbean.

Inchauste, G., J. P. Azevedo, B. Essama-Nssah, S. Olivieri, T. Van Nguyen, J. Saavedra-Chanduvi, and H. Winkler (2014). 'Understanding Changes in Poverty: Directions in Development'. Washington, DC: World Bank.

International Monetary Fund (2015). World Economic Outlook database. Available at <http://www.imf.org/external/pubs/ft/weo/2014/02/weodata/index.aspx>, accessed November 2015.

López Calva, L. and N. Lustig (2010). *Declining Inequality in Latin America: A Decade of Progress?* Washington, DC: Brookings Institution and UNDP.

OECD (2012). *OECD Employment Outlook 2012*. Paris: OECD Publishing.

OECD (2015). *OECD Employment Outlook 2015*. Paris: OECD Publishing.

Pagés, C., G. Pierre, and S. Scarpetta (2009). *Job Creation in Latin America and the Caribbean: Recent Trends and Policy Challenges*. Basingstoke: Palgrave Macmillan.

Roberts, K. (2014). 'The Politics of Inequality and Redistribution in Latin America's Post-Adjustment Era', in G. A. Cornia (ed.), *Falling Inequality in Latin America: Policy Changes and Lessons*. New York: Oxford University Press, 49–69.

Stampini, M. and L. Tornarolli (2012). 'The Growth of Conditional Cash Transfers in Latin America and the Caribbean: Did They Go Too Far?'. IZA Policy Paper 49. Bonn: Institute for the Study of Labour.

Stiglitz, J. E. (2012). *The Price of Inequality*. New York: W. W. Norton & Company.

Stiglitz, J. E. (2015). *The Great Divide: Unequal Societies and What We Can Do About Them*. New York: W.W. Norton & Company.

Weller, J. (2014). 'Aspects of Recent Developments in the Latin American and Caribbean Labour Markets', *CEPAL Review* 114: 8–28.

World Bank (2013a). 'Jobs'. World Development Report 2013. Washington, DC: World Bank.

World Bank (2013b). 'Shifting Gears to Accelerated Shared Prosperity in Latin America and the Caribbean'. Document of the World Bank 78507. Washington, DC: World Bank.

World Bank (2014). World Development Indicators. Available at <http://data.worldbank.org/data-catalog/world-development-indicators>, accessed April 2014.

World Bank (2015a). 'Working to End Poverty in Latin America and the Caribbean: Workers, Jobs, and Wages'. Document of the World Bank. Washington, DC: World Bank.

World Bank (2015b). World Development Indicators. Available at <http://data.worldbank.org/data-catalog/world-development-indicators>, accessed November 2015.

2

Data and Methodology

2.1 Data Sources

This study is based on microeconomic data from more than 150 household surveys, five million households, and eighteen million persons contained in the SEDLAC—Socio-Economic Database for Latin America and the Caribbean (CEDLAS and World Bank 2014). These data cover the following sixteen Latin American countries: Argentina, Bolivia, Brazil, Chile, Colombia, Costa Rica, Dominican Republic, Ecuador, El Salvador, Honduras, Mexico, Panama, Paraguay, Peru, Uruguay, and Venezuela. Based on these household surveys and the SEDLAC harmonization methodology, we constructed comparable time series for a wide range of labour market, poverty, and income inequality indicators. In Chapters 3–4, we focus mainly on the changes from the initial to the final year in the period under study, listed for each country in Table 2.1. We present the indicators' time series for each country in Appendix 1. For some countries, the period under study in this cross-country paper differs from the time period analysed in the corresponding country papers. The reason for using a different time period is the lack of comparability between the initial and final-year surveys. That was the case for Costa Rica, where we used 2000–9 as the period of analysis for all the labour market and income inequality indicators in this paper. For other countries, we used a different time period only for some particular indicators. Appendix 1 indicates with a vertical line when the country changed a classification so that it is not possible to use a consistent definition throughout the full time period.

In this book, we also employ aggregate macroeconomic indicators from two sources: the World Bank's World Development Indicators (World Bank 2014) and the United Nations Economic Commission for Latin America and the Caribbean's database on social expenditure (UN-ECLAC 2015).

Table 2.1 Latin American household surveys and period under study by country

Country	Isocode (two digits)	Initial year	Final year	Name of household survey
Argentina	AR	2000	2012	Encuesta Permanente de Hogares (2000–2) Encuesta Permanente de Hogares-Continua (2003–12)
Bolivia	BO	2000	2012	Encuesta de Hogares—MECOVI
Brazil	BR	2001	2012	Pesquisa Nacional por Amostra de Domicilios
Chile	CL	2000	2011	Encuesta de Caracterización Socioeconómica Nacional
Colombia	CO	2002	2013	Encuesta Continua de Hogares (2000–5) Gran Encuesta Integrada de Hogares (2008–13)
Costa Rica	CR	2001	2009	Encuesta de Hogares de Propósitos Múltiples
Dominican Republic	DO	2000	2012	Encuesta Nacional de Fuerza de Trabajo
Ecuador	EC	2003	2012	Encuesta de Empleo, Desempleo y Subempleo
Honduras	HN	2001	2012	Encuesta Permanente de Hogares de Propósitos Múltiples
Mexico	MX	2000	2012	Encuesta Nacional de Ingresos y Gastos de los Hogares
Panama	PA	2001	2012	Encuesta de Hogares
Peru	PE	2003	2012	Encuesta Nacional de Hogares
Paraguay	PY	2001	2013	Encuesta Integrada de Hogares (2001) Encuesta Permanente de Hogares (2002–13)
El Salvador	SV	2000	2012	Encuesta de Hogares de Propósitos Múltiples
Uruguay	UY	2000	2012	Encuesta Continua de Hogares
Venezuela	VE	2000	2012	Encuesta de Hogares Por Muestreo

Note: Venezuela's surveys over 2000–6 are part of SEDLAC. From 2007 onwards, we carried out our own processing.
Source: SEDLAC (CEDLAS and World Bank 2014).

2.2 Labour Market Indicators

The main purposes of the analysis are to determine whether each labour market indicator has improved or deteriorated over time on a country-by-country and cross-country basis, and what are the determinants and correlates of these changes. We use, in total, sixteen labour market indicators which we assign to one of two different categories: employment and earnings indicators, and poverty and income inequality indicators. For the employment and earnings indicators, we judge a welfare improvement to have taken place if we find:

Unemployment:

- A decrease in the unemployment rate.

Occupational composition:

- A decrease in the share of low-earnings occupations.
- An increase in the share of high-earnings occupations.[1]

[1] The residual category is the share of medium-earning occupations.

- An increase in the share of wage/salaried employees.
- A decrease in the share of self-employment.
- A decrease in the share of unpaid family workers.[2]
- A decrease in the share of workers in low-earnings sectors.
- An increase in the share of workers in high-earnings sectors.[3]
- A decrease in the share of workers with low levels of education.
- An increase in the share of workers with high levels of education.[4]
- An increase in the share of workers registered with the social security system.

Labour earnings:

- An increase in mean labour earnings.

For the poverty and income inequality indicators, we judge a welfare improvement to have taken place if we find:

Poverty and inequality:

- A decrease in the 4 dollars-a-day poverty rate.
- A decrease in the 2.5 dollars-a-day poverty rate.
- A decrease in Gini coefficient of household per capita income.
- A decrease in Gini coefficient of labour income.

More specifically, these indicators are defined as follows.

The unemployment indicator is defined following the ILO guidelines: it represents the share of unemployed persons divided by the number of persons in the labour force. A person is unemployed if s/he is 15 years old or more and during the reference period (usually one month, but it depends on the survey of each country), s/he was without work, available for work, and seeking work. A fall in the unemployment rate is classified as an improvement in the labour market.

Occupational groups are defined by means of a two-step process. First, for each country, we identify the following occupational categories:[5] management; professionals; technicians and associate professionals; clerical; service and sales workers; agricultural, forestry, and fishery workers; craft and related trades workers; plant and machine operators and assemblers; elementary and armed forces. Second, we classify them into low-earnings, medium-earnings, and high-earnings occupations. For each country, the low-earnings occupations are defined as the three occupational categories with the lowest mean earnings

[2] The residual category is the share of employers.

[3] The residual category is the share of medium-earning sectors.

[4] The residual category is the share of medium-educated workers.

[5] This is the International Standard Classification of Occupations of 2008 (ISCO-08) at a one-digit level. In the case of Argentina, this classification cannot be obtained from household survey data. Argentina is then excluded from the analysis of changes in the occupational composition of the employed population.

during the analysed period, the high-earnings occupational categories are the three occupations with the highest mean incomes, and the rest are classified as medium-earnings occupations. A fall in the share of low-earnings occupations and an increase in the share of high-earnings occupations imply an improvement in the labour market.

Occupational position is classified into four categories: employer, wage/salaried employee, self-employed, and unpaid worker. Given the nature of labour markets in Latin America, the analysis of the employment structure according to occupational positions identifies as improvements in the labour market the following situations: a decrease of self-employment, a decrease in the share of unpaid family workers, and an increase in the share of wage/salaried employees.

Sector of employment is also classified by means of a two-step procedure. We first identify ten sectors: primary activities; low-tech industry; high-tech industry;[6] construction; commerce; utilities and transportation; skilled services; public administration; education and health; and domestic workers. We further classify the sectors according to the shares of workers in low-, medium-, and high-earnings sectors, using the same criteria as in the case of the occupational groups. An increase in the share of high-earnings sectors and a decrease in the share of low-earnings sectors represent improvements in the labour market in our analysis.

With respect to the educational level of employed workers, we define three categories for the analysis: low (eight years of schooling or less); medium (from nine to thirteen years of schooling); and high (more than thirteen years of schooling). An increase in the education of the employed population is considered an improvement in the labour market, as the share of workers that are expected to receive high levels of earnings increases and the share of workers with low earnings levels decreases.

We also classify the employed population according to whether they are registered with the social security system or not. In some of the countries, only wage and salaried employees are asked about registration in the social security system. We assume that it is better for employed workers to be registered, and thus an increase in this indicator is classified as an improvement in the labour market.

Labour earnings are expressed on a monthly basis in 2005 purchasing power parity (PPP) dollars. Higher earnings represent an improvement in the labour market.

Poverty and inequality are calculated as follows. Poverty rates are based on the international poverty lines of 4 dollars a day and 2.5 dollars a day (all in

[6] For Bolivia and Paraguay, we cannot distinguish between low- and high-tech industries.

PPP dollars), and represent the poverty and extreme poverty levels respectively, often used in Latin America. These poverty indicators are based on household income per capita. Household income is the sum of labour income plus non-labour income, which includes capital income, pensions, public and private transfers, and the imputed rent from own-housing. Income inequality is calculated using the Gini coefficient of household per capita income and of labour earnings among employed workers. Some caveats should be stated regarding the use of household surveys to calculate inequality indices as the Gini coefficient. Household surveys suffer from non-response to income questions, underreporting of incomes, and lack of coverage of very high incomes. All these problems may have impacts on calculated inequality levels and trends. In this book we use income variables from SEDLAC databases which are based on 'raw data' from household surveys, without applying any adjustment or correction procedure.

To sum up, changes in labour market indicators in Latin American countries during the 2000s are evaluated using the following criteria. Improvements in labour market conditions are associated with: a decrease in unemployment; increases in the shares of high-earnings occupations, wage/salaried employees, workers in high-earnings sectors, and workers with high levels of education; an increase in monthly labour earnings; declines in the shares of low-paid occupations, unpaid family workers, self-employed, low-earnings sectors, and workers with low levels of education; and declines in poverty rates and inequality indicators. Worsenings in labour market conditions are associated with changes in labour indicators in the opposite direction.

2.3 Macroeconomic Indicators

We also use data on macroeconomic variables to correlate them to the changes in labour market indicators described in section 2.2. These data come from two sources. First, from the World Bank's World Development Indicators (WDI), we use: GDP per capita in the initial year; agriculture as a percentage of GDP; industry as percentage of GDP; services as a percentage of GDP; final consumption expenditure as a percentage of GDP; exports as a percentage of GDP; terms of trade; foreign direct investment as a percentage of GDP; and revenues from natural resources as a percentage of GDP. Second, from the United Nations Economic Commission for Latin America and the Caribbean (UN-ECLAC 2015) database on social expenditure, we use: expenditure in education and health as a percentage of GDP; public expenditure in social security as a percentage of GDP; and stock of public debt as a percentage of GDP. For all macroeconomic variables with the exception of GDP per capita in the initial year, we use data on the initial and final years and calculate the annualized change.

2.4 Variables and Notations

We denote each of the K labour market indicators as Y_k and each of the j macroeconomic variables as X_j. In the following analysis, we will use this notation:

X_{ijt}: Macroeconomic variable k for country i at time t.
Y_{ikt}: Labour market indicator k for country i at time t.
$\%\Delta X_{ij}$: Annualized percentage change of macroeconomic variable j for country i from initial to final year.
ΔX_{ij}: Annualized change in percentage points of macroeconomic variable j for country i from initial to final year.
$\%\Delta Y_{ik}$: Annualized percentage change of labour market indicator k for country i from initial to final year.
ΔY_{ik}: Annualized change in percentage points in labour market indicator k for country i from initial to final year.
Z_i : Percentage of labour market indicators that improved for country i from initial to final year.

Note that the operator $\%\Delta$ embodies an annualized percentage change. We calculate annualized percentage changes for GDP per capita, labour earnings, Gini coefficients, and terms of trade. For the rest of the indicators, the operator Δ is used, indicating annualized changes in percentage points. For example, annualized changes in percentage points include the change in unemployment, in the share of workers registered with the social security system, or in industry's share of GDP.

We calculate these changes as follows. Let initial year be t_0 and final year be t_1. Then:

$$
\begin{aligned}
\%\Delta X_{ij} &= \left[\left(\frac{X_{ijt_1}}{X_{ijt_0}}\right)^{1/(t_1-t_0)} - 1\right] * 100, \\
\%\Delta Y_{ik} &= \left[\left(\frac{Y_{ikt_1}}{Y_{ikt_0}}\right)^{1/(t_1-t_0)} - 1\right] * 100, \\
\Delta X_{ij} &= \left(\frac{X_{ijt_1} - X_{ijt_0}}{t_1 - t_0}\right), \\
\Delta Y_{ik} &= \left(\frac{Y_{ikt_1} - Y_{ikt_0}}{t_1 - t_0}\right). \qquad (1)
\end{aligned}
$$

As a way to summarize the evolution of the large number of indicators covered in each country study, we devised a measure Z_i based on the percentage of the available labour market indicators for each country over the period under study which exhibited a statistically significant improvement at the 5 per cent level.[7] We express Z_i as a percentage instead of the actual number of indicators that increased because not all indicators are available for all countries in every year. This measure provides a general direction of change in the labour market. The costs of this simple synthetic index are that it implicitly assigns an equal weight to each indicator, and it does not take into account the magnitude of the changes (only if the change was statistically significant or not). Nonetheless, this index provides a handy summary indicator of labour market improvements in each country, and so we make extensive use of it in the analysis that follows.

2.5 A Note on Causality versus Correlation

The change in a macroeconomic variable j (ΔX_j or $\%\Delta X_j$) and the change in a labour market indicator k (ΔY_k or $\%\Delta Y_k$) may be associated with each other either because ΔX_j causes ΔY_k or because the two of them are caused by a third factor. An example of ΔX_j causing ΔY_k would be a situation in which a shock in terms of trade brings about an increase in the demand for labour and in mean labour earnings. An example of ΔX_j and ΔY_k being caused by a third factor would be a situation in which training more workers in occupations where shortages exist results in higher exports and an improvement in employment composition in favour of high-earnings occupations.

We implicitly assume throughout the analysis that there is not reverse causation: that is, that changes in labour market indicators do not affect macroeconomic variables (or at least not directly). It is a judgement call whether to make causal interpretations or to be more cautious and choose wording in terms of correlations between variables, and we have done some of each.

References

CEDLAS and World Bank (2014). SEDLAC—Socio-Economic Database for Latin America and the Caribbean. Centro de Estudios Distributivos, Laborales y Sociales, Facultad de Ciencias Económicas, Universidad Nacional de La Plata and World Bank Poverty Group LCR. Available at <http://sedlac.econo.unlp.edu.ar/eng/index.php>, accessed 2014.

[7] The significance of changes is computed as a mean difference test between the initial and the final year for each country in the sample.

UN-ECLAC (2015). CEPALSTAT, United Nations, Economic Commission for Latin America and the Caribbean. Available at <http://estadisticas.cepal.org/cepalstat/WEB_CEPALSTAT/Portada.asp?idioma=i>, accessed April 2015.

World Bank (2014). World Development Indicators. Available at <http://data.worldbank.org/data-catalog/world-development-indicators>, accessed April 2014.

Part II

Cross-Country Analysis

3

Changing Labour Market Indicators and the Rate of Economic Growth in Latin America during the 2000s

3.1 Economic Growth Rate and Changes in Labour Market Indicators in the Latin American Region as a Whole

The Latin American region exhibited an outstanding performance in terms of GDP per capita growth and improvements in labour market indicators over the 2000s. Figure 3.1 provides the evolution over time of the unweighted average (counting each country with a weight of 1 regardless of the size of its population) of GDP per capita at 2005 PPP, and of each of the sixteen labour market indicators, from 2000 to 2012.

Between 2000 and 2012, average GDP per capita grew by 35.2 per cent in the Latin American region, a growth rate nearly three times larger than in developed countries. The corresponding figures for OECD countries and the United States in particular were 12.4 and 10.7 per cent respectively (World Bank 2014). All employment and earnings indicators improved for the average of the region during the 2000s. Just to mention a few examples, the average unemployment rate across the sixteen countries fell from 8.7 per cent in 2000 to 5.7 per cent in 2012, the share of registered workers increased from 40.2 to 46.9 per cent over the same period, and the share of unpaid family workers in total employment declined from 6.8 to 5.5 per cent. All poverty and income inequality indicators improved as well. The moderate and extreme poverty rates exhibited sharp reductions from 2000 to 2012. The 4 dollars-a-day poverty rate fell from an average of 40.4 per cent in 2000 to 20.4 per cent in 2012, while the 2.5 dollars-a-day poverty rate decreased from 23.9 to 12.8 per cent over the same period. The Gini coefficient of household per capita income decreased from 0.531 in 2000 to 0.477 in 2012 and the Gini coefficient of labour earnings from 0.515 to 0.468.

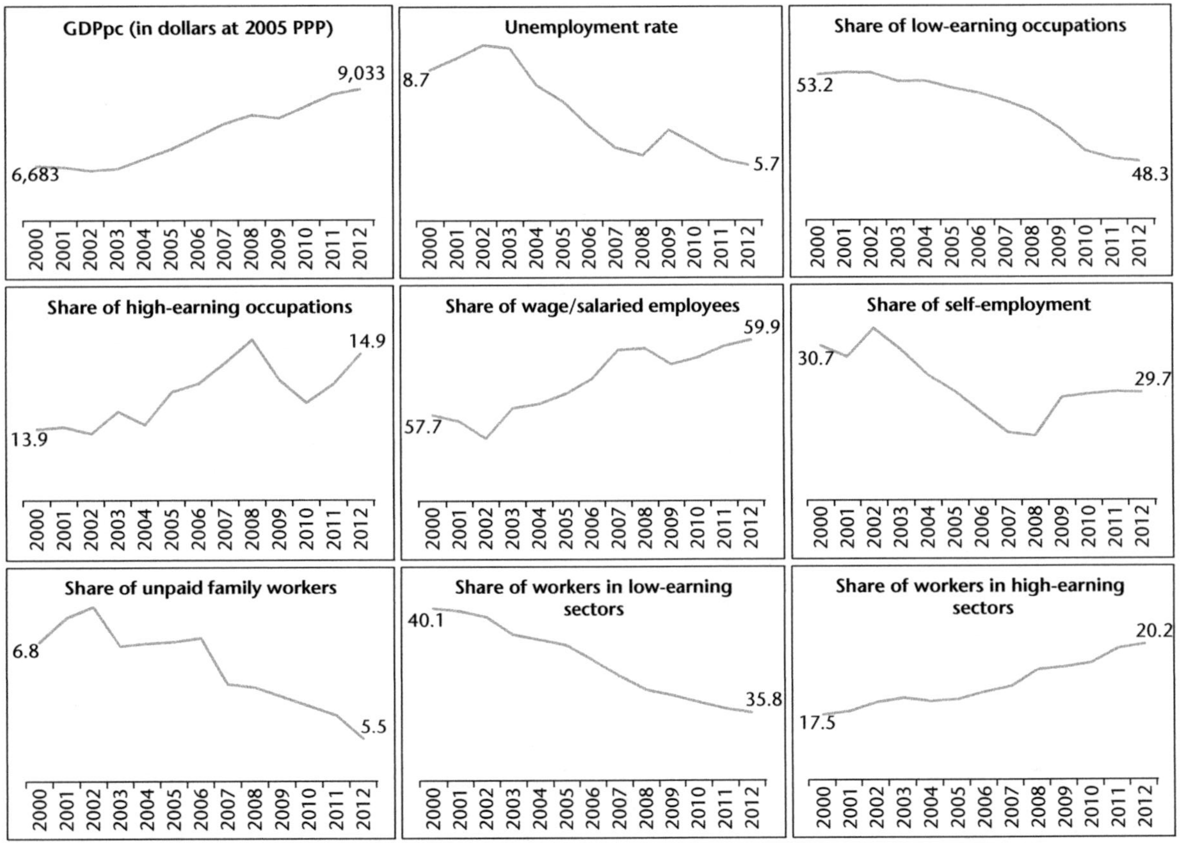

Figure 3.1 Evolution of GDP per capita and labour market indicators in the Latin American region: Unweighted average 2000–12

Note: All series represent the unweighted averages across the sixteen Latin American countries in our sample. In the years when we do not have data for a particular country, we use a linear extrapolation. In the cases where we do not have data for the initial or final year, we impute the value of the following or previous year.

Source: Authors' calculations based on SEDLAC (CEDLAS and World Bank 2014) and World Development Indicators (World Bank 2014).

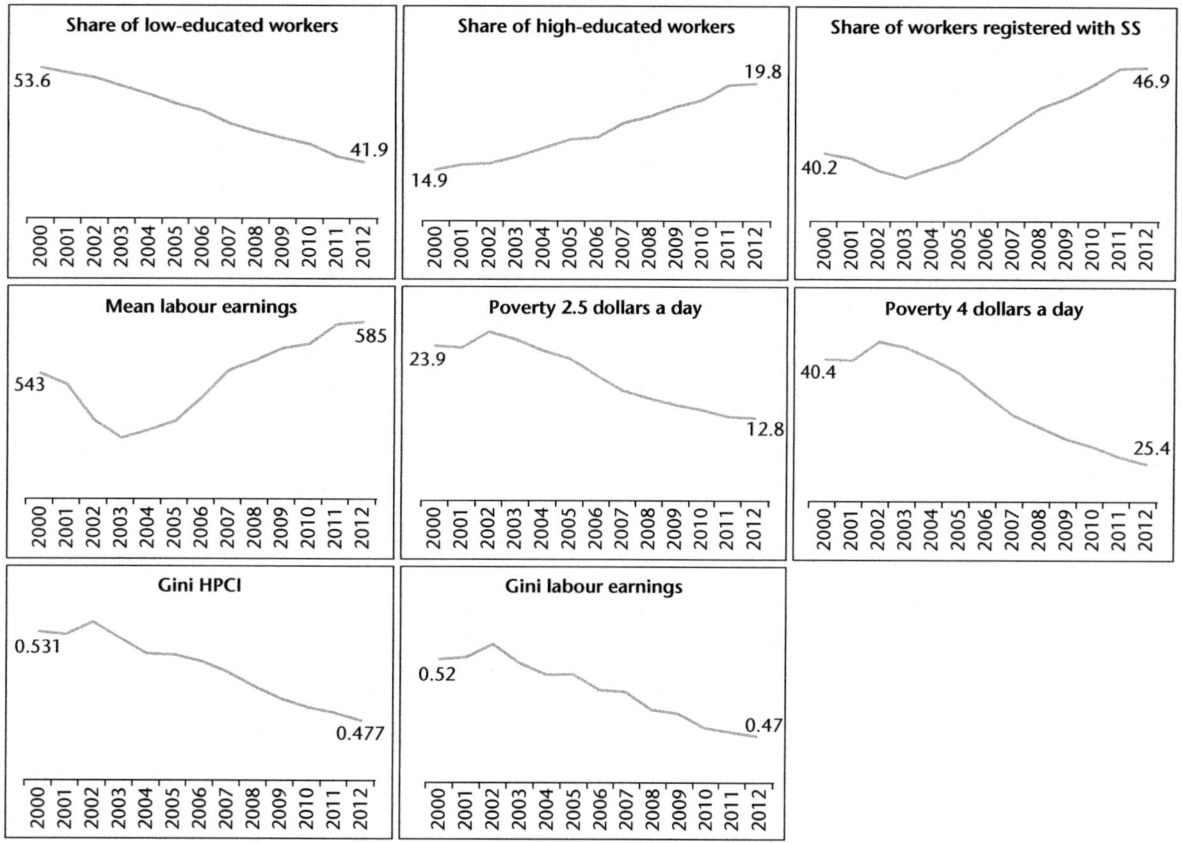

Figure 3.1 Continued

Other studies have also documented these trends. Weller (2014) studies the experience of most countries in Latin America and the Caribbean for the years 2003–12. The author documents the remarkable growth experience of the region, as well as improvements in labour market outcomes over the same period: an important reduction in the unemployment rate; an improvement in employment quality indicators, such as wages, share of workers registered with social security, share of self-employed and wage/salaried employees, sectoral composition of employment, and level of education of employed workers; and a reduction in the wage gap between highly and low-educated workers. The World Bank (2015) report documents similar trends in GDP and labour market indicators (labour earnings, educational level of the workforce, and employment position for the sample of low-educated workers). ECLAC-ILO (2015) also relates the remarkable progress in reducing poverty during 2002–12 in the Latin America region to labour market trends, highlighting the importance of strong job creation (especially in wage/salaried positions) and public policies, such as minimum-wage increases, formalization of workers, and expanding coverage of education and social protection systems.

In summary, from beginning to end in the region as a whole, GDP per capita grew, all employment and earnings indicators improved, and poverty and inequality indicators fell remarkably.

3.2 Economic Growth Rate and Changes in Labour Market Indicators Country by Country

The growth experience during the 2000s was positive for all Latin American countries: all countries in the region experienced an increase in their GDP per capita. Each of the country chapters presents an overview of other studies covering national growth trajectories over this period. Table 3.1 presents annualized growth rates of GDP per capita for each country in our sample for the years for which we have detailed labour market indicators (starting in *c.*2000 and up to *c.*2012). The figures in the table indicate positive growth rates overall, with most countries close to the region's average growth rate of 2.9 per cent per year. However, a small number of countries grew at comparatively modest rates (0.8 per cent per year in Mexico, 1.4 per cent per year in El Salvador, and 1.7 per cent per year in Venezuela), while others experienced particularly large growth rates by Latin American standards (5.6 per cent in both Panama and Peru).

Increases in GDP per capita were accompanied by generalized improvements in labour market indicators over time for most countries in our sample. The rest of this section details these improvements: we succinctly describe the

Table 3.1 Annualized growth rates of GDP per capita (at PPP 2005) for different time periods by country

Country	Initial year	Final year	Annualized growth rate of GDP per capita				
			Initial–final	2000–12	2000–8	2008–9	2009–12
AR	2000	2012	3.57	3.57	3.25	−0.03	4.22
BO	2000	2012	2.24	2.24	1.98	1.71	2.33
BR	2001	2012	2.41	2.20	2.42	−1.22	2.07
CL	2000	2011	2.96	3.10	3.13	−1.97	3.55
CO	2002	2013	3.18	2.76	2.79	0.21	2.63
CR	2001	2009	2.92	2.69	3.11	−2.49	2.49
DO	2000	2012	3.62	3.62	3.68	2.05	2.99
EC	2003	2012	2.96	2.63	2.74	−1.10	2.68
HN	2001	2012	2.14	2.01	2.94	−4.36	1.30
MX	2000	2012	0.85	0.85	0.92	−5.89	2.23
PA	2001	2012	5.59	5.12	4.50	2.06	5.81
PE	2003	2012	5.56	4.58	4.63	−0.15	4.51
PY	2001	2013	2.40	1.22	1.29	−5.65	2.56
SV	2000	2012	1.45	1.45	2.19	−3.63	0.91
UY	2000	2012	3.13	3.13	2.19	1.89	4.53
VE	2000	2012	1.67	1.67	2.71	−4.77	0.85
Average			**2.92**	**2.68**	**2.78**	**−1.46**	**2.85**

Note: The column Initial–Final shows the annualized growth rate for the period we have household surveys data available for each country. The following columns provide the annualized growth rate for comparable periods across countries.
Source: Authors' calculations based on World Development Indicators (World Bank 2014).

evolution of each of the sixteen labour market indicators in each country. We do so in two ways, first by presenting the changes in the indicators one by one ($\%\Delta Y_{ik}$ or ΔY_{ik}, i=*AR, BO,...,VE* and k=*1,...,16*) and then by aggregating them into an index Z_i.

Table 3.2 presents the qualitative changes over time in each of the sixteen selected labour market indicators for each country. We define these changes so that a positive value always signifies a welfare improvement (e.g. decrease in unemployment rate instead of change in the unemployment rate). The '+' sign in a cell indicates that for that indicator and country, there was a change in the welfare-improving direction from the first survey year to the last and this change was statistically significant at the 5 per cent level. The '−' sign indicates the opposite, that is, the labour market indicator changed in the welfare-worsening direction for that country over the years under study, and that change was statistically significant at the 5 per cent level. Finally, the 'NC' in a cell refers to no statistically significant change.

Figure 3.2, in turn, depicts the evolution over time for each specific labour market indicator in each country. Here, the data are presented untransformed, so that for example the unemployment rate in Argentina first rose and then fell, ending up much lower at the end of the period than at the beginning.

Table 3.2 Qualitative changes in labour market indicators from initial to final year by country

Indicator	AR	BO	BR	CL	CO	CR	DO	EC	HN	MX	PA	PE	PY	SV	UY	VE
Unemployment																
Decrease in the unemployment rate	+	+	+	+	+	–	*NC*	+	+	–	+	+	+	+	+	+
Occupations																
Decrease in the share of low-earnings occupations		+	+	–	+	+	–	+	*NC*	+	+	+	+	+	+	+
Increase in the share of high-earnings occupations		+	+	+	+	+	+	+	*NC*	+	+	+	*NC*	–	+	+
Occupational position																
Increase in the share of wage/salaried employees	+	+	+	+	–	+	–	–	–	+	+	+	+	*NC*	+	+
Decrease in the share of self-employment	+	+	+	*NC*	–	+	–	–	*NC*	–	+	+	+	+	+	*NC*
Decrease in the share of unpaid family workers	+	+	+	+	*NC*	+	*NC*	*NC*	–	+	*NC*	+	+	–	+	+
Economic Sector																
Decrease in the share of workers in low-earnings sectors	*NC*	+	+	–	–	+	+	+	–	+	+	+	+	+	+	+
Increase in the share of workers in high-earnings sectors	+	+	+	+	+	+	+	+	*NC*	+	+	+	+	*NC*	*NC*	+
Education																
Decrease in the share of low-educated workers	+	+	+	+	+	+	+	+	+	+	+	+	+	+	+	+
Increase in the share of high-educated workers	+	+	+	+	+	+	+	+	+	+	+	+	+	+	+	+
Workers registered with SS																
Increase in the share of workers registered with SS	+	+	+	+	+	+	+	+	–	–	+	+	+	–	+	*NC*
Earnings																
Increase in mean labour earnings	+	+	+	+	+	+	–	+	–	–	+	+	+	–	–	+
Poverty																
Decrease in 4 dollars-a-day poverty	+	+	+	+	+	+	+	+	–	+	+	+	+	+	+	+
Decrease in 2.5 dollars-a-day poverty	+	+	+	+	+	+	+	+	–	+	+	+	+	+	+	+
Inequality																
Decrease in GINI of household per capita income	+	+	+	+	+	*NC*	+	+	–	+	+	+	+	+	+	+
Decrease in GINI of labour earnings	+	+	+	+	+	*NC*	+	+	–	+	+	+	+	+	+	+
Number of improving indicators	*13*	*16*	*16*	*13*	*12*	*13*	*10*	*13*	*3*	*12*	*15*	*16*	*15*	*10*	*14*	*14*
Total number of indicators	*14*	16	16	16	16	16	16	16	16	16	16	16	16	16	16	16
% of improving indicators	*93*	*100*	*100*	*81*	*75*	*81*	*63*	*81*	*19*	*75*	*94*	*100*	*94*	*63*	*88*	*88*

Note: The table summarizes the changes in each labour market indicator from initial to final year of the period indicated in Table 3.1, except for some countries where the classification of occupations and/or the definition of registered workers are not comparable over the entire period. See each country chapter for more details. References: + denotes improvement; – denotes worsening; NC denotes no changes. All the improvements and worsenings are statistically significant at 5 per cent level.

Source: Authors' calculations based on SEDLAC (CEDLAS and World Bank 2014).

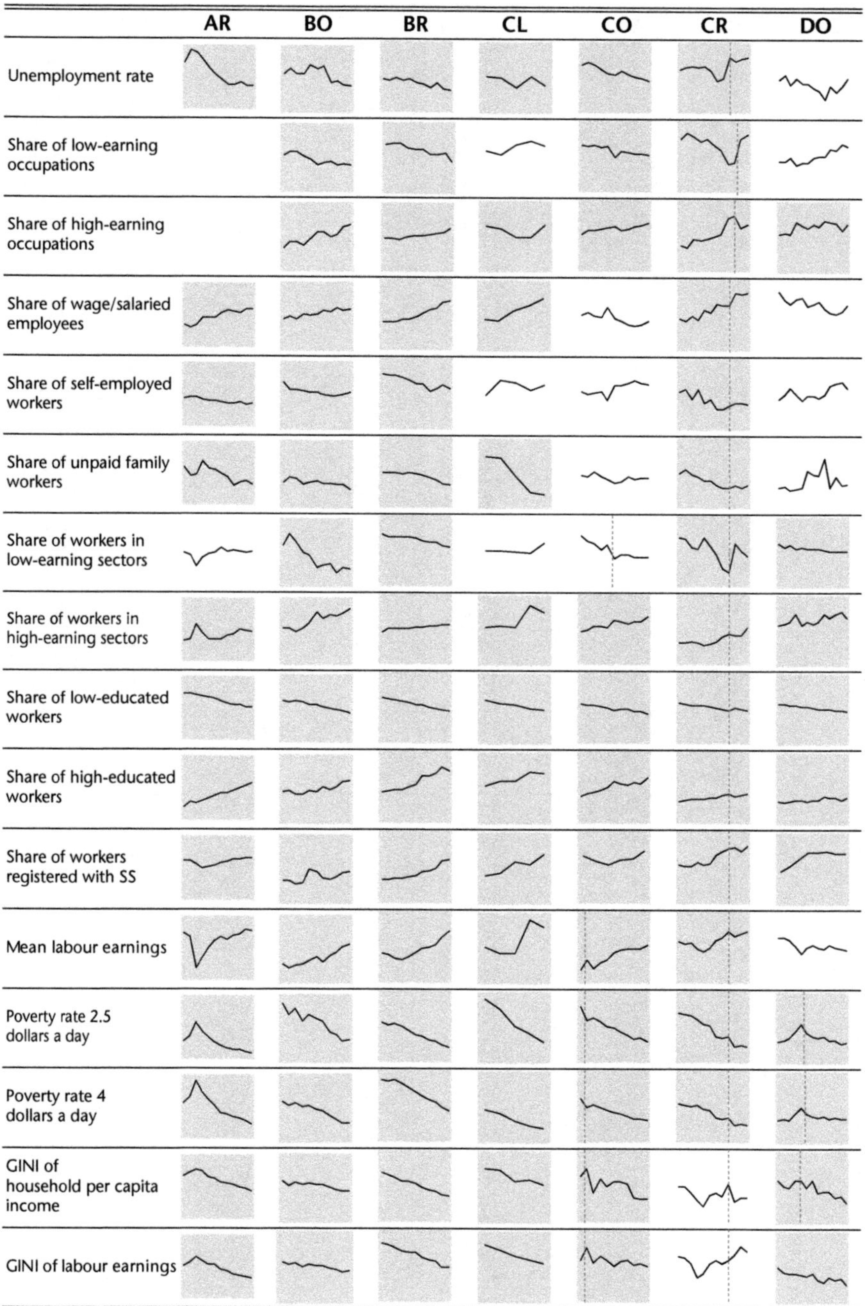

Figure 3.2 Evolution of labour market indicators over time by country

Note: Shaded figures indicate that there was an improvement from initial to final year that was statistically significant at 5 per cent level. Vertical lines indicate that the series to the left and the right are not fully comparable. In these cases, the shadow corresponds to the larger comparable period for each indicator–country cell.

Source: Authors' calculations based on SEDLAC (CEDLAS and World Bank 2014).

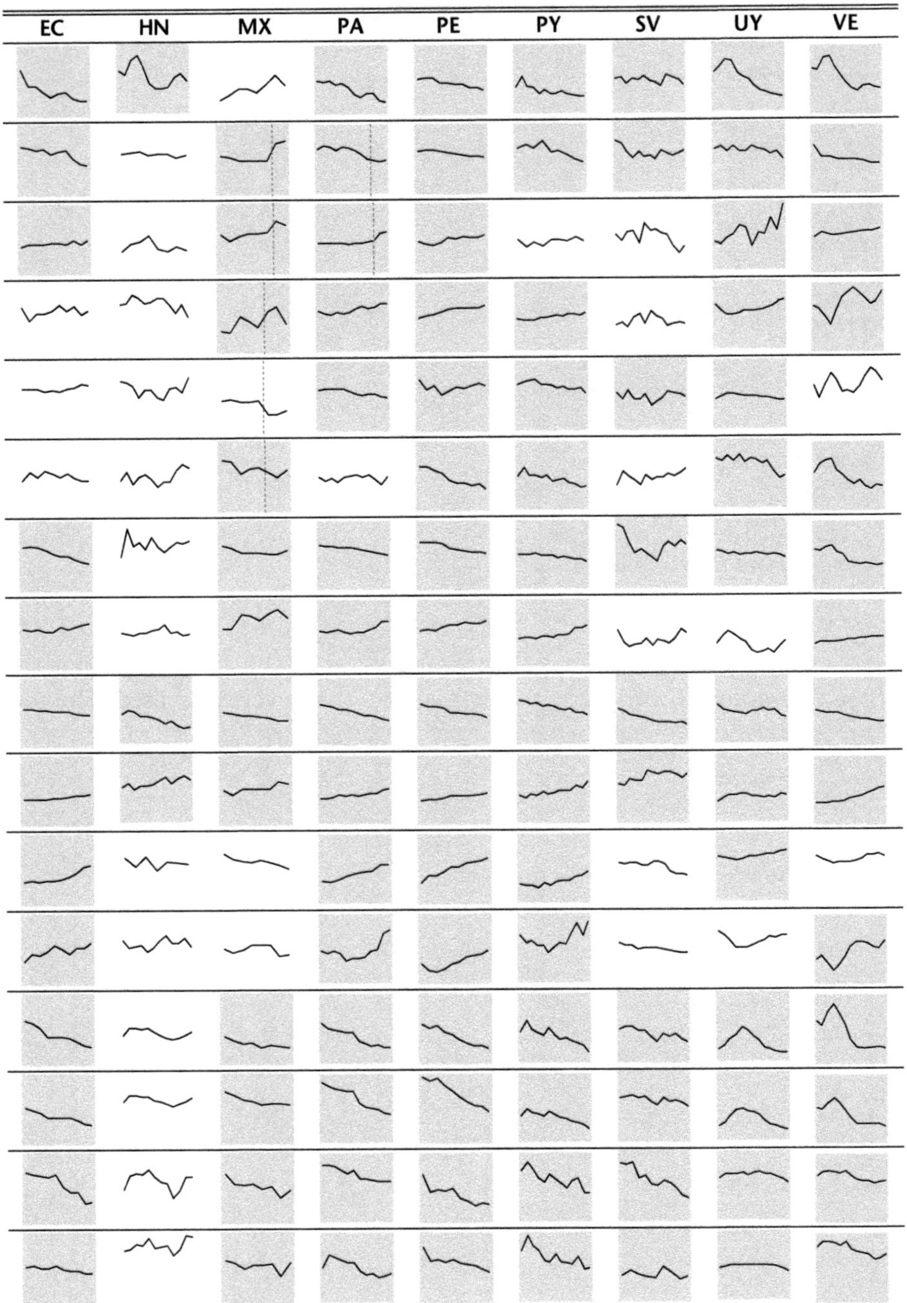

Figure 3.2 Continued

Adding yet further detail, we include the underlying time series to each graph; please see Appendix 1 for country-by-country presentations.

3.2.1 *Analysis of the Labour Market Indicators One by One (Y_k)*

Looking at the employment and earnings indicators, here is how they changed over time.

Unemployment rates fell in most of the countries (thirteen out of sixteen countries over the 2000s); they were Argentina, Bolivia, Brazil, Chile, Colombia, Ecuador, Honduras, Panama, Peru, Paraguay, El Salvador, Uruguay, and Venezuela. However, there were statistically significant increases in unemployment in Costa Rica and Mexico and no significant change in the Dominican Republic.

There was also a generalized improvement in the job mix in most countries in the sample for which these indicators are available (the distributions of workers among occupations, occupational positions, sectors, and educational levels). The most consistent changes in the job mix were the improvement in the educational level of the employed population and in the distribution of employment by economic sector. The educational level of the employed population improved in all countries in the sample: the share of employed workers with low educational levels diminished at the same time that the share of employed workers with high educational levels increased. The sectoral composition of employment improved in thirteen countries (Argentina, Bolivia, Brazil, Costa Rica, Dominican Republic, Ecuador, Mexico, Panama, Peru, Paraguay, El Salvador, Uruguay, and Venezuela): either the share of low-earnings sectors decreased (with no change in the share of high-earnings sectors) or the share of high-earnings sectors increased (with no change in the share of low-earnings sectors) or both. For ten countries (Bolivia, Brazil, Costa Rica, Dominican Republic, Ecuador, Mexico, Panama, Peru, Paraguay, and Venezuela), there was both a decline in the share of low-earnings sectors and an increase in the share of high-earnings sectors. For two countries, only the share of low-earnings sectors improved (El Salvador and Uruguay), and for one country (Argentina), there was only an increase in the share of high-earnings sectors. For the remaining three countries that did not follow the general trend, the changes were ambiguous for Chile and Colombia (where there were increases in both shares), and there was a deterioration for Honduras (there was an increase in the share of low-earnings sectors and no change in the share of high-earnings sectors).

The distribution of employment by occupation improved in eleven countries (Bolivia, Brazil, Colombia, Costa Rica, Ecuador, Mexico, Panama, Peru, Paraguay, Uruguay, and Venezuela): either the share of low-earnings occupations decreased (with no change in the share of high-earnings occupations) or the share of high-earnings occupations increased (with no change in the share of low-earnings occupations) or both. For ten countries (Bolivia, Brazil, Colombia, Costa Rica, Ecuador, Mexico, Panama, Peru, Uruguay, and Venezuela), there was both a decline in the share of low-earnings occupations and an increase in the share of high-earnings occupations. For only one country (Paraguay) did the share of low-earnings occupations decrease with no change in the share of high-earnings occupations. For the remaining four countries, three exhibited a mixed change (Chile, Dominican Republic, and El Salvador), i.e. an improvement in one of the indicators jointly with deterioration in the other one, while in only one country (Honduras) there were no significant changes in the employment composition by occupation during the period.

The distribution of the employed population by occupational position improved significantly in ten countries in our sample (Argentina, Bolivia, Brazil, Chile, Costa Rica, Panama, Peru, Paraguay, Uruguay, and Venezuela): the share of wage/salaried employees increased and the shares of self-employed and unpaid family workers fell or did not change significantly. The distribution by occupational position deteriorated in four countries, with a fall in the share of wage/salaried employees and an increase (or no significant change) in the shares of the self-employed and of unpaid family workers (Colombia, Dominican Republic, Ecuador, and Honduras). The pattern of change was ambiguous for El Salvador, where the change in the share of wage/salaried employees was not statistically significant, the share of the self-employed fell, and that of unpaid family workers increased, and for Mexico where the share of wage/salaried employees increased, the share of unpaid family workers fell, but the share of self-employment grew.

In most of the countries in our sample (twelve out of sixteen countries: Argentina, Bolivia, Brazil, Chile, Colombia, Costa Rica, Dominican Republic, Ecuador, Panama, Peru, Paraguay, and Uruguay), there was also an increase in the share of workers registered with the social security system. The evolution of this indicator, however, was negative in three countries in our sample—the registration of workers fell significantly in Honduras, Mexico, and El Salvador—and we do not observe a statistically significant change for Venezuela.

Average labour earnings increased in eleven out of sixteen countries, although they fell significantly for the remaining five. Increases in labour earnings took place in Argentina, Bolivia, Brazil, Chile, Colombia, Costa Rica, Ecuador, Panama, Peru, Paraguay, and Venezuela, with decreases in labour earnings taking place in the Dominican Republic, Honduras, Mexico, El Salvador, and Uruguay. It should be noted, however, that this indicator evolved differently over time in different countries. For instance, average earnings fell at the beginning of the period under study and then grew steadily in Argentina, Chile, Costa Rica, Panama, Paraguay, Peru, and Uruguay, but the overall change was positive for all except Uruguay. On the other hand, labour earnings grew over most of the period in Bolivia, Brazil, Colombia, and Ecuador, and fell steadily in El Salvador. Finally, labour earnings moved erratically over the period in the Dominican Republic, Honduras, Mexico, and Venezuela.

Turning now to the poverty and income inequality indicators, poverty rates measured by both the 2.5 and 4 dollars-a-day international lines declined in fifteen out of sixteen countries in our sample, with the sole exception of Honduras, where both indicators increased.

The poverty-reducing pattern in the region goes hand-in-hand with the upward trend in labour earnings and with the reduction in the unemployment rate in most countries. Interestingly, the reduction in poverty indicators occurred also in countries where mean labour earnings fell (Dominican Republic, Mexico, El Salvador, and Uruguay) and/or unemployment increased (Costa Rica and Mexico). This finding brings the role of public expenditure in social security systems as a potential factor to explain the reduction in poverty in Latin America. The relationship between changes in public expenditure in social security and in education and health, and changes in poverty indicators is analysed in section 3.4. In the same section, a detailed analysis of the relationship between changes in poverty and changes in employment and earnings indicators is also presented.

Inequality of household per capita income and of labour income fell in fourteen out of sixteen countries in our sample (Argentina, Bolivia, Brazil, Chile, Colombia, Dominican Republic, Ecuador, Mexico, Panama, Peru, Paraguay, El Salvador, Uruguay, and Venezuela). All countries exhibited significant reductions in the Gini coefficient of household per capita income and labour earnings with the exceptions of Costa Rica (where inequality of labour earnings increased and inequality of household per capita income remained unchanged) and Honduras (where both inequality indicators grew). The inequality-reducing pattern that took place in most countries indicates that increases in labour earnings, the main source of income of households in Latin America (as in other parts of the world), were accompanied by welfare-improving inequality changes. In sum, in the 2000s, in most of the countries nearly all labour market indicators improved, Honduras being the exception to this general trend. Unemployment rates fell in the majority of the countries, as did poverty and inequality. The job mix and labour earnings also improved in the great majority of countries.

3.2.2 *Analysis of the Percentage of Labour Market Indicators that Changed in the Welfare-Improving Direction (Z)*

As a way to summarize the evolution of the large number of indicators covered in each country study, we devised a measure based on how many of these indicators exhibited a statistically significant improvement, calculated as a percentage of the available indicators for each country over the period of study.[1] This measure provides a general direction of change in the labour market. The calculations using this measure are presented in the bottom row of Table 3.2. Our results indicate that 75 per cent or more of our selected labour market indicators improved in the following thirteen countries: Argentina, Bolivia, Brazil, Chile, Colombia, Costa Rica, Ecuador, Mexico, Panama, Peru, Paraguay, Uruguay, and Venezuela. Of the remaining countries, 62.5 per cent of indicators improved in the Dominican Republic and El Salvador. Honduras is the only Latin American country that experienced a generalized worsening of labour market indicators (an improvement in only three out of sixteen available indicators).[2]

3.2.3 *Summary*

In sum, our systematic evidence reveals that all countries in the region experienced an increase in their GDP per capita during the 2000s, and nearly all countries experienced substantial improvements over time in most labour market indicators.

3.3 The 2008 Economic Crisis and Changes in Labour Market Indicators

Up to now, we have analysed changes in GDP per capita and labour market indicators between the start of our data series (the year 2000 in most countries) and the end (most commonly, 2012). Of course, this period includes the international crisis of 2008. In this section, we analyse how this crisis affected labour markets in Latin American countries, whether they recovered fully or partially, and how speedy was the recovery (or how long-lasting was the crisis).

Throughout the world, the international economic crisis brought about negative economic growth of greater or lesser severity, followed by recovery. Focusing on a comparison between Latin America and some developed countries, the countries in our study suffered a reduction, on average, of 1.5 per cent in GDP per capita between 2008 and 2009. The average fall for the group of OECD countries was 3.95 per cent in GDP per capita, whereas the loss for the

[1] We express this as a percentage instead of the actual number of indicators that increased because not all indicators are available for all countries in every year.

[2] Most of the worsening changes in Honduras took place during and after the international crisis and coincided with a military coup. See Chapter 16 on Honduras for more details and references.

United States was 3.65 per cent over the same period (World Bank 2014). The OECD countries as a whole and the United States in particular recovered the pre-crisis GDP per capita level in 2012.

The impact of the economic crisis on labour markets was heterogeneous across developed countries. In some European countries, such as Luxembourg, Denmark, and Germany, the effects were short-lived, while in others, such as Spain, Cyprus, Greece, and Ireland, dramatic losses of employment and increases in unemployment rates were observed, and by 2012 data tended to show a reintensification of the negative effects of the crisis (ECB 2012). The United States exhibited larger employment losses compared to Europe despite the similar reduction in GDP. In fact, the unemployment rate more than doubled in the United States during the crisis with a considerable increase in long-term unemployment (Elwell 2013). The increase in the unemployment rate in the United States was long-lived: it recovered its pre-crises level only by 2015 (Bureau of Labour Statistics 2015). Additionally, following the international crisis, labour markets became increasingly polarized with the share of low-earnings occupations increasing by more than the share of high-earnings occupations (Autor and Dorn 2013).

Some recent studies for Latin America have analysed the impact of the Great Recession on growth and labour market outcomes. The World Bank (2015) report documents the fall in GDP and the relative worsening in several labour market indicators from 2008 to 2009, highlighting the difference between the subperiods, 2003–8 and 2008–13. While GDP increased (with the exception of 2008–9) and labour market outcomes improved during both subperiods, leading to reductions in poverty, the impact of improved labour market conditions on poverty was stronger during 2003–8 than during 2008–13. ECLAC-ILO (2015) also documents similar trends, and highlights the role of rising real wages in 2009, which the report considers to have been an important factor in stabilizing domestic demand and in turn fostering the rapid recovery from the impacts of the international crisis.

Our evidence also indicates the same underlying trends in Latin American countries. At the time of negative economic growth in 2008–9 (Table 3.1), GDP per capita fell on average by 1.5 per cent in the region, less than half of the reduction in the OECD countries. The impact of the crisis was heterogeneous across countries in Latin America. Mexico, Paraguay, Venezuela, Honduras, and El Salvador were all severely affected, with reductions in GDP per capita of 4 to 6 per cent. GDP per capita fell by 1 to 3 per cent in Brazil, Chile, Costa Rica, and Ecuador; it virtually remained unchanged in Argentina, Colombia, and Peru, while it still increased by about 2 per cent in Bolivia, the Dominican Republic, Panama, and Uruguay.

After 2008–9, recovery quickly ensued. In the post-crisis period, all countries once again achieved positive economic growth rates and recovered their pre-crisis GDP per capita levels by 2010, two years earlier than most of the OECD countries. Table 3.1 shows that the annualized growth rates in the post-crisis period were positive for all Latin American countries, and for seven of the sixteen countries in our sample, the annualized growth rate in the post-crisis period (2009–12) was larger than in the pre-crisis period (2000–8).

How did labour market indicators change during the crisis and its aftermath in Latin America? As shown above, we know from studies from other regions that labour market indicators worsened and then recovered to a greater or lesser degree.

In Latin America, starting with the crisis period, labour markets in most countries of the region were affected adversely by the international crisis, with a great deal of heterogeneity across countries in the number of labour market indicators that worsened during the crisis. Table 3.3 summarizes the changes in indicators for each country between 2008 and 2009, using again the '+', '–', and 'NC' signs to denote changes in the welfare-improving direction, changes in the welfare-worsening direction, and non-significant changes, as in the previous tables. The most widespread negative change was the increase in the unemployment rate (for twelve out of sixteen countries), followed by a fall in the share of wage/salaried employees (seven out of sixteen countries) and an increase in self-employment (seven out of sixteen countries).

The evidence in Table 3.3 indicates that Colombia and Honduras were the most affected, with negative changes in ten labour market indicators. In Bolivia, Peru, and Uruguay, we do not observe a deterioration in any of the labour market indicators, although they experienced a slowdown in the improving trend in most of them. The rest of the countries suffered a deterioration in at least one labour market indicator during the international crisis, with different degrees of exposure. For instance, in Brazil and Paraguay only the unemployment rate increased substantially, whereas Ecuador and El Salvador experienced negative changes in several other indicators.

Figure 3.3 illustrates the relationship between the percentage of labour market indicators that worsened during the crisis and the change in GDP per capita between 2008 and 2009. There is a negative relationship (reductions in GDP per capita are associated with a larger percentage of indicators moving in the worsening direction), but only marginally significant between the two variables, with an R-squared of only 0.11. The patterns are, again, heterogeneous across countries. The three countries in which labour market indicators were not affected by the crisis (Bolivia, Peru, and Uruguay) experienced positive levels of growth. The Dominican Republic grew at similar rates, but suffered a deterioration of several labour market indicators during the crisis. At the other extreme, the countries with the largest fall in GDP per capita (Panama, Paraguay, and Venezuela) suffered a deterioration in about the same

Table 3.3 Qualitative changes in labour market indicators during the international crisis of 2008 by country

Indicator	AR	BO	BR	CL	CO	CR	DO	EC	HN	MX	PA	PE	PY	SV	UY	VE
Unemployment																
Decrease in the unemployment rate	–	*NC*	–	–	–	–	–	–	*NC*	–	–	*NC*	–	–	+	–
Occupations																
Decrease in the share of low-earnings occupations		+	*NC*	–	–	*NC*	–	–	–		+	+	*NC*	*NC*	+	*NC*
Increase in the share of high-earnings occupations		*NC*	+	+	–	*NC*	*NC*	–	–		+	+	–	*NC*	+	+
Occupational position																
Increase in the share of wage/salaried employees	*NC*	+	+	+	–	*NC*	*NC*	–	–		–	*NC*	–	–	*NC*	–
Decrease in the share of self-employment	–	*NC*	*NC*	*NC*	*NC*	*NC*	–	–	–		–	*NC*	*NC*	–	*NC*	–
Decrease in the share of unpaid family workers	–	+	+	+	–	*NC*	+	–	*NC*		*NC*	*NC*	*NC*	–	*NC*	+
Economic Sector																
Decrease in the share of workers in low-earnings sectors	*NC*	*NC*	*NC*	*NC*	–	*NC*	+	*NC*	–	*NC*	*NC*	+	*NC*	*NC*	+	*NC*
Increase in the share of workers in high-earnings sectors	+	*NC*	*NC*	+	*NC*	*NC*	–	*NC*	–	+	+	+	*NC*	*NC*	*NC*	*NC*
Education																
Decrease in the share of low-educated workers	+	+	+	+	–	+	+	*NC*	–	+	*NC*	*NC*	+	*NC*	+	+
Increase in the share of high-educated workers	+	+	+	+	–	*NC*	–	*NC*	–	+	*NC*	*NC*	*NC*	*NC*	+	+
Workers registered with SS																
Increase in the share of workers registered with SS	+	*NC*	+	–	–	*NC*	+	*NC*	–	–	+	+	*NC*	–	+	+
Earnings																
Increase in mean labour earnings	+	*NC*	+	+	+	+	+	–	–	–	*NC*	+	*NC*	*NC*	+	–
Poverty																
Decrease in 4 dollars-a-day poverty	*NC*	+	+	+	+	–	+	–	+	–	+	+	–	+	+	–
Decrease in 2.5 dollars-a-day poverty	+	+	+	+	+	*NC*	+	+	+	–	+	+	+	+	+	*NC*

(*continued*)

Table 3.3 Continued

Indicator	AR	BO	BR	CL	CO	CR	DO	EC	HN	MX	PA	PE	PY	SV	UY	VE
Inequality																
Decrease in GINI of household per capita income	+	+	*NC*	*NC*	*NC*	–	*NC*	+	+	+	*NC*	*NC*	+	+	*NC*	*NC*
Decrease in GINI of labour earnings	*NC*	+	*NC*	+	–	*NC*	*NC*	+	+	+	*NC*	*NC*	+	*NC*	+	+
Number of worsening indicators	***3***	***0***	***1***	***3***	***10***	***3***	***5***	***8***	***10***	***5***	***3***	***0***	***4***	***5***	***0***	***5***
Total number of indicators	***14***	**16**	**16**	**16**	**16**	**16**	**16**	**16**	**16**	**11**	**16**	**16**	**16**	**16**	**16**	**16**
% of worsening indicators	***21.4***	***0.0***	***6.3***	***18.8***	***62.5***	***18.8***	***31.3***	***50.0***	***62.5***	***45.5***	***18.8***	***0.0***	***25.0***	***31.3***	***0.0***	***31.3***

Note: The table summarizes the changes in each labour market indicator during 2008–9 except for Chile (2006–9) and Mexico (2006–10). In the case of Chile, there is no household survey in between the years 2006 and 2009. Mexico was already in recession in the year 2008, so we considered 2006 as the base year (there was no survey in 2007).

References: + denotes improvement; – denotes worsening; NC denotes no changes. All the improvements and worsenings are statistically significant at 5 per cent.

Source: Authors' calculations based on SEDLAC (CEDLAS and World Bank 2014).

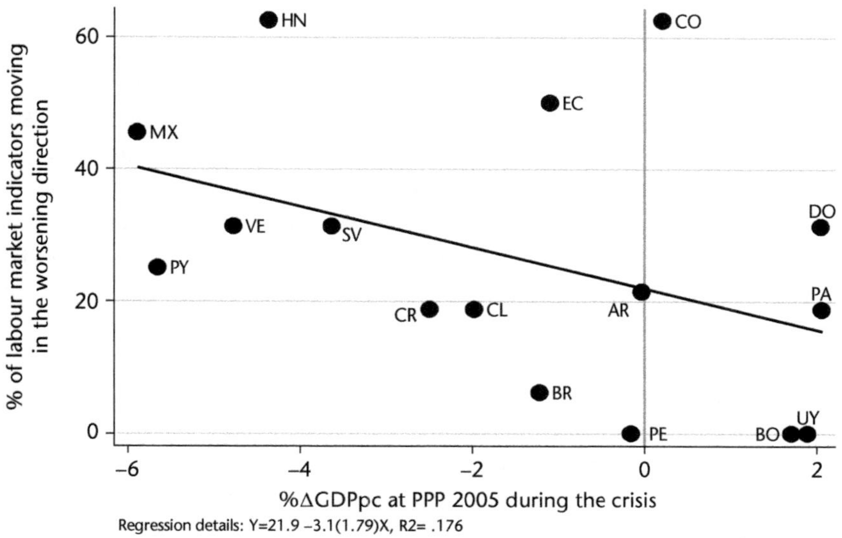

Figure 3.3 Cross-country relationship between the percentage of labour market indicators moving in the welfare-worsening direction and growth rate of GDP per capita during the international crisis

Note: This figure displays the percentage of labour market indicators that change in the welfare-worsening direction according to Table 3.4 and the growth rate of GDP per capita during the international crisis. The economic crisis period is 2008–9, except for Chile (2006–9) and Mexico (2006–10). The line represents the linear regression specified at the bottom of the figure. Robust standard error of the slope coefficient between parentheses.

Source: Authors' calculations based on SEDLAC (CEDLAS and World Bank 2014).

number of labour market indicators as the Dominican Republic, but far from the generalized deterioration in Colombia, with almost no change in GDP per capita during the crisis.

Paying particular attention to the growth–employment–poverty nexus, it is interesting to observe that poverty rates increased in only a few countries during the crisis: moderate poverty (computed with the 4 dollars-a-day poverty line) increased in five countries, and extreme poverty (computed with the 2.5 dollars-a-day poverty line) increased in only one country. The small effect of the crisis on poverty rates can be related to the small effect the crisis had on labour earnings. Table 3.3 shows that only four countries suffered a reduction in labour earnings during the crisis (Ecuador, Honduras, Mexico, and Venezuela). To see more clearly the connection between labour earnings and poverty, of the four countries where labour earnings fell during the crisis, three also exhibited increases in their poverty rates (Ecuador, Mexico, and Venezuela). However, unemployment rates increased in twelve out of sixteen countries, indicating that during the crisis, employment declined with a small effect on wages. Section 3.4 presents a more in-depth analysis of the relationship between poverty indicators and employment and earnings indicators. Most countries reacted quickly during the crisis, implementing or expanding cash transfers and emergency programmes, thereby mitigating the effect of the increase in unemployment on poverty (Veras Soares 2009; Cecchini and Madariaga 2011). The accompanying country case studies describe some of the interventions of the governments in the region during the aftermath of the crisis. Just to mention a few of them: Argentina increased social expenditure during and after the international crisis through the creation (and subsequent rise in levels) of the *Asignacion Universal por Hijo* cash transfer programme, and also increased public works and public employment; Costa Rica expanded the coverage of the cash transfer programme *Avancemos* and also increased non-contributory pensions; El Salvador implemented cash and in-kind transfers and financial support to local producers; Mexico introduced and expanded employment programmes such as *Programa de Preservación del Empleo* and *Programa Temporal de Empleo*, and also expanded the *Oportunidades* cash transfer programme. The only two countries which did not implement any countercyclical policy during the international crisis were Honduras (which was facing political instability) and Venezuela (which suffered reduced oil revenues during the crisis).

Turning now to the post-crisis period, labour market indicators fully or partially recovered in most countries. Table 3.4 presents the post-crisis evolution of the labour market indicators that deteriorated during the crisis. We distinguish between total and partial recoveries: total recoveries ('++' sign in the table) signify that the indicator surpassed its pre-crisis level; partial recovery ('+') indicates that the indicator improved from the worst year of the crisis, but not by enough to achieve its pre-crisis level. Figure 3.4 shows for each country the distribution of labour market indicators that were affected and not affected during the crisis.[3] Most labour market indicators had fully or partially recovered in most countries by 2012–13. The share of low-earnings occupations, the share of low-educated workers, and the moderate and extreme poverty rates recovered fully or partially in all countries which suffered a deterioration in these indicators during the crisis. Other labour market indicators recovered in at least half of the countries that faced a worsening during the crisis. These indicators were the unemployment rate, the share of high-earnings occupations, the shares of wage/salaried employees, self-employment, and unpaid family workers, the share of low-earnings sectors, the share of high-educated workers, the share of registered workers, mean labour earnings, and the Gini coefficient of labour earnings. The only labour

[3] Some labour market indicators improved during the crisis and deteriorated in the post-crisis period. Since the purpose of this section is to assess the impact of the crisis and the ensuing recovery, in Figure 3.4 we classified these cases as indicators that were not affected by the crisis.

Table 3.4 Qualitative changes after the international crisis of 2008 in labour market indicators which worsened during the crisis by country

Indicator	AR	BO	BR	CL	CO	DO	EC	HN	MX	PA	PE	PY	SV	UY	VE
Unemployment															
Decrease in the unemployment rate	++		++	+	++	–	++		+	++		++	+		+
Occupations															
Decrease in the share of low-earnings occupations				++	+	+	++	+							
Increase in the share of high-earnings occupations					++		++	–							
Occupational position															
Increase in the share of wage/salaried employees					+		–	–		++		++	+		++
Decrease in the share of self-employment	++					+	–	–		++			+		–
Decrease in the share of unpaid family workers	++				+		++			++			–		
Economic Sector															
Decrease in the share of workers in low-earnings sectors					+			–							
Increase in the share of workers in high-earnings sectors						–		–							
Education															
Decrease in the share of low-educated workers					++			++							
Increase in the share of high-educated workers					++	–		+							
Workers registered with SS															
Increase in the share of workers registered with SS				++	++			+	–				–		
Earnings															
Increase in mean labour earnings							++	–	+						++
Poverty															
Decrease in 4 dollars-a-day poverty							++		++			++			++
Decrease in 2.5 dollars-a-day poverty									+						

(continued)

Table 3.4 Continued

Indicator	AR	BO	BR	CL	CO	DO	EC	HN	MX	PA	PE	PY	SV	UY	VE
Inequality															
Decrease in GINI of household per capita income															
Decrease in GINI of labour earnings					++					–					
Total number of indicators affected by the crises	*3*	*0*	*1*	*3*	*10*	*5*	*8*	*10*	*5*	*5*	*0*	*3*	*5*	*0*	*5*
Number of continued deterioration	*0*	*0*	*0*	*0*	*0*	*3*	*2*	*6*	*1*	*1*	*0*	*0*	*2*	*0*	*1*
Number of partial recoveries	*0*	*0*	*0*	*1*	*4*	*2*	*0*	*3*	*3*	*0*	*0*	*0*	*3*	*0*	*1*
Number of total recoveries	*3*	*0*	*1*	*2*	*6*	*0*	*6*	*1*	*1*	*4*	*0*	*3*	*0*	*0*	*3*
% of total recoveries	**100.0**	–	**100.0**	**66.7**	**60.0**	**0.0**	**75.0**	**10.0**	**20.0**	**80.0**	–	**100.0**	**0.0**	–	**60.0**

Note: The table summarizes the changes in labour market indicators that worsened during the crisis according to Table 3.3. Estimations correspond to: Argentina 2008–12, Bolivia 2008–12, Brazil 2008–12, Chile 2006–11, Colombia 2008–13, Dominican Republic 2008–12, Ecuador 2008–12, Honduras 2008–12, Mexico 2006–12, Panama 2008–12, Peru 2008–12, Paraguay 2008–13, El Salvador 2008–12, Uruguay 2008–12, and Venezuela 2008–12. In Paraguay, the classification of occupations during 2010–13 cannot be compared with the classification before 2010. Costa Rica does not appear in this table since from 2010 onwards household surveys are not comparable to previous surveys.

References: ++ denotes total recovery: the indicator improved after 2009 above the pre-crisis level of 2008; + denotes partial recovery: the indicator improved after 2009 but did not recover its pre-crisis level of 2008; – denotes continued deterioration: the indicator continued worsening after 2009. All the improvements and worsenings are statistically significant at 5 per cent.

Source: Authors' calculations based on SEDLAC (CEDLAS and World Bank 2014).

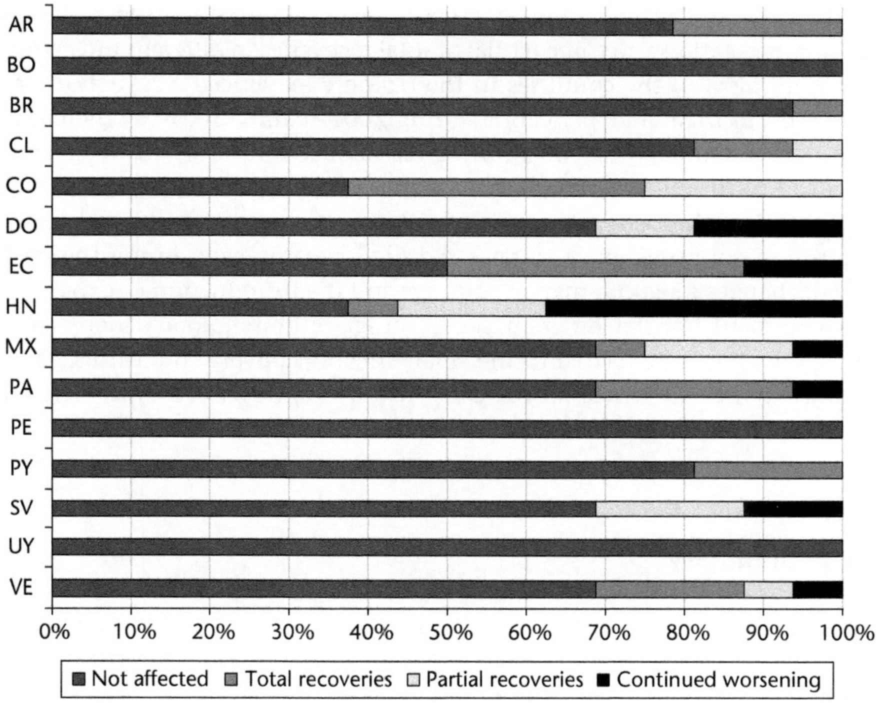

Figure 3.4 Distribution of labour market indicators according to the post-crisis path by country

Note: 'Not affected' indicates the percentage of indicators that did not worsen during the international crisis. 'Total recoveries' denotes the percentage of indicators that improved after 2009 surpassing the pre-crisis level. 'Partial recoveries' denotes the percentage of indicators that improved after 2009 but the recovery was not enough to reach its pre-crisis level of 2008. 'Continued worsening' denotes the percentage of indicators that continued to worsen after the crises.

Source: Authors' calculations based on SEDLAC (CEDLAS and World Bank 2014).

market indicator that did not recover in the aftermath of the crisis was the share of workers in high-earnings sectors.

Besides the three countries whose labour market indicators were not affected by the crisis (Bolivia, Peru, and Uruguay), three other countries (Argentina, Brazil, and Paraguay) recovered completely from the deterioration suffered during the crisis (i.e. the indicators were better in the final year than in the pre-crisis year). Chile and Colombia experienced a mix of total and partial recoveries in their indicators (i.e. the situation was better than during the crisis but not always better than in the pre-crisis year). Honduras continued to have a generalized deterioration in its labour market indicators following the crisis. The bad performance of Honduras during and after the crisis was related to the political instability (the country suffered a military coup in 2009) that prevented the country from adopting the measures needed to counteract the effects of the global recession. The remaining seven countries experienced a mixed evolution, with a deterioration and some partial or total recoveries in different indicators.

In sum, most of the countries in the region experienced a reduction or a stagnation in their GDP per capita during 2008–9 and a recovery thereafter. Following an initial worsening of labour market indicators in most Latin American countries, the majority recovered or surpassed their pre-crisis levels by the end of the period for which we have data (typically 2012).[4] In the majority of countries, poverty rates did *not* increase, even during the crisis period; changes in labour market earnings and the introduction or expansion of government transfer programmes to mitigate the temporary increases in unemployment were related to the small effect on poverty indicators. Thus, contrary to the experiences of the OECD countries, the effects of the crisis in Latin America were generally short-lived.

3.4 In Summary

Summing up, the review of our aggregate evidence reveals three main results. First, GDP per capita grew in the Latin American region as a whole during the 2000s, all employment and earnings indicators improved, and poverty and inequality indicators fell.

Second, on a country-by-country basis, all Latin American countries exhibited positive GDP per capita growth rates during the 2000s. Most countries experienced substantial improvements in labour market conditions over the period, Honduras being the only exception to this general pattern. The unemployment rate fell in thirteen out of sixteen countries. There was a generalized improvement in the distribution of employed workers by occupations, occupational positions, sectors, and educational levels. The share of workers registered with the social security system increased in twelve out of sixteen countries. Labour earnings increased in eleven out of sixteen countries, although they fell significantly for the remaining five. Poverty and extreme poverty fell significantly in all countries but one. Inequality of household per capita income and of labour income also fell in fourteen out of sixteen countries.

Finally, the growth rates of most countries in the region were negatively affected by the economic crisis of 2008, which also affected several labour market indicators in the worsening direction: most notably, a generalized increase in the unemployment rate, a fall in the share of wage/salaried

[4] The limited impact of the international crisis on Latin American labour markets was also reported in World Bank (2012) and ECLAC-ILO (2012).

workers, and an increase in self-employment. A remarkable finding about the crisis is that poverty rates increased in only five of the sixteen countries, and extreme poverty rates in only one. In light of the evidence presented in this section and in the country studies, the small effect of the crisis on poverty rates can be related, first, to the small effect of the crisis on labour earnings. In fact, three of the countries that suffered an increase in the moderate poverty rate during the crisis are among the four countries in our sample that exhibited a reduction in labour earnings (Ecuador, Mexico, and Venezuela). Second, most of the countries in the region implemented countercyclical policies to reduce the negative impacts of the crisis, including the implementation and expansion of cash transfer programmes, mitigating the adverse effect on poverty of the increase in unemployment. The effect of the crisis on labour market indicators was short-lived: most countries' labour market indicators had fully or partially recovered by 2012–13.

References

Autor, D. H. and D. Dorn (2013). 'The Growth of Low-Skill Service Jobs and the Polarization of the US Labour Market', *American Economic Review* 103 (5): 1553–97.

Bureau of Labour Statistics (2015). United States Department of Labour. Available at <http://www.bls.gov/>, accessed June 2015.

Cecchini, S. and A. Madariaga (2011). 'Conditional Cash Transfer Programs: The Recent Experience in Latin America and the Caribbean'. Cuadernos de la CEPAL 95. Santiago de Chile: Economic Commission for Latin America and the Caribbean.

CEDLAS and World Bank (2014). SEDLAC—Socio-Economic Database for Latin America and the Caribbean. Centro de Estudios Distributivos, Laborales y Sociales, Facultad de Ciencias Económicas, Universidad Nacional de La Plata and World Bank Poverty Group LCR. Available at <http://sedlac.econo.unlp.edu.ar/eng/index.php>, accessed 2014.

ECB (2012). 'Euro Area Labour Markets and the Crisis'. Ocasional Paper Series 138. Frankfurt am Main: European Central Bank.

ECLAC-ILO (2012). 'The Employment Situation in Latin America and the Caribbean'. Number 6. Santiago de Chile: Economic Commission for Latin America and the Caribbean.

ECLAC-ILO (2015). 'Employment Situation in Latin America and the Caribbean: Universal Social Protection in Labour Markets with High Levels of Informality'. Santiago de Chile: Economic Division of the Economic Commission for Latin America and the Caribbean and Office for the Southern Cone of Latin America of the International Labour Organization.

Elwell, K. C. (2013). 'Economic Recovery: Sustaining U.S. Economic Growth in a Post-Crisis Economy'. CRS Report for Congress. Washington, DC: Congressional Research Service.

Veras Soares, F. (2009). 'Do CCTs Lessen the Impact of the Current Economic Crisis? Yes, but . . . '. One Pager 96. Brasilia: International Policy Center for Inclusive Growth.
Weller, J. (2014). 'Aspects of Recent Developments in the Latin American and Caribbean Labour Markets', *CEPAL Review* 114: 8–28.
World Bank (2012). *The Labour Market Story behind Latin America's Transformation*. Washington, DC: World Bank.
World Bank (2014). World Development Indicators. Available at <http://data.worldbank.org/data-catalog/world-development-indicators>, accessed April 2014.
World Bank (2015). 'Working to End Poverty in Latin America and the Caribbean: Workers, Jobs, and Wages'. Document of the World Bank. Washington, DC: World Bank.

4

Cross-Country Analysis of the Growth–Employment–Poverty Nexus

4.1 Cross-Country Patterns: Economic Growth Rate and Changes in Labour Market Indicators

Chapter 3 showed that the improvements in labour market indicators during the 2000s were remarkably widespread in the Latin American countries. In this chapter, we analyse whether the improvements in labour market indicators were directly related to the rate of economic growth across countries.

Cross-country analysis of the role of the rate of economic growth in determining improvements in labour market indicators is presented in two complementary parts. First, we analyse how the rate of economic growth is related to the percentage of labour market indicators that moved in the welfare-improving direction during the 2000s in each of the sixteen countries. Second, we perform cross-country analysis separately for each labour market indicator.

Previous literature has covered this topic only partially, presenting the correlation between cross-country changes in labour market indicators and the GDP per capita growth rate for a limited subset of indicators. Pagés, Pierre, and Scarpetta (2009) provide an example of this type of analysis linking the annual growth rate of employment for some Latin American and other developing countries during 1980–2004 to the annual GDP per capita growth rate. For this time period (longer but out of date compared to our analysis), the authors find that Latin American countries outperformed many of the comparator countries, as they had higher rates of employment growth for a given GDP per capita growth rate. However, the authors claim that jobs were created at the same rate that labour supply increased, leading to small increases in the employment rate and even unemployment rate rises for some countries.

Weller and Kaldewei (2013) and Weller (2014) perform a similar exercise, correlating changes in the shares of wage/salaried employees and self-employed workers with the GDP growth rate for the Latin American and the Caribbean region overall during the 1995–2012 period. The analysis is performed on a year-by-year basis and indicates a strong positive correlation between changes in the share of wage/salaried employees and the GDP growth rate. For the share of self-employed workers, the authors find a less clear relationship with the GDP growth rate; in several years of the analysed period self-employment behaved countercyclically, while in some other years it behaved procyclically.

Finally, ILO (2013) analyses the cross-country relation between annual growth in both GDP and employment before the international crisis (1997–2007) and after that episode (2008–11). The correlation was positive in both subperiods, but stronger before the crisis. This last result is explained by the fact that in Central American and the Caribbean countries, whose economies are strongly connected to the North American market, the recovery was slower than in South American countries. We turn now to our analysis.

4.1.1 *Analysis of the Percentage of Labour Market Indicators that Changed in the Welfare-Improving Direction (Z)*

What is the relationship between improvements in labour market indicators and the rate of economic growth? Figure 4.1 presents a scatterplot. We see in the figure that over the 2000s, GDP per capita increased in every country and that more than 60 per cent of the labour market indicators increased in every country except for Honduras, which suffered a generalized worsening of labour market conditions.

Across these countries, does a higher economic growth rate result in a higher percentage of labour market indicators improving? Let Z_i be the percentage of labour market indicators with a statistically significant improvement in country *i*, and $\%\Delta GDPpc_i$ be the annualized percentage change of GDP per capita in country *i*. To quantify the association between the two variables in the figure, we estimate the following regression:

$$Z_i = C + \beta \ \%\Delta GDPpc_i + \mu_{i.} \qquad (2)$$

We observe a positive but weak relationship (R-squared of 0.112 and statistically insignificant) between the percentage of labour market indicators that improved during the 2000s and the rate of economic growth. Upon removing Honduras, which is the only country in our sample with a generalized worsening in labour market indicators over the period, the R-squared increases slightly to 0.120, but the slope coefficient is smaller and still not statistically significant. The reason for the lack of relationship between the percentage of improving indicators and the rate of economic growth is the limited variation in the evolution of labour market indicators, since for most countries in our sample and regardless of their annualized rates of economic growth we

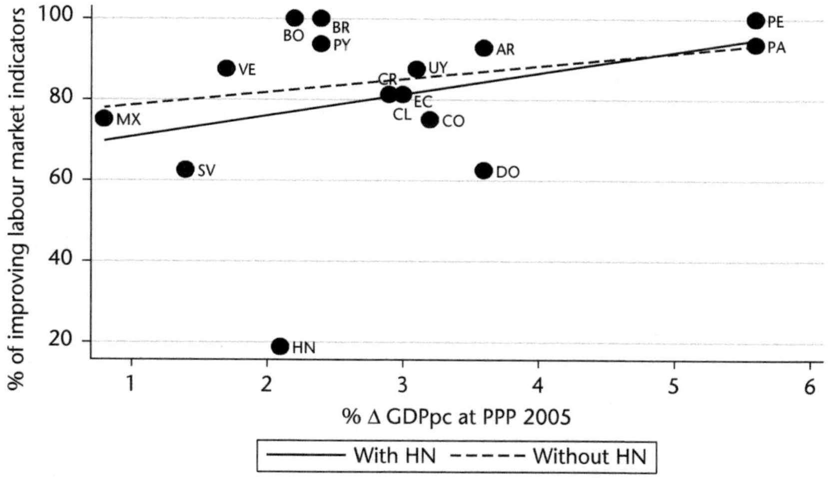

Regression details:
With HN: Y=65.4+5.26(3.95)X, R2= .112
Without HN: Y=75.3+3.24(2.43)X, R2= .12

Figure 4.1 Cross-country relationship between the percentage of labour market indicators moving in the welfare-improving direction and growth rate of GDP per capita during the 2000s

Note: This figure displays the percentage of labour market indicators that changed in the welfare-improving direction according to Table 3.2 and the annualized growth rate during the period under study according to Table 3.1. The line represents the linear regression specified at the bottom of the figure. Robust standard error of the slope coefficient between parentheses.

Source: Authors' calculations based on SEDLAC (CEDLAS and World Bank 2014).

observe that 75 per cent or more of these indicators improved during the period under study.

4.1.2 *Analysis of the Labour Market Indicators One by One (Y_k)*

The weak relationship between the percentage of labour market indicators that improved in each country (Z_i) and the rate of economic growth ($\%\Delta GDPpc_i$) may be due to the type of aggregation implicit in our index of the percentage of labour market indicators that improved over the period. Rather than constructing alternative indices, which would also be arbitrary in terms of the indicators included, the weight assigned to each one, etc., we can instead extend this analysis beyond our aggregate measure of improvement of labour markets and study the relationship between economic growth and each of the underlying indicators one by one.

Our results indicate that faster growth is associated with larger improvements in labour market indicators, but the goodness of fit of most of the relationships analysed is generally low. This conclusion is based on Figure 4.2, which displays the scatterplots for each country's annualized change in the

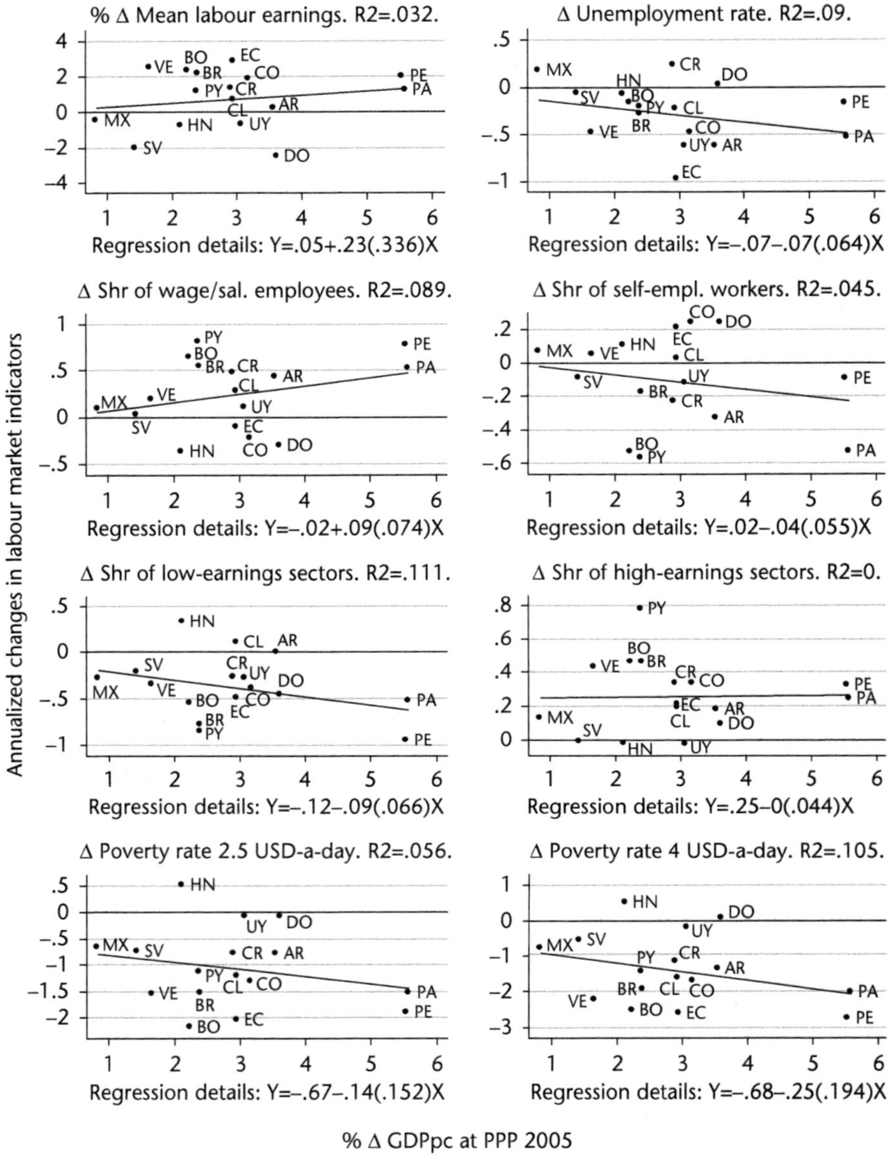

Figure 4.2 Cross-country relationship between the annualized changes in labour market indicators and annualized growth rate of GDP per capita during the 2000s

Note: The vertical axes display the annualized change in each labour market indicator. Δ denotes changes in percentage points and % Δ denotes percentage changes. The line in each figure represents the linear regression specified at the bottom. Robust standard error of the slope coefficient between parentheses. R-squared of the regression indicated along the title of each figure.

Source: Authors' calculations based on SEDLAC (CEDLAS and World Bank 2014) and World Development Indicators (World Bank 2014).

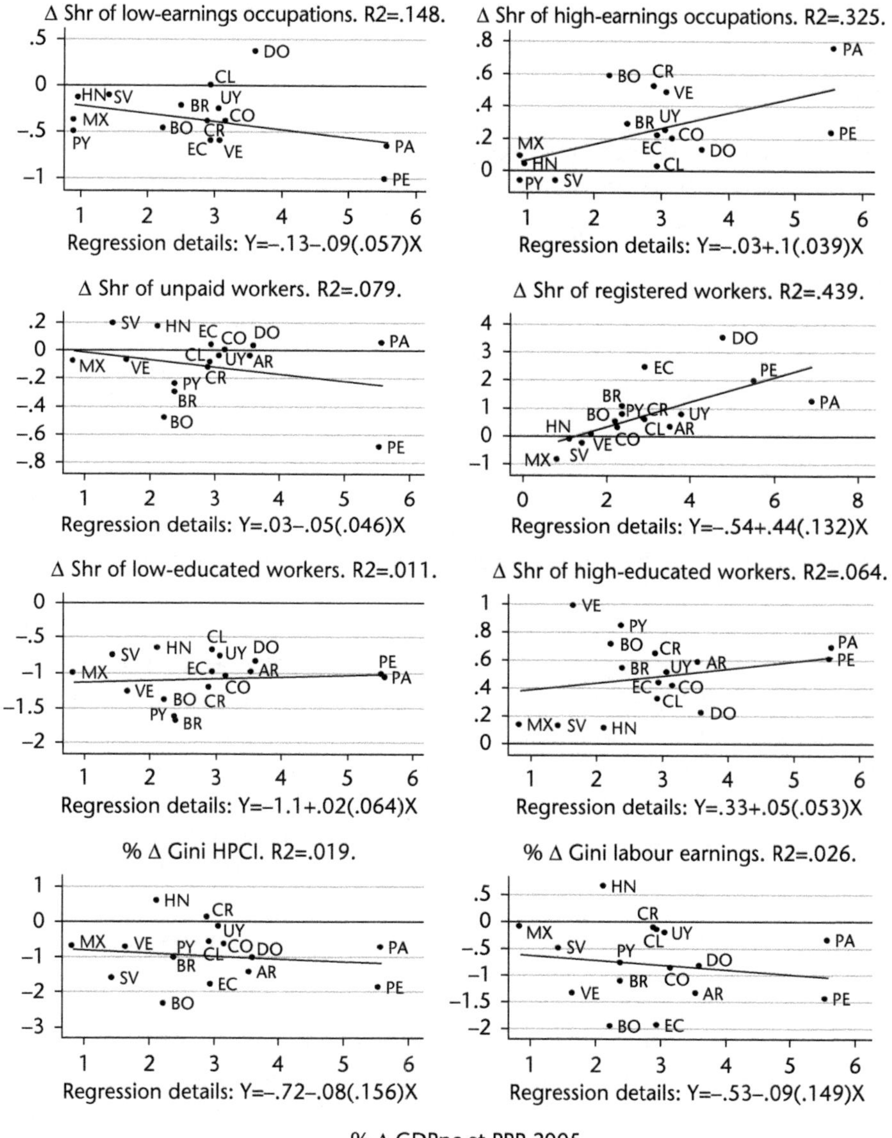

Figure 4.2 Continued

k'th labour market indicator and its rate of economic growth (one plot for each labour market indicator). Let $GDPpc_i$ be GDP per capita in country i, Y_{ik} be the labour market indicator k for country i, Δ be the annualized change in percentage points, and $\%\Delta$ be the annualized percentage change. We quantify the underlying relationship between the variables in the plots by estimating one of the following regressions, depending on the units of the indicators:

$$\Delta Y_{ik} = C + \beta\,\%\Delta GDPpc_i + \varepsilon_{ik} \text{ or } \%\Delta Y_{ik} = C + \beta\,\%\Delta GDPpc_i + \varepsilon_{ik} \qquad (3)$$

We consider a relationship to be tight if the R-squared is above the arbitrary threshold of 0.15. The R-squared was chosen instead of other commonly used statistics as the slope or an F test of statistical significance, since we wanted to capture how much of the variation in Y_k can be explained by changes in GDP per capita.

Among the employment and earnings indicators, only three exhibited a relatively tight relationship between their changes during the 2000s and the rate of economic growth. These indicators were the share of registered workers, the share of high-earnings occupations, and the share of low-earnings occupations. There thus seems to be a significant relationship between the rate of economic growth and different aspects of the occupational mix. More specifically, countries that grew faster experienced larger declines in the share of low-earnings occupations, and higher increases in the share of highly paid occupations in total employment (R-squareds of 0.15 and 0.33, respectively). Moreover, the share of workers registered with social security tended to increase more in countries with stronger economic growth, and this is the tightest of the relationships we computed (R-squared of 0.44). The increase in the share of registered workers is a manifestation of the procyclicality of registered employment, which has been extensively documented and discussed before for the region as a whole, and for most countries in the region over time (Gasparini and Tornarolli 2009).

For the remaining employment and earnings indicators, as well as for the poverty and inequality indicators, we find no statistically significant relationship or only a weak relationship between the annualized change in the labour market indicator and the rate of economic growth (R-squared lower than 0.15). For instance, there is a weak positive relationship between growth and the change in the share of wage/salaried employees (R-squared of 0.09). There are also weak negative relationships between the rate of economic growth and the changes in the unemployment rate, in the moderate poverty rate, and in the shares of unpaid workers and of low-earnings sectors.

These mostly weak relationships between the rate of economic growth and the substantial majority of indicators of labour market performance seem to be driven by the experiences of the countries which grew at moderate rates by Latin American standards. The two fastest-growing economies (Panama and Peru) exhibited widespread and large improvements in their labour market indicators, and the two slowest-growing economies (Mexico and El Salvador) showed among the smallest improvements (and even some deteriorations) in labour market indicators over the 2000s. However, these changes and deteriorations were not extreme, which accounts partially for the modest slopes of the aggregate relationships across all sixteen countries. Moreover, the other twelve countries in the middle of the growth scale exhibited a large degree of variability in the magnitudes of the changes in labour market indicators despite having similar economic growth rates. For instance, Bolivia, Brazil, and Honduras had nearly the same economic growth, and while in Bolivia and Brazil all labour market indicators improved and in some cases the improvements were larger than for Panama or Peru (the two fastest-growing economies), Honduras had by far the worst performance among the sixteen countries (Table 3.2 in Chapter 3). Some other countries exhibited larger economic growth rates when compared to Bolivia and Brazil, but smaller improvement in labour market indicators. That was the case of the Dominican Republic.

4.2 Cross-Country Patterns: Beyond Economic Growth

The analysis in sections 4.1.1 and 4.1.2 revealed that labour market conditions improved substantially in all but one of the sixteen Latin American countries covered in this study. These improvements, though widespread, occurred in countries with high and low rates of economic growth. This lack of a systematic cross-country relationship between economic growth and improvements in the labour market as measured either by the aggregate index Z or by the individual labour market indicators Y_k motivates the analysis in this chapter, in which we attempt to move beyond aggregated indicators such as economic growth and delve into more detailed macroeconomic variables.

The analysis of the role of macroeconomic variables other than the rate of economic growth in determining changes in labour market indicators proceeds as follows. To determine whether the richer Latin American countries differed from the poorer ones in terms of their labour market trajectories, we first study the relationship between countries' changes in labour market conditions and their initial level of GDP. Next, we study the changes in each labour market indicator as a function of the country's initial level of this indicator, to uncover any potential convergence effect in these indicators. Then we analyse a number of other macroeconomic variables which might be significant correlates of changes in labour market conditions. These variables are changes in: agriculture as a percentage of GDP; industry as a percentage of GDP; services as a percentage of GDP; domestic consumption expenditure as a percentage of GDP; exports as a percentage of GDP; terms of trade; foreign direct investment as a percentage of GDP; revenues from natural resources as a percentage of GDP; expenditure in education and health as a percentage of GDP; public expenditure in social security as a percentage of GDP; and the stock of public debt as a percentage of GDP. Finally, we look to see whether the changes in certain labour market indicators are linked systematically to the changes in others: for example, whether countries with more rapidly rising real wages are those with more rapidly rising unemployment or whether real earnings and employment move together.

Some of these topics have been studied in the previous literature although in a more limited way—typically, for a smaller group of labour market indicators, for a smaller group of countries, or for a different time period. For instance, World Bank (2012) highlights the role of the increasing terms of trade for the net commodity-exporting countries in the region to explain the increase in the relative demand for low-skilled workers and then the reduction in labour income inequality (measured by the returns to secondary and higher education) between 2000 and 2009–10. Similarly, World Bank (2015) relates real wage increases, reductions in household income inequality (measured by the Gini coefficient), and reductions in the poverty rate (measured by the 4 dollars-a-day international line) in the Latin American region during 2003–12 to improving terms of trade, because countries experiencing a commodity boom did much better in these labour market indicators than non-commodity-boom countries.

Tsounta and Osueke (2014) analyse the determinants of falling income inequality in Latin America from 1990 to 2012. The authors present evidence of convergence in the Gini coefficient of household per capita income across Latin American countries (eighteen countries) over the period. They also find a negative cross-country correlation between changes in tax revenues as a share of GDP and changes in household income inequality (where changes correspond to the difference between the years 2000 and 2012), and a negative cross-country correlation between changes in government spending on education as a share of GDP and changes in income inequality.

Finally, Damill and Frenkel (2014) estimate the effect of annual changes in the real exchange rate on annual changes in the unemployment rate for a panel of eighteen Latin American countries from 1990 to 2010. They find that a more depreciated real exchange rate tends to reduce unemployment. In a similar exercise, they relate the poverty rate to unemployment and the inflation rate and find that increases in the unemployment rate and in the inflation rate tend to increase the poverty rate.

4.2.1 *Initial GDP per Capita*

An ongoing debate in the modern theory of economic growth is whether there is convergence or divergence in growth rates: that is, whether poorer countries tend to grow at higher rates than richer ones (thus tending to converge in terms of GDP) or not. We start our analysis with the related question of whether the improvement in labour market indicators over the period under study was correlated with each country's initial GDP per capita. This relationship could be either positive or negative: poorer economies could have more room to improve in the labour market, so that these countries might exhibit larger improvements in related indicators, or alternatively initially richer economies may have better conditions to channel the economic growth during the period under study in the direction of improved conditions in the labour market.

Examining these competing views empirically, we find that there is no important cross-country relationship between initial GDP per capita and aggregate changes in labour market conditions. Figure 4.3 plots initial GDP per capita in 2005 PPP dollars and the percentage of improving labour market indicators for each country. Let GDP_{it_0} be the GDP per capita at 2005 PPP in the first period under study for country *i*, and Z_i be the percentage of labour market indicators that experienced an improvement in the period under study. To quantify the cross-country relationship, we estimate the following regression:

$$Z_i = C + \beta \, GDP_{it_0} + \mu_i \tag{4}$$

The relationship is positive, indicating that initially richer countries enjoyed larger improvements in labour market indicators measured by *Z*, but weak (R-squared of 0.11). However, even this low association is entirely driven by Honduras, which is a clear outlier: without Honduras, the R-squared and slope of the fitted line are virtually equal to zero.

Our finding of a lack of relationship between initial GDP per capita level and labour market conditions across countries means that there were substantial improvements in labour markets both in initially poorer and in initially richer countries, and that countries with similar initial levels of GDP per capita exhibited very different patterns in the number of labour market indicators that improved over the period under study. For instance, Peru and the Dominican Republic had almost the same level of initial GDP per capita, but the Peruvian experience was markedly more successful: all sixteen labour market indicators improved in Peru, but only ten improved in the Dominican Republic.

While there does not seem to be a relationship between initial GDP per capita and the percentage of indicators that improved, there could still be a relationship between the magnitude of changes in some of the individual labour market indicators and the initial level of GDP per capita. In Figure 4.4, we present this relationship for each of the sixteen labour market

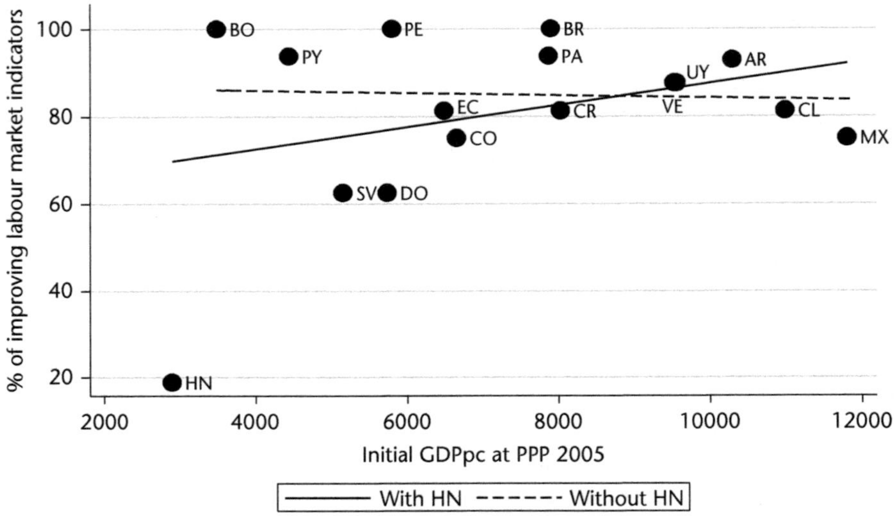

Regression details:
With HN: Y=62.6+2.5(1.93)X, R2= .106
Without HN: Y=87.1–.29(1.38)X, R2= .003

Figure 4.3 Cross-country relationship between the percentage of labour market indicators moving in the welfare-improving direction during the 2000s and initial GDP per capita

Note: This figure displays the percentage of labour market indicators that changed in the welfare-improving direction according to Table 3.2 and GDP per capita of the initial year at PPP 2005. The line represents the linear regression specified at the bottom of the figure. Robust standard error of the slope coefficient between parentheses.

Source: Authors' calculations based on SEDLAC (CEDLAS and World Bank 2014) and World Development Indicators (World Bank 2014).

indicators. Let GDP_{it_0} be the GDP per capita at 2005 PPP in the initial year under study for country i, Y_{ik} be the labour market indicator k for country i, Δ be the annualized change in percentage points, and let $\%\Delta$ be the annualized percentage change. We quantify these relationships estimating regressions of the form:

$$\Delta Y_{ik} = C + \beta\ GDP_{it_0} + \varepsilon_{ik} \text{ or } \%\Delta Y_{ik} = C + \beta\ GDP_{it_0} + \varepsilon_{ik}. \qquad (5)$$

Using equation (5), we also fail to find a relationship between initial GDP per capita and changes in individual labour market indicators. The results displayed in Figure 4.4 indicate that we can reject the hypothesis of an association between the initial level of GDP per capita and the changes in each of the labour market indicators. All the R-squareds are lower than 0.06, and the slopes are practically

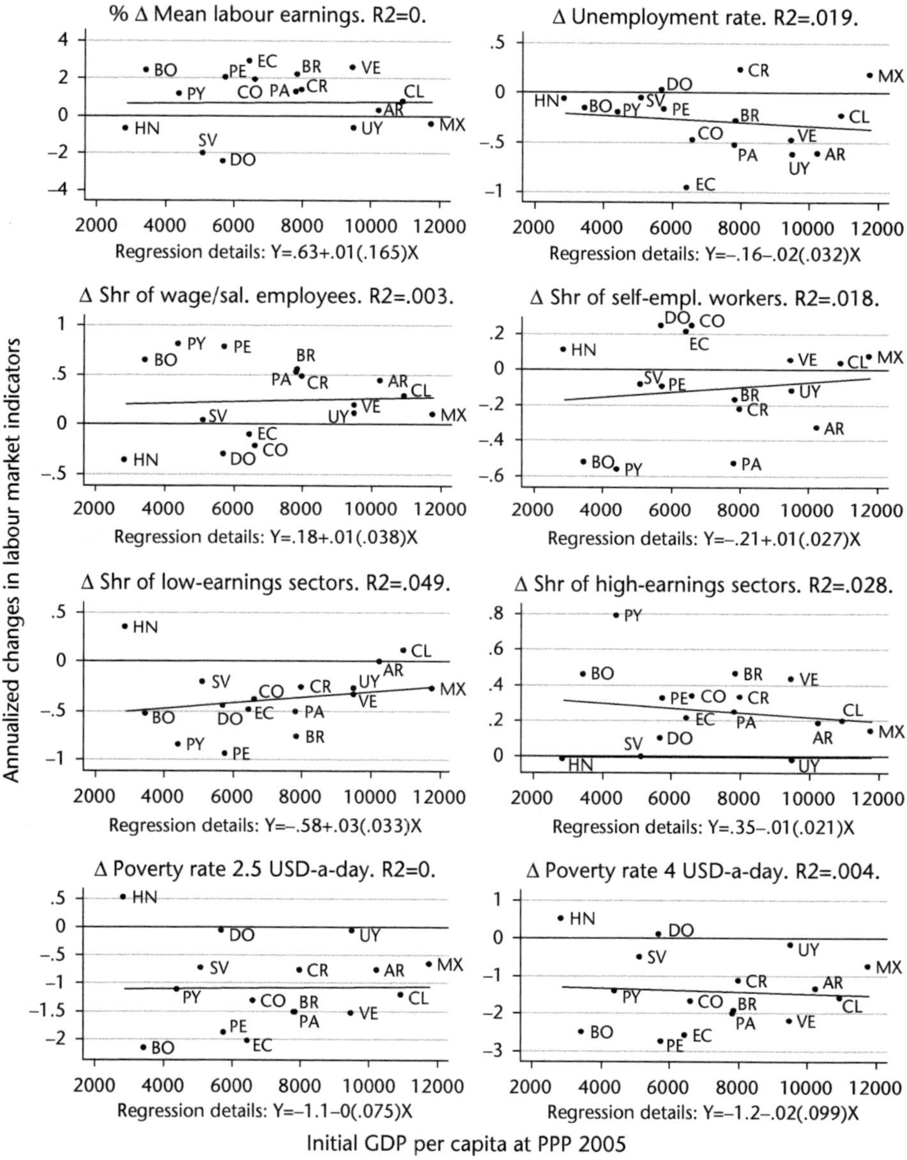

Figure 4.4 Cross-country relationship between the annualized changes in labour market indicators during the 2000s and initial GDP per capita

Note: The vertical axes display the annualized change in each labour market indicator. Δ denotes changes in percentage points; % Δ denotes percentage changes. The line represents the linear regression specified at the bottom of the figure. Robust standard error of the slope coefficient between parentheses. R-squared of the regression indicated along the title of each figure.

Source: Authors' calculations based on SEDLAC (CEDLAS and World Bank 2014) and World Development Indicators (World Bank 2014).

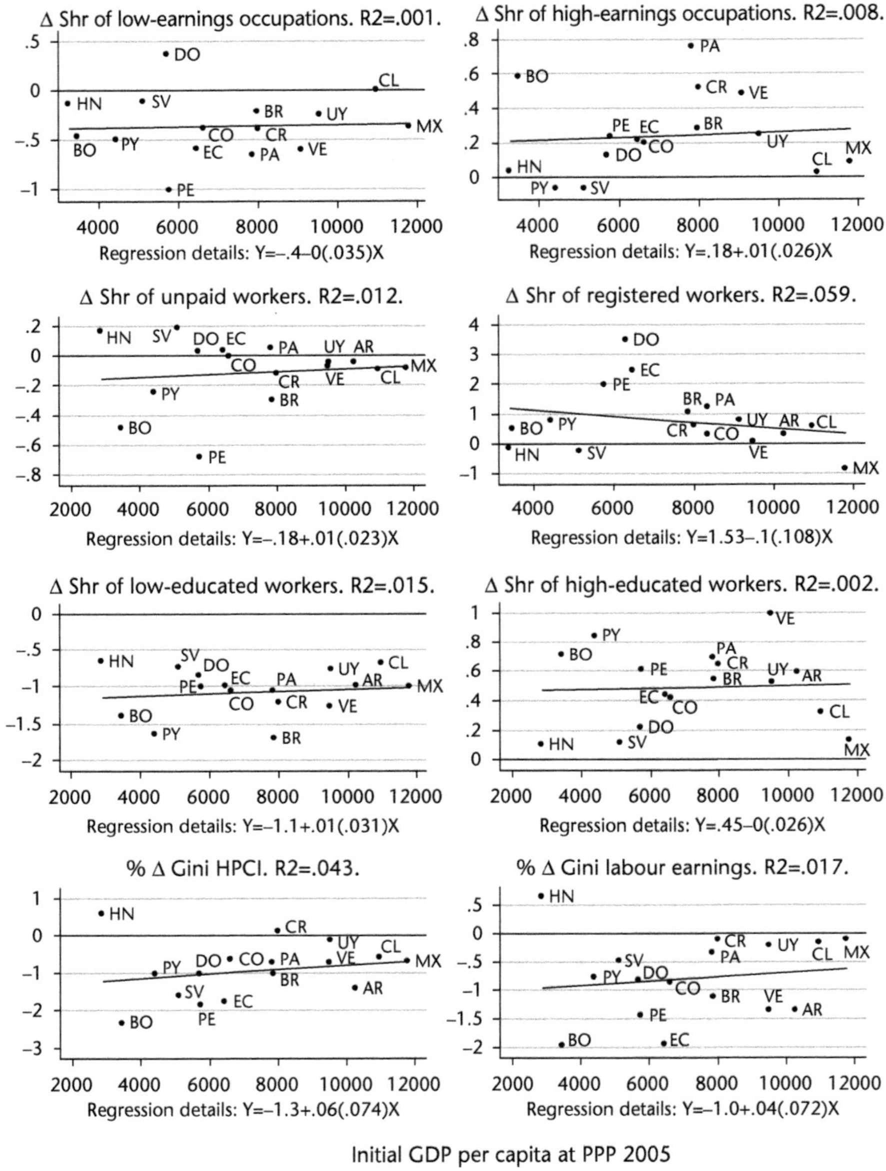

Figure 4.4 Continued

equal to 0. In brief, initial GDP per capita does not make an important difference to the rate of change of any of the labour market indicators.

4.2.2 *Convergence/Divergence Patterns in Labour Market Indicators*

In this section, we study how, across countries, the change in each of the sixteen labour market indicators is related to the initial level of that indicator. In order to do that, let Y_{ikt_0} be the value of the labour market indicator *k* in the initial year under study for country *i*, Y_{ik} be the labour market indicator *k* for country *i*, and let Δ be the annualized change in percentage points, and $\%\Delta$ be the annualized percentage change. We estimate regressions of the form:

$$\Delta Y_{ik} = C + \beta\, Y_{ikt_0} + \varepsilon_{ik} \text{ or } \%\Delta Y_{ik} = C + \beta Y_{ikt_0} + \varepsilon_{ik}. \quad (6)$$

We define convergence and divergence as follows: given the initial value of the *k*'th labour market indicator, a convergent (divergent) relationship is one where the countries with worse (better) initial values tend to have larger subsequent improvements. Convergent patterns would reflect some sort of decreasing marginal returns to growth or to improvements in a given indicator, i.e. it is harder to achieve large reductions when the labour market indicator is already high (in a welfare-increasing direction). Alternatively, divergent patterns would signal the presence of 'traps' or absorbent states in that once the labour market indicator is at a low level, it is hard for the country to bring it up.

Figure 4.5 presents the relationship between the changes in each labour market indicator and its initial value. There seems to be convergence for about a third (five out of sixteen) of our selected indicators, namely: the unemployment rate, the share of unpaid family workers, the poverty and extreme poverty rates, and the inequality of household per capita income. The relationships are especially tight for the unemployment rate, and for the share of unpaid family workers (R-squareds of about 0.73 and about 0.5, respectively). That is, countries with higher initial unemployment rates and higher shares of unpaid family workers exhibited much larger reductions in these indicators than other countries; these countries are not stuck with high unemployment rates or high shares of workers in unpaid family jobs. The results in Figure 4.5 also reveal some weak convergent patterns: for example, the share of low-earnings occupations and the share of workers with low levels of education converged, but not as much as the unemployment rate and the share of unpaid family workers did (R-squareds of 0.06 and 0.09). For the other indicators, no discernible convergence/divergence patterns appeared.

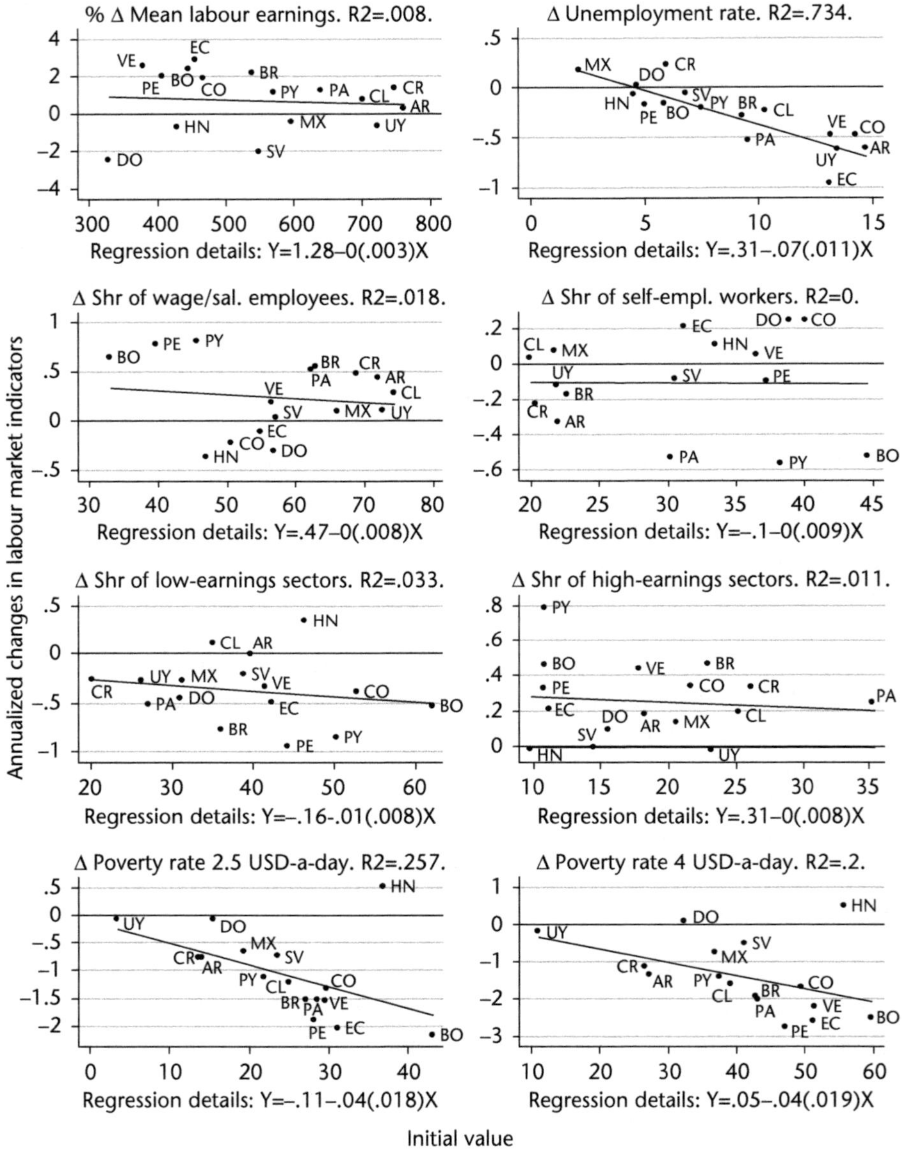

Figure 4.5 Cross-country relationship between the annualized changes in labour market indicators during the 2000s and the initial value of labour market indicators

Note: The vertical axes display the annualized change in each labour market indicator. Δ denotes changes in percentage points; % Δ denotes percentage changes. The line represents the linear regression specified at the bottom of the figure. Robust standard error of the slope coefficient between parentheses. R-squared of the regression indicated along the title of each figure.

Source: Authors' calculations based on SEDLAC (CEDLAS and World Bank 2014).

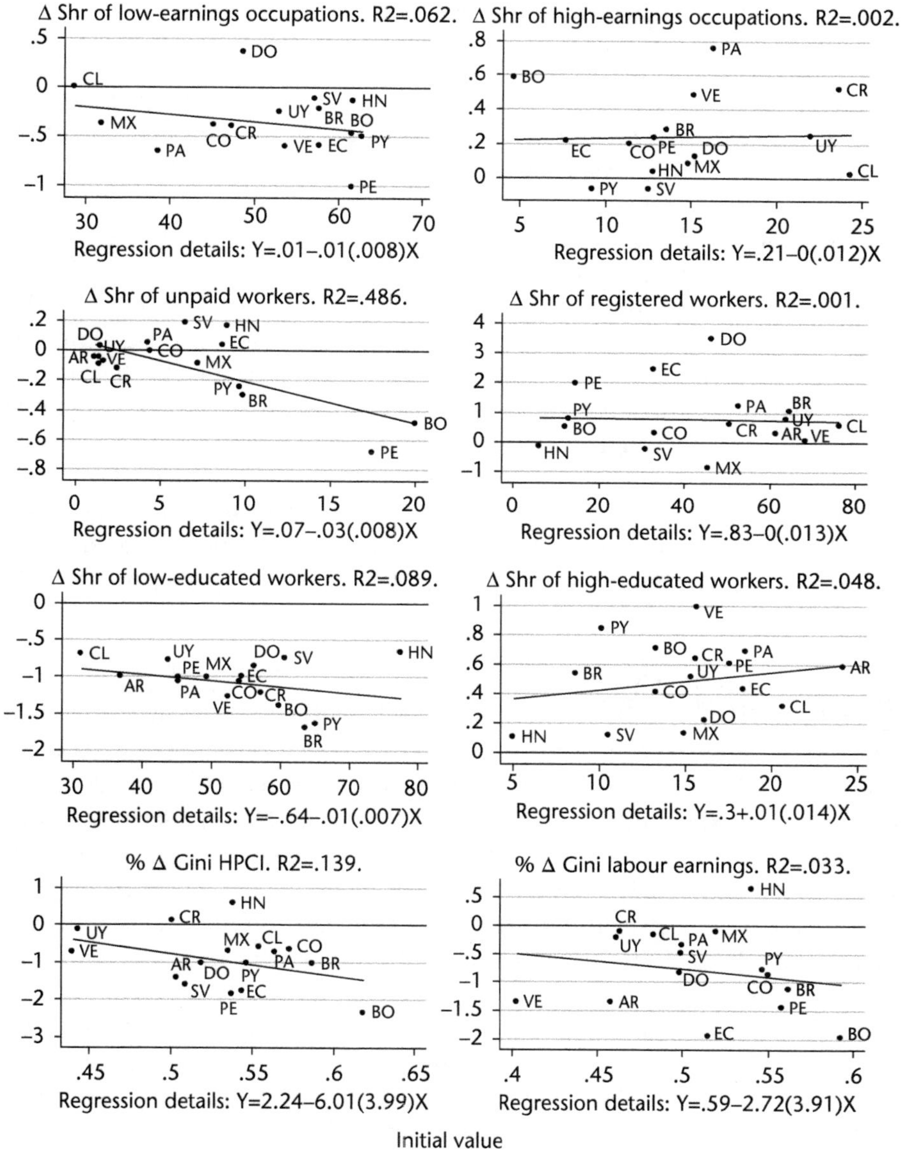

Figure 4.5 Continued

4.2.3 *Other Potential Macroeconomic Correlates of Changing Labour Market Indicators*

In this section, we turn to other macroeconomic variables besides the rate of economic growth and the initial level of national income, and study which, if any, are significantly correlated with improvements in the labour market. The macroeconomic variables analysed here fall into two categories. Most have to do with the composition of GDP. These variables, expressed as changing percentages of GDP, include the share of agriculture, the share of industry, the share of service, the share of domestic consumption expenditure, the share of expenditure in education and health, the share of expenditure in social security, the share of exports, the share of foreign direct investments, the share of revenues of natural resources, and the share of the stock of public debt. We also consider the changes in the country's terms of trade; this variable is not a share of GDP (Appendix 3 provides the macroeconomic variables time series for each country). Let Z_i be the share of improving labour market indicators for country i, and X_{ij} be the macroeconomic variable j in country i. To quantify the association between the two variables we estimate the following regression:

$$Z_i = C + \beta\ \Delta X_{ij} + \varepsilon_{ik} \text{ or } Z_i = C + \beta\ \%\Delta X_{ij} + \varepsilon_{ik}. \tag{7}$$

These bivariate tests yield several strong relationships. Most notably, the share of labour market indicators that improved was larger in countries with larger increases in exports as a percentage of GDP, larger reductions in domestic consumption expenditure as a percentage of GDP, and larger falls in the stock of public debt as a percentage of GDP (when excluding Honduras, an outlier as discussed in section 4.1.1) (Figure 4.6). There appear to be some weak positive relationships also between the share of labour market indicators that improved and the change in terms of trade and in revenues from natural resources as a percentage of GDP.

Besides these relationships between changes in these macroeconomic aggregates and the share of labour market indicators that improved over the period under study, we can also study the relationship between these macroeconomic variables and the sixteen individual labour market indicators. To gauge their importance, we perform a series of regressions between the change in labour market indicator and the changes in the macroeconomic variables. Let Y_{ik} be the labour market indicators k for country i, and X_{ij} be the macroeconomic variable j in country i. To quantify the association between the two variables we estimate the following regression:

$$\Delta Y_{ik} = C + \beta\ \Delta X_{ij} + \varepsilon_{ik} \text{ or } \%\Delta Y_{ik} = C + \beta \Delta X_{ij} + \varepsilon_{ik}, \tag{8}$$

and

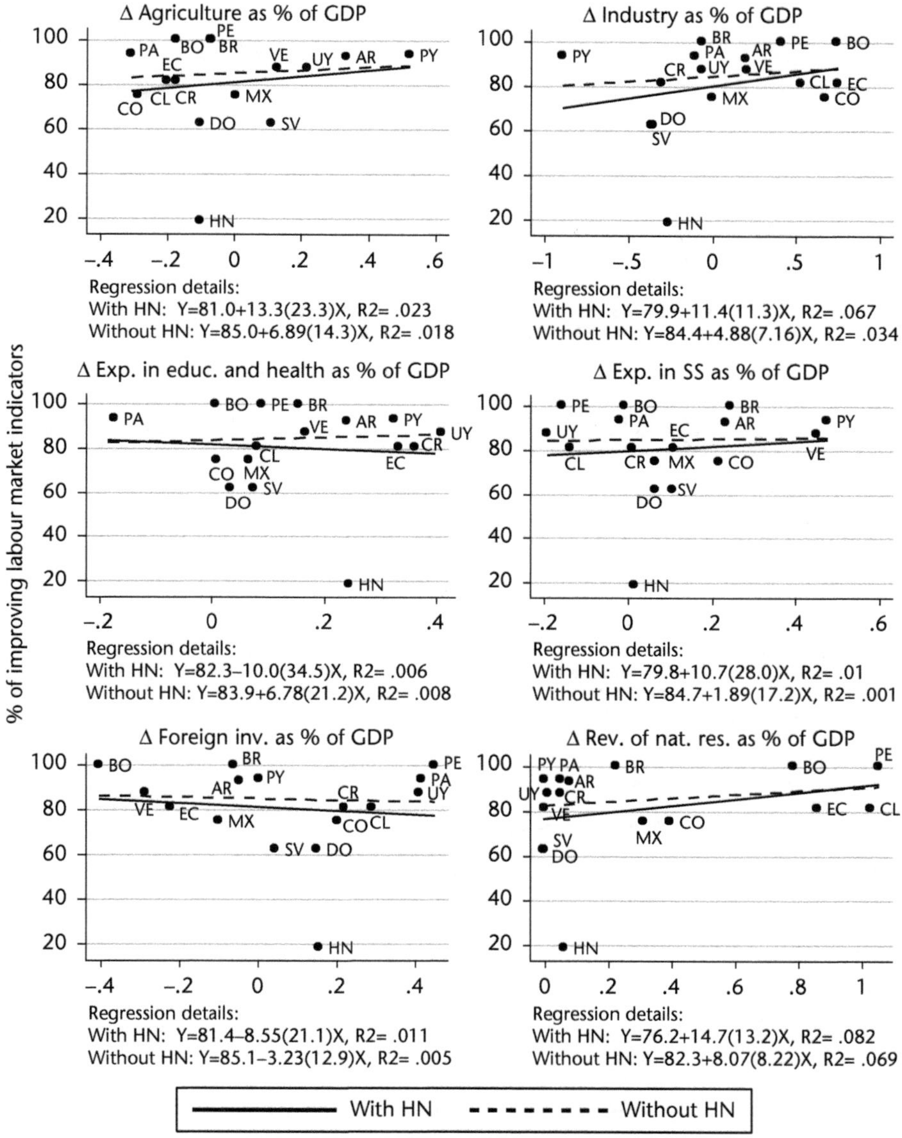

Figure 4.6 Cross-country relationship between the percentage of improving labour market indicators and the annualized changes in macroeconomic variables during the 2000s

Note: The vertical axes display the annualized change in each labour market indicator. Δ denotes changes in percentage points; % Δ denotes percentage changes. The line represents the linear regression specified at the bottom of the figure. Robust standard error of the slope coefficient between parentheses. R-squared of the regression indicated along the title of each figure.

Source: Authors' calculations based on SEDLAC (CEDLAS and World Bank 2014), World Development Indicators (World Bank 2014), and CEPALSTAT (UN-ECLAC 2015).

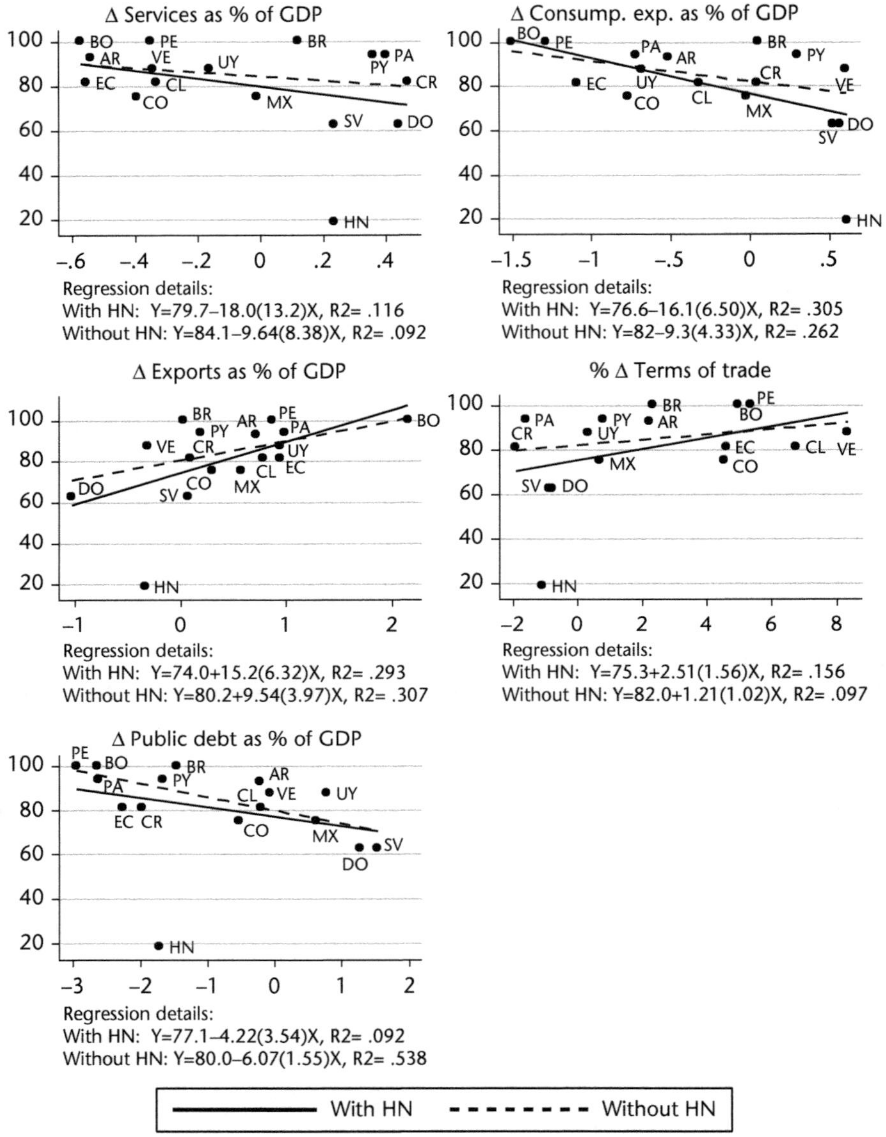

Figure 4.6 Continued

$$\Delta Y_{ik} = C + \beta\ \%\Delta X_{ij} + \varepsilon_{ik} \text{ or } \%\Delta Y_{ik} = C + \beta\%\Delta X_{ij} + \varepsilon_{ik}. \qquad (9)$$

With sixteen indicators and eleven macroeconomic variables, we have 176 regressions to estimate. The results are summarized in Table 4.1. In Table 4.1, *Positive* indicates that the R-squared is above 0.15 and that an increase in the macroeconomic variable is associated with an improvement in the labour indicator; and similarly *Negative* indicates that the relationship is also significant, but an increase in the macro variable is related to a deterioration in the indicator;*NR* (No relationship) indicates a regression with an R-squared of less than 0.15. In Table 4.2, we present the R-squared for each regression, and Appendix 2 presents the figures corresponding to each of these individual regressions.

The results are mixed, with some robust positive and negative relationships and several instances of no clear pattern of association. The change in the share of industry in GDP has a positive association with a number of indicators—an increase in labour earnings, a decline in the unemployment rate, and better distributional indicators (i.e. lower levels of poverty, extreme poverty, and inequality of household per capita income and labour earnings)—and no statistically discernible association with other labour market indicators. The change in exports as a percentage of GDP is positively associated with an increase in mean earnings and in improvements in the labour mix (decline in the share of low-earnings occupations, increase in the share of wage/salaried employees, fall in the share of self-employment and unpaid family workers), as well as improved distributional indicators. The change in terms of trade and the change in revenues from natural resources as a percentage of GDP have a similar pattern of relationships with labour market indicators as the change in exports.

Other macroeconomic variables appear to have a negative association with some of our selected labour market indicators (i.e. increases in the macroeconomic variables seem related to worsenings in these indicators). This is the case for the change in the share of services in GDP, the change in domestic expenditure as a percentage of GDP, and the change in the stock of public debt as a percentage of GDP. Increases in the share of services in GDP are associated with smaller increases/declines in mean labour earnings, smaller declines/increases in the unemployment rate, and a worsening in distributional indicators (i.e. higher levels of poverty and inequality). Similarly, increases in domestic expenditure as a percentage of GDP are associated with smaller increases/declines in mean labour earnings, smaller declines/increases in unemployment, and a worsening in distributive indicators. Increases in the stock of public debt are associated with a general worsening in labour market outcomes (with the exception of the unemployment rate, the share of registered workers, and levels of inequality).

Table 4.1 Direction of the cross-country relationship between annualized changes in macroeconomic variables and annualized changes in labour market indicators and GDP per capita growth during the 2000s

Indicator	Share of agriculture in GDP	Share of industry in GDP	Share of services in GDP	Domestic expenditure (% of GDP)	Public expend. in education and health (% of GDP)	Public expend. in social security (% of GDP)	Exports (% of GDP)	Terms of trade	Foreign direct investment (% of GDP)	Revenues from natural resources (% of GDP)	Stock of public debt (% of GDP)
Unemployment											
Decrease in the unemployment rate	NR	**Positive**	**Negative**	**Negative**	NR	NR	NR	**Negative**	NR	NR	NR
Occupations											
Decrease in the share of low-earnings occupations	NR	NR	NR	**Negative**	NR	NR	**Positive**	NR	NR	**Positive**	**Negative**
Increase in the share of high-earnings occupations	NR	NR	NR	NR	NR	NR	NR	NR	NR	NR	**Negative**
Occupational position											
Increase in the share of wage/salaried employees	NR	NR	NR	NR	NR	NR	**Positive**	NR	NR	NR	**Negative**
Decrease in the share of self-employment	NR	NR	NR	NR	NR	NR	**Positive**	NR	NR	NR	**Negative**
Decrease in the share of unpaid family workers	NR	NR	NR	**Negative**	NR	NR	**Positive**	**Positive**	NR	**Positive**	**Negative**
Economic sector											
Decrease in the share of workers in low-earnings sectors	NR	NR	NR	NR	NR	NR	NR	NR	NR	NR	**Negative**
Increase in the share of workers in high-earnings sectors	NR	NR	NR	NR	NR	**Positive**	NR	NR	NR	NR	**Negative**
Education											
Decrease in the share of low-educated workers	NR	NR	NR	NR	NR	**Positive**	NR	NR	**Negative**	NR	**Negative**
Increase in the share of high-educated workers	NR	NR	NR	NR	NR	**Positive**	NR	NR	NR	NR	**Negative**
Workers registered with SS											
Increase in the share of workers registered with SS	NR	NR	NR	NR	NR	NR	NR	NR	**Positive**	NR	NR

Earnings											
Increase in mean labour earnings	NR	**Positive**	**Negative**	**Negative**	NR	NR	**Positive**	**Positive**	NR	**Positive**	**Negative**
Poverty											
Decrease in 4 dollars-a-day poverty	NR	**Positive**	**Negative**	**Negative**	NR	NR	**Positive**	**Positive**	NR	**Positive**	**Negative**
Decrease in 2.5 dollars-a-day poverty	NR	**Positive**	**Negative**	**Negative**	NR	NR	**Positive**	**Positive**	NR	**Positive**	**Negative**
Inequality											
Decrease in GINI of household per capita income	NR	**Positive**	**Negative**	**Negative**	NR	NR	**Positive**	**Positive**	**Negative**	**Positive**	NR
Decrease in GINI of labour earnings	NR	**Positive**	**Negative**	**Negative**	NR	NR	**Positive**	**Positive**	**Negative**	**Positive**	NR
Economic growth											
Increase in GDPpc at PPP 2005	NR	NR	NR	**Negative**	NR	**Negative**	NR	NR	**Positive**	NR	**Negative**
Number of relationships with labour market indicators	**0**	**6**	**6**	**8**	**0**	**3**	**9**	**7**	**4**	**7**	**12**
Percentage of total indicators	**0.0**	**37.5**	**37.5**	**50.0**	**0.0**	**18.8**	**56.3**	**43.8**	**25.0**	**43.8**	**75.0**

Note: Positive denotes an increase of the macroeconomic variable is associated with a change in the labour market indicator in the welfare-improving direction. Negative denotes an increase of the macroeconomic variable is associated with a change in the labour market indicator in the welfare-worsening direction. NR denotes no relationship, that is the R-squared of a linear regression is smaller than 0.15.

Grey shading implies that the R-squared is higher than 0.15 and the relationship is Positive. Bold typeface with no shading implies that the R-squared is larger than 0.15 and the relationship is Negative.

Source: Authors' calculations based on SEDLAC (CEDLAS and World Bank 2014), World Development Indicators (World Bank 2014), and CEPALSTAT (UN-ECLAC 2015).

Table 4.2 Tightness of the cross-country relationship (R-squared) between annualized changes in macroeconomic variables and annualized changes in labour market indicators and GDP per capita growth during the 2000s

Indicator	Share of agriculture in GDP	Share of industry in GDP	Share of services in GDP	Domestic expenditure (% of GDP)	Public expend. in education and health (% of GDP)	Public expend. in social security (% of GDP)	Exports (% of GDP)	Terms of trade	Foreign direct investment (% of GDP)	Revenues from natural resources (% of GDP)	Stock of public debt (% of GDP)
Unemployment											
Decrease in the unemployment rate	0.00	**0.21**	**0.32**	**0.20**	0.02	0.02	0.11	**0.15**	0.01	0.03	0.02
Occupations											
Decrease in the share of low-earnings occupations	0.00	0.06	0.09	**0.19**	0.01	0.01	**0.18**	0.10	0.00	0.01	**0.55**
Increase in the share of high-earnings occupations	0.09	0.02	0.01	0.11	0.08	0.03	0.06	0.03	0.01	**0.04**	**0.27**
Occupational position											
Increase in the share of wage/salaried employees	0.08	0.01	0.00	0.12	0.00	0.01	**0.23**	0.02	0.00	0.04	**0.28**
Decrease in the share of self-employment	0.11	0.08	0.02	0.06	0.00	0.01	**0.24**	0.04	0.00	0.02	**0.19**
Decrease in the share of unpaid family workers	0.00	0.07	0.10	**0.27**	0.00	0.01	**0.20**	**0.18**	0.00	**0.29**	**0.28**
Economic sector											
Decrease in the share of workers in low-earnings sectors	0.01	0.00	0.00	0.11	0.02	0.04	0.03	0.02	0.00	0.03	**0.15**
Increase in the share of workers in high-earnings sectors	0.05	0.00	0.00	0.01	0.00	**0.36**	0.02	0.12	0.11	0.01	**0.25**
Education											
Decrease in the share of low-educated workers	0.05	0.02	0.00	0.00	0.00	**0.37**	0.01	0.02	**0.20**	0.01	**0.18**
Increase in the share of high-educated workers	0.07	0.00	0.04	0.06	0.02	**0.17**	0.07	0.14	0.04	0.00	**0.22**

Workers registered with SS											
Increase in the share of workers registered with SS	0.12	0.05	0.00	0.06	0.00	0.06	0.00	0.00	**0.16**	0.04	0.06
Earnings											
Increase in mean labour earnings	0.06	**0.30**	**0.25**	**0.29**	0.00	0.06	**0.21**	**0.40**	0.09	**0.24**	**0.53**
Poverty											
Decrease in 4 dollars-a-day poverty	0.07	**0.34**	**0.26**	**0.39**	0.09	0.02	**0.33**	**0.41**	0.12	**0.38**	**0.31**
Decrease in 2.5 dollars-a-day poverty	0.05	**0.36**	**0.31**	**0.41**	0.05	0.02	**0.31**	**0.46**	0.07	**0.38**	**0.38**
Inequality											
Decrease in GINI of household per capita income	0.00	**0.16**	**0.23**	**0.27**	0.09	0.01	**0.23**	**0.16**	**0.19**	**0.24**	0.03
Decrease in GINI of labour earnings	0.00	**0.29**	**0.39**	**0.28**	0.00	0.08	**0.15**	**0.36**	**0.30**	**0.19**	0.09
Economic growth											
Increase in GDPpc at PPP 2005	0.08	0.02	0.00	**0.25**	0.08	**0.15**	0.04	0.00	**0.42**	0.06	**0.21**

Note: Grey shading implies that the R-squared is higher than 0.15 and the relationship is Positive according to Table 4.1. Bold typeface with no shading implies that the R-squared is larger than 0.15 and the relationship is Negative according to Table 4.1.

Source: Authors' calculations based on SEDLAC (CEDLAS and World Bank 2014), World Development Indicators (World Bank 2014), and CEPALSTAT (UN-ECLAC 2015).

We find little or no consistent pattern of association of labour market indicators with the following macroeconomic variables: change in the share of agriculture in GDP, change in public expenditure on education and health as a percentage of GDP, change in public expenditure on social security as a percentage of GDP, and change in foreign direct investment as a percentage of GDP.

Looking at the experiences of countries with widespread labour market improvements in Latin America, we find that there is no unique configuration of macroeconomic factors associated with the number of welfare-improving changes in labour market indicators. On the one hand, there is a group of countries which benefited from better external conditions: higher terms of trade, increased exports, and related to that, increasing revenues from natural resources, and increasing share of industry in GDP. That was the case, for example, for Bolivia and Peru. For these countries, increases in exports seem to have resulted in a shift to the right of the labour demand for high-earnings occupations and wage/salaried employees (improving the mix of jobs), raising labour earnings, and reducing poverty. Some of these countries took advantage of the favourable external conditions, and translated them into higher levels of investment (proxied by the reduction in consumption's share of GDP) and to an improved fiscal balance (as indicated by the fall in the stock of public debt as a percentage of GDP). On the other hand, there is a group of countries where the better external conditions were not present, but the labour market conditions also improved. That was the case of Panama and Costa Rica, which exhibited some of the largest increases in the share of services in GDP and some of the largest reductions in terms of trade and in the stock of public debt as a percentage of GDP. These countries were successful in increasing the labour demand in the service sector, the driving force of these economies.

Our next step is to add the GDP per capita growth rate as a second explanatory variable in the previous models. Our objective is to test the robustness of some of the results obtained in this section: (1) faster growth is associated with larger improvements in labour market indicators, but the relationship is weak; and (2) some macroeconomic variables were associated with changes in labour market conditions always in the welfare-improving direction and some others always in the welfare-reducing direction. The reason for adding the GDP per capita growth rate as an additional regressor to the bivariate models where the explanatory factor is a macroeconomic variable is that the two variables (GDP per capita growth rate and macroeconomic variable) could be correlated, e.g. countries with larger increases in terms of trade enjoy larger increases in GDP per capita. Including the two of them as regressors allows us to separate, at least partially, the effect of the GDP per capita growth rate on the change in labour market indicators from the effect of macroeconomic factors.

We perform a series of regressions for the change in labour market indicators on the changes in the macroeconomic variables and the change in GDP per capita. Let Y_{ik} be the labour market indicators k for country i, X_{ij} be the macroeconomic variable j in country i, and $GDPpc_i$ be GDP per capita in country i. We estimate the following regression for two employment and earnings indicators (the hange in the unemployment rate and the change in mean labour income), and two poverty indicators (changes in the 2.5 and 4 dollars-a-day poverty rates):

$$\Delta Y_{ik} = C + \beta \Delta X_{ij} + \gamma \% \Delta GDP\rho c_i + \varepsilon_{ik} \text{ or}$$
$$\% \Delta Y_{ik} = C + \beta \Delta X_{ij} + \gamma \% \Delta GDP\rho c_i + \varepsilon_{ik} \tag{10}$$

and

$$11 \Delta Y_{ik} = C + \beta \% \Delta X_{ij} + \gamma \% \Delta GDP\rho c_i + \varepsilon_{ik} \text{ or}$$
$$\% \Delta Y_{ik} = C + \beta \% \Delta X_{ij} + \gamma \% \Delta GDP\rho c_i + \varepsilon_{ik}. \tag{11}$$

Our results are presented in Table 4.3. Model 1 uses GDP per capita growth rate as the only regressor and replicates the results obtained in section 4.1. Model 2 uses the changes in macroeconomic variables as regressors (one at a time) and replicates the results obtained previously in this section. Finally, Model 3 includes both the GDP per capita growth rate and the changes in macroeconomic variables as explanatory factors. In general, the magnitudes of the coefficients and standard errors of the estimations in the multivariate model (Model 3) are similar to those obtained in the bivariate models (Models 1 and 2). The details of these findings are as follows. First, from the forty-four regressions (eleven macroeconomic variables × four labour market indicators), in only four cases did the macroeconomic variables move from being not statistically significant in the bivariate model (Model 2) to being significant at the 5 per cent level in the multivariate model (Model 3). In all four cases, the sign of the relationship remained the same when moving from the bivariate model to the model that also includes the change in GDP per capita as a control variable. Second, in no case did a macroeconomic variable that was significant in statistical terms in the bivariate model (Model 2) turn to insignificance in the multivariate model (Model 3). Third, out of the forty-four regressions, in only six cases was the GDP per capita growth rate a significant factor explaining changes in labour market indicators across countries in the multivariate model (Model 3) when it was not in the bivariate model (Model 1), and the sign of the relationship was always the same as the one obtained in the bivariate regression. In conclusion, the weakness of the relationship between changes in labour market indicators and the GDP per capita growth rate across countries is not related to the effect

Table 4.3 Cross-country relationship between annualized changes in labour market indicators and annualized changes in macroeconomic variables and in GDP per capita during the 2000s

Part A

	Δ Unemployment rate							Δ% Mean labour earnings						
	(1)		(2)		(3)			(1)		(2)		(3)		
	GDPpc growth rate coefficient	R-squared	ΔX variable coeff.	R-squared	ΔX variable coeff.	GDPpc growth rate coefficient	R-squared	GDP pc growth rate coefficient	R-squared	ΔX variable coeff.	R-squared	ΔX variable coeff.	GDP pc growth rate coefficient	R-squared
Δ% GDP per capita	−0.075	0.090						0.228	0.032					
	(0.05)							(0.254)						
Δ Exports (% of GDP)			−0.143	0.105	−0.121	−0.061	0.162			1.033	0.209	0.992	0.114	0.217
			(0.108)		(0.108)	(0.058)				(0.505)**		(0.546)*	(0.259)	
Δ% Terms of trade			−0.039	0.151	−0.040	−0.078	0.248	0.000	0.000	0.322	0.398	0.325	0.254	0.437
			(0.022)		(0.022)	(0.063)				(0.109)**		(0.107)**	(0.19)	
Δ Share of services in GDP			0.467	0.316	0.466	−0.075	0.405		0.000	−2.124	0.249	−2.123	0.228	0.281
			(0.197)*		(0.187)*	(0.068)				(1.019)*		(1.056)*	(0.217)	
Δ Share of industry in GDP			−0.313	0.205	−0.287	−0.058	0.259		0.000	1.938	0.300	1.885	0.122	0.309
			(0.166)		(0.176)	(0.059)				(0.908)*		(0.954)*	(0.215)	
Δ Share of agriculture in GDP			−0.070	0.003	−0.208	−0.086	0.110		0.000	−1.665	0.055	−1.417	0.154	0.068
			(0.316)		(0.318)	(0.057)				(1.374)		(1.39)	(0.27)	
Δ Public expend. in education and health (% of GDP)			−0.313	0.024	−0.522	−0.093	0.150		0.000	0.389	0.001	0.983	0.262	0.040
			(0.651)		(0.625)	(0.057)				(2.341)		(2.68)	(0.289)	
Δ Public expend. in social security (% of GDP)			−0.223	0.018	−0.493	−0.104	0.165		0.000	2.013	0.056	3.082	0.411	0.144
			(0.298)		(0.395)	(0.045)*				(1.394)		(1.533)**	(0.274)	
Δ Domestic expenditure (% of GDP)			0.204	0.198	0.180	−0.025	0.205		0.000	−1.255	0.286	−1.398	−0.155	0.297
			(0.12)		(0.148)	(0.073)				(0.547)*		(0.602)*	(0.26)	
Δ Foreign direct investment (% of GDP)			0.108	0.008	0.599	−0.152	0.223		0.000	−1.945	0.092	−4.596	0.820	0.332

			(0.327)		(0.517)	(0.076)*				(1.312)		(1.216)**	(0.292)**	
Δ Revenues from natural resources (% of GDP)			−0.138	0.029	−0.086	−0.068	0.100		0.000	2.025	0.238	1.959	0.087	0.242
			(0.215)		(0.243)	(0.057)				(0.859)*		(0.926)*	(0.268)	
Δ Stock of public debt (% of GDP)			0.033	0.022	0.003	−0.073	0.090		0.000	−0.813	0.527	−0.914	−0.252	0.558
			(0.055)		(0.069)	(0.064)				(0.177)**		(0.21)**	(0.235)	

Part B

	Δ 2.5 dollars-a-day poverty							Δ 4 dollars-a-day poverty						
	(1)		(2)		(3)			(1)		(2)		(3)		
	GDP pc growth rate coefficient	R-squared	ΔX variable coeff.	R-squared	ΔX variable coeff.	GDP pc growth rate coefficient	R-squared	GDP pc growth rate coefficient	R-squared	ΔX variable coeff.	R-squared	ΔX variable coeff.	GDP pc growth rate coefficient	R-squared
Δ% GDP per capita	−0.138 (0.097)	0.056						−0.249 (0.138)	0.105					
Δ Exports (% of GDP)			−0.589 (0.191)**	0.325	−0.563 (0.193)**	−0.073 (0.081)	0.340			−0.753 (0.26)**	0.308	−0.692 (0.266)***	−0.170 (0.123)	0.355
Δ% Terms of trade			−0.149 (0.051)**	0.410	−0.151 (0.045)**	−0.150 (0.095)	0.475			−0.208 (0.065)**	0.462	−0.212 (0.053)**	−0.266 (0.105)*	0.582
Δ Share of services in GDP			0.991 (0.423)*	0.260	0.991 (0.427)*	−0.138 (0.095)	0.315			1.409 (0.527)**	0.305	1.408 (0.51)**	−0.249 (0.116)*	0.410
Δ Share of industry in GDP			−0.947 (0.391)*	0.343	−0.910 (0.413)*	−0.087 (0.088)	0.365			−1.276 (0.499)*	0.361	−1.197 (0.524)*	−0.182 (0.113)	0.416
Δ Share of agriculture in GDP			0.826 (0.601)	0.065	0.659 (0.707)	−0.103 (0.122)	0.093			0.936 (0.739)	0.048	0.583 (0.819)	−0.219 (0.163)	0.123
Δ Public expend. in education and health (% of GDP)			1.400 (1.063)	0.086	1.178 (1.202)	−0.098 (0.114)	0.112			1.380 (1.354)	0.049	0.884 (1.523)	−0.219 (0.158)	0.124

(continued)

Table 4.3 Continued

Part B

	Δ 2.5 dollars-a-day poverty							Δ 4 dollars-a-day poverty						
	(1)		(2)		(3)			(1)		(2)		(3)		
	GDP pc growth rate coefficient	R-squared	ΔX variable coeff.	R-squared	ΔX variable coeff.	GDP pc growth rate coefficient	R-squared	GDP pc growth rate coefficient	R-squared	ΔX variable coeff.	R-squared	ΔX variable coeff.	GDP pc growth rate coefficient	R-squared
Δ Public expend. in social security (% of GDP)			−0.579	0.022	−1.109	−0.204	0.125			−0.748	0.022	−1.650	−0.347	0.194
			(0.783)		(0.877)	(0.126)				(1.099)		(1.096)	(0.162)*	
Δ Domestic expenditure (% of GDP)			0.668	0.388	0.724	0.060	0.396			0.899	0.407	0.896	−0.004	0.408
			(0.226)**		(0.23)**	(0.081)				(0.3)**		(0.314)**	(0.109)	
Δ Foreign direct investment (% of GDP)			1.003	0.117	2.481	−0.457	0.475			1.045	0.074	3.169	−0.657	0.502
			(0.767)		(0.639)**	(0.141)**				(1.019)		(0.708)**	(0.166)**	
Δ Revenues from natural resources (% of GDP)			−1.176	0.384	−1.133	−0.056	0.393			−1.543	0.383	−1.432	−0.146	0.418
			(0.36)**		(0.401)**	(0.115)				(0.458)**		(0.484)**	(0.137)	
Δ Stock of public debt (% of GDP)			0.287	0.314	0.293	0.016	0.314			0.413	0.378	0.397	−0.041	0.381
			(0.089)**		(0.136)*	(0.141)				(0.105)**		(0.162)*	(0.179)	

Note: ** significant at 1% level, * significant at 5% level.

Source: Authors' calculations based on SEDLAC (CEDLAS and World Bank 2014), World Development Indicators (World Bank 2014), and CEPALSTAT (UN-ECLAC 2015).

of macroeconomic variables added one at a time. Similarly, the finding of a tight relationship between changes in labour market indicators and changes in some macroeconomic factors is not related to the rate of GDP per capita growth.

In summary, increases in some macroeconomic variables were associated with changes in labour market conditions in Latin America during the 2000s, some of them always in the welfare-improving direction and some others always in the welfare-reducing direction. There is no unique configuration of macroeconomic variables that was associated with the several successful experiences among our sample of sixteen countries. Finally, the correlation between the change in GDP per capita and the change in macroeconomic variables seemed to be small enough so as not to affect in general the magnitudes of the coefficients and standard errors in the estimations of the relationships between changes in labour market indicators and the rate of GDP per capita growth on the one hand, and changes in macroeconomic variables on the other hand.

4.2.4 *Relationship between Labour Market Indicators*

Another question is whether the labour market indicators tend to improve or worsen together, or whether there are pairs of indicators such that a higher rate of improvement in one is associated with a lower rate of improvement or a worsening of the other. For example, a higher rate of earnings growth could be associated with a higher increase in unemployment due to employers moving up along a single downward-sloping labour demand curve.

Our findings indicate that labour market indicators either improved jointly or worsened jointly. Table 4.4 displays the cross-country correlations between the changes or percentage changes in each of our sixteen labour market indicators. In particular, we estimate the following sets of correlations:

$$Corr(\Delta Y_{ik}, \Delta Y_{im}) \text{ or } Corr(\Delta Y_{ik}, \%\Delta Y_{im}) \quad \text{or}$$

$$Corr(\%\Delta Y_{ik}, \%\Delta Y_{im})$$

for

$$k \neq m \tag{12}$$

A correlation coefficient between 0.4 and 1 implies that, in a regression of the annualized changes in two labour market indicators, the R-squared is larger than 0.15 (which corresponds with the cut-off value we used previously), and that the association between the two variables is positive. Conversely, a coefficient between −1 and −0.4 indicates a negative relationship.

Table 4.4 Cross-country correlation matrix between the annualized changes in labour market indicators during the 2000s

Part A

		Occupations		Occupational position			Economic sector	
	Decline in unemployment	Declined in share of low-earnings occupations	Increase in share of high-earnings occupations	Increase in the share of wage/salaried employees	Decrease in the share of self-employment	Decrease in the share of unpaid family workers	Decline in the share of workers in low-earnings sectors	Increase in the share of workers in high-earnings sectors
Unemployment								
Decrease in the unemployment rate	**1.00**	0.33	0.20	−0.06	−0.03	−0.15	0.07	0.01
Occupations								
Decrease in the share of low-earnings occupations	0.33	**1.00**	**0.43**	**0.57**	0.37	**0.53**	**0.52**	**0.44**
Increase in the share of high-earnings occupations	0.20	**0.43**	**1.00**	0.35	**0.42**	0.23	0.22	0.21
Occupational position								
Increase in the share of wage/salaried employees	−0.06	**0.57**	0.35	**1.00**	**0.82**	**0.75**	**0.57**	**0.67**
Decrease in the share of self-employment	−0.03	0.37	**0.42**	**0.82**	**1.00**	0.39	0.32	**0.50**
Decrease in the share of unpaid family workers	−0.15	**0.53**	0.23	**0.75**	0.39	**1.00**	**0.66**	**0.58**
Economic sector								
Decrease in the share of workers in low-earnings sectors	0.07	**0.52**	0.22	**0.57**	0.32	**0.66**	**1.00**	**0.66**
Increase in the share of workers in high-earnings sectors	0.01	**0.44**	0.21	**0.67**	**0.50**	**0.58**	**0.66**	**1.00**
Education								
Decrease in the share of low-educated workers	−0.02	0.35	0.31	**0.64**	**0.52**	**0.53**	**0.68**	**0.89**
Increase in the share of high-educated workers	0.32	**0.61**	**0.60**	**0.68**	**0.58**	**0.48**	**0.50**	**0.75**
Workers registered with SS								
Increase in the share of workers registered with SS	0.23	−0.08	0.10	−0.03	−0.16	0.18	**0.46**	0.05
Earnings								
Increase in mean labour earnings	**0.42**	**0.72**	**0.51**	**0.48**	0.22	**0.52**	**0.44**	**0.67**

Poverty								
Decrease in 4 dollars-a-day poverty	0.36	**0.65**	**0.44**	**0.55**	0.28	**0.58**	**0.62**	**0.61**
Decrease in 2.5 dollars-a-day poverty	**0.41**	**0.73**	**0.47**	**0.59**	0.28	**0.61**	**0.58**	**0.61**
Inequality								
Decrease in GINI of household per capita income	0.23	0.32	0.07	0.38	0.24	**0.48**	**0.55**	0.29
Decrease in GINI of labour earnings	**0.47**	**0.43**	0.29	0.33	0.13	**0.50**	**0.58**	**0.46**

Part B

	Education				Poverty		Inequality	
	Decrease in the share of low-educated workers	Increase in the share of high-educated workers	Workers registered with SS	Increase in mean labour earnings	Decline in 4-dollar-a-day poverty	Decline in 4-dollar-a-day poverty	Decline in GINI of household per capita income	Decline in GINI of labour earnings
Unemployment Decrease in the unemployment rate	−0.02	0.32	0.23	**0.42**	0.36	**0.41**	0.23	**0.47**
Occupations								
Decrease in the share of low-earnings occupations	0.35	**0.61**	−0.08	**0.72**	**0.65**	**0.73**	0.32	**0.43**
Increase in the share of high-earnings occupations	0.31	**0.60**	0.10	**0.51**	**0.44**	**0.47**	0.07	0.29
Occupational position								
Increase in the share of wage/salaried employees	**0.64**	**0.68**	−0.03	**0.48**	**0.55**	**0.59**	0.38	0.33
Decrease in the share of self-employment	**0.52**	**0.58**	−0.16	0.22	0.28	0.28	0.24	0.13
Decrease in the share of unpaid family workers	**0.53**	**0.48**	0.18	**0.52**	**0.58**	**0.61**	**0.48**	**0.50**

(*continued*)

Table 4.4 Continued

Part B

	Education				Poverty		Inequality	
	Decrease in the share of low-educated workers	Increase in the share of high-educated workers	Workers registered with SS	Increase in mean labour earnings	Decline in 4-dollar-a-day poverty	Decline in 4-dollar-a-day poverty	Decline in GINI of household per capita income	Decline in GINI of labour earnings
Economic sector								
Decrease in the share of workers in low-earnings sectors	**0.68**	**0.50**	**0.46**	**0.44**	**0.62**	**0.58**	**0.55**	**0.58**
Increase in the share of workers in high-earnings sectors	**0.89**	**0.75**	0.05	**0.67**	**0.61**	**0.61**	0.29	**0.46**
Education								
Decrease in the share of low-educated workers	**1.00**	**0.67**	0.01	**0.60**	**0.53**	**0.51**	0.28	**0.46**
Increase in the share of high-educated workers	**0.67**	**1.00**	0.07	**0.68**	**0.56**	**0.63**	0.20	**0.49**
Workers registered with SS								
Increase in the share of workers registered with SS	0.01	0.07	**1.00**	0.04	0.17	0.17	0.30	**0.40**
Earnings								
Increase in mean labour earnings	**0.60**	**0.68**	0.04	**1.00**	**0.83**	**0.88**	0.28	**0.58**
Poverty								
Decrease in 4 dollars-a-day poverty	**0.53**	**0.56**	0.17	**0.83**	**1.00**	**0.98**	**0.70**	**0.77**
Decrease in 2.5 dollars-a-day poverty	**0.51**	**0.63**	0.17	**0.88**	**0.98**	**1.00**	**0.62**	**0.75**
Inequality								
Decrease in GINI of household per capita income	0.28	0.20	0.30	0.28	**0.70**	**0.62**	**1.00**	**0.85**
Decrease in GINI of labour earnings	**0.46**	**0.49**	**0.40**	**0.58**	**0.77**	**0.75**	**0.85**	**1.00**

Note: The grey shading indicates a positive correlation larger than 0.4. Correlations for occupations do not include Argentina for which we do not have data.

Source: Authors' calculations based on SEDLAC (CEDLAS and World Bank 2014).

The shaded cells in Table 4.4 indicate a strong relationship between two labour market indicators.

We find that most of our labour market indicators tend to move together, with not even one instance of a substantial trade-off between changes in our selected labour market indicators, i.e. improvements in one do not come at the cost of worsening in others. Specifically, of the 120 correlations we computed, we find that seventy-one (59 per cent of the total) of the pairs of indicators have a positive and significant association, while for the forty-nine remaining pairs we found only weak but generally positive associations. Finally, there is not even a single value in the matrix with a negative sign and above (in absolute value) our cut-off value equal to −0.4, which will indicate a trade-off between two labour market indicators: the lower value is equal to −0.16.

Several labour market indicators are highly correlated among them, with a few exceptions (Table 4.4). On the one hand, labour earnings, the sectoral and educational composition of employment, and the distributive indicators have a significant correlation with at least ten other labour market indicators. On the other hand, the unemployment rate, the share of self-employed, the share of registered workers, the Gini of household per capita income, and the share of high-earnings occupations do not co-vary as much with other indicators (they are significantly correlated with six or fewer of the others).

Some clear patterns of correlations appear from this evidence. The results from Table 4.4 and Figure 4.7 indicate that changes in labour earnings tend to be highly correlated with changes in the job mix (i.e. the occupational, positional, sectoral, and educational composition of the employed population). There may be a simple explanation for these relationships: a rightward shift of the labour demand curve, such that in order to attract more workers into the better job categories, employers must raise wages. Average earnings may also increase just by a composition effect: in a context of high unemployment, a rightward shift of the labour demand curve may lead to an increase in the share of better paying occupations, and thus in average earnings, with fixed hourly wages. As expected, increases in labour earnings are also highly correlated with reductions in poverty: countries in which labour earnings increased were generally ones in which poverty fell, which indicates the importance of labour earnings in the total income of the household. Increases in labour earnings are also related to reductions in the inequality of their distribution, indicating that the process of growth was also inequality-reducing. The evidence of improvements in the job mix, of increases in labour earnings, and of reductions in earnings inequality suggests that workers moved on average to better-paying jobs.

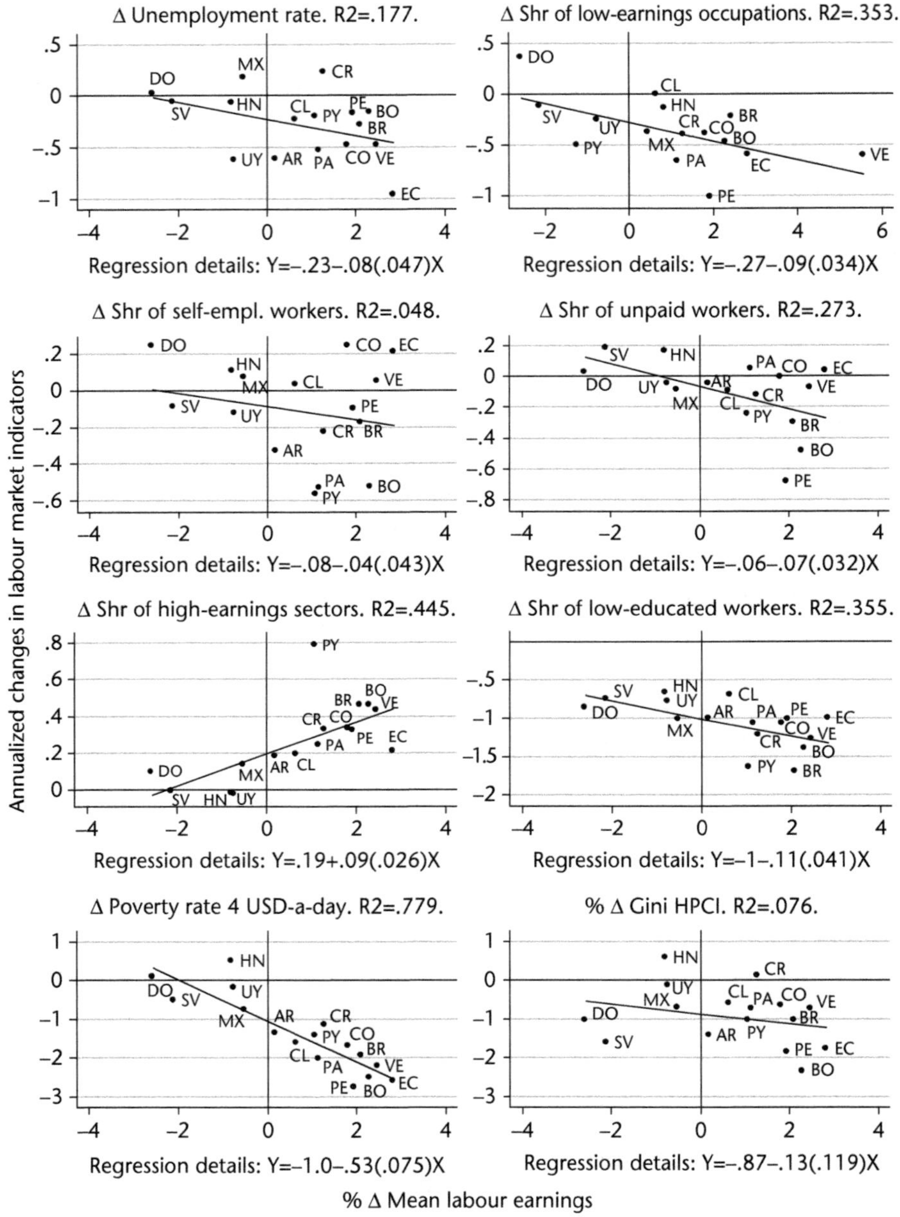

Figure 4.7 Cross-country relationship between annualized changes in labour market indicators and annualized changes in mean labour earnings during the 2000s

Note: The vertical axes display the annualized changes in each labour market indicator.Δdenotes changes in percentage points; % Δ denotes percentage changes. The line represents the linear regression specified at the bottom of the figure. Robust standard error of the slope coefficient between parentheses. R-squared of the regression indicated along the title of each figure.

Source: Authors' calculations based on SEDLAC (CEDLAS and World Bank 2014).

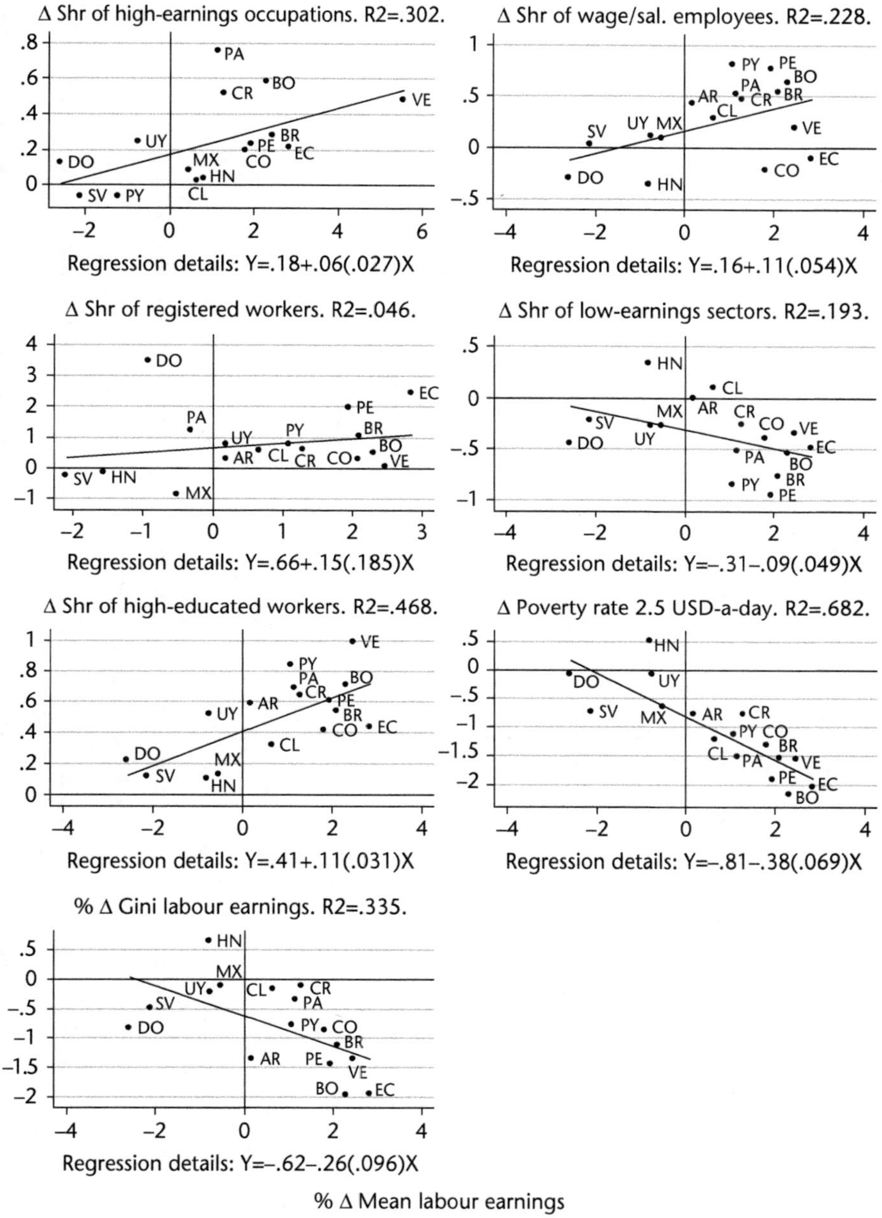

Figure 4.7 Continued

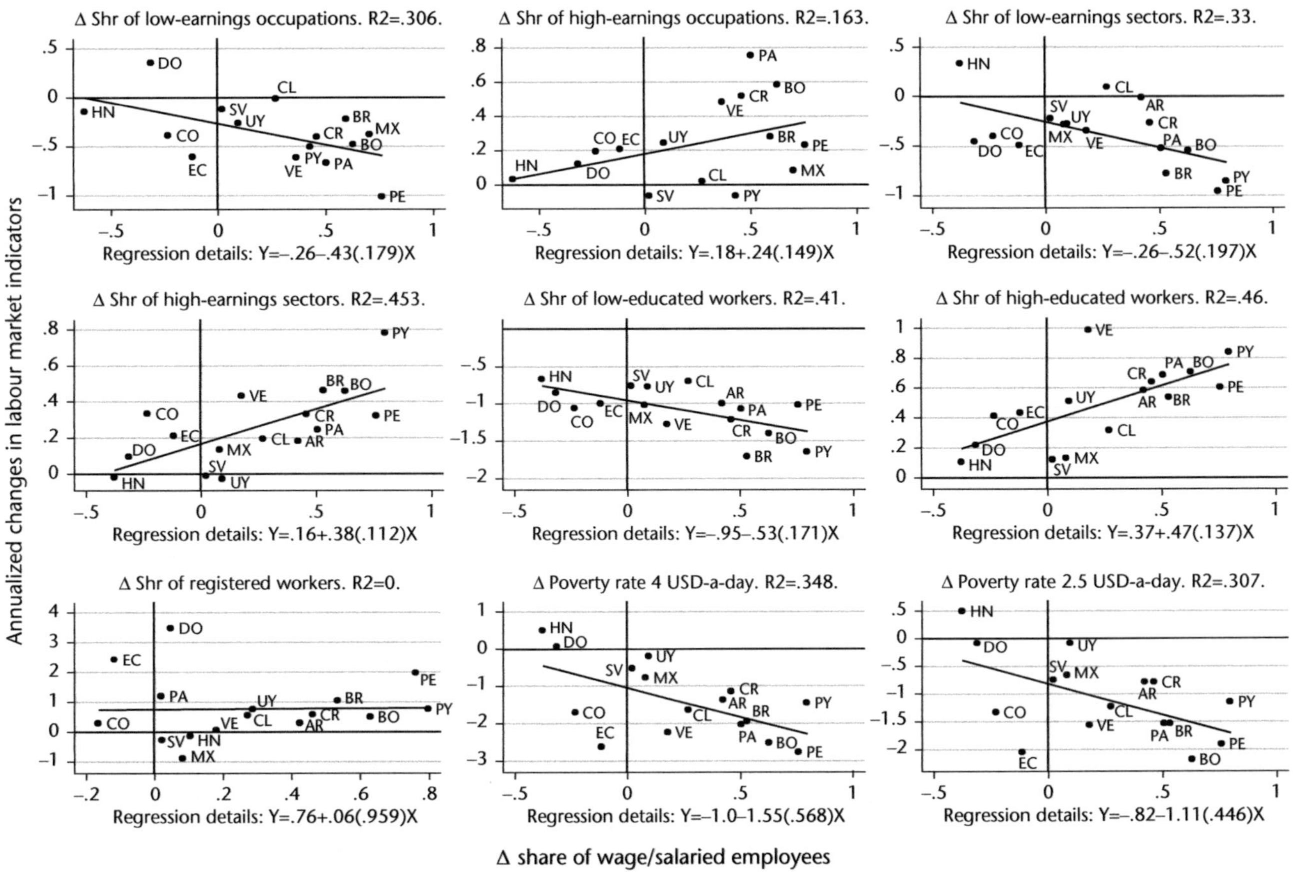

Figure 4.8 Cross-country relationship between annualized changes in selected labour market indicators and annualized changes in the share of wage/salaried employees in total employment during the 2000s

Note: The vertical axes display the annualized changes in each labour market indicator. Δ denotes changes in percentage points; % Δ denotes percentage changes. The line represents the linear regression specified at the bottom of the figure. Robust standard error of the slope coefficient between parentheses. R-squared of the regression indicated along the title of each figure.

We now turn to analyse the relationship between the share of wage/salaried employees and some selected indicators, illustrated in Figure 4.8.[1] An increase in the share of wage/salaried employees is associated with a general improvement in the labour market. Not only is the share of wage/salaried employees related to reductions in moderate and extreme poverty, but also with increases in the shares of high-earnings occupations and high-earnings sectors, as well as reductions in the shares of low-earnings occupations and sectors. These findings are also consistent with a rightward shift of labour demand in wage/salaried jobs, which seem to have a high incidence in high-earnings occupations and sectors, increasing their shares of employment and reducing poverty.

4.3 Cross-Country Patterns: Changing Employment, Earnings, and Inequality Indicators and Changes in Poverty

Our results in Chapter 3 indicated that real GDP per capita grew substantially in all Latin American countries in the 2000s, with an average per capita growth rate of approximately 3 per cent a year. We also reported that poverty, extreme poverty, and inequality also fell substantially in all but one of the sixteen countries in the region in the 2000s. At the same time, while employment and earnings indicators also improved in most countries, they did so more in some countries than in others. In this section, we analyse in more detail the relationship between changes in employment and earnings indicators, and changes in poverty indicators. We aim to establish whether larger improvements in employment and earnings are associated with larger reductions in poverty, over and above the rate of economic growth. We present here a cross-country analysis of the employment and earnings–poverty relationships based on sixteen data points (one for each country) representing the annualized changes between the initial and the final years for each country.

Although poverty reduction in the region is a well-documented fact, the studies that analyse its labour market determinants are scarcer and they only focus on a small group of labour market variables to explain the fall in the poverty rates during the 2000s. An example is ECLAC-ILO (2015), which relates the remarkable progress in reducing poverty during the period 2002–12 in the Latin America region to labour market trends. The main factors mentioned in this study are: the strong job creation, especially in wage/salaried positions, and public policies, such as minimum wages increases, formalization of workers, and expanding coverage of social protection systems and education. Other papers rely on decomposition approaches to disentangle

[1] We provide a detailed analysis of the cross-country relationship between poverty indicators and employment and earnings indicators in section 4.3.1.

the importance of different labour market outcomes in reducing poverty. This is the case of World Bank (2015), which uses different decomposition approaches to investigate the role played by different income sources in reducing poverty. The study finds that changes in labour earnings were the most important factor in explaining poverty reduction in the region during 2003–8 and 2008–13, but its importance was lower in the post-international-crisis period than before. ECLAC (2014) points out that the most important factor explaining the decline in poverty during the 2000s was the combined increase in employment and wages, although in general, labour earnings increases had a greater impact than employment growth on household income changes. This is consistent with Beccaria et al. (2011), World Bank (2013), and Inchauste et al. (2014), who also decompose changes in the poverty rate and report increases in labour income as the main channel to poverty reductions.

4.3.1 *Response of Poverty to Employment and Earnings Indicators*

Our evidence reveals a strong and consistent cross-country pattern of association between reductions in poverty and extreme poverty, and improvements in earnings and employment indicators. These relationships are illustrated in the scatter plots presented in Figure 4.9 (for poverty based on the 2.5 dollars-a-day poverty line) and Figure 4.10 (for poverty based on the 4 dollars-a-day poverty line). We find that eleven out of fourteen of the associations in Figure 4.9 and twelve out of fourteen of the associations in Figure 4.10 (excluding the relationship between the two poverty indicators in both cases) present an R-squared above a 0.15 threshold, and in almost all cases, whether the relationships are above this threshold or not, the sign of correlation is in the expected direction, i.e. improvements in earnings and employment indicators are associated with reductions in poverty rates.

Among employment and earnings indicators, there is a very strong negative cross-country correlation between changes in mean earnings and changes in moderate and extreme poverty rates during the period under study, with a stronger relationship for moderate poverty: that is, mean earnings rose faster while poverty fell faster. The relationships between changes in the two poverty rates and the percentage change in mean labour earnings are the strongest in both Figures 4.9 and 4.10. In both cases, larger increases in labour earnings are associated with larger reductions in poverty levels, with a somewhat stronger relationship for moderate poverty in Figure 4.9 (R-squared of 0.78), than for extreme poverty in Figure 4.10 (R-squared of 0.68). The correlations between percentage changes in mean labour earnings and changes in the two poverty measures, however, are both very strong, and the difference between the two is only a matter of degree. This result is consistent with the discussion

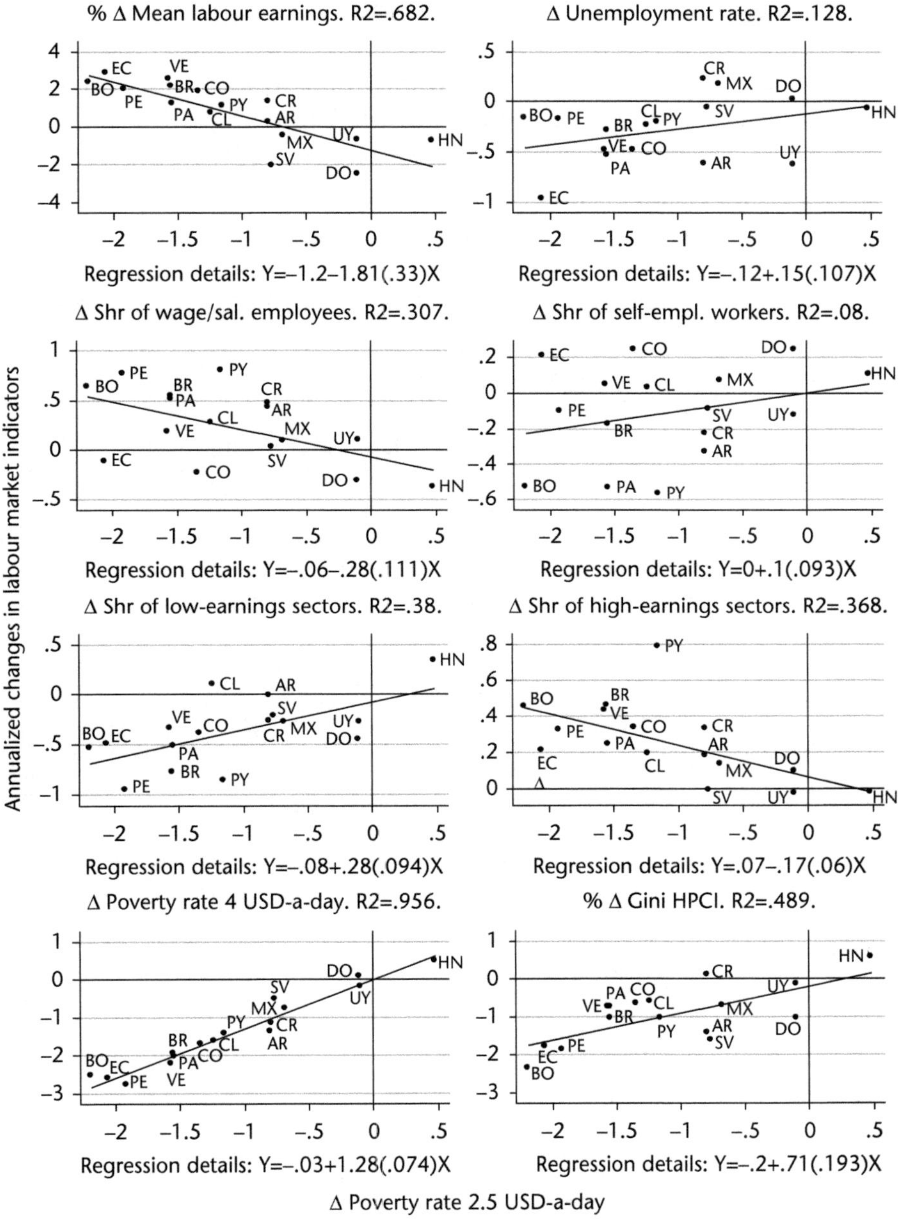

Figure 4.9 Cross-country relationship between annualized changes in labour market indicators and annualized changes in the 2.5 dollars-a-day poverty rate during the 2000s

Note: The vertical axes display the annualized changes in each labour market indicator. Δ denotes changes in percentage points; % Δ denotes percentage changes. The line represents the linear regression specified at the bottom of the figure. Robust standard error of the slope coefficient between parentheses. R-squared of the regression indicated along the title of each figure.

Source: Authors' calculations based on SEDLAC (CEDLAS and World Bank 2014).

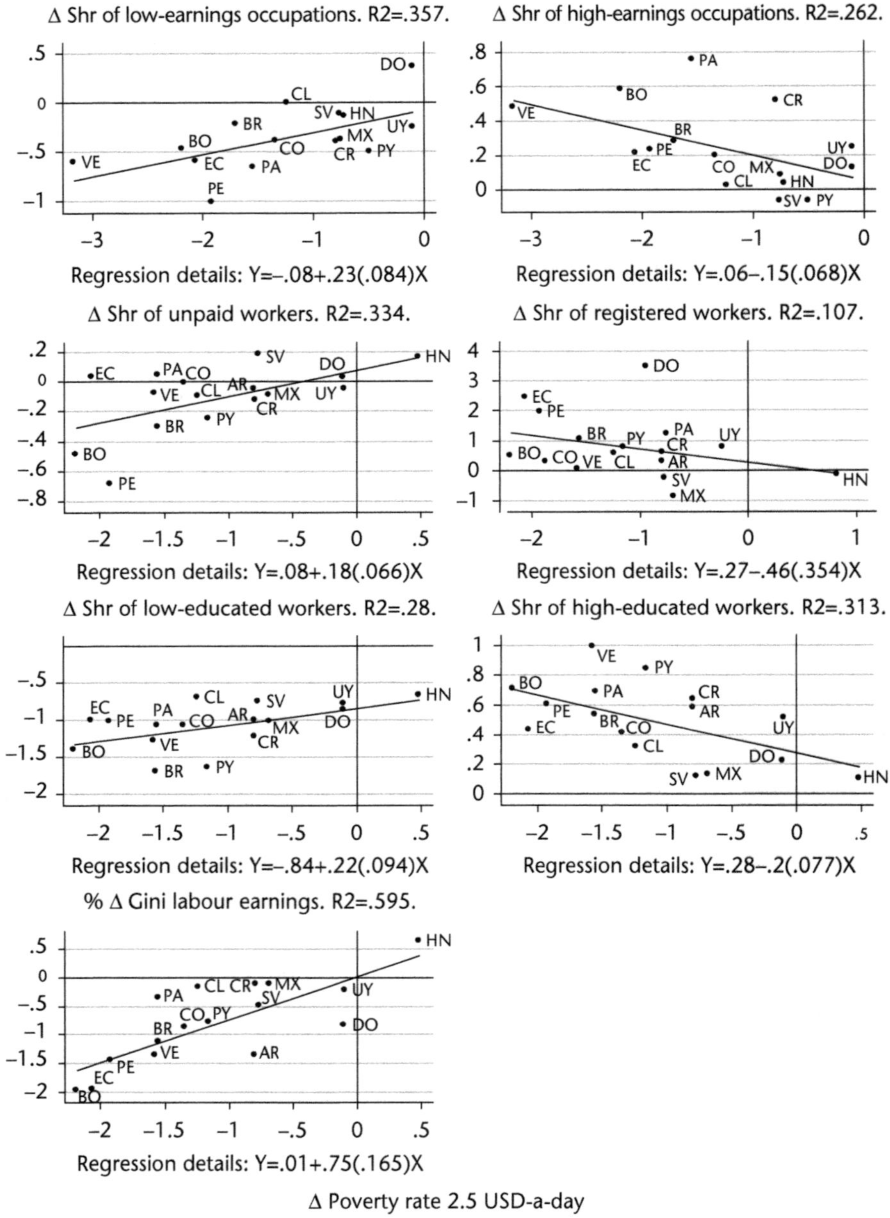

Figure 4.9 Continued

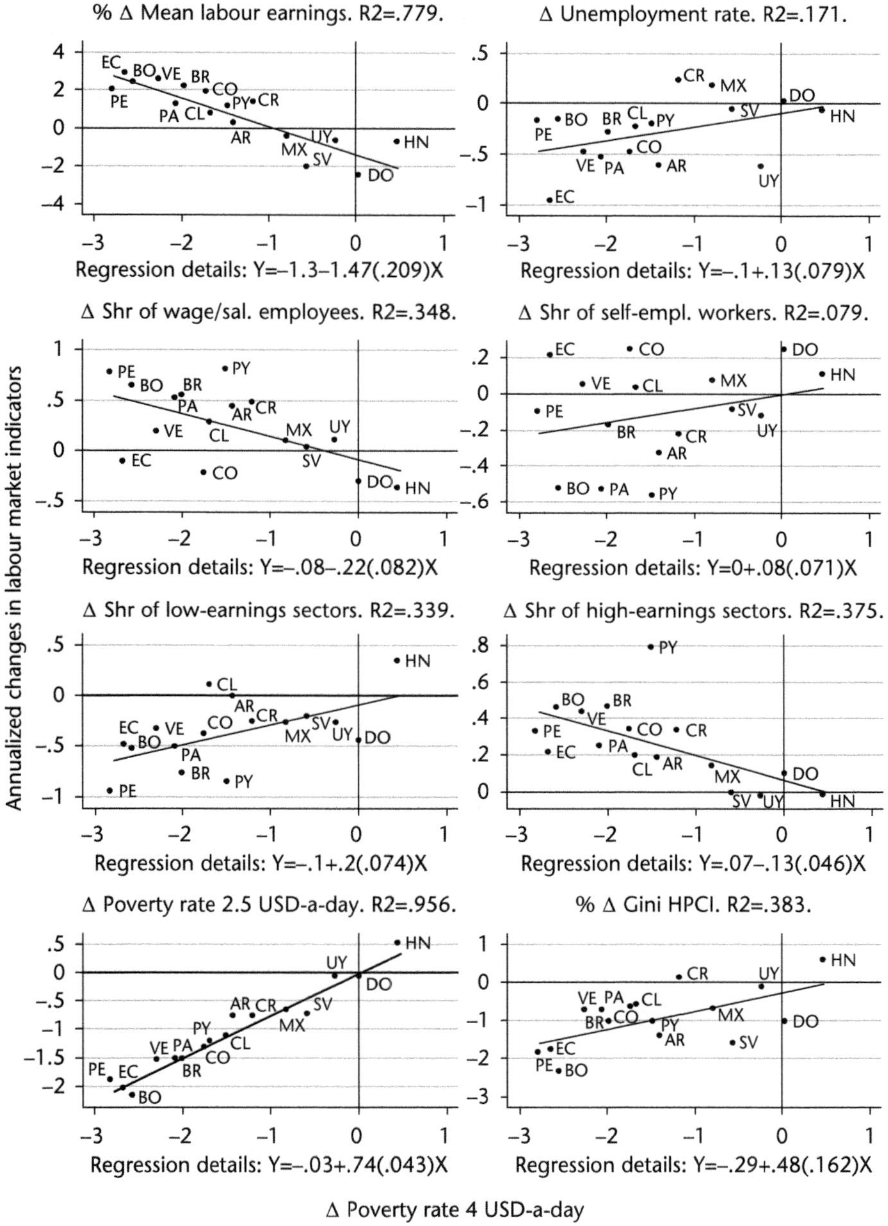

Figure 4.10 Cross-country relationship between annualized changes in labour market indicators and annualized changes in the 4 dollars-a-day poverty rate during the 2000s

Note: The vertical axes display the annualized changes in each labour market indicator. Δ denotes changes in percentage points; % Δ denotes percentage changes. The line represents the linear regression specified at the bottom of the figure. Robust standard error of the slope coefficient between parentheses. R-squared of the regression indicated along the title of each figure.

Source: Authors' calculations based on SEDLAC (CEDLAS and World Bank 2014).

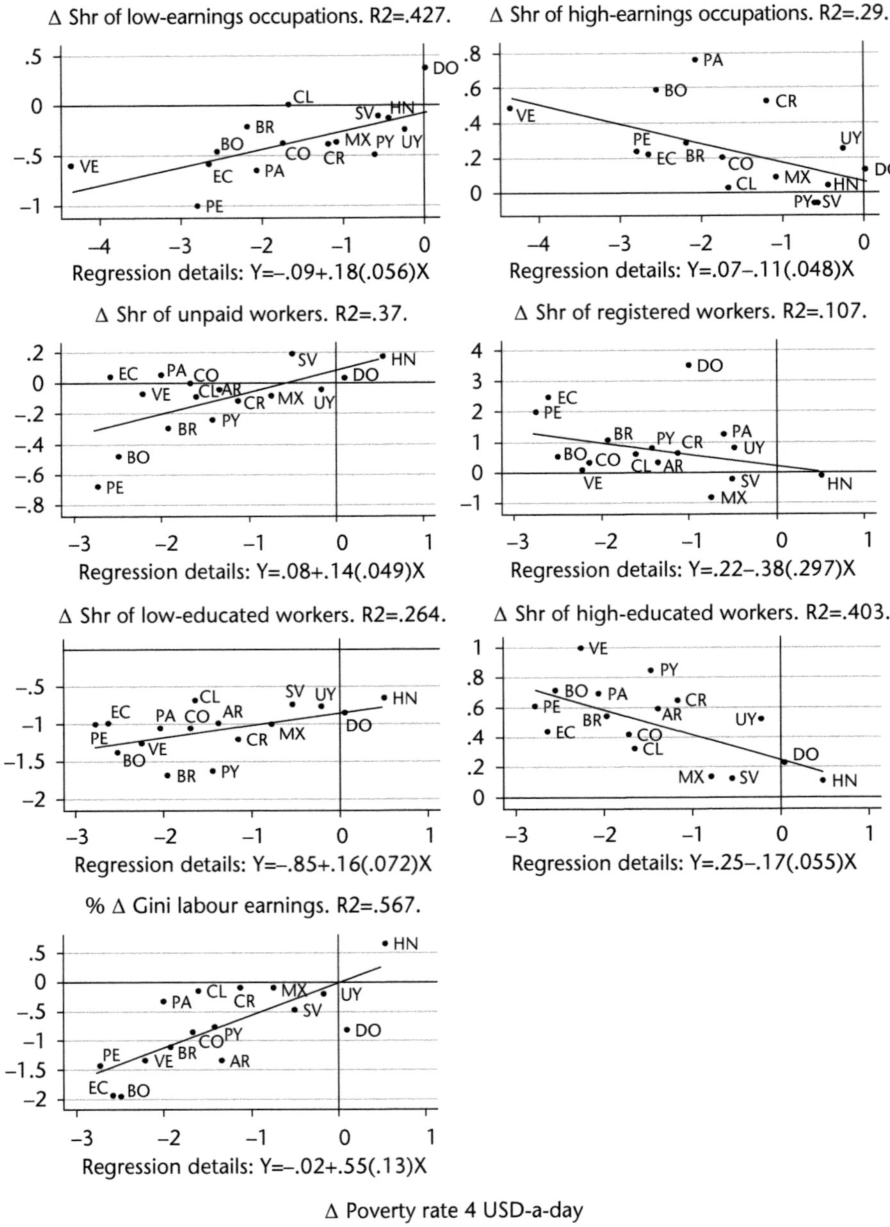

Figure 4.10 Continued

in the literature for Latin America stressing that the extreme poor do not benefit as much as those closer to the moderate poverty line from the trickle-down of economic growth (and the subsequent increase in labour earnings), which implies that improving the living conditions of those harder to reach needs more government-based redistribution than those relatively better-off among the poor (see, for instance, Cruces and Gasparini 2013, and references therein). This is also apparent in the weaker relationship between poverty rates and unemployment that we analyse in the following paragraph.

There is a positive but relatively weak correlation between changes in moderate and extreme poverty rates and changes in the unemployment rate, with a somewhat stronger relationship for moderate poverty. Whereas we found a very strong and tight association between changes in labour earnings and changes in poverty rates, the scatter plots in Figures 4.9 and 4.10 for the unemployment rate evidence a much weaker relationship. For the extreme poverty rate, the R-squared is only about 0.13, and this weak relationship is evident in the figure: for instance, Argentina, Colombia, Panama, Uruguay, and Venezuela all experienced an annualized reduction in unemployment of about 0.5 percentage points a year, but the changes in extreme poverty differed vastly between these countries, with almost no change for Uruguay and reductions from about 0.75 (Argentina) to about 1.5 percentage points (Colombia, Panama, Venezuela). Moreover, countries with about the same change in extreme poverty also experienced quite dissimilar changes in unemployment: for instance, Argentina, Costa Rica, El Salvador, and Mexico all saw annualized reductions in extreme poverty of about 0.75 percentage points, but unemployment fell by about 0.6 percentage points a year in Argentina, remained mostly unchanged in El Salvador, and increased by about 0.2 percentage points a year in Costa Rica and Mexico. The R-squared for the relationship between changes in unemployment and changes in moderate poverty (Figure 4.10) is higher, at about 0.17, but there is a similar dispersion of countries around the regression line, evidencing a weaker relationship.

There is a consistent and relatively strong cross-country pattern of association between reductions in poverty and extreme poverty, and improvements in the job mix (distributions of workers among occupations, occupational positions, sectors, and educational levels). The correlations in Figures 4.9 and 4.10 are qualitatively and quantitatively similar for moderate and extreme poverty, although slightly tighter for the moderate poverty rate. We thus report them together, citing the R-squared for extreme poverty (Figure 4.9) first and then that for moderate poverty (Figure 4.10). Specifically, we find a clear pattern of a positive correlation between changes in poverty and changes in the share of low-earnings occupations (R-squared of 0.36 for extreme poverty and of 0.43 for moderate poverty), and a corresponding negative correlation between changes in poverty and changes in the share of high-earnings occupations (R-squared of 0.26 and 0.29). Similarly, reductions in the share of low-earnings sectors are associated with reductions in the poverty rates (R-squared of 0.38 and 0.34), whereas increases in the share of high-earnings sectors over the period are correlated negatively with changes in the poverty rates (R-squared of 0.37 and 0.38). The share of workers with low educational levels tended to fall over this period, while that of workers with high educational levels tended to increase, and both changes were associated with reductions in the poverty rates (R-squared of 0.26 and 0.28 for the share of workers with low educational levels and R-squared of 0.40 and 0.31 for the share of workers with high educational levels). Finally, the pattern for occupational position is not as clear as in the cases of occupations, sectors, and education. We observe a negative correlation between poverty changes and changes in the share of wage/salaried employees over the period (R-squared of 0.31 and 0.35), and also a relatively strong positive correlation between poverty changes and changes in the share of unpaid workers (R-squared of 0.33 and 0.37). However, we do not find a meaningful pattern between poverty changes and changes in the share of self-employed workers, with positive but weak correlations (R-squared of 0.08 in both cases). The same is true, perhaps surprisingly, for the changes in the share of workers registered with social security. While the correlations between changes in this indicator and changes in poverty measures are negative, as expected, the relationships are relatively flat and not very tight (R-squared of 0.11 in both cases).

The negative cross-country correlation between percentage changes in mean earnings and changes in moderate and extreme poverty rates in Latin America in the 2000s is robust: it is still present after controlling for changes in unemployment and changes in GDP per capita. We check the robustness of the bivariate relationship between changes in mean earnings and changes in poverty by also performing multivariate regressions. We regress the percentage changes in extreme and moderate poverty rates on the percentage changes in labour earnings, GDP per capita, and unemployment. The analysis is limited since we only have sixteen observations when studying cross-country correlations over the 2000s, but we can still probe whether the correlation between changes in the poverty rates and in mean earnings is present conditional on one or two other relevant variables.

The top panel of Table 4.5 presents the results of these regressions for the extreme poverty rate. In line with the previous discussion about the lack of trickle-down effects of growth at the very bottom of the income distribution and the results in section 4.1, the relationship between changes in GDP per capita and changes in extreme poverty is not statistically significant. According to the results in column 2 of Table 4.5, there seems to be a negative and statistically significant elasticity between extreme poverty and unemployment (in contrast with the regression in changes instead of percentage

Table 4.5 Cross-country poverty elasticities with respect to GDP per capita, unemployment rate, and labour earnings during the 2000s

	Dependent variable: %Δ 2.5 dollars-a-day poverty						
	(1)	(2)	(3)	(4)	(5)	(6)	(7)
%Δ GDP per capita	−0.778			−0.381	−0.438		−0.469
	(0.407)			(0.616)	(0.254)		(0.306)
%Δ Unemployment rate		0.320		0.265		0.046	−0.024
		(0.14)*		(0.196)		(0.076)	(0.091)
%Δ Labour earnings			−1.550		−1.489	−1.496	−1.513
			(0.286)**		(0.294)**	(0.342)**	(0.376)**
R-squared	0.098	0.173	0.638	0.191	0.668	0.640	0.668
Observations	16	16	16	16	16	16	16
	Dependent variable: %Δ 4 dollars-a-day poverty						
	(1)	(2)	(3)	(4)	(5)	(6)	(7)
%Δ GDP per capita	−0.890			−0.553	−0.608		−0.625
	(0.338)**			(0.505)	(0.181)**		(0.189)**
%Δ Unemployment rate		0.305		0.225		0.080	−0.014
		(0.113)**		(0.156)		(0.08)	(0.071)
%Δ Labour earnings			−1.319		−1.234	−1.225	−1.247
			(0.185)**		(0.198)**	(0.233)**	(0.249)**
R-squared	0.183	0.223	0.656	0.278	0.739	0.669	0.739
Observations	16	16	16	16	16	16	16

Note: Poverty elasticities are calculated using the percentage change in the poverty rates, GDP per capita, the unemployment rate, and mean labour earnings between the initial and the final years in each country. Robust standard errors in parentheses.
** significant at 1% level, * significant at 5% level.
Source: Authors' calculations based on SEDLAC (CEDLAS and World Bank 2014).

changes in unemployment in Figure 4.9) of about 0.32, with a relatively low R-squared of 0.17. However, these relationships do not seem to be very robust: when including both variables in the same regression (column 4), the two are not statistically significant. Finally, and as expected from previous results, the labour earnings extreme-poverty elasticity is strongly significant, with a regression coefficient of −1.55 and R-squared of about 0.64 (column 3). The results in columns 5 to 7 in the top panel of Table 4.5 confirm the robustness of this elasticity: controlling for percentage changes in GDP per capita (column 5), for percentage changes in unemployment (column 6), or for both, none of the additional variables is statistically significant, and the labour earnings elasticity remains virtually unchanged around −1.5, and still strongly significant (which is all the more remarkable again with the limited number of observations available).

The corresponding results for the moderate poverty elasticities are presented in the bottom panel of Table 4.5. The elasticity with respect to labour earnings is again strongly significant but somewhat lower in absolute value (between −1.22 and −1.32), and also robust to the inclusion of percentage changes in GDP per capita and unemployment as conditioning variables. The elasticity between moderate poverty and unemployment is again significant when unconditional (column 2), but not statistically significant when either change in GDP per capita or change in labour earnings or both are included (columns 4, 6, and 7). The main difference with respect to the results for the extreme-poverty elasticities is the elasticity coefficient between moderate poverty and GDP per capita: the coefficient for this variable is significant when included on its own (column 1), but also when controlling for labour earnings (column 5) and labour earnings and unemployment (column 7). The unconditional elasticity is −0.890, and it is reduced to −0.625 when including the additional controls. The elasticity with respect to labour earnings also falls (although only slightly) when including the additional controls. The fact that the two variables are jointly statistically significant in the conditional regression presented in column 7 suggests that while related, the two operate also through separate channels. In other words, poverty seems to fall when labour earnings increase over and above the effect of GDP per capita growth, and vice versa. Besides the robustness of the effect of the percentage change in labour earnings on moderate and extreme poverty, the pattern of results suggests that GDP per capita growth reaches the bottom of the distribution through its effect on mean labour earnings but not through other channels.

4.3.2 *Response of Poverty to Inequality Indicators*

Moving now to the inequality indicators, there is a strong positive cross-country correlation between changes in poverty rates and changes in income and labour earnings inequality. Figures 4.9 and 4.10 present the scatter plots of changes in extreme and moderate poverty and percentage changes in the Gini coefficient of household per capita income and in the Gini coefficient of labour earnings. Both correlations appear to be stronger for the Gini of labour earnings (R-squared of 0.60 for extreme poverty and 0.57 for moderate poverty) than for the Gini of household per capita income (R-squared of 0.49 and 0.38, respectively). While there is a mechanical component, which implies that other incomes remaining equal, reductions in poverty imply reductions in inequality, the strong associations illustrate the overall improvement in the income distribution (besides poverty only) in Latin America during the 2000s.

4.4 In Summary

In this chapter, we looked at the cross-country link between growth, employment, and poverty. First, we found that faster growth is associated with larger improvements in employment and earnings indicators and in poverty and inequality indicators, but the relationships were in general weak. For only three out of sixteen indicators did we obtain a strong relationship between the rate of improvement of the indicator and the rate of economic growth. These three indicators were the share of low-earnings occupations, the share of high-earnings occupations, and the share of registered workers, all of which moved in the welfare-improving direction significantly more in countries that experienced higher rates of growth.

Second, we looked at four correlates of cross-country changes in labour market indicators beyond economic growth. The first question was, were the changes in labour market indicators across countries related to initial GDP per capita? We found no substantial relationship between either the share of labour market indicators that improved or the change in individual labour market indicators on the one hand and initial GDP per capita on the other. The second was whether other macroeconomic factors could help explain the differences across countries in labour market indicators. We found that increases in seven macroeconomic factors were related to changes in labour market indicators, some in the welfare-improving direction (exports as a percentage of GDP, terms of trade, revenues from natural resources as a percentage of GDP, and the share of industry in GDP) and some in the welfare-reducing direction (stock of public debt as a percentage of GDP, domestic consumption as a percentage of GDP, and the share of services in GDP). The third issue was whether changes in individual labour market indicators were related to their initial level. For five indicators (the unemployment rate, the share of unpaid family workers, the poverty and extreme poverty rates, and the inequality of household per capita income), we found that worse initial levels were associated with larger improvements. For the other indicators, no relationship surfaced. The fourth issue was whether some labour market indicators tended to move together with others and, if so, in which direction. We found that 59 per cent of the pairs improved significantly together and no significant relationship appeared between the other 41 per cent of the pairs; no indicator improved while another one worsened.

Finally, we studied the cross-country relationship between improvements in employment and earnings indicators and poverty changes. Our evidence revealed a generally strong and consistent cross-country pattern of association between reductions in poverty and extreme poverty on the one hand, and improvements in earnings and employment indicators on the other. From a multivariate analysis we concluded: (1) poverty, measured by the 4 dollars-a-day poverty line, fell when labour earnings increased over and above the effect of GDP per capita growth, and vice versa; and (2) GDP per capita growth did not reach the bottom of the distribution beyond its effects on labour earnings.

References

Beccaria, L., R. Maurizio, A. L. Fernández, P. Monsalvo, and M. Álvarez (2011). 'Dynamics of Poverty, Labor Market and Public Policies in Latin America'. PMMA Working Paper 2011–05. Nairobi: Poverty and Economic Policy Research Network.

CEDLAS and World Bank (2014). SEDLAC—Socio-Economic Database for Latin America and the Caribbean. Centro de Estudios Distributivos, Laborales y Sociales, Facultad de Ciencias Económicas, Universidad Nacional de La Plata and World Bank Poverty Group LCR. Available at <http://sedlac.econo.unlp.edu.ar/eng/index.php>, accessed 2014.

Cruces, G. and L. Gasparini (2013). 'Políticas sociales para la reducción de la desigualdad y la pobreza en América Latina y el Caribe: Diagnóstico, propuesta y proyecciones en base a la experiencia reciente'. CEDLAS Working Paper 142. La Plata: Centro de Estudios Distributivos, Laborales y Sociales.

Damill, M. and R. Frenkel (2014). 'Macroeconomic Policies, Growth, Employment, Poverty, and Inequality in Latin America', in G. A. Cornia (ed.), *Falling Inequality in Latin America: Policy Changes and Lessons*. New York: Oxford University Press, 213–33.

ECLAC (2014). 'Social Panorama of Latin America, 2014'. LC/G 2635-P. Santiago de Chile: Economic Commission for Latin America and the Caribbean.

ECLAC-ILO (2015). 'Employment Situation in Latin America and the Caribbean: Universal Social Protection in Labour Markets with High Levels of Informality'. Report prepared jointly by the Economic Division of the Economic Commission for Latin America and the Caribbean and the Office for the Southern Cone of Latin America of the International Labour Organization. Santiago de Chile.

Gasparini, L. and L. Tornarolli (2009). 'Labour Informality in Latin America and the Caribbean: Patterns and Trends from Household Survey Microdata', *Revista Desarrollo y Sociedad* 63 (1): 13–80.

ILO (2013). 'Global Wage Report 2012/13: Wages and Equitable Growth'. Geneva: International Labour Office.

Inchauste, G., J. P. Azevedo, B. Essama-Nssah, S. Olivieri, T. Van Nguyen, J. Saavedra-Chanduvi, and H. Winkler (2014). 'Understanding Changes in Poverty: Directions in Development'. Washington, DC: World Bank.

Pagés, C., G. Pierre, and S. Scarpetta (2009). *Job Creation in Latin America and the Caribbean: Recent Trends and Policy Challenges*. Basingstoke: Palgrave Macmillan.

Tsounta, E. and A. I. Osueke (2014). 'What Is Behind Latin America's Declining Income Inequality?'. IMF Working Paper 124. Washington, DC: International Monetary Fund.

UN-ECLAC (2015). CEPALSTAT, United Nations, Economic Commission for Latin America and the Caribbean. Available at <http://estadisticas.cepal.org/cepalstat/WEB_CEPALSTAT/Portada.asp?idioma=i>, accessed April 2015.

Weller, J. (2014). 'Aspects of Recent Developments in the Latin American and Caribbean Labour Markets', *CEPAL Review* 114: 8–28.

Weller, J. and C. Kaldewei (2013). 'Empleo, crecimiento sostenible e igualdad'. Serie Macroeconomía del Desarrollo 145. Santiago de Chile: United Nations.

World Bank (2012). 'The Labour Market Story behind Latin America's Transformation'. Washington, DC: World Bank.

World Bank (2013). 'Shifting Gears to Accelerated Shared Prosperity in Latin America and the Caribbean'. Document of the World Bank 78507. Washington, DC: World Bank.

World Bank (2014). World Development Indicators. Available at <http://data.worldbank.org/data-catalog/world-development-indicators>, accessed April 2014.

World Bank (2015). 'Working to End Poverty in Latin America and the Caribbean: Workers, Jobs, and Wages'. Document of the World Bank. Washington, DC: World Bank.

5

Within-Country Analysis of the Growth–Employment–Poverty Nexus

Additional Evidence

5.1 Assessing the Response of Labour Market Indicators to Growth using Growth Elasticities

During the 2000s, there was a clear correlation over time between poverty and GDP per capita, labour earnings, and unemployment in the Latin American region: in general, poverty fell when GDP per capita increased, labour earnings increased, and unemployment decreased. This is clearly apparent in Figure 3.1 in Chapter 3, which shows the evolution of the unweighted averages for sixteen Latin American countries of the sixteen labour market indicators and GDP per capita over the period 2000–12. Average GDP per capita in the region was stagnant from 2000 to 2003, but then increased every year afterwards except for the 2008 international crisis. Mean labour earnings among the employed decreased from 2000 to 2003 but then increased every year after that, even during the international crisis, ending about 10 per cent higher in 2012 than in 2000. Unemployment increased from 2000 to 2002 and then fell every year afterwards except for an increase during the international crisis. Other employment indicators follow a similar improving pattern over the period. The 4 dollars-a-day poverty rate at first increased from 40.4 per cent in 2000 to 43.0 per cent in 2002, but then poverty declined in every year, reaching 25.4 per cent in 2012. Notably, the average poverty rate among Latin American countries did *not* increase during the international crisis of 2008, which is consistent with our previous finding of an increase in poverty in only five out of the sixteen countries during the crisis, while poverty fell during the crisis in eight countries (Table 3.3 in Chapter 3).

In this section, we analyse in more detail the nexus between growth, on the one hand, and labour market indicators—employment and earnings indicators and poverty and inequality indicators—on the other. Our analysis is based on the estimation of labour market indicators' elasticities with respect to GDP per capita growth for each country in our sample and for the Latin American region as a whole.

We use year-by-year data for each country in contrast to Chapters 2–4 where we used the annualized changes between the initial and the final years for each country. This procedure means moving from using sixteen data points (one for each country) to 169 data points (an average of eleven per country) when we compute the average year-by-year elasticities for the region. This calls for a note on interpretation of the results from these different procedures. For instance, we might find with the year-by-year results a negative and statistically significant poverty–growth elasticity, which might seem to contradict our previous evidence of weak cross-country association between GDP growth rates and changes in the poverty rate between the initial and the final year. However, the two results are complementary. In our calculations in Chapter 4, the question we answered was: across countries, were differences in progress in reducing poverty between 2000 and 2012–13 linked to differences in economic growth rates? Our answer, according to the evidence in that chapter, was that countries with higher economic growth rates experienced larger reductions in poverty but the relationship was weak. On the other hand, the calculation of poverty–growth elasticities in this section answers a different question: if a country grows faster, what is the effect of faster growth on the change in its poverty rate? Our answer, based on the year-by-year regressions presented in section 5.1.2, is that economic growth reduces poverty but at different rates in different countries.

The literature on this topic has mainly focused on the effect of economic growth on poverty by estimating poverty–growth elasticities. In a recent review of poverty–growth elasticities, Alvaredo and Gasparini (2015: 784) present evidence on these elasticities for 114 developing countries over the period 1981–2010. They find that the change in poverty is closely and negatively related to economic growth, either in per capita gross national income (from national accounts) or per capita consumption/income growth (as measured in household surveys). Their estimations of the poverty elasticities with respect to per capita gross national income over the period 1999–2010 are (in absolute value) 1.2 and 1.9 for moderate and extreme poverty respectively. In other recent papers, Fosu (2011) and the World Bank (2011) estimate poverty–growth elasticities for Latin America for extreme and moderate poverty, based on regressions over the period 1980–2007 in the case of Fosu (2011) and 2003–10 in the case of the World Bank (2011). Estimates from Fosu's study are 0.8 and 1.2 for moderate and extreme poverty rate, while the World Bank's estimates are 1.6 and 2.0 respectively. These findings are consistent with previous studies, which find that poverty generally falls when economic growth takes place, and that poverty tends not to fall in countries where economic growth has not taken place (Fields 2001).

Regarding the elasticity of other labour market indicators with respect to growth, the previous evidence for the region is more scattered. One example is Weller (2014) who estimates elasticities of the share of wage/salaried workers and share of self-employed with respect to GDP growth during the period 1995–2012 for fourteen Latin American countries. The study finds that a 1 per cent increase in GDP is associated with an increase in the share of wage/salaried employees of 0.5 per cent and a reduction in the share of self-employed by 0.27 per cent.

We compute the elasticities by regressing the year-by-year percentage change in the relevant dependent variable on the year-by-year percentage change in GDP per capita. Let $\%\Delta Y_{ikt}$ be the year–by-year percentage change in indicator k for country i in period t. Let GDP_{it} be GDP per capita for country i at time t. Let C_i be country-fixed effects which are included only in aggregate regressions η_k for the region, but not in country-specific regressions; we call these aggregate regressions 'stacked regressions' which means that all the observations for all the countries are stacked. And let e_{it} be the error term. We estimate the growth elasticity η_k for indicator k in the stacked regressions as follows:

$$\Delta\%\ Y_{ikt} = C_i + \eta_k\ \Delta\%\ GDP_{it} + e_{it,} \tag{13}$$

with i = *{AR, BO, . . . , VE}*
k = *{labour earnings, unemployment rate, etc.}*
t = *2001, . . . , 2012/2013.*

For country *i* (*i* = *{AR, BO, . . . , VE}*) we estimate the country-specific growth elasticity η_k for indicator *k* as:

$$\Delta\%\ Y_{kt} = C + \eta_k\ \Delta\%\ GDP_t + e_{t,} \tag{14}$$

with *k* = *{labour earnings, unemployment rate, etc.}*
t = *2001, . . . , 2012/2013.*

We present the results from these growth elasticities in Table 5.1, with the aggregate elasticity from the stacked regression in the first column (for a total of 169 country–year observations from sixteen countries), and then in the remaining columns, we present the time series regression for each country, with a more limited number of observations (eleven on average for each country).

5.1.1 *Response of Employment and Earnings to Growth*

We start by analysing the aggregate elasticity of labour earnings with respect to GDP per capita (stacked regression column in Table 5.1 and mean labour

Table 5.1 Labour market indicators' elasticities with respect to GDP per capita during the 2000s by country and for the Latin American region

Indicator	Stacked regression	*AR*	*BO*	*BR*	*CL*	*CO*	*CR*	*DO*	*EC*	*HN*	*MX*	*PA*	*PE*	*PY*	*SV*	*UY*	*VE*
Unemployment																	
Elasticity coefficient	−1.953	−1.340	−1.921	−2.790	−6.659	−0.385	−6.694	−3.790	−1.284	−2.270	−5.609	−1.893	−0.396	−1.001	−3.301	−1.704	−1.663
	(0.331)**	(0.786)	(2.507)	(0.755)**	(2.718)*	(0.654)	(1.858)**	(1.704)*	(2.388)	(1.609)	(1.732)**	(1.435)	(0.434)	(0.979)	(1.356)*	(0.312)**	(0.404)**
Share of low-earnings occupations																	
Elasticity coefficient	−0.118		0.086	0.102	0.517	−1.311	−0.163	0.213	−0.007	−0.130	0.020	−0.014	−0.041	−0.083	−0.075	0.003	−0.195
	(0.111)		(0.517)	(0.096)	(0.719)	(0.203)**	(0.161)	(0.218)	(0.285)	(0.184)	(0.471)	(0.237)	(0.33)	(0.181)	(0.128)	(0.116)	(0.146)
Share of high-earnings occupations																	
Elasticity coefficient	0.208		0.995	−0.493	−1.047	0.299	−0.005	−0.421	−0.431	2.077	2.352	−0.053	0.134	2.039		−0.043	0.097
	(0.231)		(4.026)	(0.321)	(2.339)	(0.482)	(0.271)	(0.487)	(1.205)	(0.265)**	(0.761)**	(0.375)	(0.655)	(0.982)*		(0.172)	(0.488)
Share of wage/salaried employees																	
Elasticity coefficient	0.156	0.055	−1.601	0.226	0.179	−0.469	0.257	−0.105	−0.485	0.474	0.267	0.407	0.074	0.594	0.495	0.195	0.237
	(0.055)**	(0.062)	(0.92)	(0.049)**	(0.081)*	(0.135)**	(0.225)	(0.266)	(0.647)	(0.205)*	(0.647)	(0.177)*	(0.172)	(0.095)**	(0.467)	(0.05)**	(0.026)**
Share of self-employment																	
Elasticity coefficient	−0.337	−0.328	1.190	0.087	−0.013	0.953	−0.851	0.322	−0.298	−1.547	−1.036	−0.814	0.353	−0.755	−0.823	−0.633	−0.343
	(0.096)**	(0.24)	(0.714)	(0.3)	(0.224)	(0.153)**	(0.585)	(0.306)	(0.832)	(0.435)**	(1.072)	(0.358)*	(0.225)	(0.179)**	(0.672)	(0.151)**	(0.071)**
Share of unpaid family workers																	
Elasticity coefficient	−0.399	−0.012	0.478	−0.962	−0.065	−1.504	−1.464	3.434	0.783	−0.641	−0.442	0.285	−1.046	−0.467	−0.542	−1.094	−0.865
	(0.309)	(0.787)	(2.15)	(0.572)	(3.549)	(0.447)**	(0.81)	(3.13)	(2.659)	(0.906)	(2.035)	(0.999)	(0.411)*	(0.631)	(1.107)	(0.512)*	(0.593)
Share of workers in low-earnings sectors																	
Elasticity coefficient	−0.019	0.468	0.299	−0.661	0.098	−0.633	−0.081	0.318	0.061	−0.348	0.591	0.047	−0.145	−0.395	−0.617	0.266	−0.208
	(0.091)	(0.12)**	(0.738)	(0.299)*	(0.318)	(0.101)**	(0.278)	(0.364)	(0.233)	(0.354)	(0.727)	(0.321)	(0.248)	(0.101)**	(0.219)**	(0.121)*	(0.048)**
Share of workers in high-earnings sectors																	
Elasticity coefficient	−0.005	−0.570	1.890	−0.005	−1.217	0.696	−0.200	0.167	0.663	1.520	−0.333	0.503	−0.475	0.394	0.228	−0.303	0.004
	(0.11)	(0.168)**	(0.99)	(0.197)	(0.85)	(0.104)**	(0.178)	(0.492)	(0.794)	(0.216)**	(0.554)	(0.34)	(0.24)*	(0.214)	(0.324)	(0.112)**	(0.114)
Share of low-educated workers																	
Elasticity coefficient	−0.046	−0.072	−0.749	−0.142	0.824	−0.612	0.140	−0.174	−0.032	−0.346	0.187	−0.010	−0.236	0.004	−0.196	0.364	−0.094
	(0.057)	(0.047)	(0.369)*	(0.098)	(0.204)**	(0.167)**	(0.091)	(0.139)	(0.285)	(0.093)**	(0.384)	(0.264)	(0.205)	(0.27)	(0.112)	(0.29)	(0.079)

(continued)

Table 5.1 Continued

Indicator	Stacked regression	*AR*	*BO*	*BR*	*CL*	*CO*	*CR*	*DO*	*EC*	*HN*	*MX*	*PA*	*PE*	*PY*	*SV*	*UY*	*VE*
Share of high-educated workers																	
Elasticity coefficient	0.250 (0.152)	0.103 (0.169)	2.758 (1.998)	1.188 (0.756)	−1.242 (0.411)**	1.007 (0.255)**	−0.167 (0.299)	0.030 (0.345)	−0.394 (0.207)	2.144 (0.561)**	−0.003 (1.659)	0.090 (0.446)	0.080 (0.423)	1.142 (0.72)	0.258 (0.641)	−0.764 (0.487)	0.108 (0.138)
Share of workers registered with SS																	
Elasticity coefficient	0.541 (0.157)**	0.402 (0.181)*	6.716 (4.752)	0.574 (0.311)	0.625 (0.143)**	1.592 (0.438)**	0.096 (0.193)	2.582 (0.687)**	−0.053 (1.084)	3.625 (3.125)	0.757 (0.513)	0.061 (0.282)	−1.124 (1.325)	0.655 (0.358)	1.175 (0.171)**	0.307 (0.106)**	0.180 (0.128)
Mean labour earnings																	
Elasticity coefficient	1.133 (0.155)**	1.597 (0.43)**	1.521 (0.634)*	0.616 (0.409)	−1.176 (1.109)	0.912 (0.331)**	0.181 (0.673)	1.741 (0.716)*	0.319 (1.093)	1.361 (0.494)**	1.238 (0.526)*	0.555 (0.41)	0.128 (0.728)	1.265 (0.251)**	0.306 (0.528)	1.055 (0.256)**	1.232 (0.258)**
2.5 dollars-a-day poverty																	
Elasticity coefficient	−2.100 (0.354)**	−3.866 (0.167)**	0.036 (2.898)	−0.904 (0.597)	−1.910 (0.605)**	0.233 (0.332)	−2.329 (1.404)	−0.436 (1.11)	−0.703 (0.772)	−0.480 (1.739)	−0.209 (0.946)	0.551 (0.962)	−0.006 (0.907)	−1.758 (0.933)	−1.623 (2.139)	−3.576 (0.549)**	−2.030 (0.613)**
4 dollars-a-day poverty																	
Elasticity coefficient	−1.427 (0.261)**	−2.578 (0.234)**	−0.655 (1.583)	−0.603 (0.41)	−0.210 (1.292)	−0.430 (0.221)	−1.471 (1.006)	−0.175 (0.762)	−1.014 (0.534)	−0.344 (0.979)	−0.004 (0.555)	−0.289 (0.699)	−0.106 (0.44)	−0.719 (0.69)	−0.341 (0.999)	−2.954 (0.483)**	−1.315 (0.419)**
Gini of household per capita income																	
Elasticity coefficient	−0.082 (0.074)	−0.253 (0.074)**	−0.233 (1.268)	−0.093 (0.031)**	−0.594 (0.075)**	0.191 (0.116)	−0.096 (0.381)	0.144 (0.669)	−0.588 (0.446)	0.516 (0.625)	0.947 (0.241)**	0.036 (0.223)	0.107 (0.423)	0.317 (0.205)	−0.485 (0.124)**	−0.292 (0.12)*	−0.058 (0.127)
Gini of labour earnings																	
Elasticity coefficient	−0.123 (0.069)	−0.363 (0.058)**	−0.387 (0.774)	−0.251 (0.064)**	−0.059 (0.036)	−0.247 (0.159)	0.202 (0.271)	−0.004 (0.174)	−0.595 (0.768)	0.418 (0.471)	0.965 (0.56)	−0.443 (0.485)	0.234 (0.358)	0.053 (0.193)	−0.247 (0.188)	−0.383 (0.131)**	−0.001 (0.167)

Note: Labour market indicators' elasticities are calculated using the year-by-year percentage change in labour market indicators and GDP per capita within each country. The first column shows the results of the regression for the sample of all countries including country-fixed effects. The country-specific regressions do not include extra controls. Robust standard errors in parentheses. ** significant at 1% level,* significant at 5% level.

Source: Authors' calculations based on SEDLAC (CEDLAS and World Bank 2014).

earnings row). We find that mean labour earnings increased more than proportionately as GDP per capita grew. The labour earnings elasticity with respect to GDP per capita is 1.13: a 1 per cent increase in GDP per capita from one year to the next is associated with an average increase of 1.13 per cent in mean labour earnings. This relationship is also statistically significant for nine countries in the region (columns 2 to 17 in Table 5.1 and mean labour earnings row): Argentina, Bolivia, Colombia, Dominican Republic, Honduras, Mexico, Paraguay, Uruguay, and Venezuela. For all but one of these nine countries the elasticities are higher than 1, whereas the elasticities for the countries for which we find no significant coefficients are all below 0.6 but still positive (with the exception of Chile, with a negative coefficient).

We find a strong negative and significant aggregate year-by-year elasticity of unemployment with respect to GDP per capita of around −2 (stacked regression column in Table 5.1 and unemployment row). We find again, however, a high degree of heterogeneity when looking at the country-specific elasticities (columns 2 to 17 in Table 5.1 and unemployment row). While the estimated coefficients are all negative, they are significant and about −3 or larger in absolute value in Brazil, Chile, Costa Rica, Dominican Republic, Mexico, and El Salvador, substantially closer to the aggregate elasticity and significant for Uruguay and Venezuela, and not significant but still negative and large for the remaining countries except for Colombia and Peru where the estimates are closer to zero.

We also find significant aggregate year-by-year elasticities of labour market indicators broadly associated with the job mix and quality of employment with respect to GDP per capita (stacked regression column in Table 5.1 and corresponding indicator row): the share of workers registered with social security, the share of wage/salaried employees (both positive), and the share of self-employment (negative). Specifically, these results indicate that the share of registered workers increased by 0.54 per cent for each 1 per cent increase in GDP per capita, whereas the elasticity for the share of wage/salaried employees is substantially smaller (0.16). At the same time, an increase of 1 per cent in GDP is related to a decrease in the share of self-employment of about 0.34 per cent. As with the previously discussed indicators, there is a large degree of heterogeneity when looking at the estimates by country (columns 2 to 17 in Table 5.1 and corresponding indicator row).

We found insignificant aggregate year-by-year growth elasticities for a series of labour market indicators (stacked regression column in Table 5.1 and corresponding indicator row). Some of these results were not as expected ex ante: for instance, the lack of a significant aggregate relationship between percentage changes in GDP per capita and percentage changes in the share of high- and low-earnings occupations, in the share of workers in low- and high-earning sectors, and in the share of unpaid family workers.

5.1.2 *Response of Poverty and Inequality to Growth*

Now we turn to the analysis of the poverty and inequality indicators' elasticities with respect to GDP per capita. The aggregate year-by-year changes in poverty and in extreme poverty are found to be strongly negatively correlated with changes in GDP per capita (stacked regression column in Table 5.1, and 2.5 and 4 dollars-a-day poverty rows). This means that for each 1 per cent increase in GDP per capita from one year to the next, poverty decreases, on average, by 1.43 per cent, and extreme poverty decreases by 2.1 per cent. Expressing these estimates in terms of percentage points rather than percentages, we find that an increase of GDP per capita of 1 per cent implies a fall of about 0.58 percentage points in moderate poverty, and of about 0.50 percentage points in extreme poverty (with respect to the unweighted average of the moderate and extreme poverty rates of the year 2000 in Figure 3.1 in Chapter 3). These values are in line with those obtained in the literature for developing countries.[1]

Table 5.1 also includes poverty–growth elasticities country by country (columns 2 to 17 in Table 5.1, and 2.5 and 4 dollars-a-day poverty rows). We find a large degree of heterogeneity across countries. In only four of the sixteen countries in our sample do we find a statistically significant (at 5 per cent level) moderate poverty–growth or extreme poverty–growth elasticity (Argentina, Chile, Uruguay, and Venezuela). It should be noted that all but three of the estimated elasticities for all countries are negative, and that the country analysis is less robust since we only have between six and thirteen observations in each case. The larger (in absolute value) and most significant elasticities are those found for countries which suffered domestic crisis at the beginning of the 2000s, and then have larger variability in their year-by-year data. That was the case for Argentina (elasticities of −3.87 for extreme poverty and −2.58 for poverty), Uruguay (−3.58 and −2.95 respectively), and Venezuela (−2.03 and −1.32 respectively).

With respect to inequality indicators, we find small negative and not significant aggregate growth elasticities for the Gini of household per capita income (HPCI) and the Gini of labour earnings (LI) (stacked regression column in Table 5.1 and Gini of household per capita income and Gini of labour earnings rows) because of great heterogeneity in country experiences (columns 2 to 17 in Table 5.1 and Gini of household per capita income and Gini of labour earnings rows). The country elasticities are negative and significant for Argentina (HPCI

[1] These values are similar to the poverty–growth elasticities estimated by Alvaredo and Gasparini (2015) for the period 1999–2010, and World Bank (2011) for the period 2003–10. Estimations from Fosu (2011) for the period 1980–2007 are smaller than our estimates, which is consistent with the increase in the level of inequality that took place in the 1980s but especially in the 1990s in the majority of the countries in the region.

and LI), Brazil (HPCI and LI), Chile (HPCI), El Salvador (HPCI), and Uruguay (HPCI and LI), and positive and significant only for Mexico (HPCI).

To finalize this section, we illustrate in Figure 5.1 some of the country-specific elasticities with respect to GDP per capita showing the year-by-year changes for some selected labour market indicators (mean labour earnings, extreme and moderate poverty rates) for some illustrative countries: Honduras, the Dominican Republic, Bolivia, and Brazil. The four countries experienced positive GDP per capita growth rates in most of the years and had relatively similar annualized growth rates: 2.1 per cent for Honduras, 3.6 for the Dominican Republic, 2.2 for Bolivia, and 2.4 for Brazil. However, their labour market experiences were dissimilar. Honduras and the Dominican Republic are relatively bad performers in terms of the evolution of poverty and labour market indicators in the 2000s, while Bolivia and Brazil present much better patterns for these variables over time (see section 5.3). With this exercise we want to look deeper into the year-by-year changes that underlie our elasticities estimations.

The top row in Figure 5.1 presents the relationship between annual percentage changes in mean labour earnings and annual percentage changes in GDP per capita. The elasticities of labour earnings with respect to GDP per capita (slope coefficient of the regression line in the bottom of each figure) are quite similar in Honduras, the Dominican Republic, and Bolivia (between 1.36 and 1.74). However, the figure allows us to discern the different evolution of labour earnings over time in each country. For both Honduras and the Dominican Republic, we observe negative percentage changes in mean labour earnings with respect to the previous year for most of the years (evidenced by the fact that many of the points are below the zero horizontal line). Moreover, these losses in average earnings occurred even in years with positive GDP per capita growth rates. On the contrary, the figure indicates that average earnings in Bolivia and Brazil increased with respect to the previous year for most of the years we analyse (e.g. most of the points are above the zero horizontal line), even in periods with no growth in GDP per capita. In conclusion, Bolivia and Brazil were more effective than Honduras and the Dominican Republic in translating GDP per capita growth into labour earnings increases. This can be clearly seen by comparing the height of the regression lines in the top row of Figure 5.1 which we reproduce for Honduras and Bolivia in the first graph of Figure 5.2.

Turning now from labour earnings to poverty, in the second row of Figure 5.1, we observe that the extreme poverty–growth elasticities were very similar in Honduras and the Dominican Republic (slope coefficient of the regression lines at the bottom of each figure: −0.48 and −0.44 respectively), but while in the Dominican Republic the poverty rate measured by the 2.5 dollars-a-day line fell in most of the years (most of the points are below the zero horizontal line), in Honduras it increased most of the time, even in times

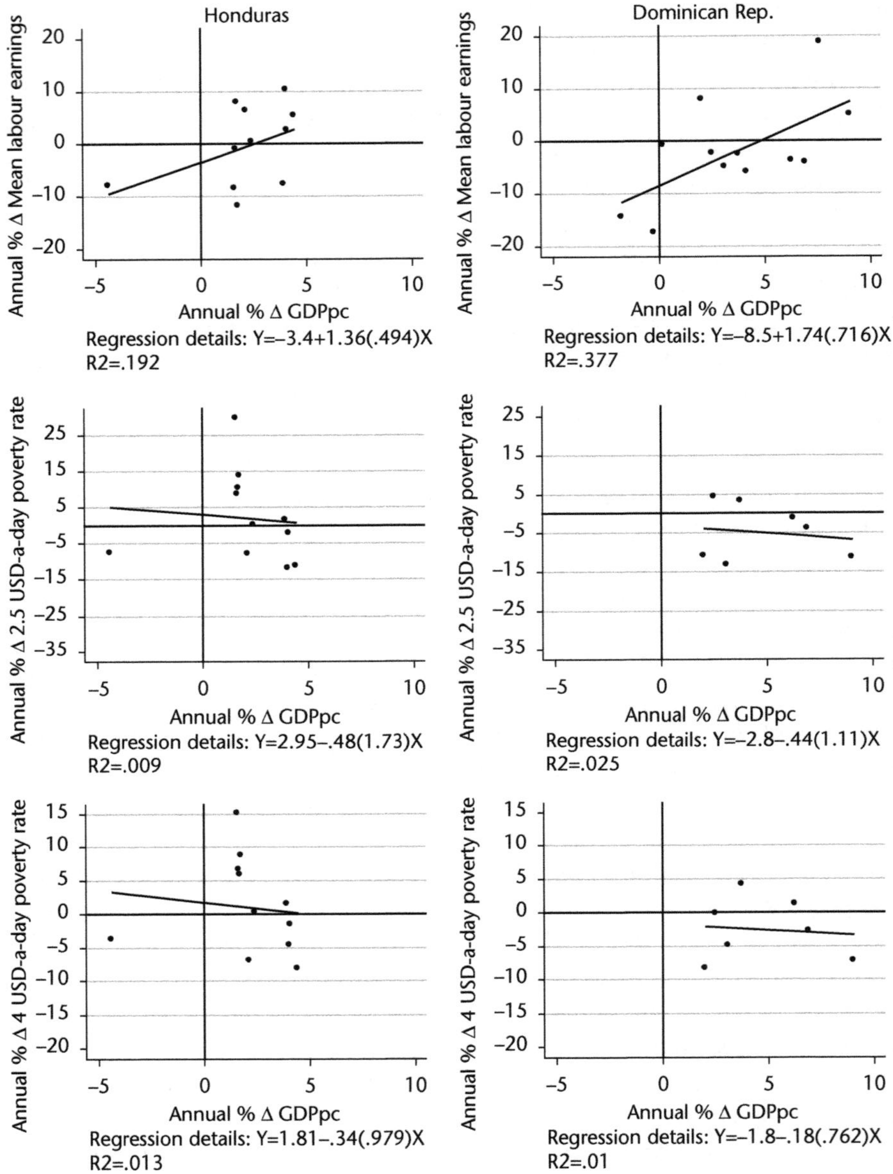

Figure 5.1 Mean labour earnings, 2.5 and 4 dollars-a-day poverty rates elasticity with respect to GDP per capita for illustrative countries

Note: The points in each figure represent year-by-year percentage changes in the labour market indicator indicated in the vertical axes and GDP per capita. The line represents the linear regression specified at the bottom of the figure. Robust standard error of the slope coefficient between parentheses.

Source: Authors' calculations based on SEDLAC (CEDLAS and World Bank 2014) and World Development Indicators (World Bank 2014).

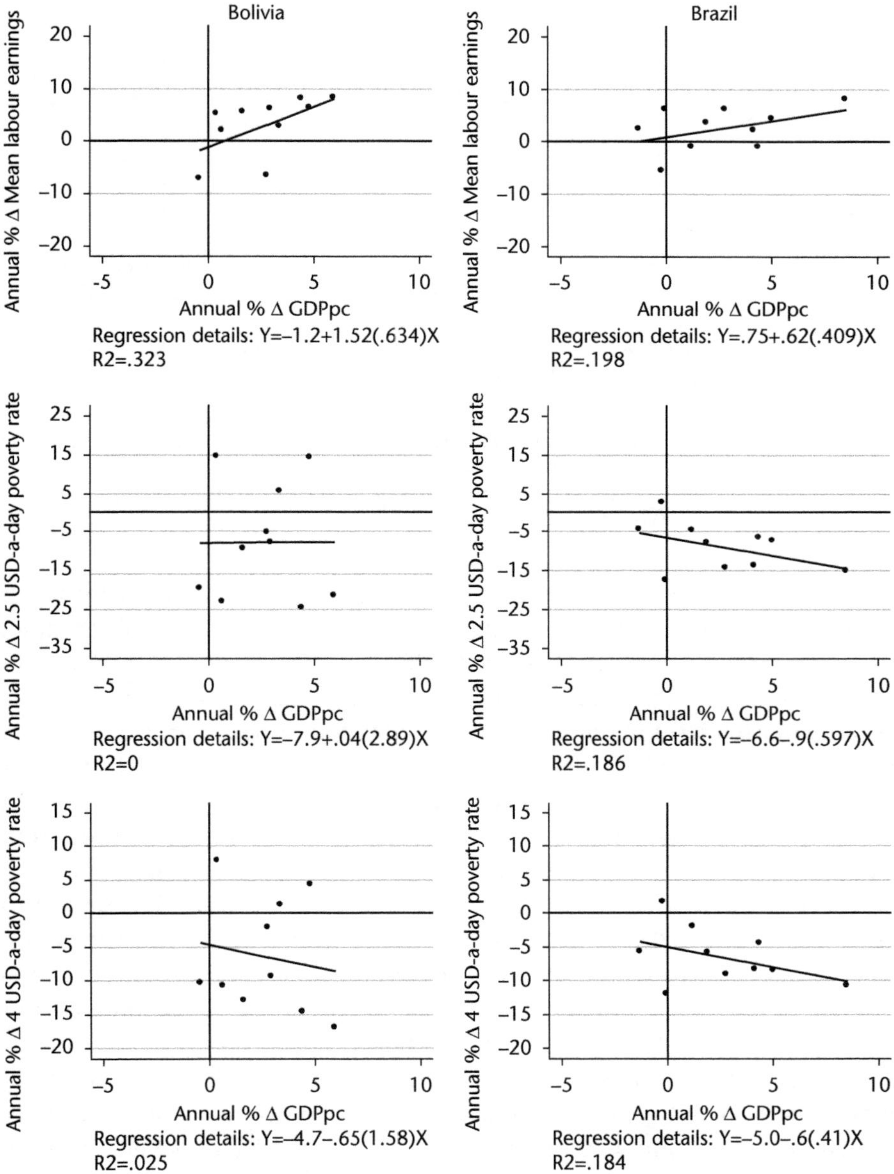

Figure 5.1 Continued

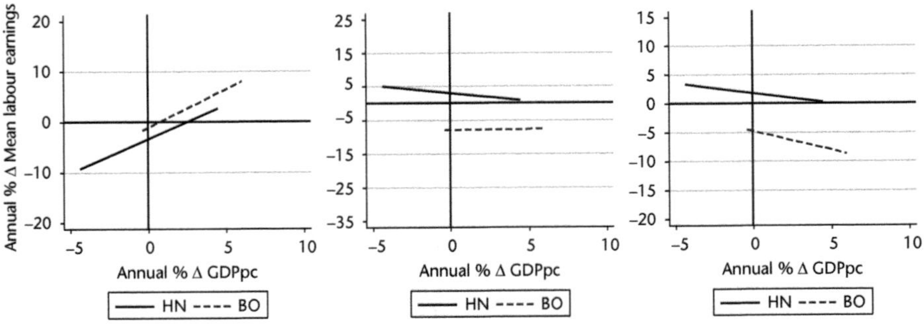

Figure 5.2 Relationship between percentage changes in mean labour earnings, 2.5 and 4 dollars-a-day poverty rates, and percentage changes in GDP per capita for illustrative countries

Note: Linear regression of the year-by-year percentage changes in each labour market indicator on year-by-year percentage changes in GDP per capita.

Source: Authors' calculations based on SEDLAC (CEDLAS and World Bank 2014) and World Development Indicators (World Bank 2014).

of positive GDP per capita growth rates. In Bolivia, the percentage changes in the extreme poverty rate were not significantly associated with GDP per capita growth. Bolivia exhibited similar reductions in the extreme poverty rate in years of low and high GDP per capita growth. Finally, in Brazil the extreme poverty rate fell most of the time and the reductions were larger the higher the GDP per capita growth, producing an estimated elasticity of −0.9. The Dominican Republic, Bolivia, and Brazil were more successful than Honduras in reducing extreme poverty (the regression lines were always below the zero horizontal line for the Dominican Republic, Bolivia, and Brazil, and always above zero for Honduras). While the Dominican Republic and Brazil seem to have translated GDP per capita growth into lower extreme poverty rates, Bolivia managed to reduce extreme poverty in both high-growth and low-growth years. The second graph in Figure 5.2 provides a clear comparison of the regression lines for Honduras and Bolivia.

Turning to moderate poverty (third row of Figure 5.1), the figures for moderate poverty elasticity are very similar to the ones of extreme poverty–growth, Bolivia being the only exception. In Bolivia, the moderate poverty rate fell most of the time and the reductions were larger when the GDP per capita grew the most.

To sum up, in the Latin American region, the year-by-year percentage changes in some employment and earnings indicators (unemployment, share of wage/salaried employees, share of self-employed, mean earnings) and poverty indicators (2.5 and 4 dollars-a-day poverty rates) were related in the welfare-improving direction to GDP per capita growth (stacked regression column of Table 5.1). The same was true for most of the countries, but the magnitudes of the effect and the patterns over time varied substantially from country to country (remaining columns of Table 5.1). The heterogeneity among countries explains why in section 4.1 we found a weak relationship across countries between improvements in the labour indicators and the rate of economic growth. It *is not* the case that economic growth was unimportant for improvements in labour market indicators. It *is* the case that more rapid economic growth improved labour market indicators in all the countries, but at a different rate in each one of them.

5.2 Response of Poverty to Employment, Earnings, and Inequality Changes

In this section, we analyse in more detail the link between employment and earnings indicators and poverty. Our analysis is based on the estimation of moderate and extreme poverty elasticities with respect to employment and earnings indicators. We compute these elasticities using year-by-year data for each country in our sample as in section 5.1 and in contrast to Chapter 4 where we used the annualized changes between the initial and the final years for each country.

There is a limited literature on the elasticities of poverty with respect to employment, earnings, and inequality indicators. Fosu (2011), Olinto et al. (2014) and Alvaredo and Gasparini (2015) have focused on the poverty elasticity with respect to inequality in household per capita income. Both papers use data from Povcalnet, which is the World Bank's computational tool available online to estimate absolute poverty and other distributional indicators (e.g. the Gini coefficient) in developing countries. Povcalnet provides an estimate of poverty and inequality indicators for each country every three years since 1981. Fosu (2011) finds a positive poverty elasticity with respect to inequality (measured by the Gini of per capita household income) for the world as a whole and in particular for the stacked data from countries of Latin American and the Caribbean for the period 1981–2007. Similar results are obtained by Olinto et al. (2014) and Alvaredo and Gasparini (2015) for a group of 100 developing countries, including those from the Latin American region for the period 1981–2010. These papers use a similar data structure to ours (stacked data for each country with many countries included), but they implement different econometric techniques than ours (e.g. instrumenting for the increase on inequality) and also use a different period of time.

An example of a study analysing the response of poverty to employment indicators is Damill and Frenkel (2014), who estimate that poverty tends to increase 0.7 percentage points for each one percentage point increase in the unemployment rate in Latin America for the period 1990–2010.

Since we are focused on the employment and poverty nexus, below we estimate poverty elasticities with respect to the mean of individuals' labour earnings. However, the previous literature—for example, Fosu (2011), Olinto et al. (2014), and Alvaredo and Gasparini (2015)—has mainly estimated the elasticity of poverty with respect to mean household per capita income, finding that poverty tends to fall with increases in mean household per capita income.

Let $P(l)_{it}$ be the poverty rate measured using the poverty line l, for country i in period t. Let K_{it} be either labour earnings, the unemployment rate, or any other employment and earnings indicator for country i at time t. Let C_i be country-fixed effects which are included only in aggregate regressions for the region, but not in country-specific regressions; as in section 5.1, we call these aggregate regressions 'stacked regressions' which means that observations of each country are stacked. And let e_{it} be the error terms. We estimate the elasticity of poverty with respect to the labour market indicator k (δ_k) in the stacked regression as follows:

$$\Delta\% \, P(l)_{it} = C_i + \delta_k \, \Delta\% \, K_{it} + e_{it}, \tag{15}$$

with l = *2.5 or 4 dollars-a-day poverty lines*
i = *{AR, BO, . . . , VE}*
t = *2001, . . . , 2012/2013*
k = *{labour earnings, unemployment rate, etc.}*.

For country i (*i* = *{AR, BO, . . . , VE}*) we estimate the country-specific elasticity of poverty with respect to the labour market indicator k (δ_k) as follows:

$$\Delta\% \, P(l)_t = C + \delta_k \, \Delta\% \, K_t + e_t, \tag{16}$$

with l = *2.5 or 4 dollars-a-day poverty lines*
t = *2001, . . . , 2012/2013*
k = *{labour earnings, unemployment rate, etc.}*.

We present the results from these estimations in Tables 5.2 (for extreme poverty) and 5.3 (for moderate poverty).

We start by analysing poverty–labour earnings elasticities. We see in the stacked regressions (stacked regression column in Tables 5.2 and 5.3 and mean labour earnings row) that the percentage changes in poverty and in extreme poverty are strongly correlated with the evolution of labour earnings in the expected direction, i.e. higher increases in labour earnings being associated with larger poverty reductions. The aggregate extreme poverty–labour earnings elasticity is −1.23, and the elasticity for moderate poverty is −0.95 (both significant at the 1 per cent level). These poverty–labour earnings elasticities are substantially smaller in absolute magnitude than the poverty–growth elasticities we estimated in section 5.1.2 (see Table 5.1). This could be expected

Table 5.2 2.5 dollars-a-day elasticity with respect to employment and earnings indicators and inequality indicators during the 2000s by country and for the Latin American region

Indicator	Stacked regression	*AR*	*BO*	*BR*	*CL*	*CO*	*CR*	*DO*	*EC*	*HN*	*MX*	*PA*	*PE*	*PY*	*SV*	*UY*	*VE*
Unemployment																	
Elasticity coefficient	0.332 (0.096)**	1.164 (0.212)**	0.391 (0.266)	0.425 (0.137)**	0.171 (0.095)	0.314 (0.445)	0.363 (0.143)*	−0.077 (0.04)	0.206 (0.118)	0.073 (0.166)	0.158 (0.186)	0.192 (0.261)	0.743 (0.418)	0.867 (0.164)**	−0.077 (0.281)	1.217 (0.848)	1.138 (0.227)**
Share of low-earnings occupations																	
Elasticity coefficient	0.318 (0.419)		−0.565 (1.235)	3.808 (2.235)	−0.900 (1.041)	−0.185 (0.173)	1.102 (1.492)	−3.172 (0.706)**	0.919 (1.464)	−0.373 (2.292)	1.232 (1.564)	1.028 (1.279)	1.449 (1.573)	4.292 (3.503)	2.986 (5.64)	−0.217 (3.202)	2.063 (1.472)
Share of high-earnings occupations																	
Elasticity coefficient	−0.132 (0.177)		0.093 (0.271)	−1.035 (0.396)**	−0.001 (0.336)	−0.226 (0.486)	0.050 (0.441)	1.096 (0.393)**	0.223 (0.254)	−0.288 (0.671)	0.308 (0.565)	−1.456 (1.088)	−0.420 (0.57)	−0.758 (0.401)		0.725 (1.424)	0.335 (1.239)
Share of wage/salaried employees																	
Elasticity coefficient	−1.501 (0.368)**	−7.447 (4.677)	−0.966 (0.786)	−4.035 (1.715)*	−9.594 (0.761)**	−0.772 (0.386)*	−3.990 (1.976)*	−0.217 (1.502)	0.117 (0.437)	−0.411 (0.624)	−0.347 (1.079)	−1.081 (1.909)	−1.443 (1.416)	−2.716 (1.371)*	−1.105 (0.933)	−12.378 (2.673)**	−6.124 (1.842)**
Share of self-employment																	
Elasticity coefficient	1.115 (0.259)**	2.492 (0.777)**	0.765 (0.706)	0.951 (1.193)	2.723 (4.172)	0.368 (0.182)*	1.127 (0.712)	−0.878 (0.576)	0.089 (0.594)	0.321 (0.445)	−0.156 (0.561)	0.504 (1.089)	1.367 (1.15)	1.724 (1.042)	0.655 (0.713)	4.174 (0.896)**	3.349 (1.172)**
Share of unpaid family workers																	
Elasticity coefficient	0.227 (0.079)**	−0.115 (0.292)	−0.087 (0.424)	0.775 (0.257)**	0.149 (0.278)	0.233 (0.202)	1.031 (0.556)	0.136 (0.033)**	−0.040 (0.157)	0.567 (0.337)	0.258 (0.33)	0.093 (0.187)	0.103 (0.438)	1.234 (0.302)**	0.217 (0.197)	0.703 (0.419)	0.274 (0.154)
Share of workers in low-earnings sectors																	
Elasticity coefficient	0.005 (0.581)	−4.864 (1.457)**	−0.914 (1.012)	1.134 (0.373)**	−1.224 (1.632)	−0.592 (0.259)*	−0.018 (0.858)	−1.558 (1.518)	2.193 (1.427)	1.292 (0.697)	0.425 (0.446)	0.870 (0.724)	1.950 (2.126)	2.034 (1.606)	2.288 (2.071)	−2.968 (1.556)	7.115 (1.6)**
Share of workers in high-earnings sectors																	
Elasticity coefficient	0.183 (0.252)	4.131 (0.899)**	−0.222 (0.361)	−0.390 (0.792)	0.553 (0.321)	0.404 (0.427)	0.386 (0.954)	0.549 (0.844)	0.179 (0.495)	−0.522 (0.766)	0.536 (1.077)	−0.738 (0.564)	−1.151 (0.863)	0.031 (0.315)	−1.164 (1.004)	1.738 (1.908)	−1.772 (1.628)
Share of low-educated workers																	
elasticity coefficient	0.264 (0.558)	4.290 (4.61)	−0.151 (1.606)	3.614 (0.9)**	−2.323 (0.376)**	0.645 (0.781)	−1.972 (1.057)	−0.441 (2.013)	2.334 (1.16)*	2.669 (2.261)	0.307 (1.024)	1.099 (0.87)	1.159 (1.536)	1.910 (1.176)	1.211 (3.828)	−2.020 (1.249)	4.051 (2.7)

(*continued*)

Table 5.2 Continued

Indicator	Stacked regression	*AR*	*BO*	*BR*	*CL*	*CO*	*CR*	*DO*	*EC*	*HN*	*MX*	*PA*	*PE*	*PY*	*SV*	*UY*	*VE*
Share of high-educated workers																	
Elasticity coefficient	−0.065	−2.869	0.058	0.150	1.208	−0.207	2.738	0.912	1.114	0.147	−0.046	0.264	−0.245	−0.823	0.698	1.211	−3.655
	(0.187)	(5.79)	(0.348)	(0.189)	(0.562)*	(0.394)	(1.719)	(0.152)**	(1.398)	(0.292)	(0.29)	(0.953)	(0.883)	(0.353)*	(0.541)	(0.66)	(2.084)
Share of workers registered with SS																	
Elasticity coefficient	−0.114	−2.457	0.138	−0.829	−2.576	−0.112	−3.503	0.112	−0.132	0.144	−0.616	−2.810	−0.208	−0.744	−1.027	−4.944	−1.513
	(0.186)	(2.265)	(0.141)	(0.193)**	(1.202)*	(0.505)	(2.799)	(0.338)	(0.365)	(0.185)	(1.031)	(1.388)*	(0.26)	(0.401)	(1.294)	(1.405)**	(1.321)
Mean labour earnings																	
Elasticity coefficient	−1.236	−1.835	0.231	−1.298	0.265	−0.452	−0.544	−0.654	−0.267	−0.905	0.342	−0.413	−0.534	−1.427	−0.960	−2.184	−1.536
	(0.171)**	(0.139)**	(0.732)	(0.156)**	(0.432)	(0.274)	(1.213)	(0.424)	(0.337)	(0.497)	(0.505)	(0.283)	(0.621)	(0.718)*	(1.347)	(0.487)**	(0.29)**
Gini of household per capita income																	
Elasticity coefficient	2.083	8.333	2.095	−0.717	2.848	−0.618	1.669	−1.041	0.061	2.334	1.235	3.517	1.186	2.818	2.867	3.573	1.394
	(0.378)**	(2.631)**	(0.291)**	(2.908)	(0.812)**	(0.991)	(1.271)	(0.611)	(0.829)	(0.719)**	(1.175)	(1.632)*	(0.847)	(1.414)*	(1.435)*	(2.263)	(1.411)
Gini of labour earnings																	
Elasticity coefficient	1.266	7.405	3.053	0.397	6.059	−0.836	−0.257	−2.060	0.360	1.481	0.395	0.354	0.860	2.014	0.409	3.529	0.519
	(0.391)**	(1.55)**	(0.428)**	(2.043)	(13.147)	(0.573)	(1.239)	(0.703)**	(0.5)	(0.338)**	(0.54)	(1.362)	(0.903)	(1.614)	(0.507)	(1.702)*	(0.846)

Note: Labour market indicators' elasticities are calculated using the year-by-year percentage change in the 2.5 dollars-a-day poverty rate and in employment and earnings indicators and inequality indicators within each country. The first column shows the results of the regression for the sample of all countries including country-fixed effects. The country-specific regressions do not include extra controls. Robust standard errors in parentheses. ** significant at 1% level, * significant at 5% level.

Source: Authors' calculations based on SEDLAC (CEDLAS and World Bank 2014).

Table 5.3 4 dollars-a-day elasticity with respect to employment and earnings indicators and inequality indicators during the 2000s by country and for the Latin American region

Indicator	Stacked regression	*AR*	*BO*	*BR*	*CL*	*CO*	*CR*	*DO*	*EC*	*HN*	*MX*	*PA*	*PE*	*PY*	*SV*	*UY*	*VE*
Unemployment																	
Elasticity coefficient	0.193	0.673	0.214	0.224	−0.100	0.168	0.188	−0.072	0.120	0.063	0.033	0.260	0.633	0.546	−0.091	1.181	0.724
	(0.066)**	(0.191)**	(0.137)	(0.115)	(0.11)	(0.158)	(0.116)	(0.027)**	(0.076)	(0.106)	(0.098)	(0.135)	(0.284)*	(0.156)**	(0.138)	(0.465)*	(0.14)**
Share of low-earnings occupations																	
Elasticity coefficient	0.587		0.080	2.080	−1.360	0.249	0.325	−1.939	0.823	0.115	0.766	0.699	1.514	3.276	1.512	3.260	1.608
	(0.295)*		(0.605)	(1.533)	(0.474)**	(0.142)	(0.911)	(0.381)**	(0.916)	(1.451)	(0.617)	(0.734)	(0.918)	(2.281)	(2.487)	(2.478)	(1.08)
Share of high-earnings occupations																	
Elasticity coefficient	−0.159		−0.012	−0.578	0.173	−0.325	−0.368	0.434	0.108	−0.304	0.075	−1.311	−0.534	−0.491		−0.901	−0.017
	(0.112)		(0.134)	(0.308)	(0.094)	(0.304)	(0.488)	(0.303)	(0.187)	(0.457)	(0.299)	(0.743)	(0.357)	(0.291)		(1.089)	(0.852)
Share of wage/salaried employees																	
Elasticity coefficient	−0.972	−4.215	−0.375	−3.289	−4.521	−0.227	−3.637	−0.500	0.001	−0.321	−0.320	−1.961	−1.026	−1.488	−0.438	−11.149	−4.449
	(0.259)**	(3.59)	(0.498)	(1.055)**	(3.059)	(0.458)	(1.201)**	(0.894)	(0.347)	(0.375)	(0.316)	(1.025)	(0.863)	(1.006)	(0.435)	(1.642)**	(1.175)**
Share of self-employment																	
Elasticity coefficient	0.802	1.415	0.176	0.306	5.546	−0.082	1.190	−0.317	0.089	0.228	0.066	0.960	0.581	0.906	0.329	3.835	2.301
	(0.181)**	(0.648)*	(0.477)	(0.689)	(0.552)**	(0.263)	(0.355)**	(0.475)	(0.407)	(0.245)	(0.178)	(0.581)	(0.841)	(0.747)	(0.32)	(0.601)**	(0.735)**
Share of unpaid family workers																	
Elasticity coefficient	0.169	−0.059	−0.099	0.570	0.361	0.230	0.710	0.106	0.016	0.295	0.135	0.111	0.242	0.814	0.060	0.388	0.207
	(0.053)**	(0.216)	(0.192)	(0.193)**	(0.028)**	(0.157)	(0.363)	(0.015)**	(0.089)	(0.184)	(0.088)	(0.075)	(0.197)	(0.246)**	(0.089)	(0.334)	(0.098)*
Share of workers in low-earnings sectors																	
Elasticity coefficient	0.098	−3.596	−0.262	0.746	1.631	0.095	0.064	−0.864	1.313	0.621	0.481	1.240	1.710	1.046	1.110	−0.458	4.181
	(0.379)	(0.979)**	(0.597)	(0.261)**	(1.059)	(0.334)	(0.801)	(1.175)	(1.145)	(0.392)	(0.174)**	(0.28)**	(1.273)	(0.997)	(0.898)	(1.398)	(1.151)**
Share of workers in high-earnings sectors																	
Elasticity coefficient	0.024	2.846	−0.207	0.004	−0.676	0.092	−0.481	0.781	−0.093	−0.409	−0.004	−0.666	−0.891	0.016	−0.305	0.066	−1.028
	(0.173)	(0.69)**	(0.206)	(0.533)	(0.224)**	(0.375)	(1.08)	(0.439)	(0.332)	(0.473)	(0.523)	(0.252)**	(0.567)	(0.204)	(0.415)	(1.648)	(1.142)
Share of low-educated workers																	
Elasticity coefficient	0.521	2.314	−0.031	2.262	−0.388	0.745	−0.088	−0.238	1.822	1.505	0.067	1.038	1.305	1.309	1.067	−0.489	2.141
	(0.409)	(3.323)	(0.998)	(0.65)**	(1.405)	(0.39)	(1.691)	(1.8)	(1.048)	(1.226)	(0.741)	(0.315)**	(0.968)	(0.729)	(1.564)	(1.163)	(2.109)

(continued)

Table 5.3 Continued

Indicator	Stacked regression	*AR*	*BO*	*BR*	*CL*	*CO*	*CR*	*DO*	*EC*	*HN*	*MX*	*PA*	*PE*	*PY*	*SV*	*UY*	*VE*
Share of high-educated workers																	
Elasticity coefficient	−0.119	−2.044	−0.006	−0.026	−0.346	−0.264	1.396	0.466	0.778	0.047	−0.024	0.276	−0.557	−0.503	0.254	0.440	−2.382
	(0.125)	(4.064)	(0.212)	(0.15)	(0.745)	(0.163)	(1.566)	(0.166)**	(0.792)	(0.17)	(0.218)	(0.792)	(0.564)	(0.241)*	(0.213)	(0.652)	(1.304)
Share of workers registered with SS																	
Elasticity coefficient	−0.104	−1.618	0.039	−0.760	0.548	−0.064	−1.745	0.051	−0.065	0.054	−0.343	−2.154	−0.074	−0.484	−0.203	−4.358	−0.738
	(0.116)	(1.638)	(0.094)	(0.151)**	(1.784)	(0.239)	(2.378)	(0.181)	(0.27)	(0.135)	(0.444)	(0.921)*	(0.199)	(0.242)*	(0.646)	(1.327)**	(0.87)
Mean labour earnings																	
Elasticity coefficient	−0.950	−1.250	−0.203	−0.955	−0.694	−0.445	−0.791	−0.626	−0.180	−0.538	−0.086	−0.323	−0.626	−0.825	−0.611	−2.015	−1.078
	(0.111)**	(0.123)**	(0.415)	(0.094)**	(0.227)**	(0.166)**	(0.751)	(0.211)**	(0.261)	(0.268)*	(0.256)	(0.227)	(0.384)	(0.489)	(0.578)	(0.275)**	(0.137)**
Gini of household per capita income																	
Elasticity coefficient	1.244	5.885	1.140	0.762	0.547	−0.704	0.684	−0.495	0.149	1.301	0.574	2.283	0.298	1.976	1.090	3.416	0.685
	(0.261)**	(2.016)**	(0.217)**	(2.027)	(1.966)	(0.809)	(1.047)	(0.419)	(0.539)	(0.386)**	(0.551)	(1.441)	(0.55)	(0.977)*	(0.698)	(1.306)**	(1.016)
Gini of labour earnings																	
Elasticity coefficient	0.891	5.457	1.753	0.783	−7.159	−0.499	−1.111	−1.179	0.319	0.967	0.266	0.875	0.099	1.511	−0.025	3.613	0.192
	(0.288)**	(0.953)**	(0.325)**	(1.171)	(13.986)	(0.615)	(1.309)	(0.449)**	(0.312)	(0.257)**	(0.314)	(0.933)	(0.691)	(1.128)	(0.235)	(1.091)**	(0.636)

Note: Labour market indicators' elasticities are calculated using the year-by-year percentage change in the 4 dollars-a-day poverty rate and in employment and earnings indicators and inequality indicators within each country. The first column shows the results of the regression for the sample of all countries including country-fixed effects. The country-specific regressions do not include extra controls. Robust standard errors in parentheses.

Source: Authors' calculations based on SEDLAC (CEDLAS and World Bank 2014).

from the trends observed in Figure 3.1 in Chapter 3, which shows that labour earnings and GDP per capita followed similar trends, but changes in labour earnings were more attenuated than those in GDP per capita.

The poverty–labour earnings elasticities differ between countries (columns 2 to 17 in Table 5.2 and Table 5.3 and mean labour earnings row). The magnitudes of the moderate poverty–earnings elasticities go from −2.0 in Uruguay to −0.09 in Mexico, while the values of the extreme poverty–earnings elasticities vary from −2.2 in Uruguay to 0.23 in Bolivia. At least one of the two elasticities (poverty or extreme poverty) is statistically significant at standard levels for nine out of sixteen countries (Argentina, Brazil, Chile, Colombia, Dominican Republic, Honduras, Paraguay, Uruguay, and Venezuela). As in the case of the poverty–growth elasticities, the poverty–labour earnings elasticities are large and highly significant for Argentina (−1.10 for moderate poverty and −1.55 for extreme poverty), Uruguay (−1.92 and −2.14 respectively), and Venezuela (−1.20 and −1.75 respectively). The results are also large and significant for Brazil (−1.07 for moderate poverty and −1.74 for extreme poverty), for which the poverty–growth elasticities were not statistically different from zero.

Turning now to the elasticity of poverty with respect to unemployment in the stacked regression, we find a strong and significant correlation between reductions in the unemployment rate and reductions in poverty and extreme poverty. Earlier we found a clear positive correlation between the unweighted averages of the unemployment rate and the poverty rates (Figure 3.1 in Chapter 3). Consistent with this, we find here significant and positive aggregate elasticities of moderate and extreme poverty rates with respect to unemployment (stacked regression column in Tables 5.2 and 5.3 and unemployment row) of 0.19 for moderate poverty (Table 5.3) and 0.33 for extreme poverty (Table 5.2), both significant at the 1 per cent level. This implies that, on average, for each 10 per cent reduction in the unemployment rate (for example, from approximately 9 per cent, the average for all sixteen countries at the beginning of the period, to 8.1 per cent), poverty falls by 1.9 per cent and extreme poverty by 3.3 per cent. Looking at the country level, as with the other elasticities discussed above, the poverty–unemployment elasticities are highly variable between countries (columns 2 to 17 in Table 5.2 and Table 5.3 and unemployment row). One or both of these elasticities (poverty or extreme poverty) are significant for Argentina, Brazil, Costa Rica, Dominican Republic, Peru, Paraguay, Uruguay, and Venezuela. The magnitudes of the elasticities are large and strongly significant for Argentina (0.67 for moderate poverty and 1.16 for extreme poverty), Paraguay (0.55 and 0.87 respectively), and Venezuela (0.72 and 1.14 respectively).

We also find a strong correlation between percentage changes in moderate and extreme poverty and percentage changes in the three labour market indicators related to the occupational position in the stacked regression (stacked regression column in Tables 5.2 and 5.3 and the corresponding indicator row). First, we find a negative and significant aggregate elasticity between extreme and moderate poverty and the share of wage/salaried employees, with a substantially higher coefficient (in absolute terms) for extreme poverty (−1.50) than for moderate poverty (about 0.97). The elasticities of poverty with respect to the occupational positions that we identified as signals of worse labour market outcomes, the share of self-employment (second) and the share of unpaid family workers (third), are positive, and substantially larger for the share of self-employment (1.12 for extreme poverty and 0.80 for moderate poverty), than for the share of unpaid workers (0.23 for extreme poverty and 0.17 for moderate poverty). As with the previous indicators, there is a high degree of heterogeneity in the magnitude of the elasticities between countries, although the signs seem to be mostly consistent among them (columns 2 to 17 in Table 5.2 and Table 5.3 and the corresponding indicator row). We did not find a significant average year-by-year poverty elasticity for the remaining employment and earnings indicators and inequality indicators, such as the share of high- and low-earnings occupations, the share of workers registered with social security, the share of workers in low- and high-earnings sectors, and the Gini coefficient of household per capita income and labour earnings.

As in section 5.1, we present in Figures 5.3 and 5.4 some of the elasticities of poverty with respect to mean labour earnings and unemployment for four countries in our sample: Honduras, the Dominican Republic, Bolivia, and Brazil. In Honduras, the extreme and moderate poverty rates increased in about half of the years under study, and the increases took place even with reductions in the unemployment rate (top row of Figure 5.3 for the extreme poverty rate and Figure 5.4 for the moderate poverty rate). That determines very small positive elasticities of moderate and extreme poverty (0.06 and 0.07 respectively) with respect to the unemployment rate, and very small R-squareds (0.02 and 0.01 respectively) (regression details in the bottom of each figure). The Dominican Republic is the only country among the four where the poverty–unemployment elasticities are negative (slope coefficient of the regression line in the bottom of each figure: −0.08 for moderate poverty and −0.07 for extreme poverty). This result is determined mainly by one year that had a large increase in the unemployment rate jointly with a large reduction in the poverty rates. In Bolivia and Brazil, both poverty rates fell most of the time, and continued to decline when the unemployment rate increased (most of the points are below the zero horizontal line). The poverty–unemployment elasticities are similar in magnitude in both countries (about 0.4 for moderate poverty and 0.2 for extreme poverty).

The analysis of the relationship between percentage changes in poverty and percentage changes in mean earnings (second row of Figure 5.3 for the

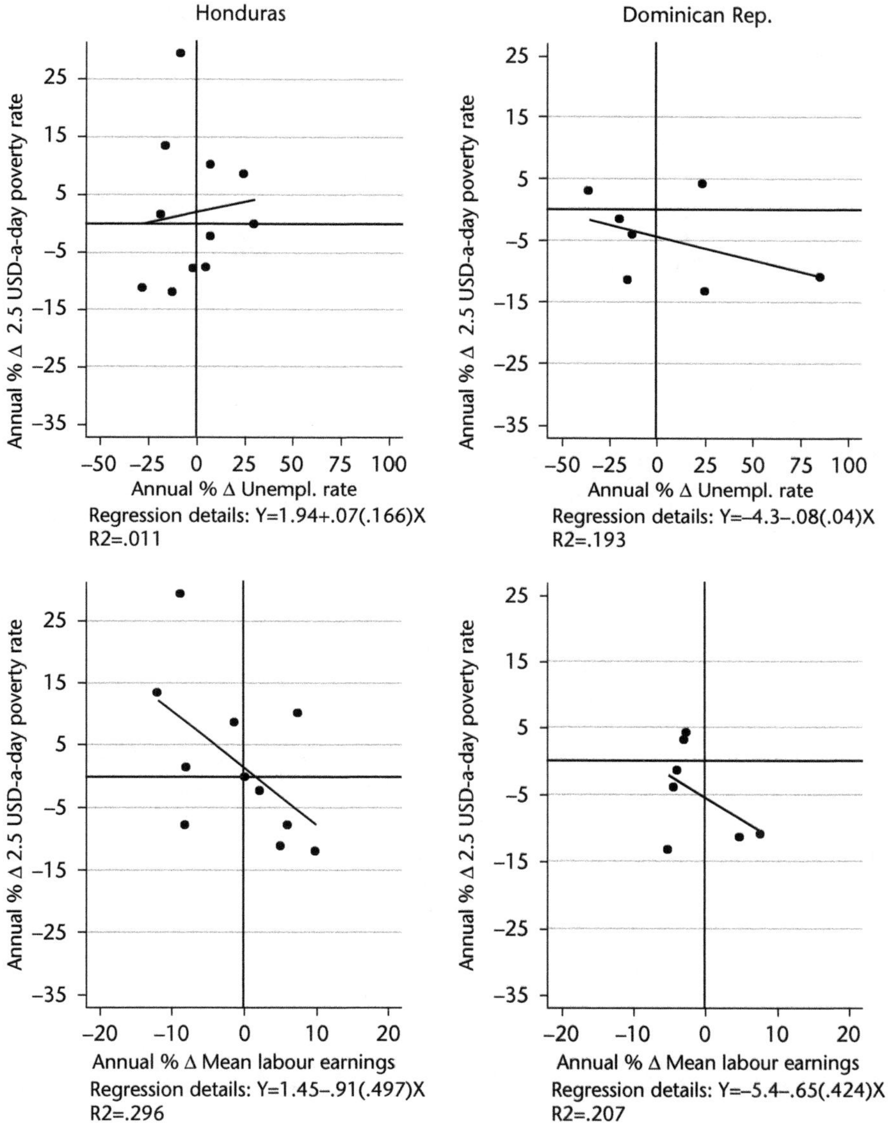

Figure 5.3 2.5 dollars-a-day poverty rates elasticity with respect to unemployment and mean earnings for illustrative countries

Note: The points in each figure represent year-by-year percentage changes in the 2.5 dollars-a-day poverty rate, and the labour market indicator indicated in the horizontal axes. The line represents the linear regression specified at the bottom of the figure. Robust standard error of the slope coefficient between parentheses.

Source: Authors' calculations based on SEDLAC (CEDLAS and World Bank 2014).

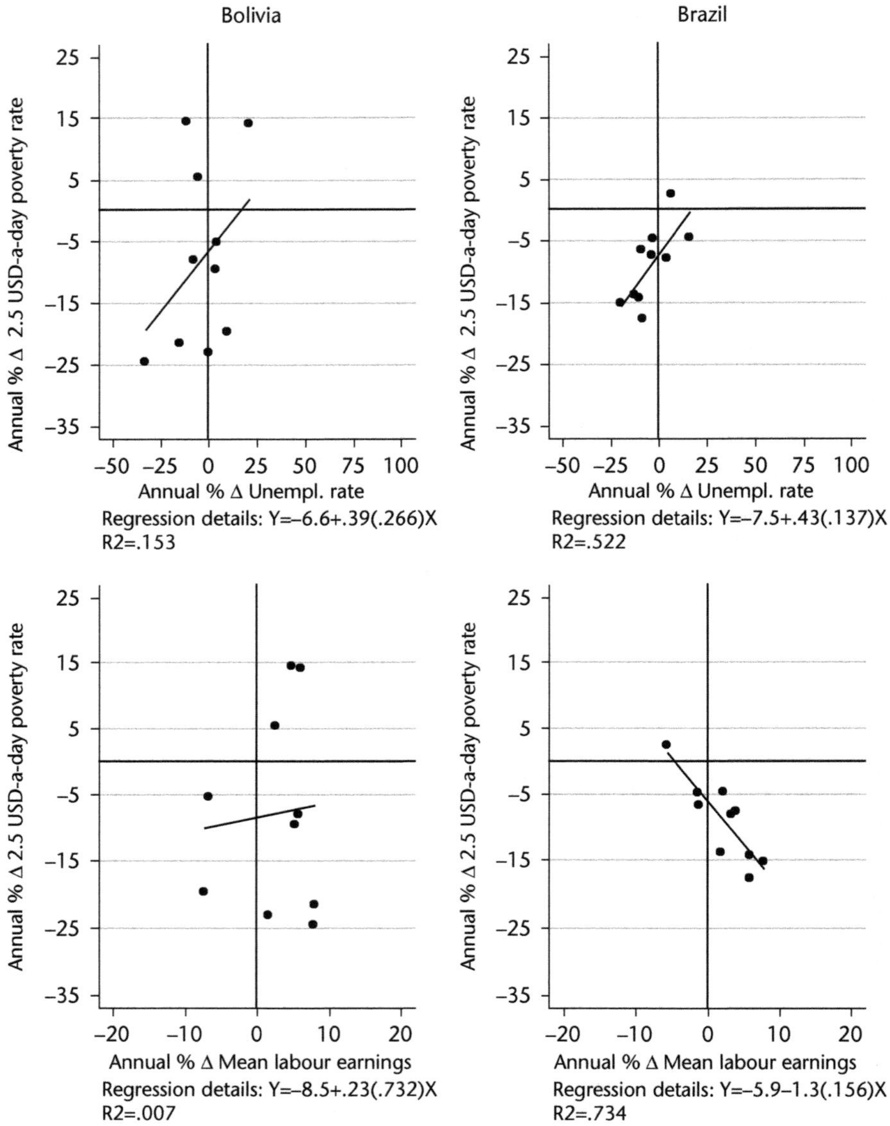

Figure 5.3 Continued

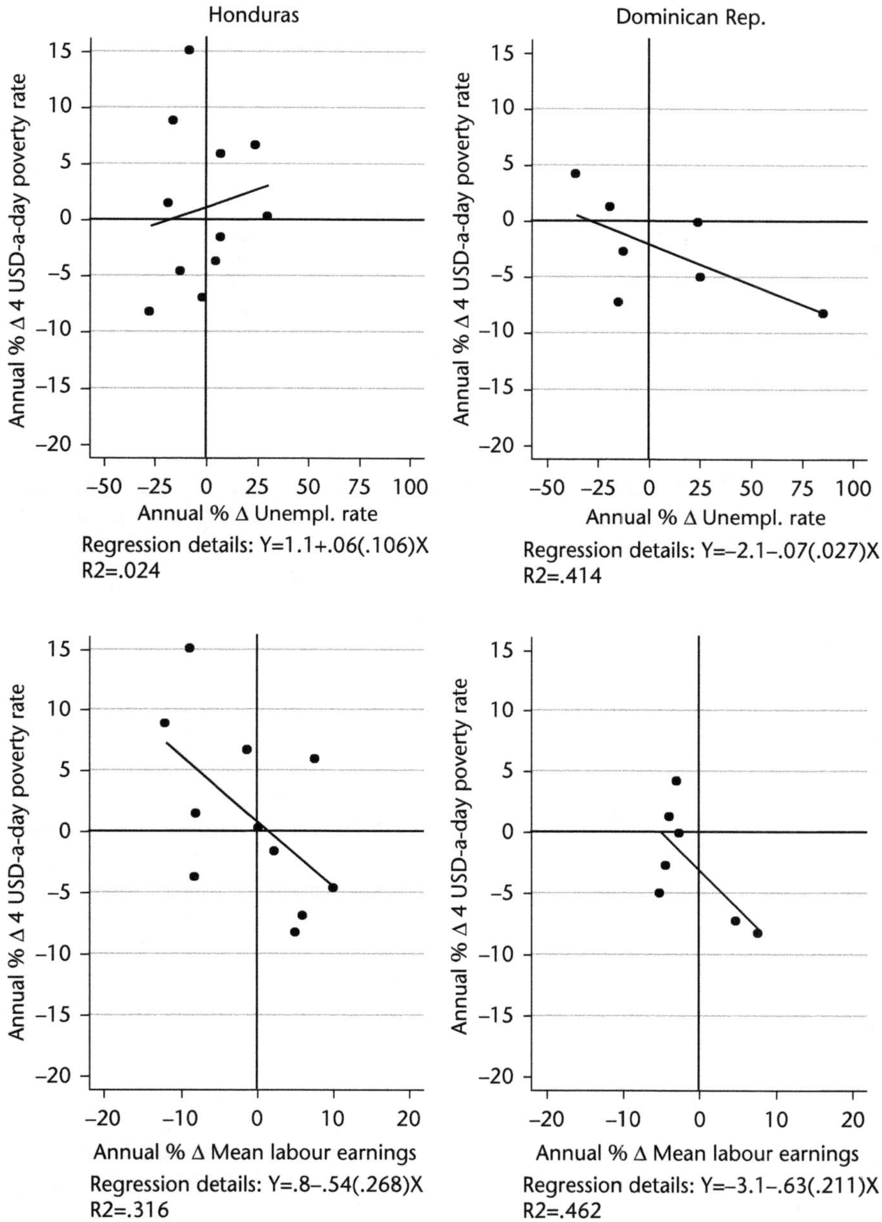

Figure 5.4 4 dollars-a-day poverty rates elasticity with respect to unemployment and mean earnings for illustrative countries

Note: The points in each figure represent year-by-year percentage changes in the 2.5 dollars-a-day poverty rate, and the labour market indicator indicated in the horizontal axes. The line represents the linear regression specified at the bottom of the figure. Robust standard error of the slope coefficient between parentheses.

Source: Authors' calculations based on SEDLAC (CEDLAS and World Bank 2014).

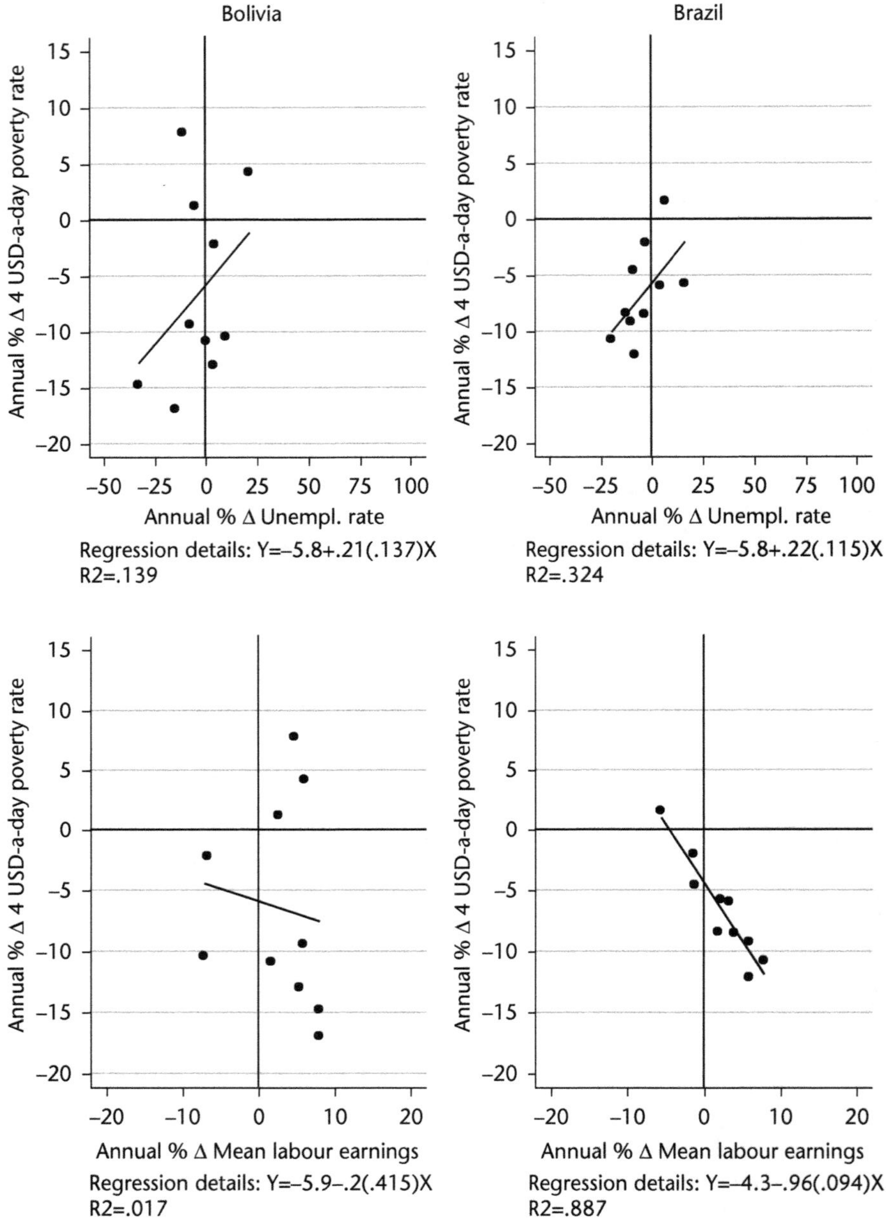

Figure 5.4 Continued

extreme poverty rate and Figure 5.4 for the moderate poverty rate) reveals that in Honduras and the Dominican Republic mean earnings fell most of the time (most of the points are to the left of the zero vertical line). In Honduras, the moderate and extreme poverty rates tended to increase when mean earnings fell and to decrease when mean earnings grew, determining a negative elasticity (slope coefficient of the regression line in the bottom of each figure: −0.54 for moderate poverty and −0.91 for extreme poverty). In the Dominican Republic, the poverty–earnings elasticities were also negative, but in this country the poverty rates continued to decrease when labour earnings fell. This specificity of the Dominican Republic case determined a regression line that is below the one for Honduras. In Bolivia, mean earnings increased most of the time, but in some of the years the poverty rates increased. This determined a negative and small moderate poverty–earnings elasticity (−0.2) and a very small R-squared (0.02). The extreme poverty–earnings elasticity was positive (0.2) with an R-squared of zero. Finally, in Brazil both poverty rates fell most of the time and mean earnings increased. The poverty reductions were larger the larger the increases in mean labour earnings. Thus, the poverty–earnings elasticities are negative (−0.96 for moderate poverty and −1.3 for extreme poverty) and the relationships very tight (R-squareds of 0.73 for extreme poverty and 0.89 for moderate poverty).

To sum up, in the Latin American region and in most of the countries, the year-by-year percentage changes in both poverty measures (2.5 and 4 dollars-a-day poverty rates) were related in the welfare-improving direction with percentage changes in some employment and earnings indicators (unemployment, share of wage/salaried employees, share of self-employed, share of unpaid workers, mean earnings), but the magnitude of the effect and the pattern over time varied substantially from country to country.

5.3 Assessing Changes of Labour Earnings across the Earnings Distribution within each Country Using Growth Incidence Curves

In this section we extend the analysis of the within-country growth–employment–poverty nexus, focusing on proportional and dollar changes in labour earnings along the earnings distribution in each country. The reason for having a section completely devoted to the analysis of labour earnings changes is that earnings are the main source of income for Latin American households, and increases in the earnings at the bottom of the income distribution have been shown to be the most important contributor to the observed decline in household per capita income inequality in the region (Azevedo et al. 2013).

We base our analysis on the construction of growth incidence curves (GICs) for labour earnings. GICs show the change in an income variable (labour earnings in our case) in percentage terms or in dollars, between two years (initial and final year in our case) by quantiles of the distribution of that income variable (deciles in our case). The purpose of this section to show the changes in labour earnings over all deciles of each country's income distribution during the 2000s.[2]

There is a limited literature on GICs of monthly labour earnings in Latin America during the 2000s. One example is Brambilla and Tortarolo (2015), who look at GICs of hourly wages and monthly incomes for six countries in Latin America (Brazil, Chile, Costa Rica, Ecuador, Honduras, and Mexico) for the period 1998–2009. They find that there was growth in labour earnings across the whole income distribution for each country and the percentage growth rate was larger for lower-income percentiles.

Most of the previous literature has looked into GICs of household per capita income. Lustig, Lopez-Calva, and Ortiz-Juarez (2013) calculated GICs for household per capita income during the period 2000–10 for Argentina, Brazil, and Mexico, while Tsounta and Osueke (2014) estimated GICs for the same sixteen Latin American countries and the same period (2000–12) studied in this book. The authors find that the incomes of all deciles increased during this period, and the poorer the decile the greater the percentage increase in household per capita income. If the reader is interested in GICs, the World Bank offers an online tool to calculate the growth incidence curves for each country in Latin America (and for the region as a whole) between any two years from 2000 to 2013.[3]

We found earlier that mean real earnings grew in most of the countries in our sample. Here, we uncover two additional findings: that the percentage gain tended to be larger for the poorer deciles, while the gain in dollars tended to be larger for the richest deciles.

Figures 5.5 and 5.6 display, for each country, the GICs for employed workers with positive earnings between the initial year and the final year. Figure 5.5 presents the percentage changes of labour earnings, while Figure 5.6 shows the dollar changes. Four main results emerge from these figures. First, as observed in section 5.3, comparing the earliest survey year with the latest, mean real labour earnings (the change in this variable is displayed as the

[2] For more on the GIC approach, see Ravallion and Chen (2003), Bourguignon (2011), and the references cited therein. As is most common in the literature, we are presenting here anonymous GICs: that is, changes in earnings for whichever individuals are in the bottom 10 per cent of the earnings distribution, next 10 per cent, and so on. We do this because so-called non-anonymous GICs require panel data, which we do not have.

[3] Available at <http://www.worldbank.org/en/topic/poverty/lac-equity-lab1/economic-growth/growth-incidence-curve>.

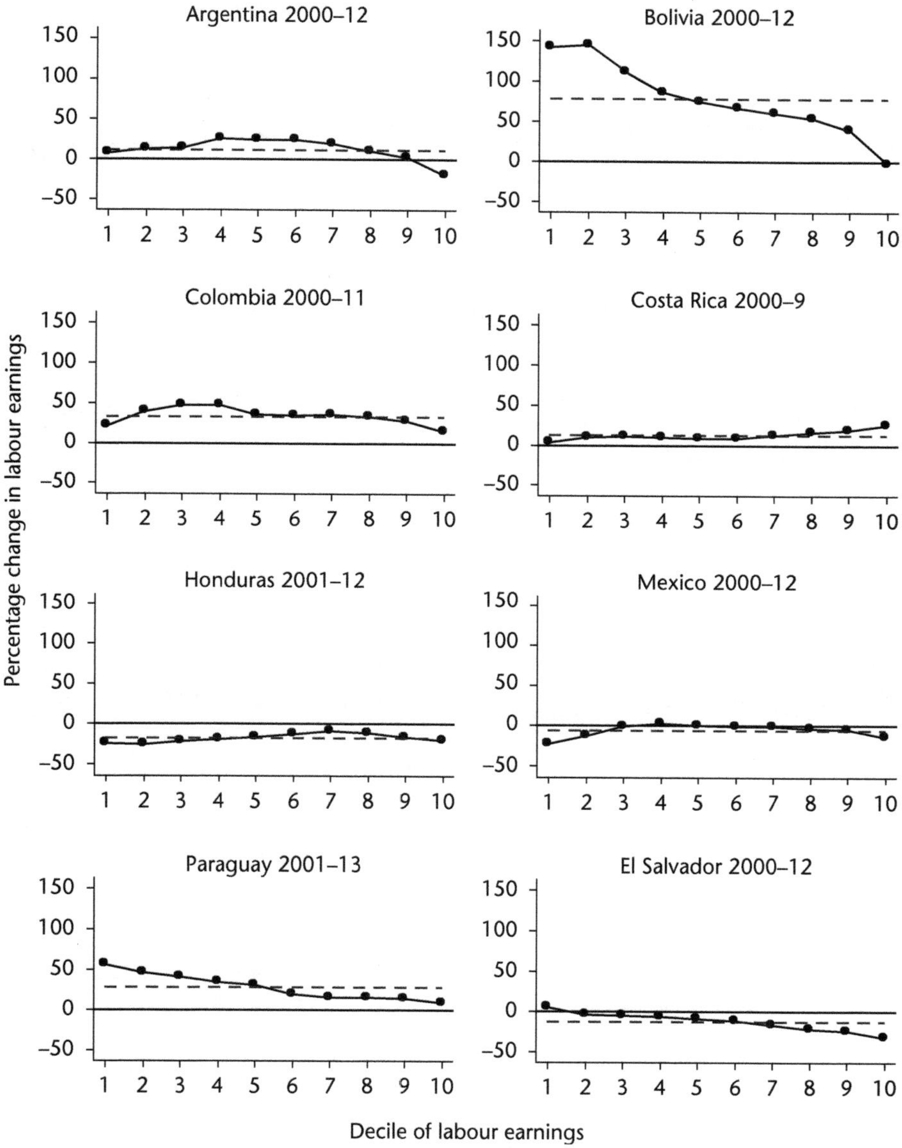

Figure 5.5 Growth incidence curves of labour earnings by country. Percentage changes for the sample of employed workers with positive labour earnings

Source: Authors' calculations based on SEDLAC (CEDLAS and World Bank 2014).

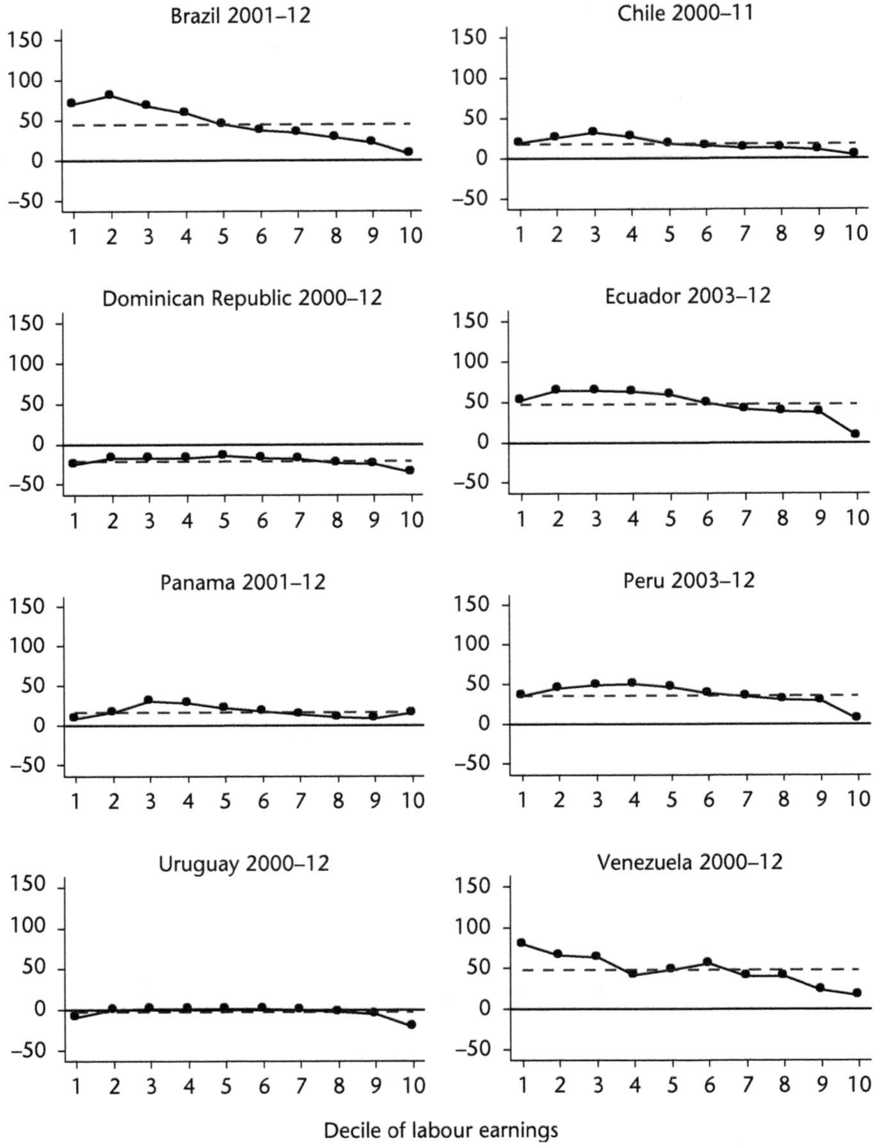

Figure 5.5 Continued

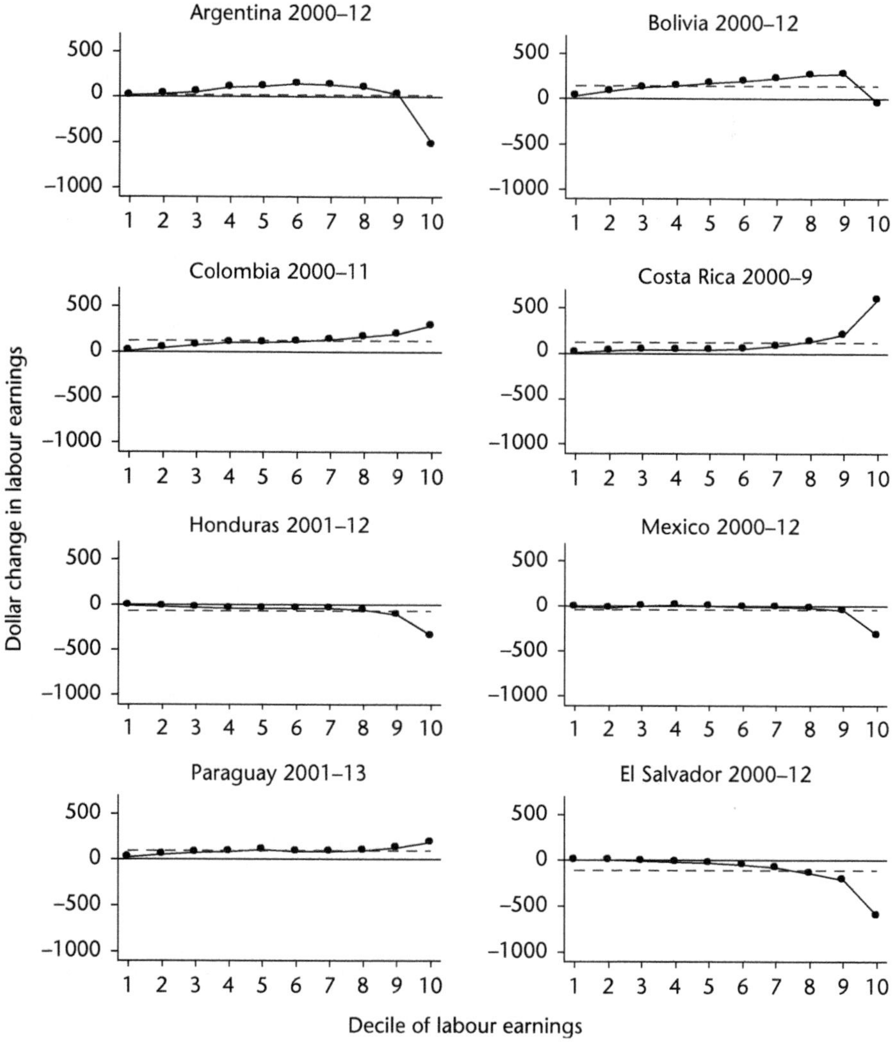

Figure 5.6 Growth incidence curves of labour earnings by country. Dollar changes for the sample of employed workers with positive labour earnings

Source: Authors' calculations based on SEDLAC (CEDLAS and World Bank 2014).

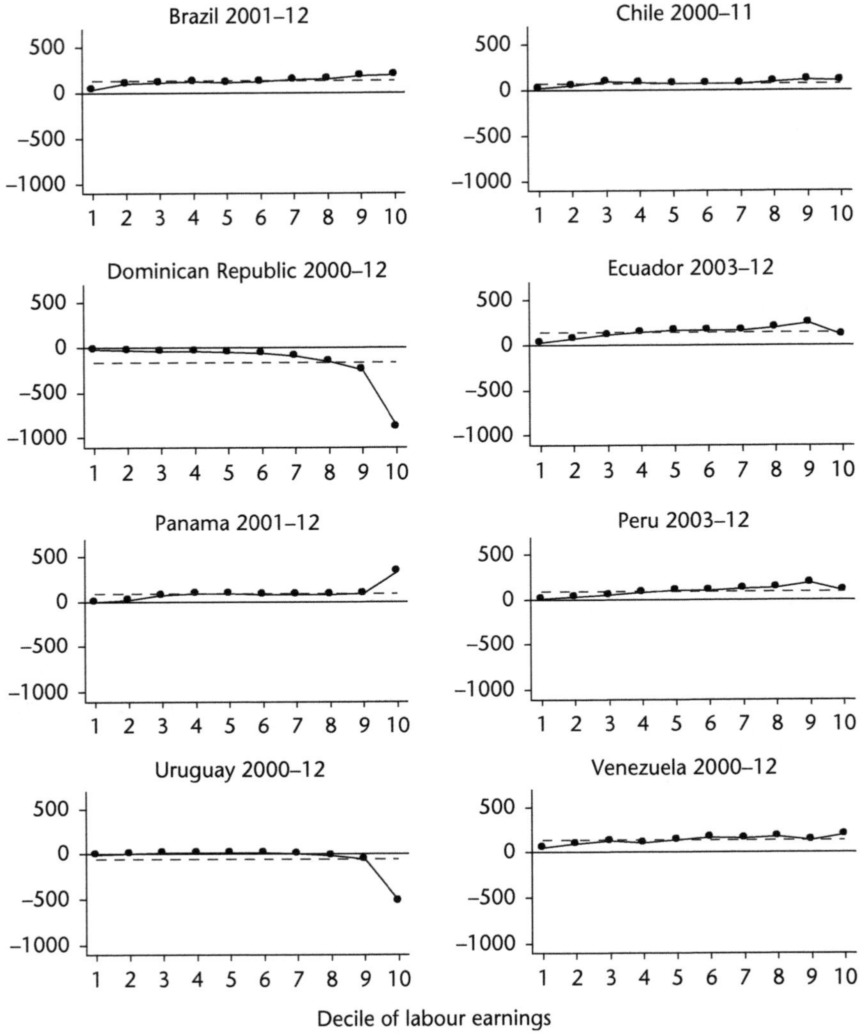

Figure 5.6 Continued

dashed horizontal line in the figures) increased in eleven countries and decreased in five (with very similar patterns for median labour earnings). Second, for more than half the countries (Brazil, Chile, Colombia, Costa Rica, Ecuador, Panama, Peru, Paraguay, and Venezuela), the GICs based on percentage earnings change are always above zero: that is, all deciles register positive earnings changes. For Argentina and Bolivia, all deciles except the top ones in each case are above zero. For Mexico and Uruguay, most deciles did not experience changes in average incomes, with reductions in the top and bottom deciles in both countries. For the remaining three countries—Dominican Republic, Honduras, El Salvador—all or nearly all of the deciles are below zero. Overall, then, most deciles in most countries experienced an increase in labour earnings. From the 160 deciles under study (ten deciles by sixteen countries), 113 (70 per cent) presented increases in labour earnings from the initial year to the final year. Note that forty-seven (30 per cent) of the country-decile cells did not experience positive earnings growth, of which forty-five belong to the five countries where mean labour earnings fell, and the remaining two to the top decile in Argentina and Bolivia. Labour earnings did not fall for the first nine deciles in any country that experienced increases in mean labour earnings. Third, in more than half of the countries, the changes in labour earnings in percentage terms were largest for the poorer deciles. In most of the remaining countries, the changes in labour earnings benefited the middle deciles the most. In only one case (Costa Rica), the percentage changes in labour earnings were largest for the richest deciles. Finally, in ten out of sixteen countries, the largest dollar increases in labour earnings took place either in the ninth or the tenth decile (i.e. the two richest). In five of the sixteen, there were losses in dollars overall, and the largest losses were in the richest decile. In one country (Argentina), the largest increase in dollars took place in the middle of the distribution. At the low end of the earnings distribution, earnings were essentially unchanged in dollars for the poorest decile in all sixteen countries. What makes these minimal dollar changes for the poor consistent with the higher percentage changes for the poor than for others is that the poor have so few dollars of earnings to begin with.

5.4 In Summary

In this chapter, we analysed the within-country growth–employment–poverty nexus in three parts. First, we studied the response of labour market indicators to economic growth. Second, we investigated the response of poverty to employment and earnings changes. Finally, we presented evidence on changes of labour earnings across the earnings distribution within each country.

The first part of the section used year-by-year data to examine whether employment and earnings indicators and poverty and inequality indicators changed in the welfare-improving direction when GDP per capita grows. We found that in the Latin American region as a whole and in most of the countries, the year-by-year percentage changes in some employment and earnings indicators (unemployment, share of wage/salaried employees, share of self-employed, mean earnings) and poverty indicators (2.5 and 4 dollars-a-day poverty rates) improved with increases in GDP per capita, but the magnitude of the effect and the pattern over time varied substantially from country to country.

In the second part of the section, we examined the year-by-year response of the moderate and extreme poverty rates to changes in employment and earnings indicators and to changes in inequality indicators. We found that in the Latin American region and in most of the countries, the year-by-year percentage changes in both poverty measures (2.5 and 4 dollars-a-day poverty rates) were related in the welfare-improving direction to percentage changes in some employment and earnings indicators (unemployment, share of wage/salaried employees, share of self-employed, share of unpaid workers, mean earnings). Again, the poverty rates were differentially responsive to changes in employment and earnings indicators in different countries. The pattern of poverty changes over time was also different across countries.

Finally, we analysed the patterns of earnings changes across different deciles of the earnings distributions in each of the countries. We used anonymous GICs to compare initial earnings (typically 2000) with final earnings (typically 2012) by decile, calculating both percentage changes and dollar changes. We found that 70 per cent of the country-decile cells exhibited positive earnings changes while the other 30 per cent either stagnated or decreased. The largest percentage increases were for the lowest deciles but the highest increases in dollars took place in the richest deciles.

References

Alvaredo, F. and L. Gasparini (2015). 'Recent Trends in Inequality and Poverty in Developing Countries', in A. Atkinson and F. Bourguignon (eds), *Handbook of Income Distribution*. Amsterdam: North-Holland, 697–805.

Azevedo, J. P., M. E. Dávalos, C. Díaz-Bonilla, B. Atuesta, and R. A. Castañeda (2013). 'Fifteen Years of Inequality in Latin America: How Have Labor Markets Helped?'. Policy Research Working Paper 6384. Washington, DC: World Bank.

Bourguignon, F. (2011). 'Non-Anonymous Growth Incidence Curves, Income Mobility and Social Welfare Dominance', *Journal of Economic Inequality* 9: 605–27.

Brambilla, I. and D. Tortarolo (2015). 'Growth in Labor Earnings across the Income Distribution: Latin America during the 2000s'. Technical Note 766. Washington, DC: Inter-American Development Bank.

CEDLAS and World Bank (2014). SEDLAC—Socio-Economic Database for Latin America and the Caribbean. Centro de Estudios Distributivos, Laborales y Sociales, Facultad de Ciencias Económicas, Universidad Nacional de La Plata, and World Bank Poverty Group LCR. Available at <http://sedlac.econo.unlp.edu.ar/eng/index.php>, accessed 2014.

Damill, M. and R. Frenkel (2014). 'Macroeconomic Policies, Growth, Employment, Poverty, and Inequality in Latin America', in G. A. Cornia (ed.), *Falling Inequality in Latin America: Policy Changes and Lessons*. New York: Oxford University Press, 213–33.

Fields, G. S. (2001). *Distribution and Development: A New Look at the Developing World.* Cambridge, MA: MIT Press and New York: Russell Sage Foundation.

Fosu, A. K. (2011). 'Growth, Inequality, and Poverty Reduction in Developing Countries: Recent Global Evidence'. WIDER Working Paper 2011/01. Helsinki: UNU-WIDER.

Lustig, N., L. F. Lopez-Calva, and E. Ortiz-Juarez (2013). 'Deconstructing the Decline in Inequality in Latin America'. Policy Research Working Paper 6552. Washington, DC: World Bank.

Olinto, P., G. Lara Ibarra, and J. Saavedra-Chanduvi (2014). 'Accelerating Poverty Reduction in a Less Poor World: The Roles of Growth and Inequality'. Policy Research Working Paper 6855. Washington, DC: World Bank.

Ravallion, M. and S. Chen (2003). 'Measuring Pro-Poor Growth', *Economics Letters* 78 (1): 93–9.

Tsounta, E. and A. I. Osueke (2014). 'What Is Behind Latin America's Declining Income Inequality?'. IMF Working Paper 124. Washington, DC: International Monetary Fund.

Weller, J. (2014). 'Aspects of Recent Developments in the Latin American and Caribbean Labour Markets', *CEPAL Review* 114: 8–28.

World Bank (2011). 'The Edge of Uncertainty: Poverty Reduction in Latin America and the Caribbean during the Great Recession and Beyond'. LAC Poverty and Labor Brief. Washington, DC: World Bank.

World Bank (2014). World Development Indicators. Available at <http://data.worldbank.org/data-catalog/world-development-indicators>, accessed April 2014.

6

Conclusions from the Cross-Country Analysis

In the 2000s, the Latin American region has witnessed an unprecedented period of growth with poverty and inequality reduction (Alvaredo and Gasparini 2015). The region also suffered from the 2008 economic crisis in Europe and the United States.

In Part II, we have synthesized the results from individual studies of sixteen Latin American countries (see the chapters in Part III) and conducted extensive new analysis, both across countries and within them. We have aimed to answer the following broad questions: Has economic growth (defined as increased output of goods and services) resulted in economic development (defined as widespread improvements in standards of living) via improved conditions in labour markets? Have these improvements halted or been reversed since the Great Recession? How do the rate and character of economic growth, changes in the various labour market indicators, and changes in poverty relate to each other?

When we embarked upon this research project, we were optimistic that we would be able to answer a wide range of questions, but we were sceptical about what the results would show. Latin America, jointly with sub-Saharan Africa, are the most unequal regions in the world, with inequality levels well above the level for East Asia and the Pacific, the Middle East and North Africa, South Asia, and Eastern Europe and Central Asia (Alvaredo and Gasparini 2015). The literature offers ample evidence that high inequality often begets even higher income inequality, possibly leading to stagnation of incomes for all but those at the very top—see, for example, Stiglitz (2015), Atkinson (2015), and Bourguignon (2015). Nor is the experience of countries such as the United States at all reassuring: economic growth took place in the 2000s except for the Great Recession and yet a wide range of indicators have not improved. The official poverty rate, median household income in real dollars, and median labour earnings in real dollars have stagnated or worsened. The official unemployment rate has only now (2015) fallen to what it was seven years ago before the Great Recession, but, of course, the official unemployment rate excludes discouraged workers and workers working part-time involuntarily, the numbers of which are at record highs in the United States. And so it seemed plausible to hypothesize that at least some Latin American countries would have followed a similar course: stagnating or worsening labour market conditions and constant or rising poverty rates despite economic growth taking place.

The positive result is that labour market conditions in fifteen of the sixteen Latin American countries followed a much more positive course from 2000 to the latest year for which data were available, typically 2012. In thirteen of the sixteen countries, 75 per cent or more of the labour market indicators improved, and in two other countries, 62.5 per cent of the labour market indicators improved. Only in Honduras did the great majority of labour market indicators *not* improve.

In all Latin American countries, economic growth rates fell as a consequence of the international crisis of 2008, some turning negative. A number of key labour market indicators—the unemployment rate, the share of wage/salaried workers in total employment, and the extent of self-employment—changed in the worsening direction for the most part. Remarkably, though, poverty rates increased in only five of the sixteen countries and extreme poverty rates in only one during the international crisis. But then, as their economies recovered, so too did these labour market indicators, so that by 2012–13, most countries' labour market indicators had recovered at least in part and in some cases in full. This newfound resilience of labour market conditions contrasts sharply with the experience of the region in the second half of the twentieth century, during which the process of 'stop and go' implied that labour markets deteriorated and economies lost most of the gains from the growth periods in the aftermath of the crises (Edwards 2008).

Looking across countries, we investigated whether the number of improvements in labour market indicators was related to the rate of economic growth, and we found a positive but weak relationship. When economic growth takes place, labour market conditions tend to improve, but at different rates in different countries. Some of the countries exhibited rapid economic growth over the 2000s when compared to the average of the region and an improvement in labour market indicators. One other country also experienced rapid economic growth, but the performance of its labour market indicators was mixed. Other countries improved their labour market indicators despite having moderate economic growth. Other countries experienced slow economic growth with mixed results in the labour market.

Continuing with the cross-country analysis, we then investigated the role of other potential correlates of changing labour market indicators beyond the rate of economic growth. First, we examined whether initial GDP per capita makes an important difference for the rate of change of any of the labour market indicators and found that it did not. Second, we asked for each labour market indicator whether its rate of improvement is related to its initial level. We found that five of the sixteen indicators converged in the sense that those countries with the worst initial values of these indicators experienced larger subsequent improvements than did countries with better initial values; the five convergent indicators were the unemployment rate, the share of unpaid family workers, the moderate poverty rate, the extreme poverty rate, and the inequality of household per capita income. Third, we studied a number of macroeconomic variables and found that improvements in labour market indicators were related to better external factors—specifically, improving terms of trade, increasing exports, increasing revenues from natural resources, and an increase in the share of industry in GDP—and to countries' success in translating those changes into export-led improvements in labour market conditions. And finally, we explored whether the changes in labour market indicators are linked systematically to other indicators across countries—for example, whether real earnings and employment move together, and if so, in which direction. We found that 59 per cent of the pairs moved together in the positive direction (for example, real earnings rising and unemployment falling), 41 per cent of the pairs did not move together in a significant way, and not even one pair of indicators moved in such a manner that one improved while the other worsened.

Our last step in the cross-country study of the growth–employment–poverty nexus was the analysis of the relationship between improvements in employment and earnings indicators and poverty changes. Our evidence revealed a generally strong and consistent cross-country pattern of association between reductions in poverty and extreme poverty on the one hand, and improvements in earnings and employment indicators on the other.

Looking within countries, we generated additional findings on the growth–employment–poverty nexus. We first used year-to-year data and found that in the Latin American region as a whole and in most of the countries, some employment and earnings indicators (unemployment, share of wage/salaried employees, share of self-employed, and mean earnings) and poverty indicators (2.5 and 4 dollars-a-day poverty rates) improved as GDP per capita increased, but the magnitudes of the effect and the pattern over time varied substantially from country to country. Second, year-by-year percentage changes in both poverty measures (2.5 and 4 dollars-a-day poverty rates) were related in the welfare-improving direction with percentage changes in some employment and earnings indicators (unemployment, share of wage/salaried employees, share of self-employed, share of unpaid workers, and mean earnings). Again, the poverty rates were differentially responsive to changes in employment and earnings indicators in different countries. Finally, we analysed the patterns of earnings changes across different deciles of the earnings distributions in each of the countries. We used anonymous GICs to compare initial earnings (typically 2000) with final earnings (typically 2012) by decile, calculating both percentage changes and dollar changes. We found that 70 per cent of the country-decile cells exhibited positive earnings changes while the other 30 per cent either stagnated or decreased. The largest percentage increases were for the lowest deciles but the highest increases in dollars took place in the richest deciles.

In brief, these results produce two main findings: first, changes in labour market conditions are related to economic growth but they are related to more than economic growth. Second, improvements in labour market conditions are strongly related to reductions in poverty. These findings suggest that on the margin, for the anti-poverty objective, research should focus less on the rate of economic growth and more on improving employment and earnings conditions in jobs where the poor are or where the poor might move to.

References

Alvaredo, F. and L. Gasparini (2015). 'Recent Trends in Inequality and Poverty in Developing Countries', in A. Atkinson and F. Bourguignon (eds), *Handbook of Income Distribution*. Amsterdam: North-Holland, 697–805.

Atkinson, A. B. (2015). *Inequality: What Can Be Done?* Cambridge, MA: Harvard University Press.

Bourguignon, F. (2015). *The Globalization of Inequality*. Princeton, NJ: Princeton University Press.

Edwards, S. (2008). 'Globalisation, Growth and Crises: The View from Latin America', *Australian Economic Review* 41 (2): 123–40.

Stiglitz, J. E. (2015). *The Great Divide: Unequal Societies and What We Can Do About Them*. New York: W.W. Norton & Company.

Part III
Individual Country Analysis

7

Argentina

7.1 Introduction

This chapter on labour markets and growth in Argentina since 2000 is one of sixteen studies of Latin American countries, each of which analyses the growth–employment–poverty nexus and aims to answer the following broad questions: Has economic growth resulted in economic development via improved labour market conditions in Latin America in the 2000s, and have these improvements halted or been reversed since the Great Recession? How do the rate and character of economic growth, changes in the various labour market indicators, and changes in poverty relate to each other?

To answer these questions, we analyse the growth experience of Argentina during the 2000s and a wide set of labour market indicators that we assign to one of two different categories: employment and earnings indicators, and poverty and income inequality indicators. More specifically, for the group of employment and earnings indicators we construct statistics on the following variables: the unemployment rate; the employment structure by employment position, economic sector, registration of workers with the social security system, and educational level; and mean labour earnings and hourly wages. We present all these indicators for the employed population as a whole and for different population groups (youth, adults, men, and women). For the group of poverty and income inequality indicators, we compute poverty rates using the official moderate and extreme poverty lines and the international lines of 2.5 and 4 dollars a day. We also calculate the Gini coefficient of household per capita income and labour earnings.

All the statistics in this chapter are obtained using microdata from the Encuesta Permanente de Hogares (EPH) for the years 2000–2, and Encuesta Permanente de Hogares-Continua (EPH-C) for the years 2003–12. In the year 2003, Argentina implemented a change in its household surveys as it moved from the EPH to the EPH-C; the two surveys—both of which are urban in scope and represent approximately two thirds of the population—are fully comparable. From 2000 to 2002 we use the October wave of the EPH, and from 2003 to 2012 we use data from the second semester with the exception of the year 2007 which has data only for the fourth quarter. The surveys were processed following a harmonization methodology and incorporated into the SEDLAC—Socio-Economic Database for Latin America and the Caribbean (CEDLAS and World Bank 2014).[1] The resulting labour market indicators were compiled into a large number of tables and figures, which are available in an earlier version of this study (henceforth, Cruces et al. 2015). Chapter 1 of this book provides the definition for each of the indicators we analyse here, while Cruces et al. (2015) includes details on definitions and classification systems used by Argentina's household surveys, and on comparability issues of these surveys over time.

7.2 Economic Growth

> Argentina experienced rapid economic growth during the 2000s overall, despite a devastating crisis at the beginning of the 2000s. The country underwent a mild recession following the international crisis of 2008, but it had completely recovered by 2010. (Cruces et al. 2015: figures 1 and 2)

From 2000 to 2012, the Argentine economy grew at an above average rate by Latin American standards. GDP per capita increased by 52.3 per cent, while the average for the region's eighteen countries was 36.2 per cent during the same period. GDP (measured in 2005 PPP dollars) grew by 69.6 per cent, and GDP per employed person rose by 17.5 per cent. While GDP per capita grew at an annual rate of 3.3 per cent, the progress of that indicator was erratic, with a minimum of −11.7 per cent in 2002 and a maximum of 8.2 per cent in 2005 and 2010 (Table 7.1).

The evolution of GDP in Argentina had a marked U-shape. At the beginning of the 2000s, Argentina underwent a major recession that ended in a severe economic, banking, and financial crisis in December 2001. Prior to the crisis, Argentina was suffering a deep recession, large levels of debt, and deficits in the fiscal and current accounts. The peso was overvalued, but devaluation was not an option without breaking the convertibility law that pegged the peso to the dollar. The country tried to restore its competitiveness through domestic deflation and by improving its fiscal accounts, but none of the efforts worked. The trigger for the crisis in Argentina was a run on the banking system which functioned mainly in dollars but lacked a lender of last resort. In the end, the

[1] See Cruces et al. (2015: table 1) for details on the size of the Argentina household surveys.

fixed exchange rate regime collapsed and the country defaulted on its sovereign debt (Kiguel 2011). GDP per capita diminished by 16.3 per cent from 2000 to 2002. In 2002, a new macroeconomic scheme was put into effect; that scheme included a high and stable real exchange rate, fiscal and current account surpluses, and a monetary policy that kept the exchange rate at high levels and re-established the health of the banking system (Cetrángolo et al. 2007). As a consequence, the Argentine economy grew substantially.

Following Argentina's crisis of 2000–2, the economy grew rapidly, registering a GDP per capita growth rate of 82.3 per cent between 2002 and 2012. The bulk of this increase took place before 2008. The years from 2002 to 2008 were characterized by rapid economic growth, with an average annual rate of 8.6 per cent. In 2007, the economic situation started to deteriorate due to the increase in the inflation rate and the expansionary fiscal policy that progressively reduced the primary surplus. The government failed to put into effect a programme of price stabilization. On the contrary, through several discretionary interventions, the government changed the way the consumer price index was calculated, damaging the credibility of its statistics (World Bank 2014a).

The Argentine economy was affected by the international crisis of 2008. GDP per capita grew by 5.8 per cent in 2008 but stopped growing completely in 2009 (0.0 per cent). At the time of the international crisis, the Argentine economy had a relatively large level of international reserves, a trade surplus, and a fiscal surplus. Additionally, the country was in a situation of financial isolation with a small volume of domestic financial intermediation. All these factors contributed to mitigate the impacts of the international crisis. However, the country suffered some negative effects from the Great Recession. First, Argentina was affected by the reduction in the international demand for its products. This impacted mainly the industrial sector, which had been the driving force of the growth period 2002–8. Second, the country suffered from the flight of capital generated by the inflationary pressures, the uncertainty resulting from the conflict between the government and the agricultural sector with regard to export taxes, and the manipulation of the official inflation statistics (Damill and Frenkel 2009). The space to apply countercyclical policies was limited after the international crisis because of the weakening of the economy. The government decided to apply trade and exchange rate restrictions to control the weakening of external balances and to nationalize the pension system in order to increase its resources. The government also raised its resources through increases in overall tax collection, which represented 18.1 per cent of GDP in 2008 and 20.8 per cent in 2012 (CEPALSTAT 2015). That allowed for increases in social expenditure, like the creation (and subsequent rise in levels) of the *Asignación Universal por Hijo* cash transfer programme, reductions in the tax burden for medium- and high-income earners, and public works (Damill and Frenkel 2009). It also allowed for an increase in public employment. The number of people employed in the public sector grew by 3.5 per cent annually between 2008 and 2012 (INDEC 2015). The pre-crisis upward growth trend resumed in 2010 and 2011, though there was a slowdown in 2012. After the crisis, annual GDP per capita growth rates were 8.2 per cent, 7.9 per cent, and 1.0 per cent in 2010, 2011, and 2012 respectively.

7.3 Unemployment

> The 2000–12 period witnessed a significant drop in the aggregate unemployment rate and in the unemployment rate for all population groups. Within this period, the unemployment rate increased in the early years of the period and diminished until 2007. It remained constant afterwards, except for a brief rise in 2009 and an equal drop in 2010.
>
> (Cruces et al. 2015: figure 3)

The unemployment rate (measured as the ratio of unemployment to labour force) decreased overall over this period, dropping from 14.8 per cent in 2000 (1,473,288 unemployed persons) to 7.3 per cent in 2012 (856,754 unemployed persons) (Table 7.1). Initially, the unemployment rate increased in conjunction with a fall in GDP from 2000 to 2002. During the economic crisis of 2001–2, unemployment increased substantially, peaking at 18.4 per cent (1,835,698 unemployed persons). The unemployment rate then fell steadily from 2002 to 2007, when it stood at 7.5 per cent. It remained at that level until 2008. The reduction in the unemployment rate was marked both by a drop in the average duration of unemployment spells and by a reduction in the rate of entry into unemployment (Beccaria and Maurizio 2008). During the Great Recession, and as GDP growth slowed, the unemployment rate increased to 8.6 per cent in 2009 (127,778 new unemployed persons). Both the number of persons in the labour force and the number of employed persons increased between 2008 and 2009 by 194,723 and 66,945 respectively. These figures suggest that the increase in the unemployment rate during the international crisis was brought about by the entry of new people into the labour market who could not find a job. A full recovery took place by 2010, when the unemployment rate returned to its pre-crisis level (7.4 per cent), where it remained in 2011 and 2012.

Looking at the disaggregated patterns and comparing 2000 with 2012, the unemployment rate decreased for youth, adults, men, and women, though it peaked in 2001–2. All groups of workers were affected negatively by the international crisis. However, the effect of the crisis on the unemployment rate was generally short-lived. The unemployment rates of all workers, regardless of age and gender, began declining in 2010, though at different paces. The rate for adults and women had returned to pre-crisis levels by 2010, whereas the rate for men did not return to pre-crisis levels until 2011; full recovery for young workers did not take place until 2012.

7.4 Job Mix

> The employment structure by occupational position improved. The percentage of paid employees in total employment increased overall, for youth, adults, men, and women. In aggregate and for all population groups, the share of paid employees diminished during the recessionary years of the early 2000s, and increased during the period of rapid economic growth which followed. The international crisis of 2008 negatively affected the composition of employment by occupational position, but that setback proved short-lived. (Cruces et al. 2015: figure 4)

The share of wage/salaried employees—the largest employment category—grew by 5.1 percentage points over the period, rising from 72.1 per cent in 2000 to 77.2 per cent in 2012. The share of the self-employed, on the other hand, decreased by 4.0 percentage points, dropping from 22.1 per cent in 2000 to 18.1 per cent in 2012. The shares of employers and of unpaid workers in total employment were small (around 4.3 and 0.9 per cent respectively) and neither one changed substantially during the 2000–12 period (Table 7.1). During the economic crisis of 2001–2, the share of wage/salaried employees hit its lowest point (71.3 per cent) and the share of self-employed workers reached its maximum (23.4 per cent). In a context of increasing and high unemployment, economic necessity may have compelled workers to take up free-entry self-employment activities. Afterwards, as the economy recovered, the share of wage/salaried employees increased steadily, reaching 76.7 per cent in 2007, almost the same level as in 2012. The share of self-employed workers decreased by up to 18.0 per cent in 2007 and kept around that level until the end of the period.

The employment structure by occupational position improved from 2000 to 2012 for youth and adult workers, men, and women, as the share of paid employees grew and the shares of self-employed and unpaid workers dropped. Within the period, the employment structure by occupational position deteriorated in the early years of the 2000s when the share of paid employees decreased for all groups. It improved in the following years until 2007–8, when it suffered a slight deterioration during the international crisis. However, the recovery was quick for all population groups.

Table 7.1 Argentina: Evolution of growth and labour market indicators over the 2000s

	2000	2001	2002	2003	2004	2005	2006	2007	2008	2009	2010	2011	2012	
Growth Indicators														
GDP per capita	10,290	9,739	8,596	9,271	10,019	10,843	11,658	12,556	13,288	13,285	14,376	15,515	15,672	
GDP per capita growth rate	−1.83	−5.36	−11.73	7.85	8.07	8.22	7.52	7.71	5.83	−0.03	8.21	7.92	1.01	
Employment and Earnings Indicators														
Employment-to-population ratio	49.50	46.44	47.60	52.67	54.35	55.36	56.06	55.85	56.25	55.68	55.89	56.58	56.49	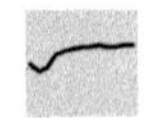
Unemployment rate	14.78	18.40	17.88	15.41	12.58	10.60	9.30	7.53	7.61	8.60	7.41	7.17	7.25	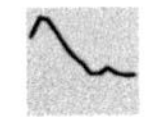
Share of employers	4.60	4.38	3.98	3.76	4.13	4.14	4.19	4.41	4.60	4.33	4.46	4.35	4.17	
Share of wage/salaried employees	72.13	71.29	72.07	74.06	74.24	74.40	75.79	76.70	76.28	75.88	76.97	77.08	77.25	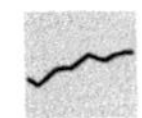
Share of self-employed workers	22.07	23.41	22.98	20.78	20.46	20.36	19.01	17.99	18.50	19.07	17.79	17.93	18.04	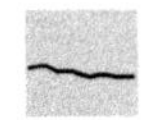
Share of unpaid family workers	1.19	0.92	0.98	1.40	1.17	1.10	1.02	0.90	0.62	0.73	0.78	0.64	0.54	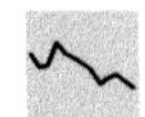
Share of workers in low-earnings sectors	39.7	39.0	35.4	38.3	39.3	39.7	41.0	39.8	40.4	39.9	39.6	39.9	39.5	
Share of workers in mid-earnings sectors	42.0	42.5	43.8	42.3	42.2	41.8	40.6	41.1	40.4	40.2	40.5	40.4	40.0	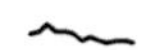
Share of workers in high-earnings sectors	18.3	18.5	20.8	19.5	18.4	18.5	18.4	19.0	19.2	19.9	19.9	19.6	20.5	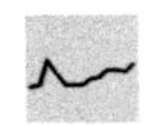
Share of low educated workers	37.04	36.17	35.51	34.55	33.59	32.76	31.18	29.09	28.37	27.58	26.38	26.13	24.93	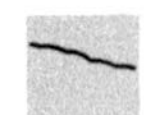

Share of medium educated workers	38.78	37.94	39.25	39.38	39.51	39.44	40.36	42.39	42.31	42.44	42.78	42.38	43.94	
Share of high educated workers	24.18	25.89	25.24	26.07	26.90	27.80	28.46	28.52	29.33	29.98	30.83	31.49	31.13	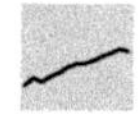
Share of workers registered with SS	61.59	61.40	55.95	50.62	52.01	54.42	57.27	60.59	62.96	64.11	65.40	65.55	65.01	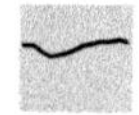
Mean labour earnings	761.7	736.0	497.8	...	578.4	646.1	705.8	732.6	718.5	747.4	756.8	799.0	781.0	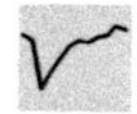
Poverty and Inequality Indicators														
Official extreme poverty rate	12.86	17.21	33.18	24.71	18.81	15.06	11.01	8.43	5.30	4.28	2.88	1.89	1.77	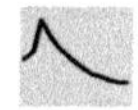
Official moderate poverty rate	39.58	44.86	64.54	52.53	45.05	39.33	32.76	27.55	18.04	15.50	12.00	8.37	6.88	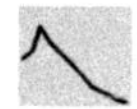
Poverty rate 2.5 dollars-a-day	14.16	18.64	29.17	22.02	16.96	13.32	10.32	8.75	8.21	8.04	6.14	4.60	4.69	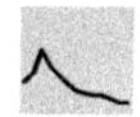
Poverty rate 4 dollars-a-day	27.46	32.86	45.54	36.44	30.96	25.80	20.62	19.54	17.26	16.31	14.07	11.55	10.84	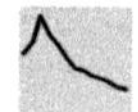
GINI of household per capita income	0.504	0.522	0.533	0.526	0.496	0.488	0.475	0.469	0.459	0.449	0.442	0.433	0.423	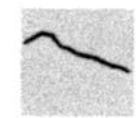
GINI of labour earnings	0.459	0.476	0.498	0.481	0.463	0.459	0.440	0.434	0.416	0.412	0.403	0.400	0.388	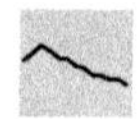

Note: The shaded labour market indicators' figures represent statistical significant improvements at 5 per cent between the initial and final years for all the employment and earnings indicators and poverty and inequality indicators. The only exceptions are the share of mid-earnings sectors and share of medium-educated workers for which we did not assign welfare evaluation criteria.

Source: SEDLAC (CEDLAS and World Bank 2014), and World Development Indicators (World Bank 2014).

> The employment composition by economic sector exhibited a slight improvement overall, as the share of high-earning sectors increased, the share of middle-earning sectors fell, and the share of low-earning sectors remained largely unchanged. The pattern of improvement in the sectoral composition of employment was not interrupted by the international crisis of 2008, but impacted on the relative shares of low- and mid-earning sectors. (Cruces et al. 2015: figure 5)

The period 2000–12 witnessed a stable pattern in the share of workers in low-earning sectors (domestic service, construction, and commerce) around 39.6 per cent both in 2000 and 2012. The share of workers in middle-earning sectors (low- and high-tech industry, utilities and transportation, and education and health) decreased from 42.0 to 40.0 per cent. Among middle-earning sectors, the share of the low-tech industry sector—the driving force of the growth period 2003–8—exhibited an increase in its share of total employment up to 2008 that was undone during the international crisis. Finally, the share in high-earning sectors (primary activities, skilled services, and public administration) rose from 18.3 to 20.5 per cent (Table 7.1).

From 2000 to 2012, the changes in the employment composition by economic sector resulted in a slight improvement for youth, adults, and men (increases in the shares of low- and high-earnings sectors coupled with reductions in the share of mid-earnings sector), while there was a full improvement for women (increase in the share of high-earnings sectors and reductions in the shares of low- and mid-earnings sectors).

The international crisis of 2008 did not affect the improving or slightly improving trend in the composition of employment by economic sector, but led to a change in the relative shares of low- and mid-earning sectors. Between 2008 and 2009, the share of low-earning sectors exhibited a larger reduction compared to the share of mid-earning sectors in the aggregate, for young workers, and for women, while the share of high-earning sectors continued to increase. For adults, the share of low-earning sectors stopped increasing and had a small reduction. For men, the pre-crisis trends in their employment composition by sector were not impacted by the international crisis.

> The educational level of the Argentine employed population improved steadily over the period, overall and for all population groups. The international crisis of 2008 had no effect on this upward trend. (Cruces et al. 2015: figure 6)

The share of employed workers with low educational levels (eight years of schooling or less) dropped from 37.0 per cent in 2000 to 24.9 per cent in 2012, while the shares of workers with medium and high educational levels (nine to thirteen years of schooling and over thirteen years of schooling) grew from 38.8 per cent in 2000 to 43.9 per cent in 2012 and from 24.2 per cent to 31.1

per cent respectively (Table 7.1).[2] We interpret this result as an improvement for the employed population as the level of education is an important predictor of labour earnings. Consequently, these changes in the employment structure by educational level implied an increase in the share of workers that tend to have high levels of earnings and a decline in the share of workers with low earnings levels.[3]

The educational level of the employed population improved between 2000 and 2012 for all population groups, although with some differences between them. For the young and adult population, the reduction in the shares of workers with low educational levels was similar, but the corresponding increase in the share of high-educated workers was larger among adults. Disaggregating by gender, the reduction in the share of workers with low levels of education was larger among men, while in the increase in the share of workers with high levels of education was larger among women.

The pattern of improvement in the educational level of the employed population in Argentina was not abated on the aggregate or on the population group level by the international crisis of 2008.

> The overall share of wage/salaried employees registered with the social security system increased between 2000 and 2012. While this indicator improved for adults, men, and women, it deteriorated for youth. Within this period, the registration rate fell in the early years of the period studied but increased in the later years. This upward trend, which started in 2004, held for all population groups; it was not interrupted by the international crisis of 2008. (Cruces et al. 2015: figure 7)

As detailed in ISSA (2014), the social security system in Argentina consists of a set of benefits covering health risks, old age pensions, unemployment insurance, family allowances, and job risks; these benefits are managed by agencies of the *Ministerio de Trabajo, Empleo y Seguridad Social* and the *Ministerio de Desarrollo Social*. There exist both contributory and non-contributory schemes. The contributory scheme is mandatory for wage/salaried employees and self-employed persons. For other workers, like persons insured under professional provincial systems and housewives, participation is voluntary. The non-contributory scheme covers persons with income below a subsistence level who are not receiving any social security benefit or support from

[2] The most frequent value of years of education for employed workers in Argentina was seven during 2000–3 (around 24.7 per cent of employed workers had seven years of education) and twelve during 2004–12 (around 26.1 per cent of employed workers had twelve years of education).

[3] The improvement in the employment structure by educational level is related to changes in the relative demand and supply of workers with high educational levels with corresponding implications for the wage gap by educational group and the unemployment rate of each educational level. We introduce a discussion about the role of these factors in Argentina in section 7.5.

family members. The non-contributory scheme is funded fully by the government.

Social security records show an increase in the percentage of wage/salaried employees registered with the contributory schemes of the system from 2000 to 2012, which rose from 61.6 per cent in 2000 (3,769,596 registered workers) to 65.1 per cent in 2012 (5,504,925 registered workers) (Table 7.1). The change, though, was not smooth. From 2000 to 2003, a period that included the severe crisis of 2001–2, the percentage of workers registered with the social security system dropped from 61.6 per cent to 50.6 per cent. The share of wage/salaried employees who were registered with the social security system then increased steadily from 2003 to 2011. This upward trend was related to several factors such as: the profitability and productivity increases of local firms driven by the high real exchange rate of the macroeconomic scheme established after the 2001–2 crisis; the set-up of a labour inspection system with the objective of monitoring compliance with labour and social security regulations; the simplification of the administrative procedures needed to register workers with the social security system; the reduction in the social security contributions paid by employers; and the implementation of specific policies for those workers most affected by unregistered employment, such as domestic workers (Novick et al. 2008; Bertranou et al. 2013). Finally, the period 2011–12 witnessed a slight decrease in the share of registered wage/salaried employees.

The rate of registration with the social security system decreased for youths and increased for adults, men, and women over the period. All population groups reached the lowest rate of registration during the period in 2003.

The international crisis did not immediately slow down the upward trend in the share of wage/salaried employees registered with the social security system among youth or adults, or among men or women. The number of registered workers increased in the aggregate by 104,751 between 2008 and 2009, while the number of unregistered workers contracted by 82,881 over the same period. However, the share of workers registered with the social security system dropped slightly from 2010 to 2012 due to the increase in the number of unregistered workers, which climbed by 135,979 workers.

7.5 Labour Earnings

> Two years of falling labour earnings from 2000 to 2002 were followed by ten years of rising labour earnings from 2002 to 2012. The increases were large enough so that labour earnings were slightly higher in 2012 than in 2000 in real terms. The pattern of falling labour earnings during 2000–02 and rising labour earnings during 2002–12 held for all population groups,

> but youth and female workers were the ones who benefited the most. In general, workers in low-earning categories experienced a larger increase in labour earnings than did workers in high-earning categories, whose labour earnings even fell for some groups. Labour earnings were not affected negatively by the 2008 crisis. (Cruces et al. 2015: figure 8)

Average monthly earnings expressed in dollars at 2005 PPP increased by 2.5 per cent, climbing from 761.7 in 2000 to 781.0 in 2012 (Table 7.1). However, the experiences within the period varied substantially. Argentina suffered an inordinate decline in average real labour earnings (−5.6 per cent) during the economic recession at the beginning of the period—that is, from 2000 to 2002; this drop was brought about by a large increase in domestic prices after the devaluation of the peso coupled with the lack of adjustment of nominal earnings in a context of high unemployment and weak unions (Gasparini and Cruces 2010). After that period, a long and steady recovery set in that brought with it an increase in labour earnings during most of the subsequent years. Starting in 2003, the government favoured successive increases in the minimum wage, and labour earnings continued to increase in a context of employment growth; by 2011, the level of labour earnings surpassed the 2000 level. The upward trend post-2002 was interrupted in 2008 when labour earnings fell by 2.0 per cent. In 2009, real earnings resumed their upward trend until 2011. Finally, labour earnings fell by 2.3 per cent in 2012.

When the analysis is broken down by population groups, women and young workers are found to be the ones who benefited the most during 2000–12. Other groups whose earnings increased substantially were wage employees, mid-earning economic sectors, and workers with low educational levels. Employers and the self-employed, workers in high-earning sectors, and workers with high educational levels experienced a drop in their labour earnings over the period.

The evidence of falling labour earnings for workers with high educational levels and increasing labour earnings for those with low and medium educational levels can be interpreted in light of previous findings of slight improvement in the employment structure by economic sector and improvement in the educational level of the employed population over the period. Changes in the employment structure by economic sector implied a reduction in the total share of sectors that can be expected to use workers with low and medium educational levels such as utilities and transportation, domestic service, high-tech industry, and commerce, and an increase in the total share of sectors that employ workers with high educational levels, such as skilled services and public administration. This evidence indicates that the demand for workers with high educational levels relative to those with low and medium educational levels increased during 2000–12. On the other hand, the educational level of people in the labour force improved over the same period, leading to an increase in the relative supply of workers with high and medium levels of education (Cruces et al. 2015: table 7). The prediction of a supply and demand analysis is that the relativewages of workers with high educational levels relative to those with low and medium educational levels will rise or fall depending on which effect dominates (increase in the relative demand versus increase in the relative supply). In the Argentinean labour market the relative wages of workers with high and medium educational levels relative to those with low educational levels fell over the period, and the relative wages of workers with high educational levels relative to those with medium educational levels also decreased (Cruces et al. 2015: table 6). The adjustment process also led to a reduction in the unemployment rate of all educational groups, with a larger reduction for workers with low levels of education (Cruces et al. 2015: table 8).

During the international crisis of 2008, and after they experienced a small decrease in 2008, labour earnings continued to grow overall and for all population groups. Some workers in specific economic sectors were negatively affected by the crisis. Labour earnings rose, on average, by 4.0 per cent during 2008–9, the year of the crisis. Increases were similar among most groups analysed, except for workers in high-tech industry (no change) and in the utilities and transportation sector (3.5 per cent decline). The crisis, then, had a mild effect on labour earnings.

7.6 Poverty and Inequality

> Despite large increases in the early 2000s, the poverty rate and the rate of working poor households decreased substantially from 2000 to 2012.
>
> (Cruces et al. 2015: figure 9)

The 4 dollars-a-day poverty rate fell from 27.5 per cent in 2000 to 10.8 per cent in 2012, after climbing to 45.5 per cent in 2002; the 2.5 dollars-a-day poverty rate dropped from 14.2 per cent to 4.7 per cent from 2000 to 2012, with a peak of 29.2 per cent in 2002; the percentage of the working poor (defined as the proportion of persons in the population living in poor households, according to the 4 dollars-a-day poverty line, where at least one member works) decreased from 14.8 to 5.7 per cent over the same period, with the highest point equal to 27.0 per cent in 2002 (Table 7.1). The downward trend in all poverty indicators was not affected by the international crisis of 2008.

Thus, poverty rates increased substantially from 2000 to 2002, a period that included the local crisis, and then decreased steadily until 2012, even during the international crisis. The poverty patterns exhibited by Argentina can be understood by examining incomes from various sources as well as government programmes. Household labour earnings, pensions, government transfers, and capital income fell substantially between 2000 and 2002 (Cruces et al. 2015: figure 10). The reduction in real earnings after the devaluation of the domestic currency at the beginning of the decade is the most important factor to explain the increase in the poverty rates to unprecedented levels for the country between 2000 and 2002 (Gasparini and Cruces 2010). The reduction in poverty indicators from 2002 to 2011 was related mainly to increases in labour earnings and employment levels. Higher labour earnings and employment levels accounted for nearly 70 per cent of the decline in the poverty rate based on the 4 dollars-a-day poverty line from 2004 to 2012. The remaining 30.0 per cent of the decline in the poverty rate was accounted for by the increase in non-labour incomes like pensions and private and public transfers (World Bank 2014a). Pensions increased steadily from 2002 to 2012, while the number of beneficiaries from government transfers exhibited a substantial increase with the implementation of the *Asignación Universal por Hijo* targeted cash transfer programme in 2008. Indeed, it is estimated that poverty measured by the 2.5 dollars-a-day poverty line in 2009 was nearly half what it would have been in the absence of progressive social spending (World Bank 2014a).

> Household per capita income inequality and labour earnings inequality increased at the beginning of the period and then started a sustained downward trend, with the result that inequality was much lower at the end of the period (2012) than it had been at the beginning (2000). The international crisis of 2008 did not affect the downward trend in inequality indices that was observed in the last ten years of the period. (Cruces et al. 2015: figure 11)

The Gini coefficient of household per capita income increased from 2000 to 2002, reaching a maximum of 0.533, and then decreased steadily to 0.423 in 2012, a much lower value than in the year 2000 (0.504). Throughout the period, the Gini coefficient of labour earnings among employed workers was lower than that of household per capita income. Its evolution mirrored the changes in the Gini coefficient of household per capita income, going from 0.459 in 2000 to 0.498 in 2002 and falling every year after, reaching 0.388 in 2012 (Table 7.1). The overall reduction in labour earnings inequality is in accord with the evidence presented in section 7.5, showing larger income increases for workers in low-earning employment categories compared to workers in high-earning categories, whose labour incomes even fell for some groups. Consequently, the reduction in labour earnings inequality in Argentina occurred at the expense of income losses for some categories.

Considering that labour earnings are the main source of income for Argentine households, its evolution could be behind the decline in household per capita income inequality. That is confirmed by Bergolo et al. (2011), who used a non-parametric decomposition method to find that the reduction in labour income inequality accounted for around three quarters of the decline in household per capita income inequality between 2001 and 2009, and the remaining 25.0 per cent was accounted for by the decline in non-labour income inequality. The decline in non-labour income inequality was caused by a more progressive fiscal policy. The initially negative (and disequalizing) effect of the devaluation of the domestic currency on real wages was in part compensated for by the expansion of progressive export taxes, which were used to finance large anti-poverty programmes like *Jefes y Jefas de Hogar Desocupados* in 2002 (Gasparini and Cruces 2010). The excise taxes also had an indirect redistributive impact because they kept domestic prices of traded goods below their international level; this was particularly important for food prices. Within the period 2002–12, the contribution of the increase in the size and progressivity of social spending to the reduction in household income inequality was more important between 2006 and 2009 compared to the period 2003–6. The reason was the introduction of a new non-contributory pension programme, the pension moratorium, in 2004 (Lustig and Pessino 2013).[4]

The literature on labour earnings inequality in Argentina provides some explanations for its decline during the 2000s. Gasparini and Cruces (2010) argue that the fall in labour income inequality over the 2000s can be accounted for by: the expansion of employment generated by the fast economic recovery; the shift of the employment structure in favour of more low-skilled labour-intensive sectors as a result of the devaluation of the Argentine peso at the beginning of the decade; the fading out of the effect of skill-based technical change on the demand for labour in the 1990s; and the rise in the influence of labour unions. All these factors caused the skills premium, measured as relative returns to tertiary education by the authors, to fall. Gasparini et al. (2011) found evidence consistent with the conclusions of Gasparini and Cruces (2010). Their analysis indicates that during the 2000s, demand and institutional factors like the minimum wage were more important for the decline in the skill premium in Argentina than the increase in the relative supply of skilled workers. Other papers analysed the contribution to the declining earnings inequality of changes in the distribution of workers' characteristics and changes in the returns to those characteristics. Azevedo et al. (2013) applied a parametric decomposition method and found that between 2000 and 2010, the changes in the distribution of workers' characteristics like

[4] The *Moratoria Previsional*, which has been translated into English as 'pension moratorium', allowed workers of retirement age to receive a pension regardless of whether they had completed the full thirty years of required social security contributions through formal employment (Lustig and Pessino 2013).

education and experience (or the 'quantity effect') and the changes in the returns to those characteristics (or the 'price effect') were inequality-reducing. However, the results of Battistón et al. (2014), who used a microsimulation approach for the period 2004–9, indicate that the quantity effect was equalizing only when levels of education are used but inequality-increasing when education is measured by years of schooling, as in Azevedo et al. (2013).

7.7 Conclusions

By Latin American standards, Argentina experienced high economic growth during the 2000s. Within the period, the pattern of economic growth was U-shaped: GDP fell dramatically during 2000–2 and then grew rapidly during 2003–12. Though the economy of Argentina stopped growing during the international crisis of 2008, it recovered the previous growth pattern by 2010.

Most labour market indicators followed the U-shaped pattern of economic growth over the period. The unemployment rate exhibited an increase in the early years of the period and a downward trend in the later years, falling overall between 2000 and 2012. The employment structure by occupational position deteriorated at the beginning of the period and then improved steadily as the share of wage/salaried employees increased and the share of self-employed and unpaid workers decreased. The educational level of the employed population increased steadily between 2000 and 2012. A reduction in the percentage of registered workers at the beginning of the period was followed by a steady upward trend after 2003. The sectoral composition of employment exhibited small changes that can be interpreted as a slight improvement. Labour earnings fell dramatically in the early years of the period and then started an upward trend. The increases were large enough in 2012 to raise labour earnings above where they had been in 2000. Workers in low-earning categories were the ones who benefited the most, while labour earnings even fell for some high-earning categories.

In accordance with the pattern of GDP growth, poverty indicators grew by a large amount at the beginning of the period and then started a downward trend. This fall was large enough to bring about a substantial reduction in poverty rates from 2000 to 2012. The Gini coefficients of household per capita income and of labour earnings decreased over the period. Inequality indices increased in the early years of the period and fell in the later years.

Some labour market indicators were affected negatively by the international crisis of 2008: the unemployment rate increased and the composition of employment by occupational position worsened. Both indicators had returned to pre-crises levels by 2010. The comparison between the effects of the international crisis of 2008 on labour market indicators and the effects generated by the 2001–2 crisis reveals that the crisis at the beginning of the 2000s impacted Argentina more strongly. The crisis of 2001–2 generated a larger reduction in GDP, a larger increase in the unemployment rate, and a larger decrease in labour earnings compared to the Great Recession. Moreover, the poverty rates measured by the international poverty lines increased during the first recessionary episode, while they continued to decrease after the international crisis of 2008. The reasons behind the smaller negative impacts of the international crisis compared to the recession at the beginning of the decade were that at the time of the international crisis, the Argentine economy had a relatively high amount of international reserves, a trade and a fiscal surplus, and the country was in a situation of financial isolation.

Young workers and women had worse labour market outcomes over the period compared to adults and men respectively, and while young workers seem to be more vulnerable to macroeconomic crises compared to adults, men were more negatively affected by the crises compared to women. The unemployment rate was higher for young compared to adult workers, the share of young employed workers in low-earning economic sectors was larger than the share of adult workers, the percentage of young workers registered with the social security system was lower when compared to adults, and labour earnings of young workers were below those of adults. On the other hand, the share of young workers in low-earning occupational positions was lower compared to adults. In addition to the generally inferior situation of young workers in the labour market compared to adults, youth labour market indicators were more adversely affected by the episodes of crises. Disaggregating by gender, we found that men had better labour market outcomes than women, with the only exception being the share of workers in low-earning positions which was larger among men. However, men were hit hardest by both crises in most labour market indicators, with the labour earning reduction during the crisis at the beginning of the period being the only exception to this pattern.

In summary, notwithstanding Argentina's massive downturn from 2000 to 2002 and the international crisis of 2008, Argentine labour market conditions were in a better state in 2012 than they were at the start of the millennium.

References

Azevedo, J. P., M. E. Dávalos, C. Díaz-Bonilla, B. Atuesta, and R. A. Castañeda (2013). 'Fifteen Years of Inequality in Latin America: How Have Labor Markets Helped?'. Policy Research Working Paper 6384. Washington, DC: World Bank.

Battistón, D., C. García-Domench, and L. Gasparini (2014). 'Could an Increase in Education Raise Income Inequality? Evidence for Latin America', *Latin American Journal of Economics—formerly Cuadernos de Economía* 51 (1): 1–39.

Beccaria, L. and R. Maurizio (2008). 'Mercado de trabajo y distribución personal del ingreso', in J. Lindenboim (ed.), *Trabajo, ingresos y políticas en Argentina: Contribuciones para pensar el siglo XXI*. Buenos Aires: EUDEBA, 71–113.

Bergolo, M., F. Carbajal, G. Cruces, and N. Lustig (2011). 'Impacto de las transferencias públicas en la década de 2000: La experiencia de los países del Cono Sur'. Unpublished manuscript. La Plata: Centro de Estudios Distributivos, Laborales y Sociales.

Bertranou, F., L. Casanova, and M. Sarabia (2013). 'Dónde, cómo y por qué se redujo la informalidad laboral en Argentina durante el período 2003–2012'. Working Paper 1. Buenos Aires: Argentine Office, International Labour Organization.

CEDLAS and World Bank (2014). SEDLAC—Socio-Economic Database for Latin America and the Caribbean. Centro de Estudios Distributivos, Laborales y Sociales, Facultad de Ciencias Económicas, Universidad Nacional de La Plata and World Bank Poverty Group LCR. Available at <http://sedlac.econo.unlp.edu.ar/eng/index.php>, accessed 2014.

CEPALSTAT (2015). Available at <http://estadisticas.cepal.org/cepalstat/WEB_CEPALSTAT/Portada.asp?idioma=i>, accessed March 2015.

Cetrángolo, O., D. Heymann, and A. Ramos (2007). 'Macroeconomía en recuperación: La Argentina post-crisis', in B. Kosakoff (ed.), *Crisis, Recuperación y Nuevos Dilemas. La Economía Argentina 2002–2007*. Buenos Aires: CEPAL, 27–61.

Cruces, G., G. Fields, D. Jaume, and M. Viollaz (2015). 'The Growth–Employment–Poverty Nexus in Latin America in the 2000s: Argentina Country Study'. WIDER Working Paper 2015/069. Helsinki: UNU-WIDER.

Damill, M. and R. Frenkel (2009). 'La Argentina y la crisis internacional'. ITF Lecturas y Policy Briefs 43. Buenos Aires: Iniciativa para la Transparencia Financiera.

Gasparini, L. and G. Cruces (2010). 'A Distribution in Motion: The Case of Argentina', in L. F. López Calva and N. Lustig (eds), *Declining Inequality in Latin America: A Decade of Progress?* Washington, DC: Brookings Institution Press, 100–33.

Gasparini, L., S. Galiani, G. Cruces, and P. Acosta (2011). 'Educational Upgrading and Returns to Skills in Latin America: Evidence from a Supply–Demand Framework, 1990–2010'. IZA Working Paper 6244. Bonn: Institute for the Study of Labor.

INDEC (2015). Available at <http://www.indec.gob.ar/>, accessed March 2015.

ISSA (2014). 'Social Security Programs throughout the World: The Americas, 2013'. SSA Publication 13–11804. Washington, DC: Social Security Administration, Office of Retirement and Disability Policy and Office of Research, Evaluation and Statistics.

Kiguel, M. (2011). 'Argentina's 2001 Economic and Financial Crisis: Lessons for Europe', in *Think Tank 20: Beyond Macroeconomic Policy Coordination Discussions in the G-20*. Washington, DC: Brookings Institution Press, 7–9.

Lustig, N. and C. Pessino (2013). 'Social Spending and Income Redistribution in Argentina in the 2000s: The Rising Role of Noncontributory Pensions'. CEQ Working Paper 5. New Orleans, LA: Center for Inter-American Policy and Research and Department of Economics, Tulane University.

Novick, M., X. Mazorra, and D. Schleser (2008). 'Un nuevo esquema de políticas públicas para la reducción de la informalidad laboral', in *Aportes a una Nueva Visión de la Informalidad Laboral en la Argentina*. Buenos Aires: World Bank and Ministerio de Trabajo, Empleo y Seguridad Social, 23–41.

World Bank (2014a). 'International Bank for Reconstruction and Development, International Finance Corporation, Multilateral Investment Guarantee Agency, and Country Partnership Strategy for the Argentine Republic'. Report 81361-AR. Washington, DC: World Bank.

World Bank (2014b). World Development Indicators. Available at <http://data.worldbank.org/data-catalog/world-development-indicators>, accessed April 2014.

8

Bolivia

8.1 Introduction

This chapter on labour markets and growth in Bolivia since 2000 is one of sixteen studies of Latin American countries, each of which analyses the growth–employment–poverty nexus and aims to answer the following broad questions: Has economic growth resulted in economic development via improved labour market conditions in Latin America in the 2000s, and have these improvements halted or been reversed since the Great Recession? How do the rate and character of economic growth, changes in the various labour market indicators, and changes in poverty relate to each other?

To answer these questions, we analyse the growth experience of Bolivia during the 2000s and a wide set of labour market indicators that we assign to one of two different categories: employment and earnings indicators, and poverty and income inequality indicators. More specifically, for the group of employment and earnings indicators we construct statistics on the following variables: the unemployment rate; the employment structure by occupational group, employment position, economic sector, registration of workers with the social security system, and educational level; and mean labour earnings and hourly wages. We present all these indicators for the employed population as a whole and for different population groups (youth, adults, men, and women). For the group of poverty and income inequality indicators, we compute poverty rates using the official moderate and extreme poverty lines and the international lines of 2.5 and 4 dollars a day. We also calculate the Gini coefficient of household per capita income and labour earnings.

All the statistics in this chapter are obtained using microdata from the Encuesta Continua de Hogares (ECH) for the years 2000 and 2003–4 and the Encuesta de Hogares (EH) for the years 2001, 2002, and 2005 to 2012. The nationwide surveys were processed following a harmonization methodology and incorporated into the SEDLAC—Socio-Economic Database for Latin

America and the Caribbean (CEDLAS and World Bank 2014).[1] The resulting labour market indicators were compiled into a large number of tables and figures, which are available in an earlier version of this study (henceforth, Cruces et al. 2015). Chapter 1 of this book provides the definition for each of the indicators we analyse here, while Cruces et al. (2015) includes details on definitions and classification systems used by Bolivia's household surveys, and on comparability issues of these surveys over time.

8.2 Economic Growth

> Bolivia experienced moderate economic growth from 2000 to 2012. The economy suffered a slowdown as a consequence of the international crisis of 2008, but GDP and GDP per capita growth rates were nonetheless positive in 2009. (Cruces et al. 2015: figures 1 and 2)

During the period 2000–12, Bolivia experienced moderate economic growth by Latin American standards. GDP per capita increased by 30.5 per cent, while the average for the eighteen Latin American countries was 36.2 per cent during the same period. GDP (measured in PPP dollars of 2005) grew by 61.2 per cent, and GDP per employed person rose by 16.8 per cent. The annual growth rate of GDP per capita was 2.1 per cent, and it varied from a minimum of −0.4 per cent in 2001 to a maximum of 4.6 per cent in 2008 (Table 8.1).

Most of the GDP growth took place in the second half of the period. At the beginning of the 2000s, Bolivia experienced low economic growth. Between 2000 and 2002, economic activity was sluggish due to a real exchange rate appreciation and a series of negative shocks such as the intensified coca eradication, the devaluation in Brazil, and the crisis in Argentina (IMF 2006). GDP growth averaged 2.2 per cent a year and GDP per capita growth rate was only 0.2 per cent annually. Starting in 2003, economic activity recovered, led by hydrocarbon and mineral exports. There was an increase in both export volumes—the result of large investments in hydrocarbon and mining sectors—and commodities prices. The royalty rate paid on hydrocarbon production also increased due to the new Hydrocarbon Law of 2005, which led to a large increase in fiscal revenues. Moreover, Bolivia benefited from a significant reduction in its external public debt and the increase of remittances by Bolivian nationals who had migrated abroad (Cali and Jemio 2010).[2] The large

[1] See Cruces et al. (2015: table 8.1) for details on the size of Bolivia household surveys.

[2] Bolivia was part of the joint IMF/World Bank Heavily Indebted Poor Countries programme that provided 100 per cent debt relief in 2006.

	2000	2001	2002	2003	2004	2005	2006	2007	2008	2009	2010	2011	2012
Growth Indicators													
GDP per capita	3,488	3,476	3,492	3,518	3,596	3,688	3,799	3,907	4,081	4,151	4,252	4,400	4,552
GDP per capita growth rate	0.42	-0.35	0.47	0.74	2.24	2.56	3.01	2.85	4.45	1.71	2.45	3.46	3.45
Employment and Earnings Indicators													
Employment-to-population ratio	66.95	70.51	68.94	70.02	...	66.38	69.47	67.53	69.94	69.97	...	70.27	67.08
Unemployment rate	5.90	6.50	5.76	5.80	...	7.05	6.53	6.85	4.62	4.81	...	4.12	3.91
Share of low-earnings occupations	61.77	63.90	63.61	60.56	...	59.48	56.03	57.33	58.11	55.91	...	56.43	56.01
Share of mid-earnings occupations	33.53	29.43	29.75	33.85	...	33.20	34.54	33.32	33.90	35.39	...	32.50	32.33
Share of high-earnings occupations	4.71	6.67	6.64	5.58	...	7.32	9.42	9.35	7.99	8.70	...	11.07	11.66
Share of employers	2.06	2.41	4.79	5.16	...	5.70	4.81	5.82	6.18	5.13	...	5.79	6.79
Share of wage/salaried employees	33.10	34.89	33.04	37.39	...	36.06	36.61	39.28	38.96	41.78	...	39.50	40.67
Share of self-employed workers	44.74	39.52	39.43	38.99	...	38.13	37.48	36.04	35.58	35.36	...	36.53	38.34
Share of unpaid family workers	20.11	23.18	22.74	18.45	...	20.11	21.10	18.85	19.29	17.73	...	18.19	14.20
Share of workers in low-earnings sectors	62.12	65.31	63.47	60.18	...	59.35	55.75	56.62	57.00	54.19	...	55.71	55.54
Share of workers in mid-earnings sectors	26.97	23.84	26.64	28.97	...	28.58	28.95	29.56	28.09	31.35	...	29.03	28.10
Share of workers in high-earnings sectors	10.91	10.85	9.89	10.86	...	12.07	15.31	13.82	14.91	14.46	...	15.26	16.36

(continued)

Table 8.1 Continued

	2000	2001	2002	2003	2004	2005	2006	2007	2008	2009	2010	2011	2012
Share of low educated workers	60.05	59.64	61.33	59.36	...	55.94	56.04	50.84	50.26	48.15	...	45.91	43.17
Share of medium educated workers	26.60	26.35	26.84	28.86	...	29.81	30.84	31.86	34.95	35.08	...	33.59	35.07
Share of high educated workers	13.35	14.02	11.83	11.78	...	14.25	13.12	17.30	14.79	16.77	...	20.50	21.76
Share of workers registered with SS	12.29	11.85	9.66	10.47	...	19.83	18.73	13.65	13.03	14.89	...	17.44	18.06
Mean labour earnings	447.3	415.4	435.7	443.6	...	471.0	498.9	466.1	503.6	530.9	...	573.8	589.3
Poverty and Inequality Indicators													
Official extreme poverty rate	42.2	30.8	36.3	27.4	...	32.4	29.1	31.1	26.0	22.6	...	17.8	18.7
Official moderate poverty rate	65.0	56.4	60.0	53.6	...	56.4	53.1	55.2	52.5	47.1	...	40.8	39.1
Poverty rate 2.5 dollars-a-day	43.25	34.72	39.70	30.50	...	34.81	32.00	30.29	22.84	20.64	...	16.19	17.05
Poverty rate 4 dollars-a-day	59.90	53.61	57.75	51.43	...	53.58	48.52	47.43	40.41	35.14	...	29.16	29.49
GINI of household per capita income	0.619	0.549	0.600	0.549	...	0.583	0.567	0.553	0.514	0.494	...	0.462	0.465
GINI of labour earnings	0.594	0.559	0.574	0.529	...	0.563	0.539	0.536	0.508	0.495	...	0.454	0.467

Note: The shaded labour market indicators' figures represent statistical significant improvements at 5 per cent between the initial and final years for all the employment and earnings indicators and poverty and inequality indicators. The only exceptions are the share of mid-earnings occupations, share of mid-earnings sectors and share of medium-educated workers for which we did not assign welfare evaluation criteria.

Source: SEDLAC (CEDLAS and World Bank 2014) and World Development Indicators (World Bank 2014).

accumulation of international reserves and significant fiscal surpluses contributed to turn Bolivia into a net external creditor (IMF 2010).

The international crisis of 2008 led to an important reduction in export prices, causing a drop in export incomes, fiscal revenues, and economic activity (Jemio and Nina 2010). However, the impact of the Great Recession on Bolivia was milder than in other Latin American countries. In fact, Bolivia was one of few countries in Latin America that sustained positive growth during the global crisis of 2008. GDP growth slowed from 6.2 per cent in 2008 to 3.4 per cent in 2009, and GDP per capita growth from 4.5 per cent to 1.7 per cent. Prudent fiscal policies during the boom allowed a sizable portion of the hydrocarbon revenue to be saved, improving the resilience of the economy to adverse external shocks (IMF 2014). The government implemented a moderately countercyclical policy to support domestic demand during the international crisis. Moreover, the financial system was barely affected due to its limited integration with international capital markets (IMF 2010). The reduction in commodity prices was only temporary, allowing the recovery of the growth rates. By 2011, GDP and GDP per capita growth rates surpassed their pre-crisis levels.

8.3 Unemployment

> The 2000–12 period witnessed a drop in the unemployment rate, which was not tightly correlated to GDP growth. The unemployment rate fell for all population groups over the period. The international crisis of 2008 led to an interruption of the overall downward trend in the unemployment rate. (Cruces et al. 2015: figure 3)

The unemployment rate (measured as the ratio of unemployment to labour force) decreased from 5.9 per cent in 2000 to 3.9 per cent in 2012 (Table 8.1). The decline in the unemployment rate was explained both by the entry of persons into the labour market (the number of persons in the labour force grew by 1,199,094 from 2000 to 2012) which mimicked the upward trend of the working-age population, and by the reduction in the number of unemployed people (reduction of 24,909 persons). The reduction in the unemployment rate was not monotonic over the period. The unemployment rate suffered an initial increase followed by a reduction between 2001 and 2003–4, while GDP was increasing, increased, and remained at the highest level of the period between 2005 and 2007 (around 6.8 per cent) when GDP was growing rapidly, and declined in the following years with a small interruption during the international crisis of 2008 (17,122 new unemployed people between 2008 and 2009). The increase in the unemployment rate between 2005 and 2007 was related to the export-based growth process of Bolivia, as the mining and hydrocarbon sectors—main export products of the country—are capital-intensive (Muriel and Jemio 2010).

Between 2000 and 2012, the unemployment rate decreased for all population groups. Young workers, adults, men, and women suffered an increase in their unemployment rates between 2005 and 2007. All population groups recovered the downward trend in the following years with an interruption during the international crisis of 2008 only for adult workers and men.

8.4 Job Mix

> The composition of employment by occupational group improved between 2000 and 2012 as workers moved from elementary and agricultural, forestry and fishery occupations to better paying occupations like management and professional jobs. All demographic groups—young and adult workers, men and women—benefited from the improvement in the occupational composition of employment over the period. The international crisis of 2008 did not affect the improving trend.
>
> (Cruces et al. 2015: figure 4)

The share of the following occupations shrank between 2000 and 2012: agricultural occupations (drop of 9.6 percentage points); crafts and trades occupations (drop of 2.9 percentage points); and technical and associate professional occupations (drop of 1.7 percentage points). The share of the following occupations grew: professional (increase of 6.7 percentage points); services and sales workers (increase of 4.3 percentage points); and plant and machine operators (increase of 3.1 percentage points). The share of the other occupational groups remained largely unchanged. These changes in the occupational composition of employment can be interpreted as an improvement since low-earning occupations (agricultural, elementary, and services and sales occupations) reduced their share in total employment by 5.8 percentage points between 2000 and 2012, while high-earning occupations (management, armed forces, and professionals) gained share in total employment (increase of 7.0 percentage points). These changes resulted in a slight reduction in the share of mid-earning occupations (technicians and associate professionals, plant and machine operators, clerical, and craft and related trade jobs) in total employment (Table 8.1).

Improvements in the occupational composition of employment between 2000 and 2012 were observed for young and adult workers, and for men and women.

The international crisis of 2008 did not affect adversely the improvement in the composition of employment by occupational group. Between 2008 and 2009 the share of low-earning occupations fell in the aggregate and for all population groups, while the share of high-earning occupations increased overall and for young, adult workers, and women. For men, though, a reduction in the share of high-earning occupations resulted in an increase in the share of mid-earning occupations during the international crisis. That share reached and surpassed the pre-crisis level by 2011.

> The employment structure by occupational position improved from 2000 to 2012 as the share of wage/salaried employees and employers in total employment increased and the share of self-employed and unpaid workers decreased. The improving trend in the employment structure by occupational position was experienced by all population groups. The international crisis of 2008 did not affect adversely the improvement in the structure of employment by occupational position overall, for adult workers, men, and women, but led to a worsening for youth. (Cruces et al. 2015: figure 5)

The structure of employment by occupational position changed over the period. In 2000 the largest category was the self-employed (44.7 per cent of total employment) followed by wage/salaried employees (33.1 per cent). By 2012, the position of these categories reversed and the largest was wage/salaried employees (40.7 per cent of total employment) followed by the self-employed (38.3 per cent) (Table 8.1). The share of unpaid workers decreased over the period from 20.1 per cent of employed persons in 2000 to 14.2 per cent in 2012, while the share of employers increased from 2.1 per cent in 2000 to 6.8 per cent in 2012. These changes in the structure of employment by occupational position can be interpreted as an improvement due to the fall in the share of low-earning categories (self-employment and unpaid workers) and the increase in the share of high-earning categories (wage/salaried employees and employers). The employment structure by occupational position improved during 2000–12 for all population groups (young and adult workers, men and women).

The international crisis of 2008 did not reverse the improvements that had been taking place for the employed labour force overall, and for adults, men, and women, but led to a worsening for young workers. The share of wage/salaried employees increased between 2008 and 2009 while the share of unpaid workers and self-employed fell. Only one occupational position indicator—the share of employers in total employment—moved in the worsening direction in 2009, but it immediately began to improve again. When we disaggregate, we find that the improving trend in the structure of employment by occupational position continued without pause in 2009 for adult workers, men, and women. For young workers, though, there was a break in the tendency described before. An increase in the share of self-employed workers and a decrease in the share of wage/salaried employees took place between 2008 and 2009. In the context of a slowdown in the economic activity, young workers in Bolivia resorted to self-employment as a strategy to continue being employed. The share of self-employed workers was again declining by 2012.

> The employment composition by economic sector improved over the course of the period studied overall and for all population groups. The international crisis of 2008 did not interrupt the decreasing trend in the share of employment in low-earning sectors, but led to a reduction in the share of high-earning sectors in total employment and an increase in the share of employment in mid-earning sectors.
> (Cruces et al. 2015: figure 6)

The period 2000–12 witnessed a reduction (from 62.1 per cent to 55.5 per cent) in the share of workers in low-earning sectors (domestic service, primary activities, and commerce). Workers employed in the mining and hydrocarbon subsectors are included in the primary activities sector in our classification. The increase in the employment share of the capital-intensive mining and hydrocarbon subsectors over the period in Bolivia was counteracted by the reduction in the employment share of the labour-intensive agricultural subsector. Interestingly, besides the reduction in the share of low-earning sectors in total employment over the period, these sectors accounted for more than half of the total employed population of the country by 2012. There was, during the same period, an increase (from 10.9 per cent to 16.4 per cent) in the share of high-earning sectors (public administration, skilled services, and utilities and transportation) in the total. These changes resulted in a slight increase in the share of mid-earning sectors (industry, construction, education, and health) in total employment (Table 8.1).

The employment composition by economic sector improved between 2000 and 2012 for young and adult workers, men and women, as they moved from low-earning sectors to high-earning sectors.

The international crisis of 2008 did not halt the downward trend in the share of low-earning sectors overall and for all population groups, but led to a reduction in the share of high-earning sectors in total employment that impacted mainly young workers and resulted in an increase in the share of mid-earning sectors in total employment. Adults and men surpassed their pre-crisis share of high-earning sectors in total employment by 2011, while for young workers and women that happened in 2012.

> The educational level of the Bolivian employed population improved steadily over the period for all population groups, and especially among young workers. The improving trend was not impacted adversely by the international crisis of 2008.
> (Cruces et al. 2015: figure 7)

The share of employed workers with low educational levels (eight years of schooling or less) dropped from 60.1 per cent in 2000 to 43.2 per cent in 2012, while the share of workers with medium and high educational levels (nine to thirteen years of schooling and over thirteen years of schooling) grew from 26.6 per cent in 2000 to 35.1 per cent in 2012 and from 13.4 per cent to 21.8 per cent respectively (Table 8.1).[3] We interpret this result as an improvement for the employed population as the level of education is an important predictor of labour earnings. Consequently, the changes in the employment structure by educational level implied an increase in the share of workers that tend to have high levels of earnings and a decline in the share of workers with low earnings levels.[4] The educational level of the employed population improved between 2000 and 2012 for all groups and especially for young workers. The pattern of improvement in the level of education of the employed population in Bolivia continued even during the international crisis of 2008, overall and for all population groups.

> The overall share of workers registered with the social security system increased between 2000 and 2012, though erratically. The improvement also took place among all population groups, especially adult workers and women. The international crisis of 2008 did not affect the upward trend of the registration rate.
>
> (Cruces et al. 2015: figure 8)

The social security system in Bolivia is composed of the short-term Mandatory Social Insurance (*Seguro Social Obligatorio*) and the Long-Term Social Insurance (*Seguro Social de Largo Plazo*). The short-term Mandatory Social Insurance covers health, life, and work contingencies. It provides medical services (attention for the affiliated members and their families), as well as in-kind and cash transfers. The Long-Term Social Insurance covers disability, old age, and death, and it is an individual capitalization system. The affiliation to this insurance is mandatory for all dependent workers and voluntary for independent workers. Besides the individual capitalization system, a non-contributory universal pension—*Bonosol*—was implemented in the 1990s for all Bolivians aged 65 or more. In 2008, the *Bonosol* was replaced by the *Renta Dignidad*, which covers all Bolivians aged 60 or more with reduced benefits for those receiving any other pension (Monterrey Arce 2013).

[3] The most frequent value of years of education for employed workers in Bolivia was five between 2000 and 2002 (around 12.4 per cent of employed workers had five years of education) and twelve between 2003 and 2012 (around 16.5 per cent of employed workers had twelve years of education).

[4] The improvement in the employment structure by educational level is related to changes in the relative demand and supply of workers with high educational levels with corresponding implications on the wage gap by educational groups and the unemployment rate of each educational level. We introduce a discussion about the role of these factors in section 8.5.

Social security records show an increase in the percentage of employed workers registered with the contributory scheme of the system between 2000 and 2012, from 12.3 per cent in 2000 (452,194 registered workers) to 18.1 per cent in 2012 (542,843 registered workers) (Table 8.1). The changes were erratic. From 2000 to 2002 the percentage of workers registered with the social security system decreased; it increased between 2002 and 2005 and fell again up to 2008. From 2009 onwards, the share of employed workers registered with the social security system increased steadily. Thus, the employed population in Bolivia has been largely informal (unregistered)—just 14.5 per cent registered over the period. Among the reasons for workers not contributing to the individual capitalization system, ignorance about how the system works and lack of economic resources are the most important (Wanderley 2009). The rate of registration with the social security system increased for all population groups (young and adult workers, men, and women).

The overall percentage of workers registered with the social security system continued to grow during the international crisis of 2008. Disaggregating, the rate of registration also continued to increase for adult workers, men, and women. For young workers, though, the rate of registration slightly decreased in 2009. This fact is in accord with our previous evidence of increase in the share of self-employment—an employment category where the registration with social security is typically low—among young workers during the international crisis.[5] By 2011 it recovered the pre-crisis level and resumed the upward trend.

8.5 Labour Earnings

> Labour earnings increased between 2000 and 2012. Within the period, there was a reduction in the early years of the period, a steady increase during 2002–06, a fall in 2007, and an upward trend in the following years. Workers were not affected negatively by the 2008 crisis. Labour earnings increased overall, for young and adult workers, and for men and women. The evidence of earning changes by employment categories over the period indicates that labour earnings increased for low-earning categories and tended to decrease for high-earning categories.
>
> (Cruces et al. 2015: figure 9)

Average monthly earnings, expressed in dollars at 2005 purchasing power parity (PPP), increased by 31.8 per cent, from US$447 in 2000 to US$589 in 2012 (Table 8.1). Labour earnings fell at the beginning of the period—2000–1—and rose in most years after that. The upward trend was interrupted

[5] The average registration rate of self-employed workers during the period 2000–12 was only 2.51 per cent, while it was 32.8 per cent for wage/salaried employees.

in 2007 when labour earnings fell by 10.1 per cent. In 2008, real earnings resumed their upward trend. Starting in 2006, the government implemented continuous increases in the minimum monthly earning. Real earnings increased even more than the growth in minimum wages and the percentage of workers earning less than the minimum monthly earnings decreased, while the percentage of workers earning more than three times the minimum monthly earnings increased (Canavire-Bacarreza and Rios-Avila 2015). Disaggregating, we find that men and women, and young and adult workers all increased their labour earnings between 2000 and 2012. The trend in their labour earnings reflected the erratic overall time path.

Mean earnings rose between 2000 and 2012 in low-earning categories and tended to fall in high-earning categories. Among occupational groups, agricultural, forestry, and fishery workers, workers in elementary occupations, and services and sales workers had an average increase in their labour earnings. Workers in management, armed forces, and professionals suffered an earning reduction. When the working population is broken down by occupational positions, the self-employed had an increase in labour earnings, while employers and paid employees slightly increased their labour earnings over the period. Domestic workers and workers from primary activities and commerce increased their labour earnings over the period. On the other hand, workers in public administration, skilled services, and utilities and transportation suffered an earnings loss. Finally, labour earnings of workers with high educational levels fell, while workers with medium and low levels of education had an increase in their labour earnings.

The evidence of falling labour earnings for workers with high educational levels and labour earnings increases for workers with medium and low educational levels can be interpreted in light of previous findings of improving employment structure by occupational group and economic sector over the period, and improving educational level of the employed population. The improving employment structure by occupational group and economic sector implied an increase in the share of occupations and sectors that can be expected to employ workers with high and medium educational levels, such as management and professional occupations, public administration, skilled services, and utilities and transportation sectors, and a reduction in the share of occupations and sectors that employ workers with low educational levels, such as elementary and agricultural occupations, and domestic workers and primary activities sectors. This evidence indicates that the demand for workers with high and medium educational levels relative to those with low educational levels increased between 2000 and 2012. On the other hand, the educational level of people in the labour force improved over the same period, indicating an increase in the relative supply of workers with high and medium levels of education (Cruces et al. 2015: table 8). The prediction of a supply and demand analysis is that the relative wages of workers with high and medium educational levels relative to those with low educational levels will rise or fall depending on which effect dominates (increase in the relative demand versus increase in the relative supply). In the Bolivian labour market the relative wages of workers with high and medium educational levels relative to those with low educational levels fell over the period, and the relative wages of workers with high educational levels relative to those with medium educational levels also decreased (Cruces et al. 2015: table 7). The adjustment process also led to a reduction in the unemployment rate of all educational levels, with a larger reduction for workers with medium levels of education (Cruces et al. 2015: table 9).

Even during the international crisis of 2008, labour earnings continued to grow overall and for all demographic groups. However, some employment categories were impacted adversely by the 2008 crisis. Among occupational groups, workers in the armed forces, agricultural, forestry, and fishery workers, professionals, management workers, and workers in elementary occupations were affected negatively by the international crisis of 2008. Among economic sectors, workers from skilled services, public administration, primary activities, domestic workers, and workers from education and health were affected negatively by the international crisis of 2008. Among educational groups, workers with high educational levels were the only ones affected adversely by the international crisis of 2008.

8.6 Poverty and Inequality

> Poverty indicators exhibited important reductions between 2000 and 2012 for all poverty lines used, with ups and downs over the period. The downward trend was not affected by the international crisis of 2008.
>
> (Cruces et al. 2015: figure 10)

The moderate poverty rate (measured by the country's official poverty line) fell from 65.0 per cent in 2000 to 39.1 per cent in 2012 (drop of 945,498 in the number of moderately poor persons); the extreme poverty rate dropped from 42.2 per cent to 18.7 per cent (drop of 1,332,796 in the number of extremely poor persons); the percentage of working poor (defined as the proportion of persons in the population living in poor households where at least one member works) decreased from 56.2 per cent to 31.6 per cent over the same period (Table 8.1). The analysis of trends based on the 2.5 and 4 dollars-a-day PPP international poverty lines shows the same trends. All of these indicators moved with ups and downs in the first half of the period analysed and decreased steadily from 2007 onwards in the case of the official poverty lines, and from 2005 onwards using the international poverty lines. The downward trends in the rates of poverty and working poor were not interrupted by the international crisis of 2008. In 2012 the moderate poverty rate and the percentage of working poor continued to decrease but at a slower pace, while the extreme poverty rate and the measures calculated using the international poverty lines showed a slight increase.

The erratic evolution of poverty indicators in the first half of the period studied has been attributed to high income inequality—high inequality slowed poverty reduction in good years and accelerated poverty in the bad years—and to the growth process based on hydrocarbons, a sector with a small share of total employment (Weisbrot and Sandoval 2007; Gray Molina and Yañez 2009). In the second half of the 2000s, labour incomes and incomes from government transfers during the international crisis explained the increase in household total income (Cruces et al. 2015: figure 11). The large availability of resources from hydrocarbon rents allowed the government to expand the social safety net through cash transfer programmes such as *Bono Juancito Pinto, Bono Juana Azurduy*, the non-contributory pension *Renta Dignidad*, as well as other social programmes, such as the undernourishment programme *Desnutrición Cero*, and the literacy programme *Yo si puedo*. However, Bolivian cash transfer programmes had only a small impact on poverty reduction (Vera Cossio 2011; Yañez et al. 2011). Some of the reasons for this include that: the programmes are not targeted to the poor (they are universal), generating significant leakages to the non-poor (Paz Arauco et al. 2013); the transfers are too small—only 4.0 per cent of the average annual consumption of a Bolivian household—(McGuire 2013); and they are poorly complemented by effective public provision of health and education, and implemented by a state with low administrative capacity (McGuire 2013).

> Household per capita income and labour earning inequality decreased between 2000 and 2012 but moved erratically over the period. The reducing trend was not interrupted by the international crisis of 2008. (Cruces et al. 2015: figure 12)

Household per capita income and labour earning inequality decreased while GDP increased over the period. The Gini coefficient of household per capita income fell from 0.619 in 2000 to 0.465 in 2012. This indicator moved erratically from 2000 to 2005 and then decreased steadily until 2011, when it stabilized at around 0.463. Throughout the period, the Gini coefficient of labour earnings among employed workers was slightly lower than that of household per capita income. Its evolution mirrored the movement of the Gini coefficient of household per capita income and fell from 0.594 in 2000 to 0.467 in 2012 (Table 8.1). The evolution of the Gini coefficient of labour earnings over the period is not surprising given the previous evidence of rising incomes for low-earning categories and decreasing incomes for high-earning categories. Consequently, the reduction in labour-earning inequality in Bolivia occurred at the expense of income losses for some categories.

Changes in household per capita income inequality in Bolivia in the first half of the 2000s have been explained mainly by factors associated with the labour market: (1) the level of education of the household head; (2) labour activity of the household (proportion of household members who are unemployed, proportion in each occupational position, and proportion in each occupational group); and to a lesser extent (3) demographic characteristics (Gray Molina and Yañez 2009). On the other hand, fiscal policy had a small effect on income inequality in the second half of the period studied. Between 2007 and 2009, social spending in Bolivia increased through a new wave of cash transfer programmes. However, none of the programmes was designed with a targeted mechanism to the poor since eligibility is not conditional on being poor. As a result, the inequality reduction in Bolivia is small once direct transfers and indirect taxes are accounted for (Lustig et al. 2011; Paz Arauco et al. 2013). Changes in labour earnings inequality between 2000 and 2010 have been explained through the reduction in the education wage premium in the labour market (or 'price effect') and changes in the distribution of the stock of education (or 'quantity effect') (Azevedo et al. 2013). The reductions in the education wage premium between 2000 and 2007 were consistent with a robust increase in the relative supply of workers with high educational levels (those with complete or incomplete college education) and a concurrent fall in its relative demand (Gasparini et al. 2011). Institutional factors have also played a role in changes in labour earnings inequality. Canavire-Bacarreza and Rios-Avila (2015) analysed the evolution of labour income inequality in Bolivia from 2000 to 2012 and reported a faster earnings growth in the lower quintiles of the earnings distribution compared to the highest quintiles. The authors associated this finding with increases in the minimum monthly earnings as well as anti-discriminatory policies. They also found that changes in demographic characteristics explain only a small portion of the observed inequality decline, while the fall in the returns to education and changes in the occupational structure of employment are the main contributors to the decline in earnings inequality over the period.

8.7 Conclusions

From 2000 to 2012, Bolivia experienced moderate economic growth by Latin American standards. The economy suffered a slowdown as a consequence of the international crisis of 2008, but Bolivia was one of the few countries in Latin America to have sustained positive growth during that episode.

All labour market indicators improved between 2000 and 2012, and that trend was, in general, not affected by the international crisis of 2008. The unemployment rate was always low and fell over the period. The composition of the employed population by occupational group improved between 2000 and 2012 as workers moved from elementary and agricultural, forestry and fishery occupations to better-paying occupations, such as management and professional jobs. The employment structure by occupational position also improved through the reduction in the share of self-employed and unpaid workers in total employment and the increase in the share of wage/salaried employees and employers. Workers moved from low-earning economic sectors like domestic service and primary activities to high-earning sectors such as public administration, skilled services, and utilities and transportation. The educational level of the Bolivian employed population improved steadily over the period, the overall share of workers registered with the social security system increased, and labour earnings grew between 2000 and 2012. Moreover, the moderate and extreme poverty rates and the rate of working poor households showed important reductions between 2000 and 2012, as did the Gini coefficient of per capita household income and labour earnings.

The international crisis of 2008 led to an interruption in the downward trend of the unemployment rate, but the pre-crisis trajectory was recovered immediately. The remaining labour market indicators were not affected by the crisis.

Young workers and women had worse labour market outcomes over the period compared to adults and men respectively, and while the effects of the international crisis were negligible in general, young workers suffered some adverse impacts. The unemployment rate was higher for young compared to adult workers, the shares of young employed workers in low-earning occupations and sectors were larger than the shares of adult workers, the percentage of young workers registered with the social security system was lower when compared to adults, and labour earnings of young workers were below those of adults. On the other hand, the share of young workers in low-earning occupational positions was below that share for adults. In addition to the generally inferior situation of young workers in the labour market, youth suffered an increase in the share of workers in low-earning positions and a decrease in the percentage of workers registered with the social security system during the international crisis. Disaggregating by gender, we found that men outperformed women in all labour market indicators over the period, and none of them suffered any adverse effect of the crisis.

In summary, notwithstanding the international crisis of 2008, Bolivian labour market conditions were in a better state in 2012 than they were at the start of the millennium.

References

Azevedo, J. P., M. E. Dávalos, C. Díaz-Bonilla, B. Atuesta, and R. A. Castañeda (2013). 'Fifteen Years of Inequality in Latin America: How Have Labor Markets Helped?'. Policy Research Working Paper 6384. Washington, DC: World Bank.

Cali, M. and L. C. Jemio (2010). 'Bolivia'. Case Study for the MDG Gap Task Force Report. London: Overseas Development Institute.

Canavire-Bacarreza, G. and F. Rios-Avila (2015). 'On the Determinants of Changes in Wage Inequality in Bolivia'. Working Paper 835. Annandale-on-Hudson: Levy Economics Institute of Bard College.

CEDLAS and World Bank (2014). SEDLAC—Socio-Economic Database for Latin America and the Caribbean. Centro de Estudios Distributivos, Laborales y Sociales, Facultad de Ciencias Económicas, Universidad Nacional de La Plata and World Bank Poverty Group LCR. Available at <http://sedlac.econo.unlp.edu.ar/eng/index.php>, accessed 2014.

Cruces, G., G. Fields, D. Jaume, and M. Viollaz (2015). 'The Growth–Employment–Poverty Nexus in Latin America in the 2000s: Bolivia Country Study'. WIDER Working Paper 2015/070. Helsinki: UNU-WIDER.

Gasparini, L., S. Galiani, G. Cruces, and P. Acosta (2011). 'Educational Upgrading and Returns to Skills in Latin America: Evidence from a Supply–Demand Framework, 1990–2010'. IZA Working Paper 6244. Bonn: Institute for the Study of Labor.

Gray Molina, G. and E. Yañez (2009). 'The Dynamics of Inequality in the Best and the Worst of Times. Bolivia 1997–2007'. Research for Public Policy Inclusive Development 16-2009. New York: RBLAC-UNDP.

IMF (2006). 'Bolivia: 2006 Article IV Consultation'. IMF Country Report 06/270. Washington, DC: International Monetary Fund.

IMF (2010). 'Bolivia: 2009 Article IV Consultation'. IMF Country Report 10/27. Washington, DC: International Monetary Fund.

IMF (2014). 'Bolivia: Staff Report for the 2013 Article IV Consultation'. IMF Country Report 14/36. Washington, DC: International Monetary Fund.

Jemio, L.C. and O. Nina (2010). 'Bolivia Phase 2'. Global Financial Crisis Discussion Series. London: Overseas Development Institute.

Lustig, N., C. Pessino, G. Gray Molina, W. Jimenez, V. Paz Arauco, E. Yañez, C. Pereira, and S. Higgins (2011). 'Fiscal Policy and Income Redistribution in Latin America: Challenging the Conventional Wisdom'. Working Paper 311. New Orleans: Tulane University Economics.

McGuire, J. (2013). 'Conditional Cash Transfers in Bolivia: Origin, Impacts and Universality'. Paper prepared for the 2013 Annual Meeting of the International Studies Association, San Francisco, 3–6 April 2013. Middletown: Wesleyan University.

Monterrey Arce, J. (2013). 'Social Protection Systems in Latin America and the Caribbean: Plurinational State of Bolivia'. ECLAC, Project Documents Collection. Santiago de Chile: United Nations.

Muriel, B. and L. C. Jemio (2010). 'Mercado laboral y reformas en Bolivia'. Serie de Documentos de Trabajo sobre Desarrollo 07/2010. La Paz: Instituto de Estudios Avanzados en Desarrollo.

Paz Arauco, V., G. Gray Molina, W. Jimenez Pozo, and E. Yañez Alguila (2013). 'Explaining Low Redistributive Impact in Bolivia'. CEQ Working Paper 6. New Orleans: Tulane University.

Vera Cossio, D. (2011). 'Matriculacion y trabajo infantil en Bolivia: Un analisis quasi experimental'. Working Paper 11/2011. La Paz: Instituto de Estudios Avanzados en Desarrollo.

Wanderley, F. (2009). 'Crecimiento, empleo y bienestar social. ¿Por qué Bolivia es tan desigual?'. Coleccion 25 Aniversario, Postgrado en Ciencias del Desarrollo, Universidad Mayor de San Andrés. La Paz: Plural Editores.

Weisbrot, M. and L. Sandoval (2007). 'La economía Boliviana y su evolucion reciente'. Informe Agosto 2007. Washington, DC: Center for Economic and Policy Research.

World Bank (2014). World Development Indicators. Available at <http://data.worldbank.org/data-catalog/world-development-indicators>, accessed April 2014.

Yañez, E., R. Rojas, and D. Silva (2011). 'The Juancito Pinto Conditional Cash Transfer Program in Bolivia: Analyzing the Impact on Primary Education'. Policy Brief, May 2011. Ottowa: Canadian Foundation for the Americas.

9

Brazil

9.1 Introduction

This chapter on labour markets and growth in Brazil since 2000 is one of sixteen studies of Latin American countries, each of which analyses the growth–employment–poverty nexus and aims to answer the following broad questions: Has economic growth resulted in economic development via improved labour market conditions in Latin America in the 2000s, and have these improvements halted or been reversed since the Great Recession? How do the rate and character of economic growth, changes in the various labour market indicators, and changes in poverty relate to each other?

To answer these questions, we analyse the growth experience of Brazil during the 2000s and a wide set of labour market indicators that we assign to one of two different categories: employment and earnings indicators, and poverty and income inequality indicators. More specifically, for the group of employment and earnings indicators we construct statistics on the following variables: the unemployment rate; the employment structure by occupational group, employment position, economic sector, registration of workers with the social security system, and educational level; and mean labour earnings and hourly wages. We present all these indicators for the employed population as a whole and for different population groups (youth, adults, men, and women). For the group of poverty and income inequality indicators, we compute poverty rates using the official moderate and extreme poverty lines and the international lines of 2.5 and 4 dollars a day. We also calculate the Gini coefficient of household per capita income and labour earnings.

All the statistics in this chapter are obtained using microdata from the Pesquisa Nacional por Amostra de Domicílios (PNAD) for the years 2001–9, 2011, and 2012. The nationwide surveys were processed following a harmonization methodology and incorporated into the SEDLAC—Socio-Economic Database for Latin America and the Caribbean (CEDLAS and World Bank

2014).[1] The resulting labour market indicators were compiled into a large number of tables and figures, which are available in an earlier version of this study (henceforth, Cruces et al. 2015). Chapter 1 of this book provides the definition for each of the indicators we analyse here, while Cruces et al. (2015) includes details on definitions and classification systems used by Brazil's household surveys, and on comparability issues of these surveys over time.

9.2 Economic Growth

> Brazil exhibited slow economic growth from 2000 to 2012. The economy stagnated from 2000 to 2003 but then experienced rapid economic growth until 2008, when it was affected by the international economic crisis. It recovered quickly in 2010, but slowed down over the next two years.
>
> (Cruces et al. 2015: figures 1 and 2)

From 2000 to 2012, Brazil's economic growth was lower than the average for the Latin American region. GDP per capita increased by 29.8 per cent, while the average for the eighteen Latin American countries was 36.2 per cent during the same period. GDP (measured in 2005 PPP dollars) grew by 47.8 per cent, and GDP per employed person experienced a 12.0 per cent rise. The annual growth rate of GDP per capita was 2.2 per cent, and it varied from −1.2 per cent in 2009 to 6.6 per cent in 2010 (Table 9.1).

In just twelve years, the Brazilian growth experience can be separated into four different stages. First, from 2000 to 2003 the economy was characterized by a volatile external environment along with concerns about the continuity of macroeconomic policies following the change in government in 2003. These factors led to a sharp decline in external capital flows, a depreciation of the local currency, and some inflationary pressures (IMF 2003). GDP per capita increased by only 1.0 per cent between 2000 and 2003, with two years in which it actually shrunk (−0.1 per cent in 2001 and −0.2 per cent in 2003). Second, rapid economic growth occurred from 2003 to 2008, with GDP per capita increasing by 19.9 per cent, equivalent to an annual growth of 3.7 per cent. The increased domestic demand (consumption and investment) was the driving force of the growth process between 2003 and 2008. Redistributive policies jointly with credit expansion encouraged the consumption of durable goods (Ferraz et al. 2010). To increase growth further, the government announced in 2007 the Growth Acceleration Program, which contains steps to increase public and private investment (IMF 2007). The country also managed to reduce the GDP volatility (a historical feature of Brazilian growth),

[1] See Cruces et al. (2015: table 1) for details on the size of Brazil household surveys.

Table 9.1 Brazil: Evolution of growth and labour market indicators over the 2000s

		2000	2001	2002	2003	2004	2005	2006	2007	2008	2009	2010	2011	2012	
Growth Indicators	GDP per capita	7,906	7,898	7,998	7,985	8,338	8,502	8,745	9,187	9,573	9,456	10,079	10,264	10,264	
	GDP per capita growth rate	2.81	−0.10	1.27	−0.17	4.42	1.97	2.85	5.06	4.20	−1.22	6.59	1.83	0.00	
Employment and Earnings Indicators	Employment-to-population ratio	...	60.76	61.66	61.23	62.46	62.88	63.21	63.02	63.69	62.89	...	61.73	61.84	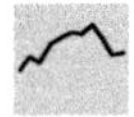
	Unemployment rate	...	9.34	9.10	9.72	8.89	9.30	8.39	8.09	7.09	8.28	...	6.69	6.15	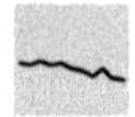
	Share of low-earnings occupations	...	...	57.83	58.00	58.09	57.39	57.22	57.20	56.51	56.48	...	56.75	55.55	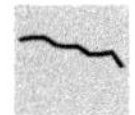
	Share of mid-earnings occupations	...	...	28.49	28.29	28.61	28.79	28.31	28.59	28.89	28.43	...	27.97	28.01	
	Share of high-earnings occupations	...	...	13.68	13.71	13.30	13.82	14.47	14.20	14.59	15.09	...	15.28	16.45	
	Share of employers	...	4.33	4.35	4.28	4.20	4.32	4.53	3.83	4.55	4.36	...	3.43	3.80	
	Share of wage/salaried employees	...	63.00	62.90	62.93	63.66	63.65	64.36	65.51	66.39	66.87	...	68.44	68.89	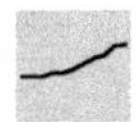
	Share of self-employed workers	...	22.72	22.63	22.67	22.27	21.95	21.49	21.41	20.44	20.66	...	21.20	20.76	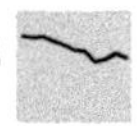
	Share of unpaid family workers	...	9.95	10.12	10.12	9.87	10.09	9.62	9.25	8.63	8.11	...	6.93	6.55	

	Share of workers in low-earnings sectors	...	36.15	34.72	34.66	35.05	34.78	33.71	32.34	31.53	31.51	...	28.52	27.59	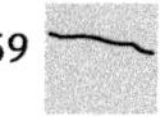
	Share of workers in mid-earnings sectors	...	40.84	40.24	40.30	39.82	40.43	40.37	41.58	41.83	41.69	...	44.06	44.36	
	Share of workers in high-earnings sectors	...	23.01	25.04	25.04	25.13	24.80	25.92	26.08	26.65	26.80	...	27.42	28.05	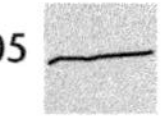
	Share of low-educated workers	...	63.79	61.96	59.97	58.56	56.83	54.69	53.05	50.72	48.93	...	46.38	44.95	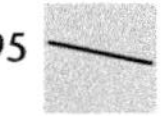
	Share of medium-educated workers	...	27.53	28.99	30.64	31.88	33.24	34.67	33.73	36.23	37.15	...	38.17	40.51	
	Share of high-educated workers	...	8.68	9.05	9.39	9.56	9.93	10.65	13.23	13.04	13.93	...	15.45	14.55	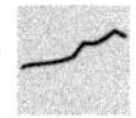
	Share of workers registered with SS	...	46.90	46.27	47.36	47.50	48.44	49.60	51.64	52.86	54.27	...	59.13	60.22	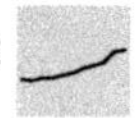
	Mean labour earnings	...	539.9	533.6	503.8	498.4	515.8	546.4	569.1	580.3	593.9		641.3	680.1	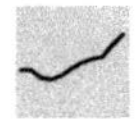
Poverty and Inequality Indicators	Poverty rate 2.5 dollars-a-day	...	27.35	26.02	26.66	24.87	22.88	19.59	18.11	15.59	14.88	...	12.60	10.37	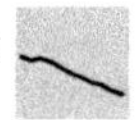
	Poverty rate 4 dollars-a-day	...	43.05	42.13	42.78	40.81	38.37	34.81	31.84	29.14	27.44	...	24.46	21.49	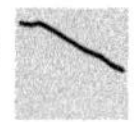

(*continued*)

Table 9.1 Continued

	2000	2001	2002	2003	2004	2005	2006	2007	2008	2009	2010	2011	2012	
GINI of household per capita income	...	0.588	0.583	0.576	0.566	0.564	0.559	0.549	0.542	0.536	...	0.527	0.523	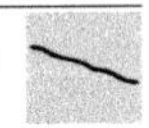
GINI of labour earnings	...	0.563	0.560	0.552	0.544	0.540	0.538	0.525	0.518	0.515	...	0.499	0.496	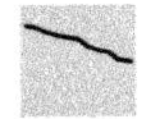

Note: The shaded figures for labour market indicators represent statistical significant improvements at 5 per cent between the initial and final years for all the employment and earnings indicators and poverty and inequality indicators. The only exceptions are the share of mid-earnings occupations, share of mid-earnings sectors, and share of medium-educated workers for which we did not assign welfare evaluation criteria.

Source: SEDLAC (CEDLAS and World Bank 2014) and World Development Indicators (World Bank 2014).

making the economy more resilient to external shocks. That was possible through several transformations (Ferraz et al. 2010). First, the stock of public external debt was reduced. Second, the historical fiscal deficit was reversed to a surplus position. Third, export growth underpinned sustained external current account surpluses which, together with strong private capital inflows, allowed the authorities to build a cushion of foreign exchange reserves (IMF 2007; Blyde et al. 2010). Fourth, prices were stabilized. The third stage in the growth experience of Brazil during the 2000s was between 2008 and 2009, when the economy suffered the impact of the international crisis. GDP per capita fell by 1.2 per cent that year. The government implemented some countercyclical measures to mitigate the negative impacts of the crisis, including an increase in wages of public-sector employees, an increase in social expenditures and in transfers to the private sector, and a reduction in taxes levied on certain goods (Mendonça de Barros 2010). Finally, the post-crisis period was characterized by a fast recovery, followed by a slowdown. In 2010, GDP per capita rose by 6.6 per cent, largely surpassing its pre-crisis level of 2008. Then, the GDP per capita growth rate slowed to 1.8 per cent in 2011 and experienced no change in 2012.

9.3 Unemployment

> The unemployment rate decreased overall, for youth and adults, and for both men and women. The unemployment rate increased during the international crisis but quickly dropped when the crisis receded, falling below its pre-crisis level by 2010. (Cruces et al. 2015: figure 3)

The unemployment rate (measured as the ratio of unemployment to labour force) fell from 9.3 per cent in 2001 (7,578,615 unemployed people) to 6.2 per cent in 2012 (6,149,025 unemployed people) (Table 9.1). This reduction was not monotonic. Unemployment stood at 9.3 per cent on average between 2001 and 2005, decreased to 7.1 per cent in 2008, went up to 8.3 per cent during the international crisis (1,299,282 new unemployed people between 2008 and 2009), and fell to 6.2 per cent in 2012, the year in which it reached its lowest level during the period of analysis. The rise in the unemployment rate during the international crisis took place in a context of an increasing number of persons in the labour force and an increasing number of employed people (1,654,748 and 355,466 persons respectively). Lay-offs grew more than hiring in 2009, leading to an increase in the number of unemployed persons and leaving new entrants into the labour market without a job (Pochmann 2009). The recovery following the international crisis was very quick and by 2011 (no data were available for 2010) the unemployment rate had dropped below its pre-crisis level.

The unemployment rate dropped for youth and adults and for both men and women. However, all groups were affected by the international crisis. By 2011, unemployment rates were lower than they had been before the crisis for all population groups.

9.4 Job Mix

> The composition of employment by occupational group improved over the period as workers moved from low-paid occupations such as elementary jobs to better paying occupations, such as professional jobs. Young and adult workers and women benefited from the improving trend, while men suffered a slight worsening. The international crisis of 2008 did not affect the improving trend in the employment structure by occupation, but impacted on the relative shares of low- and mid-paid occupations.
>
> (Cruces et al. 2015: figure 4)

From 2002 (the first year for which occupational breakdowns are available) to 2012, the share of low-earning occupations (elementary, plant and machine operators, and services and sales occupations) fell by 2.3 percentage points, while there was an increase of 2.8 percentage points in the share of high-paid occupations (management, professional, and armed forces) and a small change in the share of mid-paid occupations (technical jobs, clerical, agricultural, forestry and fishery occupations, and crafts and related trades) which declined by 0.5 percentage points (Table 9.1). The occupations that exhibited the largest reduction of shares over the period were: elementary occupations which shrank steadily from 25.8 to 18.3 per cent (7.5 percentage points), and agricultural, forestry, and fishery workers (a middle-paid occupation in Brazil) which fell from 6.8 per cent to 4.7 per cent (2.1 percentage points). On the other hand, the occupations whose shares increased were professionals (3.0 percentage points), services and sales workers (2.8 percentage points), plant and machine operators (2.4 percentage points), and clerical (2.2 percentage points). The international crisis led to a pause in the downward trend of the share of low-paid occupations in total employment. The share of mid-paid occupations continued to decrease, while the share of high-paid occupations exhibited a small increase between 2008 and 2009. The previous configuration, with a downward trend in the share of low-paid sectors, an upward trend in the share of high-paid sectors, and a share of mid-paid sectors with small annual changes, was recovered in 2012.

The improvements in occupational composition were especially large for youth and women, but there was also an improvement for adults and a slight worsening for men. The downward trend in the share of low-paid occupations stalled during the international crisis for young and adult workers and for women, the share of middle-paid occupations suffered a small reduction, and consequently the share of high-paid occupations increased for them. On the other hand, the pre-crisis trends in the male occupational structure of employment were not affected by the international crisis. Young and adult workers and women recovered the pre-crisis trends in 2012.

> The employment structure by occupational position improved, with workers moving from unpaid jobs to paid ones. This occurred for all population groups, especially among youth and women. The international crisis impacted negatively on the downward trend of the share of self-employed workers.
>
> (Cruces et al. 2015: figure 5)

From 2001 to 2012, there were changes in the employment structure by occupational position, especially in the shares of unpaid workers and wage/salaried employees. The share of the largest category—wage/salaried employees—increased from 63.0 per cent to 68.9 per cent, while the share of unpaid workers decreased from 10.0 per cent to 6.6 per cent. The share of the self-employed also dropped from 22.7 per cent in 2001 to 20.8 per cent in 2012, while the share of employers shrank from 4.3 per cent to 3.8 per cent (Table 9.1). These changes in the structure of employment by occupational position can be interpreted as an improvement as the share of high-earning positions (wage/salaried employees and employers) increased (rise of 5.4 percentage points) and the share of low-earning positions (self-employed and unpaid workers) fell. The international crisis negatively affected the downward trend of the share of self-employed workers in total employment. Between 2008 and 2009, the share of self-employed workers stopped decreasing and suffered a slight increase that was counterbalanced by a smaller increase in the share of wage/salaried employees and a small reduction in the share of employers. That could be explained by the absence of a guaranteed income system for all the new unemployed persons that emerged during the crisis and led some of them to develop activities as self-employed workers (Pochmann 2009). By 2012, the downward trend was recovered but the share of self-employed workers was still above the pre-crisis level.

The employment structure by occupational position improved for all population groups over the period. The international crisis of 2008 led to a temporary increase in the share of self-employed workers for all of them. By 2012, all groups recovered the previous downward trend but for adult workers and men the shares of self-employed were still above their pre-crisis levels. Young workers and women recovered their pre-recessionary levels.

> The employment composition by economic sector improved over the course of the period studied. Youth particularly benefited, but so did women, adults, and men. The international crisis brought this trend to a standstill.
> (Cruces et al. 2015: figure 6)

The period from 2001 to 2012 was marked by major changes in the sectoral composition of employment in Brazil. The share of workers in low-earning sectors (domestic service, primary activities, and low-tech industry) diminished by 8.6 percentage points from 2001 to 2012. On the other hand, there were increases in the shares of mid-earning sectors (high-tech industry, construction, commerce, and utilities and transportation) and high-earning sectors (public administration, skilled services, and education and health) of 3.5 and 5.0 percentage points respectively (Table 9.1). The sectors that registered the largest reductions over the period were primary activities and domestic workers (drop of 5.8 percentage points and 3.4 percentage points respectively), while skilled services showed the largest increase (5.0 percentage points). During the international crisis of 2008, the trends described above stalled, but they resumed during the post-crisis period. Consistent with evidence showing that the industry sector suffered the largest negative impact on its value added during the international crisis (compared to the agricultural and service sectors) (Cruces et al. 2015: table 2), low- and high-tech industry sectors exhibited among the largest declines in their shares in total employment during that episode. This impact was counteracted by the increase in the share of commerce in total employment. The different situation of the commerce sector in comparison to the industry sectors was due to increases in real wages and expenditure, and led consequently to a small total change in the share of mid-earning sectors in total employment during the international crisis.

Turning now to demographic disaggregation, youth was the group that most benefited from the reduction in the share of low-earning sectors, followed by women, men, and adults. The international crisis of 2008 affected all groups equally by bringing the reducing trend in the share of low-earning sectors to a standstill, but the previous trends resumed for all groups after the crisis.

> The educational level of the employed population improved over the period for all population groups, especially young workers. The economic crisis did not have an effect on this trend. (Cruces et al. 2015: figure 7)

The share of employed workers with low educational levels (eight years of schooling or less) dropped from 63.8 per cent in 2001 to 45.0 per cent in 2012, while the share of employed workers with middle and high educational levels (nine to thirteen years of schooling and over thirteen years of schooling) grew from 27.5 per cent in 2001 to 40.5 per cent in 2012 and from 8.7 per cent to 14.6 per cent respectively (Table 9.1). This improving trend in the educational level of the employed population was not affected by the international crisis.[2] We interpret this result as an improvement for the employed population as the level of education is an important predictor of labour earnings. Consequently, the changes in the employment structure by educational level implied an increase in the share of workers that tend to have high levels of earnings and a decline in the share of workers with low earnings levels.[3]

All population groups benefited from the increase in the educational level of the employed population over the period. None of them was affected by the international crisis.

> The overall share of employed workers registered with the social security system increased as a whole and for all population groups. The international crisis did not affect this upward trend. (Cruces et al. 2015: figure 8)

The social security system in Brazil is composed of three contributory regimes, one semi-contributory scheme for rural workers, and non-contributory benefits (Robles and Mirosevic 2013). The contributory regimes are the *Regime Geral de Previdência Social* (RGPS), *Regime Próprio de Previdência Social* (RPPS), and the complementary social security. The RGPS is mandatory for private workers, while the RPPS is mandatory for public workers and the military. Both are publicly administered and financed with contributions made by employers, employees, and the state. The complementary social security is voluntary and privately administered by for-profit and not-for-profit entities which invest the contributions made by the affiliated members. The semi-contributory scheme for rural workers appeared to guarantee an equal treatment between urban and rural workers. In order to receive its benefits, it is not necessary to have made prior contributions. Finally, the non-contributory benefits include the *Benefício de Prestação Continuada da Assistência Social*. This programme is an unconditional cash transfer targeted at poor families (family income below a fourth of the minimum wage) with an elderly or disabled member, and sets the household income at the level of the minimum wage.

The social security records show a major increase in the percentage of workers registered with the contributory regimes over the period. The share of employed workers registered with social security grew steadily from 46.9 per cent in 2001 (34,481,096 registered workers) to 60.2 per cent in 2012 (56,554,251 registered workers) (Table 9.1). The upward trend continued

[2] The most frequent value of years of education for employed workers in Brazil was eleven for the entire period under study (around 23.4 per cent of employed workers had eleven years of education).

[3] The improvement in the employment structure by educational level is related to changes in the relative demand and supply of workers with high educational levels with corresponding implications for the wage gap by educational group and the unemployment rate of each educational level. We introduce a discussion about the role of these factors in Brazil in section 9.5.

even during the international crisis of 2008. Several factors have been presented as determinants of the sustained increase in the share of registered workers in Brazil during the 2000s (Berg 2010; ILO 2011; Maurizio 2014). First, the sustained economic growth process allowed for a more foreseeable functioning of the labour market, favouring the growth of long-term contracts, and reducing the expected probability of lay-offs and consequently the probability of employers having to face relatively higher costs when firing a formal worker compared to an informal one. Second, the implementation of programmes and incentives for formalization. The Individual Entrepreneur Law of 2009 enabled self-employed workers to access the social security system at an affordable cost, and gave them a tax identification number to access credit and business transactions in the formal economy. Third, the cost of non-registration faced by employers increased as a result of the strengthening of labour inspections in the country.

The aggregate pattern of increased enrolment in social security also applies when the employed population is broken down by age and gender. That was especially true for young workers, who increased their share of registered workers by more than adult workers. Besides the reasons presented above, another explanation for the increase in the registration rate for young workers lies in the process of demographic transition that Brazil is experiencing. The decrease in the number of youths in the overall population and in the labour market, coupled with the incentives to poor families to keep their adolescent children in school through the *Bolsa Familia* programme, resulted in a labour market with less supply pressure from youths and fewer precarious jobs (Berg 2010). The upward trend in the share of registered workers continued even during the international crisis for all population groups.

9.5 Labour Earnings

> Real labour earnings increased steadily from 2001 to 2012, with only a slowdown during the 2008 international crisis. This applied to almost all groups, especially the most disadvantaged ones. (Cruces et al. 2015: figure 9)

Average monthly earnings, expressed in dollars at 2005 PPP, increased by 26.0 per cent, from US$540 in 2001 to US$680 in 2012 (Table 9.1). This increase was not even throughout this period. Labour earnings decreased by 7.7 per cent between 2001 and 2004 and increased by 36.5 per cent during 2004–12, with an average annual increase of 4.6 per cent. The years of the international crisis (2008 and 2009) were marked by a slowdown in yearly growth, but it was still positive and above 2.0 per cent (labour earnings increased by 2.0 per cent and 2.3 per cent in 2008 and 2009 respectively). The continuous adjustments in the minimum wage over the period were responsible for the increase in labour earnings. In the first half of the 2000s, the minimum wage increased in real terms by 3.8 per cent annually. Between 2005 and 2011, the increases were 3.0 per cent a year (Robles and Mirosevic 2013). In 2007, a policy was set in place to adjust the minimum wage according to both the variation of GDP and inflation (IPEA 2011). In 2009, as part of the efforts to alleviate the impacts of the crisis, the minimum wage was also nominally adjusted by 12.0 per cent (Berg 2009).

When broken down by population groups and employment categories, labour earnings increased for almost all groups. The only groups that experienced a drop in their earnings were workers with high educational levels and workers in the skilled services sector. The groups with the largest increase in earnings were: women among gender groups; youth among age groups; self-employed workers among employment positions; workers in the primary activities sector and construction among economic sectors; workers with low educational levels among educational groups; and workers in elementary occupations, workers in armed forces, plant and machine operators and assemblers, workers in crafts and related trades, agricultural, forestry, and fishery workers, and services and sales workers among occupational groups.

The evidence of falling labour earnings for workers with high educational levels and labour earnings increases for workers with medium and low levels of education can be interpreted in light of previous findings of improving employment structure by occupational group and economic sector over the period and improving educational level of the employed population. The improving employment structure by occupational group and economic sector implied an increase in the share of occupations and sectors that can be expected to use workers with high and medium educational levels, such as professional and clerical occupations, and public administration and skilled services sectors, and a reduction in the share of occupations and sectors that employ workers with low educational levels, such as elementary, agricultural, and craft and trades occupations, and domestic service and primary activity sectors. This evidence indicates that the demand for workers with high and medium educational levels relative to those with low educational levels increased during 2001–12. On the other hand, the educational level of people in the labour force improved over the same period, indicating an increase in the relative supply of workers with high and medium levels of education (Cruces et al. 2015: table 8). The prediction of a supply and demand analysis is that the relative wages of workers with high and medium educational levels relative to those with low educational levels will rise or fall depending on which effect dominates (increase in the relative demand versus increase in the relative supply). In the Brazilian labour market, the relative wages of workers with high and medium educational levels relative to those with low educational levels fell over the period, and the relative wages of workers with high educational levels relative to those with medium educational levels also decreased (Cruces et al. 2015: table 7). The adjustment process also led to a reduction in the unemployment rate of all educational groups that was larger for workers with medium and low levels of education compared to the reduction for workers with high levels of education (Cruces et al. 2015: table 9).

The international crisis led to a drop in labour earnings of some specific groups, but earnings increased for the great majority. Those who were negatively affected by the international crisis recovered their pre-crisis level of income by 2011.

9.6 Poverty and Inequality

> The poverty rate and the rate of working poor households decreased substantially between 2001 and 2012. (Cruces et al. 2015: figure 10)

The poverty rate based on the 4 dollars-a-day international line fell from 43.1 per cent in 2001 to 21.5 per cent in 2012; the poverty rate based on the 2.5 dollars-a-day line went from 27.4 per cent to 10.4 per cent, and the percentage of the working poor (defined as the proportion of persons in the population living in poor households, according to the 4 dollars-a-day poverty line, where at least one household member works) decreased from 29.1 to 12.3 per cent over the same period (Table 9.1). These poverty indicators decreased steadily between 2001 and 2012, even during the international crisis. The downward trend of all poverty indicators during the Great Recession is consistent with the previous finding of increasing labour earnings during that episode due to minimum wage and nominal wage increases, and with the use of the minimum wage as a reference value for social security benefits and anti-poverty programme adjustments. Pochmann (2009) also highlighted that the recession was concentrated in the industrial sector where, in general, work conditions are better. As such, the increase in unemployment during the international crisis affected mainly non-poor families.

Cash transfer programmes have played an important role from the late 1990s in poverty reduction in Brazil (Ravallion 2009). They included a series of programmes, which were later consolidated under *Bolsa Familia*—the main conditional cash transfer programme—and the unconditional cash transfer *Benefício de Prestação Continuada*. Both seem to be extraordinarily well-targeted and have helped decisively to reduce income inequality and poverty (Ferreira de Souza 2012). Ferreira et al. (2010) estimated that in the absence of these transfer policies the poverty rate in Brazil would have been about 5.0 percentage points higher in 2004. Soares et al. (2010) showed that *Bolsa Familia* was responsible for a reduction of 16.0 per cent and 33.0 per cent in extreme and moderate poverty between 2003 and 2010.

The pattern of reducing poverty in Brazil over the 2000s can be understood by examining incomes from various sources. Household labour earnings, pensions, and government transfers all increased substantially over the period studied (Cruces et al. 2015: figure 11). Within the period, the increase in labour earnings and pensions started in 2004. Incomes from government transfers increased especially during the international crisis of 2008, and incomes from capital were erratic.

> Inequality of household per capita income and labour earnings diminished substantially over the period studied, and this trend did not change with the international crisis. (Cruces et al. 2015: figure 12)

The Gini coefficient of household per capita income fell from 0.588 in 2001 to 0.523 in 2012, dropping with each consecutive year. The Gini coefficient of labour earnings among employed workers declined from 0.563 in 2001 to 0.496 in 2012 (Table 9.1). It also decreased with each passing year and was always below the Gini for household per capita income. This reduction in labour earnings inequality is in keeping with the fact that earnings increased more for most disadvantaged employment categories such as self-employed workers, workers with low educational levels, and workers in the primary activity sector and in elementary jobs. However, it is interesting to notice that earnings declined for some high-earning employment categories. Consequently, the reduction in labour earnings inequality over the period in Brazil occurred at the expense of income losses for some categories. The crisis did not alter the downward trend: during the international crisis, inequality fell for both household per capita income and labour earnings at the same rates as they had before.

Changes in household per capita income inequality in Brazil during the 2000s have been explained by changes in both labour and non-labour incomes at the household level, with both having approximately equal weight. Barros et al. (2010) found that 51.0 per cent of the decline in household per capita income inequality between 2001 and 2006 was explained by the growth in average labour income per adult worker and a small decline in its inequality. The remaining 49.0 per cent was due to a reduction in the inequality of household non-labour incomes. Among non-labour incomes, government transfers had an equalizing and large effect, while changes in the distribution of incomes from assets and private transfers were unequalizing. Bergolo et al. (2011) confirmed the equalizing effect of government transfers for the period 2001–8 that stemmed primarily from the expansion in their coverage. Azevedo et al. (2013b) extended the analysis of the decline in household per capita income inequality for the 2001–11 period. Through a decomposition approach they found an equalizing effect of labour incomes, incomes from transfers, incomes from pensions, and other non-labour incomes, along with an equalizing effect of the share of adults in the household.

The literature on labour earnings inequality in Brazil provides some explanations for its decline during the 2000s. Barros et al. (2010) for the period 2001–6 and Azevedo et al. (2013a) for the period 2001–9 used decomposition approaches and found: (1) a reduction in the wage differential between workers of different educational levels ('price effect'); and (2) a fall in the inequality of the distribution of educational levels ('quantity effect'). Gasparini et al. (2011) explained the fall in the skill premium during 2001–9 through the increase in the relative supply of skilled workers, combined with a reduction in their relative demand and institutional factors, such as increases in the minimum wage. Maurizio (2014) added the increase in the registration rate of workers as an inequality-reducing factor. Regarding the finding of a more equal distribution of educational levels, there is a discrepancy in the literature. Battistón et al. (2014), who used a microsimulation approach for the period 2002–9, found an inequality-increasing quantity effect.

9.7 Conclusions

During the 2000s, Brazil has exhibited a rare mix: slow economic growth accompanied by substantial improvements in labour market indicators. During the period 2001 to 2012, Brazil achieved less economic growth than the average Latin American country: GDP per capita increased by 29.8 per cent while the average growth for the eighteen Latin American countries was 36.2 per cent.

The labour market exhibited a marked improvement from 2001 to 2012. The unemployment rate decreased while the composition of jobs improved for all of the indicators used in this chapter. The distribution of employment by occupational group showed a decline in the share in elementary occupations and an increase in the share in better-paying occupations. There was an increase in the share of wage/salaried employees and a reduction in the share of self-employed and unpaid workers. The share of workers in low-earning sectors diminished, while the share of workers in mid- and high-paid sectors rose. Moreover, the educational composition of the employed population improved steadily. The share of workers registered with the social security system increased. Average labour earnings rose. Poverty and inequality diminished substantially.

The Brazilian economy was affected by the international economic crisis of 2008, from which it recovered quickly. During this period, the unemployment rate increased, the employment structure by occupational position deteriorated slightly, the improving trend in the composition of employment by economic sector hit an impasse, and the upward trend in labour earnings slowed down. However, all labour market indicators had recovered either their pre-crisis level or were heading in that direction by 2011.

Young workers and women had worse labour market outcomes over the period compared to adults and men respectively, but all population groups were evenly affected by the international crisis. The unemployment rate was higher for young compared to adult workers, the shares of young employed workers in low-earning economic occupations and sectors were larger than the shares of adult workers, the percentage of young workers registered with the social security system was lower when compared to adults, and labour earnings of young workers were below those of adults. On the other hand, the share of low-earning positions among young workers was below the share for adult workers. The international crisis of 2008 impacted more adversely on the unemployment rate of young workers compared to adults, but the temporary worsening in the employment structure by occupational position was larger for adults compared to youths. Disaggregating by gender, we found that men had better labour market outcomes than women, with the exceptions of the share of workers in low-earning positions that was larger among men and the share of registered workers that was similar for both gender groups. Men and women were evenly affected by the international crisis. While the unemployment rate suffered a larger increase for women, the worsening in the structure of employment by occupational position was larger for men.

In summary, notwithstanding the slow economic growth exhibited by Brazil during the 2000s and the international crisis of 2008, Brazilian labour market conditions were in a better state in 2012 than they were at the start of the millennium.

References

Azevedo, J. P., M. E. Dávalos, C. Díaz-Bonilla, B. Atuesta, and R. A. Castañeda (2013a). 'Fifteen Years of Inequality in Latin America: How Have Labor Markets Helped?'. Policy Research Working Paper 6384. Washington, DC: World Bank.

Azevedo, J. P., G. Inchauste, and V. Sanfelice (2013b). 'Decomposing the Decline in Income Inequality in Latin America'. Policy Research Working Paper 6715. Washington, DC: World Bank.

Barros, R., M. De Carvalho, S. Franco, and R. Mendonça (2010). 'Markets, the State and the Dynamics of Inequality in Brazil', in L. F. Lopez-Calva and N. Lustig (eds),

Declining Inequality in Latin America: A Decade of Progress? Washington, DC: Brookings Institution and UNDP, 134–74.

Battistón, D., C. García-Domench, and L. Gasparini (2014). 'Could an Increase in Education Raise Income Inequality? Evidence for Latin America', *Latin American Journal of Economics*—formerly *Cuadernos de Economía* 51 (1): 1–39.

Berg, J. (2009). 'Brazil: The Minimum Wage as a Response to the Crisis'. ILO Notes on the Crisis. Brasilia: International Labour Office.

Berg, J. (2010). 'Laws or Luck? Understanding Rising Formality in Brazil in the 2000s'. ILO Working Paper 5. Brasilia: International Labour Office.

Bergolo, M., F. Carbajal, G. Cruces, and N. Lustig (2011). 'Impacto de las transferencias públicas en la década de 2000: La experiencia de los países del Cono Sur'. Unpublished manuscript. La Plata: Centro de Estudios Distributivos, Laborales y Sociales.

Blyde, J., A. Castelar Pinheiro, C. Daude, and E. Fernandez-Arias (2010). 'Competitiveness and Growth in Brazil'. Technical Notes 113. Washington, DC: Inter-American Development Bank.

CEDLAS and World Bank (2014). SEDLAC—Socio-Economic Database for Latin America and the Caribbean. Centro de Estudios Distributivos, Laborales y Sociales, Facultad de Ciencias Económicas, Universidad Nacional de La Plata and World Bank Poverty Group LCR. Available at <http://sedlac.econo.unlp.edu.ar/eng/index.php>, accessed 2014.

Cruces, G., G. Fields, D. Jaume, and M. Viollaz (2015). 'The Growth–Employment–Poverty Nexus in Latin America in the 2000s: Brazil Country Study'. WIDER Working Paper 2015/071. Helsinki: UNU-WIDER.

Ferraz, J. C., F. E. Pires de Souza, and D. Kupfer (2010). 'Trayectorias para el Desarrollo Brasileño', *Boletin Informativo Techint* 333: 38–54. Buenos Aires: Techint Group.

Ferreira, F. H. G., P. G. Leite, and M. Ravallion (2010). 'Poverty Reduction without Economic Growth? Explaining Brazil's Poverty Dynamics, 1985–2004', *Journal of Development Economics* 93 (1): 20–36.

Ferreira de Souza, P. (2012). 'Poverty, Inequality and Social Policies in Brazil, 1995–2009'. IPEA Working Paper 87. Brasilia: Institute for Applied Economic Research.

Gasparini, L., S. Galiani, G. Cruces, and P. Acosta (2011). 'Educational Upgrading and Returns to Skills in Latin America: Evidence from a Supply–Demand Framework, 1990–2010'. IZA Working Paper 6244. Bonn: Institute for the Study of Labor.

ILO (2011). 'Share of Formal Employment Continues to Grow'. G20 Country Policy Briefs—Brazil. Geneva: International Labour Office.

IMF (2003). 'IMF Concludes 2003 Article IV Consultation with Brazil'. Public Information Notice 03/38. Washington, DC: International Monetary Fund.

IMF (2007). 'IMF Executive Board Concludes 2007 Article IV Consultation with Brazil'. Public Information Notice 07/114. Washington, DC: International Monetary Fund.

IPEA (2011). 'Boletim de políticas sociais: Acompanhamento e análise 19'. Brasilia: Instituto de Pesquisa Econômica Aplicada.

Maurizio, R. (2014). 'Labour Formalization and Declining Inequality in Argentina and Brazil in 2000s: A Dynamic Approach'. ILO Research Paper 9. Geneva: International Labour Office.

Mendonça de Barros, J. R. (2010). 'El impacto de la crisis internacional en Brasil'. Analisis del Real Instituto 38. Madrid: Real Instituto Elcano.

Pochmann, M. (2009). 'Work in the Economic Crisis in Brazil: First Signs', *Estudos Avançados* 23 (66): 41–52. São Paulo: Instituto de Estudos Avançados, Universidade de São Paulo.

Ravallion, M. (2009). 'A Comparative Perspective on Poverty Reduction in Brazil, China and India'. Policy Research Working Paper 5080. Washington, DC: Development Research Group, World Bank.

Robles, C. and V. Mirosevic (2013). 'Social Protection Systems in Latin America and the Caribbean: Brazil'. ECLAC, Project Documents Collection. Santiago de Chile: United Nations.

Soares, S., P. H. G. F. Souza, R. G. Osório, and F. G. Silveira (2010). 'Os impactos do benefício do programa Bolsa Família sobre a desigualdade e a pobreza', in J. A. Castro and L. Modesto (eds), *Bolsa Família 2003–2010: Avanços e desafios*, vol. 2. Brasilia: Instituto de Pesquisa Econômica Aplicada, 27–52.

World Bank (2014). World Development Indicators. Available at <http://data.worldbank.org/data-catalog/world-development-indicators>, accessed April 2014.

10

Chile

10.1 Introduction

This chapter on labour markets and growth in Chile since 2000 is one of sixteen studies of Latin American countries, each of which analyses the growth–employment–poverty nexus and aims to answer the following broad questions: Has economic growth resulted in economic development via improved labour market conditions in Latin America in the 2000s, and have these improvements halted or been reversed since the Great Recession? How do the rate and character of economic growth, changes in the various labour market indicators, and changes in poverty relate to each other?

To answer these questions, we analyse the growth experience of Chile during the 2000s and a wide set of labour market indicators that we assign to one of two different categories: employment and earnings indicators, and poverty and income inequality indicators. More specifically, for the group of employment and earnings indicators we construct statistics on the following variables: the unemployment rate; the employment structure by occupational group, employment position, economic sector, registration of workers with the social security system, and educational level; and mean labour earnings and hourly wages. We present all these indicators for the employed population as a whole and for different population groups (youth, adults, men, and women). For the group of poverty and income inequality indicators, we compute poverty rates using the official moderate and extreme poverty lines and the international lines of 2.5 and 4 dollars a day. We also calculate the Gini coefficient of household per capita income and labour earnings.

All the statistics in this chapter are obtained using microdata from the Encuesta de Caracterización Socioeconómica Nacional (CASEN). The CASEN is a nationwide and regionally representative household survey conducted every three or four years. The information in this chapter is derived from all the surveys conducted in the 2000s, that is, surveys from the years 2000, 2003, 2006, 2009, and 2011. The nationwide surveys were processed following a harmonization methodology and incorporated into the SEDLAC—Socio-Economic Database for Latin America and the Caribbean (CEDLAS and World Bank 2014).[1] The resulting labour market indicators were compiled into a large number of tables and figures, which are available in an earlier version of this study (henceforth, Cruces et al. 2015). Chapter 1 of this book provides the definition for each of the indicators we analyse here, while Cruces et al. (2015) includes details on definitions and classification systems used by Chile's household surveys, and on comparability issues of these surveys over time.

10.2 Economic Growth

> Chile experienced rapid economic growth from 2000 to 2012. The economy underwent a recession as a consequence of the international crisis of 2008 but returned to pre-recession GDP and GDP per capita levels in 2010. (Cruces et al. 2015: figures 1 and 2)

From 2000 to 2012, Chile experienced rapid economic growth by Latin American standards. GDP per capita increased by 44.2 per cent, while the average for the region's eighteen countries was 36.2 per cent during the period. GDP (measured in PPP dollars of 2005) grew by 62.9 per cent, and GDP per employed person rose by 17.4 per cent. Annual GDP per capita grew in real terms by an average of 3.1 per cent, ranging from a low of −2.0 per cent in 2009 to a high of 4.9 per cent in 2004 and 2011 (Table 10.1).

Chile has adhered since the 1980s to a policy framework based on trade openness, inflation targeting, and achievement of a structural surplus in the accounts of the central government (IMF 2004). These policies were successful at fostering growth and macroeconomic stability despite the high exposure of Chile to external shocks. The vulnerability of Chile to external shocks is explained by the significant degree of trade openness and financial integration, and the large participation of commodities—mainly minerals—in its exports (De Gregorio and Labbé 2011; IMF 2012). From 2000 to 2002, Chile faced a weak domestic demand and an adverse external environment characterized by the Argentine crisis of 2001–2 and a fall in terms of trade. GDP and GDP per capita growth rates slowed down between 2000 and 2002 but were nonetheless positive. From 2003 to 2008, Chile's GDP grew at an annual rate of 4.7 per cent, while GDP per capita grew at a rate of 3.7 per cent.

[1] See Cruces et al. (2015: table 1) for details on the size of Chile household surveys.

Table 10.1 Chile: Evolution of growth and labour market indicators over the 2000s

		2000	2001	2002	2003	2004	2005	2006	2007	2008	2009	2010	2011	2012	
Growth Indicators	GDP per capita	10,990	11,224	11,337	11,655	12,228	12,773	13,201	13,746	14,061	13,784	14,443	15,149	15,848	
	GDP per capita growth rate	3.22	2.13	1.00	2.81	4.91	4.46	3.35	4.12	2.30	–1.97	4.78	4.89	4.61	
Employment and Earnings Indicators	Employment-to-population ratio	49.92	...	...	51.41	...	...	53.11	...	...	50.04	...	51.62	...	
	Unemployment rate	10.37	...	...	9.98	...	...	7.32	...	...	10.22	...	7.73	...	
	Share of low-earnings occupations	42.81	...	...	41.64	...	...	44.45	...	...	45.57	...	44.13	...	
	Share of mid-earnings occupations	40.53	...	...	42.20	...	...	42.14	...	...	40.68	...	38.79	...	
	Share of high-earnings occupations	16.65	...	...	16.17	...	...	13.42	...	...	13.75	...	17.08	...	
	Share of employers	4.13	...	...	3.88	...	...	3.07	...	...	3.11	...	1.90	...	
	Share of wage/salaried employees	74.39	...	...	74.28	...	...	75.67	...	...	76.28	...	77.42	...	
	Share of self-employed workers	20.00	...	...	20.40	...	...	20.34	...	...	20.13	...	20.29	...	
	Share of unpaid family workers	1.48	...	...	1.45	...	...	0.91	...	...	0.47	...	0.40	...	
	Share of workers in low-earnings sectors	35.15	...	...	35.15	...	...	34.93	...	...	34.78	...	36.17	...	
	Share of workers in mid-earnings sectors	39.59	...	...	39.43	...	...	39.77	...	...	36.85	...	36.48	...	
	Share of workers in high-earnings sectors	25.25	...	...	25.42	...	...	25.30	...	...	28.37	...	27.35	...	

	Share of low-educated workers	31.29	...	...	28.02	...	...	27.01	...	...	24.47	...	23.55	...
	Share of medium-educated workers	48.01	...	...	49.98	...	...	50.96	...	...	51.13	...	52.33	...
	Share of high-educated workers	20.69	...	...	21.99	...	...	22.03	...	...	24.40	...	24.12	...
	Share of workers registered with SS	62.77	...	...	63.65	...	...	66.66	...	...	66.03	...	68.76	...
	Mean labour earnings	702.6	...	...	686.6	...	...	685.0	...	...	780.0		756.8	...
Poverty and Inequality Indicators	Official extreme poverty rate	4.67	...	...	3.90	...	...	2.63	...	...	3.11	...	2.43	...
	Official moderate poverty rate	18.9	...	...	17.1	...	...	12.7	...	...	14.1	...	13.5	...
	Poverty rate 2.5 dollars-a-day	8.89	...	...	7.64	...	...	5.12	...	...	4.09	...	2.88	...
	Poverty rate 4 dollars-a-day	22.99	...	...	20.58	...	...	15.62	...	...	11.56	...	9.88	...
	GINI of household per capita income	0.552	...	...	0.547	...	...	0.517	...	...	0.519	...	0.508	...
	GINI of labour earnings	0.560	...	...	0.546	...	...	0.532	...	...	0.522	...	0.510	...

Note: The shaded figures for labour market indicators represent statistical significant improvements at 5 per cent between the initial and final years for all the employment and earnings indicators and poverty and inequality indicators. The only exceptions are the share of mid-earnings occupations, share of mid-earnings sectors, and share of medium-educated workers for which we did not assign welfare evaluation criteria.

Source: SEDLAC (CEDLAS and World Bank 2014) and World Development Indicators (World Bank 2014).

The international crisis of 2008 led to an important reduction in export prices, export volumes, and domestic aggregate demand (Contreras and Ffrench-Davis 2012). GDP and GDP per capita contracted by 1.0 per cent and 2.0 per cent respectively in 2009. Notwithstanding, the Chilean economy recovered rapidly and, by 2010, the 2008 levels of GDP and GDP per capita had been reached. The quick recovery of the Chilean economy from the international crisis was based on its strong policy frameworks such as a fiscal rule and inflation targeting, a sound banking system, and a strong policy response (IMF 2011). The policy response included the implementation of anticyclical measures by the Central Bank of Chile and a stimulus plan funded by a fiscal buffer (*Fondo de Estabilización Económico y Social*). From 2010 to 2012, the aggregate GDP grew at an annual rate of 5.7 per cent and GDP per capita at a rate of 4.8 per cent.

10.3 Unemployment

> The unemployment rate fell between 2000 and 2011, overall and for all population groups. The downward trend was affected negatively by the international crisis of 2008, and the unemployment rate did not return in 2011 to its pre-crisis level in the aggregate and for any of the population groups. (Cruces et al. 2015: figure 3)

The unemployment rate (measured as the ratio of unemployment to labour force) fell from 10.4 per cent in 2000 (618,066 unemployed persons) to 7.7 per cent in 2011 (579,050 unemployed persons) (Table 10.1). This reduction was not monotonic. The unemployment rate decreased from 2000 to 2006 by 3.1 percentage points. It increased from 2006 to 2009, a period that included the Great Recession, when it reached 10.2 per cent (235,895 new unemployed persons). Both the number of people in the labour force and the number of employed persons increased over the same period by 294,451 and 58,556 respectively. These figures suggest that the increase in the unemployment rate in Chile between 2006 and 2009 was explained by the new entrants into the labour market that could not find a job. In 2011, it dropped once again to 7.7 per cent, though that does not represent a full recovery since that figure is higher than the pre-crisis level.

Between 2000 and 2011, the unemployment rate decreased for all population groups following the aggregate trend. All groups were negatively affected by the international crisis. Despite the reduction in the unemployment rate for all population groups at the end of the period, none of them returned to its pre-crisis level by 2011.

10.4 Job Mix

> The composition of employment by occupational group exhibited a slight worsening between 2000 and 2011. This trend held for adult workers and women, while young workers experienced an improvement in their employment structure by occupational group and men exhibited little changes. The international crisis of 2008 did not have an effect on the occupational composition of the employed population overall, and for young and adult workers, but led to a worsening for men and an improvement for women. (Cruces et al. 2015: figure 4)

The share of the following occupations shrank between 2000 and 2011: agricultural, forestry, and fishery occupations (drop of 1.9 percentage points); management (drop of 1.6 percentage points); clerical (drop of 0.8 percentage points); and plant and machine operators (drop of 0.8 percentage points). The share of the following occupations grew: professionals (increase of 2.3 percentage points); elementary (increase of 1.7 percentage points); and services and sales workers (increase of 1.5 percentage points). The share of the other occupational groups remained largely unchanged. These changes in the occupational composition of employment can be interpreted as a slight worsening since low-earning occupations (elementary, agricultural, forestry and fishery occupations, and services and sales occupations) increased their share in total employment by 1.3 percentage points between 2000 and 2011, while high-earning occupations (professionals, management, and armed forces) exhibited a smaller increase (increase of 0.4 percentage points). As a consequence, mid-earning occupations reduced their share in total employment (Table 10.1).

Disaggregating, between 2000 and 2011 the composition of employment by occupational group improved for young workers, exhibited a slight worsening for adult workers and women, and remained essentially unchanged for men.

The international crisis of 2008 did not affect the pre-crisis trends in the employment structure by occupational group overall and for young and adult workers, but led to a worsening for men and an improvement for women. By 2011, men recovered the pre-crisis structure of employment by occupational group.

> The employment structure by occupational position improved overall and for young, adult workers, and men between 2000 and 2011, while it remained unchanged for women. The international crisis of 2008 did not affect the improving trend in the aggregate and for young workers, adults, and men, and led to a reduction in the share of low-earning positions in total employment for women.
> (Cruces et al. 2015: figure 5)

The share of wage/salaried employees—the largest category in Chile—increased from 74.4 per cent in 2000 to 77.4 per cent in 2011. The share of employers, on the other hand, fell from 4.1 per cent to 1.9 per cent over the same period, and the share of unpaid workers decreased from 1.5 per cent to 0.4 per cent. The share of self-employment barely changed over the period (increase of 0.3 percentage points) (Table 10.1). These changes in the structure of employment by occupational position can be interpreted as an improvement due to the fall in the share of low-earning categories (self-employment and unpaid workers) and the increase in the share of high-earning categories (employers and wage/salaried employees).

The composition of employment by occupational position improved for youth, adults, and men, while it remained unchanged for women during 2000–11.

The international crisis of 2008 did not affect the previously improving trend in the employment structure by occupational position overall and for youth, adults, and men, and led to an improvement for women. Despite the increase in the unemployment rate during the Great Recession, the share of low-earning positions in total employment kept on decreasing in the aggregate and for young, adult workers, and men between 2006–9. Economic necessity may compel workers to take up free-entry self-employment activities in a context of increasing unemployment. However, the unemployment insurance in Chile allowed unemployed workers to look for a new job avoiding low-remunerated activities.[2] For women, the share of low-earning categories fell from 2006 and 2009 and continued with that trend in 2011.

> The employment composition by economic sector improved slightly over the period studied. All population groups benefited from the improvement in the employment structure by economic sector, and young workers and women benefited more than adults and men. The international crisis did not have an adverse effect on the composition of employment by economic sector in the aggregate or for any of the population groups. (Cruces et al. 2015: figure 6)

The period 2000–11 witnessed an increase (from 25.3 per cent to 27.3 per cent) in the share of workers in high-earning sectors (skilled services, public administration, education, and health). There was, during the same period, an increase (from 35.2 per cent to 36.2 per cent) in the share of low-earning sectors in total employment (domestic service, commerce, low-tech industry). Consequently, the share of mid-earning occupations (primary activities, construction, high-tech industry, utilities, and transportation) in total employment decreased

[2] The unemployment insurance is part of the contributory schemes of the social security system in Chile which covered around 65.0 per cent of the employed population during the period studied. Employees and employers contribute on a monthly basis to an individual account which activates if the event of unemployment occurs (Robles 2011).

(Table 10.1). Workers employed in the mining subsector are included in the primary activities sector in our classification. An increase in the employment share of the mining subsector over the period in Chile was counteracted by the reduction in the employment share of the agricultural and fishing subsectors. These changes in the employment structure by economic sector can be interpreted as a slight improvement since the increase in the share of high-earning sectors over the period was larger than the increase in the share of low-earning sectors in total employment.

The employment composition by economic sector improved between 2000 and 2011 for young workers and women, and exhibited a slight improvement for adults and men.

The international crisis of 2008 did not negatively affect the structure of employment by economic sector overall or for all population groups. Between 2006 and 2009, the share of high-earning sectors in total employment kept on increasing, while the shares of low- and mid-earning sectors exhibited a decrease. The sectors that led to the reduction in the shares of low- and mid-earning sectors were the low-tech industry sector, and the primary activities and high-tech industry sectors respectively. This result is in accord with evidence showing that the agricultural and industry sectors were hit hardest by the international crisis compared to the service sector (Cruces et al. 2015: table 2).

> The educational level of the Chilean employed population improved steadily over the period for all population groups, and especially among young workers. The improving trend was not impacted adversely by the international crisis of 2008.
>
> (Cruces et al. 2015: figure 7)

The share of employed workers with low educational levels (eight years of schooling or less) dropped from 31.3 per cent in 2000 to 23.6 per cent in 2011, while the share of employed workers with medium and high educational levels (nine to thirteen years of schooling and over thirteen years of schooling) grew from 48.0 per cent in 2000 to 52.3 per cent in 2011 and from 20.7 per cent to 24.1 per cent respectively (Table 10.1).[3] We interpret this result as an improvement for the employed population as the level of education is an important predictor of labour earnings. Consequently, the changes in the employment structure by educational level implied an increase in the share of workers that tend to have high levels of earnings and a decline in the share of workers with low earnings levels.[4] The improvement in the educational

[3] The most frequent value of years of education for employed workers in Chile was nine over the entire period (around 31.9 per cent of employed workers had nine years of education).

[4] The improvement in the employment structure by educational level is related to changes in the relative demand and supply of workers with high educational levels with corresponding implications for the wage gap by educational group and the unemployment rate of each educational level. We introduce a discussion about the role of these factors in Chile in section 10.5.

level of the employed population in Chile is associated with the reform to the education system implemented in 1994. The reform led to an increase in the basic and medium education enrolment rates and a reduction in drop-out rates, and it was accompanied by an improvement in the education infrastructure (Robles 2011).

The educational level of the employed population improved between 2000 and 2011 for all groups and especially for young workers. The pattern of improvement in the level of education of the employed population in Chile continued even during the international crisis of 2008, overall and for all population groups.

> The share of employed workers registered with the social security system increased between 2000 and 2011 overall and for all population groups. While the rate diminished during the international crisis, the pre-crisis level had been exceeded by 2011. (Cruces et al. 2015: figure 8)

The Chilean pension system was reformed in 2008. Up to 2008, the system had a contributory scheme and a non-contributory scheme. The contributory scheme was financed by workers who contributed to individual accounts, while the government funded the pensions of those who were affiliated to the old public pay-as-you-go pension system.[5] The non-contributory scheme comprised two programmes which aimed to assure a minimum pension (*Pensión Mínima Garantizada* and *Programa de Pensiones Asistenciales*). The reform of 2008 established three components of the pension system: a contributory component which is mandatory, a voluntary component, and a non-contributory component. The non-contributory component is the *Sistema de Pensiones Sociales* which replaced the previous two non-contributory programmes (*Pensión Mínima Garantizada* and *Programa de Pensiones Asistenciales*). The health system in Chile comprises three components: (1) the public system (FONASA), which covers the majority of Chilean workers; (2) the private system (ISAPRE); and (3) the Armed Forces system. Wage/salaried workers and self-employed are obligated to contribute to the health system, which also receives funding from the government. Finally, the unemployment insurance works as a contributory scheme in the Chilean social security system. Dependent workers and their employers contribute on a monthly basis to individual accounts which activate if the event of unemployment occurs (Robles 2011).

Social security records show an increase between 2000 and 2011 in the percentage of registered workers with the contributory scheme of the system. The share of workers registered grew from 62.8 per cent (3,411,843 registered workers) in 2000 to 68.8 per cent in 2011 (5,068,291 registered workers)

[5] The Chilean public pension system was replaced in 1981 by a private capitalization accounts system.

(Table 10.1). Before the onset of the international crisis, the percentage of workers registered with the social security system had increased, reaching 66.7 per cent in 2006. During the crisis the rate dropped slightly to 66.0 per cent in 2009. Interestingly, between 2006 and 2009, both the number of registered and unregistered workers increased by 114,941 and 352,821 respectively. The upward trend resumed as registered employment increased by 2.7 percentage points from 2009 to 2011, surpassing the pre-crisis level. This upward trend in the share of registered workers over the period was related to several policies designed to improve working conditions. Those measures included the simplification of procedures to register workers with the social security system; the replacement of labour inspection fines with information and education about labour regulations (*Multas por capacitación*); the improving access to formal financial services for micro and small firms with a resulting increase in their ability to comply with labour regulations; the passing of the Law of Subcontracting which obligates all the companies in the subcontracting chain to meet labour regulations (ILO 2014).

The aggregate pattern of increased enrolment in the social security system over the period held for all population groups. While young workers were the least likely to be registered with the social security system, they were the group that experienced the largest increase in the registration rate. Male workers were more likely to be registered with the social security system than women, and they benefited more than women from the upward trend.

The international crisis led to a small reduction in the percentage of registered workers overall and for all population groups. By 2011, the share of registered workers surpassed the pre-crisis level overall and for all population groups.

10.5 Labour Earnings

> Labour earnings increased between 2000 and 2011. Within the period, labour earnings fell from 2000 to 2006, grew from 2006 to 2009, and decreased once again in 2011. Workers were not affected negatively by the 2008 crisis. Disaggregating, the increase in labour earnings between 2000 and 2011 held for young and adult workers, and for men and women. The evidence of earning changes for different employment categories over the period indicates that labour earnings tended to increase more for low-earning categories compared to high-earning categories.
>
> (Cruces et al. 2015: figure 9)

Average monthly earnings, expressed in dollars at 2005 PPP, increased by 7.7 per cent, from US$703 in 2000 to US$757 in 2012 (Table 10.1). The increase in labour earnings was far below the increase in GDP per capita over the period which was 44.2 per cent. Labour earnings fell at the beginning of the period—between 2000 and 2006—while GDP was growing, rose between 2006 and 2009—a period that included the Great Recession and during which GDP fell—and increased once again in 2011. The rise in labour earnings over the period was due mostly to the increase of 27.7 per cent in real hourly wages between 2000 and 2011 (Cruces et al. 2015: table 7). The increase in hourly wages over the period was related to Chile's wage policy, which included regular adjustments in the minimum wage (Castex and Sepúlveda 2014).

Disaggregating, we find that men, women, and young and adult workers all increased their labour earnings between 2000 and 2011. The trend in their labour earnings followed the erratic path for the aggregate, with reductions in 2000–6, gains from 2006 to 2009, and a decrease in 2011.

Mean earnings rose between 2000 and 2011 for workers employed in low-earning categories, and their earning gains tended to be larger than labour income increases for workers employed in high-earning categories. Among occupational groups, elementary occupations, agricultural, forestry and fishery workers, and workers in services and sales jobs had an average increase in their labour earnings larger than the one exhibited by professionals, and workers in management and armed forces. When the working population is broken down by occupational position, the self-employed experienced an increase in labour earnings, while employers and paid employees slightly decreased their labour incomes over the period. Domestic workers and workers from commerce and low-tech industries increased their labour earnings over the period by a lower magnitude compared to workers in skilled services, public administration, and education and health. Finally, labour earnings of workers with high educational levels fell, while workers with low and medium levels of education experienced an increase in their labour earnings.

The evidence of falling labour earnings for workers with high educational levels, and labour earnings increases for workers with medium and low levels of education can be interpreted in light of previous findings of improving educational levels of the Chilean employed population, slight worsening in the employment structure by occupational group, and slight improvement in the employment structure by economic sector over the period. The slight improvement in the composition of employment by economic sector implied an increase in the share of sectors that can be expected to employ workers with high and medium educational levels, such as skilled services, public administration, and education and health, and a smaller increase in the share of sectors that employ workers with low educational levels, such as commerce. On the other hand, the slight worsening in the employment structure by occupational group implied an increase in the share of occupations that are expected to employ workers with low educational levels, such as elementary, and services and sales occupations, and a smaller increase in the share of occupations that are expected to employ workers with high and medium educational levels, such as professional jobs. This evidence indicates that the direction of the change in the demand for workers with high and medium educational levels relative to those with low educational levels was ambiguous between 2000 and 2011. On the labour supply side, the educational level of people in the labour force improved over the same period, indicating an increase in the relative supply of workers with high and medium educational levels (Cruces et al. 2015: table 8). The prediction of a supply and demand analysis is that the relative wages of workers with high and medium educational levels relative to those with low educational levels will rise or fall depending on which effect dominates (increase/decrease in the relative demand versus increase in the relative supply). In the Chilean labour market the relative wages of workers with high and medium educational levels fell over the period relative to the wages of workers with low educational levels, and the relative wages of workers with high educational levels relative to those with medium educational levels also decreased (Cruces et al. 2015: table 7). The adjustment process also led to a reduction in the unemployment rates of workers with medium and low educational levels and no change for workers with high educational levels (Cruces et al. 2015: table 9).

The international crisis of 2008 did not have a negative effect on labour earnings in the aggregate or for any of the population groups and employment categories. Between 2006 and 2009, labour earnings increased overall, for young and adult workers, men, and women, and for all employment categories. The period from 2006 to 2009 is the only one in which labour incomes increased in Chile.

10.6 Poverty and Inequality

> The poverty rates, regardless of the poverty lines used and the rate of working poor households, decreased substantially between 2000 and 2011. The moderate and extreme poverty rates based on official poverty lines increased during the international crisis and recovered their downward trend in 2011. The poverty rates based on international poverty lines and the rate of working poor households diminished even during the Great Recession (Cruces et al. 2015: figure 10)

The moderate poverty rate (measured by the country's official poverty line) fell from 19.0 per cent in 2000 to 13.5 per cent in 2011; the extreme poverty rate decreased from 4.7 per cent to 2.4 per cent; the percentage of working poor (defined as the proportion of persons in the population living in poor households where at least one member works) decreased from 11.3 per cent to 7.1 per cent over the same period (Table 10.1). The moderate poverty rate fell by 6.2 percentage points from 2000 to 2006, increased by 1.3 percentage points from 2006 to 2009 (328,158 new poor persons), a period that included the international crisis, and declined again, by 0.5 percentage points, during the post-crisis period. By 2011, moderate poverty remained above its 2006 level. The pattern for the extreme poverty rate was similar. Part of the increase in the moderate and extreme poverty rates between 2006 and 2009 can be explained by the rise in food prices (Contreras and Ffrench-Davis 2012). When the analysis is based on the 2.5 and 4 dollars-a-day PPP international poverty lines, the trends show that the poverty rates decreased steadily over the period. The same pattern of steadily decreasing trend held for the percentage of working poor households. These differing patterns of poverty indicators between 2006 and 2009 can be explained by the different procedure applied to adjust the poverty lines over time. International lines are constant in real terms using the CPI. Official poverty lines are constant in real terms using the FPI. In Chile, inflation began to accelerate in 2007 due to increases in international food and energy prices, and also due to domestic supply shocks of these products (IMF 2008). The increase in food prices determined a more rapid increase in the official poverty lines compared to the international lines in current pesos. Consequently, poverty rates measured by the official poverty lines increased between 2006 and 2009, while poverty indicators based on international poverty lines decreased.

The poverty patterns reported in the last paragraph can be interpreted by examining incomes from various sources. The analysis of sources of household total income indicates that labour income and government transfers increased between 2000 and 2011 (Cruces et al. 2015: figure 11). On the other hand, income from pensions decreased over the period. The largest increase in labour earnings occurred between 2003 and 2006, when all poverty indicators exhibited the largest reductions. Government transfers surged between 2006 and 2009, a period that included the Great Recession. The government of Chile implemented an extraordinary cash transfer in 2009 as a consequence of the international crisis (*Bono de Apoyo a la Familia*) (Robles 2011).

> The inequality of household per capita income fell over the period studied, as did the inequality of labour earnings. The inequality of household per capita income stopped decreasing during the international crisis, but recovered its downward trend by the end of the period. The downward trend of the inequality of labour earnings was not affected by the international crisis. (Cruces et al. 2015: figure 12)

The Gini coefficient of household per capita income fell from 0.552 in 2000 to 0.508 in 2011. Between 2006 and 2009, it stopped decreasing, but recovered the falling trend in 2011. Throughout the period, the Gini coefficient of labour earnings among employed workers was slightly higher than that of per capita household income. The Gini coefficient of labour earnings decreased from 0.560 in 2000 to 0.510 in 2011 (Table 10.1). This reduction in labour earnings inequality is in keeping with the fact that earnings tended to increase more for low-earning employment categories compared to high-earning categories. However, it is interesting to notice that earnings declined for some high-earning groups. Consequently, the reduction of labour earning inequality in Chile occurred at the expense of income losses for some categories.

Changes in household per capita income inequality in Chile have been related mainly to changes in labour income. Azevedo et al. (2013b) decomposed the change in the Gini coefficient of household per capita income for the period 2003–9 and found that changes in labour incomes contributed the most to inequality reduction over this period (the Gini coefficient of household per capita income decreased from 0.547 to 0.519 between 2003 and 2009). On the other hand, changes in non-labour incomes, such as government transfers, and demographic changes, such as the share of adults per household, were also inequality-reducing. Larrañaga and Herrera (2008) and more recently Contreras and Ffrench-Davis (2012) have found that the decrease in inequality of household per capita income is a consequence of less inequality in labour earnings, which represent nearly 80 per cent of total family incomes. Other studies have analysed the factors behind the evolution of labour income inequality. Azevedo et al. (2013a) used a decomposition approach and found that changes in the education wage premium (or the 'price effect') and in the distribution of the stock of education (the 'quantity effect') were inequality-reducing in Chile between 2000 and 2009. Gasparini et al. (2011) found a reduction in the gap between the wages of skilled workers (those with complete or incomplete college education) and unskilled workers (those who have completed secondary education or less) in Chile between 2000 and 2011. The shrinking educational earnings gap can be explained by factors related to supply and demand: the relative supply of skilled workers increased steadily while the relative demand for those workers fell according to the authors.

10.7 Conclusions

From 2000 to 2012, Chile experienced rapid economic growth by Latin American standards. The economy suffered a recession as a consequence of the international crisis of 2008, but Chile returned to the pre-recession GDP and GDP per capita levels in 2010.

Most labour market indicators improved between 2000 and 2011. The unemployment rate fell. The employment structure by occupational position improved through the reduction in the share of self-employed and unpaid workers in total employment and the increase in the share of paid employees and employers. The employment composition by economic sector also improved as the share of higher-paying sectors like skilled services, public administration, and education and health in total employment increased by more than the share of lower-paying sectors like domestic service, commerce, and low-tech industry. The educational level of the Chilean employed population and the percentage of workers registered with the social security system in total employment improved over the period. Labour earnings increased between 2000 and 2011, and the evidence of earning changes by employment categories over the period indicated that labour income tended to increase more for low-earning categories compared to high-earning categories. The only labour market indicator that did not improve over the period was the employment structure by occupational group, which suffered a slight worsening. All poverty indicators fell between 2000 and 2011, and the Gini coefficient of per capita household income and labour earnings also decreased.

The labour market indicators that were affected negatively by the international crisis of 2008 were the unemployment rate, the percentage of workers registered with the social security system, the poverty rates based on official poverty lines, and the Gini coefficient of household income. The unemployment rate increased during the crisis and did not return to its pre-recession level by 2011. The share of registered workers fell during the crisis, but exceeded its pre-recession level in 2011. The moderate and extreme poverty rates based on official poverty lines increased in 2009, but resumed the downward trend in 2011. Finally, the inequality of per capita household income measured by the Gini coefficient stopped decreasing during the international crisis, but resumed its falling trend in 2011.

Young workers and women had worse labour market outcomes over the period compared to adults and men respectively, but they have not been more vulnerable to the international crisis. The unemployment rate was higher for young compared to adult workers, the shares of young employed workers in low-earning occupational groups and economic sectors were larger than the shares of adult workers, the percentage of young workers registered with the social security system was lower when compared to adults, and labour earnings of young workers were below those of adults. On the other hand, the share of young workers in low-earning occupational positions was lower when compared to adults. Despite the generally inferior situation of young workers in the labour market in comparison to adult workers, both age groups were equally affected by the international crisis of 2008. The increases in the unemployment rate and in the share of workers in low-earning sectors were larger for young workers, while the increases in the shares of unregistered workers and workers employed in low-earning occupational groups were larger for adults. Disaggregating by gender, we found that men were better than women in most labour market indicators, e.g. the male unemployment rate was lower, the share of male workers in low-earning occupational groups and sectors were lower compared to women, the share of unregistered workers was lower for men compared to women, and labour earnings of men were higher than labour earnings of women. However, the negative impacts of the crisis affected men more than women.

In summary, notwithstanding the international crisis of 2008, Chilean labour market conditions were in general in a better state in 2011 than they were at the start of the millennium.

References

Azevedo, J. P., M. E. Dávalos, C. Díaz-Bonilla, B. Atuesta, and R. A. Castañeda (2013a). 'Fifteen Years of Inequality in Latin America: How Have Labor Markets Helped?'. Policy Research Working Paper 6384. Washington, DC: World Bank.

Azevedo, J. P., G. Inchauste, and V. Sanfelice (2013b). 'Decomposing the Recent Inequality Decline in Latin America'. Policy Research Working Paper 6715. Washington, DC: World Bank.

Castex, G. and F. Sepúlveda (2014). 'Caracterización del mercado laboral en Chile y su evolución en los últimos 25 años'. Working Paper 728. Santiago de Chile: Central Bank of Chile.

CEDLAS and World Bank (2014). SEDLAC—Socio-Economic Database for Latin America and the Caribbean. Centro de Estudios Distributivos, Laborales y Sociales, Facultad de Ciencias Económicas, Universidad Nacional de La Plata and World Bank Poverty Group LCR. Available at <http://sedlac.econo.unlp.edu.ar/eng/index.php>, accessed 2014.

Contreras, D. and R. Ffrench-Davis (2012). 'Policy Regimes, Inequality, Poverty and Growth: The Chilean Experience, 1973–2010'. WIDER Working Paper 2012/04. Helsinki: UNU-WIDER.

Cruces, G., G. Fields, D. Jaume, and M. Viollaz (2015). 'The Growth–Employment–Poverty Nexus in Latin America in the 2000s: Chile Country Study'. WIDER Working Paper 2015/072. Helsinki: UNU-WIDER.

De Gregorio, J. and F. Labbé (2011). 'Copper, the Real Exchange Rate, and Macroeconomic Fluctuations in Chile'. Working Paper 640. Santiago de Chile: Central Bank of Chile.

Gasparini, L., S. Galiani, G. Cruces, and P. Acosta (2011). 'Educational Upgrading and Returns to Skills in Latin America: Evidence from a Supply–Demand Framework, 1990–2010'. IZA Working Paper 6244. Bonn: Institute for the Study of Labor.

ILO (2014). 'Policies for the Formalization of Micro and Small Enterprises in Chile'. FORLAC: Programme for the Promotion of Formalization in Latin America and the Caribbean. Geneva: Regional Office for Latin America and the Caribbean, International Labour Organization.

IMF (2004). *Chile: 2004 Article IV Consultation*. IMF Country Report No. 04/291. Washington, DC: International Monetary Fund.

IMF (2008). *Chile: Selected Issues Paper*. IMF Country Report No. 08/239. Washington, DC: International Monetary Fund.

IMF (2011). *Chile: 2011 Article IV Consultation*. IMF Country Report No. 11/260. Washington, DC: International Monetary Fund.

IMF (2012). *Chile: Selected Issues*. IMF Country Report No. 12/266. Washington, DC: International Monetary Fund.

Larrañaga, O. and R. Herrera (2008). 'Los recientes cambios en la desigualdad y la pobreza en Chile', *Estudios Públicos* 109: 149–86. Santiago de Chile: Centro de Estudios Públicos.

Robles, C. (2011). 'El sistema de protección social de Chile: Una mirada desde la igualdad'. ECLAC, Project Documents Collection. Santiago de Chile: United Nations.

World Bank (2014). World Development Indicators. Available at <http://data.worldbank.org/data-catalog/world-development-indicators>, accessed April 2014.

11

Colombia

11.1 Introduction

This chapter on labour markets and growth in Colombia since 2000 is one of sixteen studies of Latin American countries, each of which analyses the growth–employment–poverty nexus and aims to answer the following broad questions: Has economic growth resulted in economic development via improved labour market conditions in Latin America in the 2000s, and have these improvements halted or been reversed since the Great Recession? How do the rate and character of economic growth, changes in the various labour market indicators, and changes in poverty relate to each other?

To answer these questions, we analyse the growth experience of Colombia during the 2000s and a wide set of labour market indicators that we assign to one of two different categories: employment and earnings indicators, and poverty and income inequality indicators. More specifically, for the group of employment and earnings indicators we construct statistics on the following variables: the unemployment rate; the employment structure by occupational group, employment position, economic sector, registration of workers with the social security system, and educational level; and mean labour earnings and hourly wages. We present all these indicators for the employed population as a whole and for different population groups (youth, adults, men, and women). For the group of poverty and income inequality indicators, we compute poverty rates using the official moderate and extreme poverty lines and the international lines of 2.5 and 4 dollars a day. We also calculate the Gini coefficient of household per capita income and labour earnings.

All the statistics in this chapter are obtained using microdata from the Encuesta Continua de Hogares (ECH) from 2001 to 2005 and Gran Encuesta Integrada de Hogares (GEIH) from 2008 to 2013. The nationwide surveys were processed following a harmonization methodology and incorporated into the SEDLAC—Socio-Economic Database for Latin America and the Caribbean

(CEDLAS and World Bank 2014).[1] The resulting labour market indicators were compiled into a large number of tables and figures, which are available in an earlier version of this study (henceforth, Cruces et al. 2015). Chapter 1 of this book provides the definition for each of the indicators we analyse here, while Cruces et al. (2015) includes details on definitions and classification systems used by Colombia's household surveys, and on comparability issues of these surveys over time.

11.2 Economic Growth

> Colombia experienced rapid economic growth between 2000 and 2013. The economy suffered a slowdown as a consequence of the international crisis of 2008, but GDP and GDP per capita growth rates were nonetheless positive in 2009. (Cruces et al. 2015: figures 1 and 2)

Between 2000 and 2012, Colombia experienced rapid economic growth by Latin American standards. GDP per capita increased by 42.4 per cent overall, while the average for the eighteen Latin American countries was 36.2 per cent during the same period. GDP (measured in PPP dollars of 2005) grew by 72.5 per cent, and GDP per employed person rose by 23.9 per cent. The annual growth rate of GDP per capita was 2.8 per cent, and it was never negative, oscillating from a minimum of 0.0 per cent in 2001 to a maximum of 5.3 per cent in 2007 (Table 11.1).

At the beginning of the 2000s, Colombia was immersed in a phase of GDP contraction that was initiated with the Asian crisis in 1997 and which led to a severe financial and banking crisis. Some other factors continued to affect the country negatively in 2000 and 2001, such as a weakening in external demand, a fall in coffee prices to historically low levels, a high level of private debt that subdued consumption, and a lack of progress in resolving internal conflicts related to the guerrilla activities (IMF 2002). In 2001, GDP and GDP per capita growth rates reached their lowest levels for the period analysed, but even then, they remained non-negative (1.7 per cent and 0.0 per cent respectively).

Starting in 2003, Colombia benefited from some external factors that contributed to the recovery of the economy (Mesa 2007). First, the increase in external demand and in the terms of trade led to a rapid growth of mineral and hydrocarbon exports. Second, remittances from abroad exhibited an unprecedented increase. Third, the reduction in the risk premium of emerging

[1] See Cruces et al. (2015: table 1) for details on the size of Colombia household surveys.

Table 11.1 Colombia: Evolution of growth and labour market indicators over the 2000s

		2000	2001	2002	2003	2004	2005	2006	2007	2008	2009	2010	2011	2012	2013	
Growth Indicators	GDP per capita	6,597	6,598	6,655	6,808	7,060	7,280	7,651	8,059	8,223	8,241	8,450	8,890	9,143	9,395	
	GDP per capita growth rate	2.68	0.02	0.87	2.29	3.71	3.12	5.10	5.32	2.05	0.21	2.53	5.21	2.85	2.76	
Employment and Earnings Indicators	Employment-to-population ratio	...	57.25	56.81	58.42	57.71	58.15	...	...	56.83	58.56	60.40	61.35	62.30	62.92	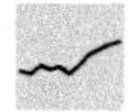
	Unemployment rate	...	13.58	14.33	13.57	12.06	11.08	...	...	10.88	11.63	10.86	9.92	9.78	9.00	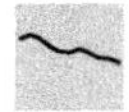
	Share of low-earnings occupations	...	46.15	45.34	46.00	45.20	45.36	...	...	39.40	42.64	42.42	41.72	41.47	41.02	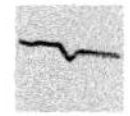
	Share of mid-earnings occupations	...	43.36	43.17	42.62	43.06	42.48	...	...	47.99	45.99	45.63	45.88	45.80	45.37	
	Share of high-earnings occupations	...	10.50	11.49	11.37	11.74	12.16	...	...	12.62	11.36	11.95	12.41	12.73	13.62	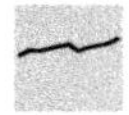
	Share of employers	...	4.41	4.61	4.58	5.16	5.30	...	...	4.67	4.98	5.01	5.04	4.95	4.58	
	Share of wage/salaried employees	...	50.00	50.77	49.58	49.35	52.00	...	...	49.06	48.50	47.36	47.07	47.28	48.25	
	Share of self-employed workers	...	40.89	40.15	40.54	40.94	38.48	...	...	42.55	42.60	43.07	43.74	43.33	42.79	
	Share of unpaid family workers	...	4.70	4.47	5.30	4.55	4.22	...	...	3.72	3.91	4.56	4.16	4.44	4.37	

(continued)

Table 11.1 Continued

		2000	2001	2002	2003	2004	2005	2006	2007	2008	2009	2010	2011	2012	2013	
	Share of workers in low-earnings sectors	...	54.03	52.79	52.18	50.58	51.94	...	...	48.08	49.01	49.07	48.40	48.45	48.39	
	Share of workers in mid-earnings sectors	...	24.59	25.41	25.11	26.48	25.56	...	...	27.47	26.85	27.56	27.49	27.41	26.18	
	Share of workers in high-earnings sectors	...	21.39	21.79	22.71	22.94	22.50	...	...	24.45	24.14	23.37	24.11	24.14	25.43	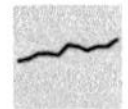
	Share of low-educated workers	...	56.11	54.36	54.24	52.70	51	...	...	47.09	48.36	48.00	45.30	45.37	42.60	
	Share of medium-educated workers	...	31.10	32.31	32.14	32.87	34.07	...	...	36.03	35.68	36.40	38.19	38.45	39.57	
	Share of high-educated workers	...	12.79	13.34	13.62	14.43	15.12	...	...	16.88	15.97	15.60	16.51	16.18	17.83	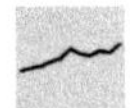
	Share of workers registered with SS	...	...	...	...	...	...	...	...	33.22	31.87	30.92	32.00	32.61	34.60	
	Mean labour earnings	...	402.0	469.3	408.1	452.6	464.9	...	...	516.9	537.1	543.5	546.0	545.6	573.5	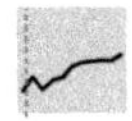
Poverty and Inequality Indicators	Official extreme poverty rate	...	...	16.09	15.61	14.62	12.80	...	...	15.46	12.97	10.86	9.09	9.56	8.34	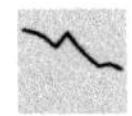
	Official moderate poverty rate	...	...	46.94	47.11	47.17	43.71	...	...	40.93	38.87	35.49	31.70	31.74	29.13	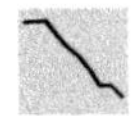

Poverty rate 2.5 dollars-a-day	...	39.04	29.84	31.05	28.37	25.30	...	...	24.45	21.92	19.56	16.97	17.50	15.16	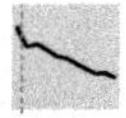
Poverty rate 4 dollars-a-day	...	60.33	49.55	51.96	49.41	45.24	...	...	41.64	39.61	36.51	33.14	32.92	30.75	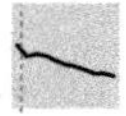
GINI of household per capita income	...	0.565	0.574	0.543	0.560	0.550	...	...	0.558	0.557	0.553	0.535	0.534	0.533	
GINI of labour earnings	...	0.517	0.551	0.510	0.530	0.519	...	...	0.502	0.514	0.516	0.504	0.506	0.499	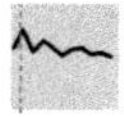

Note: The shaded figures for labour market indicators represent statistical significant improvements at 5 per cent between the initial and final years for all the employment and earnings indicators and poverty and inequality indicators. The only exceptions are the share of mid-earnings occupations, share of mid-earnings sectors, and share of medium-educated workers for which we did not assign welfare evaluation criteria. The vertical lines indicate that series are not fully comparable before and after that line. For mean labour earnings and poverty and inequality indicators, the comparison was made between 2002 and 2013.

Source: SEDLAC (CEDLAS and World Bank 2014) and World Development Indicators (World Bank 2014).

economies encouraged the arrival of foreign direct investment, while lower interest rates and increased liquidity stimulated local investment (Núñez and González 2011). On the domestic side, macroeconomic stability was achieved with prudent fiscal management, inflation targeting, a flexible exchange rate, and effective financial supervision and regulation (IMF 2013). From 2003 to 2008, the economy grew rapidly at 5.2 per cent a year, while GDP per capita increased at 3.5 per cent annually.

The international crisis led to a slowdown of the economy, but even then GDP and GDP per capita growth rates were positive. The policy response to the international crisis comprised countercyclical measures mainly related to interest rates management, prioritization of already planned government spending on infrastructure, and precautionary securing of public debt financing (Argüello 2011). The growth rate of GDP was 3.6 per cent in 2008 and 1.7 per cent in 2009, and those figures for GDP per capita were 2.1 and 0.2 per cent respectively. The economy recovered previous growth rates quickly, based on the boom of mineral exports and despite the severe floods of 2010 and the loss of Venezuela as an export market (OECD 2013). The country surpassed the pre-crisis growth rates by 2010 and kept on growing up to the end of the period.

11.3 Unemployment

> The 2001–13 period witnessed a reduction in the aggregate unemployment rate and in the unemployment rate for all population groups. Within this period, the unemployment rate increased in the early years and during the international crisis of 2008, but otherwise decreased.
>
> (Cruces et al. 2015: figure 3)

The unemployment rate (measured as the ratio of unemployment to labour force) dropped from 13.6 per cent in 2001 (2,433,367 unemployed people) to 9.0 per cent in 2013 (2,070,065 unemployed people) (Table 11.1). Initially, the unemployment rate increased in conjunction with the slowdown of GDP from 2001 to 2002, growing from 13.6 to 14.3 per cent. In 2002, the unemployment rate began a downward trend. The reduction that took place between 2002 and 2004 was related to changes in labour market regulations, such as the reduction in payment of overtimes and the lack of any obligation to pay pension contributions for learning contracts (Núñez 2005). The reducing trend was interrupted by the international crisis of 2008, when the aggregate unemployment rate increased from 10.9 per cent in 2008 to 11.6 per cent in 2009 (279,599 new unemployed people). Both the number of people in the labour force and the number of employed persons increased between 2008 and 2009 by 1,147,974 and 868,375 respectively. These figures suggest that the increase in the unemployment rate during the international crisis was brought about by the entry of new people into the labour market who could not find a job. The unemployment rate resumed a falling trend in 2010 and kept on decreasing through the end of the period studied, reaching 9.0 per cent in 2013. Even when the unemployment rate fell over the period analysed, the reduction was small compared to economic growth of the country (Núñez and González 2011). The reasons are: the increasing hiring costs of labour over the decade (minimum wage and non-salaried costs) despite the reduction in some components of labour costs in the first years; the decreasing costs of capital; and the growth process based on mineral and hydrocarbon exports, which is typically a capital-intensive activity.

Between 2001 and 2013, the unemployment rate decreased for young and adult workers, men and women. The international crisis led to an increase in the unemployment rate of all population groups, but it recovered the downward trend in 2010 for all of them.

11.4 Job Mix

> The composition of employment by occupational group improved between 2001 and 2013 as workers moved from agricultural, forestry and fishery occupations, and craft and trade jobs to better paying occupations like professional, armed forces, and management. All population groups—young and adult workers, men and women—benefited from the improvement in the composition of employment by occupational group over the period. The international crisis of 2008 led to a worsening in the structure of employment by occupational groups from which the labour market did not completely recover by 2013. (Cruces et al. 2015: figure 4)

The share of the following occupations shrank between 2001 and 2013: agricultural, forestry and fishery occupations (drop of 4.4 percentage points); plant and machine operators (drop of 1.4 percentage points); and craft and trade occupations (drop of 0.8 percentage points). The share of the following occupations grew: elementary (increase of 3.0 percentage points); armed forces (increase of 2.3 percentage points); technicians (increase of 0.8 percentage points); and professionals (increase of 0.7 percentage points). The share of the other occupational groups changed only a little (Cruces et al. 2015: table 3). These changes in the occupational composition of employment can be interpreted as an improvement since low-earning occupations (agricultural, forestry and fishery occupations, craft and trade jobs, and service and sales occupations) reduced their share in total employment by 5.1 percentage points between 2001 and 2013, while high-earning (professional, armed forces, and management) and mid-earning occupations (technical occupations, clerical jobs, plant and machine operators, and elementary occupations) gained shares in total employment (increases of 3.1 and 2.0 percentage points respectively) (Table 11.1). The improvements in the occupational composition of employment between 2001 and 2013 were observed for young and adult employed workers and for men and women.

The international crisis of 2008 adversely affected the composition of employment by occupational group in the aggregate and for all population groups. Between 2008 and 2009, the share of low-earning occupations in total employment grew, while the share of high-earning occupations fell. The share of low-earning occupations began a downward trend in the aggregate and for all population groups in 2010. Young workers and men returned to their pre-crisis shares of low-earning occupations in 2012 and 2013 respectively, while the shares in the aggregate and for adults and women never recovered their pre-crisis level. The share of high-earning occupations began an upward trend in 2010 for all population groups, and while young workers, adults and men returned to their pre-crisis shares in 2010, 2012, and 2011 respectively, women never recovered. In the aggregate, the share of high-earning occupations in total employment recovered the pre-crisis level in 2012.

> The employment structure by occupational position deteriorated between 2001 and 2013 for the employed population as a whole and for youth, adults, and women. The worsening trend in the employment structure by occupational position continued during the international crisis of 2008 in the aggregate and for young, adult workers, and women, while men experienced a slight improvement.
>
> (Cruces et al. 2015: figure 5)

Between 2001 and 2013, the share of wage/salaried employees in total employment—the largest category—dropped from 50.0 to 48.3 per cent. The share of unpaid workers also decreased, from 4.7 to 4.4 per cent. On the other hand, the shares of the self-employed and employers increased from 40.9 to 42.8 per cent and from 4.4 to 4.6 per cent respectively (Table 11.1). These changes can be characterized as a deterioration of the employment structure by occupational position, as the share of low-earning categories (self-employment and unpaid employment) increased by a total of 1.6 percentage points and the share of high-earning categories (paid employees and employers) decreased.

Between 2001 and 2013, the employment structure by occupational position deteriorated for young and adult workers, and women. For men, the structure of employment by occupational position remained essentially unchanged over the period. The worsening in the structure of employment by occupational position is striking in a growing economy where the unemployment rate is declining. However, the reduction in the unemployment rate during the 2000s was small compared to economic growth in Colombia, and that was related to increasing labour costs and a growth process based on capital-intensive sectors (Núñez and González 2011). In this context, the rise in the share of self-employment can be understood as a response to the rigidities in the creation/preservation of wage/salaried jobs.

The international crisis of 2008 did not affect the worsening trend in the employment structure by occupational position in the aggregate and for young, adult workers, and women, while a slight improvement for men took place during the crisis. Between 2008 and 2009, the share of low-earning positions in total employment continued to increase in the aggregate and for youth, adults, and women. Men, on the other hand, experienced an increase in the share of employers in total employment and a decrease in the share of the self-employed, which can be interpreted as a slight improvement. Men kept the share of low-earning positions in total employment below the pre-crisis value up to the end of the period studied.

> The employment composition by economic sector improved over the course of the period studied overall and for young and adult workers, men, and women. The international crisis of 2008 led to a worsening in the structure of employment by economic sector in the aggregate and for all population groups from which young, adult workers, and men recovered completely, but women did not.
>
> (Cruces et al. 2015: figure 6)

The share of the following sectors fell between 2001 and 2013: primary activities (drop of 4.3 percentage points); domestic workers (drop of 2.7 percentage points); and low-tech industries (drop of 1.5 percentage points). The mining and hydrocarbon subsector, the main driving force of the Colombian economy during the period analysed, is included in the primary activities sector in our classification. The mining and hydrocarbon subsector is capital-intensive and does not employ a large share of workers. The increase in its share of total employment over the period was counteracted by the reduction in the employment share of the agricultural subsector. The share of the following sectors grew: skilled services (increase of 3.4 percentage points); construction (increase of 1.7 percentage points); commerce (increase of 1.4 percentage points); utilities and transportation (increase of 1.4 percentage points); and education and health (increase of 0.6 percentage points). The share of the other sectors changed only a little. These changes in the employment composition by economic sector can be interpreted as an improvement, since low-earning sectors (domestic service, primary activities, and commerce) reduced their share in total employment by 5.6 percentage points between 2001 and 2013, while high-earning (public administration, skilled services, and education and health) and mid-earning sectors (high-tech industry, utilities and transportation, construction, and low-tech industry) gained share in total employment (increase of 4.0 and 1.6 percentage points respectively) (Table 11.1). Broken down by population groups, the employment composition by economic sector improved between 2001 and 2013 for young and adult workers, men, and women, as they moved from low-earning sectors to high-earning sectors.

The international crisis of 2008 led to a worsening in the employment structure by economic sector overall and for all population groups. Between 2008 and 2009, the share of low-earning sectors in total employment increased, while the share of employed workers in high-earning sectors fell. Young workers, adult workers, and men recovered their pre-crisis shares of employment in low- and high-earning sectors in the following years, while women recovered the share of working in high-earning sectors, but not the share of working in low-earning sectors.

> The educational level of the employed population in Colombia improved from 2001 to 2013 for the entire population and for youth, adults, men, and women. The international crisis of 2008 led to a worsening in the employment structure by educational level in the aggregate and for all population groups, but all of them recovered the pre-crisis structure in the following years.
>
> (Cruces et al. 2015: figure 7)

The share of employed persons with low educational levels (eight years of schooling or less) dropped from 56.1 per cent in 2001 to 42.6 per cent in 2013, while the share of employed persons with medium and high educational levels (nine to thirteen years of schooling and over thirteen years of schooling) grew from 31.1 per cent in 2001 to 39.6 per cent in 2013 and from 12.8 per cent to 17.8 per cent respectively (Table 11.1).[2] We interpret this result as an improvement for the employed population as the level of education is an important predictor of labour earnings. Consequently, the changes in the employment structure by educational level implied an increase in the share of workers that tend to have high levels of earnings and a decline in the share of workers with low earnings levels.[3] The improvement in the educational level of the employed population reflects the improvement in access to education for the entire population of Colombia. However, the quality of education is low; the enrolment rates in tertiary education are low and the inequality high;

[2] The most frequent value of years of education for employed workers in Colombia was eleven for the entire period under study (around 23.8 per cent of employed workers had eleven years of education).

[3] The improvement in the employment structure by educational level is related to changes in the relative demand and supply of workers with high educational levels with corresponding implications for the wage gap by educational group and the unemployment rate of each educational level. We introduce a discussion about the role of these factors in Colombia in section 11.5.

and a substantial gap between education levels of the poor and the rest of the population exists (World Bank 2009). The educational level of the employed population improved between 2001 and 2013 for all population groups, and especially for young workers.

The pattern of improvement in the educational level of the employed population in Colombia was affected by the international crisis of 2008. The share of employed persons with low educational levels increased in 2009 in the aggregate and for all population groups, with a corresponding reduction in the share of employed workers with medium and high educational levels. A possible explanation for this worsening in the employment structure by educational level can be found in the previous evidence of increasing unemployment and worsening employment structure by occupational position during the international crisis. Better-educated workers could afford to remain unemployed during the crisis, while the less-educated workers were compelled by economic necessity to take up free-entry self-employment activities or unpaid family work. By 2011, the share of employed workers with low educational levels recovered the pre-crisis value in the aggregate and for all population groups. The share of workers with medium levels of education returned to its pre-crisis level in 2010 overall and for all groups, while the share of the employed population with high educational levels reached its pre-crisis level in 2013.

> The share of workers registered with the social security system increased from 2008 (the earliest year with data on this indicator) to 2013 in the aggregate and for adults and male workers, while it decreased for young workers and women. Within this period, the registration rate fell from 2008 to 2010, a period that included the Great Recession, and increased from 2010 to 2013.
>
> (Cruces et al. 2015: figure 8)

The social security system in Colombia is comprised of a contributory scheme and a non-contributory scheme. The contributory pension scheme contains two different regimes: the *Régimen Solidario de Prima Media con Prestación Definida* (a defined contributions regime) and the *Régimen de Ahorro Individual con Solidaridad* (an individual accounts regime). Affiliation to the pension system is compulsory for both dependent and independent workers, although they may choose their preferred regime and change it once every five years. The contributory pension scheme is financed through contributions made by employees and employers. The non-contributory pension scheme, *Fondo de Solidaridad Pensional*, provides pension subsidies to those persons who cannot afford to make contributions, and is financed by the government. The non-contributory pension scheme covers informal workers, and disabled and unemployed workers. Cash or in-kind transfers are also provided for the protection of elders, such as *Programa de Protección Social al Adulto Mayor* and

Programa Nacional de Alimentación al Adulto Mayor. The contributory health scheme is available to persons with greater payment capacity, including formal and independent workers, employers, and pensioners. The non-contributory health scheme provides attention to persons lacking payment capacity. The financing of the contributory regime is made through contributions charged to the employers and employees (Mina Rosero 2013).

The percentage of workers registered with the contributory scheme of the social security system increased by 1.4 percentage points between 2008 and 2013 (Table 11.1). From 2008 to 2010, a period that included the Great Recession, the share of registered workers fell from 33.2 per cent to 30.9 per cent. Interestingly, the number of registered workers increased between 2008 and 2010, from 5,644,701 to 5,818,439. The fall in the registration rate was explained by the more rapid increase in the number of employed persons compared to the increase in the number of registered workers during this period. From 2010 to 2013, the share of registered employment grew steadily, reaching 34.6 per cent in 2013 (1,298,793 new registered workers between 2010 and 2013). Despite the Colombian growth in the last years of the period analysed, the registration rate is still very low. Non-salary labour costs in the formal sector are very high in Colombia, even when compared to OECD standards (OECD 2013). The increased labour costs, along with the universal coverage of basic public services like health, discouraged the registration of workers (Parra Torrado 2010).

The Colombian government implemented some measures aimed at increasing the registration rate, especially in the last years of the period analysed. In 2010, it decreased social security contributions for new firms and for those who create employment for young workers, women aged 40 years or more, and disabled workers (OECD 2013; ILO 2014). In 2013, the government implemented deductions for taxes that firms pay on salaries and social security contributions for workers they formalize; it created the protection mechanism for dismissed workers which guarantees social protection of workers in the event of unemployment, including continued health and pension coverage; and it increased the number of inspectors (ILO 2014).

The percentage of workers registered with the social security system increased for adult employed workers and men, and fell for young workers and women between 2008 and 2013. For all population groups, the percentage of registered workers decreased at the beginning of the analysed period, from 2008 to 2010, and increased in the later years.

The decreasing trend in the share of registered workers that took place at the beginning of the analysed period continued during the international crisis of 2008 in the aggregate and for all population groups. Young workers and women never returned to their pre-crisis share of registered employment, while adults and men surpassed their pre-crisis level in 2012.

11.5 Labour Earnings

> Real labour earnings increased between 2002 (the earliest year for which we can compare earnings from the ECH with earnings from the GEIH) and 2013 in the aggregate, for all population groups, and for almost all employment categories. Labour earnings fell in the first year (during which economic growth was zero) and then began an almost steady upward trend that continued as the economy grew even during the international crisis of 2008 and its aftermath. The upward trend held overall, for all population groups and for almost all employment categories.
>
> (Cruces et al. 2015: figure 9).

Average monthly earnings, expressed in dollars at 2005 PPP, grew by 22.2 per cent, from US$469 in 2002 to US$574 in 2013 (Table 11.1). Labour earnings fell between 2002 and 2003 and rose in the following years for the employed population as a whole. The upward trend in real labour earnings is partly explained by increases in the minimum wage. The minimum wage has been used as a political instrument sometimes, in pre-electoral years for instance, leading to increases larger than the inflation rate (Parra Torrado 2010; OECD 2013). However, it is worth noticing that a large percentage of employed workers are unregistered and do not benefit from the minimum wage legislation.

Labour earnings grew between 2002 and 2013 for all population groups, and for employed workers in almost all employment categories. All of them suffered a reduction between 2002 and 2003 (a time of non-growth) and an upward trend after that (during which economic growth was positive and above the Latin American average). Labour earnings gains were larger for low-earning categories compared to high-earning categories. The only employment categories that suffered a reduction of labour earnings between 2002 and 2013 were workers in the armed forces, employers, workers in the skilled services sector, and workers with high educational levels. All other employment categories enjoyed increases in their labour incomes between 2002 and 2013.

The evidence of falling labour earnings for workers with high educational levels and increasing labour earnings for workers with low and medium educational levels can be interpreted in light of previous findings of improvements in the employment structure by occupational group, economic sector, and educational level over the period. The improving employment structure by occupational group and economic sector implied an increase in the share of occupations and sectors that can be expected to employ workers with high and medium educational levels, like management, professional occupations, and armed forces, skilled services, education, and health, and public administration sectors, and a reduction in the share of occupations and sectors that employ workers with low educational levels, like agricultural, and craft and trades occupations, and domestic service and primary activities sectors. This evidence indicates that the demand for workers with high and medium educational levels relative to those with low educational levels increased between 2001 and 2013. On the other hand, the educational level of people in the labour force improved over the same period, indicating an increase in the relative supply of workers with high and medium educational levels (Cruces et al. 2015: table 8). The prediction of a supply and demand analysis is that the relative wages of workers with high and medium educational levels relative to those with low educational levels will rise or fall depending on which effect dominates (increase in the relative demand versus increase in the relative supply). In the Colombian labour market, the relative wages of workers with high and medium educational levels relative to those with low educational levels fell over the period, and the relative wages of workers with high educational levels relative to those with medium educational levels also decreased (Cruces et al. 2015: table 7). The adjustment process also led to a reduction in the unemployment rate of all educational groups with a larger decrease for workers with medium levels of education (Cruces et al. 2015: table 9).

The international crisis of 2008 did not have a negative effect on the upward trend in labour earnings that began in 2003, a trend that held true in the aggregate and for all population groups. Some employment categories, however, were adversely affected by the 2008 crisis. Among occupational groups, earnings fell for workers in craft and trade occupations and for agricultural and forestry and fishery workers. Among economic sectors, workers from primary activities were affected by a reduction in their labour earnings during the international crisis. Agricultural, forestry, and fishery workers, and workers from primary activities recovered their pre-crisis levels of labour income in 2010, while craft and trade workers never recovered their pre-crisis level.

11.6 Poverty and Inequality

> The moderate and extreme poverty rates based on the country's official line and on international poverty lines fell between 2002 and 2013, as did the rate of working poor households. Within this period, poverty indicators experienced a small increase in the first year (from 2002 to 2003), a reduction in the following years (from 2003 to 2011), and a slight increase at the end of the period (from 2011 to 2012). The international crisis of 2008 did not affect negatively the poverty indicators.
>
> (Cruces et al. 2015: figure 10)

The moderate poverty rate (measured by the country's official poverty line) fell from 46.9 per cent in 2002 to 29.1 per cent in 2013; the extreme poverty rate decreased from 16.1 per cent to 8.3 per cent; the percentage of working poor (defined as the proportion of persons in the population living in poor households where at least one member works) dropped from 35.0 per cent to 19.5 per cent over the same period. When the poverty rate is analysed on the basis of the 2.5 and 4 dollars-a-day PPP international poverty lines, there is also a drop in poverty between 2002 and 2013. When the 2.5 dollars-a-day poverty line is used, the poverty rate drops from 29.8 per cent in 2002 to 15.2 per cent in 2013; when poverty is calculated using the 4 dollars-a-day poverty line, the drop is from 49.6 per cent to 30.8 per cent over the same period (Table 11.1). The figures for all these indicators increased between 2002 and 2003 (except for the extreme poverty rate based on the official line) and then began a downward trend that was interrupted in 2012 when all the indicators increased (except for the poverty rate based on the 4 dollars-a-day international line). In 2013, all the indicators resumed the downward trend.

The poverty patterns reported in the last paragraph can be interpreted by examining incomes from various sources. The analysis of sources of household total income indicates that labour income, pensions, and income from capital increased between 2002 and 2013 (Cruces et al. 2015: figure 11). On the other hand, remittances declined from 2008 (the earliest we have data on this variable) to 2013. Colombia has experienced strong flows of emigration and remittances in the last two decades (UNFPA 2011). However, during the international crisis, the amount of remittances received by the country has been falling and a change is expected in the pattern of migration, with emigrants returning to Colombia and fewer persons leaving the country. Data on income from poverty alleviation programmes is not available in Colombia's national household surveys. There is evidence indicating they have been successful in increasing school enrolment and attendance, and health and nutritional status mainly among children (Attanasio et al. 2005; Attanasio and Mesnard 2006). Moreover, coverage of these programmes has increased during the international crisis of 2008 (Núñez and González 2011).

> Household per capita income inequality and labour earnings inequality decreased between 2002 and 2013, though erratically. The international crisis of 2008 led to an increase in the inequality of labour earning, while the inequality of household per capita income remained unchanged. (Cruces et al. 2015: figure 12)

From 2002 to 2013, the Gini coefficient of household per capita income fell from 0.574 to 0.533. The Gini coefficient of labour earnings among employed workers decreased from 0.551 in 2002 to 0.499 in 2013 (Table 11.1); this reduction in labour earnings inequality is in keeping with the fact that earnings increased more for low-earning employment categories compared to high-earning categories. However, it is interesting to note that earnings declined for some high-earning employment categories. Consequently, the reduction in labour earning inequality in Colombia occurred at the expense of income losses for some categories. The reduction in household per capita income and labour earnings inequality was not steady. The Gini coefficient moved erratically over the period for both income variables. During the international crisis of 2008, the Gini coefficient of labour earnings increased from 0.502 in 2008 to 0.516 in 2010 and returned in 2011 to its pre-crisis level. The Gini coefficient of household per capita income held steady during the crisis.

Changes in household per capita income inequality in Colombia have been related to changes in labour and non-labour incomes. Azevedo et al. (2013b) decomposed the change in the Gini coefficient of household per capita income for the period 2002–10 and found that changes in labour incomes contributed the most to the inequality reduction over this period (the Gini coefficient of household per capita income decreased from 0.574 to 0.553 between 2002 and 2010). Demographical factors, such as the share occupied by adults and the share of adults, and incomes from transfers also contributed to the reduction in household per capita income inequality. On the other hand, incomes from pensions and capital were inequality-increasing. Other studies have analysed the factors behind the evolution of labour income inequality. Azevedo et al. (2013a) used a decomposition approach and found that changes in the education wage premium (or the 'price effect') were inequality-reducing in Colombia between 2002 and 2010 (the Gini coefficient of labour earnings decreased from 0.551 to 0.516 between 2002 and 2010), while changes in the distribution of the stock of education (the 'quantity effect') were inequality-increasing although the effect was small. Gasparini et al. (2011) found a reduction in the gap between the wages of skilled workers (those with complete or incomplete college education) and unskilled workers (those who have completed secondary education or less) in Colombia between 2001 and 2007. The shrinking educational earnings gap can be explained mainly by the increase in the relative supply of skilled workers, while the relative demand remained unchanged.

11.7 Conclusions

By Latin American standards, Colombia experienced rapid economic growth between 2000 and 2013. The economy suffered a slowdown at the beginning of the period and after the international crisis of 2008. During both slowdowns, the growth rates were nonetheless positive.

Most labour market indicators improved between 2001 and 2013. Most of them followed the pattern of economic growth over the period, with a worsening in the early years and an improvement in the following years, interrupted by the international crisis of 2008. The unemployment rate fell between 2001 and 2013. Within this period, the unemployment rate increased in the first year of the series and during the international crisis of 2008, from which it fully recovered. The composition of employment by occupational group improved between 2001 and 2013 as workers moved from agricultural, forestry and fishery occupations, and craft and trade jobs to better-paying occupations like professional, armed forces, and management. The international crisis of 2008 adversely affected the structure of employment by occupational group, from which the labour market only partially recovered by 2013. The employment composition by economic sector also improved over the course of the period studied but was negatively impacted by the international crisis of 2008. The sectoral composition of employment did not completely recover by 2013. The educational level of the Colombian employed population improved from 2001 to 2013. Even though the international crisis of 2008 led to a worsening in the employment structure by educational level, the labour market recovered the pre-crisis structure in the following years. The share of workers registered with the social security system increased from 2008 to 2013 (the earliest year with data on this indicator) but was negatively affected by the international crisis of 2008. Real labour earnings increased between 2002 (the earliest year for which we can compare earnings from the ECH with earnings from the GEIH) and 2013. They fell during the first year and then began an almost steady upward trend that was not interrupted by the international crisis of 2008.

The moderate and extreme poverty rates, the poverty rates based on international poverty lines, and the rate of working poor households all fell between 2002 and 2013. Within this period, poverty indicators exhibited a small increase at the beginning, a reduction in the following years, and a small increase by the end of the period. Household per capita income inequality and labour earnings inequality also decreased between 2002 and 2013, though erratically. The international crisis of 2008 did not negatively affect the poverty indicators, nor the inequality of household per capita income, but led to an increase in the inequality of labour earnings.

The only labour market indicator that did not improve between 2002 and 2013 is the employment structure by occupational position, as the share of low-paying positions in total employment increased and the share of high-earning positions fell. The worsening trend in the employment structure by occupational position continued during the international crisis of 2008.

Young workers and women had worse labour market outcomes over the period compared to adults and men respectively, but they have not been more vulnerable to the international crisis. The unemployment rate was higher for young compared to adult workers, the shares of young employed workers in low-earning occupational groups and economic sectors were larger than the shares of adult workers, the percentage of young workers registered with the social security system was lower when compared to adults, and labour earnings of young workers were below those of adults. On the other hand, the share of young workers in low-earning occupational positions was lower when compared to adults. Despite the generally inferior situation of young workers in the labour market in comparison to adult workers, both age groups were equally affected by the international crisis of 2008. The increases in the unemployment rate and in the shares of workers in low-earning positions and occupations were larger for adult workers, while the increase in the share of unregistered workers and workers employed in low-earning sectors was larger for youth. Disaggregating by gender, we found that men were better than women in most labour market indicators, e.g. the male unemployment rate was lower, the share of male workers in low-earning occupational groups and positions was lower compared to women, and labour earnings of men were higher than labour earnings of women. On the other hand, the share of workers in low-earning sectors was larger among men, while the share of unregistered workers was similar among both gender groups. The negative impacts of the crisis affected men and women similarly. Women suffered a larger increase in their unemployment rate and in the share of workers in low-earning positions; men exhibited a larger increase in the share of workers in low-earning sectors; and both groups suffered a similar increase in the shares of unregistered workers and workers in low-earning occupations.

In summary, notwithstanding the international crisis of 2008, Colombian labour market conditions were in a better state in 2013 than they were at the start of the millennium.

References

Argüello, R. (2011). 'The International Economic Crisis and the Colombian Economy'. Serie Documentos de Trabajo 98. Bogotá: Facultad de Economía, Universidad del Rosario.

Attanasio, O., E. Battistin, E. Fitzsimons, A. Mesnard, and M. Vera Hernández (2005). 'How Effective Are Conditional Cash Transfers? Evidence from Colombia'. Briefing Note 54. London: Institute for Fiscal Studies.

Attanasio, O. and A. Mesnard (2006). 'The Impact of a Conditional Cash Transfer Programme on Consumption in Colombia', *Fiscal Studies* 27 (4): 421–42.

Azevedo, J. P., M. E. Dávalos, C. Díaz-Bonilla, B. Atuesta, and R. A. Castañeda (2013a). 'Fifteen Years of Inequality in Latin America: How Have Labor Markets Helped?'. Policy Research Working Paper 6384. Washington, DC: World Bank.

Azevedo, J. P., G. Inchauste, and V. Sanfelice (2013b). 'Decomposing the Recent Inequality Decline in Latin America'. Policy Research Working Paper 6715. Washington, DC: World Bank.

CEDLAS and World Bank (2014). SEDLAC—Socio-Economic Database for Latin America and the Caribbean. Centro de Estudios Distributivos, Laborales y Sociales, Facultad de Ciencias Económicas, Universidad Nacional de La Plata and World Bank Poverty Group LCR. Available at <http://sedlac.econo.unlp.edu.ar/eng/index.php>, accessed 2014.

Cruces, G., G. Fields, D. Jaume, and M. Viollaz (2015). 'The Growth–Employment–Poverty Nexus in Latin America in the 2000s: Colombia Country Study'. WIDER Working Paper 2015/073. Helsinki: UNU-WIDER.

Gasparini, L., S. Galiani, G. Cruces, and P. Acosta (2011). 'Educational Upgrading and Returns to Skills in Latin America: Evidence from a Supply–Demand Framework, 1990–2010'. IZA Working Paper 6244. Bonn: Institute for the Study of Labor.

ILO (2014). 'Trends in Informal Employment in Colombia: 2009–2013'. FORLAC: Programme for the Promotion of Formalization in Latin America and the Caribbean. Geneva: Regional Office for Latin America and the Caribbean, International Labour Organization.

IMF (2002). 'Colombia: Third Review under the Extended Arrangement'. IMF Country Report 13/35. Washington, DC: International Monetary Fund.

IMF (2013). 'Colombia 2012: IV Article Consultation'. IMF Country Report 02/15. Washington, DC: International Monetary Fund.

Mesa, F. (2007). 'El crecimiento económico y sus sostenibilidad en Colombia ¿Qué dicen las estadísticas?'. Revista CIFE 12. Bogotá: Centro de Investigaciones Facultad de Economía, Universidad Santo Tomás.

Mina Rosero, L. (2013). 'Social Protection Systems in Latin America and the Caribbean: Colombia'. ECLAC, Project Documents Collection. Santiago de Chile: United Nations.

Núñez, J. (2005). 'Éxitos y fracasos de la reforma laboral'. Documento CEDE 2005–43. Bogotá: Centro de Estudios sobre Desarrollo Económico, Universidad de los Andes.

Núñez, J. and N. González (2011). 'Colombia', in M. Sanchez and P. Sauma (eds), *Vulnerabilidad económica externa, protección social y pobreza en América Latina*. Quito: FLACSO, CEPAL, Departamento de Asuntos Económicos y Sociales de las Naciones Unidas (UN/DESA), 209–62.

OECD (2013). 'Estudios económicos de la OCDE: Colombia 2013'. Paris: OECD Publishing.

Parra Torrado, M. (2010). 'Análisis y perspectiva del desempleo en los ultimos 12 años'. Bogotá: Fedesarrollo, Centro de Investigación Económica y Social.

UNFPA (2011). 'The Global Financial Crisis in Colombia and the ICPD Agenda'. RIVAF Research Project 2010/2011. Bogotá: United Nations Population Fund.

World Bank (2009). 'Integrating the Poor into Labor Markets: Policy Recommendations for Colombia'. Report 48522-CO. Washington, DC: World Bank.

World Bank (2014). World Development Indicators. Available at <http://data.worldbank.org/data-catalog/world-development-indicators>, accessed April 2014.

12

Costa Rica

12.1 Introduction

This chapter on labour markets and growth in Costa Rica since 2000 is one of sixteen studies of Latin American countries, each of which analyses the growth–employment–poverty nexus and aims to answer the following broad questions: Has economic growth resulted in economic development via improved labour market conditions in Latin America in the 2000s, and have these improvements halted or been reversed since the Great Recession? How do the rate and character of economic growth, changes in the various labour market indicators, and changes in poverty relate to each other?

To answer these questions, we analyse the growth experience of Costa Rica during the 2000s and a wide set of labour market indicators that we assign to one of two different categories: employment and earnings indicators, and poverty and income inequality indicators. More specifically, for the group of employment and earnings indicators we construct statistics on the following variables: the unemployment rate; the employment structure by occupational group, employment position, economic sector, registration of workers with the social security system, and educational level; and mean labour earnings and hourly wages. We present all these indicators for the employed population as a whole and for different population groups (youth, adults, men, and women). For the group of poverty and income inequality indicators, we compute poverty rates using the official moderate and extreme poverty lines and the international lines of 2.5 and 4 dollars a day. We also calculate the Gini coefficient of household per capita income and labour earnings.

All the statistics in this chapter are obtained using microdata from the Encuesta de Hogares de Propósitos Múltiples (EHPM) from 2001 to 2009, and Encuesta Nacional de Hogares (ENAHO) from 2010 to 2012. The nationwide surveys were processed following a harmonization methodology and incorporated into the SEDLAC—Socio-Economic Database for Latin America and the Caribbean (CEDLAS and World Bank 2014).[1] The resulting labour market indicators were compiled into a large number of tables and figures, which are available in an earlier version of this study (henceforth, Cruces et al. 2015). Chapter 1 of this book provides the definition for each of the indicators we analyse here, while Cruces et al. (2015) includes details on definitions and classification systems used by Costa Rica's household surveys, and on comparability issues of these surveys over time.

12.2 Economic Growth

> Costa Rica achieved moderate and sustained economic growth in the 2000s, except for the international crisis of 2008, from which it quickly recovered, surpassing pre-crisis GDP levels by 2010.
>
> (Cruces et al. 2015: figures 1 and 2)

From 2000 to 2012, the Costa Rican economy grew at an average rate by Latin American standards. GDP per capita (measured in 2005 PPP dollars) increased by 37.4 per cent, while the average for the region's eighteen countries was 36.2 per cent during the same period. GDP (measured in 2005 PPP dollars) grew by 68.1 per cent, and GDP per employed person rose by 21.1 per cent. The annual growth rate of GDP per capita was 2.5 per cent, and it varied from a minimum of −2.5 per cent in 2009 to a maximum of 7.0 per cent in 2006 (Table 12.1).

The early part of the period was marked by minimal growth in the Costa Rican economy. GDP growth rates were 1.8 and 1.1 per cent in 2000 and 2001, while GDP per capita fell by 0.5 and 1.0 per cent during the same period. The poor performance of the Costa Rican economy reflected the deterioration in the terms of trade, the end of the construction phase of a large foreign direct investment project by INTEL, and the effect of high real interest rates on domestic demand (IMF 2002). The economy gained momentum quickly. Exports, mainly those from offshore manufacturing and service activities with high technological content, led the rise in output, followed by domestic demand, which increased through a substantial acceleration of private investment and consumption, and by the boom in construction (IMF 2006, 2008). The average annual growth rate of GDP per capita was 4.2 per cent from 2002 to 2007, while GDP increased by 6.0 per cent a year during the same period.

The international crisis of 2008, referred to below as the Great Recession, had an impact on the Costa Rican economy. There was a slowdown in 2008, when GDP per capita grew by just 1.2 per cent, and negative growth rates in 2009, when GDP per capita fell by 2.5 per cent and overall GDP by 1.0 per cent.

[1] See Cruces et al. (2015: table 1) for details on the size of Costa Rica household surveys.

Table 12.1 Costa Rica: Evolution of growth and labour market indicators over the 2000s

		2000	2001	2002	2003	2004	2005	2006	2007	2008	2009	2010	2011	2012
Growth Indicators	GDP per capita	8,116	8,032	8,102	8,462	8,666	9,019	9,649	10,250	10,369	10,110	10,456	10,763	11,156
	GDP per capita growth rate	−0.48	−1.04	0.88	4.43	2.41	4.08	6.99	6.22	1.16	−2.49	3.42	2.94	3.65
Employment and Earnings Indicators	Employment-to-population ratio	. . .	56.62	56.01	56.06	55.09	57.19	57.09	58.65	57.90	55.75	54.79	56.02	55.42
	Unemployment rate	. . .	6.04	6.39	6.65	6.44	6.63	5.92	4.55	4.93	7.82	7.29	7.66	7.77
	Share of low-earnings occupations	. . .	47.48	48.26	47.86	47.17	47.51	46.58	45.98	43.95	44.27	47.46	48.15	. . .
	Share of mid-earnings occupations	. . .	28.79	28.34	27.66	28.46	28.03	28.55	28.75	28.53	27.89	26.50	25.20	
	Share of high-earnings occupations	. . .	23.73	23.40	24.48	24.37	24.46	24.87	25.26	27.52	27.85	26.04	26.65	. . .
	Share of employers	. . .	8.03	7.93	8.65	8.16	7.50	7.75	7.26	7.52	7.22	3.37	3.72	3.56
	Share of wage/salaried employees	. . .	69.06	68.53	69.58	68.84	71.56	70.85	73.17	72.95	72.77	76.11	76.00	76.09
	Share of self-employed workers	. . .	20.38	20.80	19.35	20.77	18.90	19.42	17.93	18.06	18.52	18.87	18.77	18.69
	Share of unpaid family workers	. . .	2.54	2.74	2.42	2.24	2.04	1.97	1.64	1.46	1.49	1.65	1.50	1.66
	Share of workers in low-earnings sectors	. . .	28.96	28.75	27.52	27.40	28.94	27.71	26.45	24.72	24.14	28.00	27.10	26.44
	Share of workers in mid-earnings sectors	. . .	44.83	44.91	45.66	46.32	45.28	46.28	46.98	47.22	47.04	43.79	44.44	43.30

	[illegible]	...	[illegible]	[illegible]	[illegible]	[illegible]	[illegible]	[illegible]	[illegible]	[illegible]	[illegible]	[illegible]	[illegible]	[illegible]
	Share of low-educated workers	...	57.32	55.40	53.23	53.27	53.38	52.25	51.06	49.08	47.55	50.03	48.80	46.53
	Share of medium-educated workers	...	27.00	28.15	29.63	29.45	29.03	29.10	30.27	30.90	31.68	30.81	31.47	32.61
	Share of high-educated workers	...	15.68	16.45	17.14	17.28	17.59	18.64	18.67	20.02	20.77	19.16	19.73	20.85
	Share of workers registered with SS	...	50.70	50.53	50.35	51.31	50.68	51.23	53.47	54.69	55.26	55.65	54.58	56.06
	Mean labour earnings	...	749.7	736.3	740.3	694.7	675.3	703.5	764.7	784.8	832.2	794.1	812.0	833.0
Poverty and Inequality Indicators	Official extreme poverty rate		7.1	7.0	6.7	6.7	5.6	5.6	3.5	4.3	5.1	5.7	5.9	5.9
	Official moderate poverty rate		20.3	20.6	18.8	20.3	20.5	19.1	15.8	17.0	18.5	25.9	25.3	24.0
	Poverty rate 2.5 dollars a day	...	13.78	13.55	13.07	12.26	10.76	10.58	7.27	6.87	7.46	4.53	5.09	4.73
	Poverty rate 4 dollars a day	...	26.72	26.45	24.87	25.93	23.07	22.98	17.88	17.01	17.42	12.70	13.01	2.18
	GINI of household per capita income	...	0.501	0.500	0.492	0.482	0.473	0.489	0.492	0.486	0.504	0.480	0.485	.485
	GINI of labour earnings	...	0.464	0.463	0.454	0.435	0.440	0.454	0.459	0.455	0.459	0.466	0.477	0.471

Note: The shaded labour market indicators' figures represent statistical significant improvements at 5 per cent between the initial and final years for all the employment and earnings indicators and poverty and inequality indicators. The only exceptions are the share of mid-earnings occupations, share of mid-earnings sectors, and share of medium-educated workers for which we did not assign welfare evaluation criteria. The vertical lines indicate that the series 2001–9 and 2010–12 are not comparable due to changes in the household survey.

Source: SEDLAC (CEDLAS and World Bank 2014) and World Development Indicators (World Bank 2014).

GDP contraction was driven by a sharp fall in exports and incomes from tourism, the sectors most dependent on external conditions (ECLAC 2009). However, Costa Rica recovered quickly. In response to the downturn, the authorities implemented a fiscal stimulus plan (*Plan Escudo*) which included the coverage expansion of the cash transfer programme *Avancemos*, interest rate reductions in the housing sector, increases in non-contributory pensions, and public works stimulus (ILO 2013). Between 2010 and 2012, the rate of GDP per capita growth stabilized at around 3.3 per cent.

The sectoral composition of GDP changed significantly from 2000 to 2012 as the share of the service sector grew and the shares of agricultural and industry sectors decreased. The service sector was by far the largest in terms of share of the GDP over the period, followed by the industrial and agricultural sectors. The share of services in GDP increased from 58.5 per cent in 2000 to 68.6 per cent in 2012 (Cruces et al. 2015: table 2). The expansion of the service sector was related to the increase in foreign direct investment directed at this sector (for instance, tourism-related companies are foreign-owned), which led to an important growth of service exports in total Costa Rican exports (Martinez et al. 2008). The share of the industrial sector declined from 32.1 per cent in 2000 to 25.1 per cent in 2012. The share of the agricultural sector shrank over the period from 9.5 per cent in 2000 to 6.3 per cent in 2012. The economic crisis of 2008 affected mainly the industrial and agricultural sectors, which lost 3.2 per cent and 2.8 per cent of their value added respectively from 2008 to 2009. By contrast, the production of the service sector increased during the crisis. Both the industrial and agricultural sectors recovered their value-added levels in 2010.

The following labour market and income distribution data for Costa Rica are analysed separately for the 2001–9 and 2010–12 periods due to comparability problems arising from a change in the household surveys' sampling frame, a change in the method for measuring incomes, and a change in the poverty lines.

12.3 Unemployment

> The unemployment rate increased from 2001 to 2009 and remained essentially unchanged from 2010 to 2012 overall and for all population groups. Within the period, the unemployment rate increased from 2001 to 2005, diminished between 2005 and 2007, increased during the international crisis, and barely changed afterwards. (Cruces et al. 2015: figure 3)

The unemployment rate (measured as the ratio of unemployment to labour force) increased overall, rising from 6.0 per cent in 2001 (98,684 unemployed persons) to 7.8 per cent in 2009 (165,510 unemployed persons), and from 7.3 per cent in 2010 (149,532 unemployed persons) to 7.8 per cent in 2012 (169,490 unemployed persons) (Table 12.1). Both the number of persons in the labour force and the number of employed persons increased from 2001 to 2009 (an increase of 480,894 and 414,068 persons respectively) and from 2010 to 2012 (a growth of 130,049 and 110,091 persons respectively). These figures suggest that the increase in the unemployment rate over the period was explained by the new entrants into the labour market who could not find a job. Initially, the unemployment rate exhibited an upward trend between 2001 and 2005; it decreased between 2005 and 2007, and peaked at 7.8 per cent during the international crisis. After the Great Recession, and as GDP growth slowed relative to the pre-recession years, the unemployment rate oscillated at around 7.6 per cent in 2010–12.

The unemployment rate increased for youth and adults and for men and women between 2001 and 2009, and remained largely unchanged between 2010 and 2012 for all population groups except for young workers who exhibited an increase in their unemployment rate. All population groups were severely affected by the international crisis and their unemployment rates increased between 2008 and 2009. Following the crisis, the unemployment rate stagnated for adult workers, men, and women, and continued to increase for young workers.

12.4 Job Mix

> The composition of employment by occupational group improved from 2001 to 2009, with workers moving from low-earning and middle-earning occupations to high-earning occupations, and polarized between 2010 and 2011 (the latest we can analyse the series of occupations). Adult workers, men, and women exhibited similar trends over the period, while young workers improved their employment structure between 2001 and 2009 but suffered a worsening between 2010 and 2011. During the international crisis, the distribution of employment by occupational group changed very little overall and for adults, men, and women, and deteriorated for young workers. (Cruces et al. 2015: figure 4)

Between 2001 and 2009, the structure of employment by occupational group improved. Specifically, the share of low-earning occupations in total employment (elementary, services and sales occupations, and agricultural, forestry, and fishery jobs) dropped from 47.5 to 44.3 per cent; the share of middle-earning occupations (clerical, crafts and related trade workers, and plant and machine operators and assemblers) decreased slightly from 28.8 to

27.9 per cent; and the share of high-earning occupations (management, professional, and technicians) rose from 23.7 to 27.9 per cent (Table 12.1). During the international crisis, between 2008 and 2009, the composition of employment by occupational group remained essentially unchanged, but after the Great Recession, some polarization occurred in the occupation space. The share of middle-earning occupations decreased, while the shares of low- and high-earning occupations increased by a similar magnitude between 2010 and 2011.

Adult workers, men, and women benefited from the improvement in the employment structure by occupational group between 2001 and 2009, exhibited small changes during the international crisis, and experienced a polarization between 2010 and 2011. Young workers exhibited an improvement in their employment composition by occupational group between 2001 and 2009, and a deterioration during and after the international crisis.

> The employment structure by occupational position improved between 2001 and 2009 overall and for all population groups. The international crisis of 2008 led to an increase in the share of low-earning positions in total employment in the aggregate and for young workers and women, but did not affect adversely the composition of employment for adults and men. The improving trend resumed between 2010 and 2012 for young workers, while the structure of employment by occupational position remained unchanged in the aggregate and for adults, men, and women. (Cruces et al. 2015: figure 5)

Between 2001 and 2009, the employment structure by occupational position improved through a reduction in the share of low-earning positions (self-employed and unpaid workers) in total employment (drop of 2.9 percentage points) and an increase in the share of high-earning positions (wage/salaried employees and employers) (Table 12.1). The improvement was explained by the increase in the share of wage/salaried employees in total employment, the main occupational position in the Costa Rican labour market. The international crisis of 2008 led to a slight deterioration in the composition of employment by occupational position through the reduction in the share of both employers and wage/salaried employees in total employment (total drop of 0.5 percentage points) and the increase in the share of self-employment. The worsening in the employment composition can be understood in the context of increasing unemployment where economic necessity may have compelled workers to take up free-entry self-employment activities. Between 2010 and 2012 the structure of employment by occupational position remained largely unchanged.

The employment structure by occupational position improved from 2001 to 2009 for all population groups and suffered a worsening during the international crisis, except for adult workers and men whose composition of employment remained essentially unchanged. Between 2010 and 2012, the structure of employment by occupational position barely changed, except for young workers who exhibited an improvement.

> The employment composition by economic sector improved over the course of the period studied. Youth particularly benefited, but so did adults, men, and women. The international crisis of 2008 did not affect adversely the improving trend in the composition of employment by economic sector overall and for all population groups, but young workers and men suffered an increase in the share of low-earning sectors. (Cruces et al. 2015: figure 6)

The share of low-earning sectors in total employment (domestic service, primary activities, and low-tech industry) diminished by 4.8 and 1.6 percentage points from 2001 to 2009 and from 2010 to 2012 respectively. At the other end of the scale, there were increases in the share of high-earning sectors in total employment (public administration, education and health, and skilled services) of 2.6 and 2.1 percentage points over the same periods. The share of middle-earnings sectors (high-tech industry, construction, commerce, and utilities and transportation) increased between 2001 and 2009 (rise of 2.2 percentage points) and suffered a slight decrease between 2010 and 2012 (drop of 0.5 percentage points) (Table 12.1). Despite the fact that the growth process of Costa Rica during the 2000s was mainly based on offshore manufacturing and services activities with a high content of technology, the share of the high-tech industry sector in total employment fell both between 2001 and 2009 and between 2010 and 2012. The reason is that the new jobs created by offshore activities for skilled workers mainly were not numerous enough to compensate for the decline of the manufacturing sector as a whole in total employment (Ernst and Sánchez-Anchorena 2008). The international crisis of 2008 did not impact on the improving trend in the employment structure by economic sector that was taking place. The share of low-earning sectors fell by 0.6 percentage points between 2008 and 2009, while the share of high-earning sectors increased by 0.8 percentage points. The continued improving trend in the employment structure by sector during the international crisis can be explained by the large impact of the crisis on the agriculture and industry sectors, which are classified as low-earning sectors in the Costa Rican economy. As such, the share of low-earning sectors in total employment continued to decrease during the crisis episode.

All population groups benefited from the improving trend in the employment composition by economic sector over the period studied, and young workers and men benefited more than adult workers and women. The international crisis of 2008 did not adversely affect the improving trend in the employment structure by economic sector for adult workers and women. Young workers and men suffered an increase in the share of low-earning sectors in total employment between 2008 and 2009, but that increase was surpassed by the increase in the share of high-earning sectors.

> The educational level of the employed population improved over the period for all population groups, especially young workers. The economic crisis did not have an effect on this improving trend. (Cruces et al. 2015: figure 7)

The share of employed workers with low educational levels (eight years of schooling or less) dropped from 57.3 per cent in 2001 to 47.6 in 2009, and from 50.0 per cent in 2010 to 46.5 per cent in 2012. The shares of employed workers with middle and high educational levels (nine to thirteen years of schooling and over thirteen years of schooling) grew from 27.0 to 31.7 per cent and from 15.7 to 20.8 per cent between 2001 and 2009 respectively. The improving trend continued between 2010 and 2012 when the share of employed workers with medium educational levels increased from 30.8 to 32.6 per cent, and the share of employed workers with high levels of education increased from 19.2 to 20.9 (Table 12.1). The improving trend in the educational level of the employed population was not affected by the international crisis of 2008.[2] We interpret this result as an improvement for the employed population as the level of education is an important predictor of labour earnings. Consequently, the changes in the employment structure by educational level implied an increase in the share of workers that tend to have high levels of earnings and a decline in the share of workers with low earnings levels.[3] Considering that the Costa Rican growth process during the 2000s was based on offshore activities in high-technology industries and services that employ highly educated workers, such as tourism, the increase in the share of workers with high levels of education in total employment seems to be low (Sánchez and Sauma 2010). This pattern of slow improvement in the educational level of the employed population could be related to the small fraction of workers employed by these activities and to their limited contribution to technological learning and upgrading in other sectors of the economy (Ernst and Sánchez-Anchorena 2008). The educational level of the employed population improved over the period studied for all population groups and especially for young workers.

The pattern of improvement in the level of education of the employed population in Costa Rica continued even during the international crisis of

[2] The most frequent value of years of education for employed workers in Costa Rica was six over the entire period (around 29.0 per cent of employed workers had six years of education).

[3] The improvement in the employment structure by educational level is related to changes in the relative demand and supply of workers with high educational levels with corresponding implications for the wage gap by educational group and the unemployment rate of each educational level. We introduce a discussion about the role of these factors in Costa Rica in section 12.5.

2008, overall and for adult workers and women. The share of employed workers with high levels of education stopped increasing between 2008 and 2009 for young workers and men, but the upward trend resumed between 2010 and 2012.

> The share of wage/salaried employees registered with the contributory schemes of the social security system increased between 2001 and 2009 in the population as a whole and for all population groups. Between 2010 and 2012 the share of registered workers remained largely unchanged overall and for adult workers and women, and suffered a slight deterioration for young workers and men. The international crisis of 2008 did not affect the upward trend in the registration rate. (Cruces et al. 2015: figure 8)

The social security system in Costa Rica is composed of contributory schemes and non-contributory schemes which provide pensions and health care as well as other benefits to workers and their families through the *Caja Costarricense de Seguridad Social*. The contributory schemes are mandatory for private- and public-sector employees and voluntary for independent workers. These schemes are funded by contributions from employers, employees, and the government. Different contributory pension schemes exist for public-sector employees, which differ in the amount of the contribution. The non-contributory schemes are directed at poor people and provide health care and pensions. They are totally funded by the government (Sánchez and Sauma 2010).

The social security system records show an increase in the percentage of wage/salaried employees registered with the contributory schemes over the period. The share of wage/salaried employees registered with the social security system grew from 50.7 per cent in 2001 (777,345 registered wage/salaried employees) to 55.3 per cent in 2009 (1,076,494 registered wage/salaried employees), and it rose slightly from 55.7 to 56.1 per cent from 2010 to 2012 (69,382 new registered workers) (Table 12.1). Within the period, the evolution of the share of registered employees was erratic from 2001 to 2005, and the share in 2005 was equal to its level in 2001. The bulk of this increase took place from 2005 to 2009. The international crisis did not affect the improving trend in the share of registered employees that increased even between 2008 and 2009.

The share of wage/salaried employees enrolled in the social security system increased between 2001 and 2009 for all population groups. Between 2010 and 2012, the share of registered workers increased for women, remained essentially unchanged for adult workers, and deteriorated slightly for youth and men. The international crisis of 2008 did not negatively affect the improving trend in the share of wage/salaried employees registered with the social security system for any of the population groups.

12.5 Labour Earnings

> Five years of falling labour earnings from 2001 to 2005 were followed by four years of rising labour earnings from 2006 to 2009. The increase was large enough to raise labour earnings in 2009 when compared to where they had started (2001). The upward trend continued between 2010 and 2012. The pattern of falling labour earnings between 2001 and 2005 and rising labour earnings from 2006 to 2009 and from 2010 to 2012 held for all population groups. The evidence of earning changes by employment categories indicates that labour earnings increases between 2001 and 2009 were larger for low-earning categories in some cases (educational position and educational level) and for high-earning categories in others (occupational group and economic sector). Labour earning changes between 2010 and 2012 tended to be positive for high-earning categories and negative for low-earning categories. The international crisis of 2008 did not impact negatively on labour earnings overall and for any of the population groups, but led to earnings reductions for some employment categories.
>
> (Cruces et al. 2015: figure 9)

Average monthly earnings expressed in dollars at 2005 purchasing power parity (PPP) increased by 11.0 per cent from 2001 to 2009 and by 5.0 per cent from 2010 to 2012, climbing from US$750 in 2001 to US$832 in 2009 and from US$794 in 2010 to US$833 in 2012 (Table 12.1). However, the experiences within the period varied substantially. From 2001 to 2005, Costa Rica suffered a decline of 10.0 per cent in average labour earnings. This reduction was explained by the high level of inflation, especially in 2004 and 2005, and the small adjustment in minimum wages (Sánchez and Sauma 2010). After that period, a long and steady recovery set in that brought with it an increase in labour earnings during all of the subsequent years; by 2007, the level of labour earnings surpassed the 2001 level. The international crisis of 2008 did not affect this upward trend.

The same U-shaped pattern for labour earnings, albeit with different degrees of intensity, appears to apply to all population groups (young and adult workers, men and women).

Among employment categories, all of them exhibited earnings increases between 2001 and 2009 that were larger for low-earning categories in some cases and for high-earning categories in others. Between 2010 and 2012, labour earnings tended to increase for high-earning categories and to decrease for low-earning categories. Among occupational groups, the increase in labour earnings between 2001 and 2009 was larger for workers in high-earning occupations (management, professional, and technicians) compared to the change for workers in low-earning occupations (elementary, agricultural, forestry and fishery occupations, and services and sales jobs). From 2001 to 2009, labour earnings of workers in low-earning positions (self-employed) exhibited a larger increase than labour income gains of workers in high-earning positions (wage/salaried employees and employers). Labour earnings increases between 2001 and 2009 were larger for workers in high-earning sectors (public administration, skilled services, education, and health) compared to workers in low-earning sectors (domestic service, primary activities, low-tech industry). Between 2001 and 2009, workers with low levels of education exhibited a larger earnings increase when compared to workers with high levels of education, but lower than the earnings gains of workers with medium levels of education. Between 2010 and 2012, workers in low-earning occupations and low-earning positions enjoyed larger earnings increases compared to workers in high-earning occupations and high-earning positions respectively. Labour earnings fell between 2010 and 2012 for workers in low-earning sectors, and increased for workers in high-earning sectors. Workers with low educational levels suffered an earnings reduction between 2010 and 2012, while workers with medium and high levels of education exhibited earnings increases.

The evidence of increasing labour earnings between 2001 and 2009 for workers with low and high levels of education and falling labour earnings for workers with medium levels of education can be interpreted in light of previous findings of improving educational levels of the Costa Rican employed population and improving employment structure by occupational group and economic sector over that period. The improving employment structure by occupational group and economic sector implied an increase in the share of occupations and sectors that can be expected to employ workers with high and medium educational levels, such as management, professional, and technical occupations, skilled services, public administration, and education and health sectors, and a reduction in the share of occupations and sectors that employ workers with low educational levels, such as elementary jobs, agricultural occupations, primary activities, and low-tech industry sectors. This evidence indicates that the demand for workers with high and medium educational levels relative to those with low educational levels increased between 2001 and 2009. On the other hand, the educational level of persons in the labour force improved over the same period, indicating an increase in the relative supply of workers with high and medium educational levels (Cruces et al. 2015: table 8). The prediction of a supply and demand analysis is that the relative wages of workers with high and medium educational levels relative to those with low educational levels will rise or fall depending on which effect dominates (increase in the relative demand versus increase in the relative supply). In the Costa Rican labour market, the relative wages of workers with high educational levels relative to those with low educational levels was essentially unchanged from 2001 to 2009; the relative wages of workers with medium to low educational levels fell over the period;

and the relative wages of workers with high educational levels relative to those with medium educational levels increased (Cruces et al. 2015: table 7). The adjustment process also led to an increase in the unemployment rate of all educational groups between 2001 and 2009 with a larger increase for workers with low levels of education (Cruces et al. 2015: table 9). For the period from 2010 to 2012 our evidence indicates an ambiguous change in the relative demand for workers with high and medium educational levels relative to those with low educational levels, i.e. the structure of employment by occupational position polarized during those years while the structure by economic sector improved together with an increase in the relative supply of workers with high and medium levels of education. The relative wages of workers with high educational levels relative to those with low and medium educational levels increased, and the relative wages of workers with medium to low educational levels also grew. The unemployment rate increased for all educational levels with the largest increases for workers with medium and low levels of education.

The international crisis of 2008 did not impact negatively on the upward trend of labour earnings overall, for any of the population groups and most of the employment categories. The only employment category that suffered a reduction in labour earnings between 2008 and 2009 was workers in low-earning sectors. Due to the comparability problems between the 2001–9 and 2010–12 series, it is not possible to assess whether workers in low-earning sectors recovered their pre-crisis earnings level in the following years.

12.6 Poverty and Inequality

> The poverty rate and the rate of working poor households decreased from 2001 to 2009 for all poverty lines. From 2010 to 2012 there was a slight increase in the extreme poverty rate and in the poverty rate measured by the US$2.5 dollars-a-day international line. All poverty indicators increased during the international crisis of 2008; because of non-comparability of the underlying survey instruments, the poverty rates for 2009 cannot be compared with the poverty rates afterwards.
>
> (Cruces et al. 2015: figure 10)

The moderate poverty rate (measured by the country's official poverty line) fell from 20.3 per cent in 2001 to 18.5 per cent in 2009, and from 25.9 per cent in 2010 to 24.0 per cent in 2012. The extreme poverty rate decreased from 7.1 per cent in 2001 to 5.1 per cent in 2009 and increased slightly from 5.7 per cent in 2010 to 5.9 per cent in 2012. The percentages of working poor (defined as the proportion of persons in the population living in poor households where at least one member works) decreased from 11.8 to 10.9 per cent between 2001 and 2009 and from 17.2 to 15.4 per cent between 2010 and 2012 (Table 12.1). Within the period, the poverty indicators decreased from 2001 to 2007, and then increased up to 2009, a period that included the Great Recession. The number of moderately poor persons increased by 118,321 and the number of extremely poor persons rose by 48,997 between 2008 and 2009. The analysis of trends based on the 2.5 and 4 dollars-a-day PPP international poverty lines shows a reduction in the poverty rates between 2001 and 2009. The poverty rate based on the 2.5 dollars-a-day international poverty line fell from 13.8 per cent in 2001 to 7.5 per cent in 2009. The reduction using the 4 dollars-a-day poverty line was from 26.7 per cent in 2001 to 17.4 per cent in 2009. Between 2010 and 2012, both poverty rates changed slightly. There was a reduction when the poverty rate is measured through the 4 dollars-a-day poverty line (from 12.7 to 12.2 per cent) and an increase using the 2.5 dollars-a-day line (from 4.5 to 4.7 per cent). Within the period, both poverty indicators decreased substantially from 2001 to 2007, increased between 2008 and 2009, and stagnated during the post-crisis period.

The poverty patterns reported in the last paragraph can be understood by examining incomes from various sources. The analysis of sources of household total income indicates that labour income and pensions increased between 2001 and 2009 (Cruces et al. 2015: figure 11). The increase in pensions (21.7 per cent between 2001 and 2008, the latest we can analyse the series of non-labour incomes over the period 2001–9) was the most important factor to explain the increase in total household income. Between 2010 and 2012, capital income exhibited the largest increase (a rise of 19.6 per cent), followed by labour incomes (an increase of 5.6). Income from government transfers and pensions fell by 4.2 and 1.0 per cent respectively during those years. However, UNDP (2014) reported that non-contributory pensions, scholarships, assistance to poor families with children, and cash transfers from the national welfare office reduced moderate poverty by 2.5 percentage points and extreme poverty by 2.9 percentage points in 2012.

> Household per capita income inequality and labour earnings inequality decreased from 2001 to 2005, and then started an upward trend from 2006 to 2009, that continued between 2010 and 2012. During the international crisis of 2008, inequality increased. (Cruces et al. 2015: figure 12)

From 2001 to 2005, household per capita income inequality measured by the Gini coefficient decreased from 0.501 in 2001 to 0.473 in 2005. From 2005 to 2009, it increased and reached 0.504 in 2009. The upward trend continued from 2010 to 2012 when the Gini coefficient of household per capita income grew from 0.480 to 0.485. The Gini coefficient of labour earnings among employed workers decreased from 0.464 to 0.440 between 2001 and 2005, rose to 0.459 in 2009, and continued with the upward trend from 2010 to 2012 when the Gini coefficient increased from 0.466 to 0.471 (Table 12.1). The increase in labour income inequality between 2010 and 2012 is consistent with the evidence of rising labour earnings for workers in high-earning employment categories and reducing labour earnings for workers in low-earning categories during this period.

Changes in household per capita income inequality in Costa Rica have been related mainly to changes in labour income. Azevedo et al. (2013b) decomposed the change in the Gini coefficient of household per capita income for the period 2004–8 and found that changes in labour incomes contributed to the inequality increase over this period (the Gini coefficient of household per capita income increased from 0.482 in 2004 to 0.492 in 2007 and closed the subperiod in 0.486). On the other hand, changes in non-labour incomes, such as government transfers and demographic changes (e.g. the share of adults per household) were inequality-reducing. Trejos and Oviedo (2012) analysed the period 2002–9, when inequality of household per capita income increased, and found through a decomposition approach that changes in labour income were inequality-reducing, while changes in non-labour incomes were inequality-increasing with the only exception of incomes from government transfers. Finally, Sauma and Trejos (2014) reported an inequality-reducing effect of social spending, taxes, and social security contributions in Costa Rica in 2010. Other studies have analysed the factors behind the evolution of labour income inequality. Azevedo et al. (2013a) used a decomposition approach and found that changes in the education wage premium (or the 'price effect') and changes in the distribution of the stock of education (the 'quantity effect') were inequality-increasing in Costa Rica between 2000 and 2009. Gasparini et al. (2011) found a reduction in the wage premium in Costa Rica between 2000 and 2009 that was associated with an increase in the relative supply and a small increase in the relative demand of skilled workers. Finally, the increase in labour earnings inequality between 2004 and 2009 has been associated with different policy measures implemented by the government of Costa Rica, such as the liberalization of trade, tax exemption, and promotion policies for exports, which became more intensive in skilled labour (Sánchez and Sauma 2010).

12.7 Conclusions

By Latin American standards, Costa Rica experienced moderate economic growth during the 2000s. The international crisis hurt the economy and there was a recession in 2009, from which the country quickly recovered, surpassing pre-crisis GDP levels by 2010.

Most labour market indicators improved from 2001 to 2009 and from 2010 to 2012 (the periods for which we could construct comparable statistics). The employment composition by occupational group improved between 2001 and 2009 as workers moved from elementary and agricultural occupations to better-paying occupations, such as management, professional, and technical jobs. The structure of employment by occupational position improved both from 2001 to 2009 and from 2010 to 2012, mainly through the increase in the share of wage/salaried employees in total employment. The employment composition by economic sector also improved between 2001 and 2009 and between 2010 and 2012, as workers moved from low-paying sectors such as primary activities and low-tech industry to better-paying sectors such as skilled services, public administration, and education and health. The share of wage/salaried employees registered with the contributory schemes of the social security system increased from 2001 to 2009. The educational level of the employed population and labour earnings grew between 2001 and 2009 and between 2010 and 2012. All poverty diminished from 2001 to 2009, and the moderate poverty rate and poverty measured by the 4 dollars-a-day poverty line also decreased from 2010 to 2012. The Gini coefficient of labour earnings fell from 2001 to 2009.

Some indicators deteriorated during the periods analysed. The unemployment rate increased from 2001 to 2009 and remained largely unchanged from 2010 to 2012. The employment structure by occupational group polarized from 2010 to 2011. The share of wage/salaried employees who contributed to the social security system remained unchanged between 2010 and 2012. The extreme poverty rate, the poverty rate measured by the 2.5 dollars-a-day international line, household per capita income, and labour earnings inequality increased between 2010 and 2012.

The international crisis of 2008 impacted negatively on some of the indicators analysed. The unemployment rate increased, the employment structure by occupational position deteriorated slightly, and all poverty and inequality indicators increased between 2008 and 2009. Due to the non-comparability of the underlying survey instruments, it was not possible to assess whether these indicators returned to their pre-crisis levels in the following years.

Young workers and women had worse labour market outcomes over the entire period compared to adults and men respectively, and seemed to be more vulnerable to the international crisis. The unemployment rate was higher for young compared to adult workers, the shares of young employed workers in low-earning occupational groups and economic sectors were larger than the shares of adult workers, the percentage of young wage/salaried employees who contributed to the social security system was lower when compared to adults, and labour earnings of young workers were below those of adults. On the other hand, the share of young workers in low-earning occupational positions was lower compared to adults. In addition to the generally inferior situation of young workers in the labour market compared to adults, youth were more affected by the international crisis: the increase in the unemployment rate between 2008 and 2009 was larger for youth than for adults, as was the increase in the share of workers in low-earning positions. Disaggregating by gender, we found that men had better labour market outcomes than women for all of the indicators analysed. Women were more affected than men by the international crisis of 2008. Women suffered a larger increase in the unemployment rate and in the share of workers in low-earning positions between 2008 and 2009.

In summary, most labour market conditions were in a better state in 2009 than they were at the start of the millennium and all population groups were quite resilient to the international crisis. From 2010 to 2012, labour market conditions had a general improvement but a larger number of deteriorations occurred in comparison to the period 2001–9.

References

Azevedo, J. P., G. Inchauste, and V. Sanfelice (2013a). 'Decomposing the Decline in Income Inequality in Latin America'. Policy Research Working Paper 6715. Washington, DC: World Bank.

Azevedo, J. P., M. E. Dávalos, C. Díaz-Bonilla, B. Atuesta, and R. A. Castañeda (2013b). 'Fifteen Years of Inequality in Latin America. How Have Labor Markets Helped?'. Policy Research Working Paper 6384. Washington, DC: World Bank.

CEDLAS and World Bank (2014). SEDLAC—Socio-Economic Database for Latin America and the Caribbean. Centro de Estudios Distributivos, Laborales y Sociales, Facultad de Ciencias Económicas, Universidad Nacional de La Plata and World Bank Poverty Group LCR. Available at <http://sedlac.econo.unlp.edu.ar/eng/index.php>, accessed 2014.

Cruces, G., G. Fields, D. Jaume, and M. Viollaz (2015). 'The Growth–Employment–Poverty Nexus in Latin America in the 2000s: Costa Rica Country Study'. WIDER Working Paper 2015/074. Helsinki: UNU-WIDER.

ECLAC (2009). 'Costa Rica: Evolución económica durante 2008 y perspectivas para 2009'. Santiago de Chile: United Nations.

Ernst, C. and D. Sánchez-Anchorena (2008). 'Offshoring and Employment in the Developing World: The Case of Costa Rica'. Employment Working Paper 4. Geneva: International Labour Organization, Economic and Labour Market Analysis Department.

Gasparini, L., S. Galiani, G. Cruces, and P. Acosta (2011). 'Educational Upgrading and Returns to Skills in Latin America: Evidence from a Supply–Demand Framework, 1990–2010'. IZA Working Paper 6244. Bonn: Institute for the Study of Labor.

ILO (2013). 'Frente a la crisis en Europa: Reflexiones para el caso de Costa Rica'. ILO Notes. Geneva: International Labour Organization, Regional Office for Latin America and the Caribbean.

IMF (2002). 'Costa Rica: Selected Issues'. IMF Country Report No. 02/89. Washington, DC: International Monetary Fund.

IMF (2006). 'Costa Rica: 2006 Article IV Consultation'. IMF Country Report No. 06/416. Washington, DC: International Monetary Fund.

IMF (2008). 'Costa Rica: 2007 Article IV Consultation'. IMF Country Report No. 08/97. Washington, DC: International Monetary Fund.

Martinez, J. M., R. Padilla, and C. Schatan (2008). 'Comercio internacional: De bienes a servicios. Los casos de Costa Rica y Mexico'. Serie Estudios y Perspectivas 97. ECLAC, Industry and International Trade Unit. Mexico, DF: United Nations.

Sánchez, M. and P. Sauma (2010). 'Implicaciones de la politica macroeconomica, los choques externos y los sistemas de proteccion social en la pobreza, la desigualdad y la vulnerabilidad en America Latina y el Caribe: Costa Rica'. ECLAC, Project Documents Collection. Mexico, DF: United Nations.

Sauma, P. and J. D. Trejos (2014). 'Gasto publico social, impuestos, redistribucion del ingreso y pobreza en Costa Rica'. CEQ Working Paper 18. New Orleans: Tulane University.

Trejos, J. D. and L. A. Oviedo (2012). 'Cambios en la distribución del ingreso familiar en Costa Rica durante la primera década del siglo XXI', *Revista de Ciencias Económicas* 30 (2): 9–29. San Jose: Universidad de Costa Rica.

UNDP (2014). 'Reducir la pobreza en Costa Rica es posible: Propuestas para la accion'. Serie Cuadernos de Desarrollo Humano. San José: United Nations Development Programme.

World Bank (2014). World Development Indicators. Available at <http://data.worldbank.org/data-catalog/world-development-indicators>, accessed April 2014.

13

Dominican Republic

13.1 Introduction

This chapter on labour markets and growth in the Dominican Republic since 2000 is one of sixteen studies of Latin American countries, each of which analyses the growth–employment–poverty nexus and aims to answer the following broad questions: Has economic growth resulted in economic development via improved labour market conditions in Latin America in the 2000s, and have these improvements halted or been reversed since the Great Recession? How do the rate and character of economic growth, changes in the various labour market indicators, and changes in poverty relate to each other?

To answer these questions, we analyse the growth experience of the Dominican Republic during the 2000s and a wide set of labour market indicators that we assign to one of two different categories: employment and earnings indicators, and poverty and income inequality indicators. More specifically, for the group of employment and earnings indicators we construct statistics on the following variables: the unemployment rate; the employment structure by occupational group, employment position, economic sector, registration of workers with the social security system, and educational level; and mean labour earnings and hourly wages. We present all these indicators for the employed population as a whole and for different population groups (youth, adults, men, and women). For the group of poverty and income inequality indicators, we compute poverty rates using the official moderate and extreme poverty lines and the international lines of 2.5 and 4 dollars a day. We also calculate the Gini coefficient of household per capita income and labour earnings.

All of the statistics in this chapter on labour market conditions and income distribution are obtained using microdata from the October wave of the Encuesta Nacional de Fuerza de Trabajo (ENFT) for the years 2000–12. In the years 2005 and 2008, the country implemented changes in its household surveys. The pre-2005 and post-2005 surveys are fully comparable except in relation to non-labour incomes. While the change does not affect comparability in terms of labour earnings, it does impede seamless comparison of per capita household income (poverty rates and Gini index). The pre-2008 and post-2008 surveys differ only in the classification of occupations. As a consequence, comparability problems in the analysis of this labour market indicator may arise between the 2000–7 and 2008–12 periods. The nationwide surveys were processed following a harmonization methodology and incorporated into the SEDLAC—Socio-Economic Database for Latin America and the Caribbean (CEDLAS and World Bank 2014).[1] The resulting labour market indicators were compiled into a large number of tables and figures, which are available in an earlier version of this study (henceforth, Cruces et al. 2015). Chapter 1 of this book provides the definition for each of the indicators we analyse here, while Cruces et al. (2015) includes details on definitions and classification systems used by Dominican Republic's household surveys, and on comparability issues of these surveys over time.

13.2 Economic Growth

> During the 2000s, the Dominican Republic experienced above average economic growth. Within the period, GDP per capita stagnated through 2004 and, for the most part, grew rapidly from 2005 through 2012. However, economic growth slowed during the international crisis of 2008 but remained positive in every year. (Cruces et al. 2015: figures 1 and 2)

From 2000 to 2012, the Dominican economy grew at an above-average rate by Latin American standards. GDP per capita increased by 53.3 per cent, while the average for the region's eighteen countries was 36.2 per cent during the same period. GDP (measured at 2005 PPP dollars) grew by 81.8 per cent and GDP per employed person rose by 41.1 per cent. GDP per capita grew at an annual rate of 3.6 per cent over the period with a minimum of −1.7 per cent in 2003 and a maximum of 9.1 per cent in 2006 (Table 13.1).

At the beginning of the 2000s, economic growth was erratic. From 2000 to 2004, GDP per capita increased by only 2.4 per cent due to years of economic growth (2000 and 2002) followed by years of decline (2003 and 2004). The export-oriented growth model that had been in place in the Dominican Republic since the 1990s faced a series of external shocks during this period, which included a rise in oil prices and the slowdown in the US and Europe in

[1] See Cruces et al. (2015: table 1) for details on the size of Dominican Republic household surveys.

Table 13.1 Dominican Republic: Evolution of growth and labour market indicators over the 2000s

		2000	2001	2002	2003	2004	2005	2006	2007	2008	2009	2010	2011	2012	
Growth Indicators	GDP per capita	5,737	5,751	5,991	5,886	5,876	6,326	6,901	7,380	7,660	7,818	8,312	8,573	8,794	
	GDP per capita growth rate	4.00	0.24	4.18	−1.75	−0.19	7.67	9.08	6.94	3.80	2.05	6.33	3.14	2.58	
Employment and Earnings Indicators	Employment-to-population ratio	53.83	52.79	53.24	52.70	53.19	52.74	54.09	54.36	54.51	52.46	53.80	54.75	55.20	
	Unemployment rate	4.72	5.49	4.11	4.92	4.21	4.25	3.64	3.20	2.07	3.85	3.14	3.94	4.92	
	Share of low-earnings occupations	48.77	48.84	49.98	47.81	48.52	48.63	49.84	50.28	50.42	52.54	52.08	53.59	52.96	
	Share of mid-earnings occupations	35.89	35.62	34.63	35.13	35.01	35.14	33.42	33.38	32.42	30.44	31.12	30.60	30.27	
	Share of high-earnings occupations	15.35	15.53	15.39	17.06	16.47	16.24	16.74	16.34	17.17	17.03	16.81	15.81	16.76	
	Share of employers	2.59	3.86	3.19	3.49	4.72	4.42	3.87	4.23	4.04	4.86	3.75	3.18	3.12	
	Share of wage/salaried employees	56.90	54.30	53.29	54.80	55.18	52.83	53.56	54.23	52.14	51.07	50.62	51.33	53.18	
	Share of self-employed workers	38.98	40.26	42.16	40.27	38.57	39.99	40.04	39.14	40.20	42.56	43.36	43.79	41.87	
	Share of unpaid family workers	1.53	1.58	1.36	1.44	1.53	2.76	2.52	2.41	3.62	1.51	2.27	1.70	1.82	
	Share of workers in low-earnings sectors	31.21	28.51	29.71	27.65	28.66	27.59	27.40	27.55	26.54	25.84	25.55	25.85	25.70	
	Share of workers in mid-earnings sectors	53.17	55.73	54.13	55.13	55.60	56.17	56.73	56.25	56.15	57.39	57.17	56.65	57.53	
	Share of workers in high-earnings sectors	15.62	15.77	16.16	17.22	15.74	16.24	15.86	16.20	17.30	16.77	17.28	17.51	16.77	
	Share of low-educated workers	56.47	57.22	55.21	54.36	53.52	53.69	52.16	50.13	49.63	49.56	48.32	47.27	46.09	

	Share of medium-educated workers	27.37	27.67	28.25	28.73	29.21	29.80	31.01	32.66	31.11	31.67	33.16	35.50	35.19	
	Share of high-educated workers	16.15	15.11	16.55	16.91	17.27	16.51	16.84	17.20	19.26	18.76	18.52	17.24	18.71	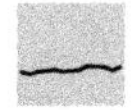
	Share of workers registered with SS	...	...	...	...	...	46.66	53.89	64.07	71.43	71.75	74.72	71.18	70.89	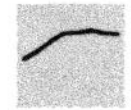
	Mean labour earnings	330.0	327.0	307.6	263.1	217.3	257.8	270.2	258.9	251.7	271.3	261.1	248.1	241.8	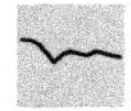
Poverty and Inequality Indicators	Official extreme poverty rate	7.77	6.79	8.84	10.42	14.50	9.40	8.09	7.31	6.89	5.92	5.25	5.43	5.35	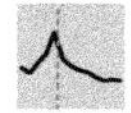
	Official moderate poverty rate	24.68	24.83	25.53	32.91	39.12	31.31	28.60	27.50	28.69	25.89	25.80	24.51	24.22	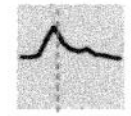
	Poverty rate 2.5 dollars a day	15.71	15.84	17.61	21.83	27.77	21.08	18.66	17.90	18.44	16.40	16.14	13.97	14.55	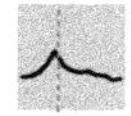
	Poverty rate 4 dollars a day	32.63	33.27	33.07	41.73	49.50	40.48	37.48	36.41	37.89	34.71	35.12	33.34	33.26	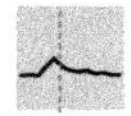
	GINI of household per capita income	0.519	0.504	0.500	0.520	0.519	0.499	0.519	0.487	0.490	0.489	0.472	0.474	0.457	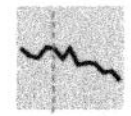
	GINI of labour earnings	0.499	0.487	0.483	0.481	0.479	0.476	0.484	0.464	0.457	0.471	0.464	0.468	0.451	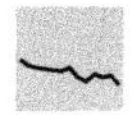

Note: The shaded figures of labour market indicators represent statistical significant improvements at 5 per cent between the initial and final years for all the employment and earnings indicators and poverty and inequality indicators. The only exceptions are the share of mid-earnings occupations, share of mid-earnings sectors, and share of medium-educated workers for which we did not assign welfare evaluation criteria. The vertical lines indicate that the series 2000–4 and 2005–12 are not comparable due to changes in the household survey. For the poverty rates and the Gini coefficient of household per capita income we compared 2005 and 2012.

Source: SEDLAC (CEDLAS and World Bank 2014) and World Development Indicators (World Bank 2014b).

2001 (Agosin 2009; Godínez and Máttar 2009).[2] However, the country faced a bigger shock in 2003 when a banking crisis arose mainly from governance problems that went undetected for many years (IMF 2003). The banking crisis contributed to the flight of capital, an increase in the inflation rate, a sharp rise in the public debt, and the devaluation of the currency (IMF 2003; Agosin 2009). GDP per capita fell by 1.8 per cent in 2003.

The government that took office in 2004 formulated a programme to address the weaknesses in macroeconomic policies. The rebound in confidence and activity led to a virtuous cycle of declining inflation and interest rates, and exchange rate stability (IMF 2005). From 2005 to 2008 the Dominican economy exhibited rapid economic growth, with an annual GDP per capita growth rate of 6.9 per cent and GDP growing at 8.4 per cent a year. The growth process was based on non-tradable sectors during this period, mainly communications, commerce, financial intermediation, construction, and transport. In particular, the growth of the communications sector was remarkable due to important foreign and domestic investments in telecommunications (Agosin 2009; ILO 2013; ILO 2014). This pattern of growth, based on non-tradable sectors, was characterized by a high capital–labour ratio, which differentiates the Dominican Republic from other Latin American countries over the period studied (Abdullaev and Estevão 2013).

In 2009, the economy suffered a slowdown as a consequence of the international crisis, with GDP per capita growth falling from 3.8 per cent in 2008 to only 2.0 per cent in 2009. The deceleration was the result of the global credit crunch, a weak external demand, and a procyclical fiscal policy, such as a reduction in social spending (IMF 2009; Lavigne and Vargas 2013). The government increased the stock of public debt to address the increasing balance of payment needs and conducted countercyclical policies (IMF 2011). The pre-crisis growth rate was surpassed in 2010 (6.3 per cent), though there were subsequent slowdowns in 2011 (3.1 per cent) and 2012 (2.6 per cent).

13.3 Unemployment

The unemployment rate fell from 2000 to 2008, increased from 2008 to 2012, and ended up slightly higher in 2012 than it had been in 2000. This V-shaped pattern was also observed for youth and adults, and for men and women. The unemployment rate was impacted adversely by the

[2] The most dynamic sectors since the 1990s had been tourism and export free zones (*maquilas*) which benefited from certain incentive policies such as preferential access to US markets, tax exemptions, and lower labour costs.

> international crisis: it increased between 2008 and 2009, dropped in 2010, though not to the pre-crisis level, and continued to rise through 2012.
> (Cruces et al. 2015: figure 3)

The unemployment rate (measured as the ratio of unemployment to labour force) increased from 4.7 per cent in 2000 (146,457 unemployed people) to 4.9 per cent in 2012 (204,390 unemployed people) (Table 13.1). The evolution of unemployment followed a V-shaped pattern: it fell from 4.7 per cent in 2000 to 2.1 per cent in 2008, the lowest value of the series, and increased to 4.9 per cent in 2012. The international crisis had an impact on unemployment that rose from 2.1 to 3.8 per cent between 2008 and 2009 (66,862 new unemployed people). The increase in the rate and number of unemployed people occurred mainly due to a reduction in the number of employed persons. From 2008 to 2009, the number of people in the labour force increased just by 17,090 persons, while the number of employed persons fell by 49,772. While there was a respite from rising unemployment in 2010, the unemployment rate grew again in 2011 and 2012, when GDP slowed down, and closed the period at 4.9 per cent, a level that is still above its pre-crisis value.

While the unemployment rate increased for youth, adults, and men between 2000 and 2012, it decreased for women between those years. The unemployment rate of all population groups mirrored the aggregate trend, with a low point in 2008. All population groups—youth, adults, men, and women—were affected by the rise in unemployment that ensued during the international crisis, and they all experienced a slight recovery in 2010, followed by further increases in unemployment in 2011 and 2012.

13.4 Job Mix

> In terms of the composition of employment by occupational group, there was a slight worsening over the period, with an increase in the shares of low-earning and high-earning occupations and a consequent decrease in the middle-earnings occupations' share. The evidence indicates a slight deterioration over time for youth, adults, men, and women. For the employed population as a whole, the share of low-earning occupations continued to increase during the international crisis and the share of high-earning occupations fell and, as of 2012, the pre-crisis level had not been reached. (Cruces et al. 2015: figure 4)

The share of the following occupations shrank between 2000 and 2012: plant and machine operators (drop of 3.7 percentage points); agricultural occupations (drop of 2.4 percentage points); and crafts and trades occupations (drop of 2.3 percentage points). The share of the following occupations grew: elementary occupations (increase of 4.9 percentage points); and services and sales jobs (increase of 1.8 percentage points).[3] The share of the other occupational groups exhibited smaller changes. These changes in the occupational composition of employment can be interpreted as a slight worsening since the share of low-earning occupations (elementary, agricultural, forestry and fishery occupations, and services and sales jobs) increased by 4.2 percentage points and the share of high-earning occupations (management, professional jobs, and technicians and associate professionals) also increased but by a smaller magnitude (rise of 1.4 percentage points). Consequently, the share of mid-earning occupations declined over the period (clerical, crafts and trades occupations, and plant and machine operators) (Table 13.1).

The evolution of employment composition by occupational group followed the aggregate pattern for all population groups who exhibited a slight worsening over the period.

During the international crisis, the composition of employment deteriorated in the aggregate and for young, adult workers, and men. The share of low-earning occupations continued to increase, while the share of high-earning occupations began a downward trend and by 2012 was still below the pre-crisis level. For women, the previous trend of slight worsening continued during the international crisis.

> The employment structure by occupational position deteriorated; the share of wage/salaried employees fell and the share of self-employed workers rose. While this trend holds true for all the population groups studied, it was particularly dramatic among young workers. The prior negative trend in this indicator continued during the international crisis. By 2012, though, the share of wage/salaried employees had surpassed its pre-crisis level. (Cruces et al. 2015: figure 5)

From 2000 to 2012, the share of wage/salaried employees—the largest occupational category—decreased from 56.9 to 53.2 per cent, while the share of the self-employed increased from 40.0 to 41.9 per cent. The share of employers and unpaid workers exhibited small increases, from 2.6 to 3.1 per cent and from 1.5 to 1.8 per cent respectively (Table 13.1). The evolution of the share of wage/salaried employees was erratic; it hovered around 55 per cent from 2000 to 2004—when the economy changed its productive structure radically—and

[3] The change in the household surveys implemented in 2008 led to a recategorization of agricultural, forestry, and fishery occupations and of elementary occupations. Of the total changes experienced by these two occupations over the period (increase in the share of elementary occupations and fall in the share of agricultural, forestry, and fishery occupations), 2.0 percentage points took place between 2007 and 2008 and are related to the change in the categorization. Since both of these categories fall into the low-earning occupations group, this recategorization does not affect our overall conclusions about the evolution of the occupational composition of the employed population.

then began a downward trend, with some ups and downs over the period. The worsening in the structure of employment by occupational position is striking considering that the unemployment rate was low and, up to 2007, exhibited a declining trend. The change in the productive structure of the economy following the episode of the banking crisis in 2003 provides an explanation. The sectors that gained share in the economy (mainly telecommunications, commerce, construction, and financial intermediation) were less labour-intensive compared to the manufacturing sector that was the driving force of the economy before the banking crisis. Consequently, economic necessity may have compelled displaced workers from the industry sectors to look for free-entry self-employment activities. The effect of the international crisis is difficult to discern since the negative trend for this indicator began in 2007, i.e. before the crisis, and continued through 2010, i.e. after the crisis had subsided.

The share of paid employees in total employment decreased for all population groups from 2000 to 2012, and the drop was greater among youth and men compared to adults and women. The crisis had a greater impact on the occupational position of adults and men than on youth and women: between 2008 and 2009, the share of wage/salaried workers increased for youth and women, while it diminished for adults and men. However, for both adults and men the decline had started in 2007.

> The employment composition by economic sector improved over the course of the period studied, overall and for all population groups. During the international crisis, the distribution of employment was squeezed, i.e. the share of mid-earning sectors increased and the shares of low- and high-earning sectors fell, and this trend continued up to the end of the period. (Cruces et al. 2015: figure 6)

The period 2000–12 witnessed major changes in the composition of employment by sector in the Dominican Republic. The share of workers in low-earning sectors (domestic service, primary activities, and low-tech industries) diminished by 5.5 percentage points, from 31.2 per cent in 2000 to 25.7 per cent in 2012. The share of workers in middle-earning sectors (high-tech industry, commerce, utilities and transportation, and education and health) increased by 4.4 percentage points, from 53.2 to 57.5 per cent. The share in high-earning sectors (construction, public administration, and skilled services) rose as well, by 1.2 percentage points, from 15.6 to 16.8 per cent (Table 13.1). Underlying the reduction in the share of low-earning sectors in total employment was the change in the productive structure of the Dominican economy. Before the severe banking crisis in 2003, the economy's growth was based on export-oriented sectors, mainly in the production of textiles by the *maquila* or export free zone, captured by the low-tech industry sector in our statistics. The low-tech industry sector's share exhibited the largest reduction among the low-earning sectors, falling by 5.1 percentage points over the period. After the episode of the banking crisis, the economy's growth switched to non-tradable sectors, mainly telecommunications, commerce, construction, and financial intermediation. But these sectors are less labour-intensive than the manufacturing sector, and their shares in total employment showed small increases during the period. The commerce, construction, and utilities and transportation sectors increased their shares by 0.6, 1.1, and 1.5 percentage points respectively. The reduction in the share of low-earning sectors in total employment was then offset mainly by the increase in the share of employment in other services sectors, like education and health, and domestic service, sectors characterized by their low productivity and low earning levels (Abdullaev and Estevão 2013; ILO 2013). During the international crisis of 2008, the distribution of employment by economic sector was squeezed: the share of mid-earning sectors increased, while the shares of low- and high-paid sectors declined by a similar magnitude. This trend continued up to the end of the period.

There was no dramatic difference between population groups (youth and adults, men and women) in the reduction in the share of low-earning sectors and in the increase in the share of high-earning sectors in total employment. The international crisis of 2008 led to an increase in the share of mid-earning sectors along with a reduction in the shares of both low- and high-earning sectors for young and adult workers and for men. This trend continued up to the end of the period for these three population groups. For women, the improving trend continued even during the international crisis.

> The educational level of the employed population improved over the period for all population groups through the increase in the share of employed workers with medium levels of education mainly. The international crisis brought this trend to a standstill. (Cruces et al. 2015: figure 7)

The share of employed workers with low educational levels (eight years of schooling or less) dropped from 56.5 per cent in 2000 to 46.1 per cent in 2012, while the shares of employed workers with middle and high educational levels (nine to thirteen years of schooling and over thirteen years of schooling) grew from 27.4 per cent in 2000 to 35.2 per cent in 2012 and from 16.1 to 18.7 per cent respectively (Table 13.1).[4] We interpret this result as an improvement for the employed population as the level of education is an important predictor of labour earnings. Consequently, the changes in the employment structure by educational level implied an increase in the share of workers that

[4] The most frequent value of years of education for employed workers in Dominican Republic was twelve over the entire period (around 14.4 per cent of employed workers had twelve years of education).

tend to have high levels of earnings and a decline in the share of workers with low earnings levels.[5] During the international crisis of 2008, the trends described above stalled, but they resumed during the post-crisis period. Along with the improving trend in the educational level of the employed population, a disproportionate increase in the share of workers with medium and high educational levels in low-skill jobs, such as sales and services occupations and elementary jobs, took place in the Dominican Republic (Abdullaev and Estevão 2013).

The educational level of all population groups (young and adult workers, men and women) improved significantly. During the international crisis of 2008, the educational distribution of employment deteriorated for young workers (the share of workers with low educational levels grew and the shares of those with medium and high educational levels declined), while it continued with the improving trend for adults, especially through a reduction in the share of workers with low educational levels and an increase in the share of those with medium levels of education. A possible explanation for the worsening in the employment structure of young workers by educational level can be found in the previous evidence of increasing unemployment and worsening employment structure by occupational position during the international crisis. Better-educated young workers could afford to remain unemployed during the crisis, while the less educated young workers were compelled by economic necessity to take up free-entry self-employment activities or unpaid family work. For men and women, there were minor changes in their distribution of employment by educational level. The previous improving trend resumed during the post-crisis period.

> As a result of a concerted effort by the government, the overall share of wage/salaried employees registered with the social security system increased dramatically among the population as a whole and among all population groups from 2005 (when data on this variable started becoming available) to 2012. While the international crisis slowed this upward trend, it resumed following the crisis.
>
> (Cruces et al. 2015: figure 8)

The social security system in the Dominican Republic includes old-age, disability and survivorship, family health, and occupational hazard insurance plans. Since 2001, the system has followed an individual capitalization account model which comprises three regimes (Lavigne and Vargas 2013). First, the contributory regime covers wage earners from the public and private

[5] The improvement in the employment structure by educational level is related to changes in the relative demand and supply of workers with high educational levels with corresponding implications for the wage gap by educational group and the unemployment rate of each educational level. We introduce a discussion about the role of these factors in the Dominican Republic in section 13.5.

sectors and the self-employed. It is funded by workers' and employers' contributions. This regime has a solidarity component (*Fondo de Solidaridad Social*) funded by employers' contributions in order to guarantee a minimum pension for all affiliated, especially those with low incomes. Second, the fully subsidized regime protects self-employed workers with unstable incomes below the minimum wage, as well as the unemployed, disabled persons, and indigents. This regime is funded by the government. Finally, the contributory-subsidized regime aims to protect self-employed professionals and technicians that receive incomes equal or superior to the minimum wage through contributions from workers and the government. This regime has not been put into practice yet.

Social security records show a major increase in the percentage of wage/salaried employees registered with the contributory regime of the system from 2005 to 2012. The share of wage/salaried employees registered with the system grew from 46.7 per cent in 2005 (725,970 registered workers) to 70.9 per cent in 2012 (1,321,044 employed workers) (Table 13.1). Most of the increase in the percentage of registered wage/salaried employees took place between 2005 and 2008 when this share grew from 46.7 per cent to 71.4 per cent (474,115 newly registered workers). This rise coincides with the system's health insurance contributory scheme coming into force in 2007. From 2008 to 2010, a period that included the Great Recession, the upward trend slowed (rising from 71.4 per cent to 74.7 per cent). Between 2010 and 2012, the percentage of wage/salaried employees registered with the social security system fell to 70.9 per cent. The registration of workers in the social security system is expected to continue with the general upward trend of the period 2005–12 when the contributory-subsidized regime comes into force. The population targeted by this scheme is about 40.0 per cent of the working population of the country, and consequently, will require a substantial subsidy from the government. That is the main reason for the delay in the implementation (ILO 2014).

The aggregate trend towards greater enrolment in the social security system holds true when the employed population is broken down by age and gender.

13.5 Labour Earnings

> Despite above-average economic growth when comparing 2000 and 2012, real labour earnings decreased at the same time. This is true for almost all the groups analysed. The effect of the international crisis on labour earnings is difficult to discern: labour earnings fell between 2007 and 2008, rose between 2008 and 2009, dropped again in 2010, and continued to decrease up to the end of the period. (Cruces et al. 2015: figure 9)

Average monthly earnings, expressed in dollars at 2005 purchasing power parity (PPP), decreased by 26.7 per cent, from US$330 in 2000 to US$242 in 2012 (Table 13.1). This decrease was not uniform over the course of the period. Labour earnings decreased by 34.2 per cent between 2000 and 2004, the year of the economic downturn. They increased by 24.3 per cent from 2004 to 2006, fell again by 6.8 per cent from 2006 to 2008 (the start of the international crisis), and increased by 7.8 per cent between 2008 and 2009. A downward trend began in 2009, lasting until the end of the period. The lack of relationship between GDP per capita and labour earnings in the Dominican Republic is striking: from 2005 to 2012, GDP per capita increased by 39.0 per cent, while labour earnings decreased by 6.2 per cent. This phenomenon is explained by two factors. First, minimum wages have declined in real terms over the period studied. In 2010, real minimum wages were 7.0 per cent lower than in 2000 (Godínez and Máttar 2009; ILO 2013). Second, workers' bargaining power has weakened over time. Labour earnings and hourly wage reductions were a common trend in all economic sectors, even in those that exhibited productivity increases such as communications, financial services, and transport (Abdullaev and Estevão 2013). Hourly wages in the sectors that increased their share in total employment, services sectors mainly, also decreased. This evidence can be interpreted as a sign of the weakened bargaining power of workers.

Labour earnings dropped overall between 2000 and 2012 for all population groups and almost all employment categories, and losses for high-earning categories tended to be larger than earning losses for low-earning categories. The drop in labour income for high-earning occupations was larger than the loss for low-earning occupations. Employers suffered the largest labour income loss among occupational positions, followed by self-employed workers and wage/salaried employees. The loss in labour income was larger for high-earning economic sectors than for low-earning economic sectors. Educational level was not an important determinant of labour income change: the labour incomes of workers with low, medium, and high educational levels dropped by a similar magnitude in percentage terms. The relative wages among educational groups show a reduction in the wages of workers with high educational levels with respect to workers with low and medium educational levels, and an increase in the relative wage of workers with medium educational levels relative to those with low educational levels (Cruces et al. 2015: table 7). These trends can be interpreted in light of the increase in the educational level of people in the labour force (Cruces et al. 2015: table 8), and changes in the productive structure of the economy. Previous evidence indicated that the sectors that increased their share in total employment increased their use of workers with medium and high educational levels despite being mainly low-productivity sectors (Abdullaev and Estevão 2013). The prediction of a supply and demand analysis is that the relative wages of workers with high and medium educational levels relative to those with low educational levels will rise or fall depending on which effect dominates (increase in the relative demand versus increase in the relative supply). In the Dominican Republic economy, the increase in the relative demand for workers with medium educational levels (with respect to workers with low educational levels) offset the increase in their relative supply, driving up the wages of workers with medium to low educational levels. The contrary occurred for workers with high educational levels, for whom their relative wages (with respect to workers with low educational levels) decreased. The adjustment process also led to a reduction in the unemployment rate of workers with high educational levels, an increase for workers with low educational levels, and no change for workers with medium educational levels (Cruces et al. 2015: table 9).[6]

The evidence regarding the effects of the international crisis is mixed. In general, for all population groups and employment categories, labour earnings fell from 2007 to 2008, grew between 2008 and 2009, and dropped once again from 2009 to 2010.

> Poverty and Inequality Poverty increased from 2000 to 2004 and decreased from 2005 to 2012. One cannot be certain whether poverty was higher or lower in 2012 than in 2000 owing to data incomparability. (Cruces et al. 2015: figure 10)[7]

The moderate and the extreme poverty rates (measured by the country's poverty lines) exhibited an upward trend from 2000 to 2004, the year of the downturn in the Dominican Republic, when the moderate and extreme poverty rates peaked at 39.1 and 14.5 per cent respectively. The percentage of working poor households (defined as the proportion of persons in the population living in poor households where at least one member works) experienced a similar trend and reached 35.7 per cent in 2004. Despite the overall reduction in labour earnings, those rates dropped almost every year from 2005 to 2012, a period that included the Great Recession. However, poverty did not decline as much as expected during a period of strong economic growth (World Bank 2014a). Analysis based on the 2.5 and 4 dollars-a-day PPP international poverty lines also shows peaks in 2004 followed by a downward trend after the Dominican crisis in 2003/4 and through 2012 (Table 13.1).

[6] These changes in the unemployment rate were obtained by making the comparison between 2000 and 2012. If the year 2010 is considered instead of 2012, which was a year of a slowdown in the activity level, a reduction in the unemployment rate of all educational groups is observed.

[7] Since the year 2005, the survey has included questions geared to better capturing non-labour incomes. The poverty rates between 2000 and 2004 are overestimated when compared to those of 2005–12. For example, had a similar set of questions been used in the 2005 and the 2004 surveys, the poverty rate of 4 dollars-a-day would have been 5.7 percentage points higher in 2005. To indicate the change in the survey instrument, lines are drawn separating the old and new questions in Cruces et al. (2015: figure 10).

The pattern of reducing poverty in the Dominican Republic since 2005 can be understood by examining incomes from various sources. Household labour earnings and remittances from abroad suffered a reduction from 2005 to 2012 (Cruces et al. 2015: figure 11). Despite this reduction, remittances have represented around 7.0 per cent of GDP during the 2000s, helping to mitigate the impacts of low wages and a weak social protection net (Ondetti 2012). On the other hand, pensions and government transfers increased from 2005 to 2012. Government transfers have improved their design, starting in 2005. Before 2005, most social programmes were poorly targeted, reinforcing the private transfers pattern, such as remittances, which are directed to non-poor households mainly. Moreover, the amount of per capita government transfers was low, limiting their impact on poverty reduction (World Bank and IDB 2006). Starting in 2005, the number of beneficiaries has increased and the target has improved. However, the funding of social protection interventions has suffered reductions, especially during downturns. During the international crisis of 2008, the Dominican Republic was the Latin American country that cut social spending the most (Lavigne and Vargas 2013).

> Inequality of labour earnings diminished overall, though erratically. Inequality of household per capita income remained unchanged between 2000 and 2004, though the Gini coefficient moved erratically during the period, and diminished from 2005 to 2012.[8] During the international crisis, there was a temporary increase in labour earnings inequality but no change in the inequality of per capita household income. (Cruces et al. 2015: figure 12)

The Gini coefficient of household per capita income was unchanged between 2000 and 2004 (0.519). However, it declined from 0.499 in 2005 to 0.457 in 2012, a period that included the Great Recession. The bulk of the decrease took place in 2007, 2010, and 2012. The Gini coefficient of labour earnings among employed workers declined from 0.499 in 2000 to 0.451 in 2012 (Table 13.1). It decreased slightly from 2000 to 2006, when it stood at 0.484; it went on to decrease rapidly until 2008, dropping as low as 0.457, only to increase to 0.471 during the international crisis. It has fallen every year since then. This reduction in labour earnings inequality is in keeping with the fact that earnings reductions were larger for high-earning employment categories compared to low-earning categories. As a consequence, the reduction in labour earning inequality in the Dominican Republic occurred at the expense of income losses for all employment categories.

Changes in household per capita income inequality in the Dominican Republic have been related to changes in labour and non-labour incomes.

[8] The changes introduced in the household survey in 2005 prevent us from making comparisons between the Gini coefficient of household per capita income before and after that year.

Azevedo et al. (2013b) decomposed the change in the Gini coefficient of household per capita income for the period 2000–10 and found that changes in labour incomes and in incomes from transfers contributed the most and equally to the inequality reduction over this period.[9] Demographical factors, such as the age structure of the labour force, had an inequality-increasing effect. Other studies have analysed the factors behind the evolution of labour income inequality. Azevedo et al. (2013a) used a decomposition approach and found that changes in the distribution of the stock of education (the 'quantity effect') were inequality-reducing in the Dominican Republic between 2000 and 2010 (the Gini coefficient of labour earnings decreased from 0.499 to 0.464 between 2000 and 2010), while changes in the education wage premium (or the 'price effect') were inequality-increasing although the effect was small.

13.6 Conclusions

By Latin American standards, the Dominican Republic experienced above-average economic growth during the 2000s. Within the 2000–12 period, GDP per capita stagnated through 2004 and, for the most part, grew rapidly from 2005 through 2012. The international crisis of 2008 led to a slowdown, but growth rates remained positive in every year.

Despite the country's high rates of economic growth, the evidence regarding the changes in labour market indicators between 2000 and 2012 is mixed. Some indicators improved while others deteriorated over the period. The improvements were as follows. The employment composition by economic sector improved over the course of the period studied: the share of workers employed in low-earning sectors decreased, and the share of workers in mid-earning sectors increased due to the change in the productive structure of the economy that moved from being export-oriented to being based on services sectors. The educational level of the employed population improved over the period. The share of wage/salaried employees registered with the social security system increased dramatically. Inequality of household per capita income and of labour earnings diminished overall. Given differences in which incomes are included before 2005 and afterwards, one cannot be certain about what happened to poverty from 2000 to 2012; what does appear clearly is that poverty increased from 2000 to 2004 and decreased from 2005

[9] The authors analyse the period 2000–10 and report a reduction in the Gini coefficient of household per capita income. However, they do not indicate if household income was adjusted to allow the comparability before and after 2005. We consider their result should be interpreted with caution.

to 2012. However, not everything improved: the unemployment rate increased between 2000 and 2012 following a V-pattern; the employment structure by occupational group exhibited a slight worsening; the composition of employment by occupational position deteriorated over the period; and real labour earnings decreased.

The international crisis of 2008 affected most labour market indicators negatively. The unemployment rate increased during the crisis and then dropped, though as of 2012 the pre-crisis rate had not been reached. The share of low-earning occupations continued with its upward trend during the crisis as well, while the share of high-earning occupations began a downward trend and its pre-crisis level had not been reached as of 2012. The composition of the employed population by occupational position continued with the worsening trend, though by 2012 the share of wage/salaried employees had returned to the pre-crisis level. Inequality of labour earnings increased between 2008 and 2009, after which inequality returned to its pre-crisis level. On the other hand, labour earnings did not fall between 2008 and 2009, but began a downward trend and continued to decrease up to the end of the period. The comparison between the effects of the international crisis of 2008 on labour market indicators and the effects generated by the banking crisis of 2003 reveals that the crisis at the beginning of the 2000s impacted the Dominican Republic more strongly. The crisis of 2003 generated a reduction in GDP, while economic growth slowed but remained positive during the international crisis of 2008. Labour earnings suffered a reduction during the domestic crisis of 2003, which led to an increase in all poverty indicators that peaked in 2004, and in household per capita income inequality. On the other hand, the international crisis of 2008 did not have an immediate impact on labour earnings, which began a downward trend in 2010; all poverty indicators fell and household per capita income inequality remained unchanged.

Young workers had worse labour market outcomes over the period compared to adults, but they do not seem to be more vulnerable to macroeconomic crises. Men and women exhibited a balanced situation in their labour market outcomes and in the negative impacts of the crises. The unemployment rate was higher for young compared to adult workers; the share of young employed workers in low-earning occupations was larger than the share of adult workers, while the share in high-paid sectors was lower; the percentage of young workers registered with the social security system was lower when compared to adults; and labour earnings of young workers were below those of adults. On the other hand, the share of young workers in low-earning occupational positions was lower compared to adults. Despite the generally inferior situation of young workers in the labour market compared to adults, both age groups were negatively affected in a similar number of labour market indicators by the economic crises faced by the country. The banking crisis of

2003 led to a larger increase in the unemployment rate and in the share of young workers in low-earning occupations, but the earnings reduction was larger for adults. The international crisis of 2008 led again to a larger increase in the unemployment rate of young workers and to a slight reduction in the share of registered young workers. On the other hand, the increase in the share of low-earning positions, i.e. self-employed workers and unpaid workers, was larger among adults. Disaggregating by gender, we found that men were better than women in some cases, e.g. the male unemployment rate was lower, the share of male workers in low-earning occupations was lower compared to women, and labour earnings of men were higher than labour earnings of women; in other cases, the opposite occurred, e.g. the percentage of workers registered with the social security system was larger for women compared to men, and the share of workers in low-earning positions and sectors was lower for women compared to men. The negative impacts of the crises affected men and women similarly. The unemployment rate increased more for men than for women during the banking crisis of 2003, but earnings losses were larger for women. During the international crisis of 2008, the unemployment rate increased more for women than for men, but the shares of low-earning occupations and positions increased by more for men.

In summary, despite the above-average economic growth for the Latin American region, changes in labour market indicators were mixed in the Dominican Republic, with the fall in real labour earnings being the more striking result.

References

Abdullaev, U. and M. Estevão (2013). 'Crecimiento y empleo en la República Dominicana: Opciones para un crecimiento generador de empleo'. IMF Working Paper 13/40. Washington, DC: International Monetary Fund.

Agosin, M. (2009). 'El desarrollo económico y social: Oportunidades y desafíos', in M. Agosin, O. Manzano, R. Rodríguez-Balza, and E. Stein (eds), *La Ruta Hacia el Crecimiento Sostenible en la República Dominicana*. Washington, DC: Inter-American Development Bank, 3–20.

Azevedo, J. P., M. E. Dávalos, C. Díaz-Bonilla, B. Atuesta, and R. A. Castañeda (2013a). 'Fifteen Years of Inequality in Latin America: How Have Labor Markets Helped?'. Policy Research Working Paper 6384. Washington, DC: World Bank.

Azevedo, J. P., G. Inchauste, and V. Sanfelice (2013b). 'Decomposing the Recent Inequality Decline in Latin America'. Policy Research Working Paper 6715. Washington, DC: World Bank.

CEDLAS and World Bank (2014). SEDLAC—Socio-Economic Database for Latin America and the Caribbean. Centro de Estudios Distributivos, Laborales y Sociales, Facultad de

Ciencias Económicas, Universidad Nacional de La Plata and World Bank Poverty Group LCR. Available at <http://sedlac.econo.unlp.edu.ar/eng/index.php>, accessed 2014.

Cruces, G., G. Fields, D. Jaume, and M. Viollaz (2015). 'The Growth–Employment–Poverty Nexus in Latin America in the 2000s: Dominican Republic Country Study'. WIDER Working Paper 2015/075. Helsinki: UNU-WIDER.

Godínez, V. and J. Máttar (eds) (2009). *La República Dominicana en 2030: Hacia una nación cohesionada*. Mexico, DF: United Nations.

ILO (2013). 'Crecimiento, empleo y cohesión social en Republica Dominicana'. Informe de la Organización Internacional del Trabajo. Geneva: International Labour Organization.

ILO (2014). 'Evolution of Informal Employment in the Dominican Republic'. Notes on Formalization. Geneva: International Labour Organization.

IMF (2003). 'IMF Concludes 2003 Article IV Consultation with the Dominican Republic'. Public Information Notice 03/123. Washington, DC: International Monetary Fund.

IMF (2005). 'IMF Executive Board Concludes 2005 Article IV Consultation with the Dominican Republic'. Public Information Notice 05/162. Washington, DC: International Monetary Fund.

IMF (2009). 'IMF Executive Board Concludes First Post-Program Monitoring Review with the Dominican Republic'. Public Information Notice 09/06. Washington, DC: International Monetary Fund.

IMF (2011). 'Dominican Republic: First Review Under the Stand-By Arrangement, Requests for Waivers of Applicability and Modification of Performance Criteria'. IMF Country Report No. 11/70. Washington, DC: International Monetary Fund.

Lavigne, M. and L. H. Vargas (2013). 'Social Protection Systems in Latin America and the Caribbean: Dominican Republic'. ECLAC, Project Documents Collection. Santiago de Chile: United Nations.

Ondetti, G. (2012). 'International Migration and Social Policy Underdevelopment in the Dominican Republic', *Global Social Policy* 12 (1): 45–66.

World Bank (2014a). 'When Prosperity Is Not Shared: The Weak Links between Growth and Equity in the Dominican Republic'. Washington, DC: World Bank.

World Bank (2014b). World Development Indicators. Available at <http://data.worldbank.org/data-catalog/world-development-indicators>, accessed April 2014.

World Bank and IDB (2006). 'Informe sobre la pobreza en la República Dominicana: Logrando un beneficio económico que beneficie a los pobres'. Washington, DC: World Bank and Inter-American Development Bank.

14

Ecuador

14.1 Introduction

This chapter on labour markets and growth in Ecuador since 2000 is one of sixteen studies of Latin American countries, each of which analyses the growth–employment–poverty nexus and aims to answer the following broad questions: Has economic growth resulted in economic development via improved labour market conditions in Latin America in the 2000s, and have these improvements halted or been reversed since the Great Recession? How do the rate and character of economic growth, changes in the various labour market indicators, and changes in poverty relate to each other?

To answer these questions, we analyse the growth experience of Ecuador during the 2000s and a wide set of labour market indicators that we assign to one of two different categories: employment and earnings indicators, and poverty and income inequality indicators. More specifically, for the group of employment and earnings indicators we construct statistics on the following variables: the unemployment rate; the employment structure by occupational group, employment position, economic sector, registration of workers with the social security system, and educational level; and mean labour earnings and hourly wages. We present all these indicators for the employed population as a whole and for different population groups (youth, adults, men, and women). For the group of poverty and income inequality indicators, we compute poverty rates using the official moderate and extreme poverty lines and the international lines of 2.5 and 4 dollars a day. We also calculate the Gini coefficient of household per capita income and labour earnings.

All the statistics in this chapter are obtained using microdata from the Encuesta de Empleo, Desempleo y Subempleo (ENEMDU) for the years 2003 to 2012. The nationwide surveys were processed following a harmonization methodology and incorporated into the SEDLAC—Socio-Economic Database for Latin America and the Caribbean (CEDLAS and World Bank 2014).[1] The resulting labour market indicators were compiled into a large number of tables and figures, which are available in an earlier version of this study (henceforth, Cruces et al. 2015). Chapter 1 of this book provides the definition for each of the indicators we analyse here, while Cruces et al. (2015) includes details on definitions and classification systems used by Ecuador's household surveys, and on comparability issues of these surveys over time.

14.2 Economic Growth

> Ecuador experienced moderate economic growth during the 2000s. The country suffered only a mild recession as a consequence of the international crisis of 2008 but the Ecuadorean economy returned to pre-recession GDP per capita level in 2010. (Cruces et al. 2015: figures 1 and 2)

During the period 2000–12, Ecuador experienced moderate economic growth by Latin American standards. GDP per capita increased by 33.9 per cent, while the average for the eighteen Latin American countries was 36.2 per cent during the same period. GDP (measured at PPP dollars of 2005) grew by 62.3 per cent, and GDP per employed person exhibited a rise of 24.7 per cent. The annual growth rate of GDP per capita was 2.4 per cent, and it varied from a minimum of −1.1 per cent in 2009 to a maximum of 6.2 per cent in 2004 (Table 14.1).

At the beginning of the 2000s, Ecuador's GDP growth rate was low (1.1 per cent in 2000) and its GDP per capita growth rate negative (−0.9 per cent in 2000) due to the economic and political crisis the country suffered at the end of the 1990s. That crisis was related to negative external shocks like El Niño, the sharp decline in the price of oil—Ecuador's largest export—and the tightening of international credit following the financial crises in Russia and Brazil. The recovery was fuelled by the adoption of the US dollar as the official currency in 2000 (IMF 2006), the increasing oil revenues, and by governmental measures such as the Fiscal Responsibility and Transparency Law that was passed in 2002, which mandated saving extra resources from increased petroleum revenues and placed limits on the growth of expenditures to provide resources for priority programmes (Giugale et al. 2012). The government also passed a series of laws that increased the flexibility of markets and allowed for greater private-sector participation in certain economic activities. One of these measures was the financing of a heavy

[1] See Cruces et al. (2015: table 1) for details on the size of Ecuador household surveys.

Table 14.1 Ecuador: Evolution of growth and labour market indicators over the 2000s

		2000	2001	2002	2003	2004	2005	2006	2007	2008	2009	2010	2011	2012
Growth Indicators	GDP per capita	6,184	6,307	6,440	6,491	6,895	7,129	7,312	7,344	7,679	7,595	7,692	8,161	8,443
	GDP per capita growth rate	−0.89	2.00	2.11	0.79	6.22	3.40	2.57	0.44	4.57	−1.10	1.27	6.10	3.46
Employment and Earnings Indicators	Employment-to-population ratio	...	...	...	61.63	65.41	64.44	65.53	64.66	62.25	61.06	59.41	59.86	59.14
	Unemployment rate	...	...	...	13.19	8.50	8.37	6.72	5.48	6.43	6.86	5.22	4.50	4.40
	Share of low-earnings occupations	...	...	...	57.88	57.42	56.80	57.12	55.56	56.22	56.75	54.43	52.91	52.42
	Share of mid-earnings occupations	...	...	...	34.34	34.07	34.64	34.44	35.48	35.02	34.63	36.15	38.60	37.93
	Share of high-earnings occupations	...	...	...	7.78	8.51	8.56	8.44	8.96	8.76	8.61	9.42	8.49	9.65
	Share of employers	...	...	...	4.88	6.70	6.29	6.01	5.21	5.29	4.20	3.48	3.52	3.77
	Share of wage/salaried employees	...	...	...	55.09	51.19	53.41	53.38	54.10	55.74	54.13	55.30	52.93	54.06
	Share of self-employed workers	...	...	...	31.29	30.64	30.53	28.90	29.76	29.08	30.68	31.64	34.82	33.16
	Share of unpaid family workers	...	...	...	8.73	11.47	9.77	11.70	10.93	9.89	10.99	9.58	8.72	9.01
	Share of workers in low-earnings sectors	...	...	...	42.39	42.61	42.35	41.55	40.68	39.90	40.07	38.76	38.13	37.92
	Share of workers in mid-earnings sectors	...	...	...	46.37	46.56	46.43	47.74	48.61	48.10	48.52	49.08	49.27	48.96
	Share of workers in high-earnings sectors	...	...	...	11.24	10.83	11.22	10.72	10.70	12.00	11.42	12.16	12.59	13.12
	Share of low-educated workers	...	...	...	54.58	55.04	53.52	52.38	51.93	50.99	50.64	48.69	46.92	45.55

	Share of medium-educated workers	...	...	...	27.03	26.16	27.74	28.99	28.86	29.46	29.22	29.93	31.78	32.20
	Share of high-educated workers	...	...	...	18.39	18.81	18.73	18.63	19.21	19.56	20.14	21.38	21.31	22.24
	Share of workers registered with SS	...	...	...	32.97	33.53	33.15	33.30	34.04	36.00	39.95	45.24	53.30	54.67
	Mean labour earnings	...	...	...	457.6	511.1	502.6	529.2	575.1	546.8	515.7	559.7	559.0	589.6
Poverty and Inequality Indicators	Official extreme poverty rate	...	...	...	23.8	21.8	19.1	14.1	14.5	13.2	13.3	10.9	9.2	8.6
	Official moderate poverty rate	...	...	...	46.6	44.2	39.1	33.6	33.6	32.3	32.5	29.0	25.1	23.7
	Poverty rate 2.5 dollars a day	...	...	...	31.33	28.81	25.61	20.00	19.81	19.29	18.85	15.88	13.55	12.85
	Poverty rate 4 dollars a day	...	...	...	51.44	48.03	43.60	38.34	38.11	36.75	37.11	33.43	29.54	27.76
	GINI of household per capita income	...	...	...	0.545	0.536	0.536	0.529	0.539	0.502	0.489	0.489	0.458	0.462
	GINI of labour earnings	...	...	...	0.515	0.527	0.501	0.489	0.524	0.482	0.466	0.463	0.436	0.431

Note: The shaded figures of labour market indicators represent statistical significant improvements at 5 per cent between the initial and final years for all the employment and earnings indicators and poverty and inequality indicators. The only exceptions are the share of mid-earnings occupations, share of mid-earnings sectors, and share of medium-educated workers for which we did not assign welfare evaluation criteria.

Source: SEDLAC (CEDLAS and World Bank 2014) and World Development Indicators (World Bank 2014).

crude-oil pipeline that facilitated an increase in oil exports from around 20,000 barrels per day in 1998 to around 350,000 barrels per day in 2005 (Giugale et al. 2012). The strong expansion of the oil sector was not accompanied by a similar economic dynamism in the rest of the economy, which made the economy even more dependent on oil production and exports than it had been before (León et al. 2010).

Dollarization and supporting policies ushered in a period of macroeconomic stability from 2000 to 2004. In 2004, Ecuador exhibited the largest growth rates of the period: the GDP and GDP per capita growth rates were 8.2 per cent and 6.2 per cent respectively. A slowdown in GDP and GDP per capita growth ensued between 2004 and 2007 as a result of some macroeconomic imbalances led by the dollarization, such as the current account deficit and the lack of credit (Larrea Maldonado 2007). The average GDP growth rate was 4.0 per cent during this period, while GDP per capita grew at 2.1 per cent annually. The economy recovered significantly in 2008 with a GDP growth rate of 7.8 per cent, due in part to high petroleum prices around the world.

The global recession, though, significantly diminished Ecuador's main sources of foreign earnings, mainly petroleum exports and remittances from abroad (Ray and Kozameh 2012). Ecuadorian exports are concentrated on a few commodities and a few markets. Exports of oil, bananas, shrimp and fish, and flowers represented approximately three quarters of total exports of the country between 2004 and 2008. Moreover, over half of total exports went to developed markets such as the US and the European Union. The global economic crisis led to an important reduction in the value of total exports (a fall of 26.0 per cent between 2008 and 2009) through the fall in oil export prices and the international demand for Ecuadorean products (Wong 2012). The international crisis also brought about a fall in remittances (drop of 12.0 per cent in 2009). Nonetheless, the country lost only 1.1 per cent of its GDP per capita in 2009, while the GDP growth rate for that year was 0.6 per cent. Ecuador recovered quickly and returned to pre-recession output levels in 2010 thanks to the implementation of expansionary fiscal policies and the use of the, albeit limited, monetary policy instruments available in a dollarized economy, such as adjusting the interest rate (Ray and Kozameh 2012). Despite the negative impact of the fall in oil prices on government finances, the country saw its budget alleviated due to the reduction in the world price of fuel as Ecuador imports fuels. That, jointly with the placement of internal debt with entities such as the Instituto Ecuatoriano de Seguridad Social (IESS) and the acquisition of new external credit in the form of prepayment for future oil sales, allowed the government to keep social programmes, infrastructure spending, and subsidies (Wong 2012; Naranjo 2013).

14.3 Unemployment

> The unemployment rate decreased substantially from 2003 overall and for all population groups. The international crisis of 2008 led to a mild increase, but in 2010 the unemployment rate was below the pre-crisis level.
> (Cruces et al. 2015: figure 3)

The unemployment rate (measured as the ratio of unemployment to labour force) followed the business cycle and fell from 13.2 per cent in 2003 (805,663 unemployed persons) to 4.4 per cent in 2012 (295,398 unemployed persons) (Table 14.1). The reduction in the unemployment rate was not monotonic and occurred jointly with a reduction in the labour force participation rate. The unemployment rate decreased from 2003 to 2008, increased slightly during the international crisis (38,796 new unemployed persons between 2008 and 2009), and recovered the downward trend to reach the low point of 4.4 per cent in 2012. The recovery was quick, and by 2010 the unemployment rate was lower than the pre-crisis level. Both the number of persons in the labour force and the number of employed persons increased between 2008 and 2009 by 158,637 and 119,841 respectively. These figures suggest that the increase in the unemployment rate during the international crisis was brought about by the entry of new persons into the labour market who could not find a job.

Unemployment trends for men, women, youth, and adults mirror the behaviour of the aggregate rate and fell over the period. The increase in unemployment between 2008 and 2009 was small and affected adult workers more than young workers and men more than women. All population groups recovered the downward trend immediately and by 2010 had an unemployment rate below the pre-crisis level.

14.4 Job Mix

> The composition of employment by occupational group improved between 2003 and 2012 as workers moved from elementary, and craft and trades occupations to better paying occupations, like professional jobs. All demographic groups—young and adult workers, men, and women—benefited from the improvement in the composition of employment by occupational group over the period. The international crisis of 2008 led to a worsening in the employment structure by occupational group in the aggregate and for adult workers and men, while young workers and women were not negatively affected. (Cruces et al. 2015: figure 4)

The share of the following occupations shrank between 2003 and 2012: elementary (drop of 4.8 percentage points); crafts and trades occupations (drop of 0.9 percentage points); technical and associate professional occupations (drop of 0.8 percentage points); and management (drop of 0.6 percentage points). The share of the following occupations grew: professionals (increase of 2.5 percentage points); clerical (increase of 1.7 percentage points); services and sales jobs (increase of 1.6 percentage points); and plant and machine operators (increase of 1.1 percentage points). The share of the other occupational groups remained largely unchanged. These changes in the occupational composition of employment can be interpreted as an improvement since low-earning occupations (elementary, agricultural, forestry, and fishery occupations, and craft and trades occupations) reduced their share in total employment by 5.5 percentage points between 2003 and 2012, while mid-earning (technicians, clerical occupations, services and sales, and plant and machine operators) and high-earning occupations (management, professionals, and armed forces) gained share in total employment (increase of 3.6 and 1.9 percentage points respectively) (Table 14.1).

The improvements in the occupational composition of employment between 2003 and 2012 were observed for young and adult workers, men, and women.

The international crisis of 2008 impacted adversely on the composition of employment by occupational group overall and for adult workers and men. Young workers and women continued with the improving trend in their employment structure by occupational group even during the Great Recession. Between 2008 and 2009, the share of low-earning occupations in total employment increased in the aggregate, for adult workers and men, while the share of high-earning occupations fell. The increase in the share of low-earning occupations was driven by the rise in agricultural occupations that overcompensated for the decline of elementary occupations in total employment—the occupational group where most workers of the oil subsector are employed. By 2010, the composition of employment by occupational group returned to the pre-crisis structure overall and for adult workers and men.

> The employment structure by occupational position deteriorated between 2003 and 2012. The percentage of high-earning categories decreased overall, for youth and adults, and for both men and women. Most of the change took place during and after the international crisis of 2008. (Cruces et al. 2015: figure 5)

The share of wage/salaried employees in total employment—the largest category—decreased by 1.0 percentage points over the period, from 55.1 per cent in 2003 to 54.1 in 2012. The share of the self-employed, on the other hand, increased by 1.9 percentage points, climbing from 31.3 per cent in 2003 to 33.2 per cent in 2012. The share of unpaid workers grew slightly (just 0.3 percentage points), while the share of employers decreased by 1.1 percentage points between 2003 and 2012 (Table 14.1). Insofar as the share of low-earning categories (self-employment and unpaid employment) increased by a total of 2.1 percentage points and the share of high-earning categories (paid employees and employers) decreased, these changes can be characterized as a worsening of the employment structure in terms of occupational position.

The employment structure by occupational position deteriorated for young workers, men, and women, while it remained unchanged for adult workers.

The deterioration in the employment structure by occupational position in the aggregate and for young workers, men, and women occurred mainly during and after the international crisis of 2008. Adult workers were also affected negatively by the international crisis but they recovered quickly. The worsening in the structure of employment by occupational position is striking considering that the unemployment rate suffered a slight increase during the crisis but recovered the downward trend immediately, and that the labour force participation rate was falling during the entire period. A closer examination of the changes indicates an increase in the share of self-employed workers and a corresponding reduction in the share of employers, with an essentially unchanged share for wage/salaried employees. These changes can be related to the changes in the employment structure by occupational groups analysed previously. Between 2008 and 2012, management was among the occupations that exhibited the largest shares' reduction of total employment and employers have a high relative weight in this occupational group. On the other hand, services and sales jobs, and agricultural occupations were among the occupations with the largest shares of increases in total employment, and self-employed workers have a high relative share of these occupations.

> The employment composition by economic sector improved over the course of the period studied overall and for all population groups. The international crisis of 2008 led to a worsening in the employment structure by economic sector in the aggregate and for adult workers, men, and women, while young workers were not negatively affected. (Cruces et al. 2015: figure 6)

The period 2003–12 witnessed a reduction (from 42.4 per cent to 37.9 per cent) in the share of workers in low-earning sectors (domestic service, primary activities, and low-tech industry). Workers employed in the oil subsector are included in the primary activities sector in our classification. The increase in the employment share of the oil subsector over the period in Ecuador was counteracted by the reduction in the employment share of the agricultural subsector. There was, during the same period, an increase (from 11.2 per cent to 13.1 per cent) in the share of high-earning sectors (public administration, skilled services, and high-tech industry) in the total. These changes resulted in an increase in the share of mid-earning sectors in total employment (utilities and transportation, education and health, construction, and commerce) which climbed from 46.4 per cent in 2003 to 49.0 per cent in 2012 (Table 14.1).

The employment composition by economic sector improved between 2003 and 2012 for young and adult workers, men, and women, as they moved from low-earning sectors to high-earning sectors. The international crisis of 2008 led to a worsening in the employment structure by economic sector overall and for adult workers, men, and women. The increase in the share of low-earning sectors in total employment during the international crisis was brought about mainly by the increase in the share of the agricultural sub-sector. The presence of contractual arrangements and the resilience of export demand for certain Ecuadorean agricultural products explain the increase in the share in total employment of the agricultural subsector between 2008 and 2009 (Wong 2012). By 2010, the pre-crisis shares were recovered. Young workers continued with the improving trend in their employment composition by economic sector even during the international crisis.

> The educational level of the employed population in Ecuador improved steadily between 2003 and 2012 for all population groups, and especially among young workers. The improving trend continued even during the international crisis of 2008. (Cruces et al. 2015: figure 7)

The share of employed workers with low educational levels (eight years of schooling or less) dropped from 54.6 per cent in 2003 to 45.6 per cent in 2012, while the share of workers with medium and high educational levels (nine to thirteen years of schooling and over thirteen years of schooling) grew from 27.0 per cent in 2003 to 32.2 per cent in 2012 and from 18.4 per cent to 22.2 per cent respectively (Table 14.1).[2] We interpret this result as an improvement for the employed population as the level of education is an important predictor of labour earnings. Consequently, the changes in the employment structure by educational level implied an increase in the share of workers that tend to have high levels of earnings and a decline in the share of workers with low earnings levels.[3] This pattern of increased educational level of the employed population continued even during the Great Recession. The improvements in the educational level of the employed population are closely related to the recovery of real public spending in education since the 1990s and the cash transfer programmes of the 2000s, which helped increase access to education (Ponce and Vos 2012).

[2] The most frequent value of years of education for employed workers in Ecuador was six during the entire period (around 26.8 per cent of employed workers had six years of education).

[3] The improvement in the employment structure by educational level is related to changes in the relative demand and supply of workers with high educational levels with corresponding implications for the wage gap by educational group and the unemployment rate of each educational level. We introduce a discussion about the role of these factors in Ecuador in section 14.5.

The educational level of the employed population improved between 2003 and 2012 for all groups and especially for young workers. This improvement in the educational level of young workers can be explained, in part, by the *Bono de Desarrollo Humano,* an unconditional cash transfer programme launched by the government of Ecuador in 2003 and targeted at poor families with children. Oosterbeek et al. (2008) and Araujo and Schady (2008) found that this programme had significant and positive effects on school enrolment.

The pattern of improvement in the level of education of the employed population in Ecuador continued even during the international crisis of 2008, overall and for all population groups.

> The overall share of wage/salaried employees registered with the social security system increased significantly between 2003 and 2012. The improvement also took place among all population groups. The international crisis of 2008 did not affect the upward trend of the registration rate. (Cruces et al. 2015: figure 8)

Social security in Ecuador is provided by five types of institutions which serve different segments of the population. The Ecuadorian Social Security Institute (IESS) is a decentralized agency and the main provider of social security for public and private workers in the country; the Social Security Institute of the Armed Forces (ISSFA) is an autonomous agency of the Armed Forces, which provides social security for military personnel; the Instituto de Seguridad Social de la Policía Nacional (ISSPOL) is an autonomous agency of the National Police, which provides social security for members of the police force; private clinics which provide emergency medical care that cannot be handled by the IESS; and private insurance companies (Naranjo 2013). These institutions provide pension insurance, rural insurance, health insurance, and occupational hazard insurance. The Ecuadorian social security system combines contributory and non-contributory schemes. Under the contributory scheme, social security benefits are financed through contributions from employees, employers, and the government. The non-contributory scheme is implemented through cash and non-cash transfers under specific programmes and is totally funded by the government.

Social security records show an increase in the percentage of wage/salaried workers registered with the system's contributory scheme between 2003 and 2012, from 33.0 per cent in 2003 to 54.7 per cent in 2012 (Table 14.1). The number of registered workers increased from 963,452 to 1,899,153 over the period. Before the onset of the international crisis, from 2003 to 2007, the percentage of wage/salaried workers registered with the social security system was stable at around 33.4 per cent. Between 2008 and 2011, the rate of registration grew annually by 10.0 per cent, though the pace of that increase dropped to 2.6 per cent in 2012. The sharp increase beginning in 2008 occurred because in 2007, the government of Ecuador instituted a set of labour policies designed to improve working conditions. Those measures included the elimination of several forms of precarious employment, such as labour subcontracting and hiring by the hour. They also included an active minimum wage policy and policies to ensure that employers comply with the obligation to register their workers in the social security system. In addition, registering with the social security system was made more attractive by increased benefits (ILO 2014). These incentives included: the expansion of health insurance for children under the age of eighteen and spouses of registered workers; the reduction from six to three months of the waiting period to obtain health insurance benefits related to the social security system; and changes in management models (health benefits rendered by clinics, hospitals, and private medical centres).

The rate of registration with the social security system increased for all population groups (young and adult workers, men, and women) over the period.

The overall percentage of workers registered with the social security system continued to grow during the international crisis of 2008. Disaggregating by population group, the rate of registration with the social security system also continued to increase for young and adult workers, men, and women.

14.5 Labour Earnings

> Labour earnings increased between 2003 and 2012. Within the period, labour earnings moved erratically. Labour earnings increased overall, for young and adult workers, and for men and women. The evidence of earning changes by employment categories over the period is mixed, with low-earning categories having larger earning increases compared to high-earning categories in some cases (economic sectors and educational levels), and high-earning categories having larger earning increases compared to low-earning categories in others (occupational positions and occupational groups). Labour earnings were negatively affected by the international crisis of 2008 overall, for adult workers, men, and women, and most employment categories, and not all of them recovered their pre-crisis level of earnings by the end of the period.
>
> (Cruces et al. 2015: figure 9)

Average monthly earnings, expressed in dollars at 2005 purchasing power parity (PPP), increased by 28.8 per cent, from US$458 in 2003 to US$590 in 2012 (Table 14.1). Labour earnings increased between 2003 and 2004, fell between 2004 and 2005, and recovered the upward trend starting in 2005. The period 2007–9 witnessed a decrease in labour earnings, which partly reflects the variations in the country's economic performance. In 2009, Ecuador had the lowest GDP and GDP per capita growth rates of the period studied. The following years—from 2010 to 2012—witnessed an average annual increase in income from labour of 4.6 per cent, which meant a return to pre-crisis levels by 2010. This latter increase in total labour earnings was due mostly to an annual increase of about 4.5 per cent in average hourly wages from 2010 to 2012. In fact, wage policy went through two distinct phases over the period. Up to 2006, wage increases were based solely on inflation. Since 2007, the government's wage policy has explicitly been aimed at improving workers' wages by more than inflation in order to achieve a 'decent' wage (Naranjo 2013).

All population groups and most employment categories experienced an increase in labour earnings over the period. Disaggregating by occupational groups, labour earnings increases were larger for high-earning groups compared to low-earning groups. Among occupational positions, low-earning categories experienced an average increase in their labour earnings that was below the gain for workers in high-earning categories. When broken down by economic sectors, labour income gains were larger for low-earning sectors compared to high-earning sectors. Among educational levels, earnings increases were larger for less educated workers.

The evidence of larger labour earnings increases for workers with low educational levels compared to those with medium and high educational levels can be interpreted in light of previous findings of improving employment structure by occupational group and economic sector over the period, and improving educational levels of the employed population. The improving employment structure by occupational group and economic sector implied an increase in the share of occupations and sectors that can be expected to employ workers with high and medium educational levels, such as professional occupations and the skilled services sector, and a reduction in the share of occupations and sectors that employ workers with low educational levels, such as elementary, craft and related trade jobs, domestic service, primary activities, and low-tech industry sectors. This evidence indicates that the demand for workers with high and medium educational levels relative to those with low educational levels increased between 2003 and 2012. It is interesting to notice that workers employed in the oil subsector—the main economic activity of Ecuador—have 9.8 years of education on average and, as such, are workers with medium levels of education. On the other hand, the educational level of people in the labour force improved over the same period, indicating an increase in the relative supply of workers with high and medium levels of education (Cruces et al. 2015: table 8). The prediction of a supply and demand analysis is that the relative wages of workers with high and medium educational levels relative to those with low educational levels will rise or fall depending on which effect dominates (increase in the relative demand versus increase in the relative supply). In the Ecuadorian labour market, the relative wages of workers with high and medium educational levels relative to those with low educational levels fell over the period, and the relative wages of workers with high educational levels relative to those with medium educational levels also decreased (Cruces et al. 2015: table 7). The adjustment process also led to a reduction in the unemployment rate of all educational groups with larger reductions for workers with low and medium levels of education (Cruces et al. 2015: table 9).

The international crisis of 2008 led to a reduction in labour earnings overall, for adult workers, men, and women, and for most employment categories, and not all of them recovered their pre-crisis level of earnings by the end of the period. Labour earnings of young workers were not impacted negatively by the international crisis. The aggregate labour earnings level was recovered in 2012. Women returned to their pre-crisis level of labour earnings in 2010, and adult workers in 2012. Men, on the other hand, had not recovered their pre-recession level of earnings by 2012. Among occupational groups, workers in management, agricultural, and clerical jobs were affected the most by the international crisis. Workers in agricultural and clerical jobs recovered their pre-recession levels of earnings in 2011 and 2012 respectively, while workers in management occupations had not returned to their pre-crisis level of labour incomes by the end of the period. Disaggregating by occupational position, employers were hit hardest by the crisis compared to the self-employed, while wage/salaried employees did not suffer an earnings reduction. The self-employed recovered their pre-crisis level of earnings in 2011, while employers had not returned to that level by 2012. When broken down by economic sector, the evidence indicates that workers in skilled services, construction, and high-tech industry sectors suffered the largest reduction in labour incomes during the international crisis. Workers in the high-tech industry sector returned to their pre-crisis level of earnings in 2010, while workers in the skilled services and construction sectors never recovered their previous level of earnings. The reductions of labour earnings during the international crisis were larger for workers with higher educational levels. Workers with low and medium educational levels returned to their pre-crisis level of earnings in 2010 and 2011 respectively, while workers with high levels of education had not fully recovered by 2012.

14.6 Poverty and Inequality

> The poverty rate and the rate of working poor households decreased substantially between 2003 and 2012. Within the period, the poverty indicators fell in the early years of the period, stopped decreasing between 2006 and 2009, and resumed the downward trend in the following years.
>
> (Cruces et al. 2015: figure 10)

The moderate poverty rate (measured by the country's official poverty line) fell from 46.6 per cent in 2003 to 23.7 per cent in 2012, the extreme poverty rate dropped from 23.8 per cent to 8.6 per cent, and the percentage of the working poor (defined as the proportion of persons in the population living in poor households where at least one member works) decreased from 37.0 per cent to 17.0 per cent over the same period (Table 14.1). A closer look at the evolution of these indicators reveals a steady downward trend at the beginning of the period, stabilization between 2006 and 2009, a period when the growth in GDP was slow, and a recovery of the downward trend in the following years. The analysis of trends based on the 2.5 and 4 dollars-a-day PPP international poverty lines shows the aforementioned trends. The poverty rate based on those measures decreased from 2003 to 2006, then levelled off until 2009 when the downward trend resumed.

The poverty patterns exhibited by Ecuador can be understood by examining incomes from various sources as well as government programmes. Between 2003 and 2012, income from labour, pensions, and government transfers, all of them measured at the household level, increased in real terms, while remittances were largely unchanged (Cruces et al. 2015: figure 11). Incomes from pensions and government transfers showed the largest increases. In fact, between 2006 and 2010 there was an important increase in social expenditure as a percentage of GDP, which went from 4.8 to 9.8 per cent. Mideros and O'Donoghue (2014) estimated that in 2012 the *Bono de Desarrollo Humano*, a cash transfer targeted at poor households, reduced the extreme and moderate poverty rates measured by the country's official poverty line by 20.8 per cent and 9.0 per cent respectively. Similar results were found by Naranjo (2008). Azevedo et al. (2013) provided additional evidence on the poverty-reducing role of government transfers. The authors broke down the observed reduction in poverty to find that the combination of cash transfer programmes and higher pensions was more responsible for the drop in extreme poverty in Ecuador, measured according to the 2.5 dollars-a-day poverty line, than changes in labour income. Remittances from abroad, which are an important source of income for poor households, also help to explain the reduction of poverty between 2003 and 2012. During the first half of the 2000s, the amount of remittances received by Ecuador was comparable to oil revenues and allowed poor households to recover from the crisis at the end of the nineties. Emigration also generated scarcity of labour in some economic sectors, wage increases, and poverty reductions (Larrea Maldonado 2007).[4]

> Household per capita income and labour earnings inequality diminished over the period studied, although erratically. (Cruces et al. 2015: figure 12)

[4] The cumulated net migration between 1996 and 2004 reached 858,374 individuals, which is very large compared to the size of the Ecuadorean labour force (Larrea Maldonado 2007).

Household per capita income and labour earnings inequality decreased as GDP increased over the period. The Gini coefficient of household per capita income fell from 0.545 in 2003 to 0.462 in 2012. The Gini increased from 0.529 to 0.539 from 2006 to 2007 as GDP growth slowed. A new, albeit minor, increase in the Gini was observed from 2011 to 2012. Throughout the period, the Gini coefficient of labour earnings among employed workers was below that of household per capita income and the decline occurred from 0.515 in 2003 to 0.431 in 2012 (Table 14.1). There was a significant increase in the Gini of labour earnings from 2006 to 2007 (0.489 to 0.524), though the downward trend resumed after that period and continued until 2012. This reduction in labour earnings inequality over the period is in keeping with our previous evidence of larger earnings gains for workers with low educational levels compared to those with high educational levels.

The reduction of income inequality during the 2000s is explained mainly by the expansion of cash transfer programmes, especially in the second half of the decade, and by rising real wages and falling unemployment. The *Bono de Desarrollo Humano* is a progressive programme and its redistributive effect has strengthened towards the end of the decade. The role of cash transfer programmes in reducing income inequality in Ecuador was reinforced by the pattern of economic recovery based on primary exports, which weakened the push for greater demand for skilled workers which had existed since the 1990s. The continued growth in the supply of workers with high levels of education coming out of the schooling system, coupled with a weakened demand for their skill level, pushed down the wage gap between skilled and unskilled workers (Ponce and Vos 2012). The same conclusion was reached by Gasparini et al. (2011), who defined skilled workers as those with some college education and unskilled workers as those up to complete secondary education, and used the Katz and Murphy (1992) framework to find that the relative supply of skilled labour increased steadily while, for certain values of elasticity of substitution between skilled and unskilled workers, the relative demand fell over the period 2003–10.[5] The trend of reducing income inequality during the 2000s was counteracted by the rise of remittances which have tended to increase income inequality (Olivié et al. 2009).

14.7 Conclusions

By Latin American standards, Ecuador experienced moderate economic growth during the 2000s. The country underwent a mild recession as a consequence of

[5] According to the educational level classification used by the authors, most workers employed in the oil sector are unskilled workers.

the international crisis of 2008, but the Ecuadorean economy returned to pre-recession GDP per capita level in 2010.

The evidence regarding the changes in labour market indicators indicated that most of these improved between 2003 and 2012. The unemployment rate fell. The composition of employment by occupational group improved between 2003 and 2012 as workers moved from elementary and craft and trades occupations to better-paying occupations, like professional, clerical, and services and sales jobs. Employment composition by economic sector improved over the course of the period studied through a reduction in the share of workers in low-earning sectors such as domestic service, primary activities, and low-tech industry, and an increase in the share of high-earning sectors like skilled services. The educational level of the employed population improved steadily over the period and the share of wage/salaried employees registered with the social security system increased. Finally, labour earnings increased between 2003 and 2012. The only labour market indicator that did not improve over the period studied is the employment structure by occupational position which deteriorated between 2003 and 2012. The moderate and extreme poverty rates, the rate of working poor households, and the Gini coefficient of per capita household income and labour earnings all decreased over the period.

Looking specifically at the international crisis of 2008, most labour market indicators were affected negatively by the crisis. The unemployment rate increased but then fell, recovering the pre-recession level by 2010. The employment composition by occupational group and economic sector worsened during the crisis but the pre-recession structures were recovered in 2010. Most of the worsening in the employment structure by occupational position took place after the international crisis. Labour earnings fell during the crisis overall and for most population groups and employment categories, and not all of them recovered the pre-crisis level of earnings by the end of the period. The poverty indicators stopped decreasing during the international crisis, but recovered the downward trend immediately.

Young workers had worse labour market outcomes over the period compared to adults, but they do not seem to be more vulnerable to macroeconomic crises. Men and women exhibited a balanced situation in their labour market outcomes, but men were most affected by the negative impacts of the crisis. The unemployment rate was higher for young compared to adult workers, the shares of young employed workers in low-earning occupational groups and economic sectors were larger than the shares of adult workers, the percentage of young workers registered with the social security system was lower when compared to adults, and labour earnings of young workers were below those of adults. On the other hand, the share of young workers in low-earning occupational positions was lower compared to adults and their educational level improved more than that of adults. Despite the generally inferior situation of young workers in the labour market compared to adults, adult workers were more affected by the international crisis of 2008 in all labour market indicators. Disaggregating by gender, we found that men were better than women in some cases, e.g. the male unemployment rate was lower, the share of male workers in low-earning positions was lower compared to women, and labour earnings of men were higher than labour earnings of women; in other cases, the opposite occurred, e.g. the percentage of workers registered with the social security system was larger for women compared to men, and the share of workers in low-earning occupations and sectors was lower for women compared to men. The negative impacts of the crisis affected men more than women in all labour market indicators.

In summary, labour market conditions in Ecuador were generally in a better situation in 2012 than they were in 2003 despite the international crisis of 2008. All population groups were affected negatively by the international crisis, but adult workers and men were more vulnerable than young workers and women.

References

Araujo, M. C. and N. Schady (2008). 'Cash Transfers, Conditions, and School Enrollment in Ecuador', *Economía* 8 (2): 43–77.

Azevedo, J. P., G. Inchauste, S. Olivieri, J. Saavedra Chanduvi, and H. Winkler (2013). 'Is Labor Income Responsible for Poverty Reduction? A Decomposition Approach'. Policy Research Working Paper 6414. Washington, DC: World Bank.

CEDLAS and World Bank (2014). SEDLAC—Socio-Economic Database for Latin America and the Caribbean. Centro de Estudios Distributivos, Laborales y Sociales, Facultad de Ciencias Económicas, Universidad Nacional de La Plata and World Bank Poverty Group LCR. Available at <http://sedlac.econo.unlp.edu.ar/eng/index.php>, accessed 2014.

Cruces, G., G. Fields, D. Jaume, and M. Viollaz (2015). 'The Growth–Employment–Poverty Nexus in Latin America in the 2000s: Ecuador Country Study'. WIDER Working Paper 2015/076. Helsinki: UNU-WIDER.

Gasparini, L., S. Galiani, G. Cruces, and P. Acosta (2011). 'Educational Upgrading and Returns to Skills in Latin America: Evidence from a Supply–Demand Framework, 1990–2010'. IZA Working Paper 6244. Bonn: Institute for the Study of Labor.

Giugale, M., V. Fretes-Cibils, and E. Somensatto (2012). 'Ecuador: An Economic and Social Agenda in the New Millennium'. Policy Note 69625. Washington, DC: World Bank.

ILO (2014). 'Trends in Informal Employment in Ecuador: 2009–2012'. Notes on Formalization. Geneva: International Labour Organization, Regional Office for Latin America and the Caribbean.

IMF (2006). 'Ecuador: Selected Issues'. Prepared by L. Abrego, E. Flores, A. Pivovarsky, and B. Rother. IMF Country Report No. 06/103. Washington, DC: International Monetary Fund.

Katz, L. and K. Murphy (1992). 'Changes in Relative Wages, 1963–1987: Supply and Demand Factors', *The Quarterly Journal of Economics* 107 (1): 35–78.

León, M., J. Rosero, and R. Vos (2010). 'Ecuador', in M. V. Sanchez, R. Vos, E. Ganuza, H. Lofgren, and C. Diaz-Bonilla (eds), *Public Policies for Human Development: Achieving the Millennium Development Goals in Latin America*. London and New York: Palgrave Macmillan, 245–77.

Larrea Maldonado, C. (2007). 'Dolarización, crisis y pobreza en el Ecuador'. Unpublished. Quito: Universidad Andina Simón Bolívar.

Mideros, A. and C. O'Donoghue (2014). 'The Effect of Unconditional Cash Transfers on Adult Labour Supply: A Unitary Discrete Choice Model for the Case of Ecuador'. UNU-MERIT Working Paper 2014–063. Maastricht: Maastricht Economic and Social Research Institute on Innovation and Technology.

Naranjo Bonilla, M. (2008). 'Ecuador: Análisis de la contribución de los programas sociales al logro de los objetivos del milenio'. ECLAC, Project Documents Collection. Santiago de Chile: United Nations.

Naranjo Bonilla, M. (2013). 'Social Protection Systems in Latin America and the Caribbean: Ecuador'. ECLAC, Project Documents Collection. Santiago de Chile: United Nations.

Olivié, I., J. Ponce, and M. Onofa (2009). 'Remesas, pobreza y desigualdad: El caso de Ecuador'. Estudios Elcano 1. Madrid: Real Instituto Elcano.

Oosterbeek, H., J. Ponce, and N. Schady (2008). 'The Impact of Cash Transfers on School Enrollment: Evidence from Ecuador'. World Bank Policy Research Working Paper Series 4645. Washington, DC: World Bank.

Ponce, J. and R. Vos (2012). 'Redistribution without Structural Change in Ecuador: Rising and Falling Income Inequality in the 1990s and 2000s'. UNU-WIDER Working Paper 2012/12. Helsinki: World Institute for Development Economic Research.

Ray, R. and S. Kozameh (2012). 'Ecuador's Economy Since 2007'. Washington, DC: Center for Economic and Policy Research.

Wong, S. (2012). 'Short-Term Macroeconomic and Poverty Impacts of the 2008 Global Economic Crisis in Ecuador'. Unpublished. Guayaquil: Escuela Superior Politécnica del Litoral.

World Bank (2014). World Development Indicators. Available at <http://data.worldbank.org/data-catalog/world-development-indicators>, accessed April 2014.

15

El Salvador

15.1 Introduction

This chapter on labour markets and growth in El Salvador since 2000 is one of sixteen studies of Latin American countries, each of which analyses the growth–employment–poverty nexus and aims to answer the following broad questions: Has economic growth resulted in economic development via improved labour market conditions in Latin America in the 2000s, and have these improvements halted or been reversed since the Great Recession? How do the rate and character of economic growth, changes in the various labour market indicators, and changes in poverty relate to each other?

To answer these questions, we analyse the growth experience of El Salvador during the 2000s and a wide set of labour market indicators that we assign to one of two different categories: employment and earnings indicators, and poverty and income inequality indicators. More specifically, for the group of employment and earnings indicators we construct statistics on the following variables: the unemployment rate; the employment structure by occupational group, employment position, economic sector, registration of workers with the social security system, and educational level; and mean labour earnings and hourly wages. We present all these indicators for the employed population as a whole and for different population groups (youth, adults, men, and women). For the group of poverty and income inequality indicators, we compute poverty rates using the official moderate and extreme poverty lines and the international lines of 2.5 and 4 dollars a day. We also calculate the Gini coefficient of household per capita income and labour earnings.

All the statistics in this chapter are obtained using microdata from the Encuesta de Hogares de Propósitos Múltiples (EHPM) from 2000 to 2012. The nationwide surveys were processed following a harmonization methodology and incorporated into the SEDLAC—Socio-Economic Database for Latin

America and the Caribbean (CEDLAS and World Bank 2014).[1] The resulting labour market indicators were compiled into a large number of tables and figures, which are available in an earlier version of this study (henceforth, Cruces et al. 2015). Chapter 1 of this book provides the definition for each of the indicators we analyse here, while Cruces et al. (2015) includes details on definitions and classification systems used by El Salvador's household surveys, and on comparability issues of these surveys over time.

15.2 Economic Growth

> El Salvador experienced slow economic growth during the 2000s. The country underwent a recession as a consequence of the international crisis of 2008. The economy of El Salvador returned to its pre-recession GDP level in 2011. (Cruces et al. 2015: figures 1 and 2)

During the period 2000 to 2012, El Salvador experienced slow economic growth by Latin American standards. GDP per capita increased by 18.8 per cent, while the average for the eighteen Latin American countries was 36.2 per cent during the same period. GDP (measured in PPP dollars of 2005) grew by 25.6 per cent, and GDP per employed person rose by 3.1 per cent. GDP per capita grew at an average annual rate of 1.5 per cent, with a minimum rate of −3.6 per cent in 2009 and a maximum rate of 3.5 per cent in 2006 (Table 15.1).

The growth experience of El Salvador was sluggish at the beginning of the decade, from 2000 to 2004, when the average GDP growth rate was 2.1 per cent. Previous crises characterized by high inflation rates and income stagnation led to the dollarization of the economy in 2001 (IMF 2005; Castillo Ponce and Rodríguez Espinosa 2009). However, the country was affected by several negative shocks during these years: the decline in the international prices of its main agricultural products, such as coffee and sugar; the competition of Chinese manufacturing products, mainly textiles; the recession in the US, its main trade partner; and some natural disasters like hurricanes and earthquakes (Monge-Naranjo and Rodríguez-Clare 2009).

From 2005 to 2007, the economy of El Salvador accelerated its growth based on the recovery of agricultural prices, government support of agricultural producers, and private consumption funded by remittances (Osorio 2009; IMF 2015). The average GDP growth rate was 3.8 per cent during this period.

The Salvadoran economy was negatively affected by the international crisis of 2008 due to its strong ties to the US economy (IMF 2010). Remittances,

[1] See Cruces et al. (2015: table 1) for details on the size of El Salvador household surveys.

Table 15.1 El Salvador: Evolution of growth and labour market indicators over the 2000s

		2000	2001	2002	2003	2004	2005	2006	2007	2008	2009	2010	2011	2012	
Growth Indicators	GDP per capita	5,155	5,220	5,322	5,425	5,506	5,682	5,880	6,080	6,129	5,906	5,953	6,048	6,125	
	GDP per capita growth rate	1.64	1.26	1.95	1.94	1.50	3.18	3.50	3.39	0.80	−3.63	0.80	1.60	1.26	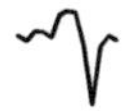
Employment and Earnings Indicators	Employment-to-population ratio	55.92	56.05	54.96	56.76	55.52	55.37	56.38	56.98	57.61	56.76	56.69	57.16	58.09	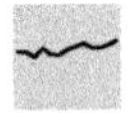
	Unemployment rate	6.86	7.00	6.20	6.95	6.78	7.19	6.50	6.39	5.92	7.34	7.04	6.64	6.06	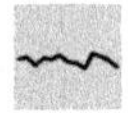
	Share of low-earnings occupations	57.32	56.97	55.78	54.94	55.73	55.11	55.19	54.76	55.86	55.56	55.21	55.54	55.86	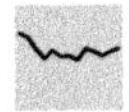
	Share of mid-earnings occupations	30.09	30.84	31.45	32.22	32.29	31.50	31.96	32.32	31.41	31.81	32.95	33.13	32.37	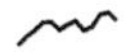
	Share of high-earnings occupations	12.59	12.19	12.77	12.84	11.98	13.39	12.85	12.91	12.73	12.63	11.83	11.34	11.78	
	Share of employers	5.54	4.76	4.75	4.78	4.38	4.53	4.46	4.49	4.33	4.27	4.06	3.70	4.17	
	Share of wage/salaried employees	57.35	58.15	56.49	59.26	60.42	57.67	61.17	59.88	58.90	56.88	57.75	57.88	57.65	
	Share of self-employed workers	30.58	28.78	31.10	28.86	28.65	29.93	27.12	28.15	29.22	30.82	30.42	30.22	29.48	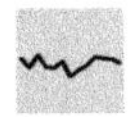
	Share of unpaid family workers	6.54	8.32	7.66	7.10	6.55	7.87	7.25	7.48	7.54	8.04	7.78	8.20	8.70	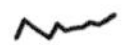
	Share of workers in low-earnings sectors	38.97	38.39	36.54	34.99	35.47	35.00	34.32	33.78	35.98	36.52	35.92	36.76	36.28	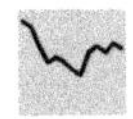
	Share of workers in mid-earnings sectors	46.46	47.89	50.09	51.42	50.90	50.98	52.17	52.27	50.21	49.79	50.06	48.56	49.28	

	Share of workers in high-earnings sectors	14.57	13.72	13.38	13.60	13.63	14.01	13.51	13.95	13.80	13.69	14.03	14.69	14.44
	Share of low-educated workers	60.88	59.21	57.68	56.92	55.89	55.65	54.05	53.49	53.63	53.58	52.46	53.27	51.69
	Share of medium-educated workers	28.55	30.36	31.14	31.97	33.06	31.97	33.92	34.62	34.18	34.10	35.64	35.37	36.36
	Share of high-educated workers	10.57	10.43	11.19	11.11	11.04	12.38	12.03	11.89	12.19	12.32	11.90	11.36	11.95
	Share of workers registered with SS	31.07	30.81	31.17	31.28	30.32	30.41	31.50	31.33	30.72	28.65	28.03	28.03	27.65
	Mean labour earnings	549.5	523.6	527.6	...	476.9	487.4	482.7	486.2	464.0	461.2	440.5	423.0	426.3
Poverty and Inequality Indicators	Poverty rate 2.5 dollars-a-day	23.78	25.32	25.16	...	22.34	22.29	18.68	15.16	20.21	18.72	19.75	16.57	14.68
	Poverty rate 4 dollars-a-day	41.35	42.29	42.76	...	41.57	41.77	38.84	35.66	40.99	38.85	39.31	37.87	34.84
	GINI of household per capita income	0.513	0.510	0.515	...	0.473	0.478	0.454	0.452	0.466	0.459	0.445	0.424	0.418
	GINI of labour earnings	0.504	0.502	0.520	...	0.472	0.489	0.475	0.471	0.466	0.498	0.480	0.462	0.470

Note: The shaded figures of labour market indicators represent statistical significant improvements at 5 per cent between the initial and final years for all the employment and earnings indicators and poverty and inequality indicators. The only exceptions are the share of mid-earnings occupations, share of mid-earnings sectors, and share of medium-educated workers for which we did not assign welfare evaluation criteria.

Source: SEDLAC (CEDLAS and World Bank 2014) and World Development Indicators (World Bank 2014).

consumption, and exports fell sharply in 2009, leading to a reduction in GDP and GDP per capita of 3.1 and 3.6 per cent respectively. The government implemented some expansionary fiscal measures (*Plan Global Anti-Crisis*) such as cash and in-kind transfers and financial support to local producers (Ministerio de Hacienda 2011). The country began a recovery in 2010, reaching the pre-crisis GDP level in 2011 and the pre-recession level of GDP per capita in 2012.

The share of the agricultural and service sectors in the economy increased between 2000 and 2012, while the share of the industrial sector diminished. The share of the service sector—the country's largest economic sector—increased from 58.1 per cent in 2000 to 61.0 per cent in 2012 (Cruces et al. 2015: table 2). The share of the agricultural sector also grew during that period, climbing from 10.5 per cent to 11.8 per cent. Within the period, the share of the agricultural sector fell from 2000 to 2004 due to the decline in the international prices of the main agricultural products of the country. In the following years, the sector recovered, based on government support to producers and increases in international prices. The share of the industrial sector, on the other hand, diminished during the same period, dropping from 31.4 per cent in 2000 to 27.2 per cent in 2012. The industry sector was affected negatively by the competition from Chinese textile products which led to the decline of the *maquila* subsector in El Salvador (Monge-Naranjo and Rodríguez-Clare 2009). All three sectors were hit by the international crisis. In 2009, the value added of the industrial sector dropped by 3.3 per cent; the figures for the agricultural and service sectors were 2.9 and 3.1 per cent respectively. The industrial and service sectors returned to pre-recession value-added levels in 2011. The agricultural sector recovered more quickly, reaching the pre-crisis value-added level in 2010.

15.3 Unemployment

> The unemployment rate dropped slightly from 2000 to 2012. It decreased for youths, adults, and men, but increased for women. While the unemployment rate increased during the international crisis, it had returned to the pre-crisis level by 2012. Throughout the period analysed, the unemployment rate varied within a narrow band of 6.0 to 7.0 per cent.
>
> (Cruces et al. 2015: figure 3)

The unemployment rate (measured as the ratio of unemployment to labour force) decreased from 6.9 per cent in 2000 to 6.1 per cent in 2012 (Table 15.1). The number of unemployed people exhibited an increase over the period, from

124,314 in 2000 to 167,515 in 2012. The reduction in the unemployment rate was then explained by the more rapid increase in the number of people in the labour force. The evolution of the unemployment rate was erratic from 2000 to 2005 with an average level of 6.8 per cent; it decreased from 2006 to 2008 and rose by 0.8 percentage points during the international crisis. Both the number of persons in the labour force and the number of employed persons increased between 2008 and 2009 by 55,488 and 15,519 respectively. These figures suggest that the increase in the unemployment rate during the international crisis was explained by the new entrants into the labour market who could not find a job. In 2010, the unemployment rate began a downward trend, and by 2012 it had returned to its pre-recession level.

From 2000 to 2012, the unemployment rate decreased for youth, adults, and men, while it increased slightly for women. The unemployment rate increased for all population groups during the international crisis. The rise between 2008 and 2009 was larger for young workers compared to adults, and for men compared to women. Adult workers and men had returned to their pre-recession unemployment rates by the end of the period studied, while young workers and women had yet to reach their pre-crisis unemployment levels.

15.4 Job Mix

> The composition of employment by occupational group improved slightly from 2000 to 2012, shifting overall from low-earning occupations such as agricultural, forestry and fishery, and craft and trade jobs to mid-earning occupations such as service and sales jobs. The employment composition by occupational group worsened for young workers and for men over the period, while it improved for adult workers and for women. The trend in employment composition by occupational group was not affected by the international crisis of 2008. This holds true on an aggregate level and when the figures are broken down by population groups.
>
> (Cruces et al. 2015: figure 4)

The occupational structure of employment improved slightly from 2000 to 2012. The share of workers in low-earning occupations (agricultural, forestry and fishery, elementary, and craft and trade occupations) decreased by 1.5 percentage points and the share of workers in high-earning occupations (management, professionals, and technicians) fell by 0.8 percentage points, which yielded an increase in the share of mid-earning occupations (clerical, services and sales jobs, plant and machine operators, and armed forces) (Table 15.1). Specifically, the share of services and sales jobs in total employment increased by 4.9 percentage points over the period (Cruces et al. 2015: table 3).

From 2000 to 2012, the employment composition by occupational group worsened for young workers and for men, while it improved for adult workers and for women.

The overall trend in the composition of employment by occupational group was not affected by the international crisis of 2008. This holds true when the analysis is broken down by population groups.

> The employment structure by occupational position deteriorated between 2000 and 2012 for the employed population as a whole, for young workers, and for men, while it improved for adult workers and remained unchanged for women. During the international crisis of 2008, the employment structure by occupational position worsened for adult workers and for women; the deterioration already underway for young workers and men at the onset of the crisis continued during the episode. (Cruces et al. 2015: figure 5).

During 2000–12, the share of paid employees in total employment—the largest category in El Salvador—was essentially unchanged, increasing slightly from 57.4 to 57.7 per cent. The share of unpaid workers increased from 6.5 to 8.7 per cent. The share of employers and of the self-employed, though, fell from 5.5 to 4.2 per cent and from 30.6 to 29.5 per cent respectively (Table 15.1). These changes can be characterized as a deterioration of the employment structure by occupational position: the share of low-earning categories (self-employment and unpaid employment) increased by a total of 1.1 percentage points while the share of high-earning categories (paid employees and employers) decreased.

Over the period 2000–12, the employment structure by occupational position deteriorated for young workers and for men, improved for adult workers, and remained essentially unchanged for women.

Among adult workers and women, a deterioration in their employment structure by occupational position set in with the international crisis of 2008. In the case of young workers and men, the crisis simply meant a continuation of pre-existing worsening trends. The increase in the share of low-earning positions for adult workers and women can be understood in the context of increasing unemployment during the Great Recession. Economic necessity may have compelled adult workers and women to take up free-entry self-employment activities. The share of low-earning positions in total employment began a downward trend in 2010 and 2011 for adult and women workers respectively, and these low-earning shares reached their pre-crisis levels by 2012. Among young workers and men, the pre-existing worsening trend in employment structure by occupational position continued during the international crisis of 2008.

> The employment composition by economic sector improved slightly over the period studied overall and for adult workers and men, while there was a slight deterioration for young workers and an improvement for women. The international crisis of 2008 brought these trends to a standstill.
>
> (Cruces et al. 2015: figure 6)

During 2000–12, the share of workers in low-earning sectors (primary activities, domestic service, and low-tech industries) dropped from 39.0 per cent to 36.3 per cent. This reduction was driven by the decline in the share of the low-tech industry sector (a drop of 3.4 percentage points over the period), which was affected negatively by the competition from Chinese textiles. The primary activities sector exhibited a decline in its share of total employment from 2000 to 2003, when the international prices of Salvadoran agricultural products were falling. In the following years, the primary activities sector recovered and ended the period with a slight increase in its share of total employment. The share of workers in high-earning sectors (public administration, skilled services, and utilities and transportation) also decreased, though only slightly during the period, from 14.6 per cent in 2000 to 14.4 per cent in 2012 (Table 15.1). As a result, the share of workers in mid-earning sectors like education and health and commerce grew during 2000–12.

The composition of the employed population by economic sector improved over the period for women, improved slightly for adults and men, and suffered a slight deterioration for young workers. During the international crisis of 2008 the trends described above stalled. Between 2008 and 2009, the share of low-earning sectors in total employment stopped decreasing in the aggregate, for young and adult workers and for men, while it continued with the downward trend for women. Construction and low-tech industry, mid- and low-earning sectors respectively, were the sectors that suffered the largest reductions in their shares of total employment during the international crisis. The increase in the share of the primary activities sector driven by the increase in international food prices kept the share of low-earning sectors in total employment unchanged. The share of high-earning sectors was largely unchanged for all population groups. Women resumed the improving trend in their employment composition by economic sector in the post-crisis period. Young and adult workers and men had not recovered their pre-recession shares of low- and high-earning sectors by 2012.

> The educational level of the employed population improved over the period, overall and for all population groups, though the improvement was particularly dramatic among young workers. The educational levels of young workers and of men deteriorated during the international crisis. (Cruces et al. 2015: figure 7)

The share of employed workers with low educational levels (eight years of schooling or less) dropped from 60.9 per cent in 2000 to 51.7 per cent in 2012, while the share of employed workers with medium and high educational levels (nine to thirteen years of schooling and over thirteen years of schooling) grew from 28.6 per cent in 2000 to 36.4 per cent in 2012 and from 10.6 per cent to 12.0 per cent respectively (Table 15.1).[2] We interpret this result as an improvement for the employed population as the level of education is an important predictor of labour earnings. Consequently, the changes in the employment structure by educational level implied an increase in the share of workers that tend to have high levels of earnings and a decline in the share of workers with low levels of earnings.[3]

While the educational level of the employed population improved for all population groups, that improvement was particularly dramatic among young workers.

The international crisis of 2008 had a negative effect on the educational levels of young and male employed workers, but no effect on the educational levels of adult or female workers. The shares of young and male employed workers with low educational levels increased between 2008 and 2009, the shares with medium educational levels declined, and the shares with high levels of education remained essentially unchanged. A possible explanation for this worsening in the employment structure by educational level can be found in the previous evidence of increasing unemployment and worsening employment structure by occupational position during the international crisis. Better-educated workers could afford to remain unemployed during the crisis, while the less educated workers were compelled by economic necessity to take up free-entry self-employment activities or unpaid family work. In 2010, both population groups returned to their pre-crisis levels of education. The international crisis did not have an adverse effect on the educational levels of adult or women employed workers.

> The overall share of workers registered with the social security system fell between 2000 and 2012. While this decline held for all population groups, it was particularly large among young workers and women. The bulk of the drop took place in the wake of the international crisis of 2008. (Cruces et al. 2015: figure 8)

The social security system in El Salvador comprises both contributory and non-contributory schemes. Specifically, the pension system is organized under four regimes (Martínez Franzoni 2013). First, the Sistema Público de Pensiones is

[2] The most frequent value of years of education for employed workers in El Salvador was twelve over the entire period under study (around 16.5 per cent of employed workers had twelve years of education).

[3] The improvement in the employment structure by educational level is related to changes in the relative demand and supply of workers with high educational levels with corresponding implications for the wage gap by educational group and the unemployment rate of each educational level. We introduce a discussion about the role of these factors in El Salvador in section 15.5.

ruled by the Instituto Salvadoreño de Seguridad Social (ISSS). Currently, it only covers public workers who decided to remain in the public system after the reform that privatized the pension system in 1998 (Rubio and Valencia 2010). Second, the individual capitalization system is mandatory for wage/salaried employees and voluntary for self-employed workers. It is funded by employers' and employees' contributions. Third, the Bienestar Magisterial regime provides mandatory insurance to teachers of private and public schools and it is funded by the Ministry of Education and teachers' contributions. Fourth, the Instituto de Previsión Social de la Fuerza Armada is mandatory for members of the armed forces. A non-contributory pension scheme was introduced in 2008 with the Pensión Básica Universal that is granted to people aged 70 and above living in extreme poverty. This pension is also combined with the Programa de Atención Integral a la Persona Adulta Mayor that grants health care for elders living in poverty. The health system in El Salvador is organized in three parts: public health, social insurance, and private services. The benefits that each system provides are highly stratified. Social security provides better-quality services than those run by the public health system, while private services are reserved for high-income earners.

Social security records show a reduction in the percentage of employed workers registered with the contributory scheme of the system during 2000–12, from 31.1 per cent in 2000 to 27.7 per cent in 2012 (Table 15.1). The bulk of the reduction took place during the international crisis of 2008. Between 2000 and 2008, the share of workers registered with the social security system was essentially unchanged. In 2009 alone, the share declined by 2.1 percentage points; this decreasing trend continued through the end of the period studied.

While the rate of registration with the social security system dropped for all population groups, the decline was greater for young workers and women. For all population groups, the downward trend in the share of workers registered with the social security system started during the international crisis of 2008.

15.5 Labour Earnings

> Labour earnings decreased from 2000 to 2012. The decrease in earnings holds true overall and for all population groups and employment categories. The percentage drop in income earnings was in general larger in high-earning categories than in low-earning categories. The pre-existing decrease in labour incomes continued during the international crisis of 2008 for all population groups and for most employment categories.
>
> (Cruces et al. 2015: figure 9)

Average monthly earnings, expressed in dollars at 2005 purchasing power parity (PPP), decreased by 22.4 per cent, dropping from US$549.5 in 2000 to US$426.3 in 2012 (Table 15.1). The declining pattern occurred despite the positive growth rates in most of the years analysed and was more accentuated in the second half of the period under study. The reduction in labour earnings was −0.4 per cent annually between 2000 and 2007 and −2.6 per cent a year from 2008 to 2012. Hourly wages followed a similar declining pattern over the period (Cruces et al. 2015: table 7). The reduction in hourly wages can be explained by the low level of minimum wages in El Salvador and their slow adjustment in comparison with the inflation rate. In 2008, the cost of a basic basket of food could not be covered by two minimum wages (Rubio and Valencia 2010). Our previous evidence of increasing share of low-earning occupations in total employment, increasing share of unregistered workers, and decreasing shares of high-earning occupations and sectors provides a possible explanation for the pattern of declining average labour incomes over the period. As the employment categories that typically obtain low levels of earnings gain share in total employment, average labour income decreases. However, as explained below, labour incomes fell for each employment category.

Labour earnings of all population groups and employment categories decreased between 2000 and 2012, with greater percentage losses in labour earnings for high-earning than for low-earning categories. The loss of labour income for workers in low-earning occupational groups was lower than the earning loss for workers in high-earning occupations. The average reduction in labour income was similar between low- and high-earning occupational positions. The reduction in labour income during 2000–12 for high-earning economic sectors was twice as large as the earnings reduction for workers in low-earning economic sectors. When broken down by educational level, the reduction in labour income was larger for workers with high educational levels when compared to workers with medium and low levels of education. The evidence of larger labour earnings reductions for workers with high educational levels compared to those with medium and low educational levels can be interpreted in light of previous findings of slight improvement in the employment structure by occupational group and economic sector over the period. In El Salvador, the slight improvement in the employment structure by occupational group and economic sector implied an increase in the share of occupations and sectors that can be expected to employ workers with medium educational levels, such as services and sales, armed forces occupations, commerce, and education and health sectors, and a reduction in the share of occupations and sectors that employ workers with low educational levels, such as craft and related trades jobs, agricultural, forestry, and fishery occupations, and low-tech industry sectors. This evidence indicates that the demand for workers with medium educational levels relative to those with low and high educational levels increased over the period 2000–12. On the other hand, the educational level of people in the labour force improved over the same period, indicating an increase in the relative supply of workers with high and medium levels of education (Cruces et al. 2015: table 8). The prediction of a supply and demand analysis is that the relative wages of workers with medium educational levels relative to those with low and high educational levels will rise or fall depending on which effect dominates (increase in the relative demand versus increase in the relative supply). In the Salvadoran labour market, the relative wages of workers with high and medium educational levels relative to those with low educational levels fell over the period, and the relative wages of workers with high educational levels relative to those with medium educational levels also decreased (Cruces et al. 2015: table 7). The adjustment process also led to an increase in the unemployment rate of all educational groups that was larger among workers with high levels of education (Cruces et al. 2015: table 9).

For all population groups and most employment categories, the pre-existing downward trend in labour earnings continued in the wake of the international crisis of 2008.

15.6 Poverty and Inequality

> The poverty rate fell, albeit erratically, over the period studied for all poverty lines used. The rate of working poor households also decreased. Poverty rates increased in 2008, perhaps as an early effect of the crisis.
>
> (Cruces et al. 2015: figure 10)

The poverty rate measured by the 4 dollars-a-day international line fell from 41.4 per cent in 2000 to 34.8 per cent in 2012; the poverty rate based on the 2.5 dollars-a-day line dropped from 23.8 per cent to 14.7 per cent over the same period (Table 15.1). The percentage of working poor households (defined as the proportion of persons in the population living in poor households, according to the 4 dollars-a-day international line, where at least one member works) also decreased from 29.7 per cent in 2000 to 25.1 per cent in 2012. These indicators increased during the period of sluggish economic growth (between 2000 and 2003), dropped between 2003 and 2007, increased again in 2008 (perhaps as an early effect of the crisis), and then began a downward trend that continued through 2010. In 2011, all poverty indicators increased once again only to fall in 2012.

The poverty patterns reported in the last paragraph can be interpreted by examining incomes from various sources. The analysis of sources of household total income indicates that labour and capital income fell during 2000–12

(Cruces et al. 2015: figure 11). Income from pensions exhibited small changes over the period. Finally, remittances increased from 2000 to 2003 when a steady downward trend began. A closer examination of the evolution of remittances indicates that the number of households receiving money from abroad grew between 2000 and 2006, fell in the following years, especially during the international crisis of 2008, and stabilized starting in 2009. Income from remittances is important in the Salvadoran economy. They represented 16.6 per cent of GDP in 2004 and are assigned to consumption, education and health mainly (Cáceres and Saca 2006). Rivera Campos and Lardé de Palomo (2002) have estimated that remittances helped to reduce the poverty rate by 4.2 per cent in 2000. Finally, government transfers from anti-poverty programmes (not available in the EHPM's surveys) have had a reducing impact on poverty (IFPRI-FUSADES 2010; Martínez et al. 2014).

> Household per capita income and labour earnings inequality decreased between 2000 and 2012. While the international crisis of 2008 led to an increase in labour earnings inequality, the country recovered in the following years.
>
> (Cruces et al. 2015: figure 12)

Between 2000 and 2012, the Gini coefficient of household per capita income fell from 0.513 to 0.418. The Gini coefficient of labour earnings among employed workers declined from 0.504 in 2000 to 0.470 in 2012 (Table 15.1). The reduction in labour earnings inequality is in keeping with the fact that earnings suffered a larger reduction for high-earning categories compared to low-earning employment categories. However, it is interesting to notice that earnings declined for all the categories. Consequently, the reduction in labour earnings inequality occurred at the expense of income losses. A year-by-year analysis shows that the inequality of household per capita income had an almost steady declining trend over the period with the exception of 2008, when it rose perhaps as an early effect of the crisis, and after which the downward trend resumed. The Gini coefficient of labour earnings exhibited a similar trend, with an increase in 2009. After the international crisis, a declining trend began that was interrupted in 2012.

Changes in household per capita income inequality in El Salvador have been related mainly to changes in labour income. Azevedo et al. (2013b) decomposed the change in the Gini coefficient of household per capita income for the period 2000–10 and found that changes in labour incomes contributed the most to the inequality reduction over this period (the Gini coefficient of household per capita income decreased from 0.513 to 0.445 between 2000 and 2010). Changes in non-labour incomes, such as government transfers, and demographical changes, like the share of adults per household, were also inequality-reducing. Other studies have analysed the factors behind the evolution of labour income inequality. Azevedo et al. (2013a) used a decomposition approach and found that changes in the education wage premium (or the 'price effect') were inequality-reducing, while changes in the distribution of the stock of education (the 'quantity effect') were inequality-increasing in El Salvador between 2000 and 2009. Gasparini et al. (2011) found large fluctuations in the gap between the wages of skilled workers (those with complete or incomplete college education) and unskilled workers (those who have completed secondary education or less) in El Salvador between 2000 and 2007, with a similar level at the end of the period compared to the beginning. The authors claim that this pattern is consistent with a volatile but roughly constant relative demand for skilled labour over the period.

15.7 Conclusions

By Latin American standards, El Salvador experienced slow economic growth during the 2000s. The country suffered a recession as a consequence of the international crisis of 2008. The pre-recession output level was reached in 2011.

The evidence on changes in labour market indicators during 2000–12 is mixed. Some improved, while others deteriorated. The unemployment rate fell from 2000 to 2012. The composition of the working population by occupational group improved slightly over the period, with an overall shift from low-earning occupations such as agricultural, forestry and fishery, and craft and trade jobs to mid-earning occupations such as service and sales jobs. The employment composition by economic sector also improved slightly during 2000–12 as workers moved from low-earning sectors such as low-tech industries to mid-earning sectors like education and health and commerce. The educational level of the employed population improved over the period. On the other hand, other labour market indicators deteriorated. The employment structure by occupational position worsened between 2000 and 2012 as the proportion of workers in high-earning categories (paid employees and employers) fell and the proportion of workers in low-earning categories (self-employed and unpaid workers) rose. The share of workers registered with the social security system dropped from 2000 to 2012. Finally, labour earnings decreased from 2000 to 2012. Poverty indicators fell over the period studied and household and labour income inequality also decreased.

The international crisis of 2008 had an adverse effect on most labour market indicators. The unemployment rate increased during the crisis and returned to pre-crisis levels in 2012. The employment structure by occupational position worsened during and after the crisis and pre-crisis levels had not been reached by the end of the period studied. The composition of employment by economic sector deteriorated during the international crisis, though the pre-crisis level had been reached in 2010. The bulk of the reduction in the percentage of workers registered with the social security system took place during and after the international crisis of 2008. Labour incomes continued the pre-existing downward trend during the Great Recession. Finally, while poverty and inequality indicators increased during the crisis, the subsequent downward trend set in almost immediately.

Young workers had worse labour market outcomes over the period compared to adults and were more vulnerable to the international crisis. Men experienced worse labour market outcomes compared to women, and suffered more from the negative impacts of the international crisis. The unemployment rate was higher for young compared to adult workers, the shares of young employed workers in low-earning occupations and economic sectors were larger than the shares of adult workers, the percentage of young workers registered with the social security system was lower when compared to adults, and labour earnings of young workers were below those of adults. In addition to the generally inferior situation of young workers in the labour market compared to adults, youth labour market indicators were more adversely affected by the episodes of crises. The youth unemployment rate increased by more than the adult unemployment rate, the shares of workers in low-earning occupations and positions increased for young workers, while they decreased for adults, and the share of registered workers decreased more for young workers than for adults. Disaggregating by gender, we found that women had better labour market outcomes than men, with the only exceptions being the share of workers in low-earning positions that was larger among women and labour earnings that were higher for men. Moreover, men were hit hardest by the international crisis, as the unemployment rate and the shares of workers in low-earning occupations and positions increased more among men.

In summary, slow economic growth during the 2000s resulted in mixed changes in labour market conditions for Salvadoran workers.

References

Azevedo, J. P., M. E. Dávalos, C. Díaz-Bonilla, B. Atuesta, and R. A. Castañeda (2013a). 'Fifteen Years of Inequality in Latin America. How Have Labor Markets Helped?'. Policy Research Working Paper 6384. Washington, DC: World Bank.

Azevedo, J. P., G. Inchauste, and V. Sanfelice (2013b). 'Decomposing the Recent Inequality Decline in Latin America'. Policy Research Working Paper 6715. Washington, DC: World Bank.

Cáceres, L. R. and N. N. Saca (2006). 'What Do Remittances Do? Analyzing the Private Remittance Transmission Mechanism in El Salvador'. Working Paper 06/250. Washington, DC: International Monetary Fund.

Castillo Ponce, R. A. and L. Rodríguez Espinosa (2009). 'La dolarización de El Salvador: ¿Una contribución negativa al crecimiento económico?', *Comercio Exterior* 59 (11): 898–909. Mexico, DF: Banco Nacional de Comercio Exterior.

CEDLAS and World Bank (2014). SEDLAC—Socio-Economic Database for Latin America and the Caribbean. Centro de Estudios Distributivos, Laborales y Sociales, Facultad de Ciencias Económicas, Universidad Nacional de La Plata and World Bank Poverty Group LCR. Available at <http://sedlac.econo.unlp.edu.ar/eng/index.php>, accessed 2014.

Cruces, G., G. Fields, D. Jaume, and M. Viollaz (2015). 'The Growth–Employment–Poverty Nexus in Latin America in the 2000s: El Salvador Country Study'. WIDER Working Paper 2015/077. Helsinki: UNU-WIDER.

Gasparini, L., S. Galiani, G. Cruces, and P. Acosta (2011). 'Educational Upgrading and Returns to Skills in Latin America: Evidence from a Supply–Demand Framework, 1990–2010'. IZA Working Paper 6244. Bonn: Institute for the Study of Labor.

IFPRI-FUSADES (2010). 'Evaluación externa del programa red solidaria: Informe de sostenibilidad del programa. Preparado para FISDL'. San Salvador: Fundación Salvadoreña para el Desarrollo Económico y Social.

IMF (2005). 'El Salvador: 2005 Article IV Consultation'. IMF Country Report 05/271. Washington, DC: International Monetary Fund.

IMF (2010). 'El Salvador: 2010 Article IV Consultation and First Review under the Stand-By Arrangement'. IMF Country Report 10/307. Washington, DC: International Monetary Fund.

IMF (2015). 'El Salvador: 2014 Article IV Consultation'. IMF Country Report 15/13. Washington, DC: International Monetary Fund.

Martínez, S., M. Pérez, and L. Tejerina (2014). 'Impacto de la pensión básica universal programa Nuestros Mayores Derechos en El Salvador'. Unpublished manuscript.

Martínez Franzoni, J. (2013). 'Social Protection Systems in Latin America and the Caribbean: El Salvador'. ECLAC, Project Documents Collection. Santiago de Chile: United Nations.

Ministerio de Hacienda (2011). 'Efectos de la crisis y medidas implementadas para enfrentarla'. Boletín Presupuestario 1. San Salvador: Ministerio de Hacienda.

Monge-Naranjo, A. and A. Rodríguez-Clare (2009). 'Crecimiento económico en El Salvador'. Pennsylvania: Pennsylvania State University.

Osorio, J. A. (2009). 'Impacto de la crisis económica internacional y respuestas de política en El Salvador'. Documento de Trabajo 2009–02. San Salvador: Banco Central de Reserva de El Salvador.

Rivera Campos, R. and A. Lardé de Palomo (2002). 'Invirtamos en educación para desafiar el crecimiento económico y la pobreza'. San Salvador: Fundación Salvadoreña para el Desarrollo Económico y Social.

Rubio, S. and A. Valencia (2010). 'Regulación y políticas activas del mercado de trabajo y esquemas de protección a trabajadores y desempleados en El Salvador', in J. Weller (ed.), *Mercado laboral y diálogo social en El Salvador*. United Nations Publications. Santiago de Chile: United Nations, 13–63.

World Bank (2014). World Development Indicators. Available at <http://data.worldbank.org/data-catalog/world-development-indicators>, accessed April 2014.

16

Honduras

16.1 Introduction

This chapter on labour markets and growth in Honduras since 2000 is one of sixteen studies of Latin American countries, each of which analyses the growth–employment–poverty nexus and aims to answer the following broad questions: Has economic growth resulted in economic development via improved labour market conditions in Latin America in the 2000s, and have these improvements halted or been reversed since the Great Recession? How do the rate and character of economic growth, changes in the various labour market indicators, and changes in poverty relate to each other?

To answer these questions, we analyse the growth experience of Honduras during the 2000s and a wide set of labour market indicators that we assign to one of two different categories: employment and earnings indicators, and poverty and income inequality indicators. More specifically, for the group of employment and earnings indicators we construct statistics on the following variables: the unemployment rate; the employment structure by occupational group, employment position, economic sector, registration of workers with the social security system, and educational level; and mean labour earnings and hourly wages. We present all these indicators for the employed population as a whole and for different population groups (youth, adults, men, and women). For the group of poverty and income inequality indicators, we compute poverty rates using the official moderate and extreme poverty lines and the international lines of 2.5 and 4 dollars a day. We also calculate the Gini coefficient of household per capita income and labour earnings.

All the statistics in this chapter are obtained using microdata from the Encuesta Permanente de Hogares de Propósitos Múltiples (EPHPM), for the years 2001 to 2012. The nationwide surveys were processed following a harmonization methodology and incorporated into the SEDLAC—Socio-Economic Database for Latin America and the Caribbean (CEDLAS and

World Bank 2014).[1] The resulting labour market indicators were compiled into a large number of tables and figures, which are available in an earlier version of this study (henceforth, Cruces et al. 2015). Chapter 1 of this book provides the definition for each of the indicators we analyse here, while Cruces et al. (2015) includes details on definitions and classification systems used by Honduras's household surveys, and on comparability issues of these surveys over time.

16.2 Economic Growth

> Honduras experienced slow economic growth during the 2000s. The country underwent a recession as a consequence of the international crisis of 2008. While GDP returned to its pre-recession output level in 2010, GDP per capita did the same in 2012. (Cruces et al. 2015: figures 1 and 2)

During the period 2000 to 2012 Honduras experienced slow economic growth by Latin American standards. GDP per capita increased by 27.0 per cent, while the average for the eighteen Latin American countries was 36.2 per cent during the same period. GDP (measured in PPP dollars of 2005) grew by 61.6 per cent, and GDP per employed person exhibited a rise of 21.3 per cent. The annual growth rate of GDP per capita was 2.2 per cent, and it varied from a minimum of −4.4 per cent in 2009 to a maximum of 4.5 per cent in 2006 (Table 16.1).

The beginning of the period was characterized by slow growth in Honduras. The economy was recovering from Hurricane Mitch that in 1998 affected four out of five Hondurans (García Merino 2009). However, the policy efforts were erratic and adulterated by institutional weaknesses which contributed to widespread social unrest (IMF 2006). In 2001, the country was also affected negatively by the slowdown of growth in the US and the collapse in world coffee prices (IMF 2001). Between 2000 and 2003, the GDP growth rate averaged 4.2 per cent and GDP per capita grew at 2.1 per cent annually.

Growth rebounded strongly in 2004, reflecting favourable external conditions that allowed for export increases and rising consumption through the strong growth in remittances (IMF 2006). From 2004 to 2008, the economy grew rapidly at 5.9 per cent a year, while GDP per capita increased at 3.8 per cent annually. Despite the strong economic growth, some social tensions re-emerged as a result of the implementation of a fiscal adjustment, of which the key element was the limitation of increases in the wage bill (IMF 2006).

[1] See Cruces et al. (2015: table 1) for details on the size of Honduras household surveys.

Table 16.1 Honduras: Evolution of growth and labour market indicators over the 2000s

		2000	2001	2002	2003	2004	2005	2006	2007	2008	2009	2010	2011	2012	
Growth Indicators	GDP per capita	2,880	2,898	2,946	3,019	3,143	3,268	3,414	3,554	3,631	3,473	3,531	3,593	3,657	
	GDP per capita growth rate	3.57	0.63	1.67	2.46	4.12	3.95	4.47	4.10	2.18	–4.36	1.67	1.76	1.78	
Employment and Earnings Indicators	Employment-to-population ratio	...	59.91	58.39	54.76	56.07	58.65	57.72	57.07	57.19	59.32	59.36	57.24	56.21	
	Unemployment rate	...	4.60	4.24	5.54	5.99	4.92	3.58	3.15	3.11	3.28	4.10	4.42	3.73	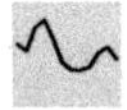
	Share of low-earnings occupations	...	...	...	...	...	61.93	62.49	63.07	61.13	62.12	61.71	59.72	61.34	
	Share of mid-earnings occupations	...	...	...	...	...	25.21	23.56	22.74	23.85	24.69	25.40	26.74	25.67	
	Share of high-earnings occupations	...	...	...	...	...	12.86	13.95	14.19	15.03	13.19	12.90	13.54	13.00	
	Share of employers	...	10.38	9.33	9.07	11.90	11.56	11.88	13.74	13.66	12.54	13.21	11.12	11.59	
	Share of wage/salaried employees	...	47.04	47.25	50.12	49.17	47.24	47.68	48.94	49.00	47.02	44.23	46.83	42.91	
	Share of self-employed workers	...	33.58	33.22	32.21	29.34	31.29	31.19	29.06	28.52	31.50	32.07	30.71	34.73	
	Share of unpaid family workers	...	9.00	10.20	8.61	9.58	9.91	9.25	8.25	8.81	8.94	10.48	11.34	10.77	
	Share of workers in low-earnings sectors	...	46.51	52.73	48.94	49.67	48.21	50.91	48.84	47.70	48.66	49.91	49.43	50.11	
	Share of workers in mid-earnings sectors	...	43.66	37.68	41.71	40.50	42.11	38.90	40.94	41.29	41.49	40.15	41.17	40.31	

	Share of workers in high-earnings sectors	...	9.83	9.59	9.35	9.83	9.68	10.19	10.22	11.01	9.84	9.94	9.40	9.59	
	Share of low-educated workers	...	77.60	79.51	79.24	76.52	76.15	75.48	74.48	72.23	73.22	70.97	69.32	70.19	
	Share of medium-educated workers	...	17.30	14.86	16.07	18.11	18.63	19.00	19.60	21.25	21.18	22.72	24.04	23.60	
	Share of high-educated workers	...	5.10	5.63	4.69	5.37	5.22	5.52	5.91	6.52	5.60	6.31	6.63	6.21	
	Share of workers registered with SS	...	...	...	...	...	...	6.19	5.00	6.34	4.40	5.63	5.42	5.21	
	Mean labour earnings	...	430.1	393.2	394.6	404.1	372.1	391.6	431.2	457.9	421.2	416.3	448.4	395.0	
Poverty and Inequality Indicators	Official extreme poverty rate	...	45.7	50.9	47.8	45.4	46.5	41.1	37.1	38.8	36.2	38.8	41.0	44.6	
	Official moderate poverty rate	...	64.7	69.5	66.7	64.5	65.5	61.0	59.6	59.7	58.2	59.8	61.2	65.3	
	Poverty rate 2.5 dollars-a-day	...	37.04	47.95	47.89	46.77	47.41	42.04	36.96	34.01	31.34	33.99	37.40	42.42	
	Poverty rate 4 dollars-a-day	...	55.91	64.28	64.38	63.29	64.16	58.80	56.00	52.05	50.04	53.30	56.39	61.28	
	GINI of household per capita income	...	0.539	0.577	0.583	0.581	0.593	0.573	0.560	0.556	0.516	0.534	0.572	0.573	
	GINI of labour earnings	...	0.541	0.545	0.558	0.556	0.575	0.546	0.553	0.554	0.526	0.543	0.582	0.580	

Note: The shaded figures of labour market indicators represent statistical significant improvements at 5 per cent between the initial and final years for all the employment and earnings indicators and poverty and inequality indicators. The only exceptions are the share of mid-earnings occupations, share of mid-earnings sectors, and share of medium-educated workers for which we did not assign welfare evaluation criteria.

Source: SEDLAC (CEDLAS and World Bank 2014) and World Development Indicators (World Bank 2014).

The international crisis of 2008 affected the country negatively, mostly in terms of a drop in exports, foreign direct investment, and remittances (Johnston and Lefebvre 2013). GDP declined by 2.4 per cent in 2009 while GDP per capita fell by 4.4 per cent the same year. Besides the international crisis, the country experienced problems stemming from a military coup in 2009. At the time of the coup, Honduras had proven itself relatively capable of responding to the recession and of stimulating growth. The debt-to-GDP ratio, debt-servicing costs, and fiscal deficit were at low levels, enabling an expansionary fiscal policy (Johnston and Lefebvre 2013). The political instability, though, prevented the country from adopting the measures needed to counteract the effects of the global recession, e.g. the new government reduced the public expenditure level (Cordero 2009). The economy returned to the pre-recession GDP level in 2010, but GDP per capita did not recover until 2012. After the crisis, annual GDP and GDP per capita growth rates stabilized at around 3.8 and 1.7 per cent respectively, led by increases in the external demand for Honduran exports, increases in their prices, and rises in remittances (Otter and Borja 2010).

16.3 Unemployment

> The unemployment rate fell from 2001 to 2012, though erratically. It decreased for youths, adults, and for men, but it had a mild increase for women. During the international crisis, the unemployment rate increased and had not fully recovered by 2012. (Cruces et al. 2015: figure 3)

The unemployment rate (measured as the ratio of unemployment to labour force) decreased from 4.6 per cent in 2001 to 3.7 per cent in 2012 (Table 16.1). The number of unemployed people, though, increased from 107,036 in 2001 to 120,832 in 2012. The downward general pattern in the unemployment rate over the period was driven by a more rapid increase in the number of people in the labour force (from 2,328,949 in 2001 to 3,237,912 in 2012).[2] The behaviour of the unemployment rate over the period was erratic. The years 2001 and 2002 witnessed a drop from 4.6 to 4.2 per cent that was followed by an increase to 6.0 per cent in 2004. The increase in the unemployment rate in 2004 took place in the context of a rapidly growing economy and an expanding labour market (GDP increased by 6.2 per cent in 2004). The more rapid increase in the number of unemployed people compared to the rise in the

[2] A more rapid increase in the number of working-age people with respect to people in the labour force determined a reducing labour force participation rate in Honduras over the period.

number of persons in the labour force indicates that the labour market was not able to absorb all new entrants. A major decline in the unemployment rate was observed in the following years. The unemployment rate fell as low as 3.1 per cent in 2008.

During and after the Great Recession and as GDP growth slowed, though, the unemployment rate increased and reached 4.4 per cent in 2011. Interestingly, the number of people in the labour force barely changed in 2011 and the number of employed persons declined (9,565 fewer employed persons), suggesting a reduction in the number of jobs. A major increase in the minimum wage implemented in 2008 is a factor that, jointly with the international crisis, had a worsening impact on the unemployment rate. There is evidence for Honduras showing that increases in the minimum wage led to disemployment effects in the private sector (Gindling and Terrell 2007). Specifically, the increase in the minimum wage in 2008 led to job losses in small and medium enterprises and in the industry sector (Villa and Lovo 2009). By 2012, a recovery took place, but the unemployment rate was still above the pre-crisis level (3.1 per cent in 2008 and 3.7 per cent in 2012).

The unemployment rate decreased for men, youth, and adult workers, while it increased slightly for women between 2001 and 2012. The effect of the international crisis on the unemployment rate was clear in 2010 and 2011. Adults and women suffered the largest increases in their unemployment rates compared to young workers and men. The unemployment rates of all population groups fell in 2012, but for adults and women they were still above their pre-crisis level of 2008.

16.4 Job Mix

> The composition of employment by occupational group exhibited little changes between 2005 (when data on this variable started becoming available) and 2012. The few changes can be interpreted as an improvement as there was a shift overall from low-earning occupations such as elementary and trades occupations to better-paying occupations such as management and services and sales jobs. All population groups benefited especially adult workers and women. During the international crisis of 2008 the composition of employment by occupational group worsened for all population groups.
>
> (Cruces et al. 2015: figure 4)

The occupational structure of employment had a mild change over the period 2005–12.[3] The few changes that did occur in the occupational composition of

[3] There was a break in the composition of employment by occupational group in 2005, when the classifications used by Honduras were changed. Despite attempts to adapt the pre- and post-2005 classifications to our preferred categories, this rupture is evident. As a result, we decided to

employment can be interpreted as an improvement insofar as the share of low-earning occupations (elementary, agricultural, and craft and trade occupations) decreased by 0.6 percentage points, while the share of mid-earning (clerical, services and sales jobs, plant and machine operators) and high-earning occupations (management, professionals, and technicians) increased by 0.5 and 0.1 percentage points (Table 16.1). The small reduction in the share of low-earning occupations is explained by a fall in the share of craft and related trades jobs (drop of 3.0 percentage points) that was counteracted by an increase in the share of agricultural, forestry, and fishery occupations (rise of 2.8 percentage points). Among high-earning occupations, management jobs increased their share by 0.6 percentage points, and this change was almost offset by a reduction in the shares of professional and technical occupations. Finally, the small increase in mid-earning jobs was related to the rise in services and sales jobs (increase of 0.8 percentage points).

Adult workers and women appear to have benefited from the changes in the structure of employment by occupational group (they experienced a slight improvement and an improvement respectively) more than young workers and men respectively (both population groups exhibited a slight worsening).

During the international crisis of 2008, the composition of employment by occupational group worsened for all population groups. The years 2008 and 2009 witnessed an increase in the share of low- and mid-earning occupations in total employment and a reduction in the share of high-earning occupations. The increase was driven by agricultural and services jobs, which is in accord with previous evidence indicating that agricultural and services sectors were slightly affected by the crisis (Cruces et al. 2015: table 2). The share of low-earning occupations in total employment recovered the pre-crisis level by 2011 for adult workers, men, and women. Young workers could not regain the pre-recession share of low-earning occupations by the end of the period. The share of high-earning occupations, on the contrary, did not recover the pre-crisis level by 2012 for any of the population groups.

> The employment structure by occupational position deteriorated between 2001 and 2012. The percentage of paid employees decreased overall, for youth and adults, and for both men and women. Most of the change took place during and after the international crisis of 2008. (Cruces et al. 2015: figure 5)

The share of wage/salaried employees—the largest category—in total employment decreased by 4.1 percentage points over the period, from 47.0 per cent in 2001 to 42.9 in 2012. The share of the self-employed, on the other hand, increased by 1.2 percentage points, climbing from 33.6 per cent in 2001 to

limit our description of the changes in the employed population by occupational group to the subperiod 2005–12.

34.7 per cent in 2012. The share of unpaid workers also grew, increasing by 1.8 percentage points over the period, as did the share of employers, which witnessed an increase of 1.2 percentage points between 2001 and 2012 (Table 16.1). Insofar as the share of low-earning categories (self-employment and unpaid employment) increased by a total of 1.5 percentage points and the share of high-earning categories (paid employees and employers) decreased, these changes can be characterized as a worsening of the employment structure in terms of occupational position.

The employment structure by occupational position deteriorated over the period for youth and adult workers and for both men and women. Between 2001 and 2012, all population groups exhibited an increase in the share of low-earning positions in total employment and a reduction in the share of high-earning categories.

The deterioration in the employment structure by occupational position in the aggregate and for all population groups occurred mainly during and following the international crisis of 2008. Between 2001 and 2008, the shares of wage/salaried employees and employers increased, while they fell during and after the international crisis (from 2008 to 2012). The share of the self-employed and the share of unpaid workers fell before the international crisis (from 2001 to 2008), while they increased during and after that event (from 2008 to 2012). The worsening in the structure of employment by occupational position is striking considering that the unemployment rate is low in Honduras—it suffered a slight increase during the crisis but recovered the downward trend by the end of the period—and that the labour force participation rate was falling over time. The changes in the structure of employment by occupational position can be interpreted in light of our previous finding related to the changes in the employment structure by occupational group. Between 2008 and 2012, services and agricultural jobs were among the occupations that exhibited the largest share of increases of total employment, and self-employed workers have a high relative weight in these occupational groups. On the other hand, technical jobs were among the occupations with the largest share of reduction in total employment, and wage/salaried employees have a high relative share in these occupations. By 2012, the employment structure by occupational position had not recovered the pre-crisis levels in the aggregate and for any of the population groups.

> The employment composition by economic sector worsened over the course of the period studied, overall and for all population groups (youth, adults, men, and women). The deterioration occurred especially during the international crisis of 2008. (Cruces et al. 2015: figure 6)

The period 2001–12 witnessed an increase from 46.5 per cent to 50.1 per cent in the share of workers in low-earning sectors (domestic services, primary activities, and low-tech industries). The increase was driven by the rise in the share of the primary activities sector. The share of workers in high-earning sectors (public administration, skilled services, and utilities and transportation) was largely unchanged over the period, shifting from 9.8 per cent in 2001 to 9.6 per cent in 2012. These changes resulted in a reduction in the share of mid-earning sectors (high-tech industry, construction, commerce, education, and health) in total employment (Table 16.1).

The employment composition by economic sector worsened for all population groups between 2001 and 2012—that is, young and adult workers, men, and women.

The international crisis of 2008 led to a worsening in the employment composition by economic sector in the aggregate and for all population groups. The growing share of workers in the primary activities sector—a low-earning sector—intensified during 2008–9. On the other hand, the share of workers in the low-tech industry sector—another low-earning sector—suffered a decline as the *maquila* was one of the subsectors most affected by the international crisis. However, the decline in the share of the low-industry sector was not enough to compensate for the increase in the share of the primary activities sector. At the other end of the scale, the share of workers in public administration and in the skilled services sectors—high-earning sectors—began a downward trend in 2008. All these changes determined a worsening in the employment structure by economic sector during the international crisis. By 2012, young workers, adult workers, and men had a worse employment composition by economic sector compared to the pre-crisis year (2008). Women finished the period with lower shares of low- and high-earning sectors than in 2008 and a larger share of mid-earning sectors.

> The educational level of the employed population improved over the period for all of the population groups, and especially among young workers. The international crisis did not have an effect on this trend. (Cruces et al. 2015: figure 7)

The share of employed workers with low educational levels (eight years of schooling or less) dropped from 77.6 per cent in 2001 to 70.2 per cent in 2012, while the share of workers with medium and high educational levels (nine to thirteen years of schooling and over thirteen years of schooling) grew from 17.3 per cent in 2001 to 23.6 per cent in 2012 and from 5.1 per cent to 6.2 per cent respectively (Table 16.1).[4] We interpret this result as an improvement for the employed population as the level of education is an important predictor of labour earnings. Consequently, the changes in the employment structure by educational level

[4] The most frequent value of years of education for employed workers in Honduras was six during the entire period (around 28.0 per cent of employed workers had six years of education).

implied an increase in the share of workers that tend to have high levels of earnings and a decline in the share of workers with low earnings levels.[5]

The improvement in the educational level of the employed population occurred for all population groups, and primarily for young workers.

The pattern of improvement in the level of education of the employed population in Honduras continued even during the international crisis of 2008. That was also the case for all population groups.

> Despite economic growth of the Honduran economy, the share of wage/salaried employees registered with the social security system exhibited a slight reduction between 2006 (when data on this variable started becoming available) and 2012, especially amongst adult workers and women. Most of the reduction took place during the international crisis of 2008. (Cruces et al. 2015: figure 8)

The social security system in Honduras is highly stratified. There are four contributory schemes and no non-contributory pension schemes (Martínez Franzoni 2013). First, the IHSS (Instituto Hondureño de Seguridad Social) grants benefits in the areas of illness, maternity, accidents at work, professional illnesses, disability, old age, death, and involuntary unemployment to workers of the private sector. Second, the INPREMA (Instituto Nacional de Previsión del Magisterio) provides life insurance, a disability pension, and a separation and retirement benefit to teachers in the public and private systems. Third, the INJUPEMP (Instituto Nacional de Jubilaciones y Pensiones de los Empleados y Funcionarios del Poder Ejecutivo) provides benefits in the case of retirement and death while in active service, as well as a disability pension to workers from the Executive branch. Finally, the IPM (Instituto de Previsión Militar) provides retirement benefits to the military, the police force, and firefighters. All contributory schemes are funded through contributions from employers and employees, and there is also a contribution from the government for the IHSS. Health care services are provided by the IHSS as part of the social security system.

Social security records show a small decrease in the percentage of wage/ salaried employees registered with the contributory schemes of the system between 2006 and 2012, from 6.2 per cent in 2006 (76,301 registered workers) to 5.2 per cent in 2012 (69,730 registered workers) (Table 16.1). Thus, the employed population in Honduras has been largely informal—just 5.5 per cent registered over the period 2006–12.

All of the population groups, and primarily adult workers and women, suffered a reduction in the share of wage/salaried workers registered with the social security system over the period.

[5] The improvement in the employment structure by educational level is related to changes in the relative demand and supply of workers with high educational levels with corresponding implications for the wage gap by educational group and the unemployment rate of each educational level. We introduce a discussion about the role of these factors in Honduras in section 16.5.

The bulk of the reduction in the share of wage/salaried workers registered with the social security system took place during the international crisis of 2008. The share of wage/salaried workers enrolled with the social security system dropped between 2008 and 2009. Those figures improved in 2010, but then resumed the downward trend. The same pattern of adjustment was observed for all population groups.

16.5 Labour Earnings

> Labour earnings decreased erratically from 2001 to 2012. Workers were affected by the 2008 international crisis and, as of 2012, earnings had not returned to pre-crisis levels. Adult workers, men, and women lost labour income between 2001 and 2012, while young workers increased their earnings. The evidence of earnings changes by employment categories indicates that labour earnings increased for low-earning categories and fell for high-earning categories in most cases. (Cruces et al. 2015: figure 9)

Average monthly earnings, expressed in dollars at 2005 purchasing power parity (PPP), decreased by 8.2 per cent, dropping from US$430 in 2001 to US$395 in 2012 (Table 16.1). For most of the period, changes in labour earnings did not reflect variations in the country's economic performance. From 2001 to 2005, labour earnings decreased while GDP grew. Much of the drop in labour earnings during the period can be attributed to a falling hourly wage pattern (an average annual reduction of 1.9 per cent) (Cruces et al. 2015: table 7). The downward trend in hourly wages was related to the implementation of a fiscal adjustment, of which the key element was the limitation of increases in the wage bill (IMF 2006). From 2005 to 2009, there was a positive relationship between changes in GDP and in labour earnings; both increased from 2005 to 2008 and then fell in 2009 during the international crisis. The increase in labour earnings between 2005 and 2008 can be explained by higher hourly wages fuelled by continuous minimum wage increases that reached their historical maximum in 2009 (Otter and Borja 2010). However, average wage increases were always below the rises in the minimum wage for two reasons. First, because only wage/salaried employees benefit by its increase and they have represented less than half of the total employed population in Honduras over the period analysed. Second, among wage/salaried employees, only two thirds of them receive a wage above the minimum established by law. There is evidence showing that in Honduras minimum wages are effectively enforced in medium- and large-scale firms, but not in small firms or for the self-employed through a lighthouse effect (Gindling and Terrell 2007). While GDP had resumed its upward trend by 2010, labour earnings continued to fall until 2011, when they increased briefly only to drop again in 2012.

Labour earnings of both men and women dropped from 2001 to 2012, as did the earnings of adults. The labour earnings of young workers, however, increased during that period. Among occupational groups, labour earnings of low-earning occupations enjoyed an average increase, while high-earning occupations suffered an average earnings reduction between 2001 and 2012. Among occupational positions, self-employed workers experienced the largest reduction in labour earnings between 2001 and 2012, followed by employers and wage/salaried employees, whose labour earnings varied only slightly. When broken down by economic sector, labour earnings increased for low-earning sectors and decreased for high-earning sectors. Disaggregating by educational levels, workers with medium levels of education experienced the largest decrease in earnings over the period. They were followed by workers with high educational levels; the earnings of workers with low educational levels exhibited a small increase over the period.

The evidence of falling labour earnings for workers with medium and high levels of education and almost no change for workers with low levels of education can be interpreted in light of previous findings of deterioration in the employment structure by occupational group and economic sector over the period. The deterioration in the employment structure by occupational group (especially during and after the international crisis) and economic sector implied a decrease in the share of occupations and sectors that can be expected to employ workers with high and medium educational levels, such as professional and technical occupations and the public administration sector, and an increase in the share of occupations and sectors that employ workers with low educational levels, such as agricultural, forestry, and fishery occupations, and the primary activities sector. This evidence indicates that the demand for workers with high and medium educational levels relative to those with low educational levels fell over the period in Honduras. On the other hand, the educational level of people in the labour force improved over the same period, indicating an increase in the relative supply of workers with high and medium levels of education (Cruces et al. 2015: table 8). The prediction of a supply and demand analysis is that the relative wages of workers with high and medium educational levels relative to those with low educational levels will fall. In the Honduran labour market, the relative wages of workers with high and medium educational levels relative to those with low educational levels fell over the period, while the relative wages of workers with high educational levels with respect to workers with medium educational levels increased slightly (Cruces et al. 2015: table 7). The adjustment process also led to a reduction in the unemployment rate of workers with low educational levels and to an increase in the unemployment rate of workers with medium educational levels.

The unemployment rate of workers with high levels of education remained essentially unchanged over the period (Cruces et al. 2015: table 9).

The international crisis of 2008 impacted negatively on labour earnings overall and for most employment categories. Labour earnings decreased between 2008 and 2009 and could not regain the pre-recession level by 2012. Workers in agricultural, forestry and fishery occupations, management, service and sales occupations, and professionals were affected negatively by the international crisis; only workers from agricultural, forestry, and fishery occupations had returned to pre-crisis levels of income by 2012. Workers from all occupational positions were impacted adversely by the international crisis. Employers had returned to pre-recession earning levels by 2011; wage/salaried employees recovered more quickly, surpassing pre-crisis levels of income by 2010. As of 2012, self-employed workers had not recovered their pre-crisis income level. Workers in most economic sectors were affected negatively by the crisis. Labour earnings in low- and high-tech industries, commerce, utilities and transportation, skilled services, and education and health services began a downward trend in 2008 and had not recovered as of 2012. The earnings of workers performing primary activities had returned to pre-crisis levels by 2011, and the earnings of domestic workers appear not to have been affected by the crisis. The earnings of workers in the construction and public administration sectors were unstable, climbing and then dropping after the crisis. Amongst educational groups, as of 2012 none of them had recovered pre-crisis levels of earnings.

16.6 Poverty and Inequality

> Whether poverty rose or fell over the period depends on the definition used. The moderate poverty rate and poverty rates based on international lines showed a mild increase between 2001 and 2012, while the extreme poverty rate fell over the same period. Within the period, poverty rates based on national and international poverty lines fell from 2002 to 2008 and increased during and after the Great Recession. The rate of working poor households was largely unchanged.
>
> (Cruces et al. 2015: figure 10)

The moderate poverty rate (measured by the country's official poverty line) increased slightly, going from 64.7 per cent in 2001 to 65.3 per cent in 2012; the extreme poverty rate declined from 45.7 per cent to 44.6 per cent; and the percentage of the working poor (defined as the proportion of persons in the population living in poor households where at least one member works) barely changed from 54.3 per cent to 54.5 per cent over the same period

(Table 16.1). The analysis based on the 2.5 and 4 dollars-a-day lines indicates that poverty rates based on international poverty lines grew over the period as a whole (5.4 percentage points using both international poverty lines).

A closer look at the evolution of these poverty indicators reveals a steady downward trend from 2002 to 2009 followed by an increase after the international crisis. The reductions in all poverty indicators from 2002 to 2008 ensued during a period of relatively quick growth and of rising social spending and minimum wages (Johnston and Lefebvre 2013). Gillingham et al. (2008) indicate that social assistance instruments such as school lunches, PRAF (programmes among beneficiaries' families) education grants, and other subsidies were all very well targeted during the poverty-reducing period, with at least two thirds of the benefits reaching the lowest two welfare quintiles. However, Honduras had difficulty implementing conditional cash transfers programmes: their impacts were limited and a duality emerged between the domestically directed and the externally financed programmes (Moore 2010). For the subperiod that spans from 2001 to 2004, Gindling and Terrell (2010) also demonstrate that an increase in the minimum wage led to a reduction in poverty. Following the international crisis of 2008, all poverty indicators began an upward trend which led to the vanishing of the improvements observed in the previous years. In fact, due to the rise at the end of the period, poverty rates based on international poverty lines grew over the period as a whole (5.4 percentage points using both international poverty lines). Poverty rate increases were associated with reductions in public spending in education, health, housing, and transport from 2010 to 2012 (Johnston and Lefebvre 2013).

The poverty patterns reported in the last paragraph can be interpreted by examining incomes from various sources. The analysis of sources of household total income indicates that labour income increased between 2002 and 2008, and decreased afterwards, mimicking the poverty indicators time trend (Cruces et al. 2015: figure 11). Incomes from pensions increased overall, especially during the poverty-reducing period (from 2002 to 2006). Income from poverty alleviation PRAF programme and *Merienda Escolar* programme mainly suffered a reduction between 2007 (the earliest we have detailed data on these variables) and 2009. In 2010, an upward trend started with the introduction of the *Bono 10.000*, a programme for education, health, and nutrition. Remittances have become an increasingly important source of income for Honduran families, especially in the first half of the 2000s. They represented around 10.0 per cent of total household income in 2007 (Villa and Lovo 2009). The explanatory factors for the increasing share of remittances in total household income are immigration to the US after Hurricane Mitch and the declining transaction costs for sending money from abroad (IMF 2006). However, remittances started a downward trend during the international crisis and had not recovered the previous levels by 2012 (Johnston and Lefebvre 2013).

> While there were some ups and downs, the period as a whole witnessed a slight increase in household per capita income inequality and labour earnings inequality.
> (Cruces et al. 2015: figure 12)

Between 2001 and 2012 the Gini coefficient of household per capita income grew from 0.539 to 0.573, while the Gini coefficient of labour earnings among employed workers increased from 0.539 to 0.573 (Table 16.1). Household per capita income and labour earnings inequality increased from 2001 to 2005, as did GDP. The Gini coefficient of household per capita income grew from 0.539 in 2001 to 0.593 in 2005 and the Gini coefficient of labour earnings increased from 0.541 in 2001 to 0.575 in 2005. The Gini fell from 2005 to 2009, reaching 0.516 in the case of household per capita income and 0.526 in the case of labour earnings. An upward trend resumed after the international crisis, with a slight recovery in 2012. Nonetheless, the inequality level measured by the Gini coefficient is still well above the pre-crisis level for both household per capita income and labour earnings.

Changes in household per capita income inequality in Honduras have been related mainly to changes in non-labour incomes. Azevedo et al. (2013b) decomposed the change in the Gini coefficient of household per capita income for the period 1999–2010 and found that changes in incomes from transfers and the share of adults by household contributed the most to the inequality reduction over this period (the Gini coefficient of household per capita income decreased from 0.543 to 0.534 between 1999 and 2010). Changes in labour incomes had only a small effect that was inequality-increasing. Otter and Borja (2010) analysed the period 2002–7 and found labour income reductions in the lower tail of the distribution of household per capita income that were compensated for by government transfers and remittances from abroad. On the other hand, there were labour income gains in the upper tail of the distribution. These structural changes resulted in a small change in the Gini coefficient of household per capita income, but made poorer people less able to improve their wellbeing through the labour market. Azevedo et al. (2013a) used a decomposition approach and found that changes in the education wage premium (or the 'price effect') were inequality-reducing, while changes in the distribution of the stock of education (the 'quantity effect') were inequality-increasing in Honduras between 1999 and 2009. However, both effects are small and most of the increase in the Gini coefficient over the period studied by these authors remained unexplained. Gasparini et al. (2011) found a reduction in the gap between the wages of skilled workers (those with complete or incomplete college education) and unskilled workers (those who have completed secondary education or less) in Honduras over the 2000s. The shrinking educational earnings gap can be explained by factors related to supply and demand: the relative supply of skilled workers increased steadily while the relative demand for those workers fell. Another factor associated with the evolution of earnings inequality is the minimum wage. Otter and Borja (2010) highlighted that increases in the minimum wage in Honduras only benefit wage/salaried workers, e.g. hourly wages of self-employed workers do not follow the trend of the minimum wage, and among wage/salaried workers one third receive less than the wage established by law, e.g. minimum wages are not completely enforced. As a result, self-employed workers end up receiving lower real wages than wage/salaried workers even in periods of economic growth.

16.7 Conclusions

By Latin American standards, Honduras experienced slow economic growth during the 2000s. The country underwent a recession as a consequence of the international crisis of 2008, and while the Honduran economy returned to the pre-recession GDP level in 2010, GDP per capita did not reach the pre-crisis level until 2012.

The evidence regarding the changes in labour market indicators between 2001 and 2012 showed more deteriorations than improvements. The improvements were as follows. The unemployment rate fell from 2001 to 2012. The composition of employment by occupational group improved slightly from 2005 to 2012, shifting overall from low-earning occupations such as elementary and trade occupations to better-paying occupations such as management and services and sales jobs. The educational level of the employed population improved over the period. On the other hand, some labour market indicators deteriorated. The employment structure by occupational position worsened during 2001–12 as the proportion of workers in high-earning categories (paid employees and employers) fell and the proportion in low-earning categories (self-employment and unpaid employment) rose. Employment composition by economic sector also worsened over the course of the period studied as the share of workers in low-earning sectors (domestic service, primary activities, and low-tech industries) increased while the share of workers in high-earning sectors (public administration, skilled services, and utilities and transportation) was largely unchanged. Despite the growth of the Honduran economy, the share of wage/salaried employees registered with the social security system experienced a slight reduction during 2006–12. Finally, labour earnings decreased from 2001 to 2012. The moderate poverty rate increased slightly from 2001 to 2012, as did household per capita income and labour earnings inequality measured by the Gini coefficient. On the other hand, the extreme poverty rate decreased over the period and the rate of working poor households was largely unchanged.

Looking specifically at the international crisis of 2008, most labour market indicators were affected negatively by the crisis. The unemployment rate increased and had not fully recovered by 2012. The employment structure by occupational group worsened during the crisis. Most of the deterioration in the employment structure by occupational position and economic sector over the period 2001–12 took place during and after the international crisis of 2008. Labour earnings were affected negatively by the crisis and, as of 2012, earnings had not returned to pre-crisis levels. The poverty rates based on national and international poverty lines and the inequality of household per capita income and labour earnings increased during the international crisis and none of them returned to their pre-recession level by 2012.

Young workers had worse labour market outcomes over the period compared to adults, and men and women exhibited a balanced situation in the labour market. The international crisis affected adult workers more than young workers, while the impacts were evenly distributed between men and women. The unemployment rate was higher for young compared to adult workers, the share of young employed workers in low-earning occupations and sectors was larger than the share of adult workers, the percentage of young workers registered with the social security system was lower when compared to adults, and labour earnings of young workers were below those of adults. On the other hand, the share of young workers in low-earning positions was lower compared to adults. Despite the generally inferior situation of young workers in the labour market compared to adults, adult labour market indicators were more adversely affected by the episode of the international crisis. Disaggregating by gender, we found that men had better labour market outcomes than women in some cases, such as the unemployment rate, the share of workers in low-earning positions, and average labour earnings, while women were better than men for other labour market indicators, such as the share of workers in low-earning occupations and sectors, and the share of unregistered workers. Both men and women were evenly impacted by the international crisis.

In summary, slow economic growth in Honduras during the 2000s was associated, in general, with labour market conditions that moved in a worsening direction. Most of them were affected adversely by the international crisis of 2008 and did not recover their pre-crisis level by 2012.

References

Azevedo, J. P., M. E. Dávalos, C. Díaz-Bonilla, B. Atuesta, and R. A. Castañeda (2013a). 'Fifteen Years of Inequality in Latin America. How Have Labor Markets Helped?'. Policy Research Working Paper 6384. Washington, DC: World Bank.

Azevedo, J. P., G. Inchauste, and V. Sanfelice (2013b). 'Decomposing the Recent Inequality Decline in Latin America'. Policy Research Working Paper 6715. Washington, DC: World Bank.

CEDLAS and World Bank (2014). SEDLAC—Socio-Economic Database for Latin America and the Caribbean. Centro de Estudios Distributivos, Laborales y Sociales, Facultad de Ciencias Económicas, Universidad Nacional de La Plata and World Bank Poverty Group LCR. Available at <http://sedlac.econo.unlp.edu.ar/eng/index.php>, accessed 2014.

Cordero, J. A. (2009). *Honduras: Recent Economic Performance*. Washington, DC: Center for Economic and Policy Research.

Cruces, G., G. Fields, D. Jaume, and M. Viollaz (2015). 'The Growth–Employment–Poverty Nexus in Latin America in the 2000s: Honduras Country Study'. WIDER Working Paper 2015/078. Helsinki: UNU-WIDER.

García Merino, F. (2009). 'Políticas e instituciones para el desarrollo económico territorial: El caso de Honduras'. Series Desarrollo Territorial 7. Santiago de Chile: Economic Commission for Latin America and the Caribbean.

Gasparini, L., S. Galiani, G. Cruces, and P. Acosta (2011). 'Educational Upgrading and Returns to Skills in Latin America: Evidence from a Supply–Demand Framework, 1990–2010'. IZA Working Paper 6244. Bonn: Institute for the Study of Labor.

Gillingham, R., D. Newhouse, and I. Yackovlev (2008). 'The Distributional Impact of Fiscal Policy in Honduras'. IMF Working Paper 08/168. Washington, DC: Intenational Monetary Fund.

Gindling, T. H. and K. Terrell (2007). 'Minimum Wages and the Welfare of Workers in Honduras'. IZA Discussion Paper 2892. Bonn: Institute for the Study of Labor.

Gindling, T. H. and K. Terrell (2010). 'Minimum Wages, Globalization, and Poverty in Honduras', *World Development* 38 (6): 908–18.

IMF (2001). 'IMF Concludes 2001 Article IV Consultation with Honduras'. Public Information Notice 01/108. Washington, DC: International Monetary Fund.

IMF (2006). 'Honduras: 2005 Article IV Consultation'. IMF Country Report 06/35. Washington, DC: International Monetary Fund.

Johnston, J. and S. Lefebvre (2013). 'Honduras Since the Coup: Economic and Social Outcomes'. Washington, DC: Center for Economic and Policy Research.

Martínez Franzoni, J. (2013). 'Social Protection Systems in Latin America and the Caribbean: Honduras'. ECLAC, Project Documents Collection. Santiago de Chile: United Nations.

Moore, C. (2010). 'The Political Economy of Social Protection in Honduras and Nicaragua', in M. Adato and J. Hoddinott (eds), *Conditional Cash Transfers in Latin America*. Baltimore, MD: International Food Policy Research Institute, 101–26.

Otter, T. and I. Borja (2010). 'Impactos económicos y sociales de la crisis internacional en Honduras'. Serie Estudios en Economía. Tegucigalpa: Programa de las Naciones Unidas para el Desarrollo en Honduras.

Villa, M. and H. Lovo (2009). 'Crisis y pobreza rural en América Latina: El caso de Honduras'. Documento de Trabajo 46. Santiago de Chile: Rimisp—Centro Latinoamericano para el Desarrollo Rural.

World Bank (2014). World Development Indicators. Available at <http://data.worldbank.org/data-catalog/world-development-indicators>, accessed April 2014.

17

Mexico

17.1 Introduction

This chapter on labour markets and growth in Mexico since 2000 is one of sixteen studies of Latin American countries, each of which analyses the growth–employment–poverty nexus and aims to answer the following broad questions: Has economic growth resulted in economic development via improved labour market conditions in Latin America in the 2000s, and have these improvements halted or been reversed since the Great Recession? How do the rate and character of economic growth, changes in the various labour market indicators, and changes in poverty relate to each other?

To answer these questions, we analyse the growth experience of Mexico during the 2000s and a wide set of labour market indicators that we assign to one of two different categories: employment and earnings indicators, and poverty and income inequality indicators. More specifically, for the group of employment and earnings indicators we construct statistics on the following variables: the unemployment rate; the employment structure by occupational group, employment position, economic sector, registration of workers with the social security system, and educational level; and mean labour earnings and hourly wages. We present all these indicators for the employed population as a whole and for different population groups (youth, adults, men, and women). For the group of poverty and income inequality indicators, we compute poverty rates using the official moderate and extreme poverty lines and the international lines of 2.5 and 4 dollars a day. We also calculate the Gini coefficient of household per capita income and labour earnings.

All the statistics in this chapter are obtained using microdata from the Encuesta Nacional de Ingresos y Gastos de los Hogares (ENIGH) for the years 2000, 2002, 2004–6, 2008, 2010, and 2012. The nationwide surveys were processed following a harmonization methodology and incorporated into the SEDLAC—Socio-Economic Database for Latin America and the Caribbean

(CEDLAS and World Bank 2014).[1] The resulting labour market indicators were compiled into a large number of tables and figures, which are available in an earlier version of this study (henceforth, Cruces et al. 2015). Chapter 1 of this book provides the definition for each of the indicators we analyse here, while Cruces et al. (2015) includes details on definitions and classification systems used by Mexico's household surveys, and on comparability issues of these surveys over time.

17.2 Economic Growth

> Mexico experienced slow economic growth from 2000 to 2012. The country's economy was affected by the 2000–01 recession in the US, and it was severely hurt by the international crisis of 2008, although by 2012 output levels had surpassed pre-crisis levels. (Cruces et al. 2015: figures 1 and 2)

During the period 2000–12, Mexico experienced slow economic growth by Latin American standards. GDP per capita increased by 10.6 per cent, while the average for the eighteen Latin American countries was 36.2 per cent during the same period. GDP (measured in PPP dollars of 2005) grew by 28.7 per cent, and GDP per employed person rose by 6.1 per cent. The annual growth rate of GDP per capita was 1.1 per cent, and it varied from a minimum of −5.9 per cent in 2009 to a maximum of 3.8 per cent in 2010 (Table 17.1).

Mexico (jointly with Guatemala) exhibited the worst economic performance among all of the countries in Latin America in terms of GDP per capita growth during the 2000s. The period under study was characterized by marked fluctuations in the growth rate which were closely related to variations in the U.S. growth rate. In fact, changes in U.S. growth have been one of the factors explaining the variation in Mexico's growth rate since the formation of the North American Free Trade Agreement (NAFTA) in 1994 (Blecker 2008).[2] A first episode of slow growth occurred from 2001 to 2003, during which Mexico's economy was affected by the 2000–1 recession in the U.S. Though GDP grew at an average rate of 0.3 per cent per year from 2001 to 2003, annual GDP per capita fell by 1.0 per cent.

The economy bounced back and resumed growth in the following years, but another sharp decline ensued in 2009 as a consequence of the economic crisis in Europe and the U.S. Indeed, Mexico was affected more by the international

[1] See Cruces et al. (2015: table 1) for details on the size of Mexico household surveys.

[2] The North American Free Trade Agreement (NAFTA) is a trilateral free trade agreement that eliminated trade and investment barriers between Canada, Mexico, and the United States.

Table 17.1 Mexico: Evolution of growth and labour market indicators over the 2000s

		2000	2001	2002	2003	2004	2005	2006	2007	2008	2009	2010	2011	2012	
Growth Indicators	GDP per capita	11,810	11,575	11,440	11,460	11,807	12,017	12,462	12,695	12,711	11,962	12,412	12,747	13,067	
	GDP per capita growth rate	3.72	−1.99	−1.17	0.17	3.03	1.78	3.70	1.86	0.13	−5.89	3.76	2.70	2.51	
Employment and Earnings Indicators	Employment-to-population ratio	59.43	...	59.89	...	59.28	59.72	62.34	...	59.43	...	57.79	...	62.48	
	Unemployment rate	2.18	...	2.95	...	3.77	3.77	3.31	...	4.48	...	5.66	...	4.23	
	Share of low-earnings occupations	32.04	...	31.26	...	28.91	28.98	29.16	...	28.98	...	41.41	...	43.08	
	Share of mid-earnings occupations	53.01	...	55.43	...	56.49	55.76	55.59	...	55.42	...	39.64	...	39.06	
	Share of high-earnings occupations	14.95	...	13.31	...	14.60	15.26	15.26	...	15.60	...	18.94	...	17.86	
	Share of employers	4.79	...	4.04	...	3.29	3.81	4.07	...	9.93	...	9.43	...	10.72	
	Share of wage/salaried employees	66.14	...	65.73	...	70.22	68.86	67.16	...	71.78	...	72.94	...	68.31	
	Share of self-employed workers	21.81	...	23.21	...	21.17	21.39	22.61	...	12.80	...	12.76	...	15.06	
	Share of unpaid family workers	7.26	...	7.02	...	5.31	5.94	6.17	...	5.49	...	4.87	...	5.91	
	Share of workers in low-earnings sectors	31.52	...	30.13	...	26.74	26.56	26.24	...	26.11	...	25.93	...	28.12	
	Share of workers in mid-earnings sectors	47.80	...	49.13	...	50.53	50.79	51.84	...	50.99	...	50.65	...	49.64	

	Share of workers in high-earnings sectors	20.67	...	20.74	...	22.74	22.65	21.92	...	22.91	...	23.43	...	22.24	
	Share of low-educated workers	49.48	...	48.48	...	45.01	44.06	42.69	...	40.98	...	37.86	...	37.19	
	Share of medium-educated workers	35.49	...	38.14	...	39.72	40.50	41.92	...	43.64	...	44.66	...	46.25	
	Share of high-educated workers	15.03	...	13.38	...	15.27	15.43	15.39	...	15.38	...	17.48	...	16.56	
	Share of workers registered with SS	45.63	...	41.58	...	40.32	39.38	40.99	...	39.61	...	37.15	...	34.94	
	Mean labour earnings	598.6	...	575.4	...	591.7	616.5	616.6	...	622.0	...	554.6	...	563.9	
Poverty and Inequality Indicators	Official extreme poverty rate	24.61	...	20.49	...	18.67	18.89	15.15	...	19.26	...	19.31	...	20.16	
	Official moderate poverty rate	55.63	...	51.59	...	47.89	47.71	44.43	...	48.51	...	50.88	...	52.00	
	Poverty rate 2.5 dollars-a-day	19.54	...	17.15	...	14.73	14.98	11.83	...	13.57	...	12.61	...	11.45	
	Poverty rate 4 dollars-a-day	36.97	...	34.10	...	30.82	29.89	27.03	...	28.54	...	28.16	...	27.65	
	GINI of household per capita income	0.536	...	0.510	...	0.507	0.509	0.495	...	0.502	...	0.472	...	0.491	
	GINI of labour earnings	0.520	...	0.515	...	0.497	0.507	0.505	...	0.508	...	0.474	...	0.512	

Note: The shaded figures of labour market indicators represent statistical significant improvements at 5 per cent between the initial and final years for all the employment and earnings indicators and poverty and inequality indicators. The only exceptions are the share of mid-earnings occupations, share of mid-earnings sectors, and share of medium-educated workers for which we did not assign welfare evaluation criteria. The vertical lines indicate that series are not fully comparable before and after that line. For occupational indicators we compared 2000 and 2008; for employment position indicators we compared 2000 and 2006.

Source: SEDLAC (CEDLAS and World Bank 2014) and World Development Indicators (World Bank 2014).

crisis than any other Latin American country. The impact of the crisis was felt in Mexico through several channels. First, the deep recession in the U.S. led to a drop in the demand for Mexico's exports. The high dependence of Mexico on exports to the U.S. (Mexican exports to the U.S. accounted for almost 80 per cent of total exports before the crisis) as well as their composition (a considerable proportion of those exports are durable goods) are factors that help explain why the growth collapse was more pronounced in Mexico compared to other countries in Latin America (Martorano 2014). Second, the global recession also led to a drop in international energy prices; because Mexico is an oil exporter, this drop coupled with a decline in domestic oil production had an unfavourable effect on Mexico's export earnings. Third, due to the labour market downturn in the U.S. Mexican migrants to the U.S. faced greater difficulties in finding and keeping jobs, which negatively affected the flow of remittances to Mexico (Sidaoui et al. 2011).[3] The effect of the international crisis was also felt through some financial channels. The crisis led to an increase in the risk premium of emerging market debt and to a reversal in capital flows to these economies. In Mexico, big conglomerates were affected the most due to their dependence on external funds for their operation. The depreciation of the Mexican peso also impacted negatively on the private sector, which owed more than 50 per cent of Mexico's external debt, a large fraction of it in foreign currency (Moreno-Brid and Paunovic 2009). GDP per capita fell by 5.9 per cent in 2009, although pre-crisis levels were regained relatively quickly by the year 2011, and economic growth continued throughout 2012.

The recovery resulted primarily from three factors. First, a rebound in manufacturing exports, mostly to the U.S. but also to other markets. Second, a strengthening internal market fuelled by a healthy domestic financial sector and the growth in employment rates.[4] Third, significant capital inflows from advanced economies seeking higher rates of return in emerging markets such as Mexico (Cañas et al. 2011; IMF 2013).

[3] Remittances represented 3.9 per cent of private consumption in 2007. Even though this figure does not seem high, the consumption of low-income families in the regions of Mexico with high migration rates depends heavily on the flow of remittances from the United States (Sidaoui et al. 2011).

[4] The stimulus package of the Mexican government included infrastructure spending, support to small- and medium-sized enterprises and to the export sector, introduction or expansion of employment programmes (*Programa de Preservación del Empleo* and *Programa Temporal de Empleo*), expansion of the *Oportunidades* cash transfer programme, regulations to facilitate the withdrawal of savings from individual pension accounts, extension of coverage of the medical insurance and maternity benefits for dismissed workers, and guaranteed pension to elderly individuals who became unemployed and had contributed for at least twenty-four years (Martorano 2014). There is no evidence indicating to what extent each of these policy measures contributed to the recovery of the economy.

17.3 Unemployment

> The unemployment rate increased substantially between 2000 and 2012 overall and for all population groups. Within the period, the unemployment rate increased from 2000 to 2004, fell from 2004 to 2006, exhibited an upward trend again until 2010, and dropped in the last year of the period. The international crisis of 2008 led to an increase in the unemployment rate. (Cruces et al. 2015: figure 3)

The unemployment rate (measured as the ratio of unemployment to labour force) grew from 2.2 per cent in 2000 (861,563 unemployed persons) to 4.2 per cent in 2012 (2,327,977 unemployed persons) (Table 17.1). Even though these unemployment rates are relatively low by developed country standards, the unemployment rate almost doubled in the twelve years under study. The movements along this increasing trend followed the business cycle. The unemployment rate rose from 2.2 per cent to 3.8 per cent between 2000 and 2004 when the country suffered the effects of the U.S. recession of 2000–1. It then stabilized at around 3.5 per cent and even decreased slightly in 2006. However, it shot up once again during and after the Great Recession, reaching a maximum for the period of 5.7 per cent in 2010 (2,816,714 unemployed persons). The increase in the unemployment rate after the international crisis was driven mainly by the destruction of jobs in the manufacturing sector (Freije et al. 2011). Unemployment fell to 4.2 per cent in 2012—while lower than the level of 2008, this is still higher than the pre-crisis rate (3.0 per cent in 2006).

Between 2000 and 2012, the unemployment rate increased for young and adult workers, and for men and women. Within the period, the unemployment rate followed the aggregate trend for each population group, with an increase in the early years of the period, a reduction between 2004 and 2006 for young workers, between 2005 and 2006 for adults and men, and between 2004 and 2005 for women, an upward trend up to 2010, and a reduction in 2012.

The international crisis led to an increase in the aggregate unemployment rate and in the unemployment rate of all population groups. Both the number of persons in the labour force and the number of employed persons increased between 2006 and 2010, indicating that the increase in the unemployment rate during the international crisis was explained by the new entrants into the labour market who could not find a job. By 2012, the youth unemployment rate and the unemployment rate for women were below the pre-crisis value of 2006; the adult unemployment rate was above the level of 2006 and 2008; the unemployment rate for men was below the level of 2008 but above the level of 2006.

17.4 Job Mix

> The employment composition by occupational group improved moderately between 2000 and 2008 in the aggregate and for all population groups, and deteriorated between 2010 and 2012 overall and for adult workers, men, and women. (Cruces et al. 2015: figure 4)[5]

The share of the following occupations shrank between 2000 and 2008: agricultural occupations (drop of 3.9 percentage points); crafts and trades occupations (drop of 1.8 percentage points); and plant and machine operators (drop of 0.7 percentage points). The share of the following occupations grew: services and sales workers (increase of 4.2 percentage points) and elementary (increase of 1.5 percentage points). The share of the other occupational groups remained largely unchanged. These changes in the occupational composition of employment can be interpreted as a slight improvement since low-earning occupations (agricultural, elementary, and plant and machine operators) reduced their share in total employment by 3.1 percentage points between 2000 and 2008, while mid-earning (crafts and trades workers, services and sales, clerical, and armed forces) and high-earning occupations (management, professionals, and technicians) gained share in total employment (increase of 2.4 and 0.7 percentage points respectively) (Table 17.1).

During the period 2000–8, young workers, adults, men, and women improved their employment structure by occupational groups.

Due to a methodological change in the household survey, the series up to 2008 is not fully comparable with the years 2010–12. Unfortunately, the effect of the crisis is difficult to disentangle from the methodological change.[6] Nonetheless, from 2010 to 2012 there was an increase in the share of low-earning occupations in total employment and a decrease in the share of high-earning occupations. The increase in the share of workers in low-earning occupations is explained mainly by the rise in the share of agricultural occupations. These changes suggest a worsening in the employment composition after the crisis, with no sign of recovery in the short term. Disaggregating by population group, the changes in the employment structure by occupational group between 2010 and 2012 show a worsening for adult workers and women, a slight worsening for men, and an improvement for young workers.

[5] A methodological change in the classification of occupations used by Mexico's household surveys in the year 2010 prevents us from comparing the series up to 2008 with the years 2010–12. See the WIDER Working Paper of this chapter for more details.

[6] Until 2010, the participation of occupations related to services and sales was the largest in relation to total employment. However, in 2010 the participation of elementary occupations increased by 12.0 percentage points in two years to become the main occupational category. The methodological change in the classification seems to be behind this evolution.

> The employment structure by occupational position remained essentially unchanged from 2000 to 2006 and worsened from 2008 to 2012, in the aggregate and for all population groups. After the international crisis of 2008, the employment structure by occupational position improved overall and for young workers, adults, and women, but it remained largely unchanged for men.
> (Cruces et al. 2015: figure 5)[7]

During 2000–6, the employment structure by occupational position exhibited small changes. The share of low-earning positions in total employment (self-employed and unpaid workers) dropped by only 0.3 percentage points. From 2008 to 2012, the employment structure by occupational position worsened, as the share of low-earning categories increased by 2.7 percentage points (Table 17.1).

Between 2000 and 2006, the employment structure by occupational position improved for young workers and men, while it remained largely unchanged for adults and women, and worsened between 2008 and 2012 for all population groups. The deterioration that took place from 2008 to 2012 is explained by the rise in the share of self-employment for all population groups. In a context of increasing unemployment, as was the period 2008–10 in Mexico, economic necessity may have compelled workers to take up free-entry self-employment activities.

During the international crisis of 2008, the employment structure by occupational position exhibited a slight improvement in the aggregate, for young and adult workers and women, and small changes for men. Between 2008 and 2010 (a comparison between 2006 and 2010 is not possible due to a methodological change in the survey), the share of low-earning positions in total employment dropped in the aggregate and for young workers, adults, and women. For young workers, men, and women, there was a substantial increase in the share of low-earning positions in total employment after the crisis (between 2010 and 2012) due to the rise in the share of self-employment.

> The employment composition by economic sector improved over the course of the period studied overall and for all population groups. The international crisis of 2008 did not interrupt the improving trend in the employment structure by economic sector in the aggregate and for young workers, adults, and women, but it led to a slight worsening for men. (Cruces et al. 2015: figure 6)

The period 2000–12 witnessed a reduction (from 31.5 per cent to 28.1 per cent) in the share of workers in low-earning sectors (domestic service, primary activities, and low-tech industry). There was, during the same period, an

[7] The comparison between the periods 2000–6 and 2008–12 is problematic because in 2008 the survey questionnaire was modified with different questions geared to identify occupational positions.

increase (from 20.7 per cent to 22.2 per cent) in the share of high-earning sectors (skilled services, public administration, and education and health) in the total. These changes resulted in an increase in the share of mid-earning sectors in total employment (from 47.8 per cent to 49.6 per cent) over the same period (Table 17.1).

The employment composition by economic sector improved during 2000–12 for young and adult workers, men, and women, as they moved from low-earning sectors to high-earning sectors.

The international crisis of 2008 did not affect the improving trend in the employment composition by economic sector in the aggregate and for young workers, adults, and women, but it led to a slight worsening for men. The continued improvement in the structure of employment by economic sector despite the international crisis in the aggregate and for young workers, adults, and women can be explained by the reduction in the share of workers in the low-tech industry sector in total employment. That occurred as a consequence of the sharp drop in exports to the U.S. (Villareal 2010). As the low-tech industry sector is a low-earning sector in Mexico, the reduction in its share in total employment implied an improvement in the labour market for those workers who remained employed.

By contrast, between 2006 and 2010, the share of low-earning sectors in total employment increased for men. The share of high-earning sectors increased as well, but by slightly less. The share of low-and high-earning sectors continued to increase by the end of the period for men, but the increase in the share of high-earning sectors was always below that of the low-earning sectors.

> The educational level of the employed population in Mexico improved steadily over the period for all population groups, and especially among young workers. The improving trend was not adversely affected by the international crisis of 2008.
>
> (Cruces et al. 2015: figure 7)

The share of employed workers with low educational levels (eight years of schooling or less) dropped from 49.5 per cent in 2000 to 37.2 per cent in 2012, while the shares of workers with medium and high educational levels (nine to thirteen years of schooling and over thirteen years of schooling) grew from 35.5 per cent in 2000 to 46.3 per cent in 2012 and from 15.0 per cent to 16.6 per cent respectively (Table 17.1).[8] We interpret this result as an improvement for the employed population as the level of education is an important predictor of labour earnings. Consequently, the changes in the employment

[8] The most frequent value of years of education for employed workers in Mexico was six in 2000 (18.9 per cent of employed workers had six years of education) and nine from 2002 to 2012 (around 21.8 per cent of employed workers had nine years of education).

structure by educational level implied an increase in the share of workers that tend to have high levels of earnings and a decline in the share of workers with low earnings levels.[9]

The educational level of the employed population improved during the period 2000–12 for all groups and especially for young workers. The more rapid reduction in the share of workers with low levels of education for youth compared to adults could be indicating that the insertion of young workers into the labour market is more difficult as they need higher education to become employed compared to adults (for whom their educational level is largely predetermined). However, Lopez-Calva et al. (2013b) indicated that the improvement in the educational level of the employed population seems to be associated with higher public spending per student in basic education and an increase in education coverage in rural areas. These factors eased supply-side constraints while the conditional cash transfer programme *Oportunidades* reduced demand-side constraints by compensating poor households for schooling costs and for the opportunity cost of children's labour.

The pattern of improvement in the level of education of the employed population in Mexico continued even during the international crisis of 2008, overall and for all population groups.

> The percentage of wage/salaried employees registered with the social security system decreased between 2000 and 2012 overall and for all population groups. The worsening trend continued during the international crisis of 2008.
>
> (Cruces et al. 2015: figure 8)

Mexico has several social security systems, which are intended to provide pensions and health care as well as other benefits to workers and their families (ISSA 2014). Some of the systems are: (1) the IMSS, which covers workers in private enterprises, and a series of full subsystems; (2) the ISSSTE, which covers public employees; (3) the ISSFAM, which covers armed forces employees; (4) Pemex (Mexico's state oil company), which covers Pemex's workers; and (5) RJP IMSS, which covers IMSS employees. In addition to these traditional institutions of contributory social security (the social security system, for short), recent programmes have provided some social insurance benefits for those not covered by the system. Most notably, the *Seguro Popular* provides health insurance only for poor persons, informal, and self-employed workers.

The benefits are provided by the social security systems through contributory and non-contributory schemes. The contributory scheme is mandatory

[9] The improvement in the employment structure by educational level is related to changes in the relative demand and supply of workers with high levels of education with corresponding implications for the wage gap by educational group and the unemployment rate of each educational level. We introduce a discussion about the role of these factors in Mexico in section 17.5.

for private-sector employees who contribute to the system jointly with employers and the government to cover health risks and old-age pensions. For other workers, like self-employed persons, household workers, and employers, the contribution is voluntary. The non-contributory schemes cover persons living in households with income below a legally defined threshold and are funded totally by the government. An intermediate system is the *Seguro Popular* that covers health risks for informal workers, the self-employed, and poor persons. The system is funded by the government and by the families according to their socioeconomic level.

Mexican social security system records show that the percentage of wage/salaried employees who are registered with traditional institutions of contributory social security fell from 45.6 per cent in 2000 to 34.9 per cent in 2012 (Table 17.1). This trend abated in 2006, but resumed at a steady rate in 2008 during the Great Recession. Indeed, in terms of registered employment, Mexico was one of the countries most affected by the economic crisis (ECLAC-ILO 2012), and there was no sign of a major recovery in this employment indicator as of 2012. There was a lower rate of registration with the social security system among wage/salaried employees in Mexico in 2012 than in 2000 for two reasons. First, registered wage/salaried employees increased much less compared to wage/salaried unregistered workers from 2000 to 2012. The number of registered workers grew by 876,414, while the number of unregistered workers increased by 9,472,012. Second, those workers who were unemployed or inactive and who wanted to enter the labour market found it more difficult to obtain registered (formal) jobs so they took up unregistered (informal) wage and salaried employment or self-employment instead (Lederman et al. 2011). Consequently, the mix of employment involved larger numbers of unregistered employees compared to the number of registered employees.

The rate of registration with the social security system dropped for all population groups (young and adult workers, men, and women). The pattern of reduction in the percentage of wage/salaried employees registered with the social security system continued during the international crisis of 2008 overall and for all population groups. The number of registered workers contracted by 136,143 between 2006 and 2010, while the number of unregistered workers increased by 3,045,103 over the same period.

17.5 Labour Earnings

Labour earnings decreased between 2000 and 2012 for workers as a whole. Within the period, there was a reduction in the early years of the period (from 2000 to 2002), an increase from 2002 to 2008, a fall in 2010, and an

> upward change in the last year. Over the full period (2000 to 2012), labour earnings decreased for adult workers and men, but increased for young workers and women. The evidence of earning changes by employment categories over the period indicates that labour earnings reductions tended to be larger in percentages for high-earning categories compared to low-earning categories. All population groups and employment categories were affected negatively by the 2008 crisis in terms of earnings.
>
> (Cruces et al. 2015: figure 9)

Average monthly earnings, expressed in dollars at 2005 purchasing power parity (PPP), decreased by 5.8 per cent, from US$599 in 2000 to US$564 in 2012 (Table 17.1). Labour earnings fell at the beginning of the period—between 2000 and 2002—rose between 2002 and 2008, fell during the international crisis, and increased in the last year of the period studied. Interestingly, in a context of moderate inflation, as was the case in Mexico during the 2000s, the adjustment of the labour market took place mainly through changes in the level of employment rather than changes in real hourly wages, in contrast to what happened in the 1980s and 1990s (Samaniego 2009; Messina and Gambetti 2014).

Disaggregating, we find that adult workers and men suffered a reduction in their labour earnings, while young workers and women enjoyed an increase between 2000 and 2012. Labour earnings fell between 2000 and 2002 for young workers, adults, and men, increased for all population groups in the following years, and experienced a new reduction during the international crisis.

Between 2000 and 2012, average earnings increased for some employment categories and decreased for others. The earnings decreases (increases) tended to be larger for workers in high-earning (low-earning) categories compared to low-earning (high-earning) categories. Among occupational groups, we can only compare 2000 with 2008 and 2010 with 2012. Agricultural, forestry and fishery workers, workers in elementary occupations, and plant and machine operators (low-earning occupational groups) had an average increase in their labour earnings between 2000 and 2008 and an earnings reduction between 2010 and 2012. Workers in management, professionals, and technicians (high-earning occupational groups) suffered an earnings reduction on average between 2000 and 2008, and an increase between 2010 and 2012. When the working population is broken down by occupational position, we can make comparisons between 2000 and 2006, and between 2008 and 2012. The self-employed had a larger increase in labour earnings than employers between 2000 and 2006, and a larger reduction between 2008 and 2012. Among economic sectors, domestic workers and workers from primary activities and low-tech industry (low-earning sectors) exhibited larger earnings gains over the period than workers in skilled services, public administration, and education and health (high-earning sectors). Finally, labour earnings of workers with high educational levels suffered a larger earnings loss than workers with medium and low levels of education.

The evidence of falling labour earnings for all educational groups can be interpreted in light of previous findings of improving educational levels of the Mexican employed population and improving employment structure by economic sector over the period. The improving employment structure by economic sector implied an increase in the share of sectors that can be expected to employ workers with high educational levels, such as skilled services, public administration, and education and health, and a reduction in the share of sectors that employ workers with low educational levels, such as primary activities and low-tech industries. This evidence indicates that the demand for workers with high and medium educational levels relative to those with low educational levels increased between 2000 and 2012. On the other hand, the educational level of people in the labour force improved over the same period, indicating an increase in the relative supply of workers with high and low levels of education (Cruces et al. 2015: table 8). The prediction of a supply and demand analysis is that the relative wages of workers with high and medium educational levels relative to those with low educational levels will rise or fall depending on which effect dominates (increase in the relative demand versus increase in the relative supply). In the Mexican labour market the relative wages of workers with high and medium educational levels relative to those with low educational levels fell over the period (Cruces et al. 2015: table 7). The adjustment process also led to an increase in the unemployment rate of all educational groups with a larger increase for workers with high levels of education (Cruces et al. 2015: table 9).

The international crisis of 2008 led to a reduction in labour earnings in the aggregate and for all population groups and employment categories. The only employment category that recovered its pre-crisis level of earnings by 2012 was the public administration sector.[10]

17.6 Poverty and Inequality

> For all poverty lines, the poverty rate was lower in 2012 than in 2000, and so too was the percentage of households classified as working poor. Within the period, the poverty indicators decreased between 2000 and 2006 and then either increased or decreased at a slower pace than before, depending on the poverty line used. (Cruces et al. 2015: figure 10)

[10] We did not include the effect of the international crisis on labour earnings by occupational categories due to comparability problems in the series.

The moderate poverty rate (measured by the country's official poverty line) fell from 55.6 per cent in 2000 to 52.0 per cent in 2012; the extreme poverty rate dropped from 24.6 per cent to 20.2 per cent (Table 17.1); the percentage of working poor (defined as the proportion of persons in the population living in poor households where at least one member works) decreased from 43.8 per cent to 40.8 per cent over the same period. The analysis of trends based on the 2.5 and 4 dollars-a-day PPP international poverty lines also shows a reduction between 2000 and 2012. A closer look at the evolution of poverty indicators based on the official poverty lines over the period under study indicates a U-shaped pattern with the lowest poverty levels in 2006. Poverty levels increased markedly with the economic crisis of 2008 and the substantial increase in food prices. The number of poor persons according to the official moderate poverty line increased from 47.6 million in 2006 to 56.8 million in 2010. Poverty indicators responded more slowly than GDP did. The moderate poverty rate continued to increase until 2012, when it reached 52.0 per cent. The patterns are very similar for the evolution of the proportion of the working poor, and for the proportion of the extreme poor. The analysis of trends based on the 2.5 and 4 dollars-a-day PPP international poverty lines shows an almost monotonic reduction over the period. These poverty rates increased slightly in 2008, and then resumed the downward trend of the previous period, although at a slower pace: the poverty rate based on the 2.5 dollars-a-day line fully recovered from the crisis (drop of 2.1 percentage points between 2008 and 2012), while the poverty level based on the 4 dollars-a-day PPP line had only partially recovered, not reaching its pre-crisis level (drop of 0.9 percentage points between 2008 and 2012).

The poverty patterns reported in the last paragraph can be interpreted by examining incomes from various sources as well as government programmes. The analysis of sources of household total income indicates that labour income and transfers from poverty alleviation programmes increased between 2000 and 2008 (Cruces et al. 2015: figure 11). There is evidence showing that half of the reduction in the moderate poverty rate measured by the official poverty line between 2002 and 2004 can be explained by the *Oportunidades* programme (del Río et al. 2011). Moreover, government transfers enabled 2.6 million persons to escape poverty in 2008 (CONEVAL 2009). On the other hand, income from capital declined from 2000 to 2008, while income from pensions was stable. Between 2008 and 2010, labour earnings exhibited a substantial decrease; capital income and transfers from poverty alleviation programmes like *Oportunidades, Programa para adultos mayores,* and other programmes suffered a small decline. However, government transfers recovered in 2012.

Despite the poverty reduction effort of Mexico's government, the poverty rates based on Mexico's official poverty lines increased between 2006 and

2012. When the analysis is based on the international poverty lines, poverty increases were smaller and temporary (they increased between 2006 and 2008 only) compared to the poverty increases based on the official lines. These differing patterns of poverty indicators between 2006 and 2012 can be explained by the different procedure applied to adjust the poverty lines over time. International lines are constant in real terms using the CPI. Official poverty lines are constant in real terms using the FPI. The increase in food prices that occurred starting in 2008 determined a more rapid increase in the official poverty lines compared to the international lines in current pesos. Consequently, poverty rates measured by the official poverty lines increased from 2006 and 2012, while poverty indicators based on international poverty lines decreased.

> Household per capita income inequality diminished over the period, while inequality of labour earnings did not change substantially.
>
> (Cruces et al. 2015: figure 12)

Household per capita income inequality decreased in conjunction with the increase in GDP up to 2006. It did not follow a clear pattern afterwards: inequality increased slightly between that year and 2008, and then dropped markedly until 2010, when it increased once again. The overall evolution is captured by the Gini coefficient, which fell from 0.536 in 2000 to 0.491 in 2012 (Table 17.1). The origin of the decline in household per capita income inequality from 2000 to 2006 has been attributed to the enactment of the North American Free Trade Agreement (NAFTA) (Esquivel 2009) and to the progressiveness of public spending (Esquivel et al. 2010; Lopez-Calva et al. 2013a). In 1994, the Mexican government launched *Procampo*, an income-support programme aimed to help farmers deal with the transition costs resulting from the opening of agricultural trade under NAFTA. *Progresa* (known as *Oportunidades* since 2002) was established in 1997. It is a large anti-poverty conditional cash transfer programme, which reached around 19.0 per cent of households in 2012. Labour markets also played an important role for the evolution of income inequality. Esquivel et al. (2010), Campos et al. (2012), Lopez-Calva et al. (2013a), and Cornia (2013) found that labour incomes contributed to income equalization during the 2000s. Remittances too proved to be equalizing in Mexico during the 2000s (Esquivel et al. 2010; Cornia 2013).

The level of inequality of labour earnings also diminished over the period under study but in a smaller magnitude. The Gini of labour earnings among employed workers was 0.520 in 2000 and 0.512 in 2012 (Table 17.1). It was mostly stable over these years, with the exception of a pronounced fall in 2010, after the economic crisis, when it reached a level of 0.474. According to our previous evidence, after the international crisis, workers with medium and low levels of education increased their earnings relative to those with high levels of education. However, it is interesting to notice that earnings declined for all workers, regardless of their level of education. Consequently, the reduction in labour earnings inequality occurred at the expense of lower labour incomes. The main driver of the reduction in labour earnings inequality during the 2000s was the reduction in the education wage premium (or the 'price effect'). The gap between the wages of skilled workers (those with secondary or higher education) and unskilled workers (those with no schooling or incomplete primary schooling) fell systematically over the period under study (Esquivel et al. 2010). This change in the wage structure has been explained by market forces—i.e. an increase in the relative supply of skilled workers along with a reduction in the relative demand for skilled labour (Gasparini et al. 2011; Campos et al. 2012; Cornia 2013)—rather than by institutional factors (Campos et al. 2012). The distribution of the stock of education (the 'quantity effect') in the labour force became more equal too (Gasparini and Lustig 2011). The reduction in the relative supply of workers with low levels of skills (measured by school attainment) might be associated with changes in public spending on education combined with the effects of the conditional cash transfer programme *Oportunidades*, which tied monetary transfers to keeping children of poor households in school. Although the distribution of educational attainment has become more equal, this change has had a disequalizing or neutral effect (Campos et al. 2012; Azevedo et al. 2013).[11] Then, the reduction of income inequality in Mexico is explained by the falling education wage premium or price effect.

17.7 Conclusions

By Latin American standards, Mexico experienced slow economic growth during the 2000s. The country was severely hurt by the international crisis of 2008, but Mexico surpassed their pre-crisis output levels by 2012.

The evidence regarding the changes in labour market indicators between 2000 and 2012 was mixed. Some of them improved while others deteriorated over the period. The improvements were as follows. The employment composition by occupational group improved moderately between 2000 and 2008 as workers moved from agricultural, forestry and fishery occupations, and occupations related to plant and machine operation to better-paying occupations like professional jobs. The employment structure by occupational

[11] This means that had the skill premium remained unchanged, educational upgrading would have been disequalizing. Because this sounds counter-intuitive, this finding is known as the 'paradox of progress'.

position improved from 2000 to 2006 through the increase in the share of employers and wage/salaried employees in total employment. The employment composition by economic sector improved from 2000 to 2012 as the share of high-earning sectors like skilled services, public administration, and education and health increased and the share of low-earning sectors like primary activities and low-tech industries diminished. The educational level of the Mexican employed population improved steadily from 2000 to 2012. The moderate and extreme poverty rates and the rate of working poor households showed important reductions between 2000 and 2012, as the Gini coefficient of per capita household income, while the Gini coefficient of labour earnings remained essentially unchanged.

The worsening was as follows. The unemployment rate increased substantially between 2000 and 2012. The employment composition by occupational group deteriorated between 2010 and 2012. The employment structure by occupational position worsened from 2008 to 2012. The percentage of wage/salaried employees registered with the social security system decreased between 2000 and 2012, and labour earnings fell.

Looking specifically at the international crisis of 2008, most labour market indicators were affected negatively. The unemployment rate increased and recovered its pre-crisis level by 2012. The employment structure by occupational group worsened between 2010 and 2012. The worsening trend in the percentage of wage/salaried employees registered with the social security system continued during the international crisis. Labour earnings fell between 2006 and 2010 and never recovered their pre-crisis level. The poverty indicators increased during the international crisis of 2008. The comparison between the effects of the international crisis of 2008 on labour market indicators and the effects generated by the recession in the US at the beginning of the period (2001–3) reveals that the Great Recession impacted Mexico more strongly. The reduction in GDP, the increase in the unemployment rate, and the decrease in labour earnings were larger during the international crisis than in the recession of 2001–3. Moreover, the moderate poverty rate (measured by the country's official poverty line) increased during the international crisis, while it continued to decrease during the first recessionary episode. The reasons behind the larger negative impacts of the international crisis compared to the recession at the beginning of the decade were the fall in the demand for Mexican exports and the domestic demand, and the reduction in remittances and the emigration of workers to the US due to the recessive labour market conditions in that country.

Young workers had worse labour market outcomes over the period compared to adults, but they do not seem to be more vulnerable to macroeconomic crises. Men and women exhibited a balanced situation in their labour market outcomes, and the negative impacts of the crises were evenly distributed among them. The unemployment rate was higher for young compared to adult workers; the shares of young employed workers in low-earning occupational groups and economic sectors were larger than the shares of adult workers; the percentage of young workers registered with the social security system was lower when compared to adults; and labour earnings of young workers were below those of adults. On the other hand, the share of young workers in low-earning occupational positions was lower than the share for adults, and their educational level improved more rapidly. Despite the generally inferior situation of young workers in the labour market, only two youth labour market indicators were more affected by the episodes of crises. They were the unemployment rate, which increased more for young workers than for adults during the recession at the beginning of the period and during the international crisis of 2008, and the percentage of registered workers, which decreased more for young workers during the international crisis. Disaggregating by gender, we found that men were better than women in some cases, e.g. the share of male workers in low-earning positions was lower compared to women, and labour earnings of men were higher than labour earnings of women; in other cases, the opposite occurred, e.g. the female unemployment rate was lower, and the percentage of workers registered with the social security system was larger for women compared to men. The negative impacts of the crises were also evenly distributed between men and women. Men were hit hardest by both crises in the case of the unemployment rate, the percentage of workers in low-earning sectors, and labour earnings. Women were the main losers during the crises episodes when we analysed the percentage of workers in low-earning occupational groups and the percentage of workers registered with the social security system.

In summary, Mexico exhibited mixed labour market changes during the 2000s and some deterioration during the international crisis of 2008, and while all population groups were vulnerable to macroeconomic crises, no group was clearly more vulnerable than any other.

References

Azevedo, J. P., G. Inchauste, S. Olivieri, J. Saavedra Chanduvi, and H. Winkler (2013). 'Is Labor Income Responsible for Poverty Reduction? A Decomposition Approach'. Policy Research Working Paper 6414. Washington, DC: World Bank.

Blecker, R. (2008). 'External Shocks, Structural Change, and Economic Growth in Mexico, 1979–2007', *World Development* 37 (7): 1274–84.

Campos, R., G. Esquivel, and N. Lustig (2012). 'The Rise and Fall of Income Inequality in Mexico, 1989–2010'. Working Paper 2012/10. Helsinki: UNU-WIDER.

Cañas, J., R. Coronado, and R. Gilmer (2011). 'Mexico Rides Global Recovery But Still Faces Hurdles', *Southwest Economy* Q3: 11–13, 20. Dallas: Federal Reserve Bank of Dallas.

CEDLAS and World Bank (2014). SEDLAC—Socio-Economic Database for Latin America and the Caribbean. Centro de Estudios Distributivos, Laborales y Sociales, Facultad de Ciencias Económicas, Universidad Nacional de La Plata and World Bank Poverty Group LCR. Available at <http://sedlac.econo.unlp.edu.ar/eng/index.php>, accessed 2014.

CONEVAL (2009). 'Evolución de la pobreza 1992–2008'. Mexico DF: Consejo Nacional de Evaluacion de la Politica Social.

Cornia, A. (2013). 'Inequality Trends and their Determinants: Latin America over 1990–2010', in A. Cornia (ed.), *Falling Inequality in Latin America: Policy Changes and Lessons*. Oxford: Oxford University Press, 23–48.

Cruces, G., G. Fields, D. Jaume, and M. Viollaz (2015). 'The Growth–Employment–Poverty Nexus in Latin America in the 2000s: Mexico Country Study'. WIDER Working Paper 2015/079. Helsinki: UNU-WIDER.

del Río, M. A., D. Manuel, and I. Islas (2011). 'Mexico', in M. Sanchez and P. Sauma (eds), *Vulnerabilidad económica externa: Protección social y pobreza en América Latina*. Quito: FLACSO, CEPAL, Departamento de Asuntos Económicos y Sociales de las Naciones Unidas (UN/DESA), 104–58.

ECLAC-ILO (2012). 'The Employment Situation in Latin America and the Caribbean'. Bulletin 5. Santiago de Chile: Economic Commission for Latin America and the Caribbean.

Esquivel, G. (2009). 'The Dynamics of Income Inequality in Mexico since NAFTA'. Document prepared for UNDP Project on Markets, the State and the Dynamics of Inequality: How to Advance Inclusive Growth.

Esquivel, G., N. Lustig, and J. Scott (2010). 'A Decade of Falling Inequality in Mexico: Market Forces or State Action?', in L. F. Lopez Calva and N. Lustig (eds), *Declining Inequality in Latin America: A Decade of Progress?* Washington, DC: Brookings Institution and UNDP, 175–217.

Freije, S., G. Lopez-Acevedo, and E. Rodriguez-Oreggia (2011). 'Effects of the 2008–09 Economic Crisis on Labor Markets in Mexico'. Policy Research Working Paper 5840. Washington, DC: World Bank.

Gasparini, L., S. Galiani, G. Cruces, and P. Acosta (2011). 'Educational Upgrading and Returns to Skills in Latin America: Evidence from a Supply–Demand Framework, 1990–2010'. IZA Working Paper 6244. Bonn: Institute for the Study of Labor.

Gasparini, L. and N. Lustig (2011). 'The Rise and Fall of Income Inequality in Latin America', in J. Ocampo and J. Ros (eds), *The Oxford Handbook of Latin American Economics*. Oxford: Oxford University Press, 218–43.

IMF (2013). *Time to Rebuild Policy Space*. Washington, DC: International Monetary Fund.

ISSA (2014). 'Social Security Programs throughout the World: The Americas, 2013'. SSA Publication 13–11804. Washington, DC: Social Security Administration, Office of Retirement and Disability Policy and Office of Research, Evaluation, and Statistics.

Lederman, D., W. Maloney, and J. Messina (2011). 'The Fall of Wage Flexibility: Labor Markets and Business Cycles in Latin America and the Caribbean since the 1990s'. World Bank Unpublished Manuscript. Washington, DC: World Bank.

Lopez-Calva, L. F., N. Lustig, and E. Ortiz-Juarez (2013a). 'Declining Inequality in Latin America in the 2000s: The Cases of Argentina, Brazil, and Mexico', *World Development* 44: 129–41.

Lopez-Calva, L. F., N. Lustig, and E. Ortiz-Juarez (2013b). 'Deconstructing the Decline in Inequality in Latin America'. Policy Research Working Paper 6552. Washington, DC: World Bank.

Martorano, B. (2014). 'Pre-Crisis Conditions and Government Policy Responses: Chile and Mexico during the Great Recession'. Office of Research Working Paper 15, Florence: UNICEF, Office of Research.

Messina, J. and L. Gambetti (2014). 'Evolving Wage Cyclicality in Latin America'. Policy Research Working Paper 6978. Washington, DC: World Bank.

Moreno-Brid, J. C. and I. Paunovic (2009). 'Crisis financier internacional y sus efectos en la economia Mexicana', *Economia: Teoria y Practica* 1: 63–80.

Samaniego, N. (2009). 'La crisis, el empleo y los salaries en Mexico'. *Economiaunam* 6 (16): 57–67. Mexico, DF: Universidad Nacional Autonoma de Mexico.

Sidaoui, J., M. Ramos-Francia, and G. Cuadra (2011). 'The Global Financial Crisis and Policy Response in Mexico'. BIS Papers 54. Basel: Bank for International Settlement.

Villareal, M. A. (2010). 'The Mexican Economy after the Global Financial Crisis'. Washington, DC: University of North Texas.

World Bank (2014). World Development Indicators. Available at <http://data.worldbank.org/data-catalog/world-development-indicators>, accessed April 2014.

18

Panama

18.1 Introduction

This chapter on labour markets and growth in Panama since 2000 is one of sixteen studies of Latin American countries, each of which analyses the growth–employment–poverty nexus and aims to answer the following broad questions: Has economic growth resulted in economic development via improved labour market conditions in Latin America in the 2000s, and have these improvements halted or been reversed since the Great Recession? How do the rate and character of economic growth, changes in the various labour market indicators, and changes in poverty relate to each other?

To answer these questions, we analyse the growth experience of Panama during the 2000s and a wide set of labour market indicators that we assign to one of two different categories: employment and earnings indicators, and poverty and income inequality indicators. More specifically, for the group of employment and earnings indicators we construct statistics on the following variables: the unemployment rate; the employment structure by occupational group, employment position, economic sector, registration of workers with the social security system, and educational level; and mean labour earnings and hourly wages. We present all these indicators for the employed population as a whole and for different population groups (youth, adults, men, and women). For the group of poverty and income inequality indicators, we compute poverty rates using the official moderate and extreme poverty lines and the international lines of 2.5 and 4 dollars a day. We also calculate the Gini coefficient of household per capita income and labour earnings.

All the statistics in this chapter are obtained using microdata from the Encuesta de Hogares (EH), for the years 2001–12. The nationwide surveys were processed following a harmonization methodology and incorporated into the SEDLAC—Socio-Economic Database for Latin America and the Caribbean (CEDLAS and World Bank 2014).[1] The resulting labour market indicators

[1] See Cruces et al. (2015: table 1) for details on the size of Panama household surveys.

were compiled into a large number of tables and figures, which are available in an earlier version of this study (henceforth, Cruces et al. 2015). Chapter 1 of this book provides the definition for each of the indicators we analyse here, while Cruces et al. (2015) includes details on definitions and classification systems used by Panama's household surveys, and on comparability issues of these surveys over time.

18.2 Economic Growth

> The Panamanian economy grew rapidly during the period 2000–12. The international crisis of 2008 did not affect the economy substantially.
> (Cruces et al. 2015: figures 1 and 2)

Panama is the Latin American economy that exhibited the highest economic growth from 2000 to 2012. The country's GDP (measured in PPP dollars of 2005) grew by 126.5 per cent, GDP per capita increased by 81.9 per cent, and GDP per person employed rose by 51.8 per cent. The annual growth of GDP per capita averaged 4.8 per cent, varying from −1.4 per cent in 2001 to 10.1 in 2007 (Table 18.1).

From 2000 to 2002, the growth of the Panamanian economy was sluggish. GDP and GDP per capita annual growth rates averaged 1.8 and −0.2 per cent respectively. The poor performance of the Panamanian economy at the beginning of the 2000s is mainly attributable to the slow growth of the developed world and also to the setback of the Latin American region in 2002. As a consequence, three out of the four sectors which depend on external demand suffered a contraction (ECLAC 2002).[2]

From 2003 to 2012, the country experienced a real boom in the economy, even during the international crisis of 2008. On average, GDP increased by 8.3 per cent per year between 2003 and 2012, while GDP per capita grew at 6.3 per cent annually over the same period. The growth of the economy took place in a context of an expanding world economy and was led by sectors that provide services to the rest of the world, such as the Panama Canal, the international banking centre, the Colon Free Trade Zone, and also by the construction, communication, and transportation sectors (ECLAC 2005; IMF 2009).

During the international economic crisis of 2008, economic growth slowed due to the contraction in domestic credit, the slowdown of private construction, and the reduction in the international demand for tourism (ECLAC 2008;

[2] The international banking centre, the Colon Free Trade Zone, and exports contracted between 2000 and 2002, while the Panama Canal continued to grow.

Table 18.1 Panama: Evolution of growth and labour market indicators over the 2000s

		2000	2001	2002	2003	2004	2005	2006	2007	2008	2009	2010	2011	2012
Growth Indicators	GDP per capita	7,869	7,758	7,776	7,947	8,383	8,819	9,396	10,346	11,192	11,424	12,067	13,154	14,320
	GDP per capita growth rate	0.66	−1.41	0.23	2.20	5.49	5.20	6.55	10.10	8.18	2.06	5.63	9.01	8.87
Employment and Earnings Indicators	Employment-to-population ratio	...	52.02	54.11	54.60	55.87	57.35	57.33	58.83	60.39	60.03	59.47	59.13	61.01
	Unemployment rate	...	9.60	9.28	9.60	8.63	8.95	7.75	5.68	5.06	6.11	6.02	4.05	3.66
	Share of low-earnings occupations	...	52.77	53.78	53.43	52.32	53.47	53.34	52.66	51.33	50.15	49.46	49.12	49.62
	Share of mid-earnings occupations	...	30.86	29.78	29.76	31.48	30.52	31.09	30.99	31.87	32.29	32.35	27.11	25.77
	Share of high-earnings occupations	...	16.37	16.45	16.82	16.20	16.01	15.57	16.35	16.80	17.56	18.19	23.77	24.61
	Share of employers	...	2.54	2.94	2.90	3.23	3.07	3.08	3.06	3.21	3.11	3.21	3.05	2.74
	Share of wage/salaried employees	...	63.20	62.45	61.71	62.63	61.77	62.99	65.33	66.06	64.67	65.89	68.00	68.06
	Share of self-employed workers	...	29.45	30.29	30.75	30.00	30.33	28.96	26.44	25.87	27.13	26.48	25.20	24.39
	Share of unpaid family workers	...	4.82	4.32	4.64	4.14	4.83	4.97	5.18	4.86	5.09	4.42	3.75	4.80
	Share of workers in low-earnings sectors	...	31.72	31.47	31.32	30.27	30.12	30.49	29.83	28.50	28.05	27.07	25.41	25.26
	Share of workers in mid-earnings sectors	...	47.62	48.22	48.06	48.81	49.64	49.39	49.67	51.13	50.77	50.99	50.86	51.28

	Share of workers in high-earnings sectors	...	20.66	20.31	20.63	20.93	20.25	20.13	20.50	20.36	21.18	21.94	23.72	23.46
	Share of low-educated workers	...	45.35	44.70	43.17	41.60	42.02	40.56	39.27	37.15	36.98	36.59	34.38	33.52
	Share of medium-educated workers	...	36.11	36.46	36.94	37.41	37.39	38.14	40.06	41.37	40.83	40.88	40.27	40.45
	Share of high-educated workers	...	18.54	18.84	19.89	20.99	20.60	21.30	20.67	21.48	22.19	22.52	25.35	26.03
	Share of workers registered with SS	...	...	...	...	52.82	51.96	53.28	55.40	57.42	58.07	58.71	61.85	62.34
	Mean labour earnings	...	641.7	630.7	637.7	626.7	596.3	605.5	606.2	610.3	637.1	643.7	715.8	730.5
Poverty and Inequality Indicators	Official extreme poverty rate	...	22.4	18.7	17.6	16.6	16.0	16.2	11.0	10.7	8.8	10.0	8.9	9.8
	Official moderate poverty rate	...	45.9	43.5	42.4	40.8	40.0	39.3	31.0	27.5	27.2	25.1	22.6	22.4
	Poverty rate 2.5 dollars-a-day	...	28.70	25.41	24.09	22.77	22.48	22.23	15.89	14.45	12.30	13.16	11.60	11.78
	Poverty rate 4 dollars-a-day	...	43.39	40.72	39.04	38.33	37.48	37.14	28.63	26.18	25.34	23.96	21.25	20.90
	GINI of household per capita income	...	0.565	0.564	0.561	0.549	0.538	0.549	0.526	0.526	0.520	0.519	0.518	0.519
	GINI of labour earnings	...	0.501	0.535	0.528	0.521	0.515	0.515	0.491	0.480	0.484	0.472	0.475	0.481

Note: The shaded figures of labour market indicators represent statistical significant improvements at 5 per cent between the initial and final years for all the employment and earnings indicators and poverty and inequality indicators. The only exceptions are the share of mid-earnings occupations, share of mid-earnings sectors, and share of medium-educated workers for which we did not assign welfare evaluation criteria. The vertical lines indicate that series are not fully comparable before and after that line. For occupational indicators we compared 2001 and 2010.

Source: SEDLAC (CEDLAS and World Bank 2014) and World Development Indicators (World Bank 2014).

IMF 2010). However, economic growth remained positive. GDP and GDP per capita grew by 3.9 and 2.1 per cent in 2009. In the following years, GDP per capita growth accelerated quickly to 5.6 per cent in 2010, 9.0 per cent in 2011, and 8.9 per cent in 2012. The recovery of high growth rates was related to public infrastructure projects, mainly the expansion of the Panama Canal, and to the increase in domestic consumption (IADB 2014).

18.3 Unemployment

> The 2001–12 period witnessed a significant drop in the aggregate unemployment rate and in the unemployment rate for all population groups. The international crisis of 2008 led to a temporary increase in the unemployment rate. (Cruces et al. 2015: figure 3)

Panama experienced a dramatic reduction in its unemployment rate during 2001–12, which was one of the main improvements in the Panamanian labour market over the period. In the year 2001, the unemployment rate stood at 9.6 per cent (111,099 unemployed persons); twelve years later, it had fallen to only 3.7 per cent (61,714 unemployed persons), less than half its original level (Table 18.1). This is undoubtedly a major labour market improvement, one which mainly took place during the period of rapid economic growth. Between 2001 and 2005, the behaviour of the unemployment rate was erratic, with several ups and downs and an average level of 9.2 per cent. Starting in 2006, the unemployment rate began to fall. The downward trend was interrupted in 2009 and 2010, a period that included the Great Recession, when the unemployment rate reached 6.1 per cent (18,011 new unemployed persons in 2009 compared to 2008). Both the number of persons in the labour force and the number of employed persons increased between 2008 and 2009 by 36,850 and 18,801 respectively. These figures suggest that the increase in the unemployment rate during the international crisis was brought about by the entry of new persons into the labour market who could not find a job. In 2011, the unemployment rate recovered the downward trend and closed the period at 4.0 per cent in 2012.

The unemployment rate decreased between 2001–12 for all population groups (youth, adults, men, and women), and all of them suffered a temporary increase in their unemployment rate during the international crisis. The unemployment rate of youth, adults, men, and women increased in 2009 and recovered the downward trend in 2010 (young workers and women) or 2011 (adults and men). By 2012, the unemployment rates of all population groups were below their pre-crisis level.

18.4 Job Mix

> The employment composition by occupational group improved between 2001 and 2010 overall, for young and adult workers, and men, while there was a slight worsening for women. The international crisis of 2008 did not affect the improving trend in the aggregate, and for young, adult workers and men, while it led to an improvement for women. Between 2011 and 2012 there was a slight improvement in the structure of employment by occupational group in the aggregate and for youth, adults, and men, and a worsening for women. (Cruces et al. 2015: figure 4).

The share of the following occupations shrank between 2001 and 2010: agricultural, forestry, and fishery jobs (drop of 3.7 percentage points) and elementary occupations (drop of 1.0 percentage points). The share of the following occupations grew: crafts and trades (increase of 1.7 percentage points); services and sales workers (increase of 1.4 percentage points); and professionals (increase of 1.2 percentage points). The share of the other occupational groups remained largely unchanged. These changes in the occupational composition of employment can be interpreted as an improvement since low-earning occupations (agricultural, elementary, and services and sales occupations) reduced their share in total employment by 3.3 percentage points between 2001 and 2010, while high-earning occupations (management, professionals, and technicians and associate professionals) gained share in total employment (increase of 1.8 percentage points). These changes resulted in an increase in the share of mid-earning occupations (clerical jobs, plant and machine operators, craft and related trades occupations) in total employment over the period (increase of 1.5 percentage points) (Table 18.1). Between 2011 and 2012, the share of low and high-earning occupations in total employment exhibited a slight increase (rise of 0.5 and 0.8 percentage points respectively), and consequently, the share of mid-earning occupations fell (drop of 1.3 percentage points).

The improvements in the occupational composition of employment between 2001 and 2010 were observed for young and adult workers and for men, while there was a slight worsening for women. Between 2011 and 2012, young workers, adults, and men exhibited a small increase in the share of both low- and high-earning occupations, while women suffered a deterioration in the structure of employment through a reduction in the share of high-earning occupations and an increase in the share of low-earning occupations.

The international crisis of 2008 did not adversely affect the improvement in the composition of employment by occupational group in the aggregate and for young workers, adults, and men, while it led to an improvement for women. Between 2008 and 2009 the share of low-earning occupations continued to fall and the share of high-earning occupations increased in the aggregate and for youth, adults, and men. For women, an improvement in their structure of employment took place between 2008 and 2009, reversing the slight deterioration of the previous years.

> The employment structure by occupational position improved between 2001 and 2012 overall, and for young, adult workers, and men, while there was a worsening for women. The international crisis of 2008 affected negatively the employment structure by occupational position mainly through a reduction in the share of wage/salaried employees in total employment, which recovered its pre-crisis level by 2011. (Cruces et al. 2015: figure 5)

Between 2001 and 2012, the employment structure by occupational position exhibited a substantial increase in the share of wage/salaried employees in total employment and a corresponding reduction in the share of self-employed. The share of wage/salaried employees in total employment—the largest employment category in Panama—increased from 63.2 per cent in 2001 to 68.1 per cent in 2012, while the percentage of self-employed diminished from 29.4 to 24.4 per cent during the same period (Table 18.1). The shares of employers and unpaid workers remained largely unchanged over the period. These changes in the employment structure by occupational position can be interpreted as an improvement since the share of high-earning positions in total employment (wage/salaried employees and employers) increased, and the share of low-earning positions (self-employed and unpaid workers) diminished.

The distribution of employment by occupational position improved for youth, adults, and men, and deteriorated for women from 2001 to 2012.

The international crisis of 2008 led to a deterioration in the employment structure by occupational position overall and for young, adult workers, and men, while it did not interrupt the deterioration that was taking place for women. Between 2008 and 2009, the share of high-earning positions in total employment decreased, mainly through the reduction in the share of wage/salaried employees. Consequently, the share of low-earning positions in total employment increased by the same magnitude. The increase in the share of low-earning positions took place through an increase in the share of self-employment. The worsening in the employment structure by occupational position is in accord with the increase in the unemployment rate, as economic necessity may compel workers to look for free-entry self-employment activities. All population groups returned to their pre-crisis structure of employment by 2010.

> The employment composition by economic sector improved over the course of the period studied overall and for all population groups. The international crisis of 2008 did not interrupt the improving trend in the structure of employment by economic sector. (Cruces et al. 2015: figure 6)

The period from 2001 to 2012 witnessed a reduction (from 31.7 per cent to 25.3 per cent) in the share of workers in low-earning sectors in total employment (domestic service, primary activities, and low-tech industry). The primary activities sector was the one that experienced the largest reduction in the share of workers in total employment, in accordance with the shrinking of the agricultural sector as a share of GDP. There was, during the same period, an increase (from 20.7 per cent to 23.5 per cent) in the share of high-earning sectors (skilled services, utilities and transportation, and public administration) in the total. Among the high-earning sectors, the skilled services sector was the one that exhibited the largest increase in the share of workers in total employment. This evidence is in keeping with the role that finance services and real estate activities had in the Panamanian growth process. All these changes resulted in an increase in the share of mid-earning sectors in total employment (education and health, construction, high-tech industry, and commerce) over the period. Construction and commerce were the sectors that led this increase (Table 18.1).

The employment composition by economic sector improved between 2001 and 2012 for young and adult workers, men, and women, as they moved from low-earning sectors to high-earning sectors.

The international crisis of 2008 did not halt the improving trend in the employment composition by economic sector overall and for adult workers, men, and women, but led to a slight worsening for youth. Between 2008 and 2009, the share of low-earning sectors continued to decrease, while the share of high-earning sectors in total employment kept on increasing in the aggregate and for adult workers, men, and women. Young workers exhibited an increase in the share of both low- and high-earning sectors in total employment between 2008 and 2009. By 2010, young workers recovered their pre-crisis structure of employment by economic sector.

> The educational level of the Panamanian employed population improved steadily over the period, overall and for all population groups. The international crisis of 2008 had no effect on this upward trend. (Cruces et al. 2015: figure 7)

The share of workers with low educational levels (eight years of schooling or less) declined from 45.4 per cent in 2001 to 33.5 per cent in 2012, while the share of workers with medium education levels (nine to thirteen years of schooling) grew from 36.1 per cent in 2001 to 40.5 per cent in 2012, and those with high levels of education (over thirteen years of schooling) increased from 18.5 to 26.0 per cent (Table 18.1).[3] We interpret this result as

[3] The most frequent value of years of education for employed workers in Panama was six from 2001 to 2009 (around 21.2 per cent of employed workers had six years of education) and twelve from 2010 to 2012 (around 22.4 per cent of employed workers had twelve years of education).

an improvement for the employed population as the level of education is an important predictor of labour earnings. Consequently, the changes in the employment structure by educational level implied an increase in the share of workers that tend to have high levels of earnings and a decline in the share of workers with low earnings levels.[4] Panama has one of the highest shares of employed workers with medium and high educational levels in the Latin American region. However, the quality of education in Panama, measured by the Programme for International Student Assessment (PISA) and national evaluations, is among the lowest in the region (Harris 2007; OECD 2010). The government has launched several programmes during the 2000s aimed at increasing coverage and improving the quality of Panamanian education, such as school nutrition programmes, delivery of resources for students, scholarships, and a curricular change programme (Rodríguez Mojica 2013).

The educational level of the employed population improved between 2001 and 2012 for all population groups (young and adult workers, men and women).

The pattern of improvement in the educational level of the employed population in Panama was not affected negatively in the aggregate or at the population group level by the international crisis of 2008.

> The share of workers registered with the social security system increased from 2004 (the earliest year with data on this indicator) to 2012, overall, for youth and adults, and for men and women. The international crisis of 2008 led to a slowdown in the upward trend of the registration rate. (Cruces et al. 2015: figure 8)

The Panamanian social security system is administered by the *Caja del Seguro Social* (CSS), which is organized in three programmes: (1) disability, old age, and death benefits; (2) health and maternity care; and (3) professional risks. A reform of the social security system in 2005 created two contributory subsystems. First, the old defined benefit system, in which affiliates at the moment of the reform could decide whether to remain or not. Second, a mixed subsystem which combines a defined-benefits component with an individual savings component. The affiliation to the CSS is mandatory for all workers employed in public and private firms and, since 2007, for independent workers. The affiliation for informal workers, domestic workers, and housekeepers is voluntary. The system is financed by employees' and employers' contributions and by government funds. The social security system also contains non-contributory programmes totally funded by the government, such as the *100 a los 70* programme (Rodríguez Mojica 2013).

[4] The improvement in the employment structure by educational level is related to changes in the relative demand and supply of workers with high levels of education with corresponding implications for the wage gap by educational groups and the unemployment rate of each educational level. We introduce a discussion about the role of these factors in Panama in section 18.5.

Social security records show an increase in the percentage of workers registered with the contributory schemes of the system, from 52.8 per cent in 2004 (632,497 registered workers) to 62.3 per cent in 2012 (1,011,130 registered workers) (Table 18.1). Between 2004 and 2008, the share of workers registered with the social security system increased by 1.2 percentage points annually. The Great Recession led to a slowdown in this upward trend and between 2008 and 2010, the share of registered workers increased by only 0.6 percentage points a year (19,078 new registered workers per year). In 2011, the share of registered workers grew rapidly (3.2 percentage points), and in 2012 it slowed down again (increase of 0.5 percentage points).

All population groups exhibited an increase in the share of workers registered with the social security system between 2004 and 2012, and the increase was larger for youth compared to adults, and for men compared to women.

The international crisis of 2008 led to a slowdown in the upward trend of registered employment overall, for young and adult workers and men, while the improving trend stalled for women.

18.5 Labour Earnings

> Real labour market earnings increased overall from 2001 to 2012. Within the period, labour earnings decreased from 2001 to 2005, and increased from 2006 to 2012, rising even during the international crisis. Labour earnings increased for all population groups over the period, and workers in low-earning categories tended to experience a larger increase in labour earnings than did workers in high-earning categories.
>
> (Cruces et al. 2015: figure 9)

Average monthly earnings, expressed in PPP dollars of 2005, increased by 13.8 per cent, from US$642 in 2001 to US$730 in 2012 (Table 18.1). However, there were substantial fluctuations in labour incomes during this period, which cannot be entirely attributed to the variations in the country's economic performance. Average labour earnings decreased slightly at the beginning of the period (from 2001 to 2002), mirroring the slow growth in GDP per capita. In the following years, from 2003 to 2005, GDP per capita rose by around 11.0 per cent while average labour earnings fell by 6.5 per cent. Galiani (2009) claims that the decrease in average real earnings during the 2001–5 period was due to a composition effect. The jobs created during this period were mainly informal (without a contract) which paid less than a formal job, bringing down average labour earnings. From 2006 to 2008, real labour earnings were stable (increase of just 0.8 per cent), while GDP per capita was increasing (growth of 19.1 per cent). From 2009 to 2012, real labour earnings increased along with GDP per capita, although at a slower pace (14.6 and 25.4 per cent respectively). An interesting characteristic of the Panamanian labour market is that the minimum wage has increased more than the mean hourly wage of the economy over the 2000s, indicating an increase in the rate of non-compliance with labour market regulations (Cruces and Galiani 2013).

When changes in earnings are analysed by population groups and employment categories, they follow the overall pattern: a reduction from 2001 to 2005 followed by a stabilization from 2006 to 2008, and an increase from 2009 to 2012. Men exhibited a larger gain in earnings compared to women, while young workers increased their labour incomes by more than adult workers. Among occupational groups, workers in low-earning occupations experienced a mild increase in labour earnings between 2001 and 2010, while workers in high-earning occupations suffered a reduction.[5] Among occupational positions, workers in low-earning positions increased their labour earnings more than workers in high-earning positions. Labour earnings of workers in low-earning sectors were largely unchanged between 2001 and 2012, while earnings of workers in high-earning sectors increased (rise of 6.0 per cent). Workers with medium educational levels experienced the largest increase in labour incomes, followed by workers with low levels of education. Workers with high levels of education suffered an earnings reduction over the period.

The evidence of falling labour earnings for workers with high educational levels and labour earnings increases for workers with medium and low levels of education can be interpreted in light of previous findings of improving employment structure by occupational group and economic sector over the period. The improving employment structure by occupational group and economic sector implied an increase in the share of occupations and sectors that can be expected to employ workers with high and medium levels of education, like professional and technical occupations, and skilled services sectors, and a reduction in the share of occupations and sectors that employ workers with low educational levels, like agricultural and elementary occupations, domestic service, primary activities, and low-tech industry. This evidence indicates that the demand for workers with high and medium educational levels relative to those with low educational levels increased between 2001 and 2012. On the other hand, the educational levels of people in the labour force improved over the same period, indicating an increase in the relative supply of workers with high and medium levels of education (Cruces et al. 2015: table 8). The prediction of a supply and demand analysis

[5] Labour earnings by occupational group can only be analysed from 2001 to 2010 and from 2011 to 2012 due to comparability problems in the classification of occupations.

is that the relative wages of workers with high and medium educational levels relative to those with low educational levels will rise or fall depending on which effect dominates (increase in the relative demand versus increase in the relative supply). In the Panamanian labour market the relative wages of workers with high and medium educational levels relative to those with low educational levels fell over the period, though slightly, and the relative wages of workers with high educational levels relative to those with medium levels of education also decreased (Cruces et al. 2015: table 7). The adjustment process also led to a reduction in the unemployment rate of all educational groups with larger reductions for workers with medium levels of education (Cruces et al. 2015: table 9).

The international crisis of 2008 did not affect the upward trend in labour earnings overall, for all population groups and most employment categories. Average labour earnings in Panama increased from 2008 to 2009. Young and adult workers, men and women also experienced an increase in their labour earnings during the international crisis. Among employment categories, some groups were hurt by the crisis. Managers and plant and machine operators suffered an earnings reduction between 2008 and 2009. By 2010, they had not reached their pre-crisis earning levels. Workers in low-tech industry, utilities and transportation, and public administration sectors exhibited a fall in earnings during the international crisis, and all of them surpassed their pre-crisis level of earning by the end of the period.

18.6 Poverty and Inequality

> Poverty fell between 2001 and 2012 for all poverty lines used. The rate of working poor households also exhibited a decreasing trend. The pattern of poverty reduction over time was slowed down or temporarily reversed during the international crisis of 2008 depending on the poverty line used.
>
> (Cruces et al. 2015: figure 10)

The moderate poverty rate (measured by the country's official poverty line) fell from 45.9 per cent in 2001 to 22.4 per cent in 2012; the extreme poverty rate decreased from 22.4 to 9.8 per cent; the percentage of the working poor (defined as the proportion of persons in the population living in poor households with at least one working member) decreased from 31.3 to 13.5 per cent over the same period. An analysis based on the 2.5 and 4 dollars-a-day PPP international poverty lines also shows a drop in the poverty rate from 2001 to 2012. The 4 dollars-a-day poverty rate fell from 43.4 per cent in 2001 to 20.9 per cent in 2012, and the 2.5 dollars-a-day poverty rate diminished from 28.7 to 11.8 per cent over the same period (Table 18.1).

Despite the superb growth performance, poverty reduction in Panama was less responsive to economic growth compared to other Latin American countries. The low growth elasticity of poverty reduction in Panama compared to the rest of the region is associated with the large contribution of indigenous population to poverty, as the indigenous poor have very low levels of human capital and skills, and are less able to take advantage of the growth process (World Bank 2011).

The international crisis of 2008 led to a slowdown in the pattern of poverty reduction measured by the moderate poverty line and the 4 dollars-a-day international poverty line, and in the percentage of working poor, while the extreme poverty rate and the 2.5 dollars-a-day poverty rate increased slightly between 2009 and 2010. The moderate poverty rate fell by only 0.4 percentage points between 2008 and 2009, while it had decreased by 2.6 percentage points a year from 2001 to 2008. Those figures were 0.8 and 2.5 percentage points for the 4 dollars-a-day poverty rate, and 0.5 and 1.9 percentage points for the percentage of working poor. The extreme and 2.5 dollars-a-day poverty rates suffered a slight increase between 2009 and 2010 (46,861 new extremely poor persons and 35,551 new poor by the 2.5 dollars-a-day poverty line). The 2.5 dollars-a-day poverty rate was below the level of 2009 by 2011. The extreme poverty rate never reached the level of 2009, but was below the level of 2008 by 2012.

The poverty patterns reported in the last paragraph can be interpreted by examining incomes from various sources. The analysis of sources of household total income indicates that labour income increased between 2001 and 2012. Government transfers increased between 2001 and 2011, but an important reduction took place in 2012 determining an overall reduction from 2001 to 2012. Incomes from pensions and capital income diminished over the same period (Cruces et al. 2015: figure 11). From 2004 to 2009, the government of Panama implemented the *Red de Oportunidades* conditional cash transfer programme, which targeted extremely poor households. During this period, government transfers captured by the EH increased at 3.4 per cent annually. The programme accounted for one quarter of the extreme poverty reduction among the indigenous population between 2003 and 2008, who make up the largest share of the extremely poor in Panama (World Bank 2011).

> Household per capita income inequality diminished substantially between 2001 and 2012, and labour earnings inequality also fell, but to a smaller extent.
>
> (Cruces et al. 2015: figure 12)

Household per capita income inequality decreased slowly but steadily from 2001 to 2012. The overall evolution is captured by the Gini coefficient, which fell from 0.565 in 2001 to 0.519 in 2010, remaining at that level until 2012.

On the other hand, the inequality of labour earnings also decreased over the period under study. The Gini of labour earnings among employed workers was 0.501 in 2001 and 0.481 in 2012. It increased from 2001 to 2002, when it peaked at 0.535, and then fell steadily until 2010, when it reached the lowest level of the twelve-year period (0.472) before rising to the level of 2012 (0.481) (Table 18.1). This reduction in labour earnings inequality is in keeping with the fact that earnings increased more for low-earning employment categories compared to high-earning categories. However, it is interesting to notice that earnings declined for some high-earning employment categories. Consequently, the reduction in labour earning inequality occurred at the expense of income losses for some categories.

Changes in household per capita income inequality in Panama have been related mainly to changes in labour income. Azevedo et al. (2013b) decomposed the change in the Gini coefficient of household per capita income for the period 2002–10 and found that changes in labour incomes contributed the most to the inequality reduction over this period (the Gini coefficient of household per capita income decreased from 0.564 to 0.519 between 2002 and 2010). Changes in non-labour incomes, such as government transfers and pensions were also inequality-reducing, while demographic changes, like the share of adults per household, were inequality-increasing. Other studies have analysed the factors behind the evolution of labour income inequality. Azevedo et al. (2013a) used a decomposition approach and found that changes in the education wage premium (or the 'price effect') were inequality-reducing, while changes in the distribution of the stock of education (the 'quantity effect') were inequality-increasing in Panama between 2001 and 2009. Gasparini et al. (2011) found a reduction in the gap between the wages of skilled workers (those with complete or incomplete college education) and unskilled workers (those who have completed secondary education or less) in Panama between 2001 and 2009. The shrinking educational earnings gap can be explained by factors related to supply and demand: the relative supply of skilled workers increased steadily while the relative demand for those workers fell.

18.7 Conclusions

The economic performance of Panama during the years 2000 to 2012 was outstanding, and it boasted the strongest economic growth in Latin America in that period. The economy suffered a slowdown as a consequence of the international crisis of 2008, but Panama was one of the few countries in Latin America to have sustained positive growth during that episode.

The result of this impressive economic growth was a clear improvement in labour market indicators. By 2012, unemployment had fallen to less than half its level in 2001. The composition of employment also improved steadily in a number of dimensions. The share of workers in agricultural and elementary occupations diminished, while the share in professional and technical jobs increased. The share of wage/salaried employees rose and the share of self-employed workers decreased. The employment composition by economic sector improved as workers moved from primary activity, domestic service, and low-tech industry to better-paying sectors, such as skilled services. The share of registered workers increased between 2004 and 2012. There was also a steady improvement in the educational level of the employed population. Average labour market earnings increased between 2001 and 2012, though not steadily. All poverty indicators decreased between 2001 and 2012, as did the Gini coefficient of household per capita income and labour earnings.

The international crisis of 2008 affected some of these indicators, even while GDP continued to rise. The unemployment rate rose, the share of paid employees fell between 2008 and 2009, and some poverty indicators increased between 2009 and 2010. The worsening of these indicators was reversed by the end of the period studied.

Young workers had worse labour market outcomes over the period compared to adults and were more vulnerable to the international crisis. Men experienced worse labour market outcomes compared to women, but women suffered more from the negative impacts of the international crisis. The unemployment rate was higher for young compared to adult workers; the share of young employed workers in low-earning occupations, positions, and economic sectors was larger than the share of adult workers; the percentage of young workers registered with the social security system was lower when compared to adults; and labour earnings of young workers were below those of adults. In addition to the generally inferior situation of young workers in the labour market compared to adults, youth labour market indicators were more adversely affected by the crisis. The youth unemployment rate increased by more than the adult unemployment rate, and the share of workers in low-earning positions increased for young workers, while it decreased for adults. Disaggregating by gender, we found that women had better labour market outcomes than men, with the only exceptions being the unemployment rate that was larger among women and labour earnings that were higher for men. However, women were hit hardest by the international crisis, as the unemployment rate and the share of workers in low-earning positions increased more among women.

In summary, Panamanian workers benefited from the impressive economic growth over the decade as their labour market conditions were in a better state in 2012 than they were at the start of the millennium.

References

Azevedo, J. P., M. E. Dávalos, C. Díaz-Bonilla, B. Atuesta, and R. A. Castañeda (2013a). 'Fifteen Years of Inequality in Latin America: How Have Labor Markets Helped?'. Policy Research Working Paper 6384. Washington, DC: World Bank.

Azevedo, J. P., G. Inchauste, and V. Sanfelice (2013b). 'Decomposing the Recent Inequality Decline in Latin America'. Policy Research Working Paper 6715. Washington, DC: World Bank.

CEDLAS and World Bank (2014). SEDLAC—Socio-Economic Database for Latin America and the Caribbean. Centro de Estudios Distributivos, Laborales y Sociales, Facultad de Ciencias Económicas, Universidad Nacional de La Plata and World Bank Poverty Group LCR. Available at <http://sedlac.econo.unlp.edu.ar/eng/index.php>, accessed 2014.

Cruces, G., G. Fields, D. Jaume, and M. Viollaz (2015). 'The Growth–Employment–Poverty Nexus in Latin America in the 2000s: Panama Country Study'. WIDER Working Paper 2015/080. Helsinki: UNU-WIDER.

Cruces, G. and S. Galiani (2013). 'Nota técnica sobre mercado laboral y seguridad social en Panamá y propuestas de política'. Unpublished manuscript.

ECLAC (2002). 'Panamá: Evolución económica durante 2002 y perspectivas para 2003'. Santiago de Chile: United Nations.

ECLAC (2005). 'Panamá: Evolución económica durante 2005 y perspectivas para 2006'. Santiago de Chile: United Nations.

ECLAC (2008). 'Panamá: Evolución económica durante 2008 y perspectivas para 2009'. Santiago de Chile: United Nations.

ECLAC (2008). 'Panamá: Pobreza y distribución del ingreso en el período 2001–07'. Santiago de Chile: United Nations.

Galiani, S. (2009). 'El mercado laboral Panameño, su performance reciente'. Unpublished manuscript. Panama: Ministry of Economics and Finances.

Gasparini, L., S. Galiani, G. Cruces, and P. Acosta (2011). 'Educational Upgrading and Returns to Skills in Latin America: Evidence from a Supply–Demand Framework, 1990–2010'. IZA Working Paper 6244. Bonn: Institute for the Study of Labor.

Harris, S. (2007). 'Panama's Great Challenge: Reforming the Educational System', in *A New Path for Panama*, Volume 25. Bethlehem: Lehigh University, Martindale Center, paper 3. Available at <http://preserve.lehigh.edu/perspectives-v25/3>.

IADB (2014). 'Documento de enfoque: Panamá 2010–2014. Evaluación del programa de país'. Washington, DC: Oficina de Evaluación y Supervisión, Inter-American Development Bank.

IMF (2009). 'Panama: 2009 Article IV Consultation'. IMF Country Report 09/207. Washington, DC: International Monetary Fund.

IMF (2010). 'Panama: 2010 Article IV Consultation'. IMF Country Report 10/314. Washington, DC: International Monetary Fund.

OECD (2010). 'PISA 2009 Results: What Students Know and Can Do. Student Performance in Reading, Mathematics and Science (Volume I)'. Paris: Organization for Economic Co-operation and Development.

Rodríguez Mojica, A. (2013). 'Social Protection Systems in Latin America and the Caribbean: Panama'. ECLAC, Project Documents Collection. Santiago de Chile: United Nations.

World Bank (2011). 'Panama Poverty Assessment: Translating Growth into Opportunities and Poverty Reduction'. World Bank Report 62955. Washington, DC: World Bank.

World Bank (2014). World Development Indicators. Available at <http://data.worldbank.org/data-catalog/world-development-indicators>, accessed April 2014.

19

Paraguay

19.1 Introduction

This chapter on labour markets and growth in Paraguay since 2000 is one of sixteen studies of Latin American countries, each of which analyses the growth–employment–poverty nexus and aims to answer the following broad questions: Has economic growth resulted in economic development via improved labour market conditions in Latin America in the 2000s, and have these improvements halted or been reversed since the Great Recession? How do the rate and character of economic growth, changes in the various labour market indicators, and changes in poverty relate to each other?

To answer these questions, we analyse the growth experience of Paraguay during the 2000s and a wide set of labour market indicators that we assign to one of two different categories: employment and earnings indicators, and poverty and income inequality indicators. More specifically, for the group of employment and earnings indicators we construct statistics on the following variables: the unemployment rate; the employment structure by occupational group, employment position, economic sector, registration of workers with the social security system, and educational level; and mean labour earnings and hourly wages. We present all these indicators for the employed population as a whole and for different population groups (youth, adults, men, and women). For the group of poverty and income inequality indicators, we compute poverty rates using the official moderate and extreme poverty lines and the international lines of 2.5 and 4 dollars a day. We also calculate the Gini coefficient of household per capita income and labour earnings.

All the statistics in this chapter are obtained using microdata from the Encuesta Integrada de Hogares (EIH) for the year 2001, and the Encuesta Permanente de Hogares (EPH) from the years 2002 to 2013. The nationwide surveys were processed following a harmonization methodology and incorporated into the SEDLAC—Socio-Economic Database for Latin America and the

Caribbean (CEDLAS and World Bank 2014).[1] The resulting labour market indicators were compiled into a large number of tables and figures, which are available in an earlier version of this study (henceforth, Cruces et al. 2015). Chapter 1 of this book provides the definition for each of the indicators we analyse here, while Cruces et al. (2015) includes details on definitions and classification systems used by Paraguay's household surveys, and on comparability issues of these surveys over time.

19.2 Economic Growth

> Paraguay experienced slow economic growth from 2000 to 2013. The growth process was erratic. Within the period, the country suffered a serious macroeconomic crisis in the early years, grew steadily from 2003 to 2008, suffered a recession induced by the international crisis of 2008, experienced a quick recovery led by agriculture, suffered a recession once again generated by a severe drought in 2012, and exhibited the largest growth rates of the period in 2013. (Cruces et al. 2015: figures 1 and 2)

During the period 2000 to 2013, Paraguay experienced low economic growth by Latin American standards. GDP per capita increased by 29.1 per cent, while the average for the eighteen Latin American countries was 36.2 per cent during the same period. GDP (measured in 2005 PPP dollars) grew by 64.2 per cent, and GDP per employed person experienced a rise of 14.0 per cent. The annual growth rate of GDP per capita was 1.6 per cent, and it varied from a minimum of –5.7 per cent in 2009 to a maximum of 11.6 per cent in 2013 (Table 19.1).

The process of economic growth in Paraguay was erratic. The volatility of the GDP growth rate in Paraguay during the 2000s was associated both with external factors, such as shocks to terms of trade and foreign demand, and domestic factors, such as weather conditions (World Bank 2013; ILO 2014). The country experienced a serious macroeconomic crisis in the first years of the period analysed. That crisis, which began in 1997, was associated with a number of factors: a domestic banking crisis and foreign economic crises (specifically in East Asian countries, Russia, Brazil, and Argentina). GDP declined by 1.1 per cent a year from 2000 to 2002, while GDP per capita fell by 3.1 per cent annually during the same period.

Starting in 2003, the economy recovered through a boom in the volume of exports and in prices despite a context of declining terms of trade (Hausmann and Klinger 2007). The upward trend in exports was related to the rapid spread

[1] See Cruces et al. (2015: table 1) for details on the size of Paraguay household surveys.

Table 19.1 Paraguay: Evolution of growth and labour market indicators over the 2000s

		2000	2001	2002	2003	2004	2005	2006	2007	2008	2009	2010	2011	2012	2013	
Growth Indicators	GDP per capita	4,572	4,442	4,353	4,453	4,544	4,554	4685	4,850	5,067	4,781	5,313	5,448	5,290	5,904	
	GDP per capita growth rate	−4.32	−2.84	−2.01	2.28	2.06	0.22	2.88	3.52	4.47	−5.65	11.13	2.54	−2.90	11.61	
Employment and Earnings Indicators	Employment-to-population ratio	...	63.91	62.12	62.93	66.61	66.64	63.31	65.60	65.62	65.65	64.44	64.75	68.37	66.81	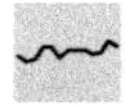
	Unemployment rate	...	7.57	10.70	7.94	7.35	5.78	6.68	5.62	5.59	6.50	5.70	5.51	4.85	5.01	
	Share of low-earnings occupations	...	62.94	64.10	63.01	64.86	61.70	62.17	61.21	59.48	58.89	...	...	...	...	
	Share of mid-earnings occupations	...	27.76	28.62	28.28	27.71	28.96	28.70	29.93	30.62	32.36	...	...	...	...	
	Share of high-earnings occupations	...	9.30	7.28	8.71	7.44	9.34	9.14	8.86	9.89	8.76	...	...	...	...	
	Share of employers	...	6.07	3.84	4.49	4.39	4.67	4.67	5.27	5.26	5.80	5.25	5.14	5.68	6.34	
	Share of wage/ salaried employees	...	45.82	44.05	45.07	44.14	47.70	47.38	49.19	51.23	49.29	52.64	53.39	52.21	55.42	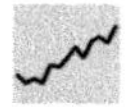
	Share of self-employed workers	...	38.35	39.99	40.38	41.32	38.36	37.83	37.47	35.06	36.05	34.18	34.06	35.57	31.50	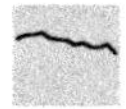
	Share of unpaid family workers	...	9.76	12.12	10.06	10.15	9.28	10.12	8.08	8.46	8.86	7.93	7.40	6.54	6.74	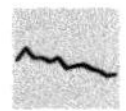

(continued)

Table 19.1 Continued

		2000	2001	2002	2003	2004	2005	2006	2007	2008	2009	2010	2011	2012	2013	
	Share of workers in low-earnings sectors	...	50.32	50.56	50.08	51.23	48.86	47.81	48.02	45.35	45.93	44.46	42.66	43.10	40.03	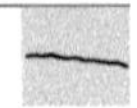
	Share of workers in mid-earnings sectors	...	38.78	37.62	38.35	37.83	38.86	39.62	40.16	41.32	40.88	41.54	38.84	38.48	39.74	
	Share of workers in high-earnings sectors	...	10.90	11.82	11.57	10.94	12.28	12.56	11.82	13.34	13.19	14.00	18.50	18.42	20.24	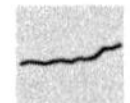
	Share of low-educated workers	...	65.22	65.08	61.07	62.21	56.48	58.23	56.23	54.11	51.54	52.89	48.13	48.84	45.35	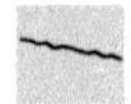
	Share of medium-educated workers	...	24.54	25.98	27.60	27.41	30.24	30.10	31.10	31.76	34.27	32.67	34.16	35.16	34.38	
	Share of high-educated workers	...	10.24	8.94	11.34	10.38	13.28	11.67	12.67	14.13	14.19	14.44	17.71	16.00	20.26	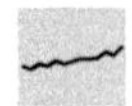
	Share of workers registered with SS	...	13.03	12.56	12.52	10.97	14.11	12.03	15.14	15.86	16.24	...	18.95	19.24	21.88	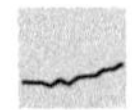
	Mean labour earnings	...	570.8	528.3	546.0	517.2	515.3	469.7	508.3	530.6	518.4	579.8	642.5	571.0	651.2	
Poverty and Inequality Indicators	Official extreme poverty rate	...	15.40	23.57	19.74	16.11	15.55	23.33	22.19	17.73	17.80	17.90	16.48	12.29	9.11	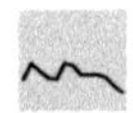
	Official moderate poverty rate	...	34.19	48.21	42.19	38.33	37.22	43.50	39.70	36.55	34.05	32.84	30.81	25.28	22.17	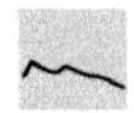
	Poverty rate 2.5 dollars a day	...	22.05	30.68	23.87	21.13	19.39	24.69	19.67	17.29	18.10	16.35	14.43	12.04	8.27	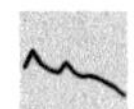

Poverty rate 4 dollars a day	...	37.67	48.52	42.29	40.33	37.60	43.69	38.69	35.69	32.99	30.69	27.75	24.08	20.20	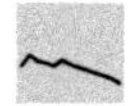
GINI of household per capita income	...	0.547	0.573	0.555	0.525	0.513	0.536	0.521	0.510	0.496	0.518	0.526	0.482	0.482	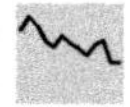
GINI of labour earnings	...	0.548	0.588	0.562	0.546	0.519	0.513	0.534	0.513	0.512	0.509	0.527	0.494	0.498	

Note: The shaded figures of labour market indicators represent statistical significant improvements at 5 per cent between the initial and final years for all the employment and earnings indicators and poverty and inequality indicators. The only exceptions are the share of mid-earnings occupations, share of mid-earnings sectors, and share of medium-educated workers for which we did not assign welfare evaluation criteria.

Source: SEDLAC (CEDLAS and World Bank 2014) and World Development Indicators (World Bank 2014b).

of soybean production thanks to innovations, such as genetically modified seeds, as well as greater meat production. Over the period 2003–8, the Paraguayan economy grew at an annual rate of 4.5 per cent while the GDP per capita growth rate averaged 2.6 per cent a year.

The country was negatively affected by the international crisis of 2008, which induced a drop in external demand, and also by the fall in international prices for agricultural products and by a drought in 2009. GDP fell by 4.0 per cent in 2009, and GDP per capita declined by 5.7 per cent that year. The growth trend quickly resumed with the growth in the agricultural sector, the better weather conditions, and the implementation of a countercyclical policy response (*Plan Estratégico*) that included public works projects, the deferral of tax increases, and agricultural subsidies (Ramírez and González 2009; CEPAL 2010; IMF 2012). GDP grew by 13.0 per cent and GDP per capita by 11.1 per cent in 2010. Later, the country was adversely affected by a severe drought that impacted on agriculture (leading to a ban on meat exports) and local negative shocks to the non-agricultural sector (IMF 2012; Castilleja et al. 2014). Growth slowed to 4.3 per cent in 2011 and fell to 1.2 per cent in 2012. In 2013, the economy bounced back sharply and that year witnessed the largest growth rate of the entire period. GDP grew by 13.5 per cent and GDP per capita by 11.6 per cent. The agricultural sector and the recovery of the meat export markets were largely responsible for that growth (Castilleja et al. 2014).

19.3 Unemployment

> The unemployment rate moved jointly with the business cycle. It decreased between 2001 and 2013 overall and for all population groups. Within the period, the unemployment rate increased in the early years, it decreased from 2003 to 2008, grew once again during the international crisis of 2008, recovered the downward trend after that episode, and had a new rise by the end of the period. The increase in the unemployment rate led by the international crisis held for all population groups.
>
> (Cruces et al. 2015: figure 3)

The unemployment rate (measured as the ratio of unemployment to labour force) fell from 7.6 per cent in 2001 (188,610 unemployed persons) to 5.0 per cent in 2013 (168,386 unemployed persons) (Table 19.1). Changes in the unemployment rate followed the business cycle. The unemployment rate increased between 2001 and 2002 when the economy was immersed in a major macroeconomic crisis, climbing from 7.6 to 10.7 per cent (66,937 new unemployed persons). From 2002 to 2008, the unemployment rate decreased, dropping to 5.6 per cent in 2008. This reduction was not steady; the unemployment rate experienced an increase in 2006. In 2009, the unemployment rate increased once again as a result of the international crisis, reaching 6.5 per cent (38,243 new unemployed persons compared to 2008). Both the number of persons in the labour force and the number of persons employed increased between 2008 and 2009 by 190,167 and 151,924 respectively. These figures suggest that the increase in the unemployment rate during the international crisis was explained by new entrants into the labour market who could not find a job. By the end of the period, the unemployment rate was decreasing in conjunction with economic recovery, though there was a slight increase in 2013, probably as a response to the recession of 2012.

From 2001 to 2013, the unemployment rate dropped for all population groups (youth and adults, men and women). The erratic evolution of the unemployment rate that was observed in the aggregate held for all population groups. Their unemployment rates increased at the beginning of the period, from 2001 to 2002, began a downward trend in 2003, but experienced new increases in 2006 and 2009. The increase of 2013 appeared only for men and adult workers.

The unemployment rate increased during the international crisis for young and adult workers, men, and women. The unemployment rate recovered the pre-recession level in 2010 for adults, in 2011 for both men and women, and in 2012 for young workers.

19.4 Job Mix

> There was a slight improvement in the composition of employment by occupational group between 2001 and 2009 (when data on this variable stopped being available) as workers moved from elementary, agricultural, and forestry and fishery occupations to better paying occupations such as service and sales, and clerical jobs. Young and adult workers, men, and women benefited from the improvement in the structure of employment by occupational group over the period. Within the period, the structure of employment suffered a worsening between 2001 and 2002 overall and for all population groups and an improvement in the following years that was not affected by the international crisis of 2008, either overall or at the population group level. (Cruces et al. 2015: figure 4)

Changes in the occupational composition of employment over the period 2001–9 showed a mild improvement. Low-earning occupations (elementary, craft and trades, and agricultural, forestry, and fishery occupations) lost share in total employment (drop of 4.1 percentage points). High-earning occupations (management, armed forces, and professionals) also reduced their share in total employment (drop of 0.5 percentage points). Mid-earning occupations (plant and machine operators, and technical, clerical, services and sales jobs), then, are those that gained share (increase of 4.6 percentage points) (Table 19.1). Within the period 2001–9, there was a worsening in the employment structure by occupational group between 2001 and 2002, when the share of low-earning occupations in total employment increased and the share of high-earning occupations decreased. Starting in 2003, the employment structure by occupational group improved, mainly through the increase in the share of mid-earning occupations in total employment. The improvement continued up to the end of the period with an interruption in 2004.

The improvements in the occupational composition of employment between 2001 and 2009 took place for young and adult workers and for men and women. All population groups suffered a worsening in the employment structure by occupational group in the early years of the period and a slight improvement after that.

The international crisis of 2008 did not affect the improving trend in the employment composition by occupational group, either overall or for any population group. The changes in employment composition by occupational groups that took place in the years following the Great Recession cannot be analysed because the classification is only available until 2009.

> The employment structure by occupational position improved from 2001 to 2013 as the shares of wage/salaried employees in total employment increased and the shares of self-employed and unpaid workers decreased. All population groups benefited from the improvement in the structure of employment by occupational position over the period. Within the period, the employment structure deteriorated in the early years overall and for all population groups, it improved in the following years, and suffered a worsening once again during the international crisis of 2008, in the aggregate and for adults, men, and women, but not for young workers. All occupational positions returned to their pre-crisis shares in 2010.
>
> (Cruces et al. 2015: figure 5)

The share of paid employees—the largest category in Paraguay—increased from 45.8 per cent in 2001 to 55.4 per cent in 2013. The share of the self-employed and unpaid workers decreased from 38.4 per cent in 2001 to 31.5 per cent in 2013 and from 9.8 per cent to 6.7 per cent respectively. The share of employers was essentially unchanged over the period (Table 19.1). These changes in the structure of employment by occupational position can be interpreted as an improvement due to the fall in the share of low-earning positions (self-employment and unpaid workers) and the increase in the share of high-earning positions (employers and wage/salaried employees). Within the period, the employment structure by occupational position deteriorated at the beginning, when the economy was immersed in a severe macroeconomic crisis, and began an improving trend in 2003 that was interrupted by the international crisis of 2008.

All population groups (young and adult workers, men, and women) benefited from the improvement in the employment structure by occupational position between 2001 and 2013. All population groups experienced a worsening in their employment structure by occupational position between 2001 and 2002. In 2003, an improving trend began for all population groups, which was interrupted in 2009 during the international crisis.

The international crisis of 2008 led to a deterioration in the employment structure by occupational position for adult workers, men, and women, while it remained largely unchanged for young workers. The deterioration in the employment structure by occupational position is in accord with the increase in the unemployment rate during the crisis, as economic necessity may compel workers to look for free-entry activities such as unpaid family jobs or self-employment. By 2010, all of the affected groups recovered their pre-crisis levels.

> The employment composition by economic sector improved over the period studied, overall and for all population groups, though erratically. The international crisis reversed this tendency for adult workers, men, and women but they recovered the previous structure of employment by 2010.
>
> (Cruces et al. 2015: figure 6)

The period 2001–13 witnessed a reduction in the share of workers in low-earning sectors (domestic service, primary activities, and industry), as the percentage of workers in those sectors dropped from 50.3 per cent in 2001 to 40.0 per cent in 2013. As mentioned above, although the agricultural sector fuelled economic growth in Paraguay from 2002 to 2008, this sector's share of total employment fell due to increased mechanization and the capital- and land-intensive characteristics of soy production, the main Paraguayan export (Hausmann and Klinger 2007; Castilleja et al. 2014). During the same period, the share of workers in high-earning sectors (skilled services, utilities and transportation, and public administration) increased from 10.9 per cent to 20.2 per cent (Table 19.1). Consequently, the share of mid-earning sectors in total employment (construction, commerce, education, and health) experienced a small change over the period (increase of 1.0 percentage point). Within the period, there was a slight deterioration in the employment structure by economic sector at the beginning, from 2001 to 2004, as the share of low-earning sectors in total employment increased along with a slight increase in the share of high-earning sectors. From 2004 and up to the end of the period, the employment structure by economic sector improved with some ups and downs in the share of each category. Specifically, low-earning sectors had a small increase during the international crisis of 2008 and rose once again in 2012, while high-earning sectors decreased slightly.

The employment composition by economic sector improved during 2001–13 for young and adult workers and for men and women as they moved from low-earning sectors to high-earning sectors. The changes in the employment structure by economic sector were erratic for all population groups. There was a worsening in the early years of the period for all of them. The employment structure by economic sector then improved steadily up to 2008 for adults, men, and women who suffered the negative effects of the international crisis. Young workers were not affected. Adults, men, and women recovered the improving trend in 2010. In 2011, adults and women suffered a worsening once again, while young workers exhibited a deterioration in their employment structure by economic sector in 2013.

The international crisis of 2008 led to a slight worsening in the employment composition by economic sector overall and for adult workers, men, and women, while young workers continued with the pre-recession trend in their employment composition. All of the affected groups recovered their pre-crisis shares by 2010.

> The educational level of the employed population improved over the period for all population groups, and especially among young workers. The international crisis of 2008 did not have an effect on the structure of employment by educational level. (Cruces et al. 2015: figure 7)

The share of workers with low educational levels (eight years of schooling or less) dropped from 65.2 per cent in 2001 to 45.4 per cent in 2013, while the share of workers with medium and high educational levels (nine to thirteen years of schooling and over thirteen years of schooling) grew from 24.5 per cent in 2001 to 34.4 per cent in 2013 and from 10.1 per cent to 20.3 per cent respectively (Table 19.1).[2] We interpret this result as an improvement for the employed population as the level of education is an important predictor of labour earnings. Consequently, the changes in the employment structure by educational level implied an increase in the share of workers that tend to have high levels of earnings and a decline in the share of workers with low earnings levels.[3] The changes in the structure of employment by educational level took place with small ups and downs over the period. The improvement in the educational level of the employed population took place simultaneously with the implementation of programmes aiming to improve access to and permanence in basic school (*Escuela Viva* since 2001)

[2] The most frequent value of years of education for employed workers in Paraguay was six during the entire period (around 22.0 per cent of employed workers had six years of education).

[3] The improvement in the employment structure by educational level is related to changes in the relative demand and supply of workers with high educational levels with corresponding implications for the wage gap by educational group and the unemployment rate of each educational level. We introduce a discussion about the role of these factors in Paraguay in section 19.5.

and literacy programmes for young and adult people (*Paraguay lee y escribe*, since 2007) (Lavigne 2012; Castilleja et al. 2014).

The improvement in the educational level of the employed population occurred for all population groups, and primarily for young workers. The pattern of improvement in the level of education of the employed population in Paraguay continued even during the international crisis of 2008, overall and for all population groups.

> The overall share of workers registered with the social security system increased between 2001 and 2013, though erratically. However, the employed population in Paraguay has been largely unregistered over the period. All population groups benefited from the improvement in the share of registered workers over the period. The improvement was not interrupted by the international crisis of 2008.
>
> (Cruces et al. 2015: figure 8)

The social security system in Paraguay is composed of a contributory scheme and a non-contributory scheme. The contributory scheme comprises a pension system and a national health system. Paraguay has eight social security institutions but two of them concentrate most of the insured population: the *Caja Fiscal* and the *Instituto de Previsión Social* (IPS). The others are administered by municipalities, railways, banks, Parliament, the national administration for electricity, and *Itaipú* (the bi-national hydroelectric power plant located between Brazil and Paraguay). The IPS is the main organization managing social security for wage earners who work in the private sector in urban areas, but in recent years it has been incorporating public-sector workers. The IPS provides both retirement pensions and health coverage for its affiliates and their families, protecting them against diverse risks, including illness, accidents, maternity, old age, and disability. The old age retirement fund is funded by employers' and employees' contributions, while the IPS contributory health insurance is also funded by the government. The non-contributory scheme comprises different programmes directed at persons in poverty and is funded totally by the government. These programmes include the *Pensión alimentaria para adultos mayores en situación de pobreza*, survivor pension, and Veterans of the Chaco War (Lavigne 2012; Higgins et al. 2013; ILO 2014).

The social security records show an increase in the percentage of workers registered with the contributory scheme between 2001 and 2013 from 13.0 per cent to 21.9 per cent (397,850 new registered workers) (Table 19.1). Despite several years of economic growth, the increase in registered employment in Paraguay was slow. The productive infrastructure based on micro and small enterprises, with a concentration of agricultural exports of little value added and very vulnerable to weather conditions and external shocks, explains the slow reduction in unregistered employment (ILO 2014). The changes were erratic. From 2001 to 2004, the percentage of workers registered with the social security system fell from 13.0 per cent to 11.0 per cent. That figure increased in 2005 to 14.1 per cent only to fall again in 2006 to 12.0 per cent. From 2007 onwards, the share of workers registered with the social security system increased steadily, and this trend was not interrupted by the international crisis of 2008. In an effort to expand coverage, the IPS launched several institutional reforms in 2003, such as the improvement and modernization of institutional management and the development of skills of IPS's human resources. Some legal reforms also had a positive effect on expanding retirement coverage. In 2004, Paraguay ratified a reciprocity agreement among Mercosur countries, by which a worker who contributed in a Mercosur member country can access social security benefits in another member country.[4] In 2009, the country also adopted reciprocity agreements between the different fiscal funds and the IPS. The exchange of information between the IPS and public-sector entities, such as the Tax Secretariat and the National Directorate of Public Contracting, also helps explain the reduced evasion and increased coverage (ILO 2014).

Disaggregating, the rate of registration with the social security system increased for all population groups (young and adult workers, men, and women) over the period. All of them suffered a reduction in the percentage of registered workers in the early years of the period, from 2001 to 2004, an increase in 2005, a fall in 2006, and a steady improvement in the following years.

The international crisis of 2008 did not affect the upward trend in the share of workers registered with the social security system that took place from 2006 onwards, overall and for any of the population groups.

19.5 Labour Earnings

> Labour earnings increased overall during the period studied, though erratically. Within the period, labour earnings experienced a downward trend in the first half (from 2001 to 2006) with some ups and downs and began an upward trend in 2006 that was interrupted by the international crisis of 2008 and by the local crisis of 2012. Though workers' earnings were affected by the 2008 international crisis, they surpassed pre-crisis levels by 2010. All population groups experienced earnings gains between 2001 and 2013, but labour incomes moved erratically for all of them. The evidence indicates that workers from low-earning categories increased their labour earnings, while workers from high-earning categories tended to suffer earnings losses over the period.
>
> (Cruces et al. 2015: figure 9)

[4] Mercosur is a regional trade agreement between Argentina, Brazil, Paraguay, and Uruguay, that was established in 1991.

Average monthly earnings, expressed in PPP dollars of 2005, increased by 14.1 per cent over the period, climbing from US$571 in 2001 to US$651 in 2013 (Table 19.1). The increase in labour earnings was just half of the increase in GDP per capita over the period that was 29.1 per cent. From 2001 to 2006, changes in labour earnings did not reflect changes in the country's economic performance. Between 2001 and 2002, GDP changed only slightly (drop of 0.02 per cent) while labour earnings decreased by 7.4 per cent. From 2003 to 2006, the economy grew at a rate of 3.8 per cent annually, while labour earnings decreased at a rate of 2.8 per cent a year. From 2007 onwards, labour earnings moved with the business cycle; GDP and earnings experienced a general upward trend during that period, with setbacks in 2009, when labour earnings fell by 2.3 per cent, and in 2012, when they fell by 11.1 per cent.

Labour earnings of young and adult workers, men, and women increased between 2001 and 2013, though erratically. All population groups suffered an earnings reduction in the first half of the period analysed (from 2001 to 2006). An upward trend began in 2007 for all groups with earnings losses in 2009 and in 2012.

Workers from low-earning categories increased their labour earnings between 2001 and 2013, while workers from high-earning categories tended to suffer earnings losses. Among occupational positions, labour earnings of the self-employed increased more than those of paid employees, while employers suffered an earnings loss. The earnings of workers in high-earning sectors (skilled services, utilities and transportation, and public administration) decreased over the period studied, while the earnings of workers in low-earning sectors (domestic service, primary activities, and industry) increased. Labour earnings of the remaining sectors (construction, commerce, and education and health) increased as well. Disaggregating by educational levels, the change in labour earnings from 2001 to 2013 favoured less educated workers. Labour earnings of workers with high and medium educational levels fell. Workers with low educational levels were the only educational group whose labour earnings increased over the period. Among occupational groups, the labour earnings of all groups decreased during 2001–9. After 2007, the aggregate trend for labour earnings was upward, but due to the international crisis of 2008, there was a negative overall change from 2001 to 2009.

The evidence of increasing labour earnings between 2001 and 2013 for workers with low educational levels, and falling labour earnings for workers with medium and high levels of education, can be interpreted in light of previous findings of improving educational levels of the Paraguayan employed population and improving employment structure by economic sector over that period. The improving employment structure by economic sector implied an increase in the share of sectors that can be expected to employ workers with high and medium educational levels, such as skilled services and public administration, and a reduction in the share of sectors that employ workers with low educational levels, such as domestic service, primary activities, and industry. This evidence indicates that the demand for workers with high and medium educational levels relative to those with low educational levels increased between 2001 and 2013. On the other hand, the educational level of persons in the labour force improved over the same period, indicating an increase in the relative supply of workers with high and medium levels of education (Cruces et al. 2015: table 8). The prediction of a supply and demand analysis is that the relative wages of workers with high and medium educational levels relative to those with low levels of education will rise or fall depending on which effect dominates (increase in the relative demand versus increase in the relative supply). In the Paraguayan labour market, the relative wages of workers with high and medium educational levels relative to those with low educational levels fell over the period, while the relative wages of workers with high educational levels relative to those with medium educational levels also decreased (Cruces et al. 2015: table 7). The adjustment process also led to a reduction in the unemployment rate of all educational groups between 2001 and 2013 that was larger for workers with medium and low levels of education compared to those with high levels of education (Cruces et al. 2015: table 9).

The international crisis of 2008 had a negative impact on labour earnings in the aggregate, for adult workers, men, and women, and for most occupational categories. Labour earnings decreased between 2008 and 2009 but recovered quickly and surpassed the pre-crisis level in 2010. In 2012, there was a new reduction in labour earnings as a consequence of the local crisis. By 2013, labour earnings were at their highest level of the entire period.

19.6 Poverty and Inequality

> The poverty rate and the rate of working poor households dropped between 2001 and 2013 for all poverty lines. Within the period, they increased in the early years (from 2001 to 2002), fell between 2002 and 2005, experienced an increase in 2006 and began a downward trend after that year. Those reducing trends were not interrupted by the international crisis of 2008 or the local crisis of 2012, except for the poverty rate measured by the US$2.5 dollars-a-day international line that suffered a slight increase between 2008 and 2009 and the extreme poverty rate that exhibited a small rise in 2010. (Cruces et al. 2015: figure 10)

The moderate poverty rate (measured by the country's official poverty line) fell from 34.2 per cent in 2001 to 22.2 per cent in 2013; the extreme poverty rate dropped from 15.4 per cent to 9.1 per cent over the period. The percentage of working poor households (defined as the proportion of persons in the population living in poor households where at least one member works) decreased from 24.4 per cent to 15.6 per cent over the same period (Table 19.1). These poverty indicators increased between 2001 and 2002, dropped between 2002 and 2005, increased again in 2006, and then began a steady downward trend that was not interrupted by the international crisis of 2008 or by the local crisis of 2012. The only exception was the extreme poverty rate that stopped decreasing in 2009 and exhibited a small increase in 2010 (rise of 0.1 percentage points). The analysis based on the 2.5 and 4 dollars-a-day PPP international poverty lines also shows a drop in the poverty rate from 2001 to 2013. The poverty rate based on the 2.5 dollars-a-day poverty line fell from 22.1 per cent in 2001 to 8.3 per cent in 2013. The reduction was from 37.7 per cent in 2001 to 20.2 per cent in 2013 for the poverty rate based on the 4 dollars-a-day poverty line (Table 19.1). Both poverty indicators followed similar trends compared to the poverty indicators based on the official poverty lines: they increased between 2001 and 2002, fell from 2002 to 2005, increased once again in 2006, and then started a downward trend up to the end of the period. The downward trend was interrupted by the international crisis of 2008 only for the poverty rate based on the 2.5 dollars-a-day poverty line (increase of 0.8 percentage points).

Rising labour incomes have been the driving force of poverty reduction during the 2000s, both because of increased earnings and increased numbers of earners (World Bank 2014a). Household labour incomes fell at the beginning of the decade, from 2001 to 2006, but exhibited an increase of 46.5 per cent between 2006 and 2013 (Cruces et al. 2015: figure 11). Non-labour incomes, such as public transfers, only started to play a significant role in 2011 due to important increases in coverage of the main social programmes. In fact, direct transfers had a small poverty-reducing effect in 2010 due to the low coverage among the poor and the low per capita transfers to those who are covered (Higgins et al. 2013). Between 2010 and 2013, incomes from government transfers at the household level grew by 87.3 per cent. The reduction in food prices also played a role in poverty reduction in the last years of the period under study (World Bank 2014a). As a result, between 2011 and 2013, all poverty indicators exhibited important reductions compared to previous years.

> Household per capita income and labour earning inequality decreased from 2001 to 2013. Changes in the inequality indices over the period were erratic: they increased at the beginning of the period (from 2001 to 2002), fell from 2002 to 2005, rose once again in 2006 and began a downward trend in 2007 that was interrupted by the international crisis of 2008. (Cruces et al. 2015: figure 12)

The Gini coefficient of household per capita income fell from 0.547 in 2001 to 0.482 in 2013 (Table 19.1). This indicator increased between 2001 and 2002, dropped between 2002 and 2005, increased again in 2006, and then entered into a downward trend that was interrupted by the international crisis of 2008. The Gini coefficient of household per capita income increased from 0.496 in 2009 to 0.526 in 2011; the downward trend resumed in 2012. The Gini coefficient of labour earnings among employed workers tended to be higher than the Gini coefficient of household per capita income over the period and dropped from 0.548 in 2001 to 0.498 in 2013 (Table 19.1); this reduction in labour earnings inequality is in accord with the evidence presented above showing earnings increases for low-earning categories and earnings reductions for high-earning categories. Consequently, the reduction in labour earnings inequality in Paraguay occurred at the expense of income losses for some categories. The Gini coefficient of labour earnings exhibited the same trends as the Gini coefficient of household per capita income over the period.

Changes in household per capita income inequality in Paraguay have been related mainly to changes in demographical factors. Azevedo et al. (2013b) decomposed the change in the Gini coefficient of household per capita income for the period 1999–2010 and found that changes in demographical factors, such as the share of adults in the population and the share of adults in the total employment, were inequality-reducing, while changes in labour and non-labour income were inequality-increasing over that period. Other studies have analysed the factors behind the evolution of labour income inequality. Azevedo et al. (2013a) used a decomposition approach and found that changes in the education wage premium (or the 'price effect') and changes in the distribution of the stock of education (the 'quantity effect') were inequality-reducing between 1999 and 2010. Gasparini et al. (2011) found a reduction in the gap between the wages of skilled workers (those with complete or incomplete college education) and unskilled workers (those who have completed secondary education or less) in Paraguay between 2003 and 2009. The shrinking educational earnings gap can be explained by factors related to supply and demand: the relative supply of skilled workers increased steadily while the relative demand for those workers fell.

19.7 Conclusions

Overall, Paraguay experienced slow economic growth by Latin American standards between 2000 and 2013. Within the period, the country suffered a serious macroeconomic crisis in the early years, grew steadily from 2003 to 2008, suffered a recession induced by the international crisis of 2008, experienced a quick recovery led by agriculture, suffered a recession once again in 2012 generated by a severe drought, and exhibited the largest growth rates of the period in 2013.

Most labour market indicators followed the erratic pattern of economic growth over the period. The unemployment rate fell overall between 2001 and 2013 and exhibited an increase in the early years of the period, a downward trend from 2003 to 2008, an increase after the international crisis, a recovery of the downward trend, and a final increase by the end of the period. The composition of employment by occupational group suffered a worsening at the beginning of the period but exhibited a slight improvement overall between 2001 and 2009 (the latest we have data on this classification) that was not affected by the Great Recession. The employment structure by occupational position improved overall from 2001 to 2013, as the shares of paid employees and employers in total employment increased and the shares of self-employed and unpaid workers decreased. Within the period, the employment structure by occupational position changed erratically, with a worsening in the early years of the period (from 2001 to 2002), an improvement in the following years, a worsening during the international crisis of 2008, and a recovery of the pre-crisis structure by the end of the period. The employment composition by economic sector changed erratically over the period and was affected negatively by the international crisis. Overall, there was an improvement between 2001 and 2013. The overall share of workers registered with the social security system increased between 2001 and 2013, with ups and downs. The improving trend was not interrupted by the international crisis of 2008. Labour earnings increased overall between 2001 and 2013. Within the period, labour earnings experienced a downward trend in the first half (from 2001 to 2006) with some ups and downs, and began an upward trend in 2006 that was interrupted by the international crisis of 2008 and by the local crisis of 2012. The evidence indicated that workers from low-earning categories increased their labour earnings, while workers from high-earning categories tended to suffer earnings losses.

All poverty indicators and the inequality of household per capita income and labour earnings dropped between 2001 and 2013. Within the period, they increased in the early years (from 2001 to 2002), fell between 2002 and 2005, experienced an increase in 2006, and began a downward trend after that year. Those reducing trends were not interrupted by the international crisis of 2008 or the local crisis of 2012 for the moderate poverty rate and the poverty rate based on the 4 dollars-a-day international line, but were affected negatively by the international crisis for the inequality indices, the extreme poverty rate, and the poverty rate based on the 2.5 dollars-a-day international line, but only slightly. The only labour market indicator that changed steadily over the period was the educational level of the employed population that improved over the period and was not affected negatively by the international crisis of 2008.

The comparison between the effects of the international crisis of 2008 on labour market indicators and the effects generated by the macroeconomic crisis at the beginning of the period (2001–2) and the recession caused by the severe drought of 2012 reveals that the 2001–2 crisis impacted Paraguay more strongly. The increase in the unemployment rate and the growth in the share of low-earning positions in total employment were larger during the 2001–2 crisis compared to the international crisis of 2008 and the 2012 recession. The share of low-earning occupations in total employment, the share of unregistered workers, and all poverty and inequality indicators increased during the 2001–2 crisis, while in general they fell during the other recessionary episodes. On the other hand, the reduction in GDP and the increase in the share of low-earning sectors in total employment were larger during the Great Recession, while the reduction in labour earnings was larger during the 2012 recession.

Young workers had worse labour market outcomes over the period compared to adults, but they do not seem to be more vulnerable to macroeconomic crises. Men and women exhibited a balanced situation in their labour market outcomes, but men were most affected by the negative impacts of the crises. The unemployment rate was higher for young compared to adult workers, the share of young employed workers in low-earning occupational groups was larger than the share of adult workers, the percentage of young workers registered with the social security system was lower when compared to adults, and labour earnings of young workers were below those of adults. On the other hand, the shares of young workers in low-earning occupational positions and sectors were lower compared to adults and their educational level improved more than that of adults. Despite the generally inferior situation of young workers in the labour market, adult workers were more affected by the episodes of crises, specifically the international crisis of 2008, in all labour market indicators, except for the increase in the unemployment rate that was larger among young workers. Disaggregating by gender, we found that men were better than women in some cases, e.g. the male unemployment rate was lower, the share of male workers in low-earning positions was lower compared to women, and labour earnings of men were higher than labour earnings of women; in other cases, the opposite occurred, e.g. the percentage of workers registered with the social security system tended to be larger for women compared to men, and the share of workers in low-earning occupations and sectors tended to be lower for women compared to men. The negative impacts of the international crisis of 2008 affected men more than women in all labour market indicators.

In summary, the growth process of Paraguay during the 2000s was volatile. Most employment and earnings indicators and poverty and inequality indicators followed the erratic pattern of economic growth, but ended the period with a general improvement relative to the starting point (the year 2000).

References

Azevedo, J. P., M. E. Dávalos, C. Díaz-Bonilla, B. Atuesta, and R. A. Castañeda (2013a). 'Fifteen Years of Inequality in Latin America: How Have Labor Markets Helped?'. Policy Research Working Paper 6384. Washington, DC: World Bank.

Azevedo, J. P., G. Inchauste, and V. Sanfelice (2013b). 'Decomposing the Recent Inequality Decline in Latin America'. Policy Research Working Paper 6715. Washington, DC: World Bank.

Castilleja, L., P. Garay, and D. Lovera (2014). 'Diagnóstico de crecimiento de Paraguay'. Nota Técnica IDB-TN-666. Washington, DC: International Development Bank, Departamento de Países del Cono Sur.

CEDLAS and World Bank (2014). SEDLAC—Socio-Economic Database for Latin America and the Caribbean. Centro de Estudios Distributivos, Laborales y Sociales, Facultad de Ciencias Económicas, Universidad Nacional de La Plata and World Bank Poverty Group LCR. Available at <http://sedlac.econo.unlp.edu.ar/eng/index.php>, accessed 2014.

CEPAL (2010). 'Economic Survey for Latin America and the Caribbean 2009–2010'. Santiago de Chile: Economic Commission for Latin America and the Caribbean.

Cruces, G., G. Fields, D. Jaume, and M. Viollaz (2015). 'The Growth–Employment–Poverty Nexus in Latin America in the 2000s: Paraguay Country Study'. WIDER Working Paper 2015/081. Helsinki: UNU-WIDER.

Gasparini, L., S. Galiani, G. Cruces, and P. Acosta (2011). 'Educational Upgrading and Returns to Skills in Latin America: Evidence from a Supply–Demand Framework, 1990–2010'. IZA Working Paper 6244. Bonn: Institute for the Study of Labor.

Hausmann, R. and B. Klinger (2007). 'Growth Diagnostic: Paraguay'. Unpublished manuscript. Cambridge, MA: Center for International Development, Harvard Kennedy School.

Higgins, S., N. Lustig, J. Ramírez, and B. Swanson (2013). 'Social Spending, Taxes, and Income Redistribution in Paraguay'. CEQ Working Paper 1311. New Orleans: Tulane University.

ILO (2014). 'Slight Decline and Key Challenges in Informal Employment in Paraguay'. FORLAC. Programme for the Promotion of Formalization in Latin America and the Caribbean. Geneva: Regional Office for Latin America and the Caribbean, International Labour Organization.

IMF (2012). 'Paraguay: Staff Report for the 2012 Article IV Consultation'. IMF Country Report 12/211. Washington, DC: International Monetary Fund.

Lavigne, M. (2012). 'Social Protection Systems in Latin America and the Caribbean: Paraguay'. ECLAC, Project Documents Collection. Santiago de Chile: United Nations.

Ramírez, J. and C. González (2009). 'Crisis y pobreza rural en América Latina: El caso de Paraguay'. Documento de Trabajo 48. Santiago de Chile: Centro Latinoamericano para el Desarrollo Rural.

World Bank (2013). 'Growth Volatility in Paraguay: Sources, Effects, and Options'. Report 78318-PY. Washington, DC: Poverty Reduction and Economic Management, Latin America and the Caribbean Region, World Bank.

World Bank (2014a). 'Volatility and Inequality as Constraints to Shared Prosperity: Paraguay Equity Assessment'. Report ACS9297. Washington, DC: Poverty and Gender Group (LCSPP), World Bank.

World Bank (2014b). World Development Indicators. Available at <http://data.worldbank.org/data-catalog/world-development-indicators>, accessed April 2014.

20

Peru

20.1 Introduction

This chapter on labour markets and growth in Peru since 2000 is one of sixteen studies of Latin American countries, each of which analyses the growth–employment–poverty nexus and aims to answer the following broad questions: Has economic growth resulted in economic development via improved labour market conditions in Latin America in the 2000s, and have these improvements halted or been reversed since the Great Recession? How do the rate and character of economic growth, changes in the various labour market indicators, and changes in poverty relate to each other?

To answer these questions, we analyse the growth experience of Peru during the 2000s and a wide set of labour market indicators that we assign to one of two different categories: employment and earnings indicators, and poverty and income inequality indicators. More specifically, for the group of employment and earnings indicators we construct statistics on the following variables: the unemployment rate; the employment structure by occupational group, employment position, economic sector, registration of workers with the social security system, and educational level; and mean labour earnings and hourly wages. We present all these indicators for the employed population as a whole and for different population groups (youth, adults, men, and women). For the group of poverty and income inequality indicators, we compute poverty rates using the official moderate and extreme poverty lines and the international lines of 2.5 and 4 dollars a day. We also calculate the Gini coefficient of household per capita income and labour earnings.

All the statistics in this chapter are obtained using microdata from the Encuesta Nacional de Hogares (ENAHO), from 2003 to 2012. The nationwide surveys were processed following a harmonization methodology and incorporated into the SEDLAC—Socio-Economic Database for Latin America and the

Caribbean (CEDLAS and World Bank 2014).[1] The resulting labour market indicators were compiled into a large number of tables and figures, which are available in an earlier version of this study (henceforth, Cruces et al. 2015). Chapter 1 of this book provides the definition for each of the indicators we analyse here, while Cruces et al. (2015) includes details on definitions and classification systems used by Peru's household surveys, and on comparability issues of these surveys over time.

20.2 Economic Growth

> The Peruvian economy performed exceptionally well between 2000 and 2012 with a growth performance that placed the country well above the regional average. The economy proved highly resilient in response to the global economic crisis of 2008. The country suffered a slowdown in 2009 and recovered quickly in 2010. (Cruces et al. 2015: figures 1 and 2)

During the period 2000–12, the Peruvian economy had one of the highest growth rates in Latin America and experienced rapid economic growth by the region's standards. GDP per capita increased by 71.1 per cent, placing Peru's growth performance at twice the average of 32.6 per cent for the eighteen Latin American countries during the same period. GDP (measured in PPP dollars of 2005) grew by 97.3 per cent, and GDP per employed person rose by 45.5 per cent. The annual growth rate of GDP per capita was 4.4 per cent, and it varied from a minimum of −1.2 per cent in 2001 to a maximum of 8.6 per cent in 2008 (Table 20.1).

Peru suffered an episode of slow growth at the beginning of the period analysed, between 2000 and 2001, as a consequence of the Russian crisis, which led to a strong reduction in capital inflows to the country and declining terms of trade (Mendoza Bellido 2013). Two factors form the basis for Peru's economic expansion from 2002 to 2012. First, growing investment, a higher rate of private consumption, and returning capital inflows fuelled the economy. Second, a favourable international environment, characterized by growing foreign demand for Peruvian products and a prolonged period of improvements in its terms of trade, laid the grounds for considerable export growth. Between 2002 and 2009, Peruvian exports grew at an average annual rate of 18.3 per cent. This was driven by an increase in both traditional and non-traditional exports (Guerra 2012). But, while the volume of Peru's traditional exports—minerals, hydrocarbon, and raw materials—increased mostly due to a price

[1] See Cruces et al. (2015: table 1) for details on the size of Peru household surveys.

Table 20.1 Peru: Evolution of growth and labour market indicators over the 2000s

		2000	2001	2002	2003	2004	2005	2006	2007	2008	2009	2010	2011	2012	
Growth Indicators	GDP per capita	5,514	5,447	5,644	5,797	6,013	6,349	6,765	7,288	7,916	7,904	8,503	8,982	9,431	
	GDP per capita growth rate	1.41	−1.20	3.62	2.71	3.71	5.60	6.56	7.72	8.62	−0.15	7.57	5.63	5.01	
Employment and Earnings Indicators	Employment-to-population ratio	...	...	...	68.47	68.02	66.98	68.69	70.42	70.45	70.78	71.14	70.72	70.52	
	Unemployment rate	...	...	...	5.06	5.18	5.16	4.54	4.55	4.41	4.29	3.90	3.77	3.45	
	Share of low-earnings occupations	...	...	...	61.74	63.18	63.25	61.84	59.37	57.92	55.69	54.82	53.82	52.59	
	Share of mid-earnings occupations	...	...	...	25.31	24.43	24.90	25.56	26.52	28.13	29.84	31.01	31.95	32.42	
	Share of high-earnings occupations	...	...	...	12.95	12.39	11.85	12.60	14.11	13.95	14.47	14.17	14.23	14.99	
	Share of employers	...	...	...	5.31	5.49	5.64	5.60	5.92	5.62	5.65	5.98	5.44	5.59	
	Share of wage/ salaried employees	...	...	...	39.78	40.96	41.33	43.22	44.58	45.09	45.31	45.22	45.26	46.64	
	Share of self-employed workers	...	...	...	37.34	36.00	36.46	35.22	35.85	36.34	36.04	36.56	36.81	36.42	
	Share of unpaid family workers	...	...	...	17.57	17.54	16.57	15.96	13.65	12.95	13.00	12.23	12.49	11.35	
	Share of workers in low-earnings sectors	...	...	...	44.44	43.97	44.08	43.02	40.17	39.21	38.04	37.10	36.83	35.83	

(continued)

Table 20.1 Continued

		2000	2001	2002	2003	2004	2005	2006	2007	2008	2009	2010	2011	2012	
	Share of workers in mid-earnings sectors	...	...	...	44.67	44.79	44.93	45.08	47.36	48.33	48.80	49.94	50.11	50.40	
	Share of workers in high-earnings sectors	...	...	...	10.89	11.24	11.00	11.90	12.47	12.46	13.16	12.96	13.07	13.76	
	Share of low-educated workers	...	...	...	45.32	44.20	44.29	42.60	39.80	39.06	38.75	38.43	37.87	36.07	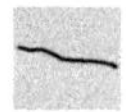
	Share of medium-educated workers	...	...	...	37.03	37.67	37.72	38.42	39.25	40.11	39.95	40.31	40.25	40.90	
	Share of high-educated workers	...	...	...	17.65	18.13	17.99	18.98	20.95	20.83	21.30	21.26	21.88	23.04	
	Share of workers registered with SS	...	...	...	14.85	20.10	19.71	22.57	25.96	26.47	28.82	29.69	30.49	32.39	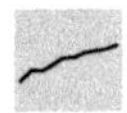
	Mean labour earnings	...	...	...	408.3	375.3	368.9	386.3	413.7	423.3	449.9	457.8	467.3	486.3	
Poverty and Inequality Indicators	Official extreme poverty rate	...	...	...	26.2	21.3	23.5	19.8	17.7	16.1	14.2	12.2	9.5	9.1	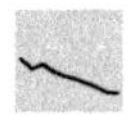
	Official moderate poverty rate	...	...	...	51.6	47.8	51.5	45.7	40.5	37.4	34.6	31.1	27.2	24.9	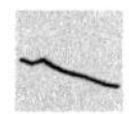
	Poverty rate 2.5 dollars-a-day	...	...	...	28.29	25.24	27.21	22.98	21.22	17.23	14.61	12.64	12.75	11.07	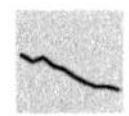
	Poverty rate 4 dollars-a-day	...	...	...	47.30	44.64	46.67	41.38	37.62	33.55	30.04	26.87	25.80	22.29	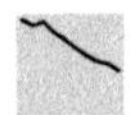

GINI of household per capita income	...	...	...	0.538	0.487	0.493	0.491	0.496	0.469	0.462	0.449	0.457	0.453	
GINI of labour earnings	...	...	...	0.559	0.518	0.522	0.514	0.524	0.513	0.509	0.506	0.496	0.489	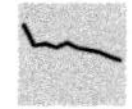

Note: The shaded figures of labour market indicators represent statistical significant improvements at 5 per cent between the initial and final years for all the employment and earnings indicators and poverty and inequality indicators. The only exceptions are the share of mid-earnings occupations, share of mid-earnings sectors, and share of medium-educated workers for which we did not assign welfare evaluation criteria.

Source: SEDLAC (CEDLAS and World Bank 2014) and World Development Indicators (World Bank 2014).

boom, exports of a few non-traditional agro-industrial products more than tripled between 2002 and 2008. According to Guerra (2012), Peru did not take advantage of the favourable international climate to further diversify its export base. Consequently, with an economic structure characterized by undiversified exports, and imports that comprised mainly of complementary goods, the country was highly vulnerable to movements in its terms of trade (Mendoza Bellido 2013). The increasing prices for Peru's products also had a pronounced effect on tax revenues through the income tax paid by the export sector. The increased revenues enabled the Peruvian government to improve public finances. Indeed, following the establishment of the Fiscal Responsibility and Transparency Law in 2001, the government achieved a significant reduction in the fiscal deficit and in the debt-to-GDP ratio (IMF 2013).

The Peruvian economy proved highly resilient in response to the global economic crisis. A deceleration was observed in 2009 when the GDP growth rate was only 0.9 per cent and GDP per capita growth −0.15 per cent. This slowdown was due to a fall in foreign demand for Peruvian products, a dramatic drop in the international prices of Peruvian exports, a reduction in remittances from abroad, and falling investment and external credit (Moron et al. 2009; Rozenberg 2009). However, the economy bounced back the following year, surpassing pre-crisis GDP and GDP per capita levels. Peru's resilience in the face of the global crisis can be explained by earlier prudent policies like the creation of fiscal and international reserve buffers and the implementation of a timely countercyclical policy response (IMF 2010; Mendoza Bellido 2013). These policies included the injection of liquidity into the system, the reduction in the interest rate by means of central bank policies, and a fiscal stimulus plan.

20.3 Unemployment

> The 2003–12 period witnessed a drop in the unemployment rate in the aggregate and for all population groups. The international crisis of 2008 did not affect the downward trend in the unemployment rate in the aggregate and for women, but led to a slight increase in the unemployment rate of men and young workers, while the adult unemployment rate remained unchanged. (Cruces et al. 2015: figure 3)

The unemployment rate (measured as the ratio of the unemployed to the labour force) fell over the period, from 5.1 per cent in 2003 (656,181 unemployed people) to 3.5 per cent in 2012 (573,560 unemployed people) (Table 20.1). The evolution of the unemployment rate can be divided into two stages. It initially kept stable at around 5.1 per cent from 2003 to 2005.

The unemployment rate then dropped significantly from 2005 to 2012, falling from 5.2 to 3.5 per cent while GDP was growing. The downward trend of the unemployment rate continued even during the Great Recession.

Despite the growth performance over the period, the unemployment rate did not experience a major decline in Peru. Osorio Amezaga (2014) finds a negative and modest association between GDP growth and the unemployment rate (which was −0.12) through the estimation of Okun's coefficient from 2001 to 2012. This fact cannot be explained by standard arguments that revolve around workers leaving the labour market as soon as they are faced with limited prospects for employment since the participation rate increased over the period analysed. On the other hand, the widespread failure to comply with laws mandating employment benefits and labour protection should encourage employers to hire more workers during periods of expansion. The author concludes that the low output elasticity of unemployment can be attributed to particularities of the Peruvian labour market.

The unemployment rate fell for young and adult workers, men, and women between 2003 and 2012. The unemployment rates of all population groups were essentially unchanged from 2003 to 2005, and began a downward trend from 2005 to 2012. The declining pattern was not interrupted by the international crisis for women, but the unemployment rate of young workers and men suffered a slight increase. By 2010, men had recovered the pre-crisis level of unemployment. Young workers returned to their pre-recession unemployment rate in 2012. The unemployment rate of adult workers stopped decreasing during the international crisis but recovered the downward trend immediately. The World Bank (2010) claims that the small effect of the international crisis on the unemployment rate in Peru could be explained by an increase in the share of unregistered or informal labour relationships in total employment, which eased the adjustment process in the presence of wage rigidities and employment protection legislation.

20.4 Job Mix

> The composition of employment by occupational group improved between 2003 and 2012 as workers moved from agricultural, forestry and fishery occupations, and elementary jobs to better paying occupations like professional and technical jobs. All demographic groups—young and adult workers, men, and women—benefited from the improvement in the occupational composition of employment over the period. The international crisis of 2008 did not affect the improving trend in the composition of employment by occupational group. (Cruces et al. 2015: figure 4)

The share of the following occupations shrank between 2003 and 2012: elementary occupations (drop of 7.8 percentage points) and agricultural, forestry, and fishery jobs (drop of 2.5 percentage points). The share of the following occupations grew: clerical (increase of 2.5 percentage points); services and sales workers (increase of 2.7 percentage points); plant and machine operators (increase of 1.9 percentage points); and technicians and associate professionals (increase of 1.2 percentage points). The share of the other occupational groups remained largely unchanged. These changes in the occupational composition of employment can be interpreted as an improvement, since low-earning occupations (agricultural, elementary, and crafts and trades occupations) reduced their share in total employment by 9.2 percentage points between 2003 and 2012, while high-earning occupations (management, professionals, and technicians and associate professionals) gained share in total employment (increase of 2.0 percentage points) (Table 20.1). These changes resulted in an increase in the share of mid-earning occupations (services and sales occupations, plant and machine operators, clerical jobs, and armed forces) in total employment over the period (increase of 7.1 percentage points).

The improvements in the occupational composition of employment between 2003 and 2012 were observed for young and adult workers and for men and women. The decrease in the rate of working in low-earning occupations in total employment was larger among youth compared to adult workers as was the increase in the rate of working in high-earning occupations. When the analysis is broken down by gender, women experienced a larger reduction in the share of employment in low-earning occupations compared to men, but a lower increase in share of high-earning occupations in total employment.

The international crisis of 2008 did not adversely affect the improvement in the composition of employment by occupational group. Between 2008 and 2009, the share of low-earning occupations continued to fall in the aggregate and for all population groups, while the share of high-earning occupations increased overall and for adult workers, men, and women. For young workers, though, a slight reduction in the share of high-earning occupations resulted in an increase in the share of mid-earning occupations. The share of high-earning occupations in total employment reached and surpassed the pre-crisis level by 2010 for young workers.

The employment structure by occupational position improved from 2003 to 2012 as the share of paid employees and employers in total employment increased and the share of self-employed and unpaid workers decreased. The improving trend in the composition of employment by occupational position was experienced by young and adult workers, men, and women. The international crisis of 2008 did

> not affect adversely the improvement in the structure of employment by occupational position for the employed population overall, for young workers, adults, and men, but led to a standstill for women. (Cruces et al. 2015: figure 5)

Between 2003 and 2012, the share of paid employees in total employment—the largest category—grew from 39.8 to 46.6 per cent. The share of employers also increased, but slightly, from 5.3 to 5.6 per cent. The shares of the self-employed and unpaid workers decreased over the period. The reduction was from 37.3 per cent in 2003 to 36.4 per cent in 2012 for the self-employed, and from 17.6 to 11.4 per cent for unpaid workers (Table 20.1). These changes can be characterized as an improvement of the employment structure by occupational position, as the share of low-earning categories (self-employment and unpaid employment) dropped by a total of 7.2 percentage points and the share of high-earning categories (paid employees and employers) increased.

The employment structure by occupational position improved between 2003 and 2012 for all population groups (young and adult workers, men, and women).

The international crisis of 2008 did not reverse the improvements that had been taking place for the employed population overall and for young workers, adults, and men, while there was a worsening for women. The share of low-earning positions recovered the previous downward trend in 2010 for women.

> The employment composition by economic sector improved over the course of the period studied overall and for all population groups. The international crisis of 2008 did not interrupt the improving trend in the structure of employment by economic sector. (Cruces et al. 2015: figure 6)

The period 2003–12 witnessed a reduction (from 44.4 per cent to 35.8 per cent) in the share of workers in low-earning sectors (primary activities, domestic service, and low-tech industry). There was, during the same period, an increase (from 10.9 per cent to 13.8 per cent) in the share of high-earning sectors (skilled services, public administration, and high-tech industry) in the total (Table 20.1). These changes resulted in an increase in the share of mid-earning sectors in total employment over the period. Despite the improvement in the employment structure by economic sector, a large portion of workers remained employed in sectors like primary activities (26.8 per cent in 2012) and commerce (26.2 per cent in 2012); these sectors tend to have a low degree of formalization and pay low wages (Guerra 2012).

The employment composition by economic sector improved between 2003 and 2012 for young and adult workers, men, and women, as they moved from low-earning sectors to high-earning sectors.

The international crisis of 2008 did not halt the improving trend in the employment composition by economic sector overall and for all population groups. Between 2008 and 2009 the share of low-earning sectors continued to decrease, while the share of high-earning sectors in total employment kept on increasing in the aggregate and for young, adult workers, men, and women. The continued improvement in the structure of employment by economic sector despite the international crisis in the aggregate and for all population groups, can be explained by the reduction in the share of workers in the primary activities sector, which includes the mining subsector in our classification, and by the reduction in the share of workers in the low-tech industry sector in total employment between 2008 and 2009. That occurred as a consequence of the drop in the exports of minerals, hydrocarbons, and agro-industrial products. As the primary activities and low-tech industry sectors are low-earning sectors in Peru, the reduction of their share in total employment implied an improvement in the labour market.

> The educational level of the Peruvian employed population improved steadily over the period for all population groups, and especially among young workers. The international crisis of 2008 led to a slowdown in the falling trend of the share of employed workers with low educational levels in the aggregate and for all population groups. (Cruces et al. 2015: figure 7)

The share of employed workers with low educational levels (eight years of schooling or less) dropped from 45.3 per cent in 2003 to 36.1 per cent in 2012, while the share of workers with medium and high educational levels (nine to thirteen years of schooling and over thirteen years of schooling) grew from 37.0 per cent in 2003 to 40.9 per cent in 2012 and from 17.7 per cent to 23.0 per cent respectively (Table 20.1).[2] We interpret this result as an improvement for the employed population as the level of education is an important predictor of labour earnings. Consequently, the changes in the employment structure by educational level implied an increase in the share of workers that tend to have high levels of earnings and a decline in the share of workers with low earnings levels.[3]

The educational level of the employed population improved between 2003 and 2012 for all groups and especially for young workers.

The international crisis of 2008 led to a slowdown in the improving trend in the structure of employment by educational level overall and for all population groups. Between 2008 and 2009, the share of employed workers with low levels of education continued to fall, but at a slower pace than before the crisis. The pattern of slowdown in the improving trend in the structure of

[2] The most frequent value of years of education for employed workers in Peru was eleven during the entire period (around 24.6 per cent of employed workers had eleven years of education).

[3] The improvement in the employment structure by educational level is related to changes in the relative demand and supply of workers with high educational levels with corresponding implications for the wage gap by educational groups and the unemployment rate of each educational level. We introduce a discussion about the role of these factors in Peru in section 20.5.

employment by educational level took place for young and adult workers, men, and women.

> The overall share of workers registered with the social security system increased over the period analysed. Nonetheless, the share of unregistered workers in Peru is still very high, despite sustained economic growth. The international crisis of 2008 led to a slowdown in the upward trend of the registration rate.
>
> (Cruces et al. 2015: figure 8)

The Peruvian social security system comprises contributory schemes and non-contributory schemes (Lavigne 2013). The contributory scheme of the pension system is composed of four regimes: (1) the *Sistema Nacional de Pensiones*, which covers both private- and public-sector employees; (2) the *Cédula Viva*, which is a special regime that covers teachers that started working before 1980, workers at state companies, and magistrates; (3) the *Sistema Privado de Pensiones*, which is an individual capitalization system; and (4) the *Fondo de Pensiones Sociales*, which is a voluntary pension system for workers who are not covered by any of the other regimes. The public contributory regimes are funded by employers, employees, and the government, while the private regime is funded by worker contributions. The Peruvian social security system also offers two non-contributory pensions for the vulnerable elderly who did not contribute to a pension fund or whose contributions do not allow them to receive a decent pension: the *Pensión Mínima de Vejez* and the *Pensión Nacional de Asistencia Solidaria*. The contributory scheme of the health insurance system is composed of two regimes, *EsSalud* and the *Sanidades de las Fuerzas Armadas y de la Policía Nacional*, which are compulsory for wage earners and members of cooperatives from both the private and public sectors and for independent workers that decide to affiliate, and for personnel from the army and police forces respectively. Finally, the *Seguro Integral de Salud* is the non-contributory scheme of the health insurance system and covers the non-insured population, with a specific focus on undernourished children and elderly living in poverty and extreme poverty.

The share of workers registered with the contributory schemes of the social security system (public and private) increased by 17.5 percentage points during the 2000s, climbing from 14.9 per cent in 2003 to 32.4 per cent in 2012 (Table 20.1). The government of Peru instituted a set of policies designed to improve working conditions over the period. Those measures included a special regime for small enterprises which provides tax incentives and reduces labour obligations, such as payment for unjustified dismissal. In addition, the *Fondo de Pensiones Sociales* (FPS) was created. Small enterprises were not obliged to contribute to any social protection system before the creation of the FPS. Since its creation in 2008, small-enterprise workers can voluntarily access the FPS which includes a government co-payment. In terms of health insurance, the obligation to contribute to *Essalud* for small-enterprise workers was eliminated and government–worker co-financing was established for affiliating workers to the *Seguro Integral de Salud* (ILO 2014). Available evidence indicates that these policies did not have an important effect on the formalization of workers (Díaz 2014). On the contrary, they may have contributed to the deterioration in working conditions. Vidal Bermúdez et al. (2012) point out that the increase in the registration of workers with the social security system during the 2000s occurred through the set-up of the *Seguro Integral de Salud*, which offers a minimum coverage with standards that are below those of the contributory health insurance scheme, and through temporary contracts. A further institutional change was the implementation of an electronic system through which employers with three or more workers must send monthly reports to the National Tax Authority indicating the number of workers, service providers, personnel in training, and outsourced workers. This administrative change increased the Ministry of Labour's capacity to supervise and monitor compliance with labour obligations. It is estimated that the introduction of the electronic system contributed to the registration of jobs (ILO 2014).

The tendency towards formalization was slightly affected by the economic crisis of 2008. The growth in the share of registered workers slowed down after the Great Recession, though not immediately. In 2009 alone, the share of registered workers rose by 2.4 percentage points, whereas the increases in 2010 and 2011 were only 0.9 and 0.8 percentage points respectively. The World Bank (2010) claims that unregistered employment in Peru may have eased the adjustment process during the Great Recession in a labour market characterized by wage rigidities and rigid labour market regulations. Despite sustained economic growth in Peru, the share of registered workers continues to be very low (32.4 per cent in 2012). Questions remain, then, about the ability of the country to turn growth in employment into an increase in employed workforce formalization (Guerra 2012). Chacaltana and Yamada (2009) also point out that the pronounced growth in employment has meant an increase in both formal and informal employment. Indeed, between 2003 and 2012, the number of registered workers increased from 2,371,403 to 6,531,140 (4,159,737 new registered workers), while the number of unregistered workers also rose from 15,612,469 to 16,231,855 (619,386 new unregistered workers).

Failure to register with the social security system is a long-standing problem in Peru. First, a demographic change at the beginning of the twenty-first century meant an increase in the economically active working-age population that could not be absorbed into the wage/salaried employment sector. As a result, there was an increase in low-productivity self-employment (Garavito 2010). Self-employed workers account for the majority of unregistered workers in the country. For this occupational position, the rate of unregistered workers fell from 96.1 per cent in 2003 to 84.1 per cent in 2012. For wage/salaried employees the rate of unregistered workers dropped from 68.7 per cent in 2003 to 47.7 per cent in 2012. Second, the Peruvian labour market has restrictive labour market regulations, which have contributed to the increase in unregistered employment (Toyama et al. 2009; World Bank 2010).

The rate of registration with the social security system increased for all population groups (young and adult workers, men, and women). Young workers are the least likely to be registered with the social security system, and while the share of young workers enrolled increased over the period, adult workers were at the forefront of the trend towards registration. Men were more likely to be registered in the system than women, and the rate of registration increased more dramatically for them compared to women over the period. The rate of registration with the social security system continued to increase for young workers, adults, men, and women during the international crisis.

20.5 Labour Earnings

> Labour earnings increased between 2003 and 2012. Within the period, there was a reduction between 2003 and 2005 and a steady increase in the following years. Labour earnings increased overall, for young and adult workers, men, and women. The evidence of earning changes by employment category over the period indicates that low-earning categories increased their earnings, while high-earning categories tended to suffer earnings reductions. Workers were not affected negatively by the 2008 crisis in the aggregate, but some employment categories suffered earnings losses. (Cruces et al. 2015: figure 9)

Average monthly earnings, expressed in PPP dollars of 2005, increased by 19.1 per cent, from US$408 in 2003 to US$486 in 2012 (Table 20.1). Labour earnings decreased at the beginning of the period—between 2003 and 2005—and grew steadily in the following years. From 2003 to 2008, GDP per capita grew by 5.8 per cent a year, but the annual increase in real labour earnings and hourly wages was just 0.7 and 0.9 per cent respectively. Two reasons have been presented to explain the real wages stagnation in Peru despite rapid economic growth. First, the increase in labour supply may have compensated for the increase in labour demand; or a highly elastic labour supply may have allowed for an increase in the employment level without increases in hourly wages (World Bank 2010). Second, the predominant type of contract in Peru is the temporal contract which limits the access of workers to trade unions, which are the main tool they have to increase their wages

(Vidal Bermúdez et al. 2012). Real labour earnings were not affected negatively by the Great Recession. In fact, in 2009 real earnings exhibited the largest annual growth rate of the period. The increase in real labour earnings during the international crisis can be explained by the reduction in the inflation rate (World Bank 2010).

Men, women, and young and adult workers all increased their labour earnings between 2003 and 2012. The trend in their labour earnings reflected the overall time path, with reductions from 2003 to 2005 and increases thereafter. Average earnings rose between 2003 and 2012 for workers employed in low-earning employment categories and tended to fall for workers in high-earning categories. Among occupational groups, agricultural, forestry, and fishery workers, workers in elementary occupations, and crafts and trades workers had an average increase in their labour earnings, while workers in management, professionals, and technicians had an average earnings reduction between 2003 and 2012. When the employed population is broken down by occupational position, the self-employed had a larger increase in labour earnings compared to employers and paid employees. Among economic sectors, workers in primary activities, domestic workers, and workers in low-tech industries increased their labour earnings over the period, while workers in high-earning sectors like skilled services, public administration, and high-tech industries suffered an earnings loss. Finally, labour earnings of workers with high educational levels fell, while workers with medium and low levels of education enjoyed an increase in their labour earnings.

The evidence of falling labour earnings for workers with high educational levels and labour earnings increases for workers with medium and low levels of education can be interpreted in light of previous findings of improving employment structure by occupational group and economic sector over the period. The improving employment structure by occupational group and economic sector implied an increase in the share of occupations and sectors that can be expected to use workers with high and medium levels of education, like professional and technical occupations, public administration, skilled services, and high-tech industry sectors, and a reduction in the share of occupations and sectors that employ workers with low educational levels, like elementary and agricultural occupations, domestic service, and primary activities sectors. This evidence indicates that the demand for workers with high and medium educational levels relative to those with low educational levels increased between 2003 and 2012. On the other hand, the educational levels of persons in the labour force improved over the same period, indicating an increase in the relative supply of workers with high and medium levels of education (Cruces et al. 2015: table 8). The prediction of a supply and demand analysis is that the relative wages of workers with high and medium educational levels relative to those with low educational levels will rise or fall depending on which effect dominates (increase in the relative demand versus increase in the relative supply). In the Peruvian labour market, the relative wages of workers with high and medium educational levels relative to those with low educational levels fell over the period, and the relative wages of workers with high educational levels relative to those with medium educational levels also decreased (Cruces et al. 2015: table 7). The adjustment process also led to a reduction in the unemployment rate of all educational groups with a larger reduction for workers with medium levels of education (Cruces et al. 2015: table 9).

Even during the international crisis of 2008, labour earnings continued to grow, overall and for all demographic groups. However, some employment categories were impacted adversely by the crisis. Among occupational groups, workers in the armed forces and technicians were affected negatively by the international crisis of 2008. Workers in both occupations recovered their pre-crisis level of earnings in 2012. Among occupational positions, employers were the only group impacted negatively by the international crisis of 2008. Employers returned to their pre-recession level of labour income in 2010. Among economic sectors, workers in the utilities and transportation sector were affected negatively by the crisis but returned in 2010 to their pre-crisis level of earnings.

20.6 Poverty and Inequality

> Poverty fell between 2003 and 2012 for all poverty lines used. The rate of working poor households also exhibited a decreasing trend. The pattern of poverty reduction over time was not interrupted by the international crisis of 2008. (Cruces et al. 2015: figure 10)

The moderate poverty rate (measured by the country's official poverty line) fell from 51.6 per cent in 2003 to 24.9 per cent in 2012; the extreme poverty rate dropped from 26.2 per cent to 9.1 per cent; the percentage of the working poor (defined as the proportion of persons in the population living in poor households where at least one member works) decreased from 42.7 per cent to 20.1 per cent over the same period (Table 20.1). These indicators decreased consistently every year but 2005, when they had an increase. Thus, in Peru there was a negative correlation between economic growth and poverty. García Carpio and Céspedes Reynaga (2011) computed growth–poverty elasticities for the period 2001–10 using Kakwani's (1990) methodology. They found that growth–poverty elasticities increased in absolute terms over the period and changed from being positive in 2001 (0.9) to negative in 2010 (−1.7). The authors also found that economic growth was pro-poor in Peru between 2001 and 2010, using the measures proposed by Kakwani and Pernia (2000) and Kakwani and Son (2002).

An analysis based on the 2.5 and 4 dollars-a-day PPP international poverty lines also shows a drop in the poverty rate from 2003 to 2012 and a negative association between the poverty rate and the growth of the economy. The poverty rate based on those measures fell between 2003 and 2004, increased from 2004 to 2005, and began a downward trend up to the end of the period. The international crisis of 2008 did not affect the pattern of poverty reduction. However, the growth–poverty elasticity was largely unchanged between 2008 and 2009 while it had shown an increasing pattern in absolute value in the previous years, and the pro-poor growth index indicates that the growth was not pro-poor during the international crisis (García Carpio and Céspedes Reynaga 2011).

The poverty patterns reported in the last paragraph can be understood by examining incomes from various sources. The analysis of sources of household total income indicates that labour income and income from transfers (public and private) increased between 2003 and 2012, while income from capital and pensions suffered a slight reduction over the same period (Cruces et al. 2015: figure 11). The increase in labour earnings (30.7 per cent between 2003 and 2012) was the most important factor to explain the increase in household total income over the period.

> Household per capita income and labour earnings inequality decreased between 2003 and 2012. The international crisis of 2008 did not affect the downward trend in the inequality indices. (Cruces et al. 2015: figure 12)

Household per capita income and labour earnings inequality decreased while GDP increased over the period. The Gini coefficient of household per capita income fell from 0.538 in 2003 to 0.453 in 2012. This indicator fell at the beginning of the period from 0.538 in 2003 to 0.487 in 2004, a level it maintained until 2007. The downward trend continued in 2007 until 2011, when a new increase set in. Throughout the period, the Gini coefficient of labour earnings among employed workers was higher than that of household per capita income, and fell from 0.559 in 2003 to 0.489 in 2012 (Table 20.1); this reduction in labour earnings inequality is in accord with the evidence presented in section 20.5 showing earnings increases for workers employed in low-earning categories and earnings reductions for workers in high-earning categories. Consequently, the reduction in labour earnings inequality in Peru occurred at the expense of income losses for some categories. The evolution of the Gini coefficient of labour earnings over time was similar to the trend shown by the Gini coefficient of per capita household income.

Several studies have found that the reduction in both labour and non-labour income inequality contributed to the reduction in household income inequality. Urrutia (2014) and Jaramillo and Saavedra (2011) presented evidence of the reduction in labour income inequality. They found that the relative wage of workers with high and medium levels of education decreased during the 2000s mainly as a result of the increase in their labour supply. The importance of non-labour income to explain the reduction in household income inequality in Peru was analysed by Yamada et al. (2012) and Jaramillo and Saavedra (2011). Yamada et al. (2012) found that 25 per cent of the reduction in the Gini coefficient of household per capita income between 2006 and 2010 can be accounted for by government transfers, like *Programa JUNTOS*. Jaramillo and Saavedra (2011) claimed that the pro-poor orientation of social spending in Peru and the improvement in access to public services were the main factors to explain the reduction in income inequality during the 2000–6 period.

20.7 Conclusions

From 2000 to 2012, the Peruvian economy performed exceptionally well, with a growth performance that placed the country well above the regional average. The economy suffered a slowdown as a consequence of the international crisis of 2008, but Peru continued to grow during that episode.

All labour market indicators improved between 2003 and 2012. The unemployment rate was always low and fell moderately. The composition of the employed population by occupational group improved over the period as workers moved from agricultural, forestry, and fishery occupations and elementary jobs to better-paying occupations like professional and technical jobs. The employment structure by occupational position also improved through the reduction in the share of self-employed and unpaid workers in total employment and the increase in the share of paid employees and employers. Workers moved from low-earning economic sectors like primary activities, domestic service, and low-tech industry to high-earning sectors such as skilled services, public administration, and high-tech industry. Moreover, the educational level of the Peruvian employed population, the overall share of workers registered with the social security system, and labour earnings all increased between 2003 and 2012. The evidence of labour income changes by employment categories indicates that low-earning categories increased their earnings, while high-earning categories tended to suffer earnings reductions. The moderate and extreme poverty rates and the rate of working poor households showed important reductions between 2003 and 2012, as did the Gini coefficient of per capita household income and labour earnings.

Looking specifically at the international crisis of 2008, the only labour market indicators that were affected by the crisis were the employment structure by educational level and the share of employment registered with the social security system which suffered a slowdown in their upward trends. The comparison between the effects of the international crisis of 2008 on labour market indicators and the effects generated by the recession at the beginning of the decade (2000–1) reveals that the crisis at the beginning of the 2000s impacted Peru more strongly. The crisis of 2000–1 generated a larger reduction in GDP per capita and increases in the unemployment rate and in the shares of workers in low-earning occupational groups and economic sectors, while the unemployment rate and the shares of workers in low-earning occupational groups and sectors continued to decrease during the Great Recession. Other labour market indicators improved during both crises. The smaller negative impacts of the international crisis compared to the recession at the beginning of the decade can be explained by the prudent policies the government implemented after the 2000–1 crisis, like the creation of fiscal and international reserve buffers, and the implementation of timely countercyclical policy responses that were not available in the first recessionary episode.

Young workers and women had worse labour market outcomes over the period compared to adults and men respectively, and while women seem to be more vulnerable to macroeconomic crises compared to men, young workers and adults were slightly and equally affected by the crises. The unemployment rate was higher for young compared to adult workers, the shares of young employed workers in low-earning occupational groups and economic sectors were larger than the shares of adult workers, the percentage of young workers registered with the social security system was lower when compared to adults, and labour earnings of young workers were below those of adults. On the other hand, the share of young workers in low-earning occupational positions was lower compared to adults. Despite the generally inferior situation of young workers in the labour market compared to adults, youth were slightly affected by the episodes of crises and the same was true for adult workers. Disaggregating by gender, we found that men had better labour market outcomes than women, with the only exception being the share of workers in low-earning occupations that was larger among men. Both men and women were slightly affected by the macroeconomic crises. The negative impacts were larger for women compared to men, as they suffered a larger increase in the unemployment rate and in the shares of workers in low-earning positions and economic sectors.

In summary, all population groups were quite resilient to macroeconomic crises, and labour market conditions were in a better state in 2012 than they were at the start of the millennium.

References

CEDLAS and World Bank (2014). SEDLAC—Socio-Economic Database for Latin America and the Caribbean. Centro de Estudios Distributivos, Laborales y Sociales, Facultad de Ciencias Económicas, Universidad Nacional de La Plata and World Bank Poverty Group LCR. Available at <http://sedlac.econo.unlp.edu.ar/eng/index.php>, accessed 2014.

Chacaltana, J. and G. Yamada (2009). 'Calidad del empleo y productividad laboral en el Perú'. IDB Working Paper 691. Washington, DC: Inter-American Development Bank.

Cruces, G., G. Fields, D. Jaume, and M. Viollaz (2015). 'The Growth–Employment–Poverty Nexus in Latin America in the 2000s: Peru Country Study'. WIDER Working Paper 2015/082. Helsinki: UNU-WIDER.

Díaz, J. J. (2014). 'Formalización empresarial y laboral', in R. Infante and J. Chacaltana (eds), *Hacia un Desarrollo Inclusive: El Caso del Perú*. United Nations Publications. Santiago de Chile: Economic Commission for Latin America and the Caribbean, 173–259.

Garavito, C. (2010). 'Mercado de trabajo: Diagnóstico y políticas', in J. Rodríguez and M. Tello (eds), *Opciones de Política Económica en el Perú 2011–2015*. Lima: Departamento de Economía, Pontificia Universidad Católica del Perú, 45–70.

García Carpio, J. M. and N. Céspedes Reynaga (2011). 'Pobreza y crecimiento económico: Tendencias durante la década del 2000'. Working Paper 2011-021. Lima: Banco Central de Reservas del Perú.

Guerra, M. L. (2012). 'Implications of the Recent Macroeconomic Policies on Employment and Labour Market Outcomes in Peru'. Employment Working Paper 134. Geneva: International Labour Organization.

ILO (2014). 'Trends in Informal Employment in Peru: 2004–2012'. FORLAC. Programme for the Promotion of Formalization in Latin America and the Caribbean. Geneva: Regional Office for Latin America and the Caribbean, International Labour Organization.

IMF (2010). 'Peru: Staff Report for the 2010 Article IV Consultation'. IMF Country Report 10/98. Washington, DC: International Monetary Fund.

IMF (2013). 'Peru: Staff Report for the 2013 Article IV Consultation'. IMF Country Report 13/45. Washington, DC: International Monetary Fund.

Jaramillo, M. and J. Saavedra (2011). 'Menos desiguales: La distribución del ingreso luego de las reformas estructurales'. GRADE Working Paper 59. Lima: Grupo de Análisis para el Desarrollo.

Kakwani, N. (1990). 'Poverty and Economic Growth with Applications to Côte d'Ivoire'. Living Standards Measurement Study Working Paper 63. Washington, DC: World Bank.

Kakwani, N. and E. Pernia (2000). 'What Is Pro-Poor Growth?', *Asian Development Review* 18 (1): 1–16.

Kakwani, N. and H. Son (2002). 'Pro-Poor Growth: Concept, Measurement, and Application'. Unpublished manuscript. Sydney: University of New South Wales.

Lavigne, M. (2013). 'Social Protection Systems in Latin America and the Caribbean: Peru'. ECLAC, Project Documents Collection. Santiago de Chile: United Nations.

Mendoza Bellido, W. (2013). 'Peruvian Miracle: Good Luck or Good Policies?'. Working Paper 371. Lima: Departamento de Economía, Ponitifica Universidad Católica del Perú.

Moron, E., J. F. Castro, and L. Villacorta (2009). 'The Global Crisis and the Peruvian Labor Market: Impact and Policy Options'. MPRA Paper 22120. Munich: Munich Personal RePEc Archive.

Osorio Amezaga, M. J. (2014). 'Unemployment and Economic Growth in Peru: 2001–2012'. New York: Columbia University.

Rozenberg, A. (2009). 'Impactos de la crisis financiera internacional en el sector externo del Perú', in G. Alarco (ed.), *Crisis: Análisis y Perspectivas de la Crisis Económica Mundial desde el Perú*. Lima: Grupo Editorial Norma, 155–90.

Toyama, J., V. R. Chávez, and T. Tostes Vieira (2009). 'Retos pendientes para incrementar la flexibilidad laboral en el Perú', in J. Weller (ed.), *El Nuevo Escenario Laboral Latinoamericano*. Siglo Veintiuno CEPAL. Buenos Aires: United Nations, 219–54.

Urrutia, P. P. C. (2014). 'Economic Growth and Wage Stagnation in Peru: 1998–2012'. Working Paper 5. Lima: Peruvian Economic Association.

Vidal Bermúdez, A., F. Cuadros Luque, and C. Sánchez Reyes (2012). 'Flexibilización laboral en el Perú y reformas de la protección social asociadas: Un balance tras 20 años'. Serie Políticas Sociales 175. Santiago de Chile: División de Desarrollo Social de 1 CEPAL.

Yamada, G., J. F. Castro, and J. L. Bacigalupo (2012). 'Desigualdad monetaria en un contexto de rápido crecimiento económico: El caso reciente del Perú', *Revista Estudios Económicos* 24: 65–77.

World Bank (2010). 'El mercado laboral Peruano durante el auge y la caída'. World Bank Country Study 50915. Washington, DC: World Bank.

World Bank (2014). World Development Indicators. Available at <http://data.worldbank.org/data-catalog/world-development-indicators>, accessed April 2014.

21

Uruguay

21.1 Introduction

This chapter on labour markets and growth in Uruguay since 2000 is one of sixteen studies of Latin American countries, each of which analyses the growth–employment–poverty nexus and aims to answer the following broad questions: Has economic growth resulted in economic development via improved labour market conditions in Latin America in the 2000s, and have these improvements halted or been reversed since the Great Recession? How do the rate and character of economic growth, changes in the various labour market indicators, and changes in poverty relate to each other?

To answer these questions, we analyse the growth experience of Uruguay during the 2000s and a wide set of labour market indicators that we assign to one of two different categories: employment and earnings indicators, and poverty and income inequality indicators. More specifically, for the group of employment and earnings indicators we construct statistics on the following variables: the unemployment rate; the employment structure by occupational group, employment position, economic sector, registration of workers with the social security system, and educational level; and mean labour earnings and hourly wages. We present all these indicators for the employed population as a whole and for different population groups (youth, adults, men, and women). For the group of poverty and income inequality indicators, we compute poverty rates using the official moderate and extreme poverty lines and the international lines of 2.5 and 4 dollars a day. We also calculate the Gini coefficient of household per capita income and labour earnings.

All the statistics in this chapter are obtained using microdata from the Encuesta Continua de Hogares (ECH) for the years 2000 to 2012. Until 2005, the ECH encompassed solely urban areas; since 2006, it has been nationwide in scope. The surveys were processed following a harmonization methodology and incorporated into the SEDLAC—Socio-Economic Database for Latin America and the Caribbean (CEDLAS and World Bank 2014).[1] The resulting labour market indicators were compiled into a large number of tables and figures, which are available in an earlier version of this study (henceforth, Cruces et al. 2015). Chapter 1 of this book provides the definition for each of the indicators we analyse here, while Cruces et al. (2015) includes details on definitions and classification systems used by Uruguay's household surveys, and on comparability issues of these surveys over time. For consistency, the analysis in this chapter focuses on the same set of urban areas for the entire period studied, although we also make remarks on the statistics at the national level for the period 2006–12.

21.2 Economic Growth

> Uruguay experienced rapid economic growth from 2000 to 2012. While economic performance slowed down following the international crisis of 2008, overall GDP and GDP per capita continued to grow in 2009.
>
> (Cruces et al. 2015: figures 1 and 2)

From 2000 to 2012, Uruguay experienced rapid economic growth by Latin American standards. GDP per capita increased by 44.7 per cent, while the average for the region's eighteen countries during the period was 36.2 per cent. GDP (measured in PPP dollars of 2005) grew by 48.0 per cent, and GDP per employed person rose by 4.5 per cent. Annual GDP per capita grew in real terms by an average of 2.8 per cent, ranging from a low of −7.8 per cent in 2002 to a high of 8.6 per cent in 2010 (Table 21.1).

At the beginning of the 2000s, from 2000 to 2002, Uruguay was affected by the devaluation of the Brazilian Real in 1999, which led to a loss of competitiveness, and by the collapse of the Argentine economy at the end of 2001, which led to a financial crisis. Uruguay was extremely vulnerable to shocks stemming from Argentina and Brazil due to the strong commercial and financial linkages between the countries (Sosa 2010). The crisis disrupted the Uruguayan banking system and caused the collapse of its currency, generating a credit crunch and a steep contraction of GDP (IMF 2003; Hausmann et al. 2005). From 2000 to 2002, average annual GDP growth was −4.5 per cent and the rate of GDP per capita annual growth was, on average, −4.7 per cent.

A package of fiscal, monetary, and banking reform measures helped the country to stabilize and to start a trend of positive growth. The external position of the country improved considerably, the peso stabilized, the inflation was brought under control, capital flight was stopped and partially reversed, and

[1] See Cruces et al. (2015: table 1) for details on the size of Uruguay household surveys.

		2000	2001	2002	2003	2004	2005	2006	2007	2008	2009	2010	2011	2012
Growth Indicators	GDP per capita	9,551	9,168	8,457	8,530	8,962	9,626	10,006	10,634	11,361	11,577	12,569	13,344	13,821
	GDP per capita growth rate	−2.28	−4.02	−7.75	0.87	5.05	7.42	3.94	6.28	6.84	1.89	8.57	6.17	3.58
Employment and Earnings Indicators	Employment-to-population ratio	52.59	52.30	49.99	49.26	51.76	52.37	54.79	57.44	58.51	59.36	59.35	61.55	60.74
	Unemployment rate	13.54	15.24	16.91	16.81	13.05	12.12	11.31	9.55	8.00	7.63	7.04	6.60	6.35
	Share of low-earnings occupations	53.17	53.78	52.63	53.76	52.59	52.60	53.95	53.24	52.88	51.62	52.41	50.25	...
	Share of mid-earnings occupations	24.74	24.37	25.00	23.65	24.23	24.38	24.38	24.05	24.52	24.66	24.69	25.00	...
	Share of high-earnings occupations	22.09	21.86	22.37	22.59	23.19	23.03	21.67	22.71	22.60	23.72	22.90	24.75	...
	Share of employers	3.71	3.94	3.70	3.42	3.53	3.94	4.32	4.43	4.62	4.48	4.52	4.59	4.25
	Share of wage/salaried employees	72.86	71.04	69.98	70.15	70.27	71.22	71.28	71.16	71.48	71.84	72.46	73.94	74.24
	Share of self-employed workers	21.99	23.65	24.81	25.07	24.65	23.53	22.97	23.00	22.60	22.31	21.95	20.61	20.59
	Share of unpaid family workers	1.44	1.37	1.50	1.35	1.56	1.31	1.43	1.41	1.29	1.37	1.06	0.87	0.92
	Share of workers in low-earnings sectors	26.48	26.10	24.68	24.93	23.60	24.05	24.30	24.70	24.27	23.60	24.12	23.38	21.70
	Share of workers in mid-earnings sectors	50.28	49.67	50.33	50.55	52.61	52.44	53.49	53.53	53.78	54.00	54.12	53.68	50.25

(continued)

Table 21.1 Continued

		2000	2001	2002	2003	2004	2005	2006	2007	2008	2009	2010	2011	2012	
	Share of workers in high-earnings sectors	23.24	24.23	24.99	24.52	23.79	23.51	22.21	21.76	21.95	22.39	21.76	22.94	23.55	
	Share of low-educated workers	43.99	39.78	38.87	38.72	37.10	36.85	39.21	39.10	41.22	39.07	40.25	35.39	34.67	
	Share of medium-educated workers	40.61	41.84	41.62	41.75	42.36	42.22	42.12	41.98	40.81	42.07	42.06	43.61	45.76	
	Share of high-educated workers	15.40	18.38	19.52	19.52	20.54	20.93	18.67	18.92	17.97	18.86	17.69	21.00	19.57	
	Share of workers registered with SS	...	64.14	62.88	60.56	59.39	61.32	64.78	65.24	66.53	67.90	68.37	72.37	73.83	
	Mean labour earnings	723.6	654.0	582.6	483.8	483.5	486.7	524.2	554.5	591.9	641.2	627.0	668.2	661.3	
Poverty and Inequality Indicators	Official extreme poverty rate	2.4	3.2	3.8	4.9	7.0	6.3	4.6	4.8	3.9	3.6	2.9	2.8	2.8	
	Official moderate poverty rate	21.4	25.8	30.4	39.1	40.0	37.5	35.4	35.7	33.1	31.8	30.9	26.9	24.9	
	Poverty rate 2.5 dollars-a-day	3.59	4.78	6.41	7.73	9.78	8.90	7.25	6.25	4.18	3.51	2.84	2.57	2.61	
	Poverty rate 4 dollars-a-day	11.22	13.92	17.78	22.76	23.72	21.60	20.76	18.94	14.17	12.00	11.28	8.85	8.32	
	GINI of household per capita income	0.444	0.462	0.466	0.462	0.471	0.459	0.473	0.478	0.465	0.464	0.454	0.436	0.415	
	GINI of labour earnings	0.462	0.485	0.495	0.500	0.505	0.499	0.504	0.507	0.502	0.495	0.479	0.450	0.420	

Note: The shaded figures of labour market indicators represent statistical significant improvements at 5 per cent between the initial and final years for all the employment and earnings indicators and poverty and inequality indicators. The only exceptions are the share of mid-earnings occupations, share of mid-earnings sectors, and share of medium-educated workers for which we did not assign welfare evaluation criteria.

Source: SEDLAC (CEDLAS and World Bank 2014) and World Development Indicators (World Bank 2014).

bank credit to the private sector began to recover (IMF 2005). From 2003 to 2008, average annual GDP and GDP per capita growth rates were 5.2 and 5.1 per cent respectively. While the international crisis of 2008 led to a slowdown in the Uruguayan economy, it continued to grow throughout the global recession. The Uruguayan economy was better prepared to face the international crisis of 2008 than it was at the beginning of the decade when it faced the Brazilian and Argentine crises. The strengths stemmed from a well-regulated banking system, a reduced debt-to-GDP ratio, and a stabilized macroeconomic scenario (IMF 2010). The rate of GDP growth dropped from 7.2 per cent in 2008 to 2.3 per cent in 2009, and GDP per capita growth rate diminished from 6.8 per cent to 1.9 per cent. The relatively mild impact of the crisis was concentrated in some export-oriented sectors; the agriculture, livestock, and energy sectors also suffered as a result of a severe drought. By 2010, though, GDP and GDP per capita growth rates had surpassed their pre-crisis levels.

All of the preceding macroeconomic data are for the Uruguayan economy as a whole. The following labour market and income distribution data focus on urban Uruguay. Some remarks are presented regarding the statistics at the national level for the period 2006–12.

21.3 Unemployment

> The 2000–12 period witnessed a significant drop in the aggregate unemployment rate and in the unemployment rate for all population groups. Within this period, the unemployment rate increased in the early years of the period and exhibited a steady downward trend in the later years. The international crisis of 2008 led to a slowdown in the downward trend in the unemployment rate. (Cruces et al. 2015: figure 3)

The urban unemployment rate (measured as the ratio of unemployment to labour force) dropped from 13.5 per cent in 2000 (158,585 unemployed persons) to 6.4 per cent in 2012 (98,719 unemployed persons) (Table 21.1). Initially, the unemployment rate increased in conjunction with a fall in GDP from 2000 to 2002, growing from 13.5 to 16.9 per cent (30,625 new unemployed persons). The downward trend in the unemployment rate began in 2003 and continued through the end of the period studied. The international crisis of 2008 did not impact adversely on the unemployment rate, but led to a drop in the pace of reduction. Between 2003 and 2008 the unemployment rate fell by 1.5 percentage points a year, while from 2009 to 2012 the reduction was only 0.4 percentage points annually. The evolution of the national unemployment rate from 2006 to 2012 exhibits the same pattern as the urban unemployment rate with a slightly lower level.

Between 2000 and 2012, the unemployment rate decreased for all population groups. All population groups exhibited the same trend as the aggregate unemployment rate with an increase at the beginning of the decade, from 2000 to 2002, and a reduction afterwards.

The international crisis of 2008 led to a slowdown in the downward trend in the aggregate unemployment rate and in the rate for all population groups.

21.4 Job Mix

> The composition of employment by occupational group improved from 2000 to 2011 (the last year for which we can construct the classification of occupations described previously) as workers moved from service and sales, and craft and trade occupations to better paying occupations such as management, professional and technical jobs. All demographic groups—youth and adult workers, men, and women—benefited from this improvement. This trend was not affected by the international crisis of 2008.
>
> (Cruces et al. 2015: figure 4)

The share of the following occupations shrank from 2000 to 2011: craft and trade occupations (drop of 3.5 percentage points); service and sales occupations (drop of 0.7 percentage points); armed forces (drop of 0.7 percentage points); and agriculture, forestry, and fishery occupations (drop of 0.5 percentage points). The share of the following occupations grew: professional jobs (increase of 1.4 percentage points); elementary occupations (increase of 1.3 percentage points); clerical positions (increase of 1.1 percentage points); and technical occupations (increase of 0.9 percentage points). The share of the other occupational groups remained largely unchanged. These changes in the composition of employment by occupational group can be interpreted as an improvement since the share of low-earning occupations (elementary, service and sales, and craft and trade occupations) diminished by 2.9 percentage points between 2000 and 2011, while the share of high-earning occupations (management, professional, and technician jobs) grew by 2.7 percentage points during the same period (Table 21.1). The structure of employment by occupational group at the national level also improved from 2006 to 2011. When the rural sector is included in the statistics, the share of mid-earning occupations in total employment is larger compared to urban figures, the share of high-earning occupations is lower, and the share of low-earning occupations is essentially the same as in urban areas. The larger share of mid-earning occupations in total employment at the national level compared to the urban area is explained by the larger share of agriculture and forestry and fishery occupations once the rural area is considered.

The improvements in occupational composition between 2000 and 2011 were observed for young and adult workers, men, and women.

The international crisis of 2008 did not have an adverse effect on the improvement in the composition of employment by occupational group. Between 2008 and 2009, the share of low-earning occupations fell in the aggregate and for all population groups, while the share of high-earning occupations increased.

> The employment structure by occupational position improved between 2000 and 2012 as the share of paid employees and employers in total employment increased and the share of self-employed and unpaid workers decreased. Within the period, the structure of employment by occupational position deteriorated from 2000 to 2003 and then improved steadily. While this trend towards improvement in employment structure by occupational position benefited young and adult workers, and men, the employment structure for women remained largely unchanged. The international crisis of 2008 did not have an adverse effect on the improvement in the structure of employment by occupational position. (Cruces et al. 2015: figure 5)

Between 2000 and 2012, the share of paid employees in total employment—the largest category in urban Uruguay—grew from 72.9 to 74.2 per cent. The share of employers also increased from 3.7 to 4.3 per cent. The shares of the self-employed and of unpaid workers, on the other hand, fell from 22.0 to 20.6 per cent and from 1.4 to 0.9 per cent respectively (Table 21.1). These changes can be characterized as an improvement in the employment structure by occupational position insofar as the share of low-earning categories (self-employment and unpaid employment) dropped by a total of 1.9 percentage points and the share of high-earning categories (paid employees and employers) increased correspondingly. Within the period, the employment structure by occupational position deteriorated from 2000 to 2003 through an increase in the share of self-employed workers and a reduction in the share of wage/salaried employees, and improved steadily in the following years. The worsening at the beginning of the decade is in keeping with the increase in the unemployment rate, as economic necessity may compel workers to look for free-entry self-employment activities. The structure of employment by occupational position at the national level also exhibited an improvement from 2006 to 2012. When the rural sector is included in the statistics, the share of low-earning positions in total employment is larger compared to urban figures, due to the larger share of both self-employed and unpaid workers.

The employment structure by occupational position improved between 2000 and 2012 for young and adult workers, and for men, while for women the structure remained largely unchanged. All population groups suffered a worsening in the employment composition by occupational positions at the beginning of the period, from 2000 to 2003, and an improvement in the following years.

The international crisis of 2008 did not bring about a reversal in the improvements that had been taking place overall and for youth, adults, and male workers. The share of paid employees increased from 2008 and 2009, while the shares of unpaid workers and of the self-employed diminished. The share of employers also decreased, though the share of that occupational position resumed growth after the crisis. When broken down by population group, the improving trend in the structure of employment by occupational position was not interrupted in 2009 for young or adult workers, or for men. Likewise, the employment structure by occupational position was largely unchanged for women through 2009.

> The employment composition by economic sector improved over the course of the period studied. While all population groups benefited from the improving trend, the improvement was larger for young workers than for adults and for women than for men. The international crisis of 2008 did not interrupt the pattern of improvement in the employment composition by economic sector.
>
> (Cruces et al. 2015: figure 6)

The period 2000–12 witnessed a drop from 26.5 per cent to 21.7 per cent in the share of workers in low-earning sectors (domestic service, construction, and low-tech industry). During the same period, there was a slight increase (from 23.2 per cent to 23.6 per cent) in the share of high-earning sectors (public administration, skilled services, and utilities and transportation) along with a larger increase (from 50.3 per cent to 54.8 per cent) in the share of mid-earning sectors (commerce, primary activities, high-tech industry, and education and health) (Table 21.1). The structure of employment by economic sector at the national level also improved from 2006 to 2012. When the rural sector is included in the statistics, the share of mid-earning sectors in total employment is larger compared to urban figures, while the shares of low- and high-earning sectors are lower. The larger share of mid-earning sectors in total employment at the national level compared to the urban level is explained by the larger share of the primary activity sector, which increases when the rural area is considered in the statistics.

Employment composition by economic sector in urban Uruguay improved between 2000 and 2012 for men, women, and for young and adult workers, though the improvement was mild in the case of adults.

The international crisis of 2008 did not reverse the downward trend in the share of employment in low-earning sectors at the aggregate level and for any population group, nor did it reverse the upward trend in the share of employment in high-earning sectors at the aggregate level and for young workers, men, and women. Indeed, there was a slight increase in the share of employment in high-earning sectors for adult workers during the crisis.

> The educational level of the urban Uruguayan employed population improved from 2000 to 2012 for the entire population and for all population groups. Within this period, there was an increase in the share of employed workers with high education levels and a reduction in the share of employed persons with low levels of education from 2000 to 2005. In the mid years of the period, between 2005 and 2010, a worsening in the educational level of the employed population took place, and a new improvement closed the period. During the international crisis of 2008, the share of employed persons with high educational levels continued with the downward trend overall and for all population groups. (Cruces et al. 2015: figure 7)

The share of employed persons with low educational levels (eight years of schooling or less) dropped from 44.0 per cent in 2000 to 34.7 per cent in 2012, while the share of employed persons with medium and high educational levels (nine to thirteen years of schooling and over thirteen years of schooling) grew from 40.6 per cent in 2000 to 45.8 per cent in 2012 and from 15.4 per cent to 19.6 per cent respectively (Table 21.1).[2] We interpret this result as an improvement for the employed population as the level of education is an important predictor of labour earnings. Consequently, the changes in the employment structure by educational level implied an increase in the share of workers that tend to have high levels of earnings and a decline in the share of workers with low earnings levels.[3]

The evolution of the shares of employed workers with low and high educational levels was not steady over the period. From 2000 to 2005, the share of employed persons with low educational levels decreased, while the share of employed workers with high levels of education increased. Between 2005 and 2010, the shares of workers with low and high educational levels grew and fell respectively. From 2010 to 2012, the trend of the first half of the decade resumed and the shares of workers with low and high educational levels fell and increased respectively. The increase in the share of employed workers with low educational levels between 2005 and 2010, and the corresponding decrease in the share of employed workers with high levels of education, reflects the change in the structure of employment by economic sector over this period. From 2005 to 2010, the share of the primary sector exhibited the largest increase among all economic sectors due to the boom in soybean production. As the primary activity sector employs mainly workers with low educational levels, the change in the structure of employment in

[2] The most frequent value of years of education for employed workers in urban and national Uruguay was six over the entire period (around 19.6 per cent of urban employed workers and 20.6 per cent of workers at the national level had six years of education).

[3] The improvement in the employment structure by educational level is related to changes in the relative demand and supply of workers with high educational levels with corresponding implications for the wage gap by educational group and the unemployment rate of each educational level. We introduce a discussion about the role of these factors in Uruguay in section 21.5.

the Uruguayan labour market between 2005 and 2010 can explain the deterioration in the educational level of the employed population over the same period.

The educational level of the employed population, considering both rural and urban areas in Uruguay between 2006 and 2012, exhibited the same trend as that of statistics for urban areas. However, the share of employed workers with low levels of education is larger in national statistics compared to urban statistics, while the shares of employed workers with medium and high levels of education are lower at the national level compared to the urban level.[4]

The educational level of the employed population improved between 2000 and 2012 for all population groups (young and adult workers, men and women).

During the international crisis of 2008, the structure of employment by educational level continued with the worsening trend that had started in 2005, overall and for all population groups. This trend was associated with the increase in the share of the primary activity sector in total employment. By 2011, the share of employed workers with high educational levels surpassed the pre-crisis value in the aggregate and for all population groups. The recovery was related to the reduction in the share of the primary activity sector in total employment due to the fall in the international prices of Uruguayan products. However, a new decrease took place in 2012 that was compensated for by the increase in the share of employed workers with medium levels of education.

> The share of workers registered with the social security system increased from 2001 (the earliest year with data on this indicator) to 2012 in urban Uruguay. Within this period, the registration rate fell between 2001 and 2004 but increased in the following years. This upward trend, starting in 2004, held for all population groups; it was not interrupted by the international crisis of 2008.
>
> (Cruces et al. 2015: figure 8)

The pension system in Uruguay is composed of a contributory scheme and a non-contributory scheme. The contributory scheme comprises two regimes. First, a mandatory pay-as-you-go regime, which is funded through payroll taxes, other taxes, and government contributions. Second, an individual capitalization regime, which is also compulsory but only for workers whose earnings are above a certain threshold. The non-contributory scheme provides economic support to all persons who lack a monetary income and who cannot

[4] The most frequent value of years of education for employed workers in urban and national Uruguay was six over the entire period (around 19.6 per cent of urban employed workers and 20.6 per cent of workers at the national level had six years of education).

support themselves due to old age or disability. The health system also comprises two regimes. First, the public health regime which provides services through the Administración de Servicios de Salud del Estado and is funded by both budgetary allocations and the contributions of people registered with the social security administration. Second, the private regime which is composed mostly of mutuals (mutual societies—similar to Health Maintenance Organaizations in the United States), which are funded by the monthly fees paid by affiliated members and transfers received through the social security system. Insured members under the public regime may opt between the services provided by the mutuals or the Administración de Servicios de Salud del Estado (Filgueira and Hernandez 2012).

The percentage of workers registered with the contributory scheme of the social security system increased by 9.7 percentage points from 2001 to 2012 (Table 21.1). Interestingly, both the number of registered and unregistered workers increased over the period. The number of workers registered with the social security system grew by 446,005 while the number of unregistered workers increased by 29,317. From 2001 to 2004, the period of the economic downturn, the share of registered workers fell from 64.1 to 59.4 per cent. From 2004 to 2012, a period that included the Great Recession, that share grew steadily, reaching 73.8 per cent in 2012. The share of workers registered with the social security system at the national level between 2006 and 2012 exhibited the same level and trend as urban figures. In 2005, the government of Uruguay started to implement a group of economic and social protection policies that can explain the increase in the percentage of registered workers (Cruces and Bergolo 2013; ILO 2014). These policies included the reactivation of collective bargaining, a tax reform that included increases in the social security contributions for some economic sectors and reductions for others, and the revision of social protection programmes which led to the extension of health insurance coverage to dependent children and spouses of registered workers. Starting in 2005 there was also a greater control exerted by the *Banco de Previsión Social* (the social security administration) and *Dirección General Impositiva* (the tax authority) on firms to detect situations of non-compliance with the registration of workers and the payment of social security contributions (Mazzuchi 2009).

The share of workers registered with the social security system increased over the period for young and adult workers, men and women. The percentage of workers registered decreased from 2001 to 2004 for all population groups, and grew in the following years.

The international crisis of 2008 did not affect the upward trend in the percentage of registered workers. Between 2008 and 2009, the share of workers registered with the social security system increased overall and for all population groups.

21.5 Labour Earnings

> Three years of falling labour earnings were followed by ten years of rising labour earnings, but the increases were not large enough in 2012 to drive labour earnings back up to where they had started (2000). The pattern of falling labour earnings between 2000 and 2003 and rising labour earnings between 2003 and 2012 held for all population groups, but while men, women, and adults had lower labour earnings in 2012 compared to 2000, young employed workers enjoyed a rise. Workers in high-earning categories experienced a larger drop in labour earnings than did workers in low-earning categories. Earnings were not affected adversely by the 2008 crisis.
> (Cruces et al. 2015: figure 9)

Average monthly earnings in urban Uruguay, expressed in PPP dollars of 2005, fell by 8.6 per cent, from US$724 in 2000 to US$661 in 2012 (Table 21.1). Labour earnings fell at the beginning of the period (from 2000 and 2004) and rose in most of the following years.[5] The recovery of labour earnings in 2005 was associated with the reactivation of collective bargaining at the sector level, which meant an increase in real wages (Mazzuchi 2009). The upward trend was interrupted in 2010 when labour earnings fell by 1.2 per cent and in 2012 when they dropped by 1.0 per cent. Average monthly earnings at the national level exhibited the same level and trend as urban monthly earnings from 2006 to 2012.

Labour earnings of adult, male, and female employed workers decreased between 2000 and 2012, while labour earnings of young employed persons increased. The pattern of falling labour earnings at the beginning of the period (2000–3) and rising labour earnings in the following years (2003–12) held for all population groups.

Mean earnings fell between 2000 and 2012 for workers in both low- and high-earning categories, but earnings of workers employed in high-earning categories dropped more than labour incomes of workers employed in low-earning categories. Employed workers from all employment categories suffered an earnings reduction from 2000 to 2003–4 and a steady earnings increase from 2004–5 to 2012. When broken down by occupational groups, labour earnings of workers in low-earning occupational groups (elementary occupations, services and sales jobs, and craft and trade occupations) decreased by less (in percentage terms) than earnings of employed workers in high-earning occupations (management, professional, and technical jobs). A breakdown of the aggregate statistics on

[5] Official statistics show a recovery of real labour earnings in 2012 compared to the level they had in 2000. This difference with respect to our statistics can be explained by the imputation of the health insurance as part of labour incomes by the statistical institute of Uruguay. We do not follow the imputation procedure to favour the comparability of statistics across countries.

labour earnings by occupational position reveals that labour earnings of the self-employed (low-earning positions) dropped by less (in percentage terms) than labour incomes of paid employees (high-earning positions). In terms of economic sectors, earnings of workers in low-earning sectors (domestic service, construction, and low-tech industries) remained largely the same during the period, while the earnings of workers in high-earning sectors (skilled services, utilities and transportation, and public administration) dropped between 2000 and 2012. Finally, labour earnings of employed workers with high educational levels fell by more (in percentage terms) than earnings of employed persons with medium and low educational levels.

The evidence of falling labour earnings for all educational groups can be interpreted in light of previous findings of improving educational levels of the Uruguayan urban employed population and improving employment structure by economic sector and occupational group over the period. The improving employment structure by economic sector and occupational group implied an increase in the share of sectors and occupations that are more likely to use workers with high and medium educational levels, such as skilled services, education and health, and professionals and technical occupations, and a reduction in the share of sectors and occupations that employ workers with low educational levels, such as domestic services, construction and low-tech industry, and elementary activities, service and sales, and craft and trade occupations. This evidence indicates that the demand for workers with high and medium educational levels relative to those with low educational levels increased between 2000 and 2012. On the other hand, the educational levels of people in the labour force improved over the same period, indicating an increase in the relative supply of workers with high and medium levels of education (Cruces et al. 2015: table 8). It is interesting to notice that between 2007 and 2010 the share of workers with low educational levels in the labour force increased. However, that share was always below the level of 2000. The prediction of a supply and demand analysis is that the relative wages of workers with high and medium levels of education relative to those with low educational levels will rise or fall depending on which effect dominates (increase in the relative demand versus increase in the relative supply). In the Uruguayan labour market, the wages of workers with high and medium educational levels relative to those with low educational levels fell over the period, while the wages of workers with high educational levels relative to those with medium educational levels also decreased (Cruces et al. 2015: table 7). The adjustment process also led to a reduction in the unemployment rate of all educational groups with a larger reduction for workers with low levels of education (Cruces et al. 2015: table 9).

The international crisis of 2008 did not have a negative effect on the upward trend in labour earnings that began in 2004; a trend that held true for the aggregate and for all demographic groups. Some occupational groups, however, were adversely affected by the 2008 crisis. Earnings of workers in agricultural, forestry, and fishery occupations and in armed forces dropped during the crisis. By 2011, the labour earnings of both occupational groups had returned to pre-crisis levels. The incomes of the other occupational categories were not adversely affected by the international crisis of 2008.

21.6 Poverty and Inequality

> All poverty indicators increased in the early years of the period studied (from 2000 to 2004) but fell steadily in the later years (from 2004 to 2012). Comparing 2012 with 2000, Uruguay registered more poverty for some poverty lines, and less poverty for others. Despite the international crisis of 2008, the downward trend in poverty indicators during the second half of the period analysed was not reversed. (Cruces et al. 2015: figure 10)

The moderate poverty rate in urban Uruguay (measured by the country's official poverty line) increased from 21.4 per cent in 2000 to 24.9 per cent in 2012; the extreme poverty rate rose from 2.4 per cent to 2.8 per cent; the percentage of working poor (defined as the proportion of persons in the population living in poor households where at least one member works) increased from 11.9 per cent to 15.5 per cent over the same period (Table 21.1). Consistent with the U-shaped pattern of GDP, the figures for all these poverty indicators increased between 2000 and 2004 while GDP was falling, and then began a steady downward trend that was not abated by the international crisis of 2008. Notwithstanding, by 2012 the levels had failed to fall below the figures for the beginning of the period. When the poverty rate is analysed on the basis of the 2.5 and 4 dollars-a-day PPP international poverty lines, there is a drop in poverty from 2000 to 2012. When the 2.5 dollars-a-day poverty line is used, the poverty rate drops from 3.6 per cent in 2000 to 2.6 per cent in 2012; when poverty is calculated using the 4 dollars-a-day poverty line, the drop is from 11.2 per cent to 8.3 per cent over the same period. According to these indicators, the period witnessed an increase in poverty from 2000 to 2004, followed by a downward trend that, by 2012, had reduced poverty rates to below the 2000 level. The post-2004 downward trend in the poverty rate and in the rate of the working poor was not interrupted by the international crisis of 2008. Poverty indicators at the national level exhibited the same trend as urban poverty indicators from 2006 to 2012, and a slightly lower level.

The poverty patterns reported in the last paragraph can be understood by examining incomes from various sources as well as government programmes.

The analysis of sources of household total income indicates that labour income, pensions, capital income, and government transfers fell at the beginning of the period, while poverty indicators increased. Labour earnings dropped from 2000 to 2003, capital income fell from 2000 to 2006, government transfers were lower in 2004 than in 2001 (the earliest year with data on this source of income), and pensions fell from 2000 to 2005 (Cruces et al. 2015: figure 11). Incomes from labour and government transfers led the recovery of household income. Among government transfers, the *PANES* emergency programme was implemented between 2005 and 2007 to reduce the effects of the economic crisis. This programme is credited with a reduction in the extreme poverty rate. In the absence of the programme, the extreme poverty rate would have been 50 per cent higher in 2006 (Reuben et al. 2008). In 2008 the government of Uruguay replaced the *PANES* with the *Plan de Equidad. Plan de Equidad* comprises the main conditional cash transfer programme of Uruguay, the *Asignaciones Familiares*. The implementation of the *Plan de Equidad* explains the increase in government transfers between 2008 and 2010.

> Household per capita income inequality and labour earnings inequality increased from 2000 to 2004, then stabilized and started a downward trend in 2007 that allowed both inequality indices to fall in 2012 below the level of 2000. The international crisis of 2008 did not affect the downward trend in inequality indices that was observed in the last years of the period.
>
> (Cruces et al. 2015: figure 12)

From 2000 to 2012, the inequality of household per capita income gauged by the Gini coefficient fell from 0.444 to 0.415. The Gini coefficient of household per capita income increased between 2000 and 2004, from 0.444 to 0.471, then stabilized around that level and began a downward trend in 2007. The Gini coefficient of labour earnings among employed workers was higher than the Gini coefficient of household per capita income over the whole period under study. The inequality of labour earnings measured by the Gini coefficient also decreased between 2000 and 2012, from 0.462 to 0.420, and exhibited a similar trend as the Gini coefficient of household per capita income (Table 21.1). The reduction of the inequality of labour earnings started in 2007, coinciding with the increase in the share of workers with low levels of education in total employment that took place from 2007 to 2010. This reduction in labour earnings inequality is also in keeping with the fact that the reduction in earnings for high-earning categories was greater than the reduction for low-earning categories. Consequently, the reduction in labour earnings inequality in Uruguay occurred at the expense of income losses for all employment categories. The Gini coefficient of household per capita income and that of labour earnings at the national level exhibited essentially the same values as the coefficients at the urban level.

Changes in household per capita income inequality in Uruguay have been related mainly to changes in labour income. Azevedo et al. (2013b) decomposed the change in the Gini coefficient of household per capita income for the period 2000–10 and found that changes in labour incomes contributed to the inequality increase over this period (the Gini coefficient of household per capita income increased from 0.444 to 0.454 between 2000 and 2010). On the other hand, changes in non-labour incomes, such as government transfers, and demographic changes (e.g. the share of adults per household) were inequality-reducing. Other studies have analysed the factors behind the evolution of labour income inequality. Azevedo et al. (2013a) used a decomposition approach and found that changes in the education wage premium (or the 'price effect') were inequality-increasing in Uruguay between 2000 and 2010, while the distribution of the stock of education (the 'quantity effect') was inequality-reducing. Gasparini et al. (2011) found a reduction in the wage premium in urban Uruguay between 2000 and 2010 that was associated with an increase in the relative supply and a decrease in the relative demand of skilled workers. Finally, the reduction in labour earnings inequality from 2007 to 2012 has been associated with different policy measures implemented by the government of Uruguay, such as the reactivation of collective bargaining in 2005, the increase in the national minimum wage in 2005, and a tax reform implemented in 2007 (Amarante et al. 2007; Amarante et al. 2011).

21.7 Conclusions

Overall, Uruguay experienced rapid economic growth by Latin American standards between 2000 and 2012. Within the period, the pattern of economic growth was U-shaped: GDP fell during 2000–2 and grew steadily during 2003–12. Growth slowed following the international crisis of 2008, but it was not reversed.

Most labour market indicators followed the U-shaped pattern of economic growth over the period. The unemployment rate exhibited an increase in the early years of the period and a downward trend in the later years, falling overall between 2000 and 2012. The composition of employment by occupational group improved from 2000 to 2011—the last year for which we can construct a consistent times series on occupations—as workers moved from service and sales, and craft and trade occupations to better-paying jobs like professional and technical positions. The employment structure by occupational position deteriorated at the beginning of the period and then improved steadily as the share of paid employees and of employers increased and the share of self-employed and unpaid workers decreased. The employment composition by economic sector improved slightly over the course of the period studied as workers moved from low-earning sectors like domestic service, construction, and low-tech industry, to better-paying sectors like education and health, skilled services, and commerce. The educational level of the Uruguayan employed population increased between 2000 and 2012, but the evolution was not steady. There was a worsening in the structure of employment by educational level in the mid-years of the period studied. The share of workers registered with the social security system increased from 2001 (the first year with data on this variable) to 2012. Within this period, there was a reduction in the percentage of registered workers at the beginning of the period and a steady upward trend from 2004. The only labour market indicator that did not improve between 2000 and 2012 is labour earnings, which dropped. The earnings of workers in high-earning categories dropped more than earnings of workers in low-earning categories. Labour earnings fell in the early years of the period and then started an upward trend, but by 2012 real labour incomes were still below their level in 2000. Poverty rates rose and then fell; whether they were higher or lower in 2012 than in 2000 depends on the poverty line used. The moderate and extreme poverty rates calculated using official poverty lines and the rate of working poor households increased between 2000 and 2012. Following the pattern of GDP growth, poverty indicators grew at the beginning of the period and then started a downward trend. However, they were still above the value of 2000. The same pattern over time appears for poverty indicators using international poverty lines, but these indicators reached a lower value in 2012 than they had in 2000. The Gini coefficient of household per capita income and of labour earnings decreased over the period. Inequality indices increased in the early years of the period and fell in the later years.

The labour market indicators that were affected negatively by the international crisis of 2008 were the unemployment rate and the employment structure by educational level. The downward trend in the unemployment rate abated and a reduction in the share of employed workers with high educational levels took place after the crisis (between 2009 and 2010) with a recovery in 2011. The reduction in poverty and inequality underway during the second half of the period analysed was not reversed by the international crisis. The comparison between the effects of the international crisis of 2008 on labour market indicators and the effects generated by the crisis at the beginning of the period, from 2000 to 2002, reveals that the crisis at the beginning of the 2000s had a stronger negative impact on Uruguay. The crisis of 2000–2 generated a reduction in GDP, increases in the unemployment rate, the share of workers in low-earning positions, and the share of unregistered workers, a decrease in labour earnings, and increases in poverty and inequality indicators. On the other hand, during the Great Recession, GDP continued to grow although at a slower pace, whereas the unemployment rate, the share of workers in low-earning positions, and the share of unregistered workers fell, labour earnings increased, and poverty and inequality indicators dropped. The Uruguayan economy seemed to be better prepared to face the international crisis of 2008, which was relatively severe, than it was at the beginning of the decade when it faced the crises of Brazil and Argentina, its main trading partners.

Young workers and women experienced worse labour market outcomes over the period compared to adults and men respectively, and while young workers seem to be more vulnerable to macroeconomic crises compared to adults, men and women were similarly affected by the episodes of crises. The unemployment rate was higher for young compared to adult workers, the share of young employed workers in low-earning occupations was larger than the share of adult workers, the share of workers in high-earning sectors and the share of workers registered with the social security system were lower for youth compared to adults, and labour earnings of young workers were below those of adults. On the other hand, the share of young workers in low-earning occupational positions was lower compared to adults. In addition to the generally inferior situation of young workers in the labour market compared to adults, youth labour market indicators were more affected by the crisis at the beginning of the 2000s and by the slowdown in the pace of reduction in the unemployment rate during the international crisis of 2008. Disaggregating by gender, we found that men had better labour market outcomes than women, with the exceptions of the share of workers in low-earning positions that was larger among men and the share of workers in low-earning occupations that was similar between men and women. Both genders were similarly affected by the crisis at the beginning of the 2000s, although the slowdown in the reduction of the unemployment rate during the Great Recession affected women more than men.

In summary, Uruguay was able to improve most labour market indicators between 2000 and 2012 despite the economic crisis at the beginning of the 2000s and the international crisis of 2008. The only exceptions were labour earnings and poverty indicators based on the official poverty lines.

References

Amarante, V., R. Arim, and G. Salas (2007). 'Impacto distributivo de la reforma impositiva'. Document prepared for the Poverty and Social Impact Analysis (PSIA) of Uruguay. Washington, DC: World Bank.

Amarante, V., M. Colafranceschi, and A. Vigorito (2011). 'Uruguay's Income Inequality and Political Regimes during 1981–2010'. WIDER Working Paper 2011/94. Helsinki: UNU-WIDER.

Azevedo, J. P., M. E. Davalos, C. Diaz-Bonilla, B. Atuesta, and R. A. Castaneda (2013a). 'Fifteen Years of Inequality in Latin America: How Have Labor Markets Helped?'. Policy Research Working Paper 6384. Washington, DC: World Bank.

Azevedo, J. P., G. Inchauste, and V. Sanfelice (2013b). 'Decomposing the Recent Inequality Decline in Latin America'. Policy Research Working Paper 6715. Washington, DC: World Bank.

CEDLAS and World Bank (2014). SEDLAC—Socio-Economic Database for Latin America and the Caribbean. Centro de Estudios Distributivos, Laborales y Sociales, Facultad de Ciencias Económicas, Universidad Nacional de La Plata and World Bank Poverty Group LCR. Available at <http://sedlac.econo.unlp.edu.ar/eng/index.php>, accessed 2014.

Cruces, G. and M. Bergolo (2013). 'Informality and Contributory and Non-Contributory Programmes: Recent Reforms of the Social-Protection System in Uruguay', *Development Policy Review* 31 (5): 531–51.

Cruces, G., G. Fields, D. Jaume, and M. Viollaz (2015). 'The Growth–Employment–Poverty Nexus in Latin America in the 2000s: Uruguay Country Study'. WIDER Working Paper 2015/083. Helsinki: UNU-WIDER.

Filgueira, F. and D. Hernandez (2012). 'Social Protection Systems in Latin America and the Caribbean: Uruguay'. ECLAC, Project Documents Collection. Santiago de Chile: United Nations.

Gasparini, L., S. Galiani, G. Cruces, and P. Acosta (2011). 'Educational Upgrading and Returns to Skills in Latin America: Evidence from a Supply–Demand Framework, 1990–2010'. IZA Working Paper 6244. Bonn: Institute for the Study of Labor.

Hausmann, R., A. Rodríguez-Clare, and D. Rodrik (2005). 'Towards a Strategy for Economic Growth in Uruguay'. Economic and Social Studies Series RE1-05-003. Washington, DC: Inter-American Development Bank.

ILO (2014). 'Reducción del empleo informal e Uruguay: Políticas y resultados'. Notes on Formalization. Geneva: International Labour Organization, Regional Office for Latin America and the Caribbean.

IMF (2003). 'Uruguay: 2003 Article Consultation and Third Review under the Stand-By Arrangement and Request for Modification and Waiver of Applicability of Performance Criteria'. IMF Country Report 03/247. Washington, DC: International Monetary Fund.

IMF (2005). 'Uruguay: Seventh Review under the Stand-By Arrangement and Request for Waiver of Nonobservance of Performance Criteria'. IMF Country Report 05/109. Washington, DC: International Monetary Fund.

IMF (2010). 'Uruguay: 2009 Article IV Consultation'. IMF Country Report 10/48. Washington, DC: International Monetary Fund.

Mazzuchi, G. (2009). 'Labour Relations in Uruguay: 2005–08'. Working Paper 6. Geneva: International Labour Organization, Industrial and Employment Relations Department.

Reuben, W., M. Miodosky, and E. Watanabe (2008). 'Building on Experience: Improving Social Protection in Uruguay and the Plan for Social Equity'. En breve 132. Washington, DC: World Bank.

Sosa, S. (2010). 'The Influence of Big Brothers: How Important Are Regional Factors for Uruguay?'. IMF Working Paper 10/60. Washington, DC: International Monetary Fund.

World Bank (2014). World Development Indicators. Available at <http://data.worldbank.org/data-catalog/world-development-indicators>, accessed April 2014.

22

Venezuela

22.1 Introduction

This chapter on labour markets and growth in Venezuela since 2000 is one of sixteen studies of Latin American countries, each of which analyses the growth–employment–poverty nexus and aims to answer the following broad questions: Has economic growth resulted in economic development via improved labour market conditions in Latin America in the 2000s, and have these improvements halted or been reversed since the Great Recession? How do the rate and character of economic growth, changes in the various labour market indicators, and changes in poverty relate to each other?

To answer these questions, we analyse the growth experience of Venezuela during the 2000s and a wide set of labour market indicators that we assign to one of two different categories: employment and earnings indicators, and poverty and income inequality indicators. More specifically, for the group of employment and earnings indicators we construct statistics on the following variables: the unemployment rate; the employment structure by occupational group, employment position, economic sector, registration of workers with the social security system, and educational level; and mean labour earnings and hourly wages. We present all these indicators for the employed population as a whole and for different population groups (youth, adults, men, and women). For the group of poverty and income inequality indicators, we compute poverty rates using the official moderate and extreme poverty lines and the international lines of 2.5 and 4 dollars a day. We also calculate the Gini coefficient of household per capita income and labour earnings.

All the statistics in this chapter are obtained using microdata from the Encuesta de Hogares por Muestreo (EPM), for the second semester of years 2000 to 2012. The nationwide surveys from 2000 to 2006 were processed following a harmonization methodology and incorporated into the SEDLAC—Socio-Economic Database for Latin America and the Caribbean (CEDLAS and World Bank 2014), while we made our own processing of the remaining surveys.[1] The resulting labour market indicators were compiled into a large number of tables and figures, which are available in an earlier version of this study (henceforth, Cruces et al. 2015). Chapter 1 of this book provides the definition for each of the indicators we analyse here, while Cruces et al. (2015) includes details on definitions and classification systems used by Venezuela's household surveys, and on comparability issues of these surveys over time.

22.2 Economic Growth

> Venezuela experienced slow economic growth during the 2000s. The country underwent a recession at the beginning of the period and during the international crisis of 2008. The Venezuelan economy surpassed its pre-recession GDP level in 2012, but GDP per capita was still below the pre-crisis level by the end of the period studied.
>
> (Cruces et al. 2015: figures 1 and 2)

During the period 2000 to 2012, Venezuela experienced low economic growth by Latin American standards. GDP per capita increased by 22.0 per cent, while the average for the eighteen Latin American countries was 36.2 per cent during the same period. GDP (measured in PPP dollars of 2005) grew by 49.7 per cent, and GDP per employed person rose by 28.4 per cent. The annual growth rate of GDP per capita was 1.2 per cent, and it varied from a minimum of −10.5 per cent in 2002 to a maximum of 16.2 per cent in 2004 (Table 22.1).

Venezuela is an economy that depends to a great extent on oil revenues and where GDP per capita follows the movements of oil prices. At the beginning of the 2000s, the Venezuelan economy was affected negatively by its political instability and a two-month strike by the state-run oil company (Alvarez and Hanson 2009). The consequence of the strike was a rapid drop in GDP of 8.3 per cent annually from 2001 to 2003. In the following years, rising international oil prices helped the economy to recover. The government regained control over the oil company after the two-month strike. The implementation of changes in the oil revenues' distribution policy along with changes in taxation allowed the government to obtain a larger amount of oil revenues and to implement an expansionary fiscal policy. Indeed, public spending was the driving force of the economy from 2003 to 2008 (Guerra and Olivo 2009). The expansionary fiscal policy was accompanied by an expansionary monetary policy, and foreign exchange rate, and price controls. GDP and GDP per capita growth rates averaged 10.5 and 8.6 per cent respectively between 2004 and 2008.

[1] See Cruces et al. (2015: table 1) for details on the size of Venezuela household surveys.

Table 22.1 Venezuela: Evolution of growth and labour market indicators over the 2000s

		2000	2001	2002	2003	2004	2005	2006	2007	2008	2009	2010	2011	2012
Growth Indicators	GDP per capita	9,527	9,667	8,650	7,835	9,104	9,869	10,658	11,396	11,799	11,237	10,894	11,173	11,623
	GDP per capita growth rate	1.72	1.47	−10.52	−9.41	16.20	8.40	7.99	6.92	3.54	−4.77	−3.05	2.56	4.02
Employment and Earnings Indicators	Employment-to-population ratio	56.06	58.94	57.98	57.82	58.69	58.80	59.47	60.13	60.75	59.85	59.31	59.65	59.37
	Unemployment rate	13.23	12.78	16.17	16.78	13.94	11.35	9.33	7.47	6.85	8.05	8.45	7.84	7.41
	Share of low-earnings occupations	...	...	...	...	53.85	50.78	50.75	50.04	49.83	49.91	49.65	49.03	48.96
	Share of mid-earnings occupations	...	...	...	...	30.90	31.75	32.59	33.24	33.18	32.68	32.28	32.85	31.96
	Share of high-earnings occupations	...	...	...	...	15.25	17.47	16.66	16.71	17.00	17.41	18.07	18.12	19.08
	Share of employers	5.10	6.62	5.53	5.08	4.80	4.89	4.49	4.17	4.09	3.78	3.46	3.48	3.26
	Share of wage/salaried employees	56.58	56.22	55.17	53.86	55.81	57.79	58.51	59.30	58.43	57.73	56.95	57.19	58.78
	Share of self-employed workers	36.60	34.81	36.69	38.34	37.43	35.72	35.77	35.55	36.30	37.72	39.00	38.46	37.19
	Share of unpaid family workers	1.71	2.34	2.61	2.72	1.96	1.60	1.22	0.98	1.18	0.77	0.59	0.88	0.77

(continued)

Table 22.1 Continued

		2000	2001	2002	2003	2004	2005	2006	2007	2008	2009	2010	2011	2012
	Share of workers in low-earnings sectors	41.54	41.39	42.58	42.64	41.13	40.39	38.31	37.87	37.52	37.86	37.56	37.03	37.35
	Share of workers in mid-earnings sectors	40.56	39.10	37.65	37.63	39.55	39.54	40.74	40.73	40.42	39.83	39.67	39.86	39.60
	Share of workers in high-earnings sectors	17.90	19.51	19.77	19.72	19.33	20.07	20.95	21.39	22.06	22.30	22.76	23.11	23.05
	Share of low-educated workers	52.55	50.59	50.37	50.25	49.37	46.21	44.18	42.95	41.24	40.02	38.35	36.75	37.19
	Share of medium-educated workers	31.73	33.13	33.42	33.35	33.71	35.73	36.20	36.81	37.32	36.60	36.55	37.03	35.30
	Share of high-educated workers	15.72	16.28	16.21	16.40	16.92	18.06	19.63	20.24	21.44	23.38	25.10	26.22	27.51
	Share of workers registered with SS	68.56	64.82	61.48	58.83	60.16	60.33	60.85	62.86	66.03	71.13	70.83	72.99	69.12
	Mean labour earnings	380.4	402.3	346.0	297.0	330.9	398.2	463.0	501.7	500.4	493.0	469.3	455.7	511.0
Poverty and Inequality Indicators	Official extreme poverty rate	13.79	15.72	21.69	27.21	24.20	18.69	10.06	7.41	8.86	8.03	8.45	8.31	7.19
	Official moderate poverty rate	37.44	42.77	50.23	58.00	55.07	44.09	31.92	25.83	30.38	28.95	29.99	29.24	23.52
	Poverty rate 2.5 dollars-a-day	29.83	27.49	36.96	42.56	36.30	28.25	18.09	12.74	11.92	11.92	12.13	12.42	11.05

Poverty rate 4 dollars-a-day	51.67	49.45	58.52	64.79	59.30	48.52	36.33	29.02	27.77	27.57	28.06	28.99	24.66	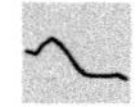
GINI of household per capita income	0.440	0.464	0.473	0.460	0.453	0.474	0.433	0.415	0.401	0.400	0.384	0.388	0.402	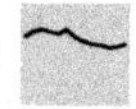
GINI of labour earnings	0.403	0.437	0.438	0.425	0.412	0.436	0.382	0.365	0.352	0.343	0.310	0.319	0.342	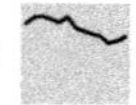

Note: The shaded figures of labour market indicators represent statistical significant improvements at 5 per cent between the initial and final years for all the employment and earnings indicators and poverty and inequality indicators. The only exceptions are the share of mid-earnings occupations, share of mid-earnings sectors, and share of medium-educated workers for which we did not assign welfare evaluation criteria.

Source: SEDLAC (CEDLAS and World Bank 2014) and World Development Indicators (World Bank 2014).

The economy was affected adversely by the international crisis of 2008, mostly through the drop in international oil prices. The reduced oil revenues prevented the government from instrumenting countercyclical policies (Guerra and Olivo 2009; Weisbrot and Johnston 2012). The public spending was reduced and taxes were increased in 2009 to face the international crisis. Moreover, the government did not increase its debt significantly despite having a low stock of public and external debt (Weisbrot and Johnston 2012). GDP fell by 3.2 per cent in 2009 while GDP per capita dropped by 4.8 per cent that year. The economy returned to its pre-crisis GDP level in 2012, helped by the recovery in oil prices and the increase in public spending starting in 2010. GDP per capita was slightly below its pre-recession value by 2012.

The share of the industry and agricultural sectors in the economy increased, while the share of the service sector diminished between 2000 and 2010 (when data on this variable stopped becoming available). The share of the industry sector, the largest one in the Venezuelan economy, increased from 49.7 per cent in 2000 to 52.2 per cent in 2010 (Cruces et al. 2015: table 2). The increase was led by the growth of the oil subsector which followed the rise in the international oil price between 2004 and 2008. Conversely, the manufacturing subsector lost share over the period due to price and exchange rate controls, and increases in imports driven by an overvalued currency (Guerra and Olivo 2009). The share of the service sector, on the other hand, diminished during the same period from 46.1 per cent in 2000 to 41.1 per cent in 2010. The agricultural sector increased its share in the total economy from 4.2 per cent in 2000 to 5.8 per cent in 2010. Turning to the year of international crisis, 2008, industry was the sector most affected by the turmoil. In 2009, the share of this sector declined by 9.9 percentage points and its value added fell by 5.0 per cent due to both the reduction in oil prices and electricity blackouts (Weisbrot and Ray 2010). The share of the industry sector in the economy and its value added had not regained their pre-crisis levels by 2010. The agricultural and service sectors suffered smaller changes in their value added compared to the industry sector between 2008 and 2009 (an increase of 1.0 per cent and a drop of 0.9 per cent respectively).

22.3 Unemployment

The unemployment rate dropped from 2000 to 2012 following the movements in the business cycle. It decreased for youths, adults, men, and women. During the international crisis, the unemployment rate increased but recovered its pre-crisis level by 2012. (Cruces et al. 2015: figure 3)

The unemployment rate (measured as the ratio of unemployment to labour force) decreased from 13.2 per cent in 2000 (1,365,752 unemployed people) to 7.4 per cent in 2012 (1,006,400 unemployed people) and moved along with the business cycle over the period (Table 22.1). Between 2001 and 2003, the unemployment rate increased from 12.8 per cent to 16.8 per cent while GDP was falling. Between 2004 and 2008, the unemployment rate decreased and reached its lowest value for the period (6.9 per cent in 2008). The international crisis of 2008 led to an increase in the unemployment rate, which rose to 8.1 per cent in 2009 and continued its upward trend until 2010. Both the number of persons in the labour force and the number of employed persons increased between 2008 and 2009 by 245,548 and 73,126 respectively. These figures suggest that the increase in the unemployment rate from 2008 to 2009 was explained by the new entrants into the labour market that could not find a job. In 2012 the unemployment rate returned to its 2007 level, but was still above the level of 2008.

The unemployment rate decreased for youth, adults, men, and women between 2000 and 2012. The international crisis hit young workers slightly harder than adult workers, and women more than men. For all population groups, the unemployment rate continued to rise until 2011, when it began declining again. By 2012, the unemployment rates of adults and men had recovered their pre-crisis levels. For youth and women, though, their unemployment rates were above the pre-recession values.

22.4 Job Mix

> The composition of employment by occupational group improved from 2004 (the earliest when we can construct the classification of occupations described previously) to 2012, shifting overall from low-earning occupations to better-paying occupations. All population groups benefited, especially women. During the international crisis of 2008, the structure of employment by occupational group slightly worsened for youth and men, improved for women, and remained unchanged for adults. Youth and men recovered the pre-crisis structure of employment by the end of the period. (Cruces et al. 2015: figure 4)

The share of the following occupations shrank between 2004 and 2012: services and sales occupations (drop of 2.4 percentage points); elementary jobs (drop of 1.5 percentage points); and agricultural, forestry, and fishery occupations (drop of 1.0 percentage points). The share of the following occupations grew: professionals (increase of 3.4 percentage points) and plant and machine operators and assemblers (increase of 1.1 percentage points). The share of the other occupational groups remained largely unchanged.

These changes in the occupational composition of employment can be interpreted as an improvement since the share of low-earning occupations (elementary, agricultural, forestry and fishery, and services and sales occupations) decreased by 4.9 percentage points, while the share of high-earning occupations (armed forces, management, and professionals) increased by 3.8 percentage points (Table 22.1). The international crisis of 2008 did not affect the employment structure by occupational group in the aggregate.

All population groups benefited from the improvement in the employment structure by occupational group, with women benefiting at the fastest rate.

During the international crisis of 2008, the occupational structure of employment slightly worsened for young workers and men, improved for women, and remained largely unchanged for adults. Young workers resumed the downward trend in the rate of working in low-earning occupations in 2010, while the recovery for men took place in 2011.

> The employment structure by occupational position remained essentially unchanged between 2000 and 2012 for the employed population as a whole. Adult workers and women exhibited an improvement in their structure of employment by occupational position; men suffered a worsening, while the structure of employment remained largely unchanged for young workers. Within the period, the employment structure by occupational position deteriorated at the beginning of the period, improved in the following years, and worsened once again during the international crisis of 2008. All population groups but young workers were impacted negatively by the Great Recession and only women recovered the pre-recession structure of employment by 2012. (Cruces et al. 2015: figure 5)

Between 2000 and 2012, the share of paid employees in total employment—the largest category—grew from 56.6 to 58.8 per cent. The share of the self-employed also increased but by less, from 36.6 to 37.2 per cent, whereas the shares of employers and unpaid workers fell from 5.1 to 3.3 per cent and from 1.7 to 0.8 per cent respectively (Table 22.1). These changes implied an unchanged structure of employment by occupational position since the shares of low-earning (self-employment and unpaid employment) and high-earning categories (paid employees and employers) exhibited small changes overall (drop and rise of 0.4 percentage points respectively). Within the period, the employment structure by occupational position suffered a worsening in the early years, when the country underwent a serious recession. It improved in the following years and deteriorated once during the international crisis of 2008. By 2012, low- and high-earning positions returned to their pre-crisis shares. In summary, in contexts of increasing unemployment and economic necessity, workers took up free-entry self-employment activities.

Between 2000 and 2012, the employment structure by occupational position deteriorated for men, improved for adult workers and women, and was essentially unchanged for young workers. All population groups suffered a worsening in their employment structure by occupational position at the beginning of the period (from 2001 to 2003) that was followed by an improvement. A new deterioration took place during the international crisis for all population groups except young workers.

The international crisis of 2008 led to a deterioration in the employment structure by occupational position for adult workers, men, and women, while there was no change for young workers. By 2012, women reached their pre-recession share of low-earning positions. Adult workers and men had not reached their pre-crisis levels by 2012.

> The employment composition by economic sector improved over the period studied, overall and for all population groups (youth, adults, men, and women). Within the period, the employment structure by economic sector deteriorated in the early years (from 2001 to 2003), improved from 2003 to 2008, and the improving trend stalled during the international crisis and resumed in 2010.
>
> (Cruces et al. 2015: figure 6)

The share of the following sectors fell between 2000 and 2012: primary activities (drop of 2.3 percentage points); high-tech industry (drop of 1.4 percentage points); commerce (drop of 1.2 percentage points); and low-tech industry (drop of 1.1 percentage points). Workers employed in the oil subsector are included in the primary activities sector in our classification. The increase in the employment share of the oil subsector in Venezuela mainly between 2004 and 2008 was counteracted by the reduction in the employment share of the agricultural subsector, resulting in a decline in the share of the primary activities sector over time. The share of the following sectors grew: public administration (increase of 2.4 percentage points); utilities and transportation (increase of 2.1 percentage points); and education and health (increase of 1.1 percentage points). The share of the other sector remained essentially unchanged. These changes clearly reveal a growth process based on public spending, i.e. the public administration sector exhibited the largest increase among all sectors, along with shrinking industry and agricultural sectors which reduced their production due to higher imports and price controls.

The employment structure by economic sector improved from 2000 to 2012 since the share of workers in low-earning sectors (domestic service, primary activities, and commerce) declined from 41.5 per cent to 37.4 per cent and the share of workers in high-earning sectors (skilled services, public administration, and utilities and transportation) grew over the period, from 17.9 per cent in 2000 to 23.1 per cent in 2012 (Table 22.1). Within the period, the employment structure by economic sector suffered a worsening at the outset (from 2001 to 2003) through an increase in the share of domestic workers (low-earning occupations) and a reduction in the share of industry sectors (mid-earning sectors), and improved in the following years (from 2003 to 2008). The improving trend stalled during the international crisis but resumed in the post-crisis period (from 2010 to 2012).

The improvement in the composition of employment by economic sector during the period took place for all population groups—that is, young and adult workers, men, and women. Within the period, all population groups suffered an initial worsening in their employment structure by economic sector (from 2001 to 2003) through an increase in the share of low-earning sectors in total employment and a decrease in the share of high-earning sectors (young workers and women), or through a larger increase in the share of low-earning sectors compared to the increase in the share of high-earning sectors (adult workers and men). An improvement took place in the following years up to 2008. The employment structure remained essentially unchanged during the international crisis of 2008 for adult workers, men, and women, while there was a slight worsening for young workers. The improving trend resumed in 2010 for adult workers, men, and women. For young workers, the worsening trend continued up to 2012.

> The educational level of the employed population improved over the period overall and for all population groups, and especially among young workers. The economic crisis did not have an effect on this trend. (Cruces et al. 2015: figure 7)

The share of employed workers with low educational levels (eight years of schooling or less) dropped from 52.6 per cent in 2000 to 37.2 per cent in 2012, while the share of employed workers with medium and high educational levels (nine to thirteen years of schooling and over thirteen years of schooling) grew from 31.7 per cent in 2000 to 35.3 per cent in 2012 and from 15.7 per cent to 27.5 per cent respectively (Table 22.1).[2] We interpret this result as an improvement for the employed population as the level of education is an important predictor of labour earnings. Consequently, the changes in the employment structure by educational level implied an increase in the share of workers that tend to have high levels of earnings and a decline in the share of workers with low earnings levels.[3]

The improvement in the educational level of the employed population took place for all population groups, and primarily among young workers.

[2] The most frequent value of years of education for employed workers in Venezuela was six from 2000 to 2007 (around 21.0 per cent of employed workers had six years of education) and eleven from 2008 to 2012 (around 22.2 per cent of employed workers had eleven years of education).

[3] The improvement in the employment structure by educational level is related to changes in the relative demand and supply of workers with high educational levels with corresponding implications for the wage gap by educational group and the unemployment rate of each educational level. We introduce a discussion about the role of these factors in Venezuela in section 22.5.

The pattern of improvement in the level of education of the employed population in Venezuela continued even during the international crisis of 2008. This was also the case for all population groups.

The share of wage/salaried employees registered with the social security system changed only slightly from 2000 to 2012. The registration rate fell in the early years of this period and increased in the later years. This pattern of change held overall and for all population groups. The international crisis of 2008 did not interrupt the upward trend that the share of registered workers exhibited in the second half of period studied (Cruces et al. 2015: figure 8).

Social security in Venezuela is provided by two types of institutions which serve different segments of the population. The Instituo Venezolano de los Seguros Sociales (IVSS) is the main provider of social security for public and private workers in the country; the Instituto de Prevision Social de las Fuerzas Armadas (IPSFA) provides social security for military personnel (Fernandez Salas 2010). These institutions provide pension insurance, health insurance, and occupational hazard insurance. Coverage is voluntary for self-employed workers, unemployed pregnant women, and persons who were previously covered (ISSA 2014). The Venezuelan social security system combines contributory and non-contributory schemes. Under the contributory scheme, social security benefits are financed through contributions from employees, employers, and the government. The non-contributory scheme (*pensiones asistenciales*) covered persons who lack contributory capacity or receive an insufficient pension from the contributory scheme (Fernandez Salas 2010). The non-contributory scheme is funded totally by the government.

The percentage of wage/salaried employees registered with the contributory scheme of the social security system changed slightly from 2000 to 2012, when it increased from 68.6 per cent to 69.1 per cent (Table 22.1). Within the period, the share of registered workers fell from 68.6 to 60.3 per cent between 2000 and 2005. From 2005 to 2011, a period that included the Great Recession, that share grew steadily and reached 73.0 per cent in 2011. A downward trend began at the end of the period and the percentage of registered workers was 69.1 per cent in 2012.

All population groups exhibited small changes in the share of workers registered with the social security system, but this variable moved erratically over the period. For all population groups, the percentage of registered wage/salaried employees fell at the beginning of the period, then increased, and then dropped again in 2012.

The international crisis of 2008 did not affect the upward trend in the percentage of registered wage/salaried employees that took place in the second half of the period analysed. Between 2008 and 2009, the share of workers registered with the social security system increased overall and for all population groups. In the following years, that share stabilized at a high level and finally fell in 2012.

22.5 Labour Earnings

> Labour earnings increased from 2000 to 2012 overall and for all population groups and employment categories. Low-earning categories had larger percentage income gains than high-earning categories. Workers were affected negatively by the 2008 crisis and not all of the groups recovered the pre-crisis level of incomes by 2012. (Cruces et al. 2015: figure 9)

Average monthly earnings, expressed in dollars at 2005 PPP, increased by 34.3 per cent, going from US$380 in 2000 to US$511 in 2012 (Table 22.1).[4] Labour earnings followed the movements of GDP over the period. They decreased in the first years, reaching a minimum of US$297 in 2003, increased steadily from 2003 to 2007, and then decreased up to 2011. In 2012, labour earnings surpassed the level of 2008. Part of the increase in labour earnings over the period can be explained by regular increases in the minimum wage which impacted mainly on the lower tail of the wage distribution (Boada and Mayorca 2011).

All population groups and employment categories experienced increases in labour earnings between 2000 and 2012. Low-earning categories (low-earning occupations, low-earning positions, and low-earning sectors) had larger percentage income gains than high-earning categories (high-earning occupations, high-earning positions, and high-earning sectors), while workers with low educational levels benefited the most from the increase in labour earnings over the period studied compared to workers with medium and high levels of education.

The evidence of larger earnings gains for workers with low and medium educational levels compared to workers with high educational levels can be interpreted in light of previous findings of improving employment structure by occupational group and economic sector over the period. The improving employment structure by occupational group and economic sector implied an increase in the share of occupations and sectors that can be expected to use workers with high and medium educational levels, such as professional occupations, and public administration, and utilities and transportation sectors, and a reduction in the share of occupations and sectors that employ workers

[4] The domestic currency of Venezuela was changed from *bolivar* to *bolivar fuerte* in January 2008 at the rate of 1 *bolivar fuerte* = 1000 *bolivares* due to inflation. We considered this change in our calculations.

with low educational levels, such as elementary, agricultural, services and sales occupations, and primary activity and commerce sectors. This evidence indicates that the demand for workers with high and medium educational levels relative to those with low educational levels increased between 2000 and 2012 (or from 2004 to 2012 according to our classification of occupations). On the other side, the educational levels of persons in the labour force improved over the same period, indicating an increase in the relative supply of workers with high and medium levels of education (Cruces et al. 2015: table 8). The prediction of a supply and demand analysis is that the relative wages of workers with high and medium educational levels relative to those with low educational levels will rise or fall depending on which effect dominates (increase in the relative demand versus increase in the relative supply). In the Venezuelan labour market, the relative wages of workers with high and medium educational levels relative to those with low educational levels fell over the period, and the relative wages of workers with high educational levels relative to those with medium educational levels also decreased (Cruces et al. 2015: table 7). The adjustment process also led to a reduction in the unemployment rate of all educational groups with larger reductions for workers with medium and low levels of education (Cruces et al. 2015: table 9).

The international crisis of 2008 had a negative impact on labour earnings overall and for most population groups and employment categories. Young, adult workers, and men suffered income reductions during the international crisis, while women were not affected negatively. Both young and adult workers and also men surpassed their pre-crisis levels of income by 2012. Among occupational groups, the categories most affected by the international crisis were management, professionals, and agriculture, forestry, and fishery workers. None of these groups regained their levels of earnings of 2008 by the end of the period. Among occupational positions, workers in high-earning categories suffered a reduction in labour earnings between 2008 and 2009, and by 2012 only wage/salaried workers returned to their pre-recession levels of income, while employers were still below that level. Workers from low-earning occupational positions were not impacted by the Great Recession. Among economic sectors, labour earnings of workers from the construction sector and high and low-tech industries exhibited the largest reductions. Workers from the construction sector had not recovered their pre-crisis level of incomes by the end of the period studied. All of the educational groups suffered income losses during the international crisis. Labour earnings of workers with high levels of education exhibited a larger reduction compared to earnings losses of workers with medium and low levels of education. High-educated workers had not recovered the pre-crisis level of earnings by 2012, while medium- and low-educated workers recovered the pre-crisis level of income that year.

22.6 Poverty and Inequality

> Poverty fell over the period studied for all poverty lines used. The rate of working poor households also exhibited a decreasing trend. The pattern of poverty reduction over time was interrupted by the international crisis of 2008 but poverty indices were again declining by 2012.
>
> (Cruces et al. 2015: figure 10)

The moderate poverty rate (measured by the country's official poverty line) decreased from 37.4 per cent in 2000 to 23.5 per cent in 2012, and the extreme poverty rate declined from 13.8 per cent to 7.2 per cent (Table 22.1). The rate of working poor households (defined as the proportion of persons in the population living in a poor household in which at least one member works) fell from 36.2 per cent to 15.3 per cent over the same period. The evolution of these indicators shows a negative association with GDP: poverty increased from the beginning of the period and up to 2003 while GDP was decreasing; fell from 2003 to 2007 while the economy was growing steadily; rose in 2008 and stabilized in the following years when the economy of Venezuela suffered the effects of the international crisis; and finally dropped in 2012 when economic growth resumed. The analysis based on the 2.5 and 4 dollars-a-day PPP international poverty lines also shows a drop in the poverty rate from 2000 to 2012 and a negative association between the poverty rate and the growth of the economy. Starting in 2009, all of the poverty indicators stopped falling, but in 2012 they were again declining.

The poverty patterns reported in the last paragraph can be interpreted by examining incomes from various sources. The analysis of sources of household total income indicates that labour incomes suffered a decline between 2001 and 2003 when all poverty indicators peaked; increased steadily from 2003 to 2007 when all poverty indicators fell; stabilized by the time of the international crisis when poverty indicators stopped decreasing; and recovered the upward trend by the end of the period when poverty indicators declined again (Cruces et al. 2015: figure 11). Incomes from capital followed a similar pattern over the period. Income from pensions did not suffer a major decline during the crisis of 2003, showed a clear upward trend between 2003 and 2006, and finally a decline that determined a similar level of pensions at the household level in 2012 compared to 2000. Finally, incomes from government transfers exhibited an erratic pattern at the beginning of the period studied, between 2000 and 2004, a stable level between 2005 and 2009, and an upward trend by the end of the period. The erratic pattern in the first years of the period can be explained by the erratic pattern of the number of beneficiaries from government transfers. Despite this erratic pattern, a clear finding emerges. The number of beneficiaries from government transfers increased dramatically after the crisis of 2003. The social programmes introduced by mid-2003 (*misiones*) were primarily focused on education, health, and work opportunities and were accompanied by a monetary transfer component that allowed the beneficiaries to escape extreme poverty and move into moderate poverty. As a result, the extreme poverty rate exhibited a drastic reduction between 2003 and 2007 (Viloria 2011).

> Household per capita income inequality and labour earnings inequality decreased over the period. The international crisis of 2008 did not affect the downward trend in the inequality indices immediately, but an upward trend began in 2010.
>
> (Cruces et al. 2015: figure 12)

Between 2000 and 2012, the Gini coefficient of household per capita income inequality fell from 0.440 to 0.402. The Gini coefficient of labour earnings among employed workers also decreased from 0.403 in 2000 to 0.342 in 2012 (Table 22.1); this reduction in labour earnings inequality is in accord with the evidence presented in section 22.5 showing larger earning increases for low-earning categories in comparison to high-earning categories. Disaggregating for different years, the inequality of household per capita income and labour earnings increased from 2000 to 2002 while GDP was decreasing, and they decreased from 2002 to 2008 when GDP was increasing with one exception: 2005 was a growth year in which inequality increased. During the international crisis, both inequality indices decreased while GDP was also falling. From 2010 until the end of the period studied, the Gini coefficient of household per capita income and labour earnings began an upward trend.

The decreasing trend in labour earnings inequality in Venezuela has been analysed by Gallo (2010). Through a decomposition approach, the author found that most of the change in labour earnings inequality (measured by the Theil index) between 1997 and 2007 remained unexplained. Among the observable factors he used in the analysis, those with greater explanatory power were the level of education, the occupational group, and the occupational position. This result implies that changes in labour earnings inequality are partly explained by changes in labour earnings inequality between educational groups, between occupational groups, and between occupational positions. Gasparini et al. (2011) analysed the period 2002–6 and found a significant fall in the education wage premium in Venezuela which is explained by an increase in the relative supply of highly educated workers (those with some college education), and a decrease in their relative demand. Some institutional factors were also at play in the decreasing trend in labour earnings inequality in Venezuela. Boada and Mayorca (2011) claimed that the continuous increases in the minimum wage mainly impacted the lower tail of the earnings distribution.

22.7 Conclusions

By Latin American standards, Venezuela experienced slow economic growth during the 2000s. The country underwent a recession in the early years of the period and during the international crisis of 2008. The Venezuelan economy returned to pre-recession GDP level in 2012, but GDP per capita was still below the pre-crisis level by the end of the period studied.

The evidence regarding the changes in labour market indicators shows that most of these improved between 2000 and 2012 and moved along with the business cycle, with a worsening at the beginning of the period (from 2001 to 2003), a following improvement, and a deterioration during the international crisis of 2008. Specifically, the unemployment rate exhibited an increase in the early years of the period, a downward trend in the following years, and a new increase during the international crisis, falling overall between 2000 and 2012. The composition of the employed population by occupational group improved from 2004 (the earliest year of that time series) to 2012, shifting overall from low-earning occupations such as elementary, agricultural, forestry and fishery, and services and sales occupations to better-paying occupations such as professional occupations, and did not suffer any impact from the international crisis in the aggregate. The employment composition by economic sector improved overall between 2000 and 2012 and exhibited a worsening at the beginning of the period and an improving trend in the following years which stalled during the international crisis and resumed in the years that followed. The educational level of the employed population improved steadily over the period. Finally, labour earnings fell in the early years of the period, improved from 2003 to 2007, deteriorated once again during the international crisis, and recovered the upward trend by the end of the period, improving overall from 2000 to 2012. The only employment and earnings indicators that did not improve over the period studied were the employment structure by occupational position and the share of registered workers with the social security system which remained essentially unchanged overall between 2000 and 2012. The moderate and extreme poverty rates, the rate of working poor households, and the Gini coefficient of household per capita income and labour earnings all decreased over the period following the movements of the business cycle.

Looking specifically at the international crisis of 2008, most labour market indicators were affected negatively by the crisis. The unemployment rate increased but then fell, recovering the pre-recession level by 2012. The employment structure by occupational position worsened during the international crisis and only some of the population groups recovered the pre-recession level by 2012. The improving trend in the employment structure by economic sector stalled during the crisis. Labour earnings were affected negatively by the crisis and, as of 2012, earnings of some employment categories had not returned to pre-crisis levels. The international crisis led to an interruption in the pattern of poverty reduction over time that was recovered in 2012 and to an increase in the Gini coefficient of household per capita income and labour earnings in 2010 that continued to the end of the period. The comparison between the effects of the international crisis of 2008 on labour market indicators and the effects generated by the domestic crisis of 2003 reveals that the crisis at the beginning of the 2000s impacted Venezuela more strongly. The crisis of 2003 generated a larger reduction in GDP, a larger increase in the unemployment rate, a larger increase in the share of low-earning positions in total employment, a decrease in the share of unregistered workers with the social security system, and a larger decrease in labour earnings compared to the Great Recession. Moreover, all poverty indicators reached a peak during the recession of 2003, while they stabilized during the international crisis of 2008.

Young workers and women had worse labour market outcomes over the period compared to adults and men respectively, and while young workers seem to be more vulnerable to macroeconomic crises compared to adults, men were more negatively affected by the crises compared to women. The unemployment rate was higher for young compared to adult workers, the shares of young employed workers in low-earning occupations and economic sectors were larger than the shares of adult workers, the percentage of young workers registered with the social security system was lower when compared to adults, and labour earnings of young workers were below those of adults. On the other hand, the share of young workers in low-earning occupational positions was lower compared to adults. In addition to the generally inferior situation of young workers in the labour market compared to adults, youth labour market indicators were more adversely affected by the episodes of crises. Disaggregating by gender, we found that men had better labour market outcomes than women, with the only exception being the share of workers registered with the social security system which was larger among women. However, men were hit hardest by both crises in most labour market indicators, with the increase in the unemployment rate during the crisis of 2003 and during the international crisis of 2008 being the only exceptions to this pattern.

In summary, notwithstanding Venezuela's massive downturn from 2001 to 2003 and the international crisis of 2008, Venezuelan labour market conditions were, in general, in a better state in 2012 than they were at the start of the millennium.

References

Alvarez, C. and S. Hanson (2009). 'Venezuela's Oil-Based Economy'. Council on Foreign Relations. Available at <http://www.cfr.org/world/venezuelas-oil-based-economy/p12089>.

Boada, A. J. and R. Mayorca (2011). 'El poder adquisitivo Venezolano desde 2000 hasta 2011: Análisis bajo dos perspectivas', *Revista Venezolana de Análisis de Coyuntura* 17 (1): 99–114.

CEDLAS and World Bank (2014). SEDLAC—Socio-Economic Database for Latin America and the Caribbean. Centro de Estudios Distributivos, Laborales y Sociales, Facultad de Ciencias Económicas, Universidad Nacional de La Plata and World Bank Poverty Group LCR. Available at <http://sedlac.econo.unlp.edu.ar/eng/index.php>, accessed 2014.

Cruces, G., G. Fields, D. Jaume, and M. Viollaz (2015). 'The Growth–Employment–Poverty Nexus in Latin America in the 2000s: Venezuela Country Study'. WIDER Working Paper 2015/084. Helsinki: UNU-WIDER.

Fernandez Salas, M. E. (2010). 'La extensión de la protección social frente a la vejez en el nuevo sistema de seguridad social Venezolano'. Paper prepared for the 6th International Conference of Policy and Research on Social Security. Maracaibo: Universidad de Zulia.

Gallo, C. R. (2010). 'Descomposición de los niveles de la desigualdad de ingresos laborales en Venezuela por factores componentes durante el periodo 1997–2007'. Colección Economía y Finanzas, Serie Documentos de Trabajo 114. Caracas: Banco Central de Venezuela.

Gasparini, L., S. Galiani, G. Cruces, and P. Acosta (2011). 'Educational Upgrading and Returns to Skills in Latin America: Evidence from a Supply–Demand Framework, 1990–2010'. IZA Working Paper 6244. Bonn: Institute for the Study of Labor.

Guerra, J. and V. Olivo (2009). 'La crisis global y su impacto en Venezuela'. Caracas: Instituto Latinoamerciano de Investigaciones Sociales.

ISSA (2014). 'Social Security Programs throughout the World: The Americas, 2013'. SSA Publication 13-11804. Washington, DC: Social Security Administration, Office of Retirement and Disability Policy and Office of Research, Evaluation and Statistics.

Viloria, C. (2011). 'Política social, desarrollo y pobreza en Venezuela'. Caracas: Instituto Latinoamerciano de Investigaciones Sociales.

Weisbrot, M. and J. Johnston (2012). 'Venezuela's Economic Recovery: Is it Sustainable?' Washington, DC: Center for Economic and Policy Research.

Weisbrot, M. and R. Ray (2010). 'Evolucion reciente de la economic Venezolana'. Washington, DC: Center for Economic and Policy Research.

World Bank (2014). World Development Indicators. Available at <http://data.worldbank.org/data-catalog/world-development-indicators>, accessed April 2014.

APPENDIX 1

Evolution of Labour Market Indicators over the 2000s by Country

Argentina

	00	01	02	03	04	05	06	07	08	09	10	11	12	13
Unemployment rate	14.78	18.40	17.88	15.41	12.58	10.60	9.30	7.53	7.61	8.60	7.41	7.17	7.25	...
Share of low-earnings occupations	...	...	...	...	...	...	...	...	...	...	...	...	...	...
Share of high-earnings occupations	...	...	...	...	...	...	...	...	...	...	...	...	...	...
Share of wage/salaried employees	72.13	71.29	72.07	74.06	74.24	74.40	75.79	76.70	76.28	75.88	76.97	77.08	77.25	...
Share of self-employed workers	22.07	23.41	22.98	20.78	20.46	20.36	19.01	17.99	18.50	19.07	17.79	17.93	18.04	...
Share of unpaid family workers	1.19	0.92	0.98	1.40	1.17	1.10	1.02	0.90	0.62	0.73	0.78	0.64	0.54	...
Share of workers in low-earnings sectors	39.7	39.0	35.4	38.3	39.3	39.7	41.0	39.8	40.4	39.9	39.6	39.9	39.5	...
Share of workers in high-earnings sectors	18.3	18.5	20.8	19.5	18.4	18.5	18.4	19.0	19.2	19.9	19.9	19.6	20.5	...
Share of low-educated workers	37.04	36.17	35.51	34.55	33.59	32.76	31.18	29.09	28.37	27.58	26.38	26.13	24.93	...
Share of high-educated workers	24.18	25.89	25.24	26.07	26.90	27.80	28.46	28.52	29.33	29.98	30.83	31.49	31.13	...
Share of workers registered with SS	61.59	61.40	55.95	50.62	52.01	54.42	57.27	60.59	62.96	64.11	65.40	65.55	65.01	...
Mean labour earnings	761.7	736.0	497.8	...	578.4	646.1	705.8	732.6	718.5	747.4	756.8	799.0	781.0	...
Poverty rate 2.5 dollars-a-day	14.16	18.64	29.17	22.02	16.96	13.32	10.32	8.75	8.21	8.04	6.14	4.60	4.69	...
Poverty rate 4 dollars-a-day	27.46	32.86	45.54	36.44	30.96	25.80	20.62	19.54	17.26	16.31	14.07	11.55	10.84	...
GINI of household per capita income	0.504	0.522	0.533	0.526	0.496	0.488	0.475	0.469	0.459	0.449	0.442	0.433	0.423	...
GINI of labour earnings	0.459	0.476	0.498	0.481	0.463	0.459	0.440	0.434	0.416	0.412	0.403	0.400	0.388	...

Source: Authors' calculations based on SEDLAC (CEDLAS and World Bank 2014).

Bolivia

	00	01	02	03	04	05	06	07	08	09	10	11	12	13
Unemployment rate	5.90	6.50	5.76	5.80	...	7.05	6.53	6.85	4.62	4.81	...	4.12	3.91	...
Share of low-earnings occupations	61.77	63.90	63.61	60.56	...	59.48	56.03	57.33	58.11	55.91	...	56.43	56.01	...
Share of high-earnings occupations	4.71	6.67	6.64	5.58	...	7.32	9.42	9.35	7.99	8.70	...	11.07	11.66	...
Share of wage/salaried employees	33.10	34.89	33.04	37.39	...	36.06	36.61	39.28	38.96	41.78	...	39.50	40.67	...
Share of self-employed workers	44.74	39.52	39.43	38.99	...	38.13	37.48	36.04	35.58	35.36	...	36.53	38.34	...
Share of unpaid family workers	20.11	23.18	22.74	18.45	...	20.11	21.10	18.85	19.29	17.73	...	18.19	14.20	...
Share of workers in low-earnings sectors	62.12	65.31	63.47	60.18	...	59.35	55.75	56.62	57.00	54.19	...	55.71	55.54	...
Share of workers in high-earnings sectors	10.91	10.85	9.89	10.86	...	12.07	15.31	13.82	14.91	14.46	...	15.26	16.36	...
Share of low-educated workers	60.05	59.64	61.33	59.36	...	55.94	56.04	50.84	50.26	48.15	...	45.91	43.17	...
Share of high-educated workers	13.35	14.02	11.83	11.78	...	14.25	13.12	17.30	14.79	16.77	...	20.50	21.76	...
Share of workers registered with SS	12.29	11.85	9.66	10.47	...	19.83	18.73	13.65	13.03	14.89	...	17.44	18.06	...
Mean labour earnings	447.3	415.4	435.7	443.6	...	471.0	498.9	466.1	503.6	530.9	...	573.8	589.3	...
Poverty rate 2.5 dollars-a-day	43.25	34.72	39.70	30.50	...	34.81	32.00	30.29	22.84	20.64	...	16.19	17.05	...
Poverty rate 4 dollars-a-day	59.90	53.61	57.75	51.43	...	53.58	48.52	47.43	40.41	35.14	...	29.16	29.49	...
GINI of household per capita income	0.619	0.549	0.600	0.549	...	0.583	0.567	0.553	0.514	0.494	...	0.462	0.465	...
GINI of labour earnings	0.594	0.559	0.574	0.529	...	0.563	0.539	0.536	0.508	0.495	...	0.454	0.467	...

Source: Authors' calculations based on SEDLAC (CEDLAS and World Bank 2014).

Brazil

	00	01	02	03	04	05	06	07	08	09	10	11	12	13
Unemployment rate	...	9.34	9.10	9.72	8.89	9.30	8.39	8.09	7.09	8.28	...	6.69	6.15	...
Share of low-earnings occupations	...	...	57.83	58.00	58.09	57.39	57.22	57.20	56.51	56.48	...	56.75	55.55	...
Share of high-earnings occupations	...	...	13.68	13.71	13.30	13.82	14.47	14.20	14.59	15.09	...	15.28	16.45	...
Share of wage/salaried employees	...	63.00	62.90	62.93	63.66	63.65	64.36	65.51	66.39	66.87	...	68.44	68.89	...
Share of self-employed workers	...	22.72	22.63	22.67	22.27	21.95	21.49	21.41	20.44	20.66	...	21.20	20.76	...
Share of unpaid family workers	...	9.95	10.12	10.12	9.87	10.09	9.62	9.25	8.63	8.11	...	6.93	6.55	...
Share of workers in low-earnings sectors	...	36.15	34.72	34.66	35.05	34.78	33.71	32.34	31.53	31.51	...	28.52	27.59	...
Share of workers in high-earnings sectors	...	23.01	25.04	25.04	25.13	24.80	25.92	26.08	26.65	26.80	...	27.42	28.05	...
Share of low-educated workers	...	63.79	61.96	59.97	58.56	56.83	54.69	53.05	50.72	48.93	...	46.38	44.95	...
Share of high-educated workers	...	8.68	9.05	9.39	9.56	9.93	10.65	13.23	13.04	13.93	...	15.45	14.55	...
Share of workers registered with SS	...	46.90	46.27	47.36	47.50	48.44	49.60	51.64	52.86	54.27	...	59.13	60.22	...
Mean labour earnings	...	539.9	533.6	503.8	498.4	515.8	546.4	569.1	580.3	593.9		641.3	680.1	...
Poverty rate 2.5 dollars-a-day	...	27.35	26.02	26.66	24.87	22.88	19.59	18.11	15.59	14.88	...	12.60	10.37	...
Poverty rate 4 dollars-a-day	...	43.05	42.13	42.78	40.81	38.37	34.81	31.84	29.14	27.44	...	24.46	21.49	...
GINI of household per capita income	...	0.588	0.583	0.576	0.566	0.564	0.559	0.549	0.542	0.536	...	0.527	0.523	...
GINI of labour earnings	...	0.563	0.560	0.552	0.544	0.540	0.538	0.525	0.518	0.515	...	0.499	0.496	...

Source: Authors' calculations based on SEDLAC (CEDLAS and World Bank 2014).

Chile

	00	01	02	03	04	05	06	07	08	09	10	11	12	13
Unemployment rate	10.37	...	...	9.98	...	...	7.32	...	...	10.22	...	7.73	...	...
Share of low-earnings occupations	42.81	...	...	41.64	...	...	44.45	...	...	45.57	...	44.13	...	...
Share of high-earnings occupations	16.65	...	...	16.17	...	...	13.42	...	...	13.75	...	17.08	...	...
Share of wage/salaried employees	74.39	...	...	74.28	...	...	75.67	...	...	76.28	...	77.42	...	...
Share of self-employed workers	20.00	...	...	20.40	...	...	20.34	...	...	20.13	...	20.29	...	...
Share of unpaid family workers	1.48	...	...	1.45	...	...	0.91	...	...	0.47	...	0.40	...	...
Share of workers in low-earnings sectors	35.15	...	...	35.15	...	...	34.93	...	...	34.78	...	36.17	...	...
Share of workers in high-earnings sectors	25.25	...	...	25.42	...	...	25.30	...	...	28.37	...	27.35	...	...
Share of low-educated workers	31.29	...	...	28.02	...	...	27.01	...	...	24.47	...	23.55	...	...
Share of high-educated workers	20.69	...	...	21.99	...	...	22.03	...	...	24.40	...	24.12	...	...
Share of workers registered with SS	62.77	...	...	63.65	...	...	66.66	...	...	66.03	...	68.76	...	...
Mean labour earnings	702.6	...	...	686.6	...	...	685.0	...	...	780.0		756.8	...	...
Poverty rate 2.5 dollars-a-day	8.89	...	...	7.64	...	...	5.12	...	...	4.09	...	2.88	...	...
Poverty rate 4 dollars-a-day	22.99	...	...	20.58	...	...	15.62	...	...	11.56	...	9.88	...	...
GINI of household per capita income	0.552	...	...	0.547	...	...	0.517	...	...	0.519	...	0.508	...	...
GINI of labour earnings	0.560	...	...	0.546	...	...	0.532	...	...	0.522	...	0.510	...	...

Source: Authors' calculations based on SEDLAC (CEDLAS and World Bank 2014).

Colombia

	00	01	02	03	04	05	06	07	08	09	10	11	12	13
Unemployment rate	...	13.58	14.33	13.57	12.06	11.08	...	...	10.88	11.63	10.86	9.92	9.78	9.00
Share of low-earnings occupations	...	46.15	45.34	46.00	45.20	45.36	...	...	39.40	42.64	42.42	41.72	41.47	41.02
Share of high-earnings occupations	...	10.50	11.49	11.37	11.74	12.16	...	...	12.62	11.36	11.95	12.41	12.73	13.62
Share of wage/salaried employees	...	50.00	50.77	49.58	49.35	52.00	...	...	49.06	48.50	47.36	47.07	47.28	48.25
Share of self-employed workers	...	40.89	40.15	40.54	40.94	38.48	...	...	42.55	42.60	43.07	43.74	43.33	42.79
Share of unpaid family workers	...	4.70	4.47	5.30	4.55	4.22	...	...	3.72	3.91	4.56	4.16	4.44	4.37
Share of workers in low-earnings sectors	...	54.03	52.79	52.18	50.58	51.94	...	... |	48.08	49.01	49.07	48.40	48.45	48.39
Share of workers in high-earnings sectors	...	21.39	21.79	22.71	22.94	22.50	...	...	24.45	24.14	23.37	24.11	24.14	25.43
Share of low-educated workers	...	56.11	54.36	54.24	52.70	50.81	...	...	47.09	48.36	48.00	45.30	45.37	42.60
Share of high-educated workers	...	12.79	13.34	13.62	14.43	15.12	...	...	16.88	15.97	15.60	16.51	16.18	17.83
Share of workers registered with SS	...	...	...	...	...	...	...	...	33.22	31.87	30.92	32.00	32.61	34.60
Mean labour earnings	...	402.0	| 469.3	408.1	452.6	464.9	...	...	516.9	537.1	543.5	546.0	545.6	573.5
Poverty rate 2.5 dollars-a-day	...	39.04	| 29.84	31.05	28.37	25.30	...	...	24.45	21.92	19.56	16.97	17.50	15.16
Poverty rate 4 dollars-a-day	...	60.33	| 49.55	51.96	49.41	45.24	...	...	41.64	39.61	36.51	33.14	32.92	30.75
GINI of household per capita income	...	0.565	| 0.574	0.543	0.560	0.550	...	...	0.558	0.557	0.553	0.535	0.534	0.533
GINI of labour earnings	...	0.517	| 0.551	0.510	0.530	0.519	...	...	0.502	0.514	0.516	0.504	0.506	0.499

Note: Vertical lines are used to indicate when the series are not fully comparable before and after that line.

Source: Authors' calculations based on SEDLAC (CEDLAS and World Bank 2014).

Costa Rica

	00	01	02	03	04	05	06	07	08	09	10	11	12	13
Unemployment rate	...	6.04	6.39	6.65	6.44	6.63	5.92	4.55	4.93	7.82	7.29	7.66	7.77	...
Share of low-earnings occupations	...	47.48	48.26	47.86	47.17	47.51	46.58	45.98	43.95	44.27	47.46	48.15	...	...
Share of high-earnings occupations	...	23.73	23.40	24.48	24.37	24.46	24.87	25.26	27.52	27.85	26.04	26.65	...	...
Share of wage/salaried employees	...	69.06	68.53	69.58	68.84	71.56	70.85	73.17	72.95	72.77	76.11	76.00	76.09	...
Share of self-employed workers	...	20.38	20.80	19.35	20.77	18.90	19.42	17.93	18.06	18.52	18.87	18.77	18.69	...
Share of unpaid family workers	...	2.54	2.74	2.42	2.24	2.04	1.97	1.64	1.46	1.49	1.65	1.50	1.66	...
Share of workers in low-earnings sectors	...	28.96	28.75	27.52	27.40	28.94	27.71	26.45	24.72	24.14	28.00	27.10	26.44	...
Share of workers in high-earnings sectors	...	26.21	26.34	26.82	26.28	25.78	26.01	26.57	28.06	28.82	28.21	28.46	30.26	...
Share of low-educated workers	...	57.32	55.40	53.23	53.27	53.38	52.25	51.06	49.08	47.55	50.03	48.80	46.53	...
Share of high-educated workers	...	15.68	16.45	17.14	17.28	17.59	18.64	18.67	20.02	20.77	19.16	19.73	20.85	...
Share of workers registered with SS	...	50.70	50.53	50.35	51.31	50.68	51.23	53.47	54.69	55.26	55.65	54.58	56.06	...
Mean labour earnings	...	749.7	736.3	740.3	694.7	675.3	703.5	764.7	784.8	832.2	794.1	812.0	833.0	...
Poverty rate 2.5 dollars-a-day	...	13.78	13.55	13.07	12.26	10.76	10.58	7.27	6.87	7.46	4.53	5.09	4.73	...
Poverty rate 4 dollars-a-day	...	26.72	26.45	24.87	25.93	23.07	22.98	17.88	17.01	17.42	12.70	13.01	12.18	...
GINI of household per capita income	...	0.501	0.500	0.492	0.482	0.473	0.489	0.492	0.486	0.504	0.480	0.485	0.485	...
GINI of labour earnings	...	0.464	0.463	0.454	0.435	0.440	0.454	0.459	0.455	0.459	0.466	0.477	0.471	...

Note: Vertical lines are used to indicate when the series are not fully comparable before and after that line.

Source: Authors' calculations based on SEDLAC (CEDLAS and World Bank 2014).

Dominican Republic

	00	01	02	03	04	05	06	07	08	09	10	11	12	13
Unemployment rate	4.72	5.49	4.11	4.92	4.21	4.25	3.64	3.20	2.07	3.85	3.14	3.94	4.92	...
Share of low-earnings occupations	48.77	48.84	49.98	47.81	48.52	48.63	49.84	50.28	50.42	52.54	52.08	53.59	52.96	...
Share of high-earnings occupations	15.35	15.53	15.39	17.06	16.47	16.24	16.74	16.34	17.17	17.03	16.81	15.81	16.76	...
Share of wage/salaried employees	56.90	54.30	53.29	54.80	55.18	52.83	53.56	54.23	52.14	51.07	50.62	51.33	53.18	...
Share of self-employed workers	38.98	40.26	42.16	40.27	38.57	39.99	40.04	39.14	40.20	42.56	43.36	43.79	41.87	...
Share of unpaid family workers	1.53	1.58	1.36	1.44	1.53	2.76	2.52	2.41	3.62	1.51	2.27	1.70	1.82	...
Share of workers in low-earnings sectors	31.21	28.51	29.71	27.65	28.66	27.59	27.40	27.55	26.54	25.84	25.55	25.85	25.70	...
Share of workers in high-earnings sectors	15.62	15.77	16.16	17.22	15.74	16.24	15.86	16.20	17.30	16.77	17.28	17.51	16.77	...
Share of low-educated workers	56.47	57.22	55.21	54.36	53.52	53.69	52.16	50.13	49.63	49.56	48.32	47.27	46.09	...
Share of high-educated workers	16.15	15.11	16.55	16.91	17.27	16.51	16.84	17.20	19.26	18.76	18.52	17.24	18.71	...
Share of workers registered with SS	...	...	...	...	...	46.66	53.89	64.07	71.43	71.75	74.72	71.18	70.89	...
Mean labour earnings	330.0	327.0	307.6	263.1	217.3	257.8	270.2	258.9	251.7	271.3	261.1	248.1	241.8	...
Poverty rate 2.5 dollars-a-day	15.71	15.84	17.61	21.83	27.77 |	21.08	18.66	17.90	18.44	16.40	16.14	13.97	14.55	...
Poverty rate 4 dollars-a-day	32.63	33.27	33.07	41.73	49.50 |	40.48	37.48	36.41	37.89	34.71	35.12	33.34	33.26	...
GINI of household per capita income	0.519	0.504	0.500	0.520	0.519 |	0.499	0.519	0.487	0.490	0.489	0.472	0.474	0.457	...
GINI of labour earnings	0.499	0.487	0.483	0.481	0.479	0.476	0.484	0.464	0.457	0.471	0.464	0.468	0.451	...

Note: Vertical lines are used to indicate when the series are not fully comparable before and after that line.

Source: Authors' calculations based on SEDLAC (CEDLAS and World Bank 2014).

Ecuador

	00	01	02	03	04	05	06	07	08	09	10	11	12	13
Unemployment rate	...	...	...	13.19	8.50	8.37	6.72	5.48	6.43	6.86	5.22	4.50	4.40	...
Share of low-earnings occupations	...	...	...	57.88	57.42	56.80	57.12	55.56	56.22	56.75	54.43	52.91	52.42	...
Share of high-earnings occupations	...	...	...	7.78	8.51	8.56	8.44	8.96	8.76	8.61	9.42	8.49	9.65	...
Share of wage/salaried employees	...	...	...	55.09	51.19	53.41	53.38	54.10	55.74	54.13	55.30	52.93	54.06	...
Share of self-employed workers	...	...	...	31.29	30.64	30.53	28.90	29.76	29.08	30.68	31.64	34.82	33.16	...
Share of unpaid family workers	...	...	...	8.73	11.47	9.77	11.70	10.93	9.89	10.99	9.58	8.72	9.01	...
Share of workers in low-earnings sectors	...	...	...	42.39	42.61	42.35	41.55	40.68	39.90	40.07	38.76	38.13	37.92	...
Share of workers in high-earnings sectors	...	...	...	11.24	10.83	11.22	10.72	10.70	12.00	11.42	12.16	12.59	13.12	...
Share of low-educated workers	...	...	...	54.58	55.04	53.52	52.38	51.93	50.99	50.64	48.69	46.92	45.55	...
Share of high-educated workers	...	...	...	18.39	18.81	18.73	18.63	19.21	19.56	20.14	21.38	21.31	22.24	...
Share of workers registered with SS	...	...	...	32.97	33.53	33.15	33.30	34.04	36.00	39.95	45.24	53.30	54.67	...
Mean labour earnings	...	...	...	457.6	511.1	502.6	529.2	575.1	546.8	515.7	559.7	559.0	589.6	...
Poverty rate 2.5 dollars-a-day	...	...	...	31.33	28.81	25.61	20.00	19.81	19.29	18.85	15.88	13.55	12.85	...
Poverty rate 4 dollars-a-day	...	...	...	51.44	48.03	43.60	38.34	38.11	36.75	37.11	33.43	29.54	27.76	...
GINI of household per capita income	...	...	...	0.545	0.536	0.536	0.529	0.539	0.502	0.489	0.489	0.458	0.462	...
GINI of labour earnings	...	...	...	0.515	0.527	0.501	0.489	0.524	0.482	0.466	0.463	0.436	0.431	...

Source: Authors' calculations based on SEDLAC (CEDLAS and World Bank 2014).

Honduras

	00	01	02	03	04	05	06	07	08	09	10	11	12	13
Unemployment rate	...	4.60	4.24	5.54	5.99	4.92	3.58	3.15	3.11	3.28	4.10	4.42	3.73	...
Share of low-earnings occupations	...	...	...	...	...	61.93	62.49	63.07	61.13	62.12	61.71	59.72	61.34	...
Share of high-earnings occupations	...	...	...	...	...	12.86	13.95	14.19	15.03	13.19	12.90	13.54	13.00	...
Share of wage/salaried employees	...	47.04	47.25	50.12	49.17	47.24	47.68	48.94	49.00	47.02	44.23	46.83	42.91	...
Share of self-employed workers	...	33.58	33.22	32.21	29.34	31.29	31.19	29.06	28.52	31.50	32.07	30.71	34.73	...
Share of unpaid family workers	...	9.00	10.20	8.61	9.58	9.91	9.25	8.25	8.81	8.94	10.48	11.34	10.77	...
Share of workers in low-earnings sectors	...	46.51	52.73	48.94	49.67	48.21	50.91	48.84	47.70	48.66	49.91	49.43	50.11	...
Share of workers in high-earnings sectors	...	9.83	9.59	9.35	9.83	9.68	10.19	10.22	11.01	9.84	9.94	9.40	9.59	...
Share of low-educated workers	...	77.60	79.51	79.24	76.52	76.15	75.48	74.48	72.23	73.22	70.97	69.32	70.19	...
Share of high-educated workers	...	5.10	5.63	4.69	5.37	5.22	5.52	5.91	6.52	5.60	6.31	6.63	6.21	...
Share of workers registered with SS	...	...	...	...	...	...	6.19	5.00	6.34	4.40	5.63	5.42	5.21	...
Mean labour earnings	...	430.1	393.2	394.6	404.1	372.1	391.6	431.2	457.9	421.2	416.3	448.4	395.0	...
Poverty rate 2.5 dollars-a-day	...	37.04	47.95	47.89	46.77	47.41	42.04	36.96	34.01	31.34	33.99	37.40	42.42	...
Poverty rate 4 dollars-a-day	...	55.91	64.28	64.38	63.29	64.16	58.80	56.00	52.05	50.04	53.30	56.39	61.28	...
GINI of household per capita income	...	0.539	0.577	0.583	0.581	0.593	0.573	0.560	0.556	0.516	0.534	0.572	0.573	...
GINI of labour earnings	...	0.541	0.545	0.558	0.556	0.575	0.546	0.553	0.554	0.526	0.543	0.582	0.580	...

Source: Authors' calculations based on SEDLAC (CEDLAS and World Bank 2014).

Mexico

	00	01	02	03	04	05	06	07	08	09	10	11	12	13
Unemployment rate	2.18	...	2.95	...	3.77	3.77	3.31	...	4.48	...	5.66	...	4.23	...
Share of low-earnings occupations	32.04	...	31.26	...	28.91	28.98	29.16	...	28.98	...	41.41	...	43.08	...
Share of high-earnings occupations	14.95	...	13.31	...	14.60	15.26	15.26	...	15.60	...	18.94	...	17.86	...
Share of wage/salaried employees	66.14	...	65.73	...	70.22	68.86	67.16	...	71.78	...	72.94	...	68.31	...
Share of self-employed workers	21.81	...	23.21	...	21.17	21.39	22.61	...	12.80	...	12.76	...	15.06	...
Share of unpaid family workers	7.26	...	7.02	...	5.31	5.94	6.17	...	5.49	...	4.87	...	5.91	...
Share of workers in low-earnings sectors	31.52	...	30.13	...	26.74	26.56	26.24	...	26.11	...	25.93	...	28.12	...
Share of workers in high-earnings sectors	20.67	...	20.74	...	22.74	22.65	21.92	...	22.91	...	23.43	...	22.24	...
Share of low-educated workers	49.48	...	48.48	...	45.01	44.06	42.69	...	40.98	...	37.86	...	37.19	...
Share of high-educated workers	15.03	...	13.38	...	15.27	15.43	15.39	...	15.38	...	17.48	...	16.56	...
Share of workers registered with SS	45.63	...	41.58	...	40.32	39.38	40.99	...	39.61	...	37.15	...	34.94	...
Mean labour earnings	598.6	...	575.4	...	591.7	616.5	616.6	...	622.0	...	554.6	...	563.9	...
Poverty rate 2.5 dollars-a-day	19.54	...	17.15	...	14.73	14.98	11.83	...	13.57	...	12.61	...	11.45	...
Poverty rate 4 dollars-a-day	36.97	...	34.10	...	30.82	29.89	27.03	...	28.54	...	28.16	...	27.65	...
GINI of household per capita income	0.536	...	0.510	...	0.507	0.509	0.495	...	0.502	...	0.472	...	0.491	...
GINI of labour earnings	0.520	...	0.515	...	0.497	0.507	0.505	...	0.508	...	0.474	...	0.512	...

Note: Vertical lines are used to indicate when the series are not fully comparable before and after that line.

Source: Authors' calculations based on SEDLAC (CEDLAS and World Bank 2014).

Panama

	00	01	02	03	04	05	06	07	08	09	10	11	12	13
Unemployment rate	...	9.60	9.28	9.60	8.63	8.95	7.75	5.68	5.06	6.11	6.02	4.05	3.66	...
Share of low-earnings occupations	...	52.77	53.78	53.43	52.32	53.47	53.34	52.66	51.33	50.15	49.46 |	49.12	49.62	...
Share of high-earnings occupations	...	16.37	16.45	16.82	16.20	16.01	15.57	16.35	16.80	17.56	18.19 |	23.77	24.61	...
Share of wage/salaried employees	...	63.20	62.45	61.71	62.63	61.77	62.99	65.33	66.06	64.67	65.89	68.00	68.06	...
Share of self-employed workers	...	29.45	30.29	30.75	30.00	30.33	28.96	26.44	25.87	27.13	26.48	25.20	24.39	...
Share of unpaid family workers	...	4.82	4.32	4.64	4.14	4.83	4.97	5.18	4.86	5.09	4.42	3.75	4.80	...
Share of workers in low-earnings sectors	...	31.72	31.47	31.32	30.27	30.12	30.49	29.83	28.50	28.05	27.07	25.41	25.26	...
Share of workers in high-earnings sectors	...	20.66	20.31	20.63	20.93	20.25	20.13	20.50	20.36	21.18	21.94	23.72	23.46	...
Share of low-educated workers	...	45.35	44.70	43.17	41.60	42.02	40.56	39.27	37.15	36.98	36.59	34.38	33.52	...
Share of high-educated workers	...	18.54	18.84	19.89	20.99	20.60	21.30	20.67	21.48	22.19	22.52	25.35	26.03	...
Share of workers registered with SS	...	...	...	...	52.82	51.96	53.28	55.40	57.42	58.07	58.71	61.85	62.34	...
Mean labour earnings	...	641.7	630.7	637.7	626.7	596.3	605.5	606.2	610.3	637.1	643.7	715.8	730.5	...
Poverty rate 2.5 dollars-a-day	...	28.70	25.41	24.09	22.77	22.48	22.23	15.89	14.45	12.30	13.16	11.60	11.78	...
Poverty rate 4 dollars-a-day	...	43.39	40.72	39.04	38.33	37.48	37.14	28.63	26.18	25.34	23.96	21.25	20.90	...
GINI of household per capita income	...	0.565	0.564	0.561	0.549	0.538	0.549	0.526	0.526	0.520	0.519	0.518	0.519	...
GINI of labour earnings	...	0.501	0.535	0.528	0.521	0.515	0.515	0.491	0.480	0.484	0.472	0.475	0.481	...

Note: Vertical lines are used to indicate when the series are not fully comparable before and after that line.

Source: Authors' calculations based on SEDLAC (CEDLAS and World Bank 2014).

Peru

	00	01	02	03	04	05	06	07	08	09	10	11	12	13
Unemployment rate	...	...	...	5.06	5.18	5.16	4.54	4.55	4.41	4.29	3.90	3.77	3.45	...
Share of low-earnings occupations	...	...	...	61.74	63.18	63.25	61.84	59.37	57.92	55.69	54.82	53.82	52.59	...
Share of high-earnings occupations	...	...	...	12.95	12.39	11.85	12.60	14.11	13.95	14.47	14.17	14.23	14.99	...
Share of wage/salaried employees	...	...	...	39.78	40.96	41.33	43.22	44.58	45.09	45.31	45.22	45.26	46.64	...
Share of self-employed workers	...	...	...	37.34	36.00	36.46	35.22	35.85	36.34	36.04	36.56	36.81	36.42	...
Share of unpaid family workers	...	...	...	17.57	17.54	16.57	15.96	13.65	12.95	13.00	12.23	12.49	11.35	...
Share of workers in low-earnings sectors	...	...	...	44.44	43.97	44.08	43.02	40.17	39.21	38.04	37.10	36.83	35.83	...
Share of workers in high-earnings sectors	...	...	...	10.89	11.24	11.00	11.90	12.47	12.46	13.16	12.96	13.07	13.76	...
Share of low-educated workers	...	...	...	45.32	44.20	44.29	42.60	39.80	39.06	38.75	38.43	37.87	36.07	...
Share of high-educated workers	...	...	...	17.65	18.13	17.99	18.98	20.95	20.83	21.30	21.26	21.88	23.04	...
Share of workers registered with SS	...	...	...	14.85	20.10	19.71	22.57	25.96	26.47	28.82	29.69	30.49	32.39	...
Mean labour earnings	...	...	...	408.3	375.3	368.9	386.3	413.7	423.3	449.9	457.8	467.3	486.3	...
Poverty rate 2.5 dollars-a-day	...	...	...	28.29	25.24	27.21	22.98	21.22	17.23	14.61	12.64	12.75	11.07	...
Poverty rate 4 dollars-a-day	...	...	...	47.30	44.64	46.67	41.38	37.62	33.55	30.04	26.87	25.80	22.29	...
GINI of household per capita income	...	...	...	0.538	0.487	0.493	0.491	0.496	0.469	0.462	0.449	0.457	0.453	...
GINI of labour earnings	...	...	...	0.559	0.518	0.522	0.514	0.524	0.513	0.509	0.506	0.496	0.489	...

Source: Authors' calculations based on SEDLAC (CEDLAS and World Bank 2014).

Paraguay

	00	01	02	03	04	05	06	07	08	09	10	11	12	13
Unemployment rate	...	...	...	5.06	5.18	5.16	4.54	4.55	4.41	4.29	3.90	3.77	3.45	...
Share of low-earnings occupations	...	...	...	61.74	63.18	63.25	61.84	59.37	57.92	55.69	54.82	53.82	52.59	...
Share of high-earnings occupations	...	...	...	12.95	12.39	11.85	12.60	14.11	13.95	14.47	14.17	14.23	14.99	...
Share of wage/salaried employees	...	...	...	39.78	40.96	41.33	43.22	44.58	45.09	45.31	45.22	45.26	46.64	...
Share of self-employed workers	...	...	...	37.34	36.00	36.46	35.22	35.85	36.34	36.04	36.56	36.81	36.42	...
Share of unpaid family workers	...	...	...	17.57	17.54	16.57	15.96	13.65	12.95	13.00	12.23	12.49	11.35	...
Share of workers in low-earnings sectors	...	...	...	44.44	43.97	44.08	43.02	40.17	39.21	38.04	37.10	36.83	35.83	...
Share of workers in high-earnings sectors	...	...	...	10.89	11.24	11.00	11.90	12.47	12.46	13.16	12.96	13.07	13.76	...
Share of low-educated workers	...	...	...	45.32	44.20	44.29	42.60	39.80	39.06	38.75	38.43	37.87	36.07	...
Share of high-educated workers	...	...	...	17.65	18.13	17.99	18.98	20.95	20.83	21.30	21.26	21.88	23.04	...
Share of workers registered with SS	...	...	...	14.85	20.10	19.71	22.57	25.96	26.47	28.82	29.69	30.49	32.39	...
Mean labour earnings	...	...	...	408.3	375.3	368.9	386.3	413.7	423.3	449.9	457.8	467.3	486.3	...
Poverty rate 2.5 dollars-a-day	...	...	...	28.29	25.24	27.21	22.98	21.22	17.23	14.61	12.64	12.75	11.07	...
Poverty rate 4 dollars-a-day	...	...	...	47.30	44.64	46.67	41.38	37.62	33.55	30.04	26.87	25.80	22.29	...
GINI of household per capita income	...	...	...	0.538	0.487	0.493	0.491	0.496	0.469	0.462	0.449	0.457	0.453	...
GINI of labour earnings	...	...	...	0.559	0.518	0.522	0.514	0.524	0.513	0.509	0.506	0.496	0.489	...

Source: Authors' calculations based on SEDLAC (CEDLAS and World Bank 2014).

El Salvador

	00	01	02	03	04	05	06	07	08	09	10	11	12	13
Unemployment rate	6.86	7.00	6.20	6.95	6.78	7.19	6.50	6.39	5.92	7.34	7.04	6.64	6.06	...
Share of low-earnings occupations	57.32	56.97	55.78	54.94	55.73	55.11	55.19	54.76	55.86	55.56	55.21	55.54	55.86	...
Share of high-earnings occupations	12.59	12.19	12.77	12.84	11.98	13.39	12.85	12.91	12.73	12.63	11.83	11.34	11.78	...
Share of wage/salaried employees	57.35	58.15	56.49	59.26	60.42	57.67	61.17	59.88	58.90	56.88	57.75	57.88	57.65	...
Share of self-employed workers	30.58	28.78	31.10	28.86	28.65	29.93	27.12	28.15	29.22	30.82	30.42	30.22	29.48	...
Share of unpaid family workers	6.54	8.32	7.66	7.10	6.55	7.87	7.25	7.48	7.54	8.04	7.78	8.20	8.70	...
Share of workers in low-earnings sectors	38.97	38.39	36.54	34.99	35.47	35.00	34.32	33.78	35.98	36.52	35.92	36.76	36.28	...
Share of workers in high-earnings sectors	14.57	13.72	13.38	13.60	13.63	14.01	13.51	13.95	13.80	13.69	14.03	14.69	14.44	...
Share of low-educated workers	60.88	59.21	57.68	56.92	55.89	55.65	54.05	53.49	53.63	53.58	52.46	53.27	51.69	...
Share of high-educated workers	10.57	10.43	11.19	11.11	11.04	12.38	12.03	11.89	12.19	12.32	11.90	11.36	11.95	...
Share of workers registered with SS	31.07	30.81	31.17	31.28	30.32	30.41	31.50	31.33	30.72	28.65	28.03	28.03	27.65	...
Mean labour earnings	549.5	523.6	527.6	...	476.9	487.4	482.7	486.2	464.0	461.2	440.5	423.0	426.3	...
Poverty rate 2.5 dollars-a-day	23.78	25.32	25.16	...	22.34	22.29	18.68	15.16	20.21	18.72	19.75	16.57	14.68	...
Poverty rate 4 dollars-a-day	41.35	42.29	42.76	...	41.57	41.77	38.84	35.66	40.99	38.85	39.31	37.87	34.84	...
GINI of household per capita income	0.513	0.510	0.515	...	0.473	0.478	0.454	0.452	0.466	0.459	0.445	0.424	0.418	...
GINI of labour earnings	0.504	0.502	0.520	...	0.472	0.489	0.475	0.471	0.466	0.498	0.480	0.462	0.470	...

Source: Authors' calculations based on SEDLAC (CEDLAS and World Bank 2014).

Uruguay

	00	01	02	03	04	05	06	07	08	09	10	11	12	13
Unemployment rate	13.54	15.24	16.91	16.81	13.05	12.12	11.31	9.55	8.00	7.63	7.04	6.60	6.35	...
Share of low-earnings occupations	53.17	53.78	52.63	53.76	52.59	52.60	53.95	53.24	52.88	51.62	52.41	50.25	...	...
Share of high-earnings occupations	22.09	21.86	22.37	22.59	23.19	23.03	21.67	22.71	22.60	23.72	22.90	24.75	...	...
Share of wage/salaried employees	72.86	71.04	69.98	70.15	70.27	71.22	71.28	71.16	71.48	71.84	72.46	73.94	74.24	...
Share of self-employed workers	21.99	23.65	24.81	25.07	24.65	23.53	22.97	23.00	22.60	22.31	21.95	20.61	20.59	...
Share of unpaid family workers	1.44	1.37	1.50	1.35	1.56	1.31	1.43	1.41	1.29	1.37	1.06	0.87	0.92	...
Share of workers in low-earnings sectors	26.48	26.10	24.68	24.93	23.60	24.05	24.30	24.70	24.27	23.60	24.12	23.38	21.70	...
Share of workers in high-earnings sectors	23.24	24.23	24.99	24.52	23.79	23.51	22.21	21.76	21.95	22.39	21.76	22.94	23.55	...
Share of low-educated workers	43.99	39.78	38.87	38.72	37.10	36.85	39.21	39.10	41.22	39.07	40.25	35.39	34.67	...
Share of high-educated workers	15.40	18.38	19.52	19.52	20.54	20.93	18.67	18.92	17.97	18.86	17.69	21.00	19.57	...
Share of workers registered with SS	...	64.14	62.88	60.56	59.39	61.32	64.78	65.24	66.53	67.90	68.37	72.37	73.83	...
Mean labour earnings	723.6	654.0	582.6	483.8	483.5	486.7	524.2	554.5	591.9	641.2	627.0	668.2	661.3	...
Poverty rate 2.5 dollars-a-day	3.59	4.78	6.41	7.73	9.78	8.90	7.25	6.25	4.18	3.51	2.84	2.57	2.61	...
Poverty rate 4 dollars-a-day	11.22	13.92	17.78	22.76	23.72	21.60	20.76	18.94	14.17	12.00	11.28	8.85	8.32	...
GINI of household per capita income	0.444	0.462	0.466	0.462	0.471	0.459	0.473	0.478	0.465	0.464	0.454	0.436	0.415	...
GINI of labour earnings	0.462	0.485	0.495	0.500	0.505	0.499	0.504	0.507	0.502	0.495	0.479	0.450	0.420	...

Source: Authors' calculations based on SEDLAC (CEDLAS and World Bank 2014).

Venezuela

	00	01	02	03	04	05	06	07	08	09	10	11	12	13
Unemployment rate	13.23	12.78	16.17	16.78	13.94	11.35	9.33	7.47	6.85	8.05	8.45	7.84	7.41	...
Share of low-earnings occupations	...	...	...	...	53.85	50.78	50.75	50.04	49.83	49.91	49.65	49.03	48.96	...
Share of high-earnings occupations	...	...	...	...	15.25	17.47	16.66	16.71	17.00	17.41	18.07	18.12	19.08	...
Share of wage/salaried employees	56.58	56.22	55.17	53.86	55.81	57.79	58.51	59.30	58.43	57.73	56.95	57.19	58.78	...
Share of self-employed workers	36.60	34.81	36.69	38.34	37.43	35.72	35.77	35.55	36.30	37.72	39.00	38.46	37.19	...
Share of unpaid family workers	1.71	2.34	2.61	2.72	1.96	1.60	1.22	0.98	1.18	0.77	0.59	0.88	0.77	...
Share of workers in low-earnings sectors	41.54	41.39	42.58	42.64	41.13	40.39	38.31	37.87	37.52	37.86	37.56	37.03	37.35	...
Share of workers in high-earnings sectors	17.90	19.51	19.77	19.72	19.33	20.07	20.95	21.39	22.06	22.30	22.76	23.11	23.05	...
Share of low-educated workers	52.55	50.59	50.37	50.25	49.37	46.21	44.18	42.95	41.24	40.02	38.35	36.75	37.19	...
Share of high-educated workers	15.72	16.28	16.21	16.40	16.92	18.06	19.63	20.24	21.44	23.38	25.10	26.22	27.51	...
Share of workers registered with SS	68.56	64.82	61.48	58.83	60.16	60.33	60.85	62.86	66.03	71.13	70.83	72.99	69.12	...
Mean labour earnings	380.4	402.3	346.0	297.0	330.9	398.2	463.0	501.7	500.4	493.0	469.3	455.7	511.0	...
Poverty rate 2.5 dollars-a-day	29.83	27.49	36.96	42.56	36.30	28.25	18.09	12.74	11.92	11.92	12.13	12.42	11.05	...
Poverty rate 4 dollars-a-day	51.67	49.45	58.52	64.79	59.30	48.52	36.33	29.02	27.77	27.57	28.06	28.99	24.66	...
GINI of household per capita income	0.440	0.464	0.473	0.460	0.453	0.474	0.433	0.415	0.401	0.400	0.384	0.388	0.402	...
GINI of labour earnings	0.403	0.437	0.438	0.425	0.412	0.436	0.382	0.365	0.352	0.343	0.310	0.319	0.342	...

Source: Authors' calculations based on SEDLAC (CEDLAS and World Bank 2014).

References

CEDLAS and World Bank (2014). SEDLAC—Socio-Economic Database for Latin America and the Caribbean. Centro de Estudios Distributivos, Laborales y Sociales, Facultad de Ciencias Económicas, Universidad Nacional de La Plata and World Bank Poverty Group LCR. Available at <http://sedlac.econo.unlp.edu.ar/eng/index.php>, accessed 2014.

APPENDIX 2

Cross-Country Relationship between Changes in Labour Market Indicators and Changes in Macroeconomic Variables during the 2000s

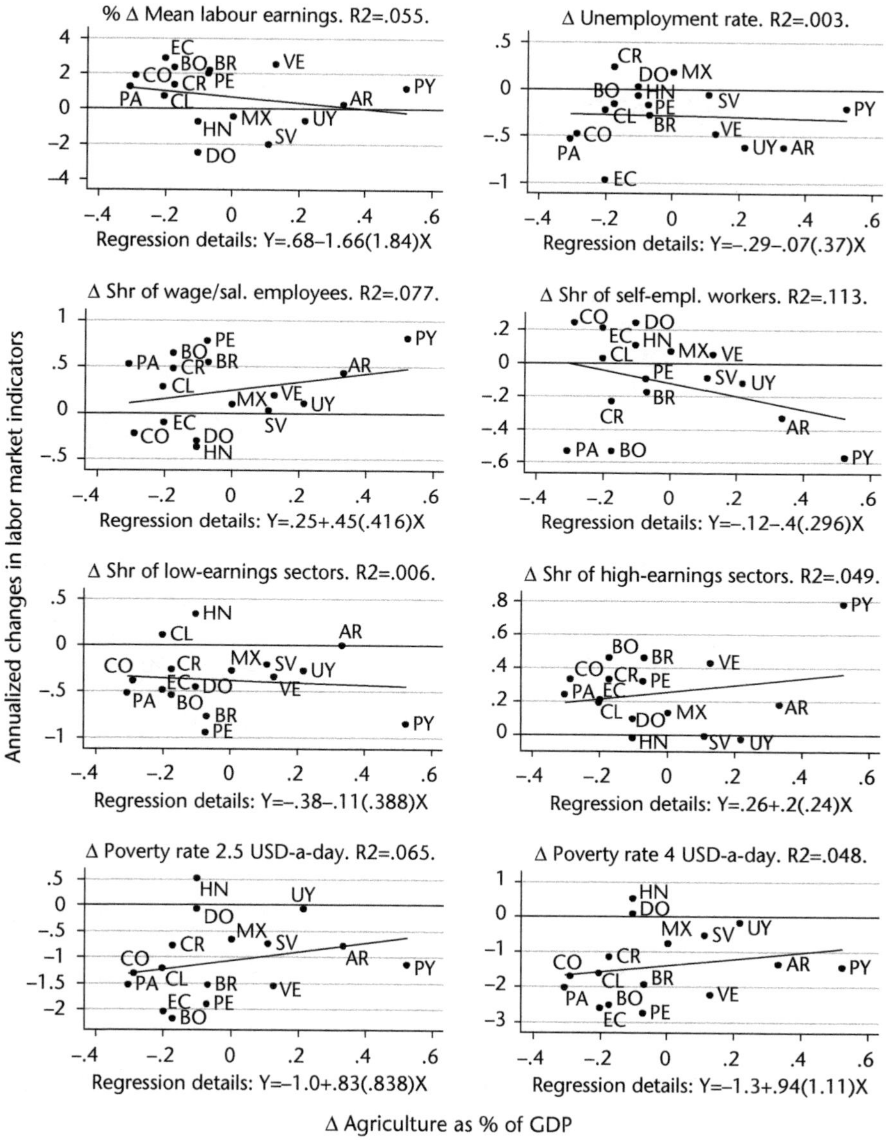

Figure A2.A Annualized change in agriculture's percentage share of GDP

Note: The vertical axes display the annualized change in each labour market indicator. Δ denotes changes in percentage points and %Δ denotes percentage changes. The line represents the linear regression specified at the bottom of the figure. Robust standard error of the slope coefficient between parentheses. R-squared of the regression indicated along the title.

Source: Authors' calculations based on SEDLAC (CEDLAS and World Bank 2014), World Development Indicators (World Bank 2014), and CEPALSTAT (UN-ECLAC 2015).

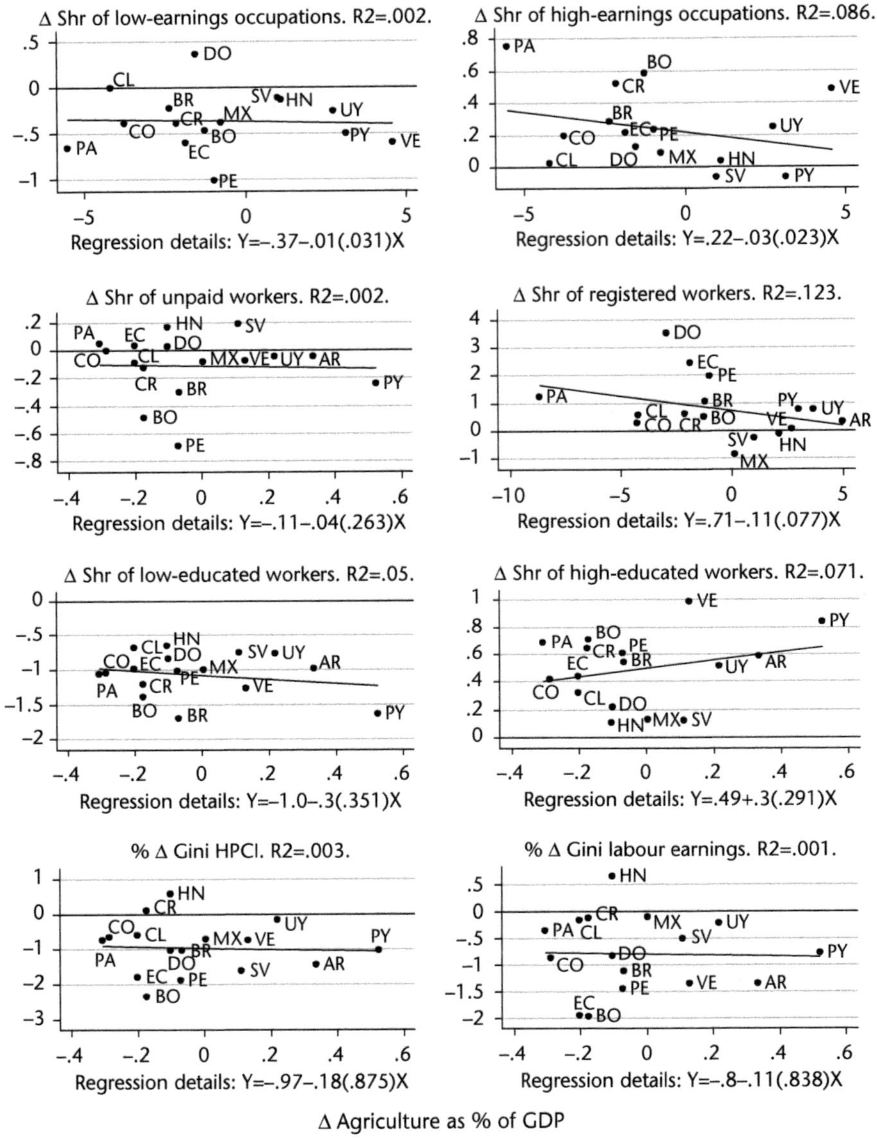

Figure A2.A Continued

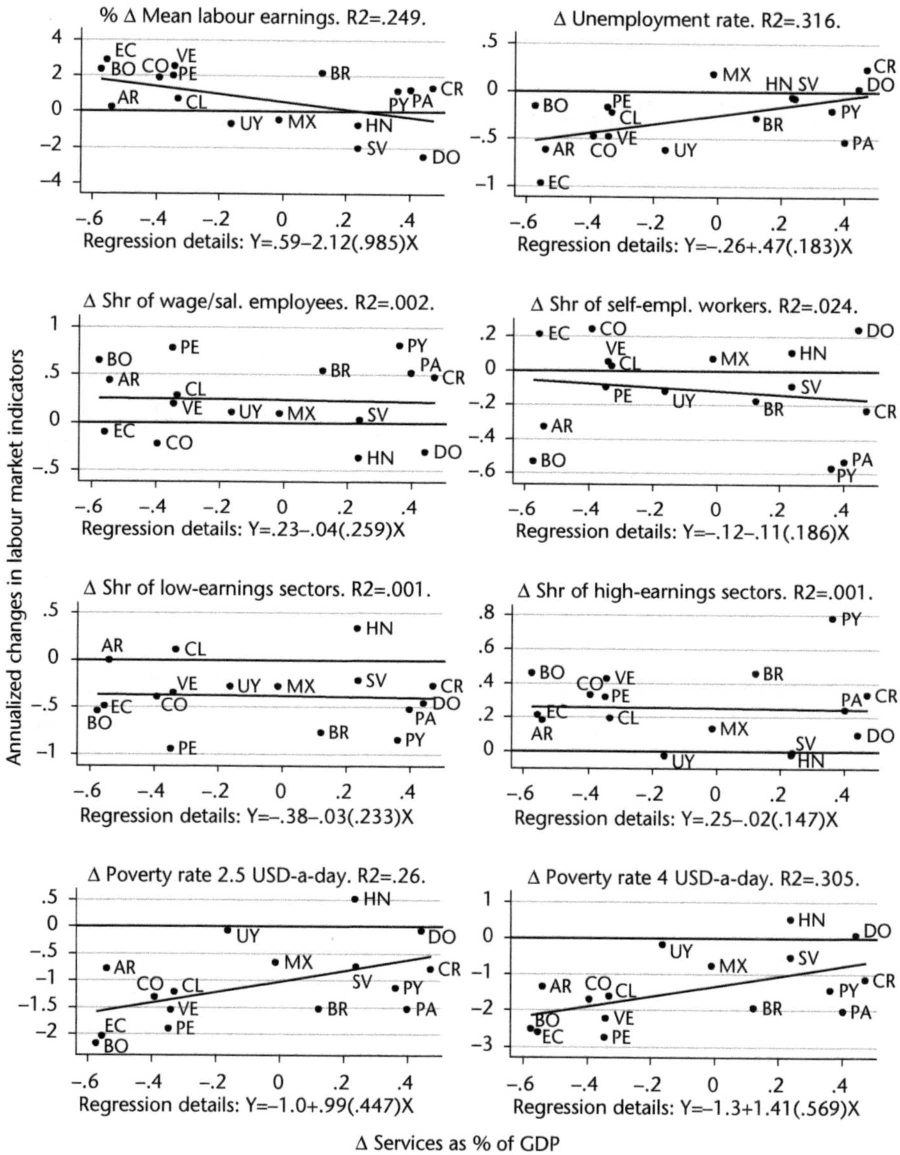

Figure A2.B Annualized change in service's percentage share of GDP

Note: The vertical axes display the annualized change in each labour market indicator. Δ denotes changes in percentage points and %Δ denotes percentage changes. The line represents the linear regression specified at the bottom of the figure. Robust standard error of the slope coefficient between parentheses. R-squared of the regression indicated along the title.

Source: Authors' calculations based on SEDLAC (CEDLAS and World Bank 2014), World Development Indicators (World Bank 2014), and CEPALSTAT (UN-ECLAC 2015).

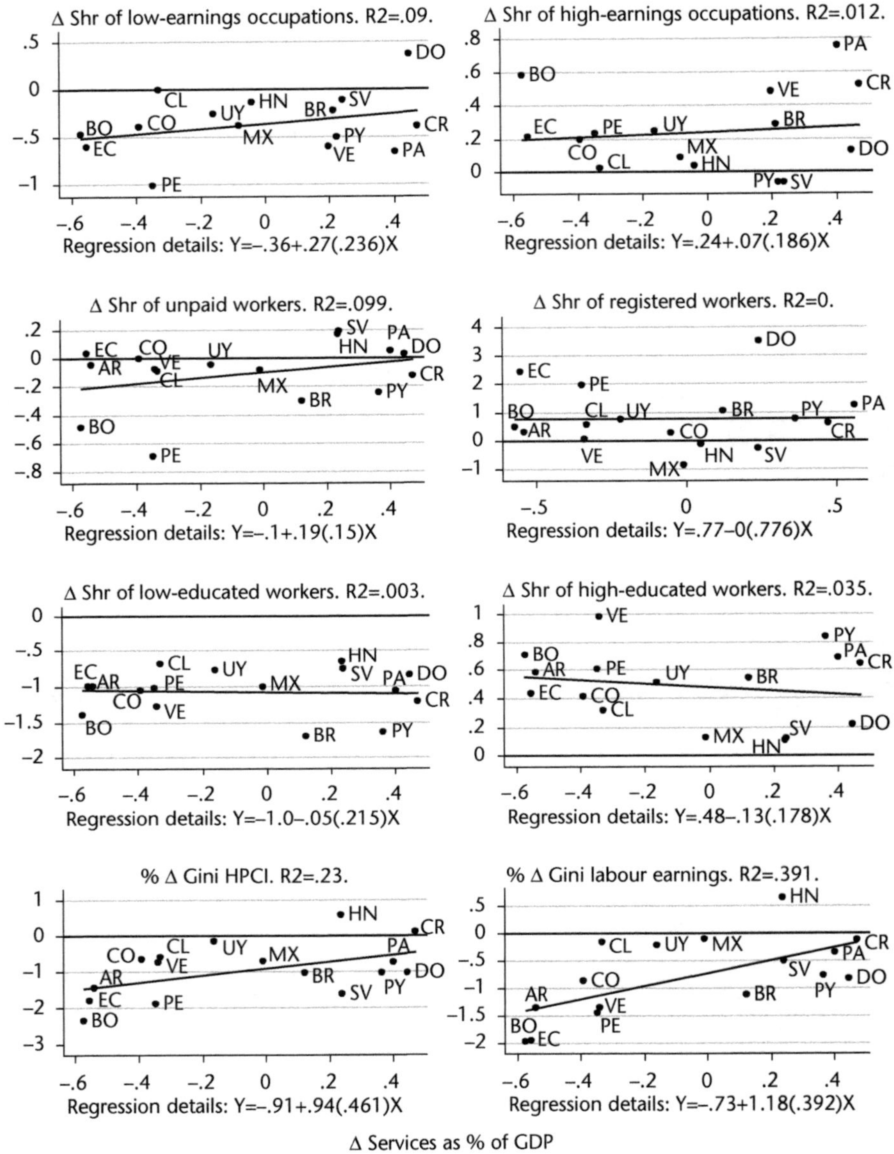

Figure A2.B Continued

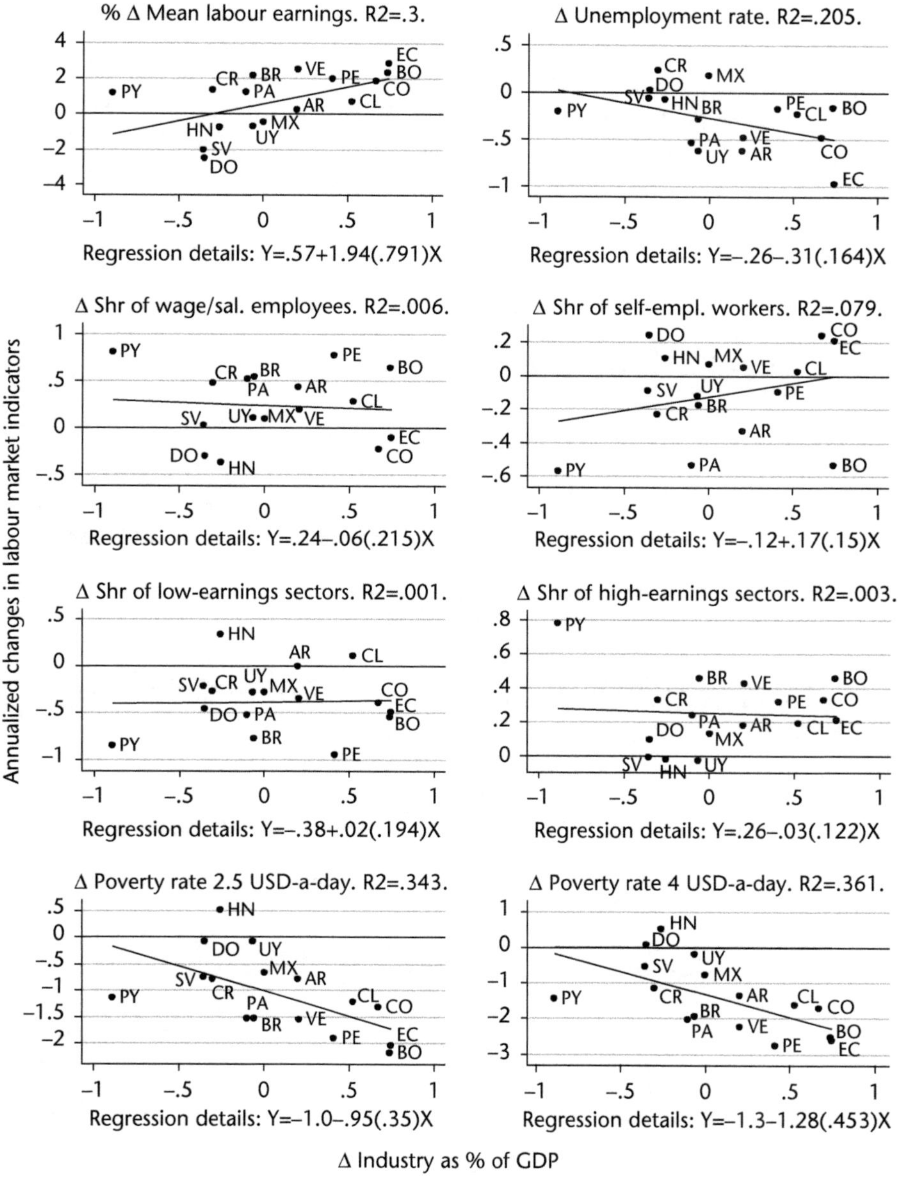

Figure A2.C Annualized change in industry's percentage share of GDP

Note: The vertical axes display the annualized change in each labour market indicator. Δ denotes changes in percentage points and %Δ denotes percentage changes. The line represents the linear regression specified at the bottom of the figure. Robust standard error of the slope coefficient between parentheses. R-squared of the regression indicated along the title.

Source: Authors' calculations based on SEDLAC (CEDLAS and World Bank 2014), World Development Indicators (World Bank 2014), and CEPALSTAT (UN-ECLAC 2015).

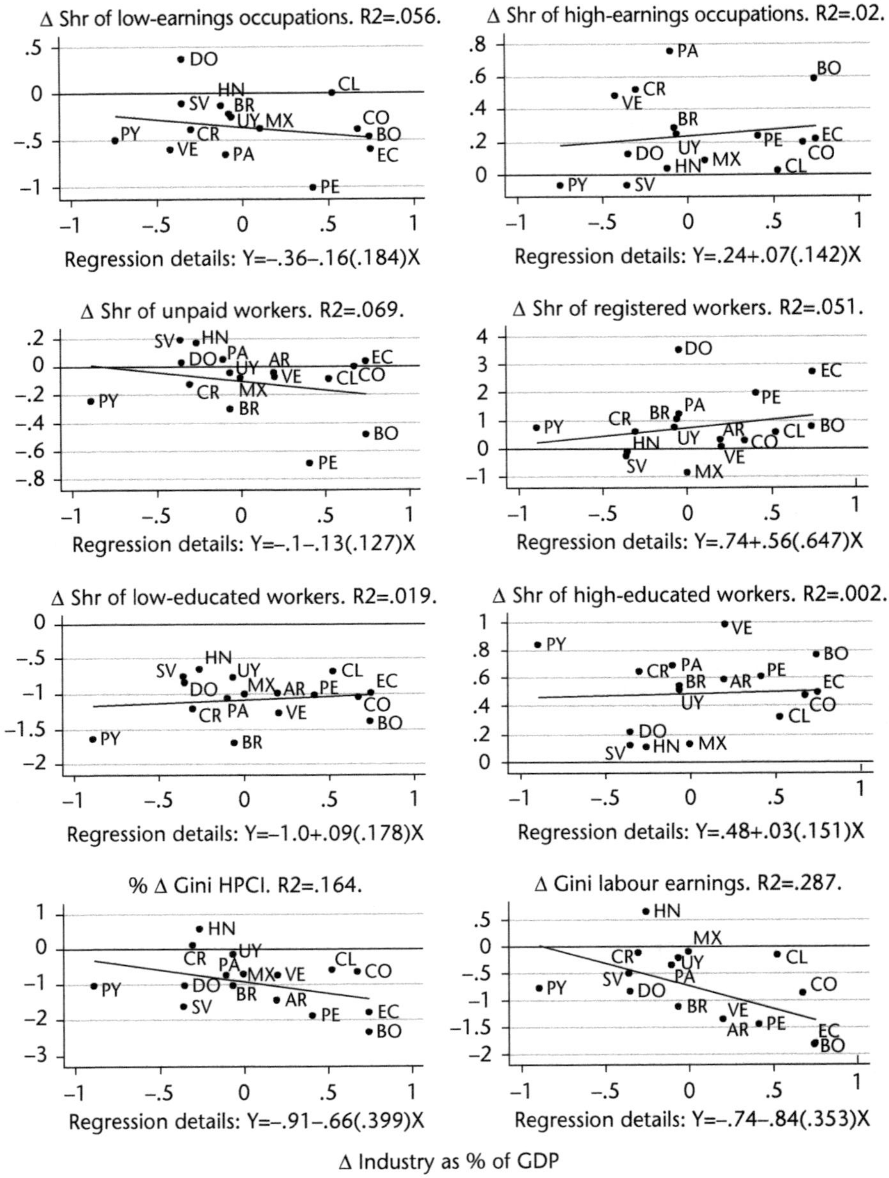

Figure A2.C Continued

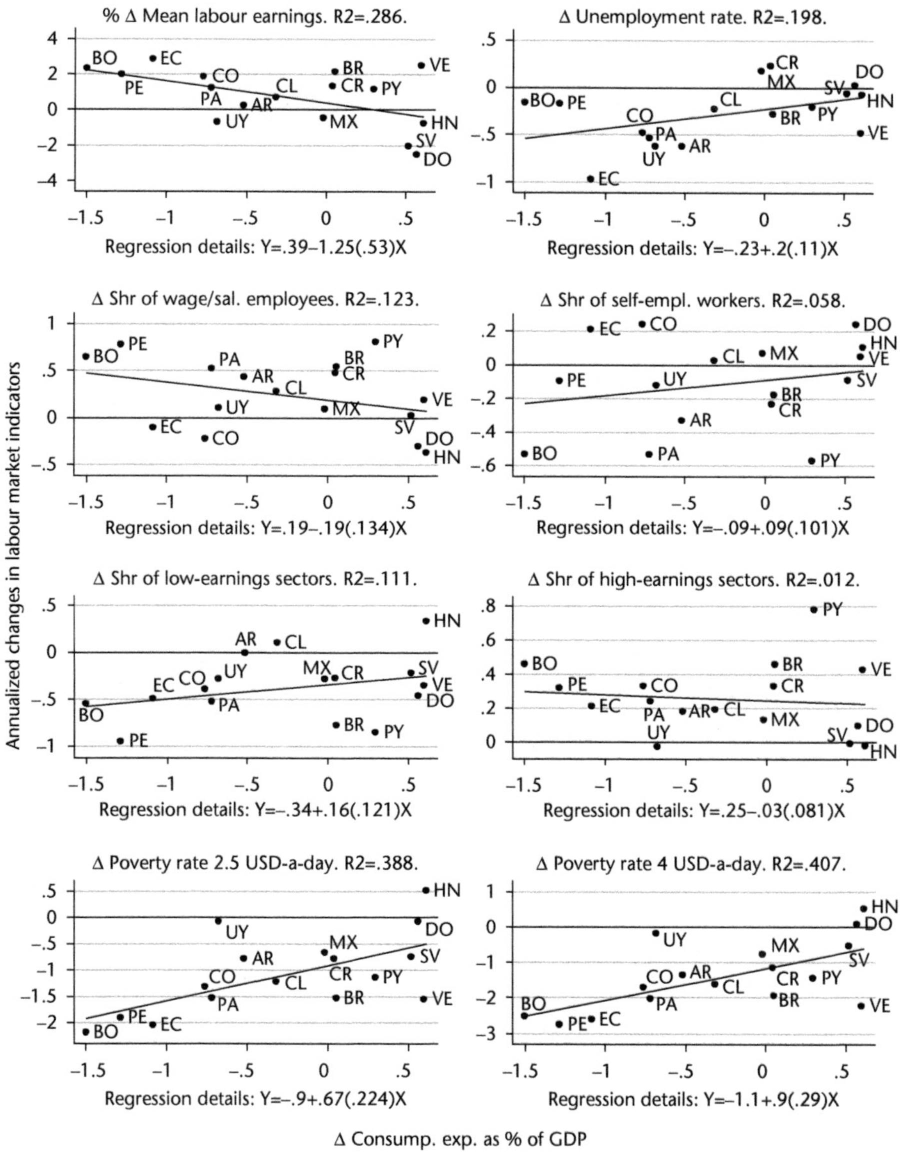

Figure A2.D Annualized change in domestic consumption as a percentage of GDP

Note: The vertical axes display the annualized change in each labour market indicator. Δ denotes changes in percentage points and %Δ denotes percentage changes. The line represents the linear regression specified at the bottom of the figure. Robust standard error of the slope coefficient between parentheses. R-squared of the regression indicated along the title.

Source: Authors' calculations based on SEDLAC (CEDLAS and World Bank 2014), World Development Indicators (World Bank 2014), and CEPALSTAT (UN-ECLAC 2015).

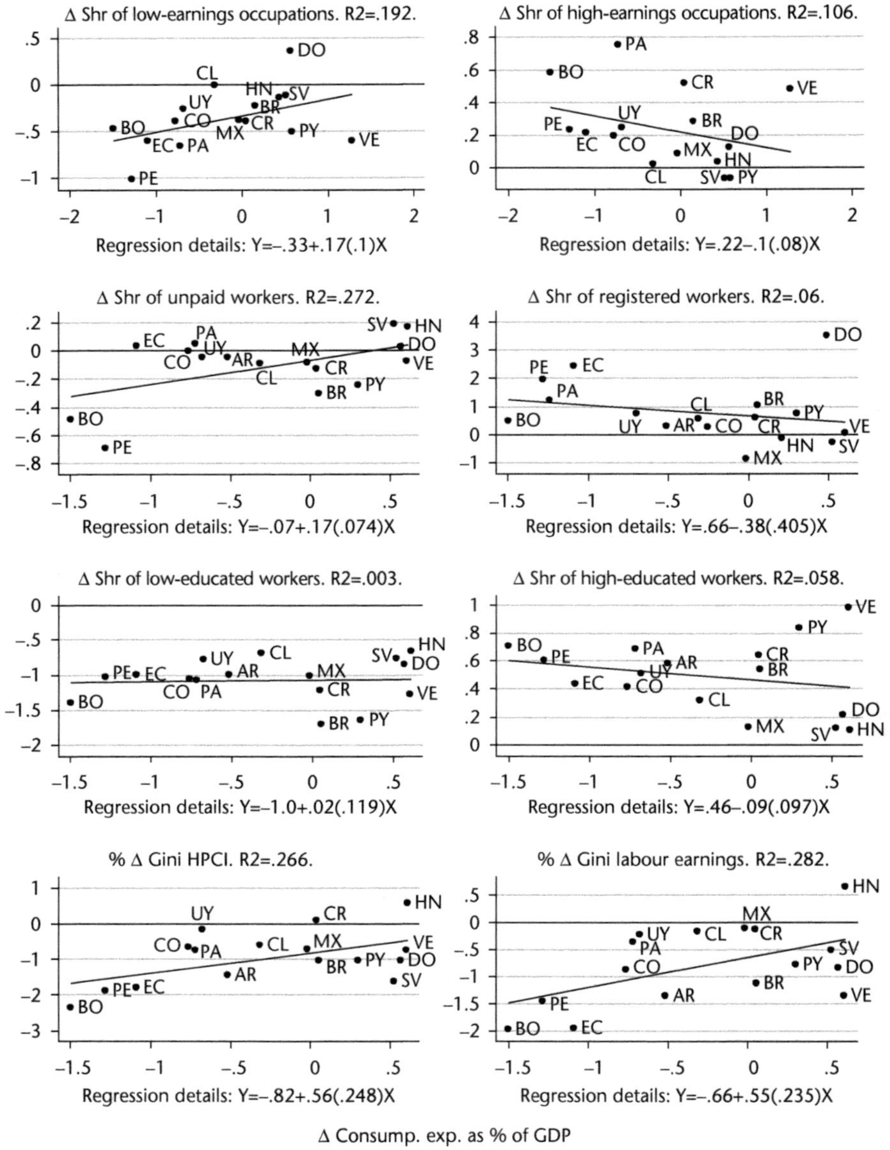

Figure A2.D Continued

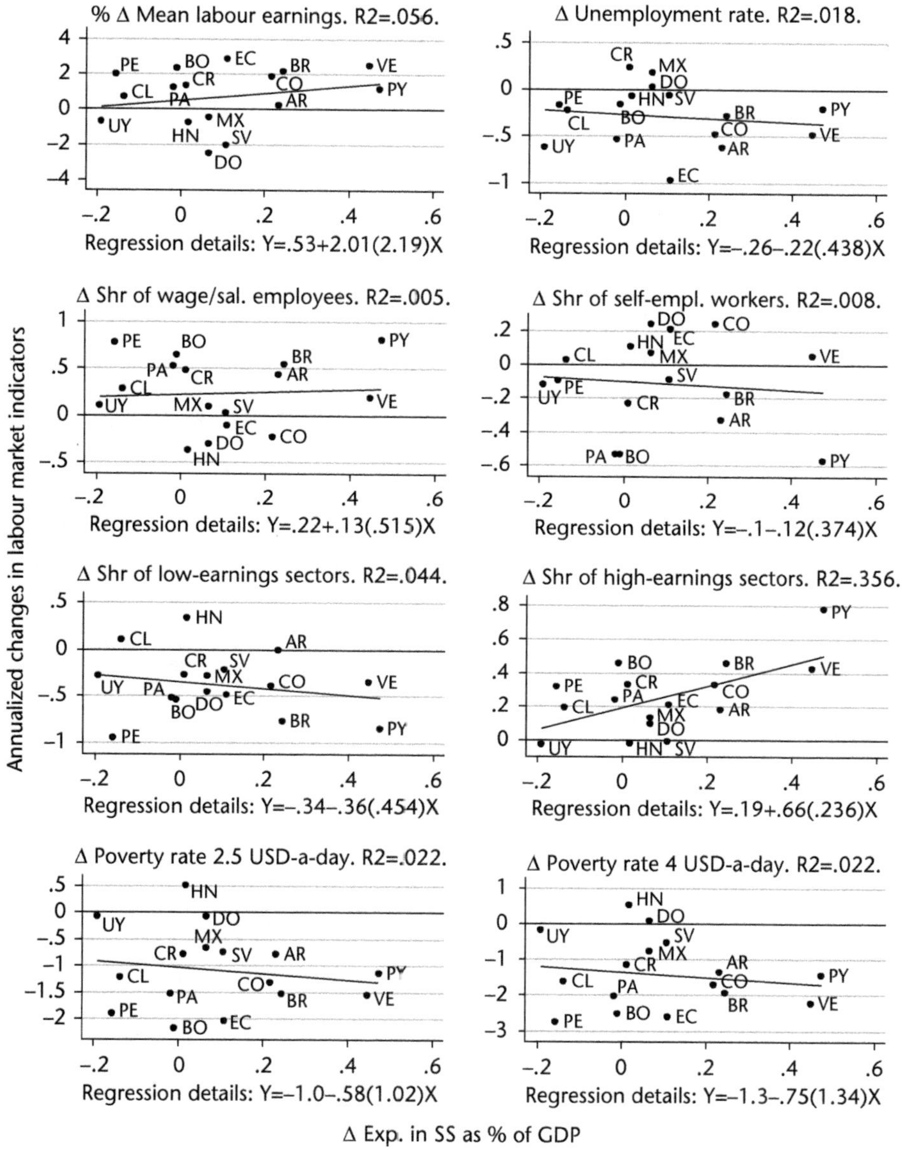

Figure A2.F Annualized change in public expenditure in social security as a percentage of GDP

Note: The vertical axes display the annualized change in each labour market indicator. Δ denotes changes in percentage points and %Δ denotes percentage changes. The line represents the linear regression specified at the bottom of the figure. Robust standard error of the slope coefficient between parentheses. R-squared of the regression indicated along the title.

Source: Authors' calculations based on SEDLAC (CEDLAS and World Bank 2014), World Development Indicators (World Bank 2014), and CEPALSTAT (UN-ECLAC 2015).

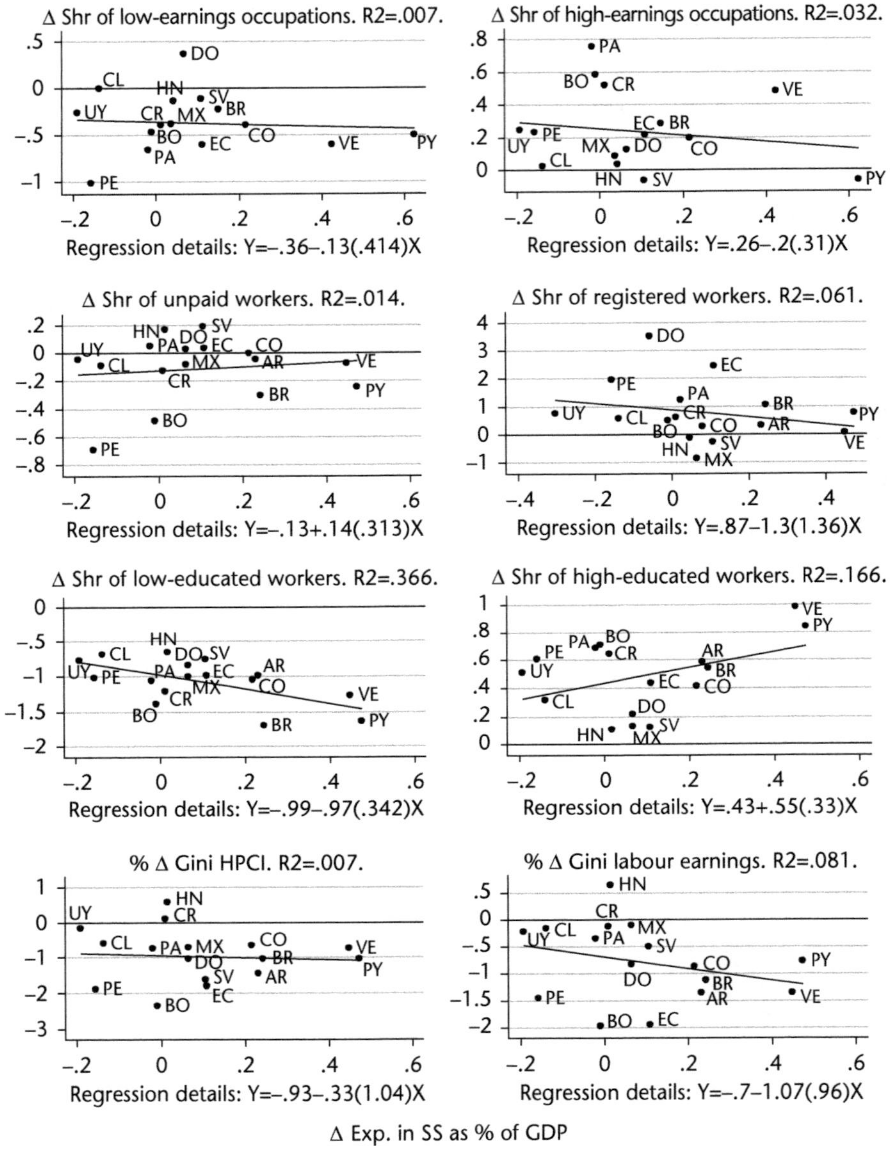

Figure A2.F Continued

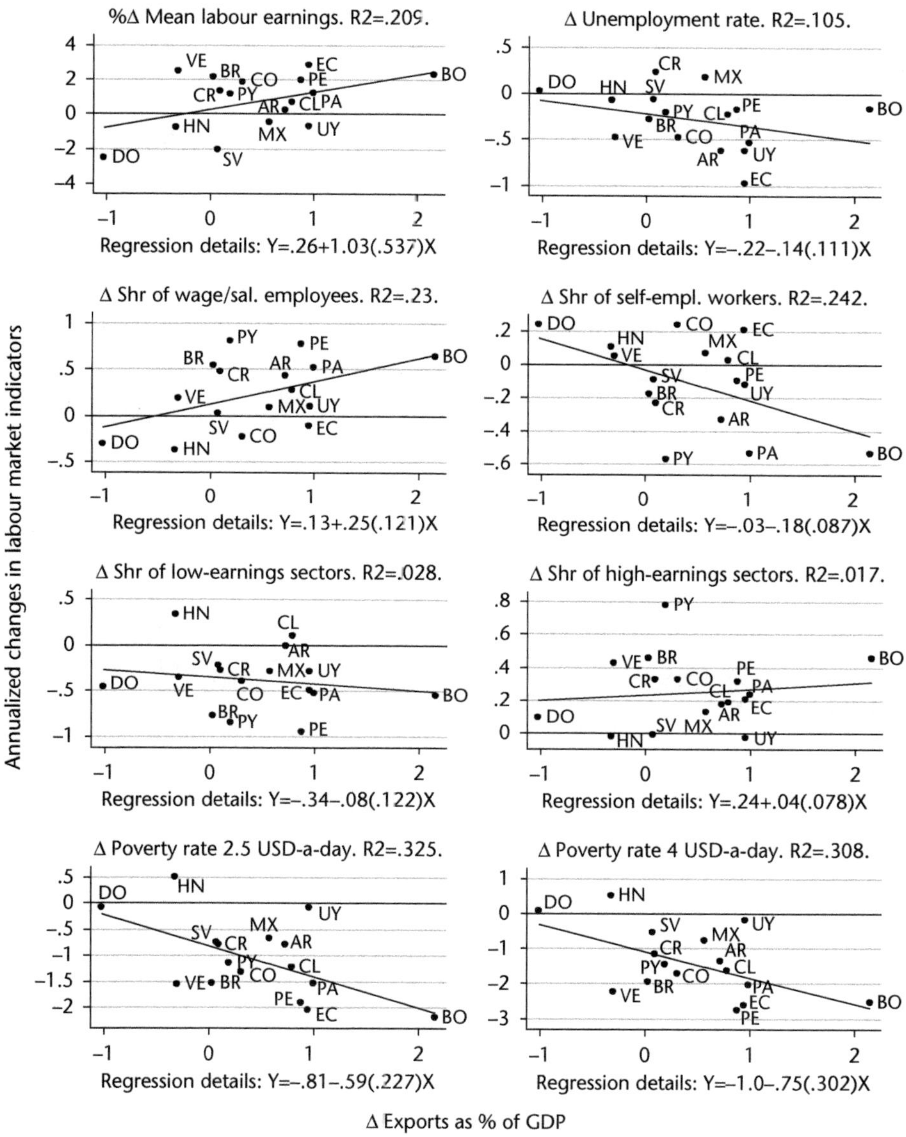

Figure A2.G Annualized change in exports as a percentage of GDP

Note: The vertical axes display the annualized change in each labour market indicator. Δ denotes changes in percentage points and %Δ denotes percentage changes. The line represents the linear regression specified at the bottom of the figure. Robust standard error of the slope coefficient between parentheses. R-squared of the regression indicated along the title.

Source: Authors' calculations based on SEDLAC (CEDLAS and World Bank 2014), World Development Indicators (World Bank 2014), and CEPALSTAT (UN-ECLAC 2015).

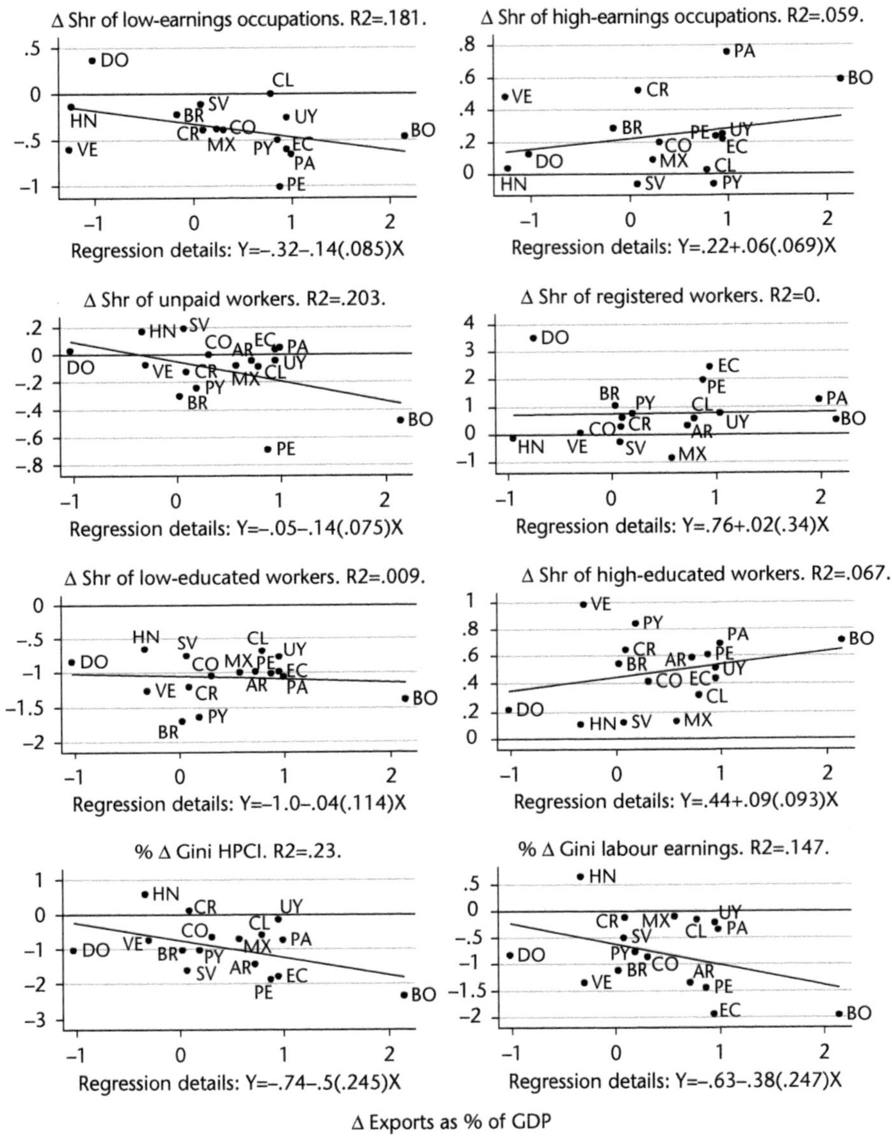

Figure A2.G Continued

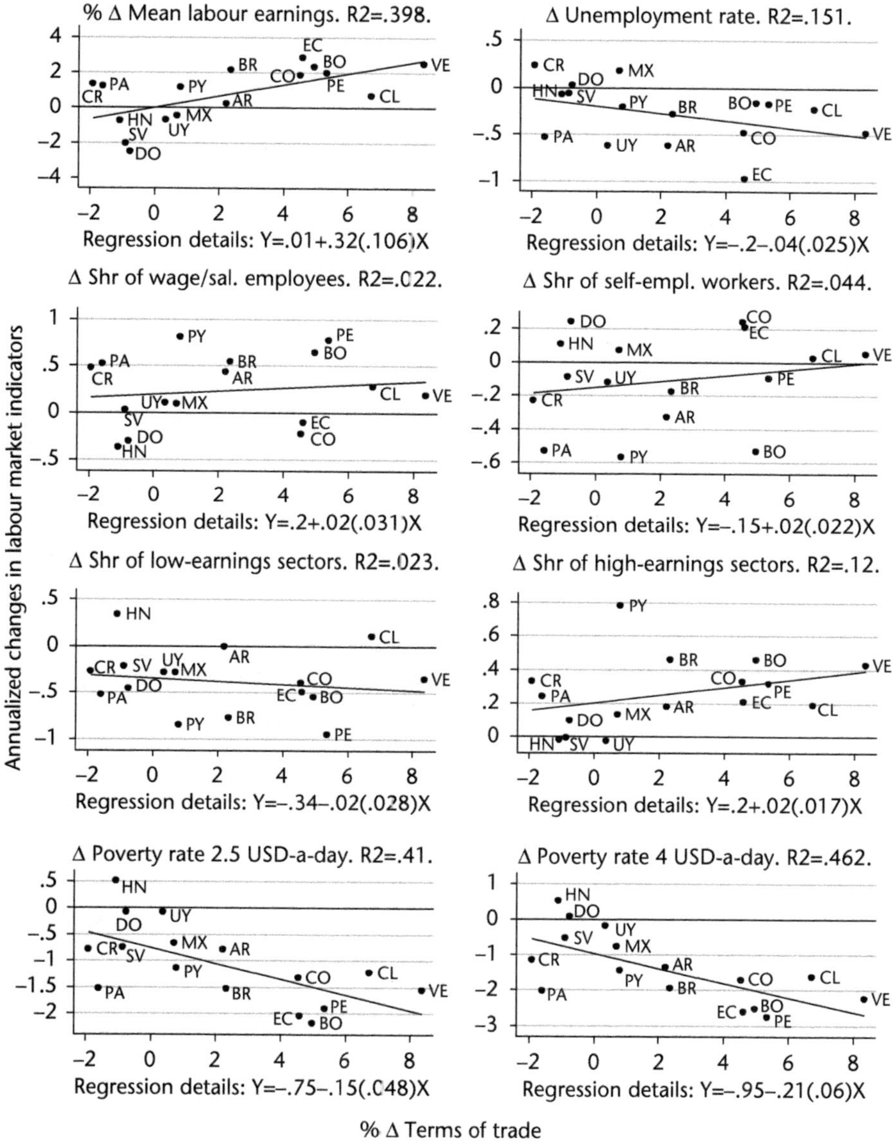

Figure A2.H Annualized change in terms of trade

Note: The vertical axes display the annualized change in each labour market indicator. Δ denotes changes in percentage points and %Δ denotes percentage changes. The line represents the linear regression specified at the bottom of the figure. Robust standard error of the slope coefficient between parentheses. R-squared of the regression indicated along the title.

Source: Authors' calculations based on SEDLAC (CEDLAS and World Bank 2014), World Development Indicators (World Bank 2014), and CEPALSTAT (UN-ECLAC 2015).

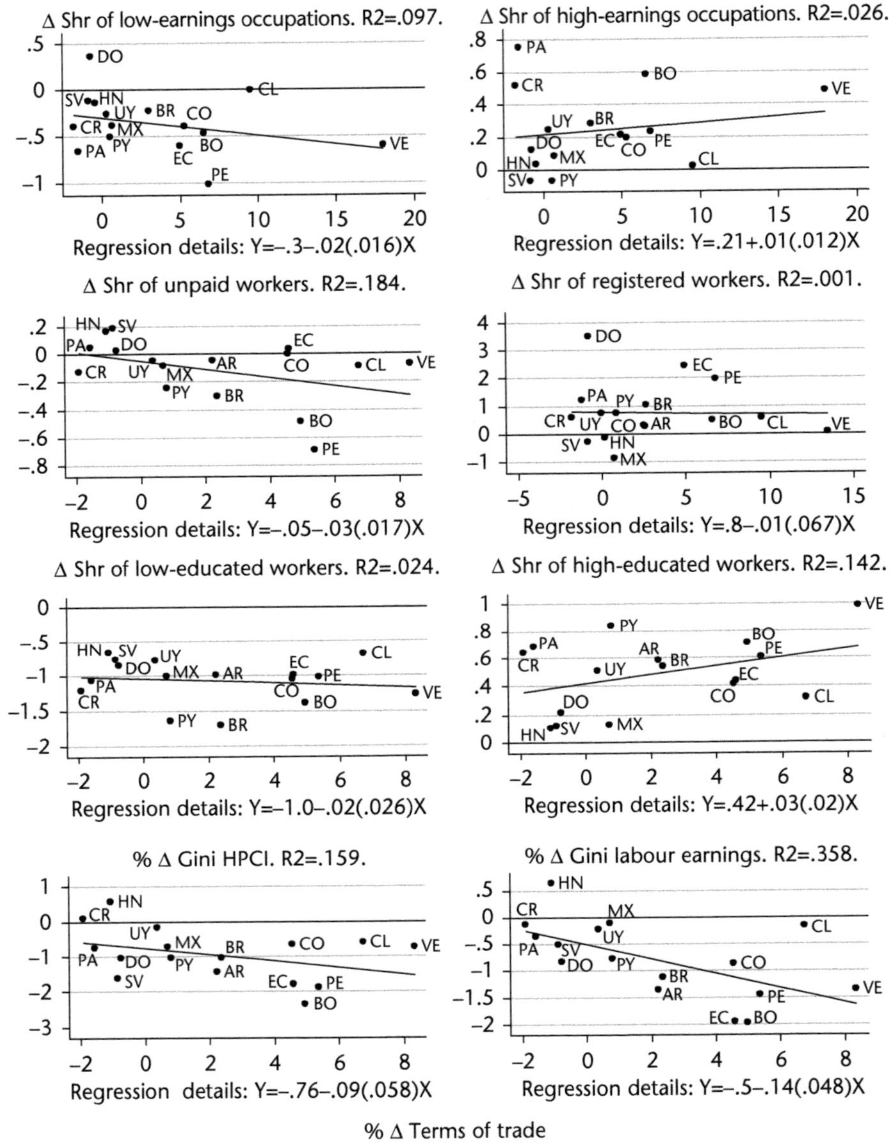

Figure A2.H Continued

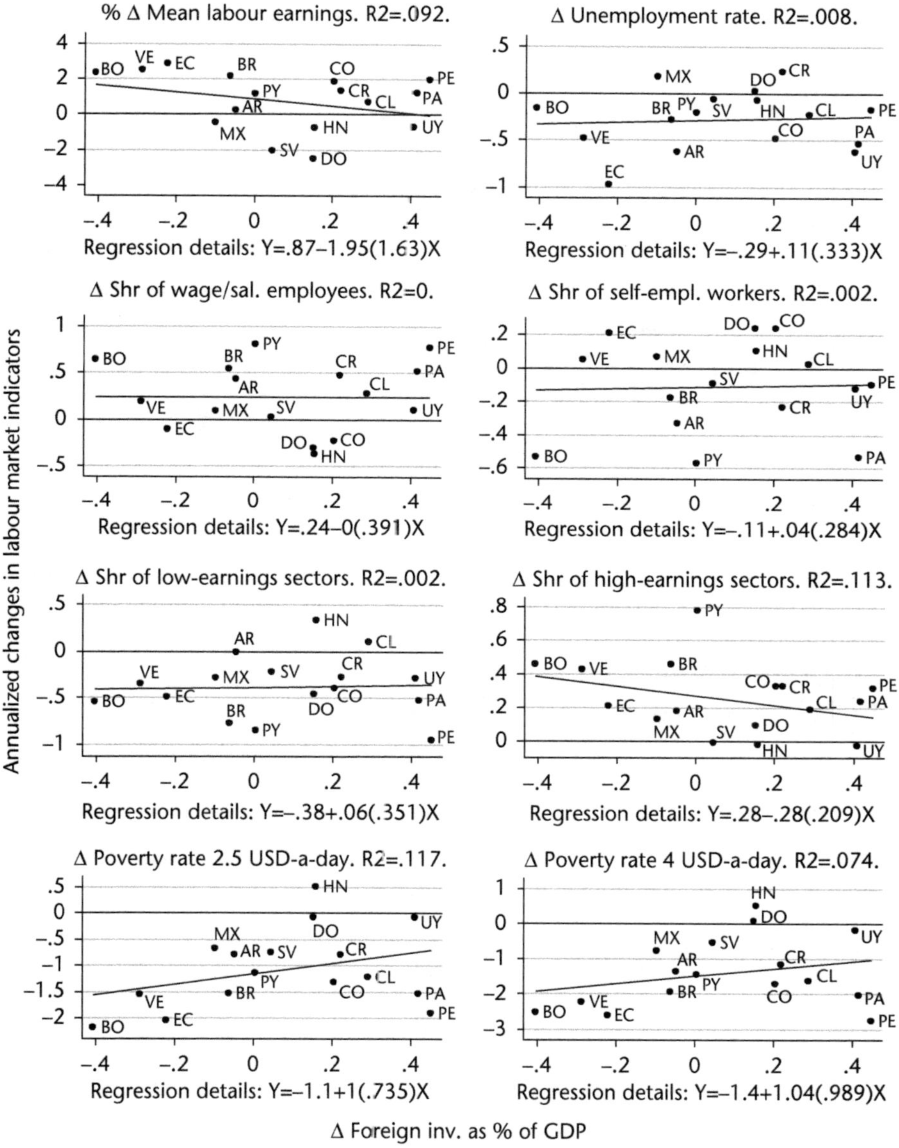

Figure A2.1 Annualized change in foreign direct investment as a percentage of GDP

Note: The vertical axes display the annualized change in each labour market indicator. Δ denotes changes in percentage points and %Δ denotes percentage changes. The line represents the linear regression specified at the bottom of the figure. Robust standard error of the slope coefficient between parentheses. R-squared of the regression indicated along the title.

Source: Authors' calculations based on SEDLAC (CEDLAS and World Bank 2014), World Development Indicators (World Bank 2014), and CEPALSTAT (UN-ECLAC 2015).

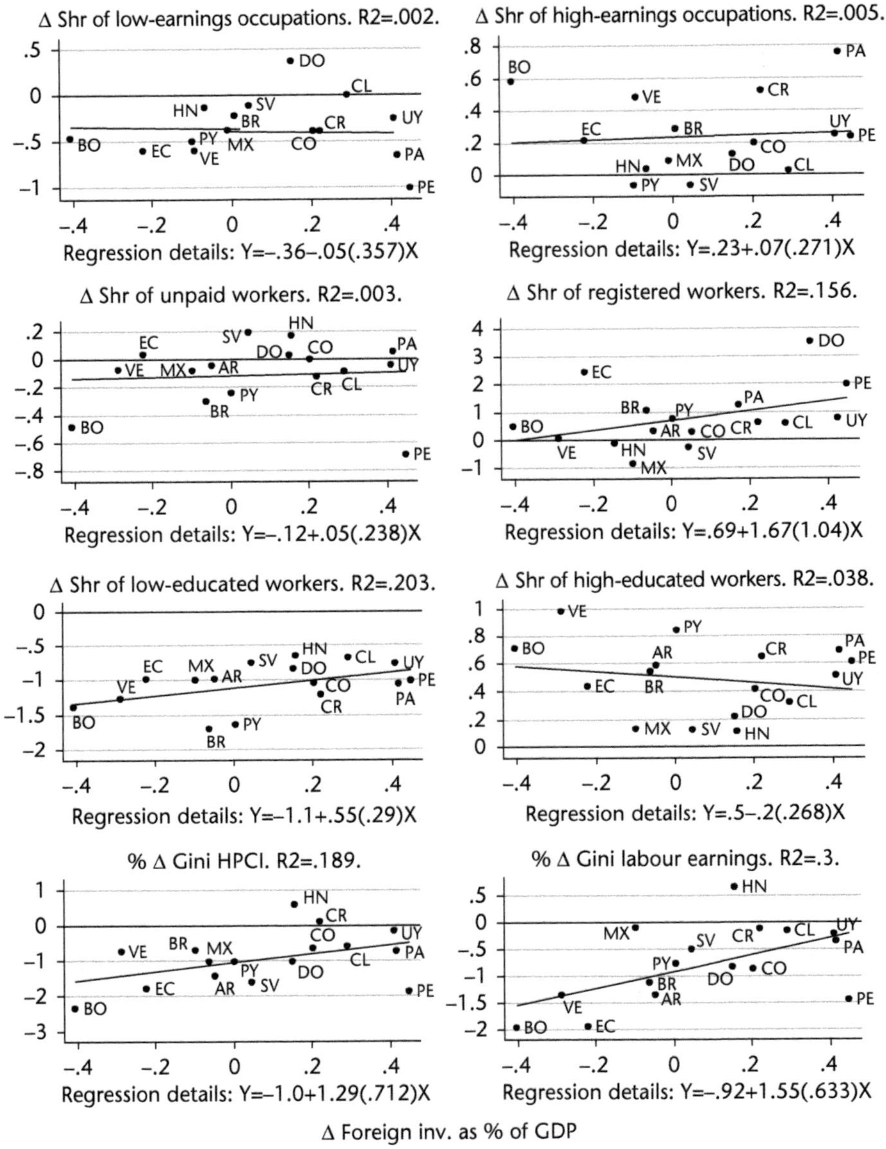

Figure A2.I Continued

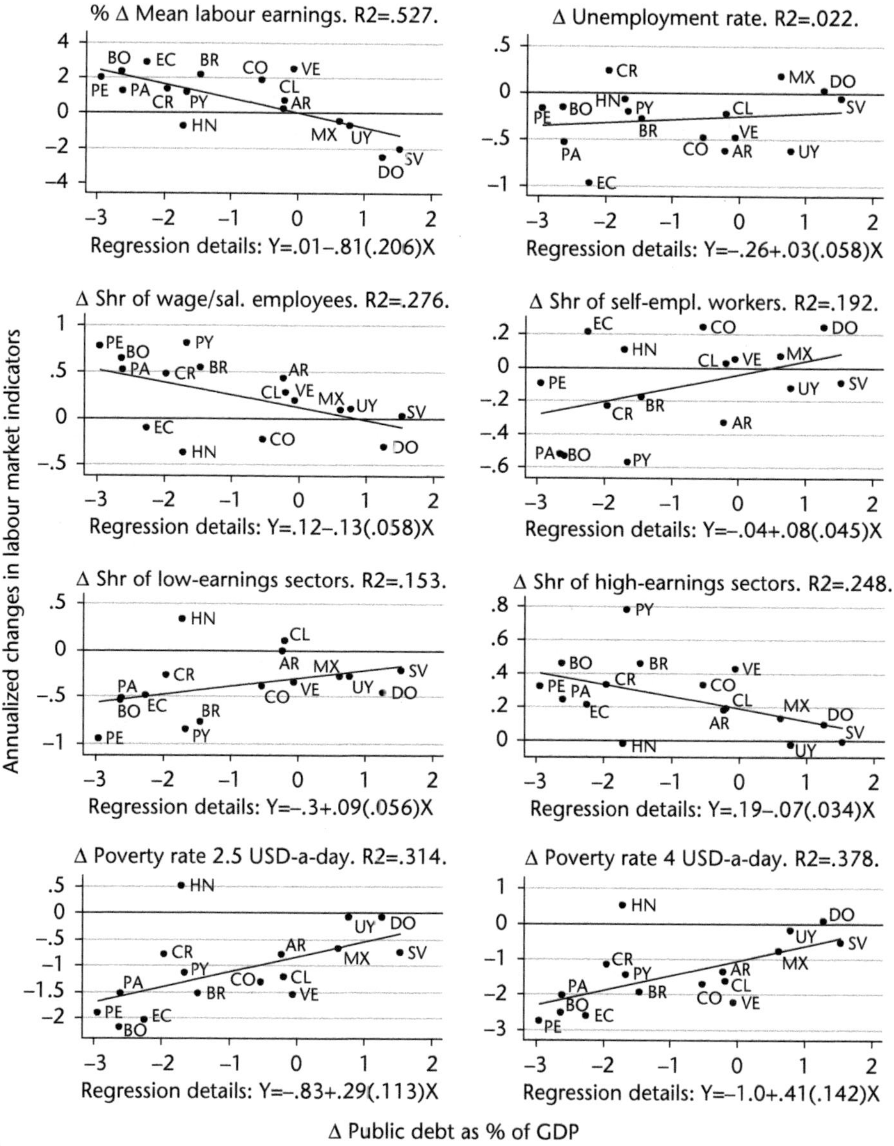

Figure A2.J Annualized change in the stock of public debt as a percentage of GDP

Note: The vertical axes display the annualized change in each labour market indicator. Δ denotes changes in percentage points and %Δ denotes percentage changes. The line represents the linear regression specified at the bottom of the figure. Robust standard error of the slope coefficient between parentheses. R-squared of the regression indicated along the title.

Source: Authors' calculations based on SEDLAC (CEDLAS and World Bank 2014), World Development Indicators (World Bank 2014), and CEPALSTAT (UN-ECLAC 2015).

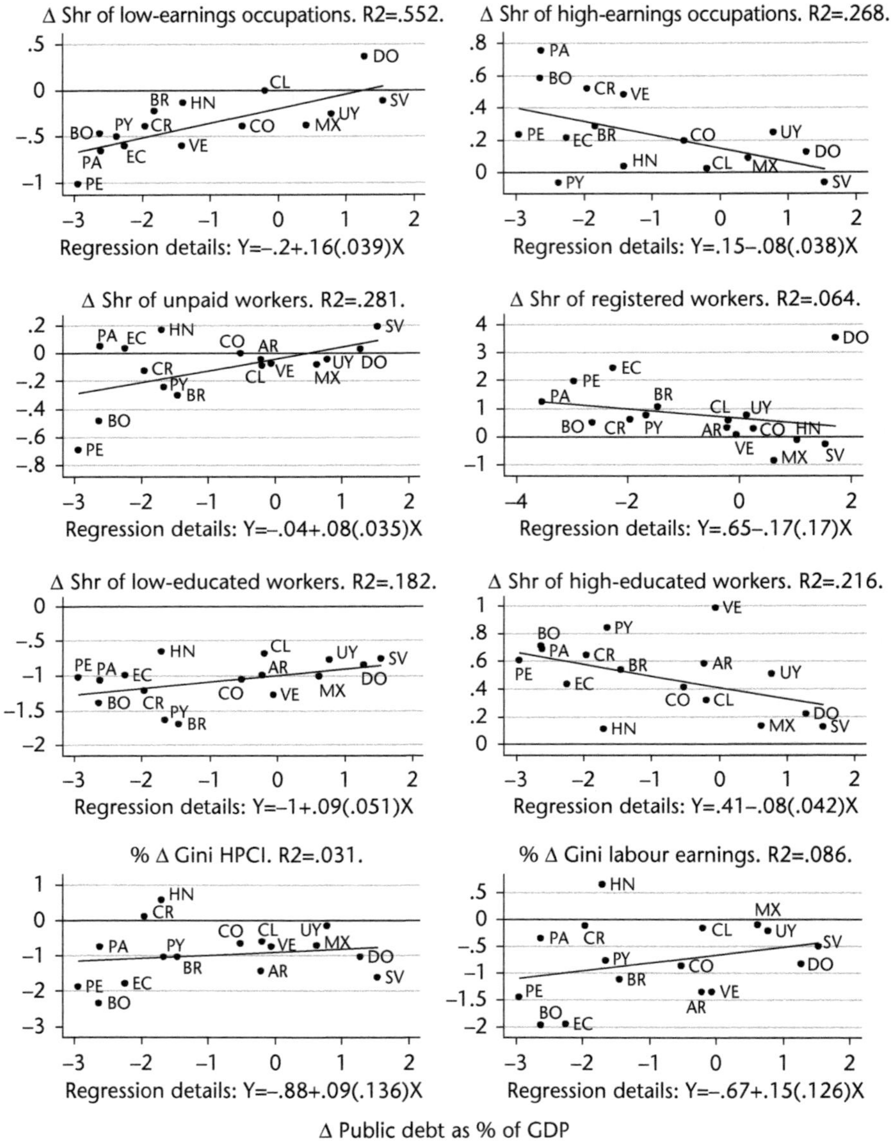

Figure A2.J Continued

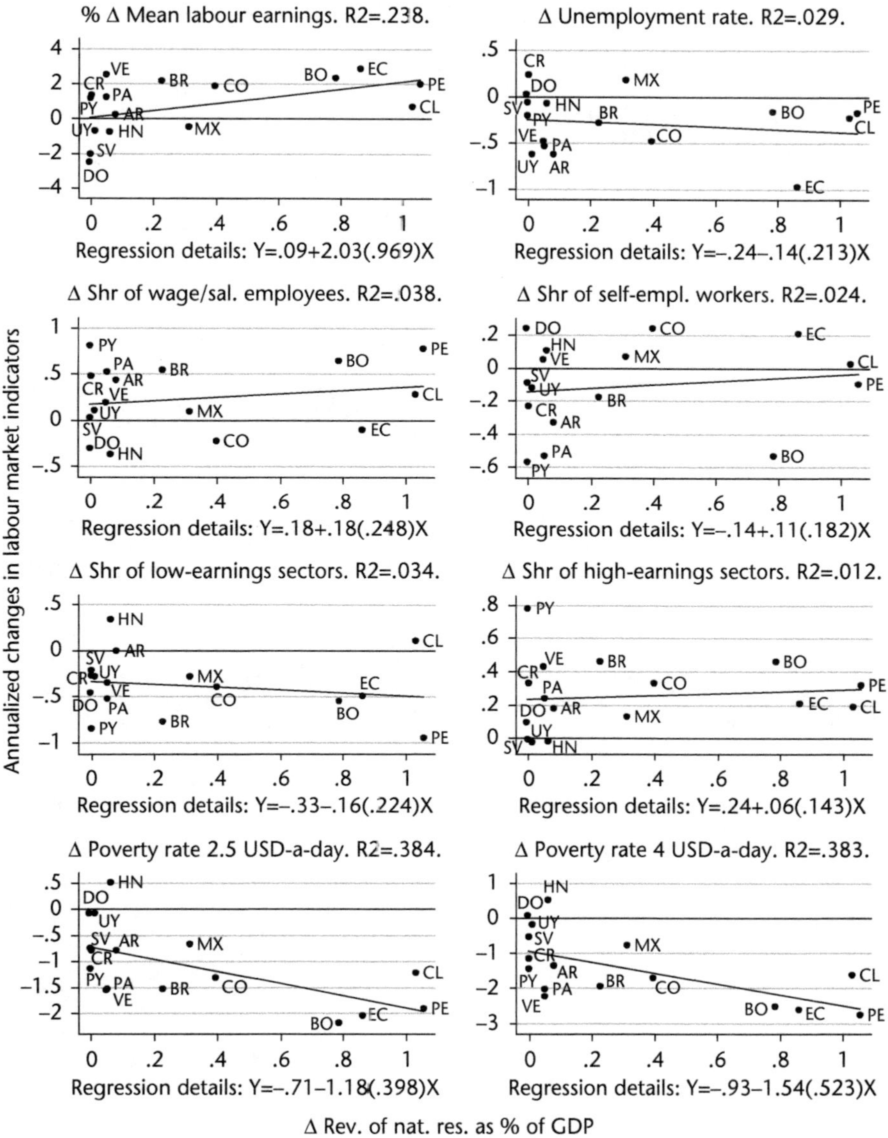

Figure A2.K Annualized change in revenues from natural resources as a percentage of GDP

Note: The vertical axes display the annualized change in each labour market indicator. Δ denotes changes in percentage points and %Δ denotes percentage changes. The line represents the linear regression specified at the bottom of the figure. Robust standard error of the slope coefficient between parentheses. R-squared of the regression indicated along the title.

Source: Authors' calculations based on SEDLAC (CEDLAS and World Bank 2014), World Development Indicators (World Bank 2014), and CEPALSTAT (UN-ECLAC 2015).

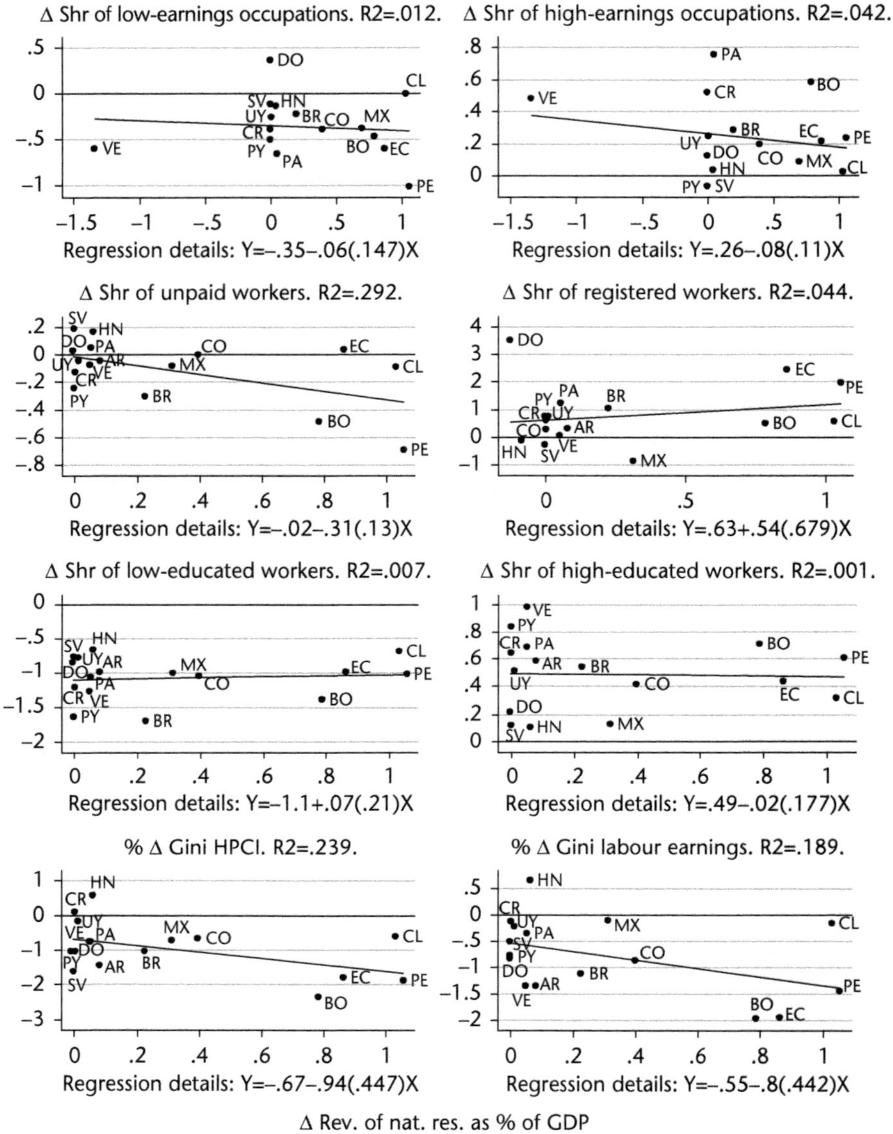

Figure A2.K Continued

References

CEDLAS and World Bank (2014). SEDLAC—Socio-Economic Database for Latin America and the Caribbean. Centro de Estudios Distributivos, Laborales y Sociales, Facultad de Ciencias Económicas, Universidad Nacional de La Plata and World Bank Poverty Group LCR. Available at <http://sedlac.econo.unlp.edu.ar/eng/index.php>, accessed 2014.

UN-ECLAC (2015). CEPALSTAT, United Nations, Economic Commission for Latin America and the Caribbean. Available at <http://estadisticas.cepal.org/cepalstat/WEB_CEPALSTAT/Portada.asp?idioma=i>, accessed April 2015.

World Bank (2014). World Development Indicators. Available at <http://data.worldbank.org/data-catalog/world-development-indicators>, accessed April 2014.

APPENDIX 3

Evolution of Macroeconomic Variables over the 2000s by Country

Argentina

	00	01	02	03	04	05	06	07	08	09	10	11	12
GDP per capita (dollars PPP 2005)	10,290	9,739	8,596	9,271	10,019	10,843	11,658	12,556	13,288	13,285	14,376	15,515	15,672
Share of agriculture in GDP	5.1	4.9	10.8	11.0	10.5	9.5	8.5	9.5	9.9	7.6	10.1	10.7	9.1
Share of industry in GDP	28.1	27.0	32.4	34.9	35.8	35.8	35.9	34.0	32.5	32.1	31.2	31.1	30.5
Share of services in GDP	66.9	68.1	56.8	54.1	53.7	54.7	55.6	56.5	57.5	60.3	58.7	58.2	60.4
Domestic expenditure (% GDP)	87.2	77.7	78.2	75.7	75.9	74.5	74.2	75.8	79.7	78.3	78.3	81.0	81.9
Public expenditure in education and health (% GDP)	10.0	10.3	8.9	8.4	8.4	9.3	9.7	10.3	11.1	12.9	...	...	...
Public expenditure in social security (% GDP)	10.1	10.5	9.8	9.7	9.2	9.1	9.3	10.7	11.1	12.9	...	...	...
Exports (% GDP)	11.0	11.6	28.4	25.9	25.7	25.1	24.8	24.6	24.5	21.4	21.7	21.8	19.7
Terms of trade	100.0	99.3	98.7	107.2	109.2	106.9	113.4	117.5	133.2	127.1	126.6	135.0	130.3
Foreign direct investment (% GDP)	3.0	0.7	1.7	1.1	2.3	2.4	2.1	2.0	2.4	1.1	1.7	1.9	2.5
Revenue from natural resources (% GDP)	3.3	3.1	7.0	7.8	8.6	10.4	9.8	8.1	9.1	5.0	4.9	5.0	4.3
Stock of public debt (% GDP)	37.6	44.9	127.8	117.6	106.0	60.2	51.7	44.2	39.0	39.6	36.1	33.3	35.1

Source: Authors' calculations based on World Development Indicators (World Bank 2014) and CEPALSTAT (UN-ECLAC 2015).

Bolivia

	00	01	02	03	04	05	06	07	08	09	10	11	12
GDP per capita (dollars PPP 2005)	3,488	3,476	3,492	3,518	3,596	3,688	3,799	3,907	4,081	4,151	4,252	4,400	4,552
Share of agriculture in GDP	15.0	15.2	14.9	15.4	15.4	14.4	13.9	12.9	13.5	13.8	12.9	12.5	13.0
Share of industry in GDP	55.2	55.6	55.8	55.2	53.7	53.6	51.0	50.7	48.2	49.9	49.9	48.5	48.3
Share of services in GDP	29.8	29.2	29.3	29.4	31.0	32.0	35.1	36.4	38.4	36.2	37.3	38.9	38.7
Domestic expenditure (% GDP)	90.9	91.0	89.8	87.5	84.2	82.3	77.1	77.3	75.5	80.2	76.1	74.7	72.9
Public expenditure in education and health (% GDP)	6.5	7.0	7.9	8.1	8.0	7.7	7.8	7.7	6.7	7.8	7.5	7.2	6.6
Public expenditure in social security (% GDP)	4.8	5.1	5.1	5.0	4.8	4.4	4.0	3.7	4.6	5.0	4.7	4.2	4.7
Exports (% GDP)	18.3	20.0	21.6	25.6	31.1	35.5	41.8	41.8	44.9	35.7	41.2	44.1	47.3
Terms of trade	100.0	95.8	96.2	98.5	104.1	111.8	139.8	142.1	143.9	139.4	157.6	175.0	179.1
Foreign direct investment (% GDP)	8.8	8.7	8.6	2.4	0.7	−2.5	2.5	2.8	3.1	2.4	3.2	3.6	3.9
Revenue from natural resources (% GDP)	8.0	8.2	8.0	13.7	20.3	38.8	37.8	36.2	39.9	16.6	18.5	21.3	17.4
Stock of public debt (% GDP)	60.6	72.6	77.1	86.4	81.0	75.4	49.7	37.2	34.0	36.3	34.6	34.5	29.1

Source: Authors' calculations based on World Development Indicators (World Bank 2014) and CEPALSTAT (UN-ECLAC 2015).

Brazil

	00	01	02	03	04	05	06	07	08	09	10	11	12
GDP per capita (dollars PPP 2005)	7,906	7,898	7,998	7,985	8,338	8,502	8,745	9,187	9,573	9,456	10,079	10,264	10,264
Share of agriculture in GDP	5.6	6.0	6.6	7.4	6.9	5.7	5.5	5.6	5.9	5.6	5.3	5.5	5.2
Share of industry in GDP	27.7	26.9	27.1	27.8	30.1	29.3	28.8	27.8	27.9	26.8	28.1	27.5	26.3
Share of services in GDP	66.7	67.1	66.3	64.8	63.0	65.0	65.8	66.6	66.2	67.5	66.6	67.0	68.5
Domestic expenditure (% GDP)	83.5	83.3	82.3	81.3	79.0	80.2	80.3	80.2	79.1	82.3	80.8	81.0	83.9
Public expenditure in education and health (% GDP)	8.8	9.2	7.9	9.3	8.9	8.9	9.3	9.9	10.0	10.9	10.9	10.9	10.9
Public expenditure in social security (% GDP)	11.2	11.1	12.3	11.6	11.9	12.3	12.9	12.8	12.8	13.8	13.8	13.8	13.8
Exports (% GDP)	10.0	12.2	14.1	15.0	16.4	15.1	14.4	13.4	13.7	11.0	10.9	11.9	12.6
Terms of trade	100.0	99.6	98.4	97.0	97.9	99.2	104.4	106.6	110.4	107.8	125.1	134.9	128.9
Foreign direct investment (% GDP)	5.1	4.1	3.3	1.8	2.7	1.8	1.8	3.3	3.1	1.9	2.5	2.9	3.4
Revenue from natural resources (% GDP)	2.5	2.6	3.1	3.6	4.1	5.3	5.5	6.3	7.1	3.7	4.9	5.4	5.1
Stock of public debt (% GDP)	63.5	76.4	78.7	73.1	70.2	67.4	56.7	58.5	58.9	61.3	53.6	53.6	60.5

Source: Authors' calculations based on World Development Indicators (World Bank 2014) and CEPALSTAT (UN-ECLAC 2015).

Chile

	00	01	02	03	04	05	06	07	08	09	10	11	12
GDP per capita (dollars PPP 2005)	10,990	11,224	11,337	11,655	12,228	12,773	13,201	13,746	14,061	13,784	14,443	15,149	15,848
Share of agriculture in GDP	5.9	5.2	5.5	5.3	4.7	4.6	4.1	3.9	3.6	3.5	3.4	3.7	3.6
Share of industry in GDP	32.2	32.8	33.1	32.7	35.3	36.9	44.2	43.0	38.0	37.6	39.1	38.0	35.5
Share of services in GDP	61.9	62.1	61.4	62.0	60.0	58.5	51.7	53.2	58.4	58.8	57.5	58.3	60.9
Domestic expenditure (% GDP)	76.6	77.7	77.5	75.1	71.7	69.9	66.0	66.9	72.1	72.1	71.3	73.1	74.9
Public expenditure in education and health (% GDP)	6.7	7.0	7.2	6.9	6.6	6.2	6.0	6.4	7.1	8.2	7.7	7.6	8.0
Public expenditure in social security (% GDP)	7.9	7.9	7.8	7.3	6.7	6.4	5.8	5.7	6.0	7.0	6.6	6.4	6.3
Exports (% GDP)	29.3	30.9	31.5	33.9	37.9	38.4	42.4	43.8	41.5	37.2	38.1	38.0	34.2
Terms of trade	100.0	93.3	97.2	102.8	124.9	139.8	183.2	189.5	164.8	166.7	204.0	205.3	182.4
Foreign direct investment (% GDP)	6.1	5.8	3.6	5.5	7.1	5.6	4.7	7.2	8.4	7.5	7.2	9.3	10.7
Revenue from natural resources (% GDP)	7.0	6.5	6.2	7.3	11.8	13.2	21.4	21.2	19.3	14.4	17.8	18.3	15.6
Stock of public debt (% GDP)	13.0	14.4	14.7	12.4	10.5	6.9	4.9	3.9	5.1	5.8	8.7	11.0	11.9

Source: Authors' calculations based on World Development Indicators (World Bank 2014) and CEPALSTAT (UN-ECLAC 2015).

Colombia

	00	01	02	03	04	05	06	07	08	09	10	11	12
GDP per capita (dollars PPP 2005)	6,597	6,598	6,655	6,808	7,060	7,280	7,651	8,059	8,223	8,241	8,450	8,890	9,143
Share of agriculture in GDP	8.9	9.0	9.2	9.0	8.6	8.4	8.1	7.8	7.5	7.5	7.1	6.9	6.5
Share of industry in GDP	29.4	29.4	29.8	31.4	32.4	32.8	33.8	33.7	35.5	34.5	35.0	37.9	37.5
Share of services in GDP	61.6	61.7	61.0	59.6	59.0	58.8	58.1	58.5	57.0	58.0	57.9	55.3	56.0
Domestic expenditure (% GDP)	80.2	82.7	82.6	81.2	80.1	81.1	79.7	80.1	82.2	83.1	82.1	83.0	82.6
Public expenditure in education and health (% GDP)	9.9	10.7	11.4	11.3	10.6	10.3	10.0	10.4	11.7	13.6	13.9	13.7	14.2
Public expenditure in social security (% GDP)	6.0	6.3	5.6	5.4	5.3	5.3	5.2	5.3	5.5	6.4	6.5	6.6	6.7
Exports (% GDP)	15.9	15.4	14.8	16.6	16.8	16.8	17.6	16.5	17.8	16.0	15.9	18.9	18.3
Terms of trade	100.0	94.2	92.5	95.2	102.3	111.0	115.2	124.4	138.1	118.8	134.4	150.2	151.1
Foreign direct investment (% GDP)	2.6	2.8	3.9	3.3	4.3	4.3	6.5	7.2	7.0	4.6	4.0	5.3	5.9
Revenue from natural resources (% GDP)	7.1	5.3	5.0	6.4	6.9	8.1	9.1	8.0	9.4	6.6	8.0	10.3	9.4
Stock of public debt (% GDP)	42.3	43.0	43.4	41.1	40.9	37.5	33.3	27.6	24.8	27.4	28.8	30.3	35.1

Source: Authors' calculations based on World Development Indicators (World Bank 2014) and CEPALSTAT (UN-ECLAC 2015).

Costa Rica

	00	01	02	03	04	05	06	07	08	09	10	11	12
GDP per capita (dollars PPP 2005)	8,116	8,032	8,102	8,462	8,666	9,019	9,649	10,250	10,369	10,110	10,456	10,763	11,156
Share of agriculture in GDP	9.5	8.8	8.5	8.7	8.6	9.0	8.9	8.5	7.2	7.4	7.2	6.5	6.3
Share of industry in GDP	32.1	29.7	29.1	28.6	29.5	79.1	29.2	29.3	28.7	27.4	26.2	25.3	25.1
Share of services in GDP	58.5	61.5	62.4	62.6	61.8	61.9	61.9	62.2	64.1	65.2	66.7	68.2	68.6
Domestic expenditure (% GDP)	80.2	82.7	82.6	81.2	80.1	81.1	79.7	80.1	82.2	83.1	82.1	83.0	82.6
Public expenditure in education and health (% GDP)	9.9	10.7	11.4	11.3	10.6	10.3	10.0	10.4	11.7	13.6	13.9	13.7	14.2
Public expenditure in social security (% GDP)	6.0	6.3	5.6	5.4	5.3	5.3	5.2	5.3	5.5	6.4	6.5	6.6	6.7
Exports (% GDP)	48.6	41.5	42.4	46.7	46.3	48.5	49.1	48.7	45.4	42.3	38.2	37.4	37.7
Terms of trade	100.0	98.4	96.9	95.5	91.9	88.3	85.8	84.9	81.7	84.4	81.1	78.1	77.7
Foreign direct investment (% GDP)	2.6	2.8	3.9	3.3	4.3	4.3	6.5	7.2	7.0	4.6	4.0	5.3	5.9
Revenue from natural resources (% GDP)	...	...	...	0.0	0.0	0.0	0.0	0.1	0.0	0.0	0.0	0.0	...
Stock of public debt (% GDP)	42.3	43.0	43.4	41.1	40.9	37.5	33.3	27.6	24.8	27.4	28.8	30.3	35.1

Source: Authors' calculations based on World Development Indicators (World Bank 2014) and CEPALSTAT (UN-ECLAC 2015).

Dominican Republic

	00	01	02	03	04	05	06	07	08	09	10	11	12
GDP per capita (dollars PPP 2005)	5,737	5,751	5,991	5,886	5,876	6,326	6,901	7,380	7,660	7,818	8,312	8,573	8,794
Share of agriculture in GDP	7.2	7.5	7.2	6.4	7.0	7.5	7.1	6.6	6.3	6.2	6.2	6.0	6.1
Share of industry in GDP	35.9	34.2	35.0	33.8	33.0	32.1	32.2	31.6	32.2	32.5	32.0	33.1	31.7
Share of services in GDP	56.8	58.4	57.8	59.8	60.0	60.5	60.8	61.9	61.5	61.3	61.7	61.0	62.2
Domestic expenditure (% GDP)	85.5	86.2	86.7	85.4	84.3	89.0	89.6	90.2	95.4	93.2	94.7	93.9	92.4
Public expenditure in education and health (% GDP)	3.8	4.2	4.6	3.2	2.6	3.4	3.4	4.1	3.9	3.8	4.3	4.2	4.2
Public expenditure in social security (% GDP)	1.0	1.4	0.8	1.1	2.0	2.2	2.3	2.0	2.6	2.2	1.8	1.8	1.8
Exports (% GDP)	37.0	33.7	32.5	43.1	42.3	30.0	30.0	28.8	25.5	22.2	23.0	25.0	24.9
Terms of trade	100.0	100.9	101.5	97.9	96.7	95.8	94.9	98.0	93.6	101.3	97.5	92.4	91.5
Foreign direct investment (% GDP)	4.0	4.3	3.5	2.9	4.1	3.3	4.3	5.5	6.0	3.6	3.6	4.0	5.8
Revenue from natural resources (% GDP)	0.7	0.3	0.4	1.2	1.9	1.6	2.6	3.7	1.1	0.1	0.1	0.9	0.7
Stock of public debt (% GDP)	17.8	19.7	23.5	40.4	24.2	21.1	20.1	18.1	24.4	28.0	28.8	30.0	33.2

Source: Authors' calculations based on World Development Indicators (World Bank 2014) and CEPALSTAT (UN-ECLAC 2015).

Ecuador

	00	01	02	03	04	05	06	07	08	09	10	11	12
GDP per capita (dollars PPP 2005)	6,184	6,307	6,440	6,491	6,895	7,129	7,312	7,344	7,679	7,595	7,692	8,161	8,443
Share of agriculture in GDP	16.3	13.7	12.2	11.7	10.4	10.0	9.9	9.8	9.3	10.5	10.7	10.4	9.9
Share of industry in GDP	35.7	31.5	31.3	30.1	31.8	33.4	35.6	36.2	39.3	34.3	34.9	36.8	36.9
Share of services in GDP	48.0	54.7	56.4	58.2	57.8	56.6	54.5	53.9	51.4	55.2	54.4	52.8	53.3
Domestic expenditure (% GDP)	73.9	82.0	82.7	82.5	81.4	79.2	76.6	76.0	73.3	76.0	75.8	72.8	72.7
Public expenditure in education and health (% GDP)	2.3	3.2	3.9	3.5	3.7	3.7	3.8	3.9	4.6	6.1	6.2	6.2	6.5
Public expenditure in social security (% GDP)	0.4	0.6	0.3	0.4	0.3	0.7	0.7	1.1	1.0	1.4	1.7	1.5	1.4
Exports (% GDP)	32.1	23.2	21.5	22.6	24.6	27.6	30.3	31.9	34.2	25.2	28.7	32.2	31.2
Terms of trade	100.0	84.6	86.8	89.8	91.5	102.4	109.9	113.0	124.0	109.7	120.8	132.9	134.7
Foreign direct investment (% GDP)	−0.1	2.2	2.7	2.7	2.3	1.2	0.6	0.4	1.6	0.5	0.2	0.8	0.7
Revenue from natural resources (% GDP)	19.3	12.0	10.1	11.5	17.4	22.8	24.7	23.8	26.8	15.1	17.7	21.4	19.3
Stock of public debt (% GDP)	63.7	49.4	43.9	40.4	36.4	32.4	26.5	25.2	20.6	14.9	17.8	17.3	20.2

Source: Authors' calculations based on World Development Indicators (World Bank 2014) and CEPALSTAT (UN-ECLAC 2015).

Honduras

	00	01	02	03	04	05	06	07	08	09	10	11	12
GDP per capita (dollars PPP 2005)	2,880	2,898	2,946	3,019	3,143	3,268	3,414	3,554	3,631	3,473	3,531	3,593	3,657
Share of agriculture in GDP	15.9	14.6	13.5	12.8	13.4	13.7	13.0	13.0	13.1	11.7	12.5	15.3	14.8
Share of industry in GDP	32.5	30.7	30.1	30.1	29.1	28.7	30.0	28.6	28.0	28.1	27.6	27.8	27.9
Share of services in GDP	51.7	54.7	56.4	57.2	57.5	57.6	57.0	58.4	58.9	60.3	59.9	56.9	57.3
Domestic expenditure (% GDP)	84.2	87.2	88.3	88.8	89.0	90.9	92.7	94.4	97.0	97.2	96.0	93.7	93.9
Public expenditure in education and health (% GDP)	7.6	8.5	8.4	10.0	9.7	9.4	9.4	9.6	9.9	11.5	11.2	...	...
Public expenditure in social security (% GDP)	0.3	0.4	0.3	0.3	0.3	0.4	0.3	0.7	0.8	0.7	0.6	...	...
Exports (% GDP)	54.0	51.4	52.7	54.1	58.4	59.0	56.1	53.5	51.3	39.5	45.8	51.3	50.4
Terms of trade	100.0	94.8	92.0	88.0	87.2	87.2	83.2	81.6	76.6	81.9	84.2	91.2	84.3
Foreign direct investment (% GDP)	5.4	4.0	3.5	4.9	6.2	6.2	6.6	7.9	8.7	3.4	3.1	5.9	5.8
Revenue from natural resources (% GDP)	0.1	0.1	0.1	0.2	0.3	0.4	1.3	1.1	0.7	0.6	0.9	0.9	0.8
Stock of public debt (% GDP)	55.5	53.6	55.3	60.5	59.5	44.7	28.7	17.4	20.1	23.9	29.2	31.5	34.9

Source: Authors' calculations based on World Development Indicators (World Bank 2014) and CEPALSTAT (UN-ECLAC 2015).

Mexico

	00	01	02	03	04	05	06	07	08	09	10	11	12
GDP per capita (dollars PPP 2005)	11,810	11,575	11,440	11,460	11,807	12,017	12,462	12,695	12,711	11,962	12,412	12,747	13,067
Share of agriculture in GDP	3.5	3.6	3.5	3.5	3.6	3.4	3.4	3.3	3.3	3.5	3.5	3.4	3.6
Share of industry in GDP	35.7	33.9	33.7	34.6	35.8	35.5	36.3	36.1	36.6	34.3	34.8	35.7	35.7
Share of services in GDP	60.8	62.5	62.7	61.9	60.7	61.2	60.3	60.6	60.2	62.2	61.7	60.9	60.7
Domestic expenditure (% GDP)	78.1	80.3	81.5	79.6	79.1	79.2	77.8	78.2	77.9	78.6	79.2	79.0	77.9
Public expenditure in education and health (% GDP)	5.4	5.8	5.7	5.9	5.6	5.9	5.9	5.9	6.0	6.7	6.5	6.6	6.2
Public expenditure in social security (% GDP)	2.3	2.3	2.1	2.2	2.2	2.2	2.3	2.5	2.6	3.0	3.1	3.3	3.1
Exports (% GDP)	26.0	23.4	23.2	24.6	26.1	26.4	27.6	27.7	27.9	27.3	30.0	31.5	32.9
Terms of trade	100.0	97.4	97.9	98.8	101.6	103.6	104.1	105.1	105.9	94.0	101.2	108.5	109.1
Foreign direct investment (% GDP)	2.6	4.1	3.2	2.6	3.2	2.8	2.2	3.1	2.6	1.9	2.2	2.0	1.5
Revenue from natural resources (% GDP)	4.5	3.6	3.5	4.8	6.1	8.0	8.6	8.4	10.0	6.4	7.3	8.7	8.3
Stock of public debt (% GDP)	20.6	20.2	21.4	21.7	20.3	19.6	20.2	20.6	24.0	27.2	27.2	27.5	28.2

Source: Authors' calculations based on World Development Indicators (World Bank 2014) and CEPALSTAT (UN-ECLAC 2015).

Panama

	00	01	02	03	04	05	06	07	08	09	10	11	12
GDP per capita (dollars PPP 2005)	7,869	7,758	7,776	7,947	8,383	8,819	9,396	10,346	11,192	11,424	12,067	13,154	14,320
Share of agriculture in GDP	7.2	7.7	7.5	7.8	8.0	7.0	6.5	6.0	5.4	5.0	4.7	4.1	3.9
Share of industry in GDP	18.9	16.8	15.8	16.9	18.2	16.6	16.6	16.5	17.8	17.2	16.9	16.7	17.8
Share of services in GDP	73.9	75.5	76.7	75.4	73.8	76.5	76.9	77.5	76.7	77.7	78.4	79.2	78.3
Domestic expenditure (% GDP)	73.1	75.6	79.1	75.9	77.6	75.2	73.3	70.6	66.0	63.9	74.6	74.2	67.7
Public expenditure in education and health (% GDP)	7.6	8.0	8.2	8.2	8.4	8.3	6.4	5.8	6.1	6.7	6.5	6.6	6.2
Public expenditure in social security (% GDP)	2.2	1.8	1.6	1.6	1.4	1.5	1.2	1.8	1.6	3.0	3.1	3.3	3.1
Exports (% GDP)	72.6	72.7	67.5	63.6	67.6	75.5	76.7	81.2	85.2	81.0	76.5	84.2	83.5
Terms of trade	100.0	102.7	101.6	97.2	95.3	93.5	90.8	90.0	85.9	90.0	88.3	86.4	86.2
Foreign direct investment (% GDP)	5.4	4.0	0.8	6.3	7.2	7.1	17.1	9.6	9.9	4.2	8.8	13.2	8.6
Revenue from natural resources (% GDP)	...	0.0	0.1	0.1	0.1	0.1	0.2	0.2	0.2	0.4	0.4	0.5	0.6
Stock of public debt (% GDP)	61.4	65.7	64.7	62.4	65.2	61.0	56.5	49.0	41.4	41.7	39.7	37.9	37.0

Source: Authors' calculations based on World Development Indicators (World Bank 2014) and CEPALSTAT (UN-ECLAC 2015).

Peru

	00	01	02	03	04	05	06	07	08	09	10	11	12
GDP per capita (dollars PPP 2005)	5,514	5,447	5,644	5,797	6,013	6,349	6,765	7,288	7,916	7,904	8,503	8,982	9,431
Share of agriculture in GDP	8.5	8.2	7.8	7.6	7.3	7.2	7.0	7.0	7.2	7.3	6.8	7.0	7.0
Share of industry in GDP	29.9	29.6	30.4	30.8	33.0	34.3	37.0	37.0	36.6	34.2	36.1	36.6	34.6
Share of services in GDP	61.6	62.2	61.8	61.5	59.7	58.5	56.0	56.0	56.2	58.5	57.2	56.4	58.4
Domestic expenditure (% GDP)	84.0	85.2	83.5	83.4	80.6	78.4	72.0	70.6	72.3	75.2	71.7	70.2	71.8
Public expenditure in education and health (% GDP)	4.4	4.4	4.5	4.5	4.5	4.5	4.3	4.4	4.7	5.4	5.0	4.9	5.3
Public expenditure in social security (% GDP)	3.6	4.3	4.4	4.3	4.4	4.3	3.8	3.6	3.0	3.3	3.2	3.0	2.9
Exports (% GDP)	16.0	15.7	16.1	17.7	21.5	25.1	28.5	29.1	27.2	23.9	25.7	28.6	25.6
Terms of trade	100.0	95.6	98.4	102.2	111.3	119.4	152.1	157.6	136.6	129.1	152.5	171.9	163.7
Foreign direct investment (% GDP)	1.6	2.2	4.0	2.3	2.4	3.5	4.0	5.4	5.7	5.3	5.7	4.8	6.4
Revenue from natural resources (% GDP)	2.4	1.7	1.5	2.1	4.3	7.0	13.9	14.7	12.9	9.4	12.2	14.4	11.7
Stock of public debt (% GDP)	37.4	35.7	44.7	45.4	41.9	38.4	31.4	27.4	25.6	25.2	22.9	20.1	18.9

Source: Authors' calculations based on World Development Indicators (World Bank 2014) and CEPALSTAT (UN-ECLAC 2015).

Paraguay

	00	01	02	03	04	05	06	07	08	09	10	11	12
GDP per capita (dollars PPP 2005)	10,290	9,739	8,596	9,271	10,019	10,843	11,658	12,556	13,288	13,285	14,376	15,515	15,672
Share of agriculture in GDP	15.8	14.8	14.9	18.3	20.4	19.6	19.1	21.2	23.5	18.9	22.5	21.4	17.4
Share of industry in GDP	35.7	38.0	40.5	37.3	34.6	34.8	33.3	31.7	29.7	32.0	30.1	27.5	28.1
Share of services in GDP	48.5	47.3	44.6	44.4	45.1	45.7	47.6	47.1	46.7	49.0	47.4	51.0	54.5
Domestic expenditure (% GDP)	75.6	74.7	67.5	67.8	70.1	70.8	73.2	74.4	79.1	79.4	80.2	80.7	81.8
Public expenditure in education and health (% GDP)	...	...	6.1	4.8	5.4	6.1	6.5	6.6	6.5	8.3	7.6	8.4	10.0
Public expenditure in social security (% GDP)	...	...	1.6	3.7	3.4	4.0	5.2	5.2	4.8	6.6	5.4	6.2	7.3
Exports (% GDP)	46.1	44.2	52.9	54.3	53.8	57.3	58.3	56.3	54.3	51.2	54.6	48.9	46.6
Terms of trade	100.0	100.2	96.7	101.4	104.3	97.4	95.5	100.1	107.3	105.0	105.0	107.5	110.5
Foreign direct investment (% GDP)	1.3	1.1	0.2	0.4	0.5	0.1	1.8	0.8	1.4	0.3	1.7	1.8	2.0
Revenue from natural resources (% GDP)	...	...	...	...	...	...	...	...	...	...	...	...	...
Stock of public debt (% GDP)	35.3	33.5	47.0	38.7	34.3	29.3	23.2	15.9	14.3	14.6	14.1	12.1	12.6

Source: Authors' calculations based on World Development Indicators (World Bank 2014) and CEPALSTAT (UN-ECLAC 2015).

El Salvador

	00	01	02	03	04	05	06	07	08	09	10	11	12
GDP per capita (dollars PPP 2005)	5,155	5,220	5,322	5,425	5,506	5,682	5,880	6,080	6,129	5,906	5,953	6,048	6,125
Share of agriculture in GDP	10.5	10.1	9.1	9.0	9.5	10.6	10.7	11.9	12.5	12.4	12.6	12.5	11.8
Share of industry in GDP	31.4	31.9	32.2	31.8	30.4	29.7	29.1	28.2	27.7	27.0	26.7	26.9	27.2
Share of services in GDP	58.1	57.9	58.7	59.2	60.0	59.7	60.2	59.9	59.7	60.6	60.7	60.6	61.0
Domestic expenditure (% GDP)	98.1	99.1	98.3	98.9	101.1	102.4	103.7	106.1	107.6	102.0	103.6	104.3	104.4
Public expenditure in education and health (% GDP)	...	...	...	...	7.0	7.1	7.4	6.9	7.0	8.1	8.0	8.0	7.9
Public expenditure in social security (% GDP)	...	...	...	...	3.5	3.8	4.0	3.6	4.3	4.1	4.2	4.7	4.8
Exports (% GDP)	27.4	25.8	26.4	27.1	27.0	25.6	25.7	25.9	26.9	23.2	25.9	28.0	28.4
Terms of trade	100.0	102.5	101.6	97.7	96.8	96.8	95.5	94.6	91.9	94.9	91.3	91.3	90.2
Foreign direct investment (% GDP)	1.3	2.0	3.3	0.9	2.3	3.0	1.3	7.7	4.2	1.8	−0.5	0.5	1.9
Revenue from natural resources (% GDP)	0.0	0.0	0.0	0.0	0.0	0.0	0.0	0.0	0.0	0.0	0.0	0.0	0.0
Stock of public debt (% GDP)	27.2	30.7	35.2	37.2	38.1	37.5	37.7	34.9	34.4	42.6	42.6	41.7	45.7

Source: Authors' calculations based on World Development Indicators (World Bank 2014) and CEPALSTAT (UN-ECLAC 2015).

Uruguay

	00	01	02	03	04	05	06	07	08	09	10	11	12
GDP per capita (dollars PPP 2005)	9,551	9,168	8,457	8,530	8,962	9,626	10006	10634	11361	11577	12569	13344	13821
Share of agriculture in GDP	7.0	6.5	8.7	11.1	12.9	10.4	10.7	10.2	10.9	8.4	7.9	9.4	8.4
Share of industry in GDP	24.5	24.5	24.3	26.1	25.6	27.1	26.4	27.2	25.8	25.6	26.1	23.9	24.7
Share of services in GDP	68.5	69.0	67.0	62.8	61.5	62.5	62.9	62.6	63.3	66.0	66.0	66.8	66.9
Domestic expenditure (% GDP)	88.9	88.4	85.7	81.7	79.8	80.4	81.9	81.5	81.6	79.6	80.6	81.4	82.3
Public expenditure in education and health (% GDP)	6.0	6.5	6.6	6.4	6.2	6.3	6.9	7.4	8.7	9.6	9.8	10.5	...
Public expenditure in social security (% GDP)	13.2	14.1	14.5	12.8	11.7	11.7	11.8	12.9	11.7	12.0	12.2	11.1	...
Exports (% GDP)	16.7	16.8	20.6	27.4	32.1	30.4	30.3	29.1	30.2	28.3	27.2	27.2	26.3
Terms of trade	100.0	104.0	102.6	103.5	99.9	90.7	88.6	88.7	94.1	96.9	100.0	101.8	104.2
Foreign direct investment (% GDP)	1.2	1.4	1.4	3.5	2.4	4.8	7.7	5.8	7.1	5.3	5.6	5.7	5.4
Revenue from natural resources (% GDP)	0.0	0.0	0.0	0.0	0.1	0.1	0.1	0.1	0.1	0.1	0.1	0.1	0.1
Stock of public debt (% GDP)	31.6	38.9	96.0	95.5	74.7	66.7	61.6	52.9	51.6	46.7	40.9	40.3	39.2

Source: Authors' calculations based on World Development Indicators (World Bank 2014) and CEPALSTAT (UN-ECLAC 2015).

Venezuela

	00	01	02	03	04	05	06	07	08	09	10	11	12
GDP per capita (dollars PPP 2005)	9,527	9,667	8,650	7,835	9,104	9,869	10,658	11,396	11,799	11,237	10,894	11,173	11,623
Share of agriculture in GDP	4.2	4.5	4.1	4.6	4.0	4.0	4.0	4.1	4.4	6.1	5.8	9.4	8.4
Share of industry in GDP	49.7	46.1	49.8	51.6	55.5	57.8	56.5	53.3	54.1	44.2	52.2	23.9	24.7
Share of services in GDP	46.1	49.4	46.1	43.9	40.5	38.2	39.5	42.6	41.5	49.7	42.1	66.8	66.9
Domestic expenditure (% GDP)	64.2	69.1	66.5	67.7	61.2	57.8	58.7	63.6	63.4	76.6	67.1	66.7	71.5
Public expenditure in education and health (% GDP)	8.5	9.3	9.6	8.8	9.9	9.0	10.7	10.8	9.9	9.8	8.7	9.9	10.5
Public expenditure in social security (% GDP)	3.8	5.0	4.3	5.9	5.8	5.7	7.5	7.7	6.8	6.9	7.1	8.7	9.2
Exports (% GDP)	29.7	22.7	30.4	33.9	36.2	39.7	36.5	31.1	30.8	18.1	28.5	29.9	26.2
Terms of trade	100.0	82.2	87.6	98.7	118.1	154.4	184.4	202.1	249.5	181.7	215.9	259.5	262.1
Foreign direct investment (% GDP)	4.0	3.0	0.8	2.4	1.3	1.9	0.1	1.1	0.4	−0.8	0.5	1.2	0.6
Revenue from natural resources (% GDP)	28.0	22.3	26.8	32.7	39.3	47.5	43.9	34.4	34.9	18.8	20.3	33.7	28.6
Stock of public debt (% GDP)	28.1	31.2	41.7	47.4	38.8	33.1	24.0	19.1	14.0	18.2	32.0	25.1	27.5

Source: Authors' calculations based on World Development Indicators (World Bank 2014) and CEPALSTAT (UN-ECLAC 2015).

References

UN-ECLAC (2015). CEPALSTAT, United Nations, Economic Commission for Latin America and the Caribbean. Available at <http://estadisticas.cepal.org/cepalstat/WEB_CEPALSTAT/Portada.asp?idioma=i>, accessed April 2015.

World Bank (2014). World Development Indicators. Available at <http://data.worldbank.org/data-catalog/world-development-indicators>, accessed April 2014.

Index

As most chapters pertain to a particular country, the sub-headings for each country have not been double-entered under main entries.